Created Equal
A History of the United States

Volume 1, To 1877

FOURTH EDITION

Jacqueline Jones
University of Texas at Austin

Thomas Borstelmann
University of Nebraska

Vicki L. Ruiz
University of California, Irvine

Peter H. Wood
Duke University

Elaine Tyler May
University of Minnesota

PEARSON

Boston   Columbus   Indianapolis   New York   San Francisco   Upper Saddle River
Amsterdam   Cape Town   Dubai   London   Madrid   Milan   Munich   Paris   Montréal   Toronto
Delhi   Mexico City   São Paulo   Sydney   Hong Kong   Seoul   Singapore   Taipei   Tokyo

Editorial Director: Craig Campanella
Editor-in-Chief: Dickson Musslewhite
Acquisitions Editor: Ed Parsons
Program Manager: Seanna Breen
Editorial Assistant: Yin Yin Lu
Director of Marketing: Brandy Dawson
Executive Marketing Manager: Wendy Albert
Senior Managing Editor: Ann Marie McCarthy
Senior Operations Supervisor: Mary Fischer
Procurement Specialist: Mary Ann Gloriande
Project Manager: Carol O'Rourke
Director of Digital Media: Bryan Hyland
Digital Media Editor: Liz Roden

Digital Media Project Manager: Michael Halas
Creative Director: Blair Brown
Art Director: Maria Lange
Interior Design: Red Kite Project
Cover Design: Red Kite Project and Maria Lange
Cover Illustration: Paul Chung
Cover Image: © ClassicStock / Alamy
Full Service Project Management and Composition:
    PreMediaGlobal
Full Service Project Manager: Greg Johnson/
    PreMediaGlobal
Printer and Binder: R.R. Donnelley / Willard
Cover Printer: Lehigh-Phoenix Color/Hagerstown

Credits and acknowledgments borrowed from other sources and reproduced, with permission, in this textbook appear on appropriate page within text.

Many of the designations by manufacturers and seller to distinguish their products are claimed as trademarks. Where those designations appear in this book, and the publisher was aware of a trademark claim, the designations have been printed in initial caps or all caps.

Library of Congress Cataloging-in-Publication Data

Jones, Jacqueline
    Created equal : a history of the United States / Jacqueline Jones University of Texas at Austin; Peter H. Wood, Duke University; Thomas Borstelmann, University of Nebraska; Elaine Tyler May, University of Minnesota; Vicki L. Ruiz, University of California, Irvine.—Fourth Edition
    pagescm
    ISBN 978-0-205-90130-2—ISBN 0-205-90130-1
    1. United States—History.   2. United States—Social conditions.   3. United States—Politics and government.   4. Cultural pluralism—United States—History.   5. Minorities—United States—History.   6. Cultural pluralism—United States—History—Sources.   7. Minorities—United States—History—Sources.   I. Title.
    E178.J767 2014
    973—dc23

                                                                          2013014699

2 3 4 5 6 7 8 9 10

Combined Volume
ISBN-13: 978-0-205-90130-2
ISBN-10: 0-205-90130-1

Exam Copy
ISBN-13: 978-0-205-90687-1
ISBN-10: 0-205-90687-7

Volume 1
ISBN-13: 978-0-20590133-3
ISBN-10: 0-205-90133-6

Volume 1 A la Carte
ISBN-13: 978-0-205-89952-4
ISBN-10: 0-205-89952-8

Volume 2
ISBN-13: 978-0-205-89954-8
ISBN-10: 0-205-89954-4

Volume 2 A la Carte
ISBN-13: 978-0-205-90006-0
ISBN-10: 0-205-90006-2

Brief Contents

Contents

Special Features

Maps

Tables

Figures

Preface

New to This Edition

The fourth edition of *Created Equal* has a greatly strengthened focus on the overarching **theme of contested equality.** This strong emphasis on one theme renders the text a strikingly **more effective pedagogical tool.** Students will be more engaged and will appreciate the chance to think critically about ongoing struggles over equal rights and shifting boundaries of inclusion and acceptance. Amid all the new challenges of the twenty-first century, this unifying theme feels more relevant than ever.

Personalize Learning with New MyHistoryLab

This text features full **integration with the new MyHistoryLab**—a rich resource that delivers proven results in helping students succeed, provides engaging experiences that personalize learning, and comes from a trusted partner with educational expertise and a deep commitment to helping students and instructors achieve their goals.

- The **Pearson eText**, with a new streamlined design for tablet devices, lets students access *Created Equal* anytime, anywhere, and any way they want—and they can listen to and download every chapter. Section tabs on the margin of every page make the text much easier to navigate. The new Pearson eText is now fully interactive and links to all the learning resources in MyHistoryLab.
- **Chapter launcher videos** introduce students to the material, helping to engage them even before they begin reading the chapter. Each chapter has a 15-minute segment, comprised of a three-minute overview and three four-minute videos on specific topics. The videos are featured on the second page, directly after the chapter opener.
- In the new **MyHistoryLibrary with audio**, students can read, listen to, annotate, download, and print over 200 of the most commonly assigned primary source documents. These documents can also be annotated by instructors.
- With the new **History Explorer**, students visualize and analyze historical evidence in a powerful mapping resource. The modules cover topics from English Colonization to the Civil Rights Movement, and each contains an assignable exercise with automated assessment. They are also featured in every chapter of the text in a special box.
- The new **automated writing assessment engine** allows students to further explore key topics by responding to them in essay form. The system offers ten formal prompts on standard topics like the American Revolution, the Lewis and Clark expedition, and the New Deal. Each assignment is based on one of MyHistoryLab's engaging **Author Video Lectures**.
- A **personalized study plan** for each student, based on Bloom's Taxonomy, promotes critical thinking skills and helps students succeed in the course and beyond.
- **Assessment** tied to videos, applications, and chapters enables instructors and students to track progress and get immediate feedback. Instructors will be able to find the best resources for teaching their students.

- **MyHistoryLab icons** are paired with images in the text for more thorough integration between the book and online resources.
- The new **Instructor's eText** makes it easier than ever for instructors to access subject-specific resources for class preparation. Housed within MyHistoryLab, it serves as the hub for all available instructor resources—including the new MyHistoryLab Instructor's Guide.
- The new **MyHistoryLab Instructor's Guide** outlines the basic steps for registering and building a course in MyHistoryLab and describes the key resources and assignments available for each chapter of *Created Equal*.
- The **Class Preparation Tool** collects the best class presentation resources in one convenient online destination. Resources include PowerPoint slides, streaming audio and video, audio clips for class tests and quizzes, and all illustrations for creating interactive lectures.

Engage Students and Improve Critical Thinking

- **Chapter introductory vignettes** provide brief firsthand accounts of individuals whose personal journeys share common ground with the themes of equality that pervade American history. Their journeys, often made more difficult, complicated, or exhausting by the struggle to achieve an inclusive definition of American citizenship, are the stories that *Created Equal* was specifically designed to tell.
- **Chapter images** are bigger, visually interesting, and instructive. New annotations that accompany all photographs encourage students to turn a critical eye on their content and style and to answer, with reasoned opinion, questions that address multiple layers of meaning.
- **Interpreting History** essays are guided historical inquiries into primary sources that directly engage students with the singular voices of America's past. Every chapter features a full-page Interpreting History essay, which relates the content of that chapter to the unique perspective of a particular person from a particular place and time.

Support Instructors

- **Learning Objective questions** highlight the important issues and themes. Each is linked to one of the chapter's main sections, and they are all emphasized in the chapter overview.
- The **Chapter Review** on the last page addresses all Learning Objective questions from the beginning of each chapter in brief answers, summarizing the important issues and themes.
- The **Thematic Timeline** ending each chapter reinforces the essential points of the narrative, as events are tied to key terms from the text.

About the Authors

Jacqueline Jones was born in Christiana, Delaware, a small town of 400 people in the northern part of the state. The local public school was desegregated in 1955, when she was a third grader. That event sparked her interest in American history. She received her undergraduate education at the University of Delaware, and her Ph.D. in history at the University of Wisconsin, Madison. Her scholarly interests have evolved over time, focusing on American labor and women's, African American, and southern history. She teaches American history at the University of Texas at Austin, where she is the Mastin Gentry White Professor of Southern History and the Walter Prescott Webb Chair in History and Ideas. Dr. Jones is the author of several books. In 2001, she published a memoir that recounts her childhood in Christiana: *Creek Walking: Growing Up in Delaware in the 1950s*. Her most recent book is titled *A Dreadful Deceit: The Myth of Race from the Colonial Era to Obama's America* (2013).

Peter H. Wood was born in St. Louis and recalls visiting the courthouse where the *Dred Scott* case originated. Emeritus professor of history at Duke University, he studied at Harvard and attended Oxford as a Rhodes Scholar. In 1974, he published the pioneering book *Black Majority*, concerning slavery in colonial South Carolina. He recently earned the Eugene Asher Distinguished Teaching Award of the American Historical Association. Topics of his articles range from the French explorer LaSalle to Gerald Ford's pardon of Richard Nixon. He has written a short overview of early African Americans, entitled *Strange New Land*, and he has published three books about the famous American painter Winslow Homer. Wood, who now lives in Longmont, Colorado, has served on the boards of the Highlander Center and Harvard University. His varied interests include archaeology, documentary film, and growing gourds. He keeps a baseball bat used by Ted Williams beside his desk.

Thomas ("Tim") Borstelmann grew up in North Carolina. His formal education came at Durham Academy, Phillips Exeter Academy, Stanford University (A.B., 1980), and Duke University (Ph.D., 1990). An avid cyclist, runner, swimmer, and skier, he taught history at Cornell University from 1991 to 2003, when he moved to the University of Nebraska-Lincoln to become the first E. N. and Katherine Thompson Distinguished Professor of Modern World History. Dr. Borstelmann's first book, *Apartheid's Reluctant Uncle: The United States and Southern Africa in the Early Cold War* (1993), won the Stuart L. Bernath Book Prize of the Society for Historians of Foreign Relations. His second book, *The Cold War and the Color Line: American Race Relations in the Global Arena*, appeared in 2001. At Cornell he won a major teaching award, the Robert and Helen Appel Fellowship. His most recent book is *The 1970s: A New Global History from Civil Rights to Economic Inequality* (2012).

Elaine Tyler May developed a passion for American history in college when she spent her junior year in Japan. As an American student in Asia, she yearned for a deeper understanding of America's past and its place in the world. She returned home to study history at UCLA, where she earned her B.A., M.A., and Ph.D. She has taught at the University of Minnesota since 1978. Her widely acclaimed *Homeward Bound: American Families in the Cold War Era* was the first study to link the baby boom and suburbia to the politics of the Cold War. The *Chronicle of Higher Education* featured *Barren in the Promised Land: Childless Americans and the Pursuit of Happiness* as a pioneering study of the history of reproduction. Her most recent book is *America and the Pill: A History of Promise, Peril and Liberation*. Professor May served as president of the American Studies Association in 1996 and president of the Organization of American Historians in 2010.

Vicki L. Ruiz grew up in Florida. For her, history remains a grand adventure, one that she began at the kitchen table, listening to the Colorado stories of her mother and grandmother. The first in her family to receive an advanced degree, she graduated from Gulf Coast Community College and Florida State University, then went on to earn a Ph.D. in history at Stanford in 1982. She is the author of *Cannery Women, Cannery Lives* and *From Out of the Shadows: Mexican Women in 20th-Century America*. She and Virginia Sánchez Korrol have co edited *Latinas in the United States: A Historical Encyclopedia*. She has participated in student mentorship projects, summer institutes for teachers, and public humanities programs. Dr. Ruiz a fellow of the Society of American Historians and the American Academy of Arts and Sciences. She is the past president of the American Studies Association and the Organization of American Historians. Since 2001, she has taught history and Chicano/Latino studies at the University of California, Irvine. The mother of two grown sons, she is married to Victor Becerra, an urban planner and community activist.

Acknowledgments

As authors, we could not have completed this project without the loving support of our families. We wish to thank Jeffrey Abramson, Lil Fenn, Lynn Borstelmann, Lary May, and Victor Becerra for their interest, forbearance, and encouragement over the course of several editions. Our own children have been a source of inspiration, as have our many students, past and present. We are grateful to scores of colleagues and friends who have helped shape this book, both directly and indirectly, in more ways than they know. Along the way, Matt Basso, Chad Cover, Jeff Manuel, Rob McGreevey, Eben Miller, Andrea Sachs, Mary Strunk, and Melissa Williams provided useful research and administrative assistance; their help was invaluable. Rob Heinrich is deserving of special thanks for his close read of the manuscript and proofs and research assistance. Louis Balizet provided careful reading of several chapter drafts.

Our friends at Pearson have continued their generous support and assistance for our efforts. We thank all the creative people associated with Pearson (and there are many) who have had a hand in bringing this book to life.

Supplementary Instructional Materials

FOR INSTRUCTORS	FOR STUDENTS
MyHistoryLab www.myhistorylab.com **Save Time. Improve Results.** MyHistoryLab is a dynamic website that provides a wealth of resources geared to meet the diverse teaching and learning needs of today's instructors and students. MyHistoryLab's many accessible tools will encourage students to read their text and help them improve their grade in their course.	**MyHistoryLab** www.myhistorylab.com **Save Time. Improve Results.** MyHistoryLab is a dynamic website that provides a wealth of resources geared to meet the diverse teaching and learning needs of today's instructors and students. MyHistoryLab's many accessible tools will encourage you to read your text and help you improve your grade in your course.
Instructor's Resource Center www.pearsonhighered.com/irc This website provides instructors with additional text-specific resources that can be downloaded for classroom use. Resources include the Instructor's Resource Manual, PowerPoint presentations and the Test Item File. Register online for access to the resources for Created Equal.	**www.coursemart.com** CourseSmart eTextbooks offer the same content as the printed text in a convenient online format—with highlighting, online search, and printing capabilities. You **save 60% over the list price** of the traditional book.
Instructor's Resource Manual Available for download at www.pearsonhighered.com/irc, the Instructor's Resource Manual contains chapter outlines, detailed chapter overviews, lecture outlines, topics for discussion, and information about audio-visual resources.	**Books à la Carte** These editions feature the exact same content as the traditional printed text in a convenient, three-hole-punched, loose-leaf version at a discounted price—allowing you to take only what you need to class. You'll **save 35% over the net price** of the traditional book.
Test Item File Available for download at www.pearsonhighered .com/irc, the Test Item File contains more than 1,500 multiple-choice, identification, matching, true-false, and essay test questions and 10–15 questions per chapter on the maps found in each chapter.	**Library of American Biography Series** www.pearsonhighered .com/educator/series/Library-of-American-Biography/10493.page Pearson's renowned series of biographies spotlighting figures who had a significant impact on American history. Included in the series are Edmund Morgan's *The Puritan Dilemma: The Story of John Winthrop*, B. Davis Edmund's *Tecumseh and the Quest for Indian Leadership*, J. William T. Youngs's, *Eleanor Roosevelt: A Personal and Public Life*, and John R. M. Wilson's *Jackie Robinson and the American Dilemma*.
PowerPoint Presentations Available for download at www.pearsonhighered.com/irc, the PowerPoints contain chapter outlines and full-color images of maps, figures, and images.	
MyTest www.pearsonmytest.com MyTest is a powerful assessment generation program that helps instructors easily create and print quizzes and exams. Questions and tests can be authored online, allowing instructors ultimate flexibility and the ability to efficiently manage assessments anytime, anywhere! Instructors can easily access existing questions and edit, create, and store using simple drag-and-drop and Word-like controls.	**Penguin Valuepacks** www.pearsonhighered.com/penguin A variety of Penguin-Putnam texts is available at discounted prices when bundled with *Created Equal, 4/e*. Texts include Benjamin Franklin's *Autobiography and Other Writings*, Nathaniel Hawthorne's *The Scarlet Letter*, Thomas Jefferson's *Notes on the State of Virginia*, and George Orwell's *1984*.

(continued)

FOR INSTRUCTORS	FOR STUDENTS
Retrieving the American Past (www.pearsoncustom.com, **keyword search | rtap**) Available through the Pearson Custom Library, the *Retrieving the American Past* (RTAP) program lets you create a textbook or reader that meets your needs and the needs of your course. RTAP gives you the freedom and flexibility to add chapters from several best-selling Pearson textbooks, in addition to *Created Equal, 4/e,* and/or 100 topical reading units written by the History Department of Ohio State University, all under one cover. Choose the content you want to teach in depth, in the sequence you want, at the price you want your students to pay.	**A Short Guide to Writing About History, 7/e** Written by Richard Marius, late of Harvard University, and Melvin E. Page, Eastern Tennessee State University, this engaging and practical text helps students get beyond merely compiling dates and facts. Covering brief essays and the documented resource paper, the text explores the writing and researching processes, identifies different modes of historical writing, including argument, and concludes with guidelines for improving style. **ISBN-10: 0205673708; ISBN-13: 9780205673704**
	Longman American History Atlas This full-color historical atlas designed especially for college students is a valuable reference tool and visual guide to American history. This atlas includes maps covering the scope of American history from the lives of the Native Americans to the 1990s. Produced by a renowned cartographic firm and a team of respected historians, the Longman American History Atlas will enhance any American history survey course. **ISBN: 0321004868; ISBN-13: 9780321004864**

MyHistoryLab

An online homework, tutorial, and assessment program, MyHistoryLab offers immersive content, tools, and experiences to engage students and help them succeed.

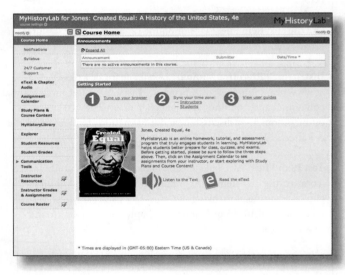

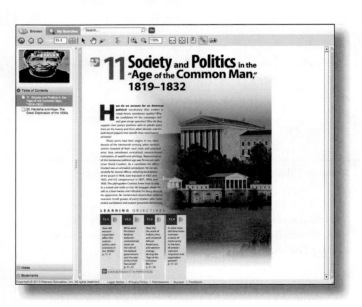

Pearson eText with Audio

Contained within MyHistoryLab, the Pearson eText enables students to access their textbook online—through laptops, iPads, and tablets. Download the free Pearson eText app to use on tablets. Students may also listen to their text with the Audio eText.

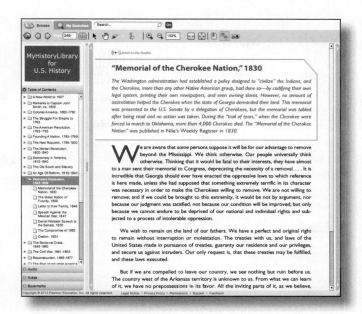

New MyHistoryLibrary

A new release of Pearson's MyHistoryLibrary contains more than 200 of the most commonly assigned primary source documents, delivered through Pearson's powerful eText platform. Each reading may also be listened to in the Audio eText companion.

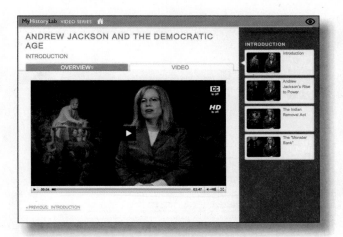

MyHistoryLab Video Series: Key Topics in US History

This comprehensive video series helps students get up-to-speed on key topics. Correlated to the chapters of *Created Equal*, each video unit reviews key topics of the period, readying students to get the most from the text narrative. The videos feature seasoned historians reviewing the pivotal stories of our past, in a lively format designed to engage and inform.

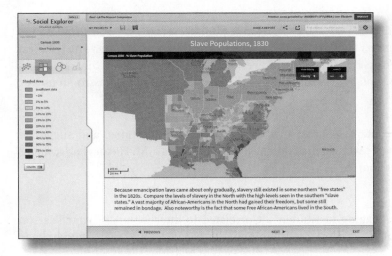

Explorer

This path-breaking new application in MyHistoryLab enables students to use dynamic maps to understand pivotal events and topics. A unique Explorer application is correlated to each chapter of *Created Equal*.

Writing Space

MyHistoryLab Writing Space provides the best way to develop and assess concept mastery and critical thinking through writing. Use Writing Space to create, track, and grade writing assignments, access writing resources, and exchange meaningful, personalized feedback quickly and easily. Plus, Writing Space includes integrated access to Turnitin, the global leader in plagiarism prevention.

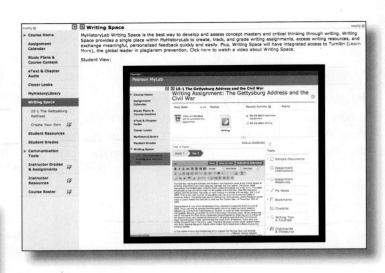

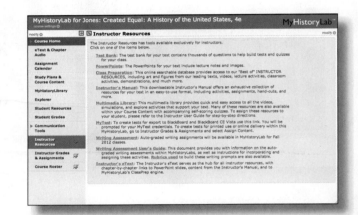

Key Supplements & Customer Support

Annotated Instructor's eText

Contained within MyHistoryLab, the *Annotated Instructor's eText* for your Pearson textbook leverages the powerful Pearson eText platform to make it easier than ever for you to access subject-specific resources for class preparation. The *AI eText* serves as the hub for all instructor resources, with chapter-by-chapter links to PowerPoint slides, content from the Instructor's Manual, and to MyHistoryLab's ClassPrep engine, which contains a wealth of history content organized for classroom use.

Instructor's Manual

The Instructor's Manual for your Pearson textbook contains chapter overviews, discussion questions, and suggested assignments for each chapter, including both general and text-specific content. It also contains a MyHistoryLab syllabus and suggestions for integrating MyHistoryLab into your course.

PowerPoint Presentations

Strong PowerPoint presentations make lectures more engaging for students. Correlated to the chapters of your Pearson textbook, each presentation includes a full lecture script, discussion questions, a wealth of images and maps, and links to the full array of MyHistoryLab media.

MyTest Test Bank

Containing a diverse set of multiple choice and essay questions, the MyTest test bank supports a variety of assessment strategies. The large pool of multiple choice questions for each chapter includes factual, conceptual, and analytical questions, so that instructors may assess students on basic information as well as critical thinking.

Customer Support

Pearson's dedicated team of local representatives will work with you not only to choose course materials but also to integrate them into your class and assess their effectiveness. Moreover, live support for MyHistoryLab users, both educators and students, is available 24/7.

1 First Founders

When and where does **American history** begin? The answer continues to change, especially in recent years, as new techniques allow scientists to dig more deeply into sparse evidence from the distant past. Human existence in the Americas is far less ancient than in Africa and Eurasia, but exploration of the earliest chapters in the story proves to be specially exciting and controversial.

Take the evidence announced in 2012 relating to rapid shifts in climate and ocean level at the end of the last Ice Age. "Our work gives a window onto an extreme event in which deglaciation coincided with a dramatic and rapid rise in global sea levels—an ancient 'mega flood'," observed Dr. Alex Thomas, part of a European team working in the Pacific. "Sea level rose more than ten times more quickly than it is rising now. It is vital,"the Oxford University scientist continued," that we look into Earth's geological past to understand rare but high-impact events, such as the collapse of giant ice sheets that occurred 14,600 years ago."

Will further research confirm this suggestion that shifts in oceanic currents and the rapid melting of ice sheets in Antarctica caused sea levels to rise more than 45 feet in a narrow span of a few centuries, while cold temperatures in the high latitudes of the Northern Hemisphere warmed drastically? And if so, how did such massive changes during several centuries spur, or disrupt, the arrival of America's first human residents?

LEARNING OBJECTIVES

1.1	1.2	1.3	1.4	1.5
What types of evidence are used to explain the arrival of humans in North America? p. 3	In the millennium before Columbus, what evidence exists for non-local trade in North America? p. 5	Why is the first voyage of Columbus in 1492 still viewed as such an earth-changing event? p. 9	What factors motivated and shaped Spain's rapid intrusion into sixteenth-century America? p. 14	How did Europe's sharp religious split influence the early colonization of North America? p. 19

Arrowheads and stone tools buried under layers of earth indicate different eras of ancient habitation. Here, archaeologists digging at Cactus Hill, Virginia, unearth artifacts that suggest human habitation before the arrival of hunters using Clovis points. The foreground objects are laid out clockwise by apparent age, with the most recent at the top. Clovis-like spearheads appear in the second group. The third and fourth groups, taken from lower layers, are older items reaching back well beyond 14,000 years. With these, it becomes difficult to separate crude human tools from natural rock fragments. How does the study of arrowheads and stone tools contribute to our understanding of American history?

Listen to Chapter 1 on MyHistoryLab

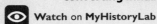 Watch the Video Series on MyHistoryLab

Learn about some key topics related to this chapter with the
MyHistoryLab Video Series: Key Topics in U.S. History.

1 **A New World: To 1607** This video surveys the history of Native Americans and includes discussion of their migrations across the Bering Strait, their adaptation to a range of environmental conditions, and the various cultures they developed. The video also reveals how the first hundred years of European colonization had an unprecedented impact on numerous Native American cultures.

 Watch on **MyHistoryLab**

The First Americans Prior to 1492, the pre-Columbian Mesoamerican cultures of Central America and Mexico, notably the Mayans and Aztecs, developed distinctive cultures and built great empires. This video describes their civilizations as well as Native American societies in North America, such as the Puebloan peoples, the Plains Indians, and the Mississippian mound-building cultures. **2**

Watch on **MyHistoryLab**

3 **The Expansion of Europe** This video discusses Columbus and other European explorers who competed to find a viable route to China and the Indies. The huge Western Hemisphere hampered Europe's westward access to the spices of Asia, but it posed new challenges—the prospect of searching for mineral wealth and converting inhabitants to Christianity.

 Watch on **MyHistoryLab**

The Protestant Reformation The first European settlers who came to North America were typically religious refugees. This video explores the Protestant Reformation, beginning with Martin Luther, a German monk. He and his followers protested against corruption in the Roman Catholic Church. They formed new Protestant denominations that spread through northern Europe and played an active role in overseas colonization. **4**

Watch on **MyHistoryLab**

Such recent discoveries follow a century of mounting study into how human beings first came to inhabit North America and what conditions they faced. In 1907, on the 300th anniversary of Jamestown, amazingly little was understood about who had lived in North America before the first successful English colonists arrived. Everyone knew that the Italian explorer Christopher Columbus had reached the Caribbean while attempting to sail to the Indies for Spain in 1492. They had learned in school that Columbus, thinking he had reached the Asian islands close to India and China ("the Indies"), mistakenly lumped America's peoples together as Indians. But most Americans still knew very little about North America before 1607.

Our expanding view of American history—relevant for the twenty-first century—now stretches back in time far before the Jamestown settlement. It reaches broadly from coast to coast, and it looks at two important starting points. For one, the earliest roots lie with the ancient Indians of the continent over many millennia. A very different, and much later, starting point involves the foreigners who suddenly intruded into portions of the Native American world in the sixteenth century, after the voyages of Christopher Columbus. They spoke Spanish, French, and occasionally English, and in retrospect they represent another significant beginning. All these people, therefore, now number among America's first founders.

Ancient America

1.1 What types of evidence are used to explain the arrival of humans in North America?

Early in the twentieth century, near Folsom, New Mexico, archaeologists found a manmade spear point resting between the rib bones of a type of ancient bison that had been extinct for 10,000 years. They named such thin projectile tips Folsom points, after the site. Their discovery proved that humans had lived and hunted on the continent far earlier than scientists had ever imagined. It sparked a revolution in North American archaeology. Soon after the Folsom find, amateurs at nearby Clovis, New Mexico, spotted some large, well-chipped spearheads. In 1932, collectors found more of these so-called Clovis points in the same vicinity, this time beside the tooth of an extinct mammoth. The points lay underneath a soil layer containing Folsom points, so they were clearly even older.

Since then, scientists have unearthed Clovis-like points throughout much of North America. According to the latest calculations, humans started creating these weapons roughly 13,900 years ago and ceased about 12,900 years ago. This means that people were hunting widely on the continent nearly 14,000 years ago. Archaeologists continue to push back and refine the estimated date for the appearance of the first people in the Americas. Recently, they have unearthed evidence suggesting the possible presence of pre-Clovis inhabitants.

The Question of Origins

Like all other peoples, the varied Native American societies retain rich accounts of their own origins. No amount of scientific data can diminish or replace tribal creation stories that serve an important cultural purpose. In these powerful sagas, America's first humans emerge from the earth, are created by other animals, or receive life from the Great Spirit. At the same time, modern researchers continue to compile evidence about the origin and migrations of the diverse peoples who inhabited the Americas for thousands of years before the arrival of Christopher Columbus.

Scientists have determined that the most recent ancestors of modern humans moved from Africa to spread across the Eurasian landmass, the area comprising Europe and Asia, scarcely 70,000 years ago. By 40,000 years ago, some of these Stone Age hunter-gatherers had already reached Australia. Others lived on the steppes of central Asia and the frozen tundra of Siberia. They had perfected the tools they needed to survive in a cold climate: flint spear points for killing mammoths, reindeer, and the woolly rhinoceros; and bone needles to sew warm, waterproof clothes out of animal skin.

Over thousands of years, bands of these northern hunters migrated east across Siberia in search of game. Eventually, they arrived at the region where the Bering Strait now separates Russia from Alaska. Between 25,000 and 11,000 years ago, cold conditions expanded Arctic ice caps, trapping vast quantities of the earth's water in the form of huge glaciers. As a result, ocean levels sank by 300 feet—enough to expose a bridge of land more than 600 miles wide between Asia and America.

The Bering Land Bridge formed part of a frigid, windswept region known as Beringia. Small groups of people could have subsisted in this cold landscape by hunting mammoths and musk oxen until Ice Age glaciers receded about 14,000 years ago. As the climate warmed and the ocean rose again, some headed farther east onto higher ground, near the headwaters of the Tanana River in eastern Alaska. These newcomers would have been cut off permanently from Siberia as water once more submerged the land bridge. But the same warming process also eventually opened a pathway through the glaciers blanketing northern America.

This ice-free corridor along the eastern slope of the Rocky Mountains could account for the sudden appearance of Clovis hunters across much of North America

Paleo-Indians The earliest human inhabitants of North America, who first migrated to the continent from Siberia more than 15,000 years ago. Faced with a warming climate and the disappearance of many large game animals roughly 10,000 years ago (8,000 B.C.E.), their descendants learned to hunt smaller animals and adapted to varied local conditions during the Archaic Period (to c. 1000 B.C.E.).

nearly 14,000 years ago. Small bands of people, armed with razor-sharp Clovis points, spread rapidly across the continent, destroying successive herds of large animals that had never faced human predators before. According to this theory, generations of hunters known as **Paleo-Indians** could have migrated as far as the tip of South America within several thousand years.

Three new developments complicate the picture. First of all, archaeologists have uncovered artifacts suggesting the presence of immediate predecessors to the Clovis people. Such finds have occurred at dispersed sites, including Cactus Hill in Virginia, Meadowcroft in Pennsylvania, and (most recently) Buttermilk Creek in central Texas. Secondly, experts now argue these earliest arrivals came by sea. Many suggest Asian bands followed the North Pacific rim and migrated down the American west coast. Others speculate coastal Europeans may have followed a comparable circum-Atlantic route to the Americas. Meanwhile, genetic comparisons of different peoples, present and past, are yielding increasingly specific, if controversial, details about early migrations and interactions. Advances in understanding ancient DNA—the genetic material that determines our physical make-up and transmits it to our offspring—may soon sharpen or change our awareness regarding the origins of the earliest Paleo-Indians.

The Archaic World

As the continent warmed further and the great glaciers receded north, more than 100 of America's largest species disappeared. These included mammoths, mastodons, horses, camels, and the great long-horned bison. Researchers debate whether these large animals were hunted to extinction, wiped out by disease, or destroyed by climate change. One theory—warmly debated in recent years—suggests that a major meteorite struck the earth some 12,900 years ago and altered the North American environment so drastically that it prompted the extinction of numerous large mammals and the swift, puzzling demise of Clovis Culture.

Some 10,000 years ago, the Paleo-Indian period in North America gradually gave way to the **Archaic** period, which lasted for roughly 7,000 years. Scientists agree that environmental shifts and major changes in wildlife forced human groups to develop new methods of survival. On the northern plains, Archaic-era bands learned to drive whole herds of bison over cliffs and use the remains for food, clothing, and tools. A weighted spear-throwing device, called an **atlatl**, let hunters bring down medium-sized game. Archaic peoples also devised nets, hooks, and snares for catching birds, fish, and small animals. By 4,000 years ago, archaic peoples were even using duck decoys in the Great Basin of Utah and Nevada.

Archaic The second long stage of North American habitation, covering about 7,000 years, from roughly 8,000 B.C.E. to 1000 B.C.E. (or from 10,000 to 3,000 years ago). During this period, inhabitants adapted to diverse local environments, gathering plants and hunting smaller animals than during the previous Paleo-Indian period.

Atlatl A weighted, handheld device that enabled early Native Americans to throw spears with added power and velocity.

Though genetically similar, these far-flung bands of Archaic Indians developed diverse cultures as they adapted to very different landscapes and environments. Nothing illustrates this diversity more clearly than speech. A few early languages branched into numerous language families, then divided further into hundreds of separate tongues. Similar cultural variations emerged in everything from diet and shelter to folklore and spiritual beliefs.

The Rise of Maize Agriculture

One condition remained common to all the various Archaic American groups, despite their emerging regional differences: they all lacked domesticated animals. Archaic Indians, like their Asian forebears, did possess dogs, and settlers in the Andes domesticated the llama over 5,000 years ago. But horses, camels, cattle, sheep, goats, and pigs were all absent; no mammals existing in the Americas could readily be made to provide humans with milk, meat, hides, and hauling power.

Although their prospects for domesticating animals were severely limited, early Americans had many more options when it came to the domestication of plants. Humans managed to domesticate plants independently in five different areas around the world, and three of those regions were located in the Americas. First, across parts of South America, inhabitants learned to cultivate root crops of potatoes and manioc (also known as cassava, which yields a nutritious starch). Second, in **Mesoamerica** (modern-day Mexico and Central America), people gradually brought squash, beans, and maize (corn) under cultivation—three foods that complement one another effectively in dietary terms. In a third region, eastern North America, Indians at dozens of Archaic sites were raising squash and sunflowers as early as 4,000 years ago.

Maize agriculture, unique to the Americas, became a crucial ingredient for the growth of complex societies, but its development and diffusion took time. Unlike wheat, the Eurasian cereal crop which offered a high yield from the start, maize took thousands of years of cultivation to evolve into an extremely productive food source.

When it came to mastering maize agriculture, the differences between Mesoamerica and North America proved substantial. Southwestern Indians began growing thumb-sized ears of maize only about 3,000 years ago (at a time of increasing rainfall), well after the crop had taken hold in Mesoamerica. More than a thousand years later, maize reached eastern North America. There, sunflowers and squash were already providing supplemental food sources for communities that subsisted primarily by hunting and gathering. Maize adapted slowly to the cooler woodland climate and shorter growing season, but gradually the crop became central to eastern agriculture during the first millennium C.E.

In Mesoamerica, meanwhile, maize cultivation had already paved the way for several powerful cultures. The earliest—the Olmec—emerged in the lowlands along the southwestern edge of the Gulf of Mexico about 3,000 years ago. Their name meant "those who live in the land of rubber," for they had learned how to turn the milky juice of several plants into an unusual elastic substance. The Olmec grew maize and manioc in abundance, and their surplus of food supported a hierarchical society. They built large burial mounds and pyramids, revered the jaguar in their religion, developed a complex calendar, and played a distinctive game with a large ball of solid rubber. Since they traded widely with people across Mesoamerica, they passed on these cultural traits, which reappeared later in other societies in the region.

Olmec traders, traveling by coastal canoe, may even have encountered and influenced the Poverty Point culture that existed in northeastern Louisiana 4,200 to 2,700 years ago. The Poverty Point culture, with a trade network on the lower Mississippi River and its tributaries, stands as a mysterious precursor to the mound-building societies of the Mississippi Valley that emerged much later. Remnants of these more extensive Mississippian cultures still existed when newcomers from Europe arrived to stay, around 1500. In many parts of North America, smaller and less stratified tribal cultures remained intact well into the era of European colonization. To subsist, they combined hunting for a variety of animals with gathering and processing local plant foods.

Here

1.1

1.2

1.3

1.4

1.5

Mesoamerica The transitional region between North and South America, composed of Mexico and Central America.

A Thousand Years of Change: 500 to 1500

1.2 In the millennium before Columbus, what evidence exists for non-local trade in North America?

The millennium stretching from the fifth century to the explorations of Columbus in the fifteenth century witnessed dramatic and far-reaching changes in the separate world of the Americas. In the warm and temperate regions on both sides of the equator, empires rose and fell as maize agriculture and elaborate irrigation systems provided food surpluses, allowing the creation of cities and the emergence of hierarchical societies.

On the coast of Peru, the expansive Inca empire emerged in the 1400s, building on previous societies. Inca emperors, ruling from the capital at Cuzco, prompted the construction of a vast road system throughout the Peruvian Andes. Stonemasons built large storage facilities at provincial centers to hold food for garrisons of soldiers and to store tribute items such as gold and feathers destined for the capital. Until the empire's fall in the 1530s, officials leading pack trains of llamas ferried goods to and from Cuzco along mountainous roadways.

Similarly, Mesoamerica also saw a series of impressive civilizations—from the Maya to the Aztec—in the millennium spanning 500 to 1500 in the Western calendar. Developments in North America in the same millennium were very different but bear enough resemblance to patterns in Mesoamerica to raise difficult questions about early contacts. Did significant migrations northward from Mesoamerica ever take place? And if not, were there substantial trade links at times, allowing certain materials, techniques, ideas, and seeds to reach North American peoples? Or did the continent's distinctive societies, such as the Anasazi in the Southwest and the Cahokia mound builders on the Mississippi River, develop almost entirely independently?

Valleys of the Sun: The Mesoamerican Empires

In Mesoamerica, the Maya and the Aztec established rich empires where worship of the sun was central to their religious beliefs. Mayan culture flourished between 300 and 900. The Maya controlled a domain stretching from the lowlands of the Yucatan peninsula to the highlands of what is now southern Mexico, Guatemala, Honduras, and El Salvador. They derived their elaborate calendar—a 52-year cycle made up of 20-day months—and many other aspects of their culture from the earlier Olmec, but they devised their own distinctive civilization. The Maya built huge stone temples and held ritual bloodletting ceremonies to appease their gods. Recently, researchers have deciphered the complex pictographs, or glyphs, that appear throughout Mayan art.

The Maya declined rapidly after 750, and dominance in Mesoamerica moved farther west, where great cities had arisen in central Mexico. The people who constructed the metropolis of Teotihuacan in the Mexican highlands remain an enigma. They appear to have traded with the Maya and perhaps with the Olmec before that. They laid out their immense city in a grid, dominated by the 200-foot Pyramid of the Sun. By 500, the city held more than 100,000 inhabitants, making it one of the largest in the world. But Teotihuacan's society declined fast, for unknown reasons, succeeded first by the Toltec and then by the Aztec.

The Aztec (or Mexica) had migrated to the central Valley of Mexico from the north in the twelfth century. Looked down upon at first by the local people, they swiftly rose to power through strategic alliances and military skill. According to legend, the Aztec's war god instructed their priests to locate the place where a great eagle perched on a cactus. They found such a spot, on a swampy island in Lake Texcoco. By the 1400s, the Aztec had transformed the island into Tenochtitlan, an imposing urban center, located on the site of modern Mexico City.

The impressive city of Tenochtitlan, surrounded by Lake Texcoco and linked to shore by causeways, became the Aztec capital. Its architecture imitated the ruined temple city of Teotihuacan, which lay 35 miles to the north. The Aztec also adopted many other features of the cultures they had displaced. They used the cyclical 52-year Mesoamerican calendar, and they worshipped the great god Quetzalcoatl, the plumed serpent associated with wind and revered by the Toltec, their predecessors in the Valley of Mexico.

Eager to expand their empire, the Aztec launched fierce wars against neighboring lands. But their primary objective was not to kill enemies or gain more territory. Instead, Aztec warriors demanded tribute and took prisoners from the people they subdued. They then sacrificed numerous captives at pyramid temples to placate the gods. These deities, they believed, would in turn protect them as they conducted further wars of capture, leading to more tribute and sacrifices.

Like the Inca of Peru, the Aztec imposed harsh treatment on the peoples they conquered, extracting heavy annual taxes. This ruthless policy caused outlying provinces to resent Aztec authority and made the centralized empire vulnerable to external attack. When a foreign assault prompted the empire's downfall in the early sixteenth century, the challenge came from a direction Aztec priests and generals could not predict.

The Anasazi: Chaco Canyon and Mesa Verde

The great urban centers of Peru and Mesoamerica had no counterparts farther north. The peoples inhabiting North America in the millennium before Columbus never developed the levels of **social stratification**, urban dynamism, architectural grandeur, astronomical study, or intensive corn agriculture that characterized the Maya, Inca, or Aztec. Yet elements of all these traits appeared in North America, especially in the Southwest and the Mississippi Valley, with the emergence of increasingly settled societies and widening circles of exchange.

In the North American Southwest, three identifiably different cultures were already well established by the year 500. The Mogollon occupied the dry, mountainous regions of eastern Arizona and southern New Mexico. These expert potters lived in sunken pit houses that were cool in summer and warm in winter. The Hohokam, their neighbors to the west in south-central Arizona, constructed extensive canal and floodgate systems to irrigate their fields from the Gila and Salt rivers. Farther north, where Utah and Colorado meet Arizona and New Mexico, lived the people remembered as the Anasazi, or "ancient ones."

By 750, the Anasazi inhabited aboveground houses of masonry or adobe clustered around a circular ceremonial room dug into the earth. They entered this sunken religious chamber, known as a kiva, by descending a ladder through the roof. The climb back up symbolized the initial ascent of humans into the Upper World from below. European explorers later used the Spanish word for town, *pueblo*, to describe the Anasazi's multiroom and multistory dwellings.

Beginning in the 850s, Chaco Canyon in northwest New Mexico emerged as the hub of the Anasazi world. Researchers at this site in the San Juan River basin have identified a north–south traffic in turquoise, highly prized in both Mexico and the Southwest. Wide, straight roads radiating out from Chaco let builders haul hundreds of thousands of logs for use as roof beams in the nine great pueblos that still dot the canyon. The largest, Pueblo Bonito, rises five stories high in places and has 600 rooms arranged in a vast semicircle.

After 1130, a prolonged drought gripped the area, and the turquoise workshops of Chaco Canyon fell silent. Gradually—with populations growing, the climate worsening, and competition for resources stiffening—many Anasazi headed north and moved into sheltered cliff dwellings. The remarkable Cliff Palace at Mesa Verde in southwestern Colorado has 220 rooms and 23 kivas. Reached only by ladders and steep trails, these pueblos offered protection from enemies and shelter from the scorching summer sun. When another prolonged drought (1276–1299) forced the Anasazi to move once again, survivors dispersed south into lands later occupied by the Hopi, Zuni, and Rio Grande peoples.

The Mississippians: Cahokia and Moundville

Earlier, in the Mississippi Valley, the Hopewell people had prospered for half a millennium before 500 C.E. (in the era of the Roman Empire in Europe). The Hopewell lived mainly in Ohio and Illinois. But their network of trade extended over much of the continent. Hopewell burial sites have yielded pipestone and flint from the Missouri River valley, copper and silver from Lake Superior, mica and quartz from Appalachia, seashells and shark teeth from Florida, and artwork made from Rocky Mountain obsidian and grizzly-bear teeth.

Hopewell trading laid the groundwork for larger mound-building societies, known as the Mississippian cultures, that emerged in the Mississippi Valley and the Southeast in roughly the same centuries as the great civilizations of Mesoamerica and the Anasazi in the Southwest. The Mississippian tradition developed gradually after 500. Then, after 900, the tradition flourished broadly for six centuries.

Shifts in technology and agriculture facilitated the rise of the Mississippians. Bows and arrows, long used in Arctic regions of North America but little known elsewhere, became widespread in the eastern woodlands around 700. At the same time, maize underwent a transformation from a marginal oddity to a central staple crop. Across the East, food supplies expanded as Native American communities planted corn in the rich

Social stratification The schematic arrangement of a population into a ranking of horizontal social layers (strata), or an identifiable hierarchy of classes within a society.

bottomland soil along the region's many rivers. With greater productivity, commercial and religious elites took advantage of farmers and asserted stronger control over the community's increasing resources.

Mississippian mound-building centers have been found as far apart as Spiro, in eastern Oklahoma, and Etowah, in northern Georgia. The largest complex was at Cahokia in the 25-mile floodplain below where the Illinois and Missouri rivers flow into the Mississippi. On Cahokia Creek, near East St. Louis, Illinois, dozens of rectangular, flat-topped temple mounds still remain after almost a thousand years. The biggest mound—indeed, the largest ancient earthwork in North America—rises 100 feet in four separate levels, covering 16 acres and using nearly 22 million cubic feet of earth. Nearby, residents erected 48 posts in a huge circle, 410 feet in diameter. This creation, now called Woodhenge after England's Stonehenge, functioned as a calendar to mark the progression of the sun throughout each year.

Cahokia's mounds rose quickly in the decades after 1050. A succession of powerful leaders reorganized the vicinity's small, isolated villages into a strong regional chiefdom that controlled towns on both sides of the Mississippi River. These towns provided the chiefdom's centralized elite with food, labor, and goods for trading. Around 1100, the population of Cahokia exceeded 15,000 people. It then waned steadily over the next two centuries as the unstable hierarchy lost its sway over nearby villages. As Cahokia declined, other regional chiefdoms rose along other rivers. The most notable appeared at Moundville in west-central Alabama, 15 miles south of modern Tuscaloosa. The site, with more than 20 flat-topped mounds, became a dominant ceremonial center in the thirteenth century. But by 1400, a century before the appearance of Europeans, Moundville's Mississippian elites had started to lose their power.

✳ Explore the Topic   Social Hierarchies in America Before Columbus

The most striking Mississippian earthwork to survive is the enigmatic Serpent Mound, built in the eleventh century by the Fort Ancient people in southern Ohio. The snake (holding an egg in its mouth) has links to astronomy because its curves are aligned toward key positions of the sun. The serpent may even represent Halley's Comet, which blazed in the heavens in 1066. Completely uncoiled, the earthwork would measure more than a quarter mile in length. What do large-scale earthworks, that can only be seen in their entirety from above, suggest regarding Mississippian beliefs about the sky?

Linking the Continents

1.3 Why is the first voyage of Columbus in 1492 still viewed as such an earth-changing event?

E stimates vary widely, but probably around one-sixth of the world's population—as many as 60 to 70 million people—resided in the Americas when Columbus arrived in 1492. Most of them lived in the tropical zone near the equator, but roughly one-tenth of the hemisphere's population (six to seven million) dwelled in North America, spread from coast to coast.

We cannot rule out the appearance in America of ancient ocean travelers on occasion. Around 400, Polynesian mariners sailed their double-hulled canoes from the Marquesas Islands in the South Pacific to the Hawaiian **archipelago**. Conceivably, in the millennium before 1500, one or two boats from Africa, Ireland, Polynesia, China, or Japan sailed—or were blown—to the American mainland. But any survivors of such a journey would have had little genetic or cultural impact, for no sustained back-and-forth contact between the societies occurred. Even the seafaring Norse from Scandinavia, known as Vikings, never established a lasting colony. Their brief settlement at L'Anse aux Meadows in northern Newfoundland a thousand years ago is now well documented, but they remained only a few years at this coastal site. Native American societies, therefore, knew nothing of the people, plants, animals, and microbes of the Eastern Hemisphere.

Archipelago A group of islands, such as the Hawaiian archipelago.

America's near isolation ended dramatically, beginning in the late fifteenth century, after innovations in deep-sea sailing opened the world's oceans as a new frontier for human exploration. Chinese sailors in the North Pacific or Portuguese mariners in the South Atlantic could well have been the first outsiders to establish ongoing contact with the peoples of the Western Hemisphere. Instead, it was Christopher Columbus, an Italian navigator in the service of Spain, who became the agent of this sweeping change. He encountered the Americas by accident and misinterpreted what he had found. But his chance encounter with a separate realm sparked new patterns of human migration, cultural transfer, and ecological exchange that would reshape the modern world.

Oceanic Travel: The Norse and the Chinese

Scandinavian settlers had colonized Ireland in the 830s and Iceland in the 870s. A century later, these seafarers—led by Erik the Red—reached Greenland in the 980s. When Erik's son Leif learned that Norse mariners blown off course had sighted land farther west, he sailed from Greenland to the North American coast. Here he explored a region near the Gulf of St. Lawrence that he named Vinland.

Around 1000, Leif Eriksson's relatives directed several return voyages to Vinland, where Norse Vikings built an outpost. The tiny colony of 160 people, including women and children, lived and grazed livestock in Vinland for several years until native peoples drove them away. The Greenlanders returned occasionally to cut timber, and they traded with inhabitants of northeastern Canada for generations. But, by 1450, Norse settlements in Greenland had died out completely.

Whether sailors in Europe knew much about Norse exploits in the North Atlantic remains a mystery. What Europeans did know, vaguely, was the existence of the distant Chinese Empire. They called the realm Cathay, a term used by Italian merchant Marco Polo, who journeyed from Venice across Asia along the fabled Silk Road in the 1270s. Polo returned to Italy in 1292 to publish his *Travels*, an account of adventures in China during the reign of Kublai Khan.

Marco Polo told of many things unknown to Europeans, including rocks that burned like wood (coal) and spices that preserved meat. Asian spices such as nutmeg, cinnamon, pepper, ginger, and cloves, if they could be obtained, would offer new preservatives. When renewed Islamic power in the Middle East cut off the Silk Road to Cathay, Europeans searched for other ways to reach that far-off region.

The desire to obtain oriental spices at their source fueled European oceanic exploration, leading eventually to the transformation of the Americas. Yet it was China, not Europe, that first mastered ocean sailing on a large scale. Chinese strength in overseas exploration and trade reached its height in the early fifteenth century under Admiral Zheng He (pronounced "Jung Huh"). Between 1405 and 1433, this brilliant officer led seven large fleets to the Indian Ocean, sailing as far as East Africa. His immense treasure ships, 400 feet long and equipped with cannon, carried strange items—even giraffes—home to Asia.

Then, abruptly, China turned away from the sea, passing up its chance to become the first global maritime power and to play a leading role in shaping the destiny of North America. Within a century of Zheng He's accomplishments, the royal court grew dismissive of foreign trade and turned inward. Chinese officials destroyed the log books of earlier voyages and curtailed production of oceangoing vessels. Instead of powerful China on the Pacific, it was tiny Portugal, overlooking the Atlantic, that emerged as the leader in maritime innovation and exploration in the fifteenth century.

Portugal and the Beginnings of Globalization

Geography and religious zeal helped to spur Portugal's unlikely rise to world prominence. Its strategic location exposed the tiny maritime country to the ongoing conflict between Christianity and Islam. The religion founded by Muhammad (born at Mecca in 570) had spread rapidly across North Africa from Arabia. By the eighth century, followers of Islam (known as Muslims, Moslems, or Moors) had crossed the Straits of Gibraltar to establish a kingdom in southern Spain. Centuries later, Spanish and Portuguese Christians rallied to force Islam out of the **Iberian** peninsula—a campaign that concluded in 1492—and to join other militant Europeans in fighting against Islamic power in the Middle East.

When Christian crusades to the Holy Land failed to defeat the Muslims and reopen overland trade routes to China, European strategists dreamed of skirting Africa by sea to reach Asia. The Portuguese were well positioned to lead this flanking movement around the areas under Muslim control. And if no such oceanic route to Asia existed, some speculated that Portuguese exploration south by sea still might provide links to a strong Christian ally. Fanciful rumors persisted regarding a wealthy black Christian ruler somewhere in Africa known as Prester John.

Intellectual and economic motives also existed for Portuguese ventures beyond the Sahara Desert, along the coast of sub-Saharan Africa. Such journeys, presenting new challenges in shipbuilding and navigation, could boost European knowledge of the unknown and open new markets. The first step involved an investment of leadership and resources, before early efforts could bear fruit and give the exploration process a momentum of it own.

Prince Henry of Portugal (1394–1460) provided these initial ingredients. In 1415, the young prince—later honored as "Henry the Navigator"—had crossed the Straits of Gibraltar to fight Muslims at Ceuta in North Africa. Committed to the campaign against Islam, Henry then waged a religiously inspired crusade-at-sea, building his headquarters at Sagres in southwest Portugal. From there, his sailors launched a far-reaching revolution in human communication and trade, perhaps the most momentous early step in a **globalization** process that continues to the present day.

Henry's innovative ships, known as caravels, pushed south along the African coast. Their narrow hulls were well suited for ocean sailing, and they used triangular lateen sails. This sail design, borrowed by Mediterranean sailors from Arab boats on the Red Sea, helped mariners maneuver against headwinds. Henry's experts at Sagres drew on the work of Jewish cartographers to develop state-of-the-art charts, astronomical tables, and navigational instruments. By the 1440s, his captains had mastered the winds and currents near West Africa. They initiated trade in gold and ivory, and, most ominously, they began buying African slaves and selling them in Europe. But when Henry died in 1460, his mariners had only sailed as far as what is now Sierra Leone.

Iberian Relating to Europe's Iberian peninsula, the location of Spain and Portugal.

Globalization The process of integration—economic, but also cultural—of different parts of the world into a more unified system of trade and communication.

📖 **Read the Document**   **Voyage from Lisbon to the Island of São Thomé (1540)**

Prince Henry of Portugal rarely went to sea himself. Instead, he established a base at Sagres, overlooking the Atlantic Ocean. From here, beginning in 1418, he sent mariners south along the African coast. They quickly laid claim to the islands of the eastern Atlantic, and by the 1440s they had initiated trade along the West African coast, carrying gold and slaves back to Portugal. How might the rugged coastline of Portugal's southern tip have prepared Henry's mariners to maneuver successfully against the headwinds off coastal Africa?

Looking for the Indies: Da Gama and Columbus

During the 1480s, following a war with Spain, the Portuguese renewed their African designs. In 1482, they erected a trading fort called Elmina Castle on the Gold Coast (modern Ghana) to guard against Spanish competition and to support exploration toward the east. Finally, in 1487, Bartolomeu Dias rounded the southernmost tip of Africa, around the Cape of Good Hope, proving that a link existed between the Atlantic and Indian oceans. The Portuguese could now sail to India and tap into the rich spice trade. Success came a decade later with the voyage (1497–1499) of Vasco da Gama. When his ship returned from India laden with pepper and cinnamon, the Portuguese had at last opened a southeastern sea route to the silk and spice markets of the East.

Meanwhile, the rulers of rival Spain gambled on finding a profitable *westward* route to the Indies. In 1492, King Ferdinand and Queen Isabella finally succeeded in driving Islam from their realm by military means. The monarchs imposed Christian orthodoxy and forced Jews into exile. That same year, they agreed to sponsor an Atlantic voyage by an Italian-born navigator, Christopher Columbus. Leaving Spain with ninety men aboard three small vessels, Columbus headed for the Canary Islands and then sailed due west on September 6. After a voyage of three or four weeks, he expected to encounter the island of Cipangu (Japan), which Marco Polo had mentioned, or to reach the coast of Asia.

Why these huge misunderstandings? The mariner made several crucial mistakes. Like other Europeans, Columbus knew the world was round, not flat. He also accepted the idea of the ancient geographer Ptolemy that by using north–south lines, one could divide the globe into 360 degrees of longitude. But he questioned Ptolemy's estimate that each degree measures 50 nautical miles at the equator. (Each actually measures 60 miles.) Instead, Columbus accepted an alternative figure of 45 miles, making the circumference of his theoretical globe 25 percent smaller than the real distance around the earth. Besides *under*estimating the world's circumference, he compounded his error by *over*estimating two other crucial distances: the breadth of the Eurasian landmass and the extent of Japan's separation from China. The first distance is actually 130 degrees of longitude, and the second is 20. Columbus used authorities who suggested 225 and 30 degrees, respectively. His estimates placed Japan 105 degrees closer to Europe, at the longitude that runs through eastern Lake Superior and western Cuba.

Early on October 12, the distressed sailors finally sighted a small island in the Bahamas, naming it San Salvador after their Christian savior. The inhabitants proved welcoming, and Columbus recorded pleasure over the "gold which they wear hanging from their noses. But I wish to go and see if I can find the island of Cipangu." He did find a large and beautiful island (Cuba, not Cipangu), and he estimated that the Asian mainland of the Great Khan was only "a 10 days' journey" farther west. He claimed a nearby island as La Isla Española, the Spanish island, or Hispaniola (current-day Haiti and the Dominican Republic). He noted stories of hostile islanders farther south called Caribs, or Caniba, who were said to devour their enemies. "I repeat," he asserted, "the Caniba are no other than the people of the Grand Khan." (Upon hearing of these fierce Caribs, Europeans soon fashioned the word *cannibal* and named the region the Caribbean.)

Bolstered by these encounters, the explorers returned hastily across the Atlantic on a more northerly route. They weathered a horrendous winter storm to reach Spain in March 1493. Columbus told the Spanish court that he had touched the Indies off the Asian coast, and he displayed several natives he called "Indians" to prove it. His three later voyages did not shake this belief, which he clung to until his death in 1506. Columbus had not reached the lands he sought, but his exploits would have immediate and extraordinary consequences.

In the Wake of Columbus: Competition and Exchange

Within months of Columbus's return, the pope in Rome issued a papal bull, or decree. This pronouncement, titled *Inter Caetera*, viewed the whole world as the rightful inheritance of Christianity. It brashly divided the entire earth between two Christian powers, Spain and Portugal, by drawing a line down through the Atlantic Ocean from the North Pole to the South Pole. West of the line, the Spanish alone could continue to seek access to Asia. East of the line, on the other half of the globe, Portugal would have a monopoly. The two Iberian powers affirmed this division of the earth in the Treaty of Tordesillas (1494).

European navigators and cartographers quickly began to comprehend the geographic reality that Columbus had so thoroughly misunderstood. When Amerigo

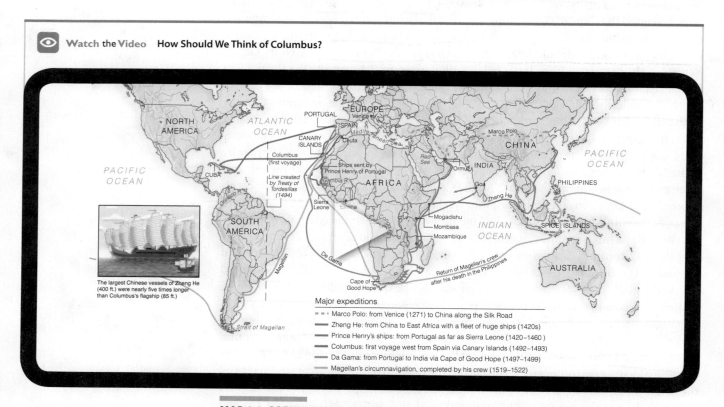

MAP 1.1 OPENING NEW OCEAN PATHWAYS AROUND THE GLOBE, 1420–1520 In the 1420s, ships from Portugal and China explored opposite coasts of Africa. But China withdrew from oceanic trade, and European mariners competed to explore the world by sea. Within a century, Magellan's ship had circled the globe for Spain. The colonization in North America is a chapter in this larger saga of global exploration.

✳ Explore Global Exploration on MyHistoryLab

HOW DID GLOBAL EXPLORATION CHANGE THE OLD AND NEW WORLDS?

Beginning in the 1400s, European explorers searched for sea routes to the silk and spice markets of Asia. Sailing west, Columbus encountered the Americas, where diverse societies existed that were unknown to Europe. Many of these cultures were large, complex, and interconnected. Over the next two centuries, Europeans attempted to conquer these Native American societies by force, set up colonies, and establish trade ties, connecting the Old World (Europe, Asia, and Africa) with the New World (the Americas). This Age of Global Exploration had a profound impact on world history and was especially destructive to societies in the Americas, as vast numbers of people in the New World succumbed to Old World diseases.

This illustration (c. 1500) of Italian origin is said to show the first European representation of people in the New World.

COMPARISON OF THE ESTIMATED PRECONTACT POPULATION IN THE AMERICAS (c. 1500) AND IN EUROPE'S FOUR EARLY COLONIAL POWERS

The Americas
(60–70 million)

Colonial Powers
(29.7 million)

Note: Each figure represents a million people.

*Colonial Powers: England, Spain, Portugal, France.

KEY QUESTIONS   Use **MyHistoryLab** *Explorer* to **answer** these **questions:**

Analysis ▶▶▶ *What global trade routes existed in the Old World prior to the Age of Global Exploration?*

Map the late medieval trade contacts between Europe, Asia, and North Africa.

Comparison ▶▶▶ *In what ways were societies in the Americas interrelated before the arrival of the Europeans?*

Map the economic interconnectedness of the New World.

Consequence ▶▶▶ *How did the new transatlantic trade connect different parts of the world?*

Map the integration of the Old and New Worlds into a single trading network.

Vespucci, another Italian in the service of Spain, crossed the South Atlantic in 1499, he described what he saw not as part of Asia but as a *Mundus Novus*, or New World. European geographers wrote his name, *America*, across their maps. Meanwhile, a third Italian navigator—John Cabot (or Caboto)—obtained a license from the English king, Henry VII, to probe the North Atlantic for access to Cathay. In 1497, Cabot sailed west from Bristol across the Atlantic to Newfoundland and perhaps Nova Scotia. Clearly, the ventures of Columbus had sparked widespread excitement and curiosity in European ports, and increasing knowledge fueled greater transatlantic contact.

After thousands of years, the long separation of the hemispheres had been broken. The destinies of the world's most divergent continents swiftly became linked. Those links fostered human migrations of an unprecedented scale. With European ships came transfers of seeds and viruses, bugs and birds, plants and animals that forever reshaped the world. Scholars call this phenomenon the **Columbian Exchange**. The term underscores the two-way nature of the flow. West across the Atlantic went horses, cows, sheep, pigs, chickens, honeybees, and important foods such as sugar cane, coffee, bananas, peaches, lemons, and oranges. But Europeans' westbound ships also carried devastating diseases unknown in the Americas, such as smallpox, measles, malaria, and whooping cough. East in the opposite direction traveled corn, potatoes, pumpkins, chili peppers, tobacco, cacao, pineapples, sunflowers, turkeys—and perhaps syphilis. The planet and all its inhabitants would never be the same again.

Columbian Exchange The significant two-way interchange of plants, animals, microbes, and people that occurred once Christopher Columbus established regular contact by sea between the Eastern and Western Hemispheres. For thousands of years before 1492, despite occasional encounters, these two separate and different "worlds" had remained isolated from each other.

Spain Enters the Americas

1.4 What factors motivated and shaped Spain's rapid intrusion into sixteenth-century America?

Throughout the sixteenth century, European mariners, inspired by the feats of Columbus and da Gama, risked ocean voyaging in hopes of scoring similar successes. Those who survived brought back novelties for consumers, information for geographers, and profits for ship owners. New wealth prompted further investment in exploration, and expanding knowledge awakened cultural changes for both explorers and the people they met. The dynamic European era known as the Renaissance owed much to overseas exploration. Returning mariners brought reports of surprising places and people. Their experiences challenged the inherited wisdom of traditional authorities and put a new premium on rational thought, scientific calculation, and careful observation of the natural world.

In turn, Europe's Renaissance, or rebirth, stimulated ever wider exploration as breakthroughs in technology and navigation yielded practical results. Sailing south around Africa and then east, Portuguese caravels reached China by 1514 and Japan by 1543. Sailing west, Spanish vessels learned first that the Caribbean did not offer a passage to Asia and then in 1522—through Magellan's global voyage—that the ocean beyond America was enormous. In the West Indies, and then elsewhere in the Western Hemisphere, Native Americans began to pay dearly for the exchange that ships from Spain had initiated.

The Devastation of the Indies

Spanish arrival in the West Indies in 1492 triggered widespread ecological and human disaster within decades. Well-armed and eager for quick wealth, the early colonizers brought havoc to the Taino Indians and Caribs who inhabited the islands. The strange newcomers killed and enslaved native peoples and extracted tribute from the survivors in the form of gold panned from streams. Spanish livestock trampled or consumed native gardens, prompting severe food shortages. Worse, European diseases ravaged countless villages. The West Indian population plummeted as island societies totaling more than one million lost nineteen of every twenty people within a generation.

This near-extinction had three consequences. First, when Dominican friars reached Cuba in 1510, these devout missionaries denounced Spanish brutality as sinful. The Indians, they argued, possessed souls that only Christian baptism could save. A

Spanish soldier named Bartholomé de Las Casas, who repented and joined the Dominican order, led the outcry for reform. In his scathing exposé, titled *The Devastation of the Indies*, he opposed genocide and urged conversion.

Second, in response to the steep drop in population, Spanish colonizers began importing slaves from Africa to replace the decimated Indian workforce. The same Christians who bemoaned Native American enslavement (including Las Casas) justified this initiative and overlooked the contradictions. The first importation of Africans came in 1502, following the Portuguese precedent in the Azores.

Third, decimation in the islands prompted the Spanish to intensify their explorations. They sought new sources of Indian labor close at hand, fresh lands to exploit, and easy passageways to the Pacific. They pushed out from the Caribbean in several directions. In 1513, Vasco Núñez de Balboa pressed across the narrow **isthmus** of Panama to glimpse the Pacific. That same year, Juan Ponce de León sailed northwest from Puerto Rico, hoping the nearby peninsula, which he named Florida, would yield new gold and slaves. But Florida's Indians were already familiar with Spanish raiders; they turned Ponce de León away after he claimed the region for Spain.

Isthmus A narrow strip of land connecting two larger land areas (such as the isthmus of Panama).

The Spanish Conquest of the Aztec

By 1519, the Spanish had determined that the Gulf of Mexico offered no easy passage to Asia. They needed fresh alternatives. In Spain, crown officials sought someone to sail

((Read the Document   **Bartolomé de Las Casas, *The Devastation of the Indies* (1565)**

As the Indian population of the Caribbean plummeted in the face of new diseases and exploitation, the Spanish began importing Africans to the New World as slaves. Many were put to work mining precious metals. Here men are forced to dig for gold nuggets beside a mountain stream, then wash them in a tub and dry them over a fire, before handing them to their Spanish master to weigh on his hand-held scale. As Spain was building its empire in the newly discovered lands of the Americas, what factors may have led the Spanish to extract mineral wealth from the continent rather than produce cash crops?

southwest, around the South American continent that Columbus and Vespucci had encountered. For this perilous task, they dispatched a Portuguese navigator named Ferdinand Magellan, who had sailed in the Indian Ocean. On his epic voyage (1519–1522), Magellan located a difficult passage through the tip of South America—now called the Strait of Magellan—and revealed the vast width of the Pacific, which covers one-third of the earth's surface. Warring factions in the Philippines killed Magellan and twenty-seven of his men, but one of his ships made it back to Spain, becoming the first vessel to circumnavigate the globe.

As news of Magellan's voyage raced through Spain in 1522, word also arrived that a Spanish soldier, or *conquistador*, named Hernán Cortés had toppled the gold-rich empire of the Aztec in central Mexico. Like other ambitious conquistadores, Cortés had followed Columbus to the Caribbean. In 1519, hoping to march overland to the Pacific as Balboa had done, Cortés established a base camp at Vera Cruz on Mexico's east coast. He quickly realized he had reached the edge of a powerful empire.

At Tenochtitlan, the Aztec emperor, Moctezuma, reacted with uncertainty to news that bearded strangers aboard "floating islands" had appeared off his coast. If the newcomers' leader was the returning god Quetzalcoatl, the court had to welcome him with the utmost care. The emperor sent basket loads of precious objects encrusted with gold to Cortés's camp. But the elaborate gifts only alerted Cortés and his men to the Aztec's wealth.

Although the Spanish numbered scarcely 600, they had several key advantages over the Aztec. Their guns and horses, unknown in America, terrified the Indians. When Cortés found coastal peoples staggering under heavy Aztec taxes, he recruited them as willing allies. An Indian woman (christened Doña Marina, or La Malinche) acted as his translator and companion. In an aggressive show of force, Cortés marched directly to the capital and seized Moctezuma as his hostage.

The Spanish still faced daunting obstacles, but sickness worked decisively to their advantage. Smallpox was a disease the Aztec had never encountered before, so they lacked any immunity. The European illness reached the mainland with the invading army, and a crushing epidemic swept the Aztec capital in 1521. The disaster let Cortés conquer Tenochtitlan (which he renamed Mexico City) and claim the entire region as New Spain.

Magellan and Cortés Prompt New Searches

Cortés's conquest of Mexico raised Spain's hopes of additional windfalls in the Americas. In 1531, Spanish raiders under Francisco Pizarro set sail from Panama for Peru, with plans to overthrow the Inca empire. Pizarro had limited resources (180 men and 37 horses), but smallpox assisted him, as it had helped Cortés, and his invaders accomplished their mission. Marching overland to Cuzco in 1533, they killed the emperor, Atahualpa, and sacked the mountain capital for the gold it contained. Meanwhile, Cortés dispatched three ships west from Mexico across the Pacific, and one actually reached the Philippines. By the 1560s, Spanish cargo ships, known as galleons, were making the lengthy round trip from Acapulco (on Mexico's west coast) to the Philippines and back across the Pacific.

In 1524, Italian navigator Giovanni da Verrazzano sailed west for the French, hoping to find a swift northern passage from Europe to Asia that was easier than Magellan's arduous southern route. He reached North America near North Carolina's Outer Banks, later cruising north to enter New York harbor before abandoning his search. In 1526, Lucas Vásquez de Ayllón led 500 men and women from the Spanish Caribbean to the Santee River region (near present-day Georgetown, South Carolina) to settle and explore. But Ayllón fell sick and died, and the colony proved short-lived.

In 1528, a rival of Cortés and Ayllón named Pánfilo de Narváez launched another ill-fated expedition from Cuba, landing near Florida's Tampa Bay. Narváez intended to bring wealth and glory to his 400 soldiers, but disease, hunger, and Indian hostilities plagued the party's journey along the Gulf Coast. Only four men—three Spanish and one North African black named Esteban—survived to make an extended trek on foot across the Southwest from Galveston Bay to Mexico City. Their leader, Àlvar Núñez Cabeza de Vaca, wrote about the remarkable odyssey after he returned to Spain in 1537. Scholars now recognize Cabeza de Vaca's *Relation* (1542) as an early classic in North American literature.

Interpreting History

"These Gods That We Worship Give Us Everything We Need"

"As for our **gods,** we will **die** before **giving** up **serving** and **worshiping** them."

T hree years after Cortés captured Tenochtitlan in central Mexico, a dozen missionaries from the Franciscan Order arrived in the city to preach Christianity to the conquered Aztec. In several meetings with principal elders and priests, they explained their beliefs and laid out their plans through a translator. Similar talks would take place throughout America in later generations.

No transcript of the 1524 conversations exists, but another Franciscan, the famous preserver of Aztec culture Bernardino de Sahagún, gathered recollections of the encounter from both sides and reconstructed the dialogue. He published his version in 1564, creating parallel texts in Spanish and Nahuatl, the Aztec language. "Having understood the reasoning and speech of the twelve, Sahagún reports, the city leaders "became greatly agitated and fell into a great sadness and fear, offering no response." The next morning, they requested a complete repetition of the unsettling message. "Having heard this, one of the principal lords arose, asked the indulgence of the twelve, . . . and made the following long speech."

The Aztecs portrayed Quetzalcoatl, their god of knowledge and patron of priests, as a feathered serpent. Here, he confronts his rival brother, Tezcatlipoca, a powerful god of war and sorcery, who is often shown with a mirror and an obsidian knife. Why would Aztecs vow to die before giving up their worship of these gods?

Our lords, leading personages of much esteem, you are very welcome to our lands and towns. . . . We have heard the words that you have brought us of the One who gives us life and being. And we have heard with admiration the words of the Lord of the World which he has sent here for love of us, and also you have brought us the book of celestial and divine words.

You have told us that we do not know the One who gives us life and being, who is Lord of the heavens and of the earth. You also say that those we worship are not gods. This way of speaking is entirely new to us, and very scandalous. We are frightened by this way of speaking because our forebears who engendered and governed us never said anything like this.

On the contrary, they left us this our custom of worshiping our gods. . . . They taught us how to honor them. And they

taught us all the ceremonies and sacrifices that we make. They told us that . . . we were beholden to them, to be theirs and to serve countless centuries before the sun began to shine and before there was daytime. They said that these gods that we worship give us everything we need for our physical existence: maize, beans, chia seeds, etc. We appeal to them for the rain to make the things of the earth grow.

These our gods are the source of great riches and delights, all of which belong to them. . . . They live in very delightful places where there are always flowers, vegetation, and great freshness, a place . . . where there is never hunger, poverty, or illness. . . . There has never been a time remembered when they were not worshiped, honored, and esteemed. . . .

It would be a fickle, foolish thing for us to destroy the most ancient laws and customs left by the first inhabitants of this land. . . . We are accustomed to them and we have them impressed on our hearts. . . . How could you leave the poor elderly among us bereft of that in which they have been raised throughout their lives? Watch out that we do not incur the wrath of our gods. Watch out that the common people do not rise up against us if we were to tell them that the gods they have always understood to be such are not gods at all.

It is best, our lords, to act on this matter very slowly, with great deliberation. We are not satisfied or convinced by what you have told us, nor do we understand or give credit to what has been said of our gods. . . . All of us together feel that it is enough to have lost, enough that the power and royal jurisdiction have been taken from us. As for our gods, we will die before giving up serving and worshiping them. This is our determination; do what you will.

Questions for Discussion

1. Why would the Aztec priests fear an uprising of the common people under these circumstances? How would you respond to a similar situation?

2. As suggested near the end of this chapter, a similar religious confrontation was taking place in Europe in 1524, during the early years of the Protestant Reformation. Contrast and compare these two situations.

SOURCE: Kenneth Mills and William B. Taylor, *Colonial Spanish America: A Documentary History*. Wilmington, DE: Scholarly Resources, 1998, pp. 21–22.

Three New Views of North America

Even before Cabeza de Vaca published his narrative, Europeans initiated three more expeditions into North America. Each probed a separate region of the continent, hoping to gauge the land's dimensions, assess its peoples, and claim its resources. Together, the three enterprises made 1534 to 1543 the most extraordinary decade in the early European exploration of North America, for Native Americans and newcomers alike.

In the Northeast, Frenchman Jacques Cartier visited the Gulf of St. Lawrence in 1534 and bartered for furs with the Micmac Indians. He returned the next year and penetrated southwest up the St. Lawrence River into Canada. (The name comes from *kanata*, the Huron–Iroquois word for "village.") After a friendly reception at the large Indian town of Hochelaga near modern Montreal, the French returned downriver to camp at Stadacona, the future site of Quebec. Following a hard winter, in which he lost twenty-five men to scurvy, the explorer and his remaining crew sailed for France.

Cartier came back to Quebec in 1541, seeking precious minerals and signs of a water passage farther west to the Pacific Ocean. He found neither, but a colonizing expedition followed in 1542, led by a nobleman named Roberval. It contained several hundred French settlers, including women for the first time. But again, scurvy and cold took a heavy toll at the Quebec campsite, and the weakened colony withdrew after a single winter. Despite a decade of effort, the French still had not established a beachhead in the New World. Nevertheless, they had demonstrated their resolve to challenge Spain's exclusive claim to American lands.

The Spanish, meanwhile, launched two intrusions of their own—one in the Southeast and one in the Southwest. News of Pizarro's 1533 triumph over the Incas in Peru helped renew the search for wealthy kingdoms to conquer. In 1537, Emperor Charles V of Spain granted one hardened veteran of the Peruvian campaign—Hernando de Soto—the right to explore in and beyond Florida, establishing a personal domain for himself. The conquistador spent most of his fortune assembling a force of more than 600 soldiers that reached Tampa Bay in 1539. The enterprise included several women and priests, along with scores of servants and African slaves, plus 200 horses. De Soto had also brought along a herd of 300 pigs that multiplied rapidly and provided food during the long march through the interior.

Over the next four years, de Soto's party traveled through parts of ten southern states. They hoped to find a city as wealthy as Cuzco in Peru or Tenochtitlan in Mexico. Instead, they encountered only scattered villages. Towns that refused to provide the intruders with porters or guides met with brutal reprisals that included the use of attack dogs. At Mabila, near modern-day Selma, Alabama, de Soto's mounted army, brandishing swords and lances, killed several thousand Native Americans who had dared to attack them with bows and arrows. Still, Spanish frustrations grew due to difficult terrain, stiff Indian resistance, and failure to find riches. After exploring beyond the Mississippi River, de Soto died of a fever in 1542. His disheartened followers escaped downstream to the Gulf of Mexico the next year, leaving epidemic sickness in their wake.

At the same time, another encounter was unfolding in the Southwest. In Mexico, speculation about gold in the north had intensified after the appearance of Cabeza de Vaca. His African companion, Esteban, guided a reconnaissance party north in 1539. Esteban was killed by the Zuni Indians, but exaggerated accounts of the region's pueblos prompted rumors about seven golden cities, including two named Cibola and Quivira. The next year, aspiring conquistador Francisco Vásquez de Coronado set out from northern Mexico to reach these wealthy towns before de Soto could. He left his post as a frontier governor and assembled a huge expedition with more than 300 Spanish adventurers and 1,000 Indian allies. However, his grandiose expectations were quickly dashed. The pueblos of the Zuni, he reported, "are very good houses, three and four and five stories high," but the fabled "Seven Cities are seven little villages."

Spanish newcomers imposed a heavy burden on the Pueblo Indians, demanding food and burning helpless towns. Desperate to get rid of Coronado, the Pueblo recruited a Plains Indian to lead the Spaniards to some far-off Quivira, hoping men and horses would starve to death. In the spring of 1541, the Indian guided Coronado's

📖 **Read the Document**   Jacques Cartier: First Contact with the Indians (1534)

1.1

1.2

1.3

1.4

1.5

Two decades after Verrazzano's explorations, this 1547 chart shows the early claims of France in North America. It depicts the men and women of Roberval's short-lived colonizing expedition as they disembarked in Canada in 1542, watched by Native Americans. Perhaps to feature the large St. Lawrence River, the European mapmaker put North at the bottom and South at the top. Hence, the Atlantic coast seems upside down to our eyes, with Florida appearing in the upper right-hand corner. Does Roberval's band of colonists and explorers seem particularly well suited for creating a New World settlement?

party northeast onto the Great Plains, past endless herds of buffalo. But mighty Quivira proved to be only a Wichita Indian village in what is now central Kansas. The irate Spanish strangled their deceitful guide and made their way back south to New Spain. As they crossed northern Texas, they even came within 300 miles of de Soto's ill-fated party in eastern Arkansas. But neither de Soto nor Coronado—nor Cartier in the north—ever discovered wealthy cities or a sea passage to the Far East.

The Protestant Reformation Plays Out in America

1.5   How did Europe's sharp religious split influence the early colonization of North America?

I n 1520, while Cortés vied with the Aztec for control in Mexico and Magellan maneuvered around South America, the pope excommunicated a German monk named Martin Luther. Three years earlier, Luther had nailed a list of ninety-five theses to the church door at Wittenberg, challenging papal authority. Luther's followers questioned lavish church spending and long-standing church practices such as the selling of religious pardons to raise money. They also rejected the church's elaborate hierarchy and criticized its refusal to translate the Latin Bible into modern languages. Luther's reform movement triggered the division of Western Christianity into competing faiths. For their written protestations against the papacy, Luther and his fellow insurgents received the enduring name *Protestants*. Their reform movement became known broadly as the Reformation. Those who opposed it, siding with Rome, launched a Counter-Reformation to defend and revitalize the Roman Catholic Church.

For the first time in history, a controversy in Europe made waves that washed onto American shores. Throughout the remainder of the sixteenth century, European national and religious conflict played out in part overseas, a pattern that repeated itself in future centuries. France and Spain, competing in Europe, wrestled to claim control of Florida. England, an upstart Protestant monarchy with a rising population and an expanding navy, seized control of Ireland and launched its first attempt to plant a colony in North America.

Reformation and Counter-Reformation in Europe

Beginning in 1517, zeal for Luther's religious reforms spread across Europe, sparking armed conflict. In Switzerland, militant priests abolished the practice of confession, condemned the church calendar full of fasts and saints' days, and defied the tradition of a celibate clergy by marrying. The Swiss Reformation found its leader in a French Protestant named John Calvin who arrived in Geneva in 1541 and ruled the city as a church-centered state for more than two decades.

Calvin imposed his own strict interpretation on Lutheranism and drew dedicated followers to his church. Offended by expensive vestments and elaborate rituals, he donned a simple black "Geneva" robe. He argued that faith alone, not "good works," would lead Christians to be saved. Salvation, he preached, was determined by God, not bought by giving **tithes** to the church. Only a select few people, Calvin explained, were destined to be members of God's chosen elect. Moreover, only an informed clergy and the careful study of scripture could reveal signs of a person's status. Soon, Calvinist doctrine helped shape Protestant communities across northern Europe: Huguenots in France, Puritans in England, Presbyterians in Scotland, and the Dutch Reformed Church in the Netherlands.

The Protestant Reformation that Luther had ignited coincided roughly with another important change in Europe: the emergence of the modern nation-state. Kings and queens gradually expanded court bureaucracies and asserted greater control over their subjects and economies. They strengthened their armies, gaining a near monopoly on the use of force, and they took full advantage of the new medium of printing. As religious ferment spread and local allegiances gave way to a broader sense of national identity, strong sovereigns moved to distance themselves from papal authority in Rome.

The emergence of England as a nation-state (under the Tudor dynasty founded by Henry VII in 1485) illustrates this shift in power away from Rome. In 1533, when the pope refused to grant England's next king an annulment of his first marriage, Henry VIII wrested control of the English church from papal hands and had Parliament approve his divorce and remarriage. The new Church of England, or Anglican Church, continued to follow much of the Catholic Church's doctrine. However, its "Protector and only Supreme Head" would now be the English monarch. During her long reign from 1558 to 1603, Henry VIII's daughter Queen Elizabeth I managed to steer the Church of England on a middle course between advocates of Catholicism and extreme Protestants.

Throughout Europe, as zealous believers on both sides of the debate staked out their positions, attempts to heal religious divisions gave way to confrontation. Challenges to the pope in Rome, whether from dissenting parishes or powerful monarchs, met with stiff resistance as Catholic leaders mobilized opposition. Their followers rallied to defend Roman Catholicism through efforts known collectively as the Counter-Reformation.

A militant new Catholic religious order called the Society of Jesus, or the Jesuits, represented one dimension of the Counter-Reformation. Led by a Spanish soldier named Ignatius Loyola and willing to give their lives for their beliefs, these dedicated missionaries and teachers helped to reenergize the Catholic faith and spread it to distant parts of the world. Another institution, the Inquisition, reflects a different side of the Counter-Reformation. In 1542, Catholic authorities established a new religious-judicial proceeding, known as the Inquisition, to help resist the spread of Protestantism. Heretics—persons accused of denying or defying church doctrine—were brought before the Inquisition's strict religious courts; those who refused to renounce their beliefs suffered severe punishment. These heresy trials made clear to Inquisition leaders that the advent of printing was helping to spread the works of Luther and his Protestant allies. In 1557, therefore, the Vatican issued an "Index" of prohibited books.

Tithe A levy or donation (generally a tenth part) given to provide support, usually for a church.

In Spain, King Philip II, who ruled from 1556 to 1598, led an Inquisition to root out Protestant heresy. The Spanish monarch came close to overpowering Protestant England as well. In 1588, he sent a fleet of warships—the Spanish Armada—to reconquer England for the Roman Catholic Church. A timely storm and hasty mobilization by the island nation foiled the Spanish king's invasion. But Philip II's confrontation with the navy of Elizabeth I epitomized the sharp new division between Catholic and Protestant power in Europe. This deepened antagonism—religious, ideological, and economic—shaped events overseas in the second half of the sixteenth century. The struggle became especially clear in Florida, the vague region claimed by Spain that encompassed Indian lands from Chesapeake Bay to the Gulf of Mexico.

Competing Powers Lay Claim to Florida

As Spain used force to obtain the dazzling wealth of New World societies, its European rivals looked on jealously. As early as 1523, French sea raiders had captured Spanish ships returning from Mexico with Cortés's Aztec bounty of gold, silver, and pearls. Ten years later, French pirates made a similar haul. To protect the flow of riches from America, the Spanish soon initiated a well-armed annual convoy to escort their wealth from Havana to Seville. Each year, Spain's huge West Indies treasure fleet made an enticing target as it followed the Gulf Stream along the Florida coast.

But France had its own designs on Florida, furthered by the special concerns of French Huguenots. Unsure of their future in a religiously divided country, these Protestants took a leading role in the colonization efforts of France. In 1562, French Huguenots established a settlement at Port Royal Sound (Parris Island, South Carolina), close to the route of Spain's annual treasure fleet. The effort lasted only two years and aroused Spanish suspicions of "Lutheran" intruders.

Undaunted, the French backed a larger colonizing effort to Florida in 1564. When French Protestants erected Fort Caroline on the St. John's River at present-day

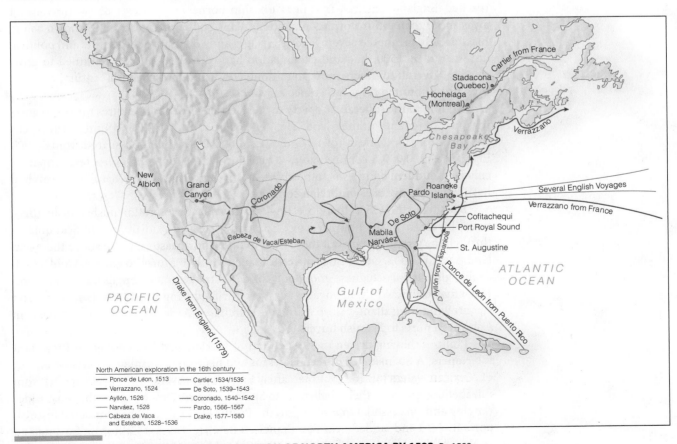

MAP 1.2 THE EXTENT OF EUROPEAN EXPLORATION OF NORTH AMERICA BY 1592 By 1592, a century after Columbus's initial voyage, European explorers and colonists had touched the edges of North America, and a few had ventured far inland. But they had not found riches or a passageway to the Pacific, and only the Spanish had managed to establish a lasting foothold along the Florida coast.

Jacksonville, the Spanish crown took swift action. In 1565, Philip II sent 300 soldiers and 700 colonists under Pedro Menéndez de Avilés to oust the French and secure Florida. Menéndez captured Fort Caroline and massacred hundreds of French Huguenots. The heretics, he feared, might attack the treasure fleet, forge alliances with Florida's Indians, or provoke revolt among slaves in the Spanish Caribbean. To prevent further French incursions on Florida's Atlantic coast, Menéndez established a new outpost at nearby St. Augustine. He also sent Juan Pardo north from Port Royal Sound to establish forts in the interior.

With French threats defeated, the Spanish at St. Augustine attempted to plant strategic missions farther north to convert Native Americans to Christianity and secure Spain's land claims. In 1570, eight missionaries from Loyola's Society of Jesus sailed north from Florida to Chesapeake Bay. There, the Jesuits established a mission to convert local Indians and looked for "an entrance into the mountains and on to China." But the friars' rules and beliefs antagonized the Native Americans. By the time Menéndez visited the region in 1572, all the missionaries had been killed. Spain's failure to secure a foothold on Chesapeake Bay soon proved costly, as a new European rival appeared on the scene. Almost overnight, Protestant England emerged as a contending force in the Atlantic world. Now English adventurers began challenging Spanish dominance in the Caribbean and along North America's southeastern coast.

The Background of English Expansion

The voyages of John Cabot and the visits of Bristol fishing vessels to Newfoundland's Grand Banks had stimulated an early English interest in the Atlantic. But for several reasons, this curiosity intensified after 1550. Henry VIII had used his power, plus the wealth he had seized from the Roman Catholic Church, to build a sizable navy before he died in 1547. The merchant fleet grew as well, carrying English wool and cloth to Antwerp and other European ports.

Demographic growth also promoted expansion. When bubonic plague first reached England in 1348 (via fleas on ship-borne rats), waves of sickness swept away more than a third of the inhabitants. This epidemic catastrophe, known as the Black Death, prompted severe labor shortages and 150 years of economic and political unrest. But by 1500, England's population had recovered, and it continued to grow steadily. Overall numbers more than doubled during the sixteenth century, creating pressure on limited resources, especially land.

Adding to the squeeze, property owners, eager to enclose pastures for sheep grazing, pushed tenants off their land. This "enclosure movement" set countless rural people adrift to seek work in towns and cities. London's population soared from 50,000 in 1500 to 200,000 a century later. When Europe's saturated woolen textile market collapsed suddenly, English cloth exports fell 35 percent in 1551. Merchants searched hastily for new avenues of foreign commerce.

Starting in the 1550s, therefore, England's overseas exploration pushed in all directions. Investors in the new Muscovy Company sent ships north around Scandinavia through the Arctic Ocean, but they failed to find a northeastern route above the Asian landmass to China. Other English vessels sailed south to Morocco and the Gold Coast, challenging the Portuguese monopoly of the African trade. English mariner John Hawkins conducted three voyages to West Africa during the 1560s. Horning in on the growing transatlantic slave traffic, he purchased Africans and then sold them in Caribbean ports to Spanish buyers.

Philip II, having driven the French out of Florida, had had enough of Protestant interlopers. A Spanish fleet forced Hawkins and his young kinsman Francis Drake out of Mexican waters in 1568. But thereafter, English sea rovers, with quiet support from Elizabeth, stepped up their challenges to Spain's empire. Drake proved the most wide-ranging and successful. On a voyage to the Pacific (1577–1580), he plundered Spanish ports in Peru and landed near San Francisco Bay. He claimed California for England as New Albion and then sailed around the globe. In the 1580s, Drake continued, in his words, "to singe the Spaniard's beard." He sacked ports in the West Indies, encouraged slave uprisings against the Spanish, and attacked the settlement at St. Augustine. He also captured numerous treasure ships, sank two dozen enemy vessels in their home port at Cadiz, and helped to defeat Philip II's Spanish Armada in 1588.

England's anti-Catholic propagandists made Drake a national hero. Moreover, they painted Spanish cruelties toward Indians in the New World in the worst possible terms. To bolster their case, they translated the vivid writings of Las Casas into English. But the English were not blameless themselves. In the Elizabethan years, they established their own pattern of violence during their brutal conquest of Ireland. Many who played leading roles in this bloody takeover came to view a colony in America as the next logical step in England's aggressive overseas expansion.

Lost Colony: The Roanoke Experience

Sir Humphrey Gilbert, who had served in Ireland, was one Elizabethan with an eye on America. In 1576, Gilbert promoted the idea of a short northwestern passage to China, and Martin Frobisher, another veteran of the Irish campaign, undertook voyages to locate such a route. Writing an essay on "How Her Majesty May Annoy the King of Spain," Gilbert proposed a colony in Newfoundland. The queen granted him a patent—a license giving him exclusive rights—for such a project. But shipwrecks and desertions doomed the venture to failure. When Gilbert died at sea on the homeward voyage, his half-brother, Walter Raleigh, obtained a similar patent to plant a colony in North America.

In 1584, Raleigh sent explorers to the Outer Banks, the string of coastal barrier islands below Chesapeake Bay that Verrazzano had glimpsed sixty years earlier. They brought back two Indian informants and positive reports about the land near Roanoke Island. The next month, Richard Hakluyt, England's foremost advocate and chronicler of overseas expansion, handed Elizabeth I an advisory paper entitled "Western Planting." The document called for the establishment of a strategic outpost on the North American coast, where the English could launch attacks against Spanish shipping, hunt for useful commodities, and convert Indians to Protestant Christianity.

Raleigh's three efforts to establish such an outpost failed in rapid succession. In 1585, he first sent Ralph Lane, a hardened veteran of the Irish campaigns, to build a fort at Roanoke Island. But storms at sea scattered his ships, and most of Lane's initial force never arrived. Those who did, including scientist Thomas Harriot and artist John White, fared badly because of scarce food, bad discipline, and hostile relations with the Indians. Francis Drake, arriving in 1586 after harassing the Spanish in the West Indies and Florida, expected to find a thriving enterprise. Instead, he carried the disheartened soldiers back to England. They had paid a price, Hakluyt commented, "for the cruelty and outrages committed by some of them against the native inhabitants of that country." A second expedition diverted to the Caribbean to prey on enemy shipping, after leaving a few men at Roanoke, who did not survive.

In May 1587, John White led a third English venture to America, with 110 people, including women and children. They planned to settle on Chesapeake Bay, but a contentious captain refused to carry them farther north after an initial stop at Roanoke Island. In August the settlers agreed to send White back to England for more supplies; they would leave a message for him if they moved. When he finally returned in 1590—delayed by England's clash with the Spanish Armada—he found the site deserted. A word carved on a post suggested that survivors had joined the nearby Croatan Indians, but the Lost Colony's fate remains a source of endless speculation. The Spanish, worried by the English foray, drew up plans for a fortification at Chesapeake Bay, but warfare between Spain and England kept both countries preoccupied elsewhere until Philip II and Elizabeth I had died.

Conclusion

Over approximately 150 centuries, people of distant Asian ancestry had explored and settled the bountiful Western Hemisphere. In every region of North America, from the Arctic North to the semitropical Florida Keys, they had adapted and prospered over countless generations. Then suddenly, in a single century, unprecedented intrusions by sea brought newcomers from foreign lands to the coasts of the Americas. Their numbers only increased with time. In the next century, the contest for European control of the Atlantic seaboard began in earnest.

John White took part in several voyages to Roanoke Island in the 1580s. A skilled artist, the Englishman made valuable firsthand drawings of Native Americans living in what is now coastal North Carolina, including the wife and daughter of a local leader. The woman kept her "haire trussed opp in a knott," had tattoos on her arms, wore "a chaine of great pearles," and often carried "a gourde full of some kinde of pleasant liquor." The girl holds an English doll, for Indian children "are greatly Delighted with puppetts . . . brought out of England." In what ways would White's drawings have shaped the way Europeans viewed America and its inhabitants?

Chapter Review

Ancient America

1.1 What types of evidence are used to explain the arrival of humans in North America? p. 3

Scientists studying climate change have examined shifting sea levels to show that an ancient land bridge once linked Siberia and Alaska. Since long-lasting spear points vary over time and space, they help archaeologists calculate human migration. Physical anthropologists comparing Asian and American skeletal remains can also now compare ancient DNA samples.

A Thousand Years of Change: 500 to 1500

1.2 In the millennium before Columbus, what evidence exists for non-local trade in North America? p. 5

For several centuries after 850, Chaco Canyon in New Mexico became a hub for north–south trade in turquoise. Hopewell burial sites in Ohio reveal goods from Florida and Lake Superior, while relics from temple mounds of the later Mississippian cultures show that Cahokia and Moundville were centers for extensive trade.

Linking the Continents

1.3 Why is the first voyage of Columbus in 1492 still viewed as such an earth-changing event? p. 9

Before 1492, Norse settlers had briefly colonized Newfoundland; European and Chinese navigators had ventured below the equator. But Columbus's first voyage from Spain established a lasting linkage between the Eastern and Western Hemispheres. The resulting exchange of plants, animals, peoples, and microbes ("the Columbian Exchange") has had a transformative impact.

Spain Enters the Americas

1.4 What factors motivated and shaped Spain's rapid intrusion into sixteenth-century America? p. 14

Invading the Americas gave the Spanish access to fresh geographical knowledge and new material wealth. Colonization provided resources for European consumers (gold, pearls, chocolate) and precluded settlement by rival European nations. Exploration might have revealed a western route to China, and conquest offered Christians new opportunities to spread their faith.

The Protestant Reformation Plays Out in America

1.5 How did Europe's sharp religious split influence the early colonization of North America? p. 19

The Protestant Reformation divided European Christendom into rival camps and intensified national rivalries at home and abroad. The Catholic Spanish established St. Augustine in 1565 to protect sea traffic from the Gulf of Mexico. Under Queen Elizabeth, the Protestant English attempted to fix a rival colony at Roanoke in 1585.

Timeline

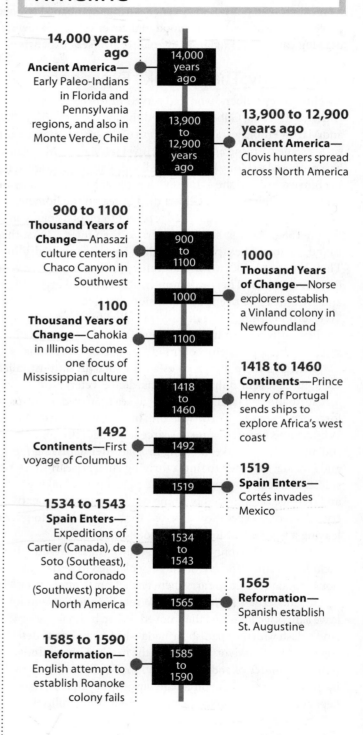

14,000 years ago
Ancient America— Early Paleo-Indians in Florida and Pennsylvania regions, and also in Monte Verde, Chile

14,000 years ago

13,900 to 12,900 years ago

13,900 to 12,900 years ago
Ancient America— Clovis hunters spread across North America

900 to 1100
Thousand Years of Change—Anasazi culture centers in Chaco Canyon in Southwest

900 to 1100

1000

1000
Thousand Years of Change—Norse explorers establish a Vinland colony in Newfoundland

1100
Thousand Years of Change—Cahokia in Illinois becomes one focus of Mississippian culture

1100

1418 to 1460

1418 to 1460
Continents—Prince Henry of Portugal sends ships to explore Africa's west coast

1492
Continents—First voyage of Columbus

1492

1519

1519
Spain Enters— Cortés invades Mexico

1534 to 1543
Spain Enters— Expeditions of Cartier (Canada), de Soto (Southeast), and Coronado (Southwest) probe North America

1534 to 1543

1565

1565
Reformation— Spanish establish St. Augustine

1585 to 1590
Reformation— English attempt to establish Roanoke colony fails

1585 to 1590

2 European Footholds in North America, 1600–1660

F atalities, friendship, stale-mate—what would result from the collision of newcomers and Native Americans? Would cultural differences be complementary or antagonistic? The first half of the seventeenth century in North America was a time of dramatic transition from occasional foreign contacts to secure colonial settlements. Although some friendships were established, each new European foothold—Jamestown, Quebec, Santa Fe, Plymouth, Boston—brought cultural shock and high attrition for all involved.

Occasionally, we can imagine these early encounters through the eyes of someone familiar with Old World and New World cultures. One such rare individual was Squanto, a Native American who befriended the English settlers arriving aboard the *Mayflower* in December 1620. He had grown up in a Patuxet Indian village beside what is now Plymouth Bay. Like others, he remembered the first French and English fishing vessels, which had appeared when he was a small boy.

But Squanto also came to know the wider Atlantic world. In 1614, he was among twenty-seven Indians taken hostage aboard an English ship. He spent time in Spain, England, and Newfoundland before managing to return home in 1619. However, it was not a happy homecoming. A foreign epidemic,

This nineteenth-century painting (shown here in detail) captures the isolation and forbidding winter weather the *Mayflower* passengers faced when they reached the American coast in December 1620. Snow coats the deck, frost hardens the sails, and floating ice hinders the oarsmen as they cautiously row ashore. Are the ominous signs of winter a commentary on the newcomers' chances of survival in North America?

SOURCE: William Halsall, *Mayflower in Plymouth Harbor* (1882).

LEARNING OBJECTIVES

2.1 ((	2.2 ((	2.3 ((	2.4 ((	2.5 ((
What motivated Spain to extend the northern borders of its New World empire? p. 27	How did the expanding beaver trade shape the French and Dutch colonies before 1660? p. 31	What factors worked for and against the early English colonization efforts in America? p. 35	How were the Puritans strengthened or weakened by seeing themselves as God's chosen people? p. 40	In what ways did the rapid spread of tobacco help or hurt the Chesapeake colonies? p. 46

((Listen to Chapter 2 on MyHistoryLab

Watch the Video Series on MyHistoryLab

Learn about some key topics related to this chapter with the *MyHistoryLab Video Series: Key Topics in U.S. History.*

1 **Beginnings of English Colonial Societies: 1607–1660** Because the lands claimed by England belonged to the crown, merchants, nobles, and others who wished to establish settlements in the New World had to petition the king (James I, or his successors) for a royal charter. This video describes the companies that established colonies in America, such as the Virginia Company and the Plymouth Company, and shows how difficult life could be for the first settlers.

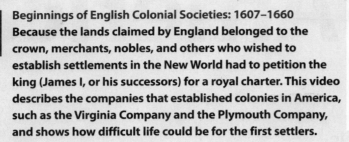 Watch on MyHistoryLab

Jamestown The colony of Jamestown, founded in the lower Chesapeake Bay by the Virginia Company in 1607, is the subject of this video. Captain John Smith, Chief Powhatan, and his daughter Pocahontas all have an important place in Jamestown's early history. So does tobacco, since this aromatic and addictive plant changed the colony's economy and, within several generations, allowed aggressive planters to amass large fortunes.

Watch on MyHistoryLab **2**

3 **New England** This video surveys the founding of New England's separatist Pilgrim colony of Plymouth and the later neighboring Puritan colonies of Massachusetts Bay, Rhode Island, and Connecticut. Seeking religious freedom, the newcomers put distance between themselves and the powerful Anglican Church in England. But they now faced new conflicts with Native Americans. When efforts at coexistence failed, wars erupted with the Wampanoag and Pequot peoples.

 Watch on MyHistoryLab

The Chesapeake As this video illustrates, the Chesapeake colonies differed from the colonies of New England both in how they were formed and in the way people lived. Maryland was a proprietary colony, the sole possession of the proprietor, George Calvert, Lord Baltimore. He wished to make the colony a refuge for Catholics persecuted in England. At times, Maryland's colonists had better relations with neighboring Indians than with the Protestant settlers of Virginia. **4**

Watch on MyHistoryLab

brought to the northeast coast by European ships, had recently killed thousands of local Indians. Unburied skulls and bones still lay aboveground.

Therefore, when the beleaguered pilgrims encountered Squanto during their first winter at Plymouth, Indians and newcomers alike were reeling from severe losses. The Indians' entire Patuxet village had been swept away by disease. Among the 102 colonists who had set out aboard the *Mayflower*, half would be dead by the time the snow melted. Those still alive were surprised and grateful to encounter a local inhabitant who could translate between English and his own Algonquian language.

In the Northeast, as elsewhere in America, death seemed to play favorites in the following years. As colonization continued, recurrent epidemics took a particularly heavy toll on Native Americans, who lacked immunity when exposed to foreign diseases for the first time. In 1622, Squanto himself fell sick and died of a fever, leaving no relatives behind. In contrast, most early survivors within the Plymouth Colony lived on to see numerous children and grandchildren thrive.

B y the middle of the seventeenth century, English settlements had taken root in both the Chesapeake region and New England. The success of these colonies would exert a lasting influence on the future direction of American society. But their stories unfolded as part of a far wider North American drama that included a diversity of European groups and embraced both the Atlantic and the Pacific shores. Whether confronting newcomers from Spain, France, Holland, or England, scores of Native American communities faced new challenges that altered traditional Indian ways of living and sometimes threatened their very survival.

Spain's Ocean-Spanning Reach

What motivated Spain to extend the northern borders of its New World empire?

n 1580, Spain's Philip II laid claim to the throne of Portugal. This consolidation (which endured until 1640) unified Europe's two richest seaborne empires but also created new problems. First, combining with Portugal put huge additional burdens on the overstretched Spanish bureaucracy. Second, the global success of the combined Iberian empires invited challenges from envious rivals in northern Europe. The new international competition came from the French, the Dutch, and the English, aspiring naval powers with imperial ambitions that touched the Pacific as well as the Atlantic.

By 1600, for example, a Dutch ship had entered the Pacific, defying Spanish claims for control of that ocean, and had reached Japan, where the new Tokugawa dynasty (1600–1868) was consolidating its control. The pilot, an Englishman named Will Adams, visited Edo—the rising military town that would grow into modern-day Tokyo. He even built a ship for the *shogun* (ruler). Adams's experience in Japan serves as a reminder that by 1600 competition for oceanic control stretched far beyond the Atlantic. Who would dominate Pacific sea-lanes to America?

Vizcaíno in California and Japan

In April 1607, a letter from the king of Spain reached Mexico City. The king commanded his viceroy in charge of affairs in Mexico (New Spain) to create an outpost on California's Monterey Bay. Spanish galleons returning from the Philippines through the North Pacific to the west coast of Mexico desperately needed a haven along the route, after crossing the immense ocean. Monterey Bay was well supplied with water, food, and timber. The sheltering harbor would provide a perfect way station, where ships could take on supplies and make repairs before heading south.

But the viceroy in Mexico City had other ideas. He diverted the necessary funds into a search for the fabled North Pacific isles of Rica de Oro ("Rich in Gold") and Rica de Plata ("Rich in Silver"). In 1611, the viceroy dispatched Sebastián Vizcaíno to hunt for these mysterious islands. The seasoned Pacific navigator found no isles of gold and silver, but he did visit Japan. When Vizcaíno returned across the Pacific in 1613 aboard a vessel built in Japan, he brought 180 Japanese with him to Mexico. Several young Japanese had made a well-publicized visit to Catholic Europe in the 1580s, and this larger delegation was bound for Spain and Italy, via America, to open doors between East and West. However, the Tokugawas soon began to persecute the European traders and Christian missionaries who had been allowed in the Japanese islands for a generation, so the frail link between Europe and Japan through Mexico never developed further.

Tokugawa officials, it seems, feared that tolerating foreigners in Japan's ports might foster the spread of Christianity and undermine their supremacy. Moreover, developing Japanese fleets might bring guns to warlords and disrupt hard-won peace. So Japan passed up an opportunity for naval expansion, just as Ming China had done two centuries earlier after the voyages of Zheng He. Instead, the new dynasty adopted a policy of commercial and cultural isolation that lasted for more than 200 years. Otherwise, the history of North America and the world would almost certainly have taken a very different path.

For the Spanish, Vizcaíno's Pacific adventure consumed crucial funds, and the possibility of a Spanish settlement at Monterey quickly disappeared. Concerned that their empire had already become overextended, Spanish officials postponed plans to colonize California's coast. In addition, Spain wondered whether to maintain its existing North American colony in Florida and its newest frontier province: New Mexico.

Oñate Creates a Spanish Foothold in the Southwest

In 1598, Juan de Oñate renewed the northern efforts of Coronado's expedition several generations earlier. Setting out from New Spain, he led 500 men, women, and children north into the upper Rio Grande valley to create the province of New Mexico. Aided by Franciscan friars (organized followers of St. Francis loyal to the pope), Oñate and his colonists expected to convert the Pueblo Indians to Christianity. Expanding outward from the compact apartment-like native towns, or pueblos, the intruders hoped to open a vast new colonial realm "greater than New Spain."

But Oñate drastically underestimated the difficulties. When embittered Indians at Acoma pueblo killed eleven of his soldiers in 1599, he retaliated by bombarding the mesa-top citadel, killing 800 inhabitants and enslaving nearly 600 others. Following the brutal repression of Acoma, neighboring pueblos reluctantly submitted to Spanish demands for labor and food. Colonial reinforcements arriving in 1600 were dismayed by the harsh conditions; Oñate needed new discoveries for the colony to prosper. In 1601, he launched an expedition east into the Great Plains, but the venture proved as futile as Coronado's earlier march had been.

To make matters worse, drought gripped the Rio Grande valley, and many of the recent settlers departed, complaining that the region lacked woods, pastures, water, and suitable land. When Oñate returned from the plains, he found that two-thirds of his tiny colony had given up and returned to Mexico. Foiled on the east and weakened along the Rio Grande, Oñate next pressed west to seek a link to the Pacific. When he reached the Gulf of California in 1605, he envisioned a possible link to the Pacific trade.

In fact, however, Oñate's new "Mexico" remained isolated and impoverished. The desperate colonists, strapped for food and clothing, pressed hard on the native peoples. They demanded tribute in the form of cotton blankets, buffalo hides, and baskets of scarce maize. In winter, ill-equipped Spanish-speaking soldiers stripped warm robes off the backs of shivering women and children; in summer, they scoured each pueblo for corn, torturing residents to find out where food was hidden.

Meanwhile, a few hundred Pueblo Indians—intimidated by the Spanish, desperate for a share of the food they had grown, and fearful of attacks by neighboring Apache—began to accept Christian baptism and seek Spanish protection. By 1608, when the crown threatened to withdraw support from the struggling province, the colony's Franciscan missionaries appealed that their converts had grown too numerous to resettle and too dependent to abandon. Their argument may have been exaggerated, but it caught the attention of authorities.

Besides, England and France were launching new colonies in Virginia and Canada. Since mapmakers still could not accurately calculate longitude (east–west position on the globe), no one was sure whether these bases created by international rivals posed a threat that was dangerously close at hand. Worried Spanish officials finally agreed with the Franciscan friars that New Mexico must carry on. They replaced Oñate with a new governor and asserted royal control over the few dozen settlers who remained in the colony.

New Mexico Survives: New Flocks Among Old Pueblos

The Spanish decision to hold on in New Mexico reshaped life for everyone in the region. At least 60,000 Indians living in nearly sixty separate pueblos found their world transformed and their survival threatened over the next half-century. In 1610, the new governor, ruling over scarcely fifty colonists, created a capital at the village of Santa Fe. Within two decades, roughly 750 colonists inhabited the remote province, including Spanish, Mexican Indians, Africans, and mixed-race children.

The racial and ethnic diversity of the New Mexico colony repeated the pattern already visible in New Spain. Similarly, labor practices and religious changes also followed models established after the conquest of the Aztec in Mexico. As in New Spain, certain privileged people in the new colony received **encomiendas**; such grants entitled the holders (known as *encomenderos*) to the labor of a set number of Native American workers. With labor in short supply throughout the Spanish colonies, settlers led

Encomienda The Spanish *encomienda* system, imposed in Spain's American empire, requiring Indian communities to supply labor or pay tribute to a local colonial overlord (identified as an *encomendero*).

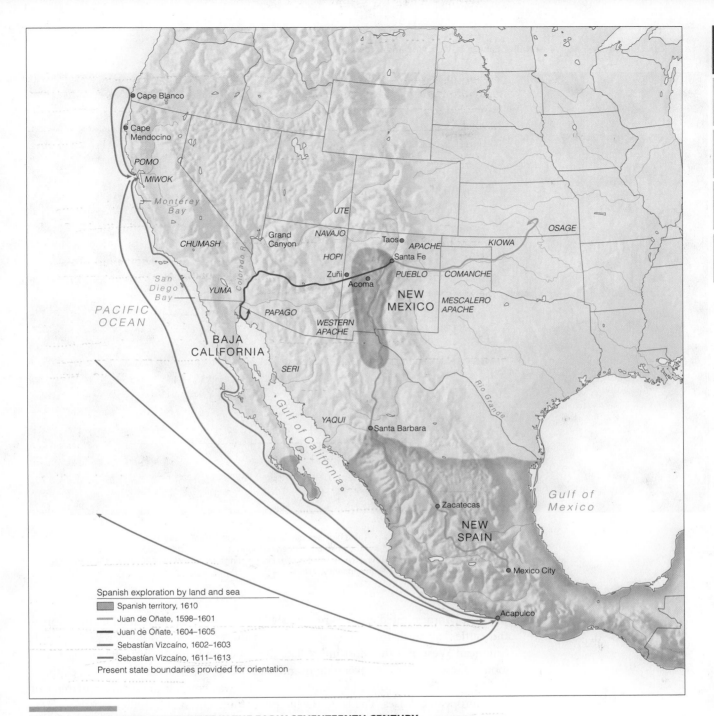

Spanish exploration by land and sea
Spanish territory, 1610
Juan de Oñate, 1598–1601
Juan de Oñate, 1604–1605
Sebastián Vizcaíno, 1602–1603
Sebastián Vizcaíno, 1611–1613
Present state boundaries provided for orientation

MAP 2.1 THE SPANISH SOUTHWEST IN THE EARLY SEVENTEENTH CENTURY

occasional raids against nomadic Plains Indians, keeping some captives and shipping others south to toil as slaves in the Mexican silver mines.

Meanwhile, the number of Franciscan missionaries rose rapidly. They forbade traditional Pueblo celebrations, known as **kachina** dances, and destroyed sacred kachina masks. Their combination of intense zeal and harsh punishments prompted many Indians to learn Spanish and become obedient converts. However, it also drove the Indians' own religious practices underground—literally, into the hidden, circular kivas that had long been a focal point for Native American spiritual activities in the region. There, people kept their traditional faith alive in secret and passed sacred rituals along to the next generation.

The Spanish brought more than Christianity to New Mexico. The newcomers also transferred novel crops (wheat, onions, chilies, peas) and planted new fruits (peaches, plums, cherries). Settlers introduced metal hoes and axes, along with donkeys, chickens,

Kachina An Indian religious system, inspired by Mexican traditions, and present in the American Southwest for more than 800 years. The kachina cult used masks for group performances associated with rain, curing, fertility, warfare, and the ancestors. Among many Pueblo and Hopi Indians, this tradition was epitomized by kachina (or katsina) dolls.

29

Acoma, often called Sky City, sits atop a high sandstone mesa west of Albuquerque, New Mexico. The name means "place that always was," and the pueblo has been continuously inhabited for roughly 1,000 years. Acoma's Native American community survived a devastating attack by Spanish colonizers in 1599. Would the mesa's steep cliffs keep the Spanish out of Acoma indefinitely?

and other domesticated animals previously unknown to the native inhabitants. Horses and cattle, led north from New Spain, eventually revolutionized life across the North American West. But the most immediate impact came from Spanish sheep. Each friar soon possessed a flock of several thousand, and Pueblo artisans wove wool into cloth.

But the Pueblo world, like Squanto's world, was eroding under the onslaught of new European diseases. The large Pueblo population, cut in half in the sixty years after Coronado's appearance, still numbered more than 60,000 in 1600. Sickness, along with warfare and famine, cut this number in half again by 1650 and in half once more by 1680.

Conversion and Rebellion in Spanish Florida

By 1600, Spanish Florida also disappointed imperial officials. Dreams of gold-filled kingdoms and a strategic passage from the Southeast to the Orient had never materialized. The Spanish government regarded the outpost at St. Augustine as an undue burden and planned to disband the colony. But as in New Mexico, Franciscan missionaries won the day. They argued that scores of Indian towns appeared ready to receive Christianity. By 1608, the crown had decided to let the colony continue.

A handful of missionaries fanned out among the Indians of northern Florida, erecting small churches and mission schools. They recruited Indian students aggressively without regard to age or sex. In 1612, Francisco de Pareja published an illustrated, bilingual confessional in Castilian Spanish and Timucuan, the earliest text in any North American

Indian language. The book enabled wary friars to ask villagers, "Have you said suggestive words?" and "Have you desired to do some lewd act with some man or woman or kin?"

Contact with Christian beliefs and books came at a steep price, for each inland village was expected to help feed the colonial garrison at St. Augustine. Native women neglected household crops to grow additional maize and grind it into meal. Annually, Spanish officials requisitioned Indian men from each village to transport the cornmeal overland to the Atlantic coast and return to the mission carrying supplies for the Franciscans. Imported candles, communion wine, and mission bells all had to be hauled inland.

Friars and Indian bearers traveling to the interior also carried sicknesses from St. Augustine. Epidemics of foreign diseases—measles, bubonic plague, malaria, typhus, smallpox, and influenza—took a devastating toll on the Native Americans. As whole villages disappeared, Hispanic entrepreneurs began to expand cattle ranching across northern Florida. Faced with encroaching farms, crushing labor demands, and frightful mortality, local native leaders saw their power reduced and their communities depleted. These conditions sparked a short-lived revolt by Indians at Apalachee in 1647. Nine years later, when the governor at St. Augustine feared a possible attack by English ships, a wider Native American uprising shook Timucua in north-central Florida.

In the end, the English threat to Spanish Florida did not materialize in 1656, but the rumor underscored how much had changed in the preceding half-century. Two generations earlier, in 1600, no European power besides Spain had possessed a solid foothold in any portion of the Americas. But over the next six decades, France, Holland, and England all asserted claims on the American mainland.

France and Holland: Overseas Competition for Spain

2.2   How did the expanding beaver trade shape the French and Dutch colonies before 1660?

At the turn of the seventeenth century, interlopers from Holland challenged Spanish colonizers in the Philippines and Portuguese traders in Japan. These Dutch efforts illustrated the growing competition between European powers for control of the world's oceans. In London, commercial leaders received a royal charter to create the English East India Company in 1600. Two years later, merchants in Amsterdam, hoping to capture Portugal's lucrative Asian trade, established the Dutch East India Company to send ships to eastern oceans. By 1652, they had founded a Dutch colony at Cape Town, near the southern tip of Africa.

The united powers of Spain and Portugal proved even more vulnerable in the Atlantic. To be sure, Spanish convoys continued to transport Mexican gold and silver to Europe annually, along with Asian silks and spices shipped to Mexico via the Pacific trade. Portuguese vessels carried Africans to the New World at a profit. But ships from rival European nations preyed on these seaborne cargoes with increasing success.

Defiantly, European competitors also laid claim to numerous islands in the Caribbean. By 1660, the English had taken control of Barbados, Providence Island, Antigua, and Jamaica; the Dutch had acquired St. Maarten, St. Eustacius, Saba, and Curaçao; and the French had claimed Guadeloupe, Martinique, Grenada, and St. Lucia. For France, however, the most promising Atlantic prospects lay farther north in Canada. There, Spanish power was absent, hopes for a Northwest Passage persisted, and French imperial claims stretched back generations.

The Founding of New France

Since the time of Jacques Cartier, **Basque** fishing boats from the coast of France had crisscrossed Newfoundland's Grand Banks. The trade increased after 1580 as crews

Basque The Basque region of southwest France, bordering the Pyrenées and the Atlantic Bay of Biscay, was famous for its fishing fleet and its experienced sailors.

built seasonal stations along the American coast for drying codfish. These stations prompted greater contact with Indians; soon Europeans were exchanging metal goods for furs on terms that pleased all. A Native American could trade a worn-out robe made from beaver skins for a highly valued iron kettle. A European artisan could craft a beaver hat that proved fashionable and profitable.

As North Atlantic fishing and trading expanded, the domestic situation in France improved. In 1598, King Henry IV issued the **Edict of Nantes**, a decree granting political rights and limited toleration to French Protestants, or Huguenots. With religious wars curtailed, the king could contemplate new colonization initiatives in America. An experienced French soldier and sailor named Samuel de Champlain emerged as a key leader in this effort. From 1602 until his death in 1635, Champlain devoted himself to the St. Lawrence River region, where Acadia on the Atlantic coast and Canada along the extensive river valley made up the anticipated realm of New France.

In 1608, Champlain and several dozen other men established an outpost at Quebec, where Cartier and Roberval had wintered generations earlier. In June 1609, Champlain joined a band of Algonquin and Huron Indians in a raid on the Iroquois in what is now upstate New York. When they engaged their Iroquois enemies in battle, Champlain fired his gun—a novelty in the region—killing several war chiefs and sparking a rout. For the powerful **Iroquois League** south of the St. Lawrence (the Five Nation confederation composed of the Seneca, Cayuga, Onondaga, Oneida, and Mohawk Indians), the defeat spawned lasting bitterness. For the French, their victory sealed good relations with the Algonquin and Huron, ensuring the survival of Quebec and spurring unprecedented commerce. Within fifteen years, Native Americans were trading 12,000 to 15,000 beaver pelts annually via the St. Lawrence River valley.

In 1627, the powerful first minister in France, Cardinal Richelieu, pressed for greater French settlement in Canada through a new private company. He banned Huguenots from participating and pushed to make sure that only Roman Catholics were allowed to migrate to Canada. But his expansive policies alarmed rival England, which captured Quebec briefly in 1629. When restored to French control several years later, the tiny outpost contained fewer than 100 people. In an effort to expand the meager settlement and populate the fertile valley upriver from Quebec, French authorities began granting narrow strips of land with river frontage to any Catholic lord who would take up residence there and bring French tenants to his estate.

Competing for the Beaver Trade

Cardinal Richelieu's power in France epitomized the ongoing Counter-Reformation. This outpouring of Catholic zeal reached as far as North America. In 1635, Jesuits founded a college in Quebec, and six nuns arrived in 1639 to begin a school for Indian girls and a hospital. Other religious workers established a station farther west in 1641 in territory recently dominated by the Iroquois; the strategic outpost marked the beginnings of Montreal. From there, the French planned to control the beaver trade as it expanded west. They also hoped to prevent the Iroquois League from diverting furs south to Holland's new colony on the Hudson River.

But the desperate Iroquois nations, facing collapse, took a stand. Increasing contact with Europeans and their contagious diseases had brought catastrophic epidemics to the Iroquois homelands below Lake Ontario. Beginning in 1633, sicknesses that were new to the region swept away some 10,000 people and cut the Five Nations' population in half within a decade, emptying the distinctive longhouses that made up Iroquois villages.

According to Iroquois tradition, mourning survivors must replace deceased individuals swiftly with captives to maintain the community's strength and continuity. Pressed by grieving families, Iroquois warriors initiated a generation of violent campaigns intended to capture and absorb neighboring groups. These so-called mourning wars are also remembered as the Beaver Wars because they included a clear economic motive. Besides captives, the Iroquois aggressors sought furs. If they could seize pelts before the valuable items reached the French, they could trade them to the Dutch for

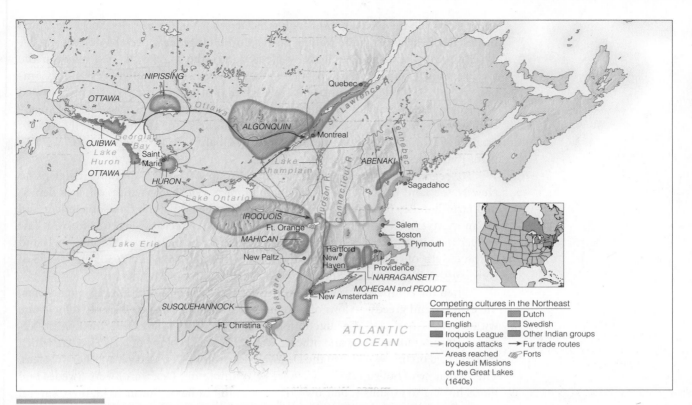

MAP 2.2 EUROPEAN AND NATIVE AMERICAN CONTACT IN THE NORTHEAST, 1600–1660
French and English colonization efforts brought devastating diseases to the Five Nations of the Iroquois League.
Eager to take captives and profit from the growing trade in furs, the Iroquois ranged north and west to make war
on the French and their Huron Indian allies.

guns and powder. Well armed, they could then engage in further wars for captives
and furs.

This spiral of aggression put the Iroquois on a collision course with the Huron and
their allies, a small band of Jesuit missionaries willing to risk martyrdom in New France.
Eager for Native American converts, the Jesuits focused their attention on the region east
of Lake Huron, where 30,000 Huron Indians lived in large villages. The Jesuits erected chapels at four of these towns and constructed a central base at St. Marie near Georgian Bay.
Having volunteered for hardship, they witnessed far more of it than they ever imagined.

First came the same foreign epidemics that had wasted the Iroquois; smallpox cut
down roughly two-thirds of the Huron population, or 20,000 people, between 1635 and
1640. Then came the Iroquois themselves, bent on capturing Huron women and children
to revitalize their longhouses, swept by disease in the 1630s. Armed by Dutch traders
eager for furs, 1,000 Iroquois warriors descended on the weakened Huron in March 1649.
They burned villages, secured captives, tortured several priests to death, and seized large
stocks of pelts. The Iroquois then launched raids on the St. Lawrence River valley, disrupting the fur trade and frightening the several thousand French inhabitants. By 1660, it
seemed that New France—thinly settled, weakly defended, and poorly supplied—might
face the same extinction that the much older and larger Huron community had suffered.

A Dutch Colony on the Hudson River

The Dutch traders who supplied firearms to the Iroquois in exchange for furs owed their
start to English-born navigator Henry Hudson. In 1609, sailing for the Dutch East India
Company, Hudson crossed the Atlantic in search of a western passage to the Orient. He
visited Chesapeake Bay and Delaware Bay, then rediscovered modern-day New York
harbor, the bay that Verrazzano had entered in 1524. Flying the Dutch flag above his
vessel, the *Half Moon*, Hudson sailed north up the broad river that now bears his name.
The Dutch moved quickly to gain a foothold in the region. Ships from Amsterdam

appeared far up the Hudson, exchanging metal goods for beaver pelts. Soon the Dutch had established a year-round trading post at Fort Orange, near present-day Albany.

In 1621, responsibility for New Netherland—the region claimed between the Delaware and Connecticut rivers—fell to the newly chartered Dutch West India Company (DWIC). Modeled on the Dutch East India Company, the DWIC concentrated on piecing together an empire in the South Atlantic. Dutch ships seized part of sugar-rich Brazil (1632), the island of Curaçao near Venezuela (1634), and Portugal's African outpost at Elmina, on the coast of modern-day Ghana (1637). But the DWIC also laid plans for a North American colony.

To begin, the company transported a group of French-speaking Belgians to New Netherland in 1624. To secure the boundaries of the province, officials deposited farm families far up the Hudson at Fort Orange and along the Connecticut and Delaware rivers. However, Peter Minuit, the colony's director from 1626 to 1631, saw danger in this dispersal. To consolidate settlement, he purchased Manhattan Island at the mouth of the Hudson from the local Indians in 1626. By 1630, the village of New Amsterdam boasted 270 settlers at the southern tip of Manhattan.

When the company threw open the Indian trade to others besides its own agents, the careless and greedy actions of unregulated traders sparked a series of violent wars with coastal tribes. Also, the Dutch squabbled constantly with neighboring English settlers over fur-trading rights and other matters. The small colony of New Sweden, which materialized on the west side of the Delaware River in 1637, posed yet another problem. The settlers who built Fort Christina (now Wilmington, Delaware) were Swedes and Finns hoping to establish their own trade with the Indians. But in 1655, these several hundred Scandinavians were obliged to surrender to a Dutch fleet.

"All Sorts of Nationalities": Diverse New Amsterdam

The symbol of Dutch power in the region, and the commander of the fleet that seized New Sweden, was Peter Stuyvesant. He ruled New Netherland aggressively for several decades before England seized the colony in 1664. Stuyvesant had served as governor

Read the Document   **Father Isaac Jogues, Description of New Amsterdam (1646)**

New Amsterdam Fort on Manhattan Island. Why did Dutch control of the Hudson River antagonize both the French and the English?

SOURCE: Collection of the New-York Historical Society, (Neg #1049)

of Dutch Curaçao, losing his right leg in a battle with the Spanish. When he arrived in New Netherland in 1647 as director general for the DWIC, he moved swiftly to assert control.

Stuyvesant limited beer and rum sales, fined settlers for promiscuity and knife fighting, and established a nine-member night watch. When a group of English Quakers, members of the newly formed Society of Friends, arrived at New Amsterdam in 1657, he attempted to expel the radical Protestants and fine any who gave them shelter. However, Dutch residents of Flushing, on Long Island, defied Stuyvesant's ban and signed a public letter of objection stressing religious toleration.

To address the colony's chronic labor shortage, Stuyvesant endorsed trade in African slaves and used his Caribbean connections to expand this traffic. When the Portuguese forced Holland out of Brazil in 1654 and closed that sugar colony to Dutch slave vessels, some of the ships brought their cargoes to New Amsterdam instead. Like the Dutch-speaking blacks already living in the colony, most of these newcomers were enslaved for life. But the DWIC, the largest importer and owner of slaves in New Netherland, granted "half-freedom" to some whom it could not employ year-round. These people, in return for an annual fee, could travel freely and marry, acquire property, and hire out their labor. By 1664, black residents made up over 10 percent of New Netherland's population and 20 percent of New Amsterdam, the colony's capital.

New Amsterdam, home to fewer than 2,000 people, also had a small Jewish contingent, the first in mainland North America. In 1654, twenty-three Sephardic Jews reached Manhattan, forced out of Brazil by the Portuguese. Stuyvesant, strident in his anti-Semitism, claimed such "blasphemers of the name of Christ" would "infect and trouble this new colony." But the DWIC, which included Jewish stockholders and was eager for newcomers of all kinds, overruled the governor's request to expel the refugees. In the end, colony officials authorized a Jewish ghetto, or segregated neighborhood, where the newcomers could pray together freely in private. At first, however, they were not allowed to construct a synagogue for public worship.

In the early 1660s, the colony continued to grow, "slowly peopled by the scrapings of all sorts of nationalities," as Stuyvesant complained. Huguenots occupied New Paltz near the Hudson; farther north, other newcomers founded Schenectady in 1661. Swedes and Finns continued to prosper along the Delaware, and numerous English had settled on Long Island. Compared with New France, New Netherland seemed far more populous, prosperous, and ethnically diverse. But whereas the French colony to the north endured for another century, the Dutch enterprise was soon absorbed by England. For despite a slow start, the English managed to outdistance all their European rivals and establish thriving North American colonies in the first half of the seventeenth century.

English Beginnings on the Atlantic Coast

2.3 What factors worked for and against the early English colonization efforts in America?

When Queen Elizabeth I passed away in 1603, several important elements were already in place to help England compete for colonial outposts. Thousands of rural tenants had been pushed off farms; these landless people, who flocked to urban centers in search of work, formed a restless supply of potential colonists. Also, the country had an expanding fleet of English-built ships, sailed by experienced mariners. In addition, England had a group of seasoned and ambitious leaders. A generation of soldiers (many of them younger sons of the property-holding elite known as the **gentry**) had fought in Europe or participated in the brutal colonization of Ireland.

Because Elizabeth I died without heirs, the king of Scotland, James Stuart, succeeded her as ruler. During the reigns of James I (1603–1625) and his son Charles I (1625–1649), religious and economic forces in Stuart England prompted an increasing

Gentry An English term for the land-owning social class of well-to-do elite who possessed wealth and power, but lacked the hereditary titles of the nobility.

number of people to consider migrating overseas. With the expansion of the country's Protestant Reformation, religious strife escalated toward civil war, which erupted in 1642. During the tumultuous 1630s, English public officials were glad to transplant Puritans and Catholics alike to foreign shores. In turn, many ardent believers—weary of conflict or losing hope for their cause at home—welcomed the prospect of a safe haven abroad. Economically, the development of joint stock organizations enabled merchants to raise capital and spread the high risk of colonial ventures by selling numerous shares to small investors. At the same time, the fluctuating domestic economy prompted many people to consider seeking their fortunes elsewhere.

The Virginia Company and Jamestown

For Richard Hakluyt, England's leading publicist for overseas expansion, the proper focus seemed clear: "There is under our noses," he wrote in 1599, "the great & ample countrey of Virginia." Great and ample, indeed, especially before the rival Dutch established New Netherland. On paper, the enormous zone that England claimed as Virginia stretched north to south from the top of modern-day Vermont to Cape Fear on Carolina's Outer Banks. From east to west, it spanned North America from the Atlantic to the Pacific, however narrow or wide the continent might prove to be.

In 1606, James I chartered the Virginia Company as a two-pronged operation to exploit the sweeping Virginia claim. Under the charter, a group of London-based merchants took responsibility for colonizing the Chesapeake Bay region. Meanwhile, merchants from the English seaports of Plymouth, Exeter, and Bristol took charge of developing the northern latitudes of the American coast. In 1607, two ships from Plymouth deposited roughly a hundred colonists at the Sagadahoc (Kennebec) River in Maine. The Sagadahoc settlers erected a fort and buildings, but frostbite, scurvy, and dwindling supplies prompted a retreat home in 1608.

A parallel effort by the Londoners proved more enduring—but just barely. In April 1607, three ships from the Thames bearing 105 men sailed into Chesapeake Bay. The newcomers disembarked on what appeared to be a secluded island near a broad river. Within months, these subjects of James I had named the waterway the James River and established a fortified village beside it called Jamestown. In June, hoping for quick rewards, they shipped to London various stones that they thought contained precious gems and gold ore.

When the rocks proved worthless, the colonists' dreams of easy wealth evaporated. So did their fantasies about pushing west to the Pacific. During the outpost's first winter, a fire destroyed the tiny settlement, and death from hunger, exposure, and sickness cut the garrison's population in half. The governor and council appointed by the Virginia Company bickered among themselves, providing poor leadership. Fully one-third of the early arrivals claimed to be gentlemen, from England's leisure class— a proportion six times higher than in England—and most proved unaccustomed to hard manual labor. Moreover, all the colonists were employees of the company, so any profits from their labor went to repay London investors.

Despite the unsuitable make-up of the garrison, conditions improved briefly with the emergence of John Smith, a vigorous leader who explored the region in a **shallop** during the summer of 1608 and created a remarkably accurate map of Chesapeake Bay. Captain Smith dealt brazenly with the local Powhatan Indian confederation, numbering more than 13,000 people. He reached a tenuous accommodation with the paramount chief, Powhatan, who had been steadily expanding his power across the Tidewater region. (Later, Smith claimed to have been assisted and protected by Powhatan's young daughter, Matoaka, whose nickname was Pocahontas.) Still, the Jamestown colony limped along with meager support, living in fear of Spanish attacks.

With hopes of a swift bonanza dashed, the London merchants decided to alter their strategy. They would salvage the venture by attracting fresh capital. Then they would recoup their high initial costs by recruiting new settlers who could produce staple products suited for export—perhaps grapes, sugar, cotton, or tobacco. In 1609, the company began to sell seven-year joint stock options to the English public. Subscribers could invest

Shallop A shallow-draft, undecked vessel, roughly 30 feet in length, holding more than a dozen sailors and suitable for rowing and sailing in rivers and bays.

Following the success of an animated film entitled *Pocahontas* (1995), Hollywood went on to create *The New World* (2005) in anticipation of Jamestown's 400th anniversary. In this iconic scene, director Terrance Malick recreated the arrival of the *Susan Constant* on the James River in 1607. Why do dramatic first encounters between widely differing cultures continue to hold such fascination for American artists and filmmakers?

money or they could sign on for service in Virginia. Company officials promised such adventurers at least a hundred acres of land when their investment matured in 1616. In June 1609, 500 men and 100 women departed for the Chesapeake aboard nine ships.

"Starving Time" and the Seeds of Representative Government

When the battered fleet arrived at Jamestown, the new arrivals found insufficient supplies. Moreover, the first settlers had failed to discover a profitable staple crop. The colonists depended heavily on the Native Americans for food, and Powhatan's Confederacy proved increasingly unwilling and unable to share its harvest. In a grim "starving time," the ill-equipped newcomers scavenged for berries and bark. Extreme hunger drove a few to cannibalize the dead before dying themselves. By the spring of 1610, seven of every eight people had died; scarcely sixty remained alive.

In June, these survivors abandoned their ghost town altogether. But as they set sail for England, they encountered three long-overdue ships entering Chesapeake Bay with fresh supplies and 300 new settlers. Reluctantly, they agreed to try again. More years of harsh discipline, Indian warfare, and scarce resources followed. A severe seven-year drought, from 1606 through 1612, also conspired against the hapless newcomers.

Relief came from an unexpected quarter: the "bewitching vegetable" known as Orinoco tobacco. The plant, grown in parts of the West Indies and South America, had captured English taste in the previous generation. Sales of this New World product in England sent profits to the Spanish crown and prompted James I to launch a vigorous antismoking campaign in 1604. But John Rolfe, reaching Jamestown in 1610,

37

Headright Under the headright system, English colonial governments granted a fixed amount of land, usually 50 acres, to any head of household for every family member or hired hand that person brought into the colony. Sometimes fewer acres were granted for women and children on the grounds that they would clear and plant less land.

Burgess A representative elected to the popular branch of the colonial legislature in either Virginia or Maryland.

wondered whether the "noxious weed" might provide the colonists with a viable staple crop. Rolfe, a smoker himself, suspected that sweet-flavored Orinoco tobacco could prosper in Virginia soil. Within a year, Rolfe had somehow managed to obtain seeds, and by 1612, his patch of West Indian tobacco was flourishing. Desperate settlers and impatient London investors were delighted by Rolfe's successful experiment. Soon production of the leaf soared at Jamestown, to the neglect of all other pursuits.

During Virginia's initial tobacco boom, recently starving settlers saw handsome profits within reach. Because land was plentiful, the only limitations to riches were the scarcity of workers and the related high cost of labor. Any farmer who could hire half a dozen field hands could increase his profits fivefold, quickly earning enough to obtain more land and import more servants. The company transported several shiploads of apprentices and servants to the labor-hungry colony. When a Dutch captain delivered twenty enslaved blacks in 1619, settlers eagerly purchased these first Africans to arrive in English Virginia. They also bid on the 100 women who disembarked the same year, shipped from England by the company to be sold as wives and workers. Still, men continued to outnumber women more than three to one for decades to come.

To encourage English migration further, the Virginia Company offered transportation and 50 acres to tenants, promising them ownership of the land after seven years of work. Men who paid their own way received 50 acres and an additional **headright** of fifty acres for each household member or laborer they transported. The Virginia Company went out of its way to assure colonists of access to such established English freedoms as the right to trial by jury and to a representative form of government. The company established civil courts controlled by English common law, and it instructed Virginia's governor to summon an annual assembly of elected **burgesses**—the earliest representative legislature in North America. First convened in 1619, the House of Burgesses wasted no time in affirming its commitment to fundamental English rights. The governor, the house said, could no longer impose taxes without the assembly's consent.

Launching the Plymouth Colony

To attract additional capital and people, the Virginia Company also began awarding patents (legal charters) to private groups of adventurers. The newcomers would live independently on a large tract, with only minimal control from the governor and his council. Two such small colonies originated among English Protestants living in exile in Holland because their separatist beliefs did not allow them to profess loyalty to the Church of England. The first group of 180, based in Amsterdam, departed for America late in 1618 on a crowded ship. Winter storms, sickness, and a shortage of fresh water destroyed the venture; scarcely fifty survivors straggled ashore in Virginia.

A second group of English Separatists, residing in the smaller Dutch city of Leiden, fared better. Most had migrated to Holland from northeast England in 1608. This group openly opposed the hierarchy, pomp, and inclusiveness of the Church of England. Instead, they wanted to return to early Christianity, where small groups of worthy (and often persecuted) believers formed their own communities of worship. After a decade in Holland, many of them had wearied of the foreign culture. They were dismayed by the effect of worldly Leiden on their children, and they also sensed, correctly, that warfare would soon break out in Europe. A few families pushed for removal to America, despite the obvious dangers of such a journey.

Possible destinations ranged from South America to Canada. But in the end, the Separatists decided to use a patent granted by the Virginia Company to a group of English capitalists. On the negative side, the migrants had to work for these investors for seven years. They also had to take along paying passengers who did not share their beliefs. On the positive side, they received financial support from backers who paid to rent a ship. Moreover, instead of having their daily affairs controlled from London, they had the power to govern themselves.

In September 1620, after costly delays, thirty-five members of the Leiden congregation and additional Separatists from England departed from Plymouth, along with

✳ Explore English Colonization on MyHistoryLab

HOW DID ENGLISH COLONIZATION TRANSFORM EASTERN NORTH AMERICA?

The early 1600s brought major changes to the eastern portion of North America. Prior to that time, Native Americans made up the overwhelming majority of the population and controlled virtually the entire region. However, as the seventeenth century began, European powers began staking claims in the region and establishing settlements up and down the coast over the following decades. Such changes shook historical Native American trading and settlement patterns. Members of some of these nations lost their land to the newcomers and others entered successful alliances with Europeans to navigate their changing world. As the seventeenth century closed, the English in particular—having absorbed competing European colonial claims of the Dutch and Swedish—pushed their settlements beyond the coastline, creating a secure and expanding foothold.

The Jethro Coffin House, a saltbox house built in 1686, is the oldest surviving structure in Nantucket, Massachusetts.

GROWTH OF THE NON-INDIAN POPULATION OF THE THIRTEEN COLONIES, 1650–1750

Colony	1650	1700	1750
New Hampshire	1,300	5,000	27,500
Massachusetts (Includes Plymouth & Maine)	16,600	55,900	188,000
Rhode Island	800	5,900	33,200
Connecticut	4,100	26,000	111,300
New York	4,100	19,100	76,700
New Jersey		14,000	71,400
Pennsylvania		18,000	119,700
Delaware	200	2,500	28,700
Maryland	4,500	29,600	141,100
Virginia	18,700	61,600	231,000
North Carolina		10,700	73,000
South Carolina		5,700	69,000
Georgia			5,200

KEY QUESTIONS Use MyHistoryLab *Explorer* to answer these questions:

Cause ▶▶▶ *During this period, where did English settlements expand in North America, causing Native Americans to suffer territorial losses?*

Chart the growth of English colonization.

Comparison ▶▶▶ *In what ways did English expansion face competition from its European rivals?*

Map the claims of other European nations in eastern North America.

Analysis ▶▶▶ *How did the Iroquois Confederacy change over this time?*

Trace the expansion of Iroquois control of new territories along its borders.

other passengers. They were crowded aboard the *Mayflower*, a 160-ton vessel bound for Virginia. But a stormy two-month crossing brought them to Cape Cod, in modern-day Massachusetts, no longer considered part of the Virginia Company's jurisdiction. Sickly from their journey and with winter closing in, they decided to disembark at the spot they called Plymouth rather than push south to Chesapeake Bay. Earlier, they had signed a solemn compact aboard the *Mayflower* binding them together in a civil community.

William Bradford, the chronicler and longtime governor of Plymouth Colony, later recalled their plight: "They had now no friends to welcome them nor inns to entertain or refresh their weather-beaten bodies . . . . Besides, what could they see but a hideous and desolate wilderness." Bradford could scarcely exaggerate the challenge. His own wife drowned (an apparent suicide) shortly after the *Mayflower* dropped anchor. And by the time the ship departed in April, an illness had swept away half the colonists. When those remaining planted barley and peas, the English seeds failed to take hold.

Still, settlers had abundant fish and wildlife, along with ample Indian corn, and soon reinforcements arrived from England bringing needed supplies. The newcomers also brought a legal patent for the land of Plymouth Plantation. With Squanto's aid, the settlers secured peaceful relations with Massasoit's villages. When a good harvest assured survival for another winter, they invited Massasoit and his Indians to join in a three-day celebration of thanksgiving so that, according to one account, all might "rejoice together after we had gathered the fruit of our labors."

The Puritan Experiment

2.4 How were the Puritans strengthened or weakened by seeing themselves as God's chosen people?

After more than a generation of costly colonization attempts, England still had little to show for its efforts when Charles I inherited the throne in 1625. Then two forces prompted rapid change: positive publicity about America and negative developments at home. John Smith, long a key promoter of overseas settlement, drew inspiration from the early efforts at Jamestown and Plymouth. In 1624, he published a best-seller predicting future success for these regions. Ironically, the book's popularity depended in large part on the grim religious, political, and economic conditions in England that suddenly gave such literature a broad appeal.

Puritan Unrest Leads to the Massachusetts Bay Company

European Christianity had taken a number of different forms since the religious upheaval sparked by Luther a century earlier. The first Protestants had demanded a reformation of the Roman Catholic Church and had questioned papal authority over Christians. Now many non-Catholic English worshippers doubted whether the Church of England (also known as the Anglican Church) had gone far enough toward rejecting the practices of Rome. They lamented what they saw as the church's bureaucratic hierarchy, ornate rituals, and failure to enforce strict observance of the Christian Sabbath each Sunday. They scoffed at the gaudy vestments of Anglican bishops, elaborate church music, and other trappings of worship unjustified by biblical scripture. Instead, they praised the stark simplicity that John Calvin had brought to his church in Geneva.

As English Calvinists grew in number, their objections to the Church of England increased. They protested that the Anglican Church, like the Catholic Church, remained inclusive in membership rather than selective. They argued for limiting participation only to the devout, and they insisted that the Church of England should be independent and self-governing rather than tied to the monarchy. This keen desire for further cleansing and purity, so common to reformers, spurred the ongoing movement known as Puritanism.

Some of the most radical members of the broad Puritan coalition (including Bradford and the Plymouth pilgrims) became known as Separatists because they were committed to an extreme position: complete separation from what they saw as the corrupt Church of England. But many more Puritans (including most of the reformers who migrated to Massachusetts Bay) resisted separation. They hoped to stay technically within the Anglican fold while taking increased control of their own congregations—a practice known as congregationalism. Unwilling to conform to practices that offended them, these nonseparating Congregationalists remained determined to save the Anglican Church through righteous example, even if it meant migrating abroad for a time to escape persecution and demonstrate the proper ways of a purified Protestant church.

An emphasis on instructive preaching by informed leaders lay at the heart of the Puritan movement. Puritans believed that the sermon should be central to the Christian worship service. Their churches resembled lecture halls, emphasizing the pulpit more than the altar. In preaching, Puritans stressed a "plain style" that the entire congregation could understand. Moreover, they urged listeners to play an active role in their faith—to master reading and engage in regular study and discussion of scripture. In response to mounting public interest in these practices, Puritan ministers intensified their preaching and published their sermons. In effect, they dared authorities to silence them.

Reprisals came swiftly, led by William Laud, bishop of London. Laud instructed all preachers to focus their remarks on biblical passages and avoid writing or speaking about controversial religious matters. As England's church grew more rigid and its monarchy more controlling, the nation's economy was taking a turn for the worse. Rents and food costs had risen more rapidly than wages, and workers paid dearly. Jobs became more scarce, and unemployed workers staged local revolts. In 1629, entrepreneurs who viewed New England as a potential opportunity teamed up with disaffected Puritans to obtain a charter for a new entity: the Massachusetts Bay Company. Through a generation of costly trial-and-error experiments, the English had amassed great expertise in colonization. And given the worsening conditions at home, especially among the Puritan faithful, proposals for overseas settlement attracted widespread attention.

"We Shall Be as a City upon a Hill"

During the next dozen years, more than 70,000 people left England for the New World. Two-thirds of them sailed to the West Indies. But a large contingent of Puritans embarked for the new Massachusetts Bay colony, adjacent to the Plymouth settlement. A loophole in the king's grant permitted them to take the actual charter with them and to hold their company meetings in America. This maneuver took them out from under the usual control of London investors and let them turn the familiar joint stock structure into the framework for a self-governing colony. By 1629, advance parties had established a post at Salem for people who "upon the account of religion would be willing to begin a foreign plantation."

In England, meanwhile, a Puritan squire named John Winthrop assumed leadership of the Massachusetts Bay Company. "God will bringe some heavy Affliction upon this lande," he predicted to his wife, but the Lord "will provide a shelter & a hidinge place for us and others." In exchange, God would expect great things from these chosen people, as from the Old Testament Israelites. "We are entered into covenant with him for this work," Winthrop told his companions aboard the *Arbella* en route to America in 1630.

Winthrop laid out this higher Calvinist standard in a memorable shipboard sermon titled "A Model of Christian Charity." Far from hiding in obscurity, dedicated Puritans must set a visible example for the rest of the world, Winthrop declared. "We shall be as a city upon a hill."

The *Arbella* was one of seventeen ships that brought more than 1,000 people to New England in 1630. The English newcomers chose Winthrop as governor and established Boston as their port. By the time civil war erupted in England in 1642, nearly 20,000 people had made the journey, eager to escape the religious persecution and governmental tyranny of Charles I. Whole congregations migrated with their ministers; other people (more than 20 percent) crossed as servants. But most came as independent families, setting up stable households where women played important parts. They took an immediate role in crucial aspects of domestic manufacture and production, and their numerous children provided additional hands where labor was in short supply.

Earlier settlers traded food, lodging, and building materials to fresh arrivals in exchange for textiles, tools, money, and labor. When new groups of church members wanted to establish a village, they applied for land to the General Court, a legislature made up of representatives elected from existing towns. Well before 1640, English settlements dotted the coast and had sprung up inland along the Connecticut River, where smallpox had decimated the Indians in 1633. There, English outposts rose at Wethersfield, Hartford, and Springfield, where English traders hoped to attract furs away from the French and Dutch.

Dissenters: Roger Williams and Anne Hutchinson

Like the biblical Hebrews before them, the Puritans—self-appointed saints—believed that God had chosen them for a special mission in the world. The Almighty, they believed, would watch carefully, punish harshly, and reward mightily. Inevitably some devout people, raised to question authority in England, continued to dissent in New England. Not everyone accepted the idea that Puritans should dominate Indians or that women should defer to men. Roger Williams, a graduate of Cambridge University, and Anne Hutchinson, the talented daughter of an English minister, stand out as two of the earliest and most effective challengers to leadership in the Massachusetts Bay colony.

When Williams arrived in Boston, his Separatist leanings angered Bay Colony authorities, who still hoped to reform the Anglican Church rather than renounce it. Williams's other contentions proved equally distressing. The young minister argued that civil authorities, inevitably corrupt, had no right to judge religious matters. He even pushed for an unprecedented separation of church and state—to protect the church. He also contended that the colony's land patent from the king had no validity. The settlers, he said, had to purchase occupancy rights from the Native Americans. Unable to silence him, irate magistrates banished Williams from Massachusetts Bay in the winter of 1635. Moving south, he took up residence among the Narragansett Indians and built a refuge for other dissenters, which he named Providence. In 1643, Williams returned to London, where he persuaded leaders of England's rising Puritan revolution to grant a charter (1644) to his independent colony of Rhode Island.

A more explosive popular challenge centered on Anne Hutchinson, who had grown up in England with a strong will, a solid theological education, and a thirst for spiritual perfection. She married a Lincolnshire textile merchant and took an active part in religious discussions while also bearing fifteen children. When her Puritan minister, John Cotton, departed for New England, Hutchinson claimed that God, in a private revelation, had instructed her to follow. In 1634, the family migrated to Boston, where Hutchinson attended Cotton's church and hosted religious discussions in her home. The popularity of these weekly meetings troubled authorities, as did her argument that the "Holy Spirit illumines the heart of every true believer." Hutchinson downplayed outward conformity—modest dress or regular church attendance—as a route to salvation. Instead, she stressed direct communication with God's inner presence as the key to individual forgiveness.

Most Puritans sought a delicate balance in their lives between respected outer works and inner personal grace. Hutchinson tipped that balance dangerously toward the latter. To the colony's magistrates, especially Winthrop, such teaching pointed toward dangerous anarchy—more troublesome when it came from a woman. These officials labeled Hutchinson and her followers as Antinomians (from *anti*, "against," and *nomos*, "law"). But the vehement faction grew, attracting merchants who chafed under economic restrictions, women who questioned men's domination of the church, and young adults who resented the strict authority of their elders. By 1636, this religious and political coalition had gained enough supporters to turn Winthrop out as governor.

((Read the Document   John Winthrop, "A Model of Christian Charity" (1630)

2.1

2.2

2.3

2.4

2.5

London port records for 1635 show that the composition of departing groups varied markedly, depending on their colonial destination. Children were much more common aboard ships heading for New England than on vessels bound for the West Indies. Also, eight of every twenty passengers for New England were women or girls. In contrast, females made up only three in twenty of those going to Virginia and one in twenty among people heading for Barbados. Why were people more likely to migrate to New England in family units than elsewhere?

Challenged by this Antinomian Crisis, members of the Puritan establishment fought back. They divided the opposition to win reelection for Winthrop, and they established Harvard College to educate ministers who would not stray from the fold. Also, they staged a flurry of trials for contempt and sedition (inciting resistance to lawful authority), and they made a special example of Hutchinson herself. After a two-day hearing in 1637, during which Hutchinson defended herself admirably, Winthrop sentenced Hutchinson to banishment as "a woman not fit for our society." Forced into exile, she moved first to Rhode Island and later to New Netherland, living at Pelham Bay near the estate of Joseph Bronk (now called the Bronx). There, Hutchinson and most of her family were killed by Indians in 1643. A river and a parkway in New York still bear her name.

Expansion and Violence: The Pequot War

Immigration to New England slowed during the 1640s because of religious and political upheaval at home. In England, Puritans and supporters of Parliament

Interpreting History

Anne Bradstreet: "THE TENTH MUSE, LATELY SPRUNG UP IN AMERICA"

Mistress **Bradstreet's male** detractors hinted that she should **put** down her **quill** pen and take up a **sewing** needle.

The Puritans who migrated to America stressed literacy and education as part of their faith. They left extensive court records, sermons, and diaries, but few of these surviving documents come from the pens of women. The poems and reflections of Anne Bradstreet provide a notable exception. "Here you may find," she told her children shortly before her death in 1672, "what was your living mother's mind."

The lifelong poet was born Anne Dudley in Lincolnshire, England, in 1612. She already "found much comfort in reading the Scriptures" by age seven. "But as I grew to be about 14 or 15," she recalled, "I found my heart more carnal, and . . . the follies of youth took hold of me. About 16, the Lord . . . smote me with the smallpox . . . and again restored me." That same year, she married Simon Bradstreet, the son of a minister. Two years later, despite a frail constitution, she sailed for Massachusetts Bay with her husband and her father (both future governors of the colony) aboard the Arbella.

Anne Bradstreet was alert to all that seemed strange and different in America. When I "came into this country," she related, "I found a new world and new manners." The young couple set up housekeeping in the town of Cambridge, on the Charles River, but life was difficult at first. Anne suffered from "a lingering sickness like a consumption." Moreover, "It pleased God to keep me a long time without a child, which was a great grief to me and cost me many prayers and tears." Finally, she bore a son in 1633, and seven more children followed.

As the family grew and moved about, the young mother wrote poems and meditations. But Mistress Bradstreet's male detractors hinted that she should put down her quill pen and take up a sewing needle. "If what I do prove well, it won't advance," she lamented in rhyme; "They'l say it's stol'n, or else it was by chance." Nevertheless, a book of her poems was published in England in 1650, hailing her as "The Tenth Muse, Lately Sprung Up in America."

Cambridge, on the Charles River near Boston, was a small village in the 1660s. The large building in the foreground is Harvard College, founded in 1636, and the smaller brick building beside it is the Indian College, built in 1655. The village was even smaller when Anne Bradstreet resided there briefly after her arrival in Massachusetts Bay. When John Smith gave a map of the region to Charles I, England's king named the Charles River for himself.

As a writer, Anne Bradstreet was more interested in spiritual improvement than literary grace. "Many speak well," she observed, "but few can do well." Throughout life, she followed a simple creed: "There is no object that we see; no action that we do; no good that we enjoy; no evil that we feel or fear, but we may make some spiritual advantage" of it. Nothing epitomizes this belief more clearly than "some verses upon the burning of our house, July 10th, 1666." Bradstreet composed the lines on an unburned scrap of paper as she groped to make sense of the calamity. The poem helped her to mourn her loss, take stock of her blessings, and renew her faith. In part, it reads,

In silent night when rest I took,
For sorrow neer I did not look,
I waken'd was with thundring nois
And Piteous shreiks of dreadfull voice. . . .

I, starting up, the light did spye,
And to my God my heart did cry. . . .
Then coming out beheld a space
The flame consume my dwelling place.

And, when I could no longer look,
I blest his Name that gave and took,
That layd my goods now in the dust:
Yea so it was, and so 'twas just. . . .

When by the Ruines oft I past,
My sorrowing eyes aside did cast,
And here and there the places spye
Where oft I sate, and long did lye.

Here stood that Trunk, and there that chest;
There lay that store I counted best:
My pleasant things in ashes lye,
And them behold no more shall I. . . .

Then streight I gin my heart to chide,
And did thy wealth on earth abide?
Didst fix thy hope on mouldring dust,
The arm of flesh didst make thy trust? . . .

Thou hast a house on high erect
Fram'd by that mighty Architect. . . .
The world no longer let me Love,
My hope and Treasure lyes Above.

Questions for Discussion

1. How might Anne Bradstreet's eventful life before age twenty have shaped her into a poet?

2. Imagine losing your home and belongings in a storm, flood, or fire. Would it deepen or weaken your religious beliefs? How about your need for material possessions?

SOURCE: Anne Bradstreet, "Verses Upon the Burning of Our House, July 10, 1666," 1666.

✳ **Explore the Topic** Leaving England for America in the 1630s

2.1

2.2

2.3

2.4

2.5

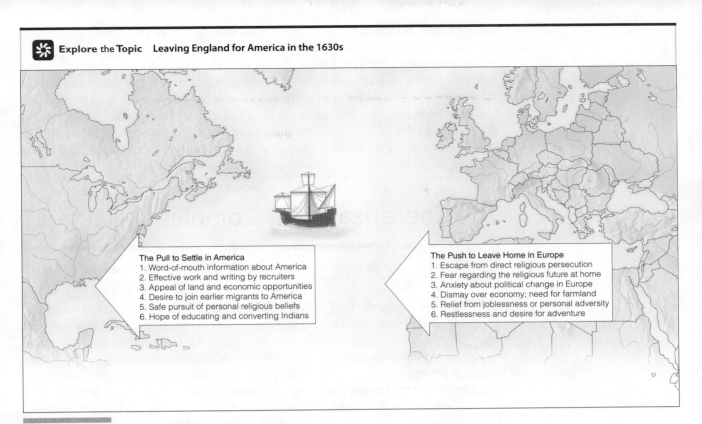

The Pull to Settle in America
1. Word-of-mouth information about America
2. Effective work and writing by recruiters
3. Appeal of land and economic opportunities
4. Desire to join earlier migrants to America
5. Safe pursuit of personal religious beliefs
6. Hope of educating and converting Indians

The Push to Leave Home in Europe
1. Escape from direct religious persecution
2. Fear regarding the religious future at home
3. Anxiety about political change in Europe
4. Dismay over economy; need for farmland
5. Relief from joblessness or personal adversity
6. Restlessness and desire for adventure

FIGURE 2.1 THE TOUGH CHOICE TO START OVER

formed an army and openly challenged royal authority during the English Civil War. After seizing power, these revolutionaries beheaded Charles I in 1649, abolished the monarchy, and proclaimed England a republican Commonwealth. Settlers in Massachusetts Bay struggled to square such sweeping developments in England with Winthrop's earlier assurance that the eyes of God and humankind would be fixed on New England.

Making matters worse, religious and economic controversies intensified as New England's next generation came of age. Needing new farmland and intellectual breathing room, fresh congregations began to hive off from the original settlements like swarms of bees. By 1640, New Hampshire, Rhode Island, and Connecticut each had at least four new towns that would provide the beginnings for independent colonies.

But the northeastern forest was not an empty wilderness, any more than the Chesapeake tidewater, the Florida interior, or the mesas of New Mexico had been. As the Hutchinsons discovered, newcomers who pushed inland were co-opting the land of longtime residents. Pressure on New England's Native Americans erupted in armed conflict in the Pequot War of 1637, at the height of the Antinomian Crisis. The Pequot Indians, English allies recently weakened by smallpox, resided near the mouth of the Connecticut River. But John Winthrop, whose son was leading a settlement effort in the area, fanned fears that the Pequot "would cause all the Indians in the country to join to root out all the English."

Recruiting Narragansett and Mohegan Indians to the English side, the colonists unleashed all-out war against the Pequot. The campaign culminated in a dawn raid on a stockaded Pequot town that sheltered noncombatants. The invaders torched the village (at Mystic, Connecticut) and shot or put to the sword almost all who tried to escape. Some 400 Indian men, women, and children died. The Puritans' Indian allies were shocked by the wholesale carnage. English warfare, they protested, "is too furious, and slaies too many men." Chastened by this intimidating display of terror and weakened by recurrent epidemics, the tribes of southern New England negotiated away much of their land over the next generation, trading furs to the rapidly multiplying colonists and seeking to understand their perplexing ways.

Having gained the upper hand, the Bible-reading English made gestures to convert their Native American neighbors. The Massachusetts General Court encouraged missionary work, forbade the worship of Indian gods, and set aside land for "praying towns" to encourage "the Indians to live in an orderly way amongst us." In Cambridge, the Reverend John Eliot labored to create and print a 1,200-page Indian Bible. Officials at Harvard, committed by their charter to the "education of the English and Indian youth of this Country," erected a well-publicized Indian College.

The Chesapeake Bay Colonies

2.5 In what ways did the rapid spread of tobacco help or hurt the Chesapeake colonies?

On Chesapeake Bay, settlers' relations with the Indians remained strained at best during the first half of the seventeenth century. In 1608, in an effort to secure the support of Indian leadership, the English performed an elaborate ceremony granting a scarlet cloak and a copper crown to Chief Powhatan. But two years later, suspicious that he was harboring runaway colonists, the English burned the nearest Indian villages and unthinkingly destroyed much-needed corn. A wife of one Indian leader, taken captive, watched English soldiers throwing her children in the river and shooting them in the head before she herself was stabbed to death.

For both sides, hopes of reconciliation rose briefly in 1614 with the match between Pocahontas, daughter of Powhatan, and John Rolfe, the prominent widower who had introduced tobacco. But the marriage proved brief; Pocahontas died in England three years later, after bearing one child. Leaders intended the wedding alliance as a diplomatic gesture toward peace. But it did little to curtail the settlers' bitterness over their lingering dependence on Indian supplies, or Native Americans' resentment regarding English encroachment and arrogance.

The Demise of the Virginia Company

Powhatan's death in 1618 brought to power his more militant younger brother, Opechancanough, the leader of the Pamunkey tribe. His encounters with the English had been frequent and unfriendly. By 1618, the English tobacco crop was booming, and more newcomers were arriving annually. Over the next three years, forty-two ships brought 3,500 people to the Chesapeake colony. The influx disheartened the Indians, and Opechancanough and his followers in the Powhatan Confederacy sought ways to end the mounting intrusion.

Briefly, disease seemed to work in the Indians' favor. Immigrants who made the long sea voyage with poor provisions often fell ill in the swampy, unhealthy environment of Jamestown. By 1622, the colony's inhabitants were dying almost as rapidly as newcomers arrived. Sickness had carried off 3,000 residents in the course of only three years. Opechancanough sensed a chance to deliver the finishing blow.

Early in 1622, the Powhatan Confederacy coordinated a sudden offensive along the lower James River. On March 22, Opechancanough's forces surprised the English, attacking the outlying settlements and sparing no one. Of the 1,240 colonists, nearly 350 lost their lives. Warned by an Indian, residents of Jamestown survived the uprising, but hope for peaceful relations ended.

The attack of 1622 fueled opposition to the Virginia Company among disgruntled English investors. In 1624, King James I annulled the company's charter, making Virginia a royal colony controlled by the crown. In the colony's first seventeen years, more than

8,500 people, almost all of them young, had embarked for the Chesapeake. By 1624, only fifteen of every 100 remained alive.

The surviving colonists placed a bounty on Opechancanough's head, but attempts to ambush or poison him failed. The Indian leader lived on, nursing his distrust of the English. In 1644, he inaugurated a second uprising that killed some 500 colonists. But the English settlement had grown too large to eradicate. By this time, old age forced the "Great General" to be carried on a litter. When the English finally captured him and brought him to Jamestown in 1646, Opechancanough was too old to walk unassisted. Still, he remained defiant until shot in the back by one of the Englishmen guarding him.

After two years of brutal warfare, the Pamunkey and their allies in the Powhatan Confederacy conceded defeat and submitted to English authority. From then on, they would pay a token annual tribute for the privilege to remain on lands that had once belonged to them. With the way cleared for Chesapeake expansion, land-hungry English settlers appeared in ever-increasing numbers in Virginia and the smaller, younger Maryland colony.

Maryland: The Catholic Refuge

Maryland owed its beginnings to George Calvert, a respected Catholic member of England's government who in 1625 was named the first Baron of Baltimore in Ireland. Calvert, now Lord Baltimore, had a keen interest in colonization, and he spent time in Newfoundland. But winter conditions were harsh at Avalon, his fishing colony at Ferryland, so in 1632 he petitioned Charles I for land in the Chesapeake. The king granted him 10 million acres adjacent to Virginia, to be named Maryland in honor of England's Catholic queen, Henrietta Maria. The Maryland charter gave the proprietor and his heirs unprecedented personal power, especially in the granting of lands to colonists without limitations based on religious belief.

Because Calvert died before the royal charter took effect, his eldest son, the second Lord Baltimore, took charge of the settlement effort. In 1634, the *Ark* and the *Dove* carried more than 200 settlers—both Protestants and Catholics—to the new colony. There, they established a capital at St. Mary's, near the mouth of the Potomac River. With the execution of the king in 1649 and the creation of an anti-Catholic commonwealth in England, the Calvert family provided a haven in Maryland for their coreligionists. However, Catholics never became a majority in the Chesapeake colony.

In 1649, Maryland's assembly passed an Act Concerning Religion, guaranteeing toleration for all settlers who professed a belief in Jesus Christ. This assertion of religious toleration, though limited, proved too broad for many to stomach. In the 1650s, supporters of the English Puritan cause seized power in Maryland, repealed the act, and briefly ended the Calverts' proprietorship. But by 1660, with the restoration of the Stuart monarchy in England, proprietary rule returned to the prosperous farming colony.

Tobacco Becomes a Way of Life

By 1660, Virginia and Maryland totaled roughly 35,000 settlers, scattered along the edges of the bay and its adjoining tidewater rivers. In contrast to New England, the Chesapeake still could not maintain its colonial population without steady infusions of newcomers. A sickly climate kept life expectancy low, and men continued to outnumber women by more than two to one. Early experiments with oranges, pineapples, and grapes led nowhere. Chesapeake lumber sold well at first, but it was John Rolfe's tobacco plant that emerged as the Tidewater's unlikely crop of choice.

Virginia's annual tobacco exports grew from a total weight of 2,000 pounds in 1615 to 500,000 in 1626. By 1630, saturated markets and stiff taxes led to slumping tobacco

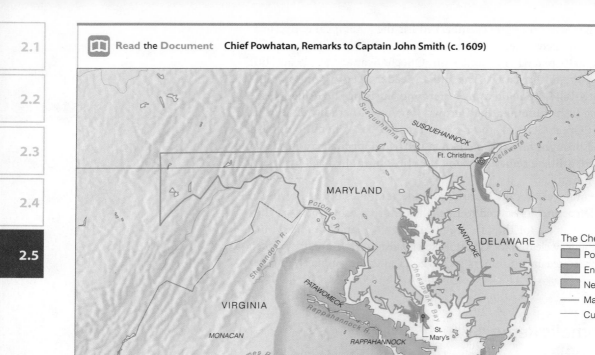

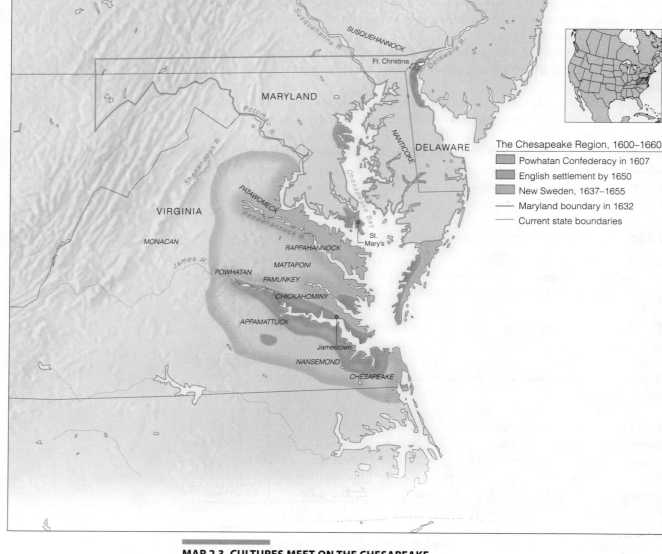

The Chesapeake Region, 1600–1660

Powhatan Confederacy in 1607

English settlement by 1650

New Sweden, 1637–1655

Maryland boundary in 1632

Current state boundaries

MAP 2.3 CULTURES MEET ON THE CHESAPEAKE

prices, so Virginians diversified their efforts. The beginning of the Massachusetts Bay colony created a demand for food that Chesapeake farmers met with well-timed coastal shipments. In 1634, they reported selling to "their zealous neighbours of New England tenne thousand bushels of corne for their releefe, besides good quantities of beeves, goats and hoggs, whereof this country hath great plentie." Such diversification proved brief, however. By 1640, London was receiving almost 1.4 million pounds of Chesapeake tobacco annually.

Though tobacco prices remained low throughout much of the seventeenth century, newcomers to Virginia and Maryland still managed to eke out a profit. They could grow the plants amid stumps in partially cleared fields. They could learn the many necessary procedures—planting, weeding, worming, suckering, topping, cutting, stripping, and curing—as the crop progressed. In short, it took hard work, but little farming experience, to bring cured tobacco to waterfront docks. Since captains charged by volume rather than weight, planters reduced shipping costs by devising a uniform barrel size and developing ways to press more leaves into each cask.

Still, the problems were formidable. Tobacco depleted the soil rapidly, so crop yields dwindled after several years. Then farmers had to leave their plots fallow, allowing them to recover, while clearing new fields for planting. This time-consuming task forced them onto marginal land that was poorly drained and less fertile. It also moved them away from navigable rivers, raising transportation costs. Storms, droughts, and crop diseases posed constant threats, and dependence on a single product in a distant and uncertain overseas market created added dangers.

By mid-century, Chesapeake tobacco planters worried about market saturation and overproduction. But by then, for better or worse, growing the noxious weed had become a way of life. Virginia and Maryland settlers found themselves enmeshed in the high-risk world of tobacco farming. Dependence on the troublesome crop would expand across the upper South for centuries to come.

Conclusion

During half a century, the French, Dutch, and English had all moved to challenge Spanish claims in North America. By 1660, all four of these maritime powers of western Europe had taken aggressive steps to establish permanent footholds on the fringes of the enormous continent. In each instance, the European colonizers benefited first from the presence of knowledgeable Native Americans and then from the sharp decline of those same people through warfare and the onslaught of new diseases.

Granted, warfare with foreign invaders and death from unknown diseases had become a part of Native American history in the preceding century. But the sixteenth century was an era of tentative European exploration. In contrast, the first half of the seventeenth century saw Europeans move beyond occasional forays to permanent colonization. Spain, France, Holland, and England each had formidable assets in Europe and on the high seas. By 1660, all had sponsored colonial settlements that had endured for several generations, and each had begun to taste the seductive fruits of empire in North America and elsewhere.

The English, slowest to become involved in overseas colonization, had caught up with their competitors by 1660. Among European countries, England had proven the most aggressive in forming expansive family-based colonies rather than military garrisons or trading outposts. As a result, by 1660 England's fledgling North American colonies had already outstripped all rivals in total population, and they were growing at an increasing pace, thanks in particular to the rapid expansion in New England. This emerging superiority in numbers would prove advantageous in the imperial clashes that lay ahead.

Chapter Review

Spain's Ocean-Spanning Reach

2.1 What motivated Spain to extend the northern borders of its New World empire? p. 27

Magellan's lengthy voyage to Asia around South America created incentives to find a much shorter east-west passageway through North America. Seeking such a route might also lead to new sources of wealth and new souls to convert. Spanish territorial claims in North America would prevent encroachment by rival European powers.

France and Holland: Overseas Competition for Spain

2.2 How did the expanding beaver trade shape the French and Dutch colonies before 1660? p. 31

As beaver diminished in the coastal Northeast, the Iroquois League fought to control the flow of pelts from the Great Lakes Region. French colonists founded Montreal in 1641 to assure beaver trade via the St. Lawrence, while the Dutch built Fort Orange, trading guns to divert pelts down the Hudson.

English Beginnings on the Atlantic Coast

2.3 What factors worked for and against the early English colonization efforts in America? p. 35

An expanding population, increasing religious and political turmoil, and rising urban unemployment made overseas settlement attractive. A growing fleet and experienced mariners made overseas colonization possible, and the desire to stake claims ahead of European rivals added incentive. Drawbacks included geographical uncertainties, Native American resistance, and harsh, unfamiliar living conditions.

The Puritan Experiment

2.4 How were the Puritans strengthened or weakened by seeing themselves as God's chosen people? p. 40

Self-righteous Puritans challenged corruption they saw in England, prompting official reprisals. But persecution reinforced their conviction that they were a "saving remnant" destined to play a key role in God's larger plan. This religious zeal provided the determination to succeed at colonization, but it also fostered intolerance and fractious debate.

The Chesapeake Bay Colonies

2.5 In what ways did the rapid spread of tobacco help or hurt the Chesapeake colonies? p. 46

John Rolfe's introduction of Orinoco tobacco in 1612 gave Jamestown a profitable staple crop that suited the climate. But growing tobacco instead of raising foodstuffs limited the self-sufficiency of Virginians and tied them to unstable foreign markets. It also depleted Chesapeake soil and—we now know—proved addictive and cancer-causing.

Timeline

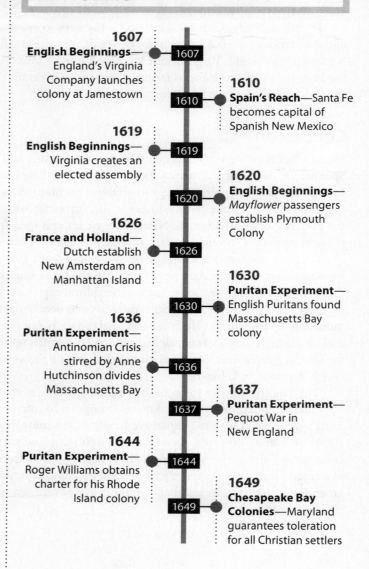

1607
English Beginnings— England's Virginia Company launches colony at Jamestown

1607

1610
1610
Spain's Reach—Santa Fe becomes capital of Spanish New Mexico

1619
English Beginnings— Virginia creates an elected assembly

1619

1620
1620
English Beginnings— *Mayflower* passengers establish Plymouth Colony

1626
France and Holland— Dutch establish New Amsterdam on Manhattan Island

1626

1630
1630
Puritan Experiment— English Puritans found Massachusetts Bay colony

1636
Puritan Experiment— Antinomian Crisis stirred by Anne Hutchinson divides Massachusetts Bay

1636

1637
1637
Puritan Experiment— Pequot War in New England

1644
Puritan Experiment— Roger Williams obtains charter for his Rhode Island colony

1644

1649
1649
Chesapeake Bay Colonies—Maryland guarantees toleration for all Christian settlers

3 Controlling the Edges of the Continent, 1660–1715

In the race for colonies, which European power would be first to explore and lay claim to North America's vast interior? By 1704, when Marguerite Messier Le Sueur set out by canoe from Montreal, planning to descend the Mississippi to Louisiana, the French had gained a clear advantage in this race, though their dominance would only last for another half century. ✗

At age twenty-eight, Marguerite had already been married half her life; she wed explorer-trader Pierre-Charles Le Sueur in 1690, when he was thirty-four and she was only fourteen. In 1702, Marguerite's husband had paddled down the Mississippi, taking furs to the new French outpost at Mobile. Before setting sail for France, he erected a house for his family and sent word to Canada for them to join him on the Gulf Coast when he returned.

So, in April 1704, Marguerite and her five children, along with her brother and a guide, left Montreal by canoe to attempt the inland journey of nearly 2,000 miles to Mobile. Traveling via the Great Lakes, they reached southern Illinois after more than a year and then descended the Mississippi. Marguerite's brother and a daughter died along the way, and when the survivors arrived at Mobile in

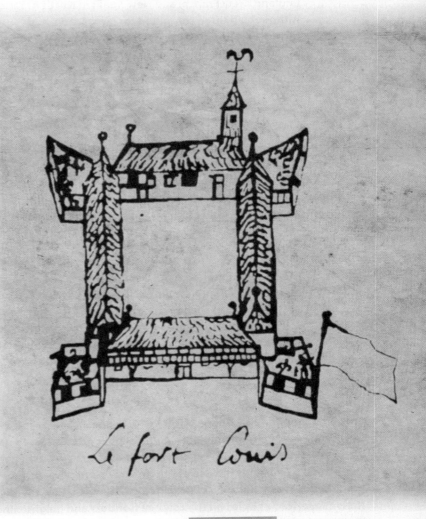

Le fort Louis

In 1702, the French constructed Fort Louis on the Mobile River to serve as a base for developing the Gulf Coast and its rich interior. The fort (near modern Biloxi, Mississippi) had four bastions, armed with cannons, to protect an adjacent village of seventy houses. Many of the newcomers had traveled a long inland route from Canada by canoe. How did early knowledge of the Mississippi River valley assist and shape French claims to the North American interior?

LEARNING OBJECTIVES

3.1	3.2	3.3	3.4	3.5
Why did France gain access to North America's interior before other European powers? p. 53	Did Indian experiences with Spanish colonization vary widely in Arizona, New Mexico, and Florida? p. 59	Why did England's varied new Restoration-Era American colonies present so many contrasts? p. 64	To what degree was colonial violence after 1670 sparked by internal tensions or by affairs in England? p. 68	How did worldly success and wartime profits contribute to colonial unrest after 1690? p. 73

Listen to Chapter 3 on MyHistoryLab

Watch the Video Series on MyHistoryLab

Learn about some key topics related to this chapter with the *MyHistoryLab Video Series: Key Topics in U.S. History.*

1 **Different Colonial Models: France, Spain and England: 1660–1715** This video explores the differences between the colonial administration and settlements of New England, New France, and New Spain in North America. Although all three competed for land, trade, and resources and pitted their Indian allies against each other, only the English sought to establish a facsimile of England in the New World. Spain and France were content to extract natural resources and relied on missionaries, soldiers, and traders more than on large civilian populations to stake their claims.

 Watch on MyHistoryLab

France and the American Interior This video focuses on New France, which, at its height, encompassed much of Canada and the North American interior. The French established key port cities along the St. Lawrence and Mississippi rivers, and their forts dotted the Great Lakes region. French policy gave priority to fur trading over settlement and stressed strong alliances with Native American partners. Coexistence with Indian allies helped to ensure the safety of French traders and missionaries.   **2**

Watch on MyHistoryLab

3 **The Spanish Empire on the Defensive** Although the Kingdom of Spain was the first to establish a vast empire in the New World, it soon competed with other European seafaring countries, especially as England and France displaced it as the leading power in Europe. This video charts Spain's imperial decline in America. New Spain lacked a mercantile tradition, focusing instead on extracting precious metals. Spain's colonial leaders exploited Native American populations under their control rather than developing a more sustainable form of colonization.

 Watch on MyHistoryLab

England's Empire Takes Shape After 1660, England took over the Dutch colony of New Netherland in North America and implemented a colonial policy that stressed greater centralization and control. This video examines this imperial change under the final Stuart monarchs (Charles II and James II) and their successors. It examines the rise of Britain's navy and other changes that resulted in English dominance in the Atlantic. The population of British North America grew rapidly in the eighteenth century, pressuring Native American peoples on the colonial frontiers and heightening tension between Great Britain and its imperial rival, France.   **4**

Watch on MyHistoryLab

August 1705, more bad news awaited them. Returning from France, Marguerite's husband had contracted yellow fever in Cuba and died before his ship reached Mobile.

Immigrants aboard the vessel, including potential brides recruited for Louisiana, brought yellow fever ashore at Mobile. The town—home to just 160 men and a dozen women—lacked food and shelter for the sickly newcomers, and the disease spread quickly, sweeping away forty residents in two months and decimating nearby Indian villages. Still, townsmen welcomed the ship's eligible young women, ages fourteen to eighteen, and priests celebrated thirteen marriages within the first three weeks. Determined to persist in this infant settlement, Marguerite moved into the house her late husband had built and played an active role in the survival of the Louisiana colony.

n the second half of the seventeenth century, European maritime powers were caught up in a global race to expand and protect their overseas empires, and the chessboard was constantly changing. By the 1670s, Dutch authorities had been forced to withdraw entirely from North America. But the Spanish, French, and English competed intensively, starting towns wherever possible in order to stake their claims.

England, a latecomer to the competition, expanded the number and size of its coastal colonies, creating new port towns along the eastern seaboard. Pushing up from the South, Spain struggled to retain its foothold in Florida and New Mexico and to lay claim to parts of Arizona and Texas as well. New Spanish towns appeared at Albuquerque, El Paso, and Pensacola. Only France, pressing west and south from the St. Lawrence Valley, managed to penetrate the interior of the continent extensively. A string of forts from the Great Lakes to the Gulf of Mexico—Detroit, Peoria, Mobile, and others—all came into being under the French flag.

Whatever the flag, every colonial foothold was separated from the European centers of empire by the vast Atlantic, and faced several fundamental questions: Who has the right to govern? What is the source of their authority and the extent of their domain? Such questions, debated earlier at Plymouth, Jamestown, and Santa Fe, expanded after 1660; vague boundaries multiplied, and structures of control proved tenuous. Far from royal authority, religious dissenters and political rebels who felt excluded or exploited could question the legitimacy of those in charge. Challenges to authority became familiar experiences over the next two generations.

France and the American Interior

3.1 Why did France gain access to North America's interior before other European powers?

The potential wealth of the North American interior had long intrigued government ministers in France. If Canadian fur traders could explore this vast domain and befriend its Indian inhabitants, France might control some of the continent's most fertile farmland and keep its extensive natural assets out of the hands of European rivals. If the French could recruit enough Native Americans as loyal allies, they might even threaten the rich Spanish silver mines in Mexico and challenge the growing English colonies east of the Appalachian Mountains. But for France to realize such wide ambitions, the French king, Louis XIV, would need to make North American colonization a national priority, and the extent of his commitment remained uncertain.

The Rise of the Sun King

King Louis XIV stood at the center of France's expanding imperial sphere. Indeed, so much seemed to revolve around him that he became known as the "Sun King." In 1661, at age twenty-two, he assumed personal control of a realm of 20 million people. During most of his long rule—until his death in 1715 at age seventy-seven—Louis dominated European affairs. Always a builder of monuments, he expanded the Louvre in Paris and then dazzled the French nobility and clergy with his opulent new palace at Versailles.

In religion, the Sun King challenged the Catholic pope on one hand and suppressed French Protestants (Huguenots) on the other. In politics, he centralized the monarchy's power as never before. Louis' administration consolidated the laws of France, strengthened the armed forces, built roads, and expanded commerce. His government ministries foreshadowed the power of modern nation-states by regulating industry and imposing tariffs and taxes.

Throughout Louis XIV's reign, his officials followed a set of policies known as **mercantilism,** a system in which a government stressed economic self-sufficiency and a favorable balance of trade. By avoiding foreign debts and drawing in valuable

Mercantilism A commercial policy that sought to achieve economic self-sufficiency and a favorable balance of trade (often by planting colonies) in order to promote a country's prosperity, strength, and independence. Rival European imperial powers favored the strategy of mercantilism in the seventeenth and eighteenth centuries.

resources from its competitors and its own colonies, a state could pay for wars abroad and costly projects at home. The French mercantilist strategy was to exploit labor efficiently and import raw materials cheaply, while exporting expensive manufactured products, such as glassware, wine, silk, and tapestries, in exchange for gold and silver. Colonists were expected to generate much-needed natural resources and to consume manufactured goods from the mother country.

In Paris, finance minister Jean-Baptiste Colbert emerged as the chief architect of this strategy of aggressive mercantilism. At home, he taxed foreign imports, removed domestic trade barriers, and improved internal transportation. Moreover, he reduced worker holidays and outlawed strikes. Colbert improved France's ports and created a code to regulate maritime shipping. He expanded the naval fleet and pressed French sailors into its service. Pushing still harder, he organized overseas trading companies and provided insurance for their expensive ventures. In addition, he sanctioned France's involvement in the African slave trade. Colbert yearned to acquire new territory to increase the empire's self-sufficiency and keep overseas resources out of enemy hands. To that end, he and his successors encouraged French exploration of North America on an unprecedented scale.

Read the Document King Louis XIV, "The Code Noir" (1685)

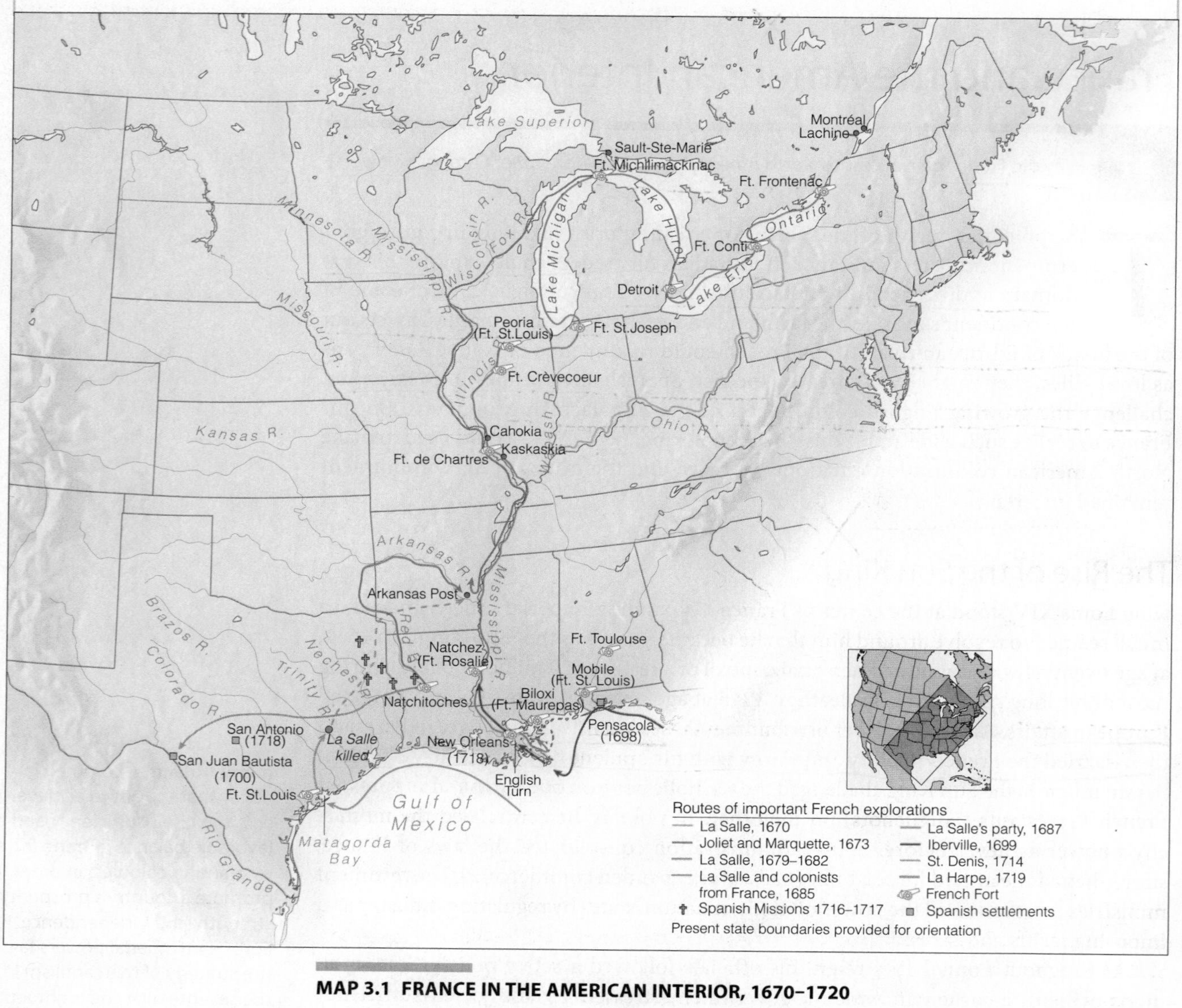

MAP 3.1 FRANCE IN THE AMERICAN INTERIOR, 1670–1720

54

The government of Louis XIV assumed direct control over New France from a private company in 1663. Colbert hoped to diversify production away from the fur trade, so he shipped artisans to the colony, plus livestock and tools. To promote domestic life and population growth, the government also transported young single women and announced cash incentives for early marriages and large families. Many of the soldiers sent to protect New France from Iroquois and English threats stayed on to establish farms.

On balance, however, Colbert's plans for a prosperous, well-populated colony in Canada failed. The small population of New France—10,000 by 1680—never grew as rapidly as French imperial strategists desired. The harsh winters and short growing seasons hindered the expansion of agriculture, and barriers imposed by Louis XIV inhibited migration. His "Code Noir" of 1685, which sanctioned slavery and restricted the activities of free Negroes, also banned Jews from French colonies, where only the practice of Roman Catholicism would be allowed. That same year, the king revoked the Edict of Nantes, which had granted Protestants their legal rights in France. Therefore, as thousands of frightened Huguenots prepared to leave the country, these dissenters found themselves prevented from traveling to France's colonies. In contrast to the English, the French did not use their overseas colonies as havens for outcasts, troublemakers, and religious dissidents.

Exploring the Mississippi Valley

Here

In New France, intrepid explorers had probed steadily across the Great Lakes, reaching the western shores of Lake Michigan in 1634. There, Winnebago Indians (today's Ho-Chunk Nation) told of a river called the "Messisipi," and rumors of this river circulated among the French for a generation. Finally, in 1673, trader Louis Jolliet, joined by a Jesuit priest named Jacques Marquette, entered the upper Mississippi and descended the great stream to the mouth of the Arkansas River. If the Mississippi waterway flowed south into the Gulf of Mexico, instead of west to the Pacific as some explorers hoped, perhaps the river could give France a path to the wealth of New Spain and provide French settlers with access to a warm-water port.

Officials in Quebec moved to exploit these western prospects, using an experienced young adventurer: René-Robert Cavelier, Sieur de La Salle. In 1679, inspired by word of Jolliet's exploits, La Salle and his men pushed west through the Great Lakes to erect forts on the Illinois River, a tributary of the Mississippi. These outposts strengthened French trading ties with local Indians and provided a launching point for exploring the Mississippi Valley. In 1682, La Salle led a contingent of French and Indians south from the Illinois to the mouth of the great river, showing that it emptied into the Gulf of Mexico. Before returning to Canada and France, he claimed the entire river basin for France, naming it Louisiana to honor his king.

But La Salle, hindered by poor maps and crude navigational instruments, miscalculated the position of the Mississippi's mouth. Therefore, when he tried to return by sea, sailing from France early in 1685 with four ships and several hundred colonists, he mistakenly disembarked on the Texas coast. Slowly, the entire colonization plan unraveled. When one ship sank near shore, the hapless settlers lost valuable supplies and any hope of relocating. Jealous lieutenants eventually killed La Salle before he could find the Mississippi River. Most of the colonists he had brought from France perished in the Texas wilderness.

In La Salle's wake, other explorers, lacking official sanction, used Indian guides to probe westward, seeking routes to the Pacific. Historians puzzle over the thin evidence several left behind. On a sketch map of the southwest, Jean Couture claimed to have traveled all the way to the Gulf of California. Baron Lahontan, a marine in his early twenties, asserted in a letter to his French patron that he journeyed up "The Long River" in the winter of 1688–1689. His small party may have proceeded down the Wisconsin to the Mississippi, hiked across northern Iowa on well-known Indian trails, and then paddled up a long portion of the Missouri River into North Dakota. But few believed Lahontan's cryptic report, so it had little influence on later exploration.

When La Salle's French expedition landed on the Texas coast in 1685, one ship ran aground and broke up; another departed quickly. La Salle's colonists only had the *Belle* (foreground), and it sank in a storm the following year. In 1995, archaeologists found the vessel in shallow water and salvaged the remains. Why was the lure of discovering a westward route to the Pacific by land or water so enduring?

King William's War in the Northeast

The lure of finding a westward route to the Pacific continued, but the French colonizers had overreached themselves. They had failed to challenge Spanish power in the Gulf of Mexico or to establish a southern port. In the East, French Canadians faced renewed Iroquois attacks along the St. Lawrence River in the 1680s. Moreover, a strengthened Protestant regime emerged in London with the ascent of William III to the English throne in 1689. This transition started more than 100 years of bitter conflict between Protestant England and Catholic France, an ideological and military struggle that often included North America.

The American hostilities began in the Northeast in 1689 when the Iroquois, well supplied with English arms, launched raids near Montreal. As King William's War escalated, the French and their Indian allies struck back, burning outposts in New York and New England. At Fort Loyal (modern Portland, Maine) raiders butchered 100 English men, women, and children who had surrendered, and they took others captive. English survivors left their dead unburied and fled south toward Salem and Boston. In Massachusetts Bay, many viewed the attack as part of a wider design to undo the Reformation and expand the authority of the Catholic Church.

After eight years of bloodshed, King William's War ended in a stalemate in 1697. Hurt by the hostilities, the Iroquois soon promised to remain neutral during any future colonial wars between France and England, a pledge they generally honored for more than half a century. The French, having strengthened their position in Canada, revived the "southern strategy" that had obsessed Colbert and La Salle for establishing a Gulf Coast colony.

A turn in European events opened the door for renewed French efforts in the American heartland. King Carlos II of Spain fell ill without an immediate heir, and the royal courts of Europe competed to determine his successor. Louis XIV, eager to acquire Spain's European realm and American dominions for France, proposed that his grandson, Philip of Anjou, receive the Spanish crown. But England supported an opposing candidate, so the War of Spanish Succession (1701–1714) broke out soon after Carlos died.

Founding the Louisiana Colony

Even before new hostilities erupted in Europe in 1701, Louis XIV and his ministers took steps to secure French claims in the Gulf of Mexico, despite Spain's naval dominance in the area. By renewing La Salle's plan for a Louisiana colony, France could strengthen its hand in the impending war over succession to the Spanish throne. A colony on the Gulf of Mexico would provide a southern outlet for the French fur trade and a strategic outpost to counter Spain's new fort at Pensacola in western Florida.

England also saw advantages to establishing a base on the lower Mississippi. Such a post could challenge Spanish and French claims to the Gulf region and increase English trade with the Chickasaw and other southern Indians. In 1698, a London promoter quietly made plans to transport a group of Huguenot refugees to the mouth of the Mississippi. Catching wind of this scheme, the French organized their own secret expedition to the Gulf of Mexico under an aspiring Canadian officer, Pierre Le Moyne d'Iberville.

Coming from a large and well-connected Montreal family, the Le Moynes, Iberville quickly drew several siblings into the gulf colonization plan, including his teenage brother, Bienville. Iberville and his party sailed for the Gulf of Mexico from the French port of Brest in 1699. Their ship entered the mouth of the Mississippi in time to repel the English expedition at a site on the river still known as English Turn. They also managed to build a fort at nearby Biloxi Bay before returning to France.

The two brothers were now well on their way to creating the Gulf Coast colony that La Salle and his followers had failed to establish. A second voyage let Iberville conduct further reconnaissance of the lower Mississippi. On a third trip, in 1702, he established Fort Louis, near Mobile Bay, giving French traders access to the Choctaw Indians. Young Bienville, placed in charge of Fort Louis, labored to sustain the tiny outpost at Mobile. Iberville himself left to pursue other schemes and died an early death in 1706.

Enmeshed in the War of Spanish Succession, France ignored its new Gulf colony. Epidemics reduced Louisiana's newcomers and took a far heavier toll on Indian neighbors. Settlers drawn from Canada, with prior wilderness experience, maintained close ties with local Native Americans and resented the incompetence and haughtiness of colonists sent from France. The latter complained about the poor living conditions and looked down on the uneducated Canadians. However, despite social friction and a chronic lack of supplies from France, the small community at Mobile survived.

Far to the north, additional posts reinforced French territorial claims, fostered the fur trade, and protected neighboring Indians against Iroquois raids. The village of Peoria sprang up on the Illinois River in 1691. Catholic missions appeared nearby at Cahokia (1697) and Kaskaskia (1703). Fort de Chartres took shape in southern Illinois in 1719. Farther north, the French established two other strategic posts. In 1689, they

Interpreting History

Large Enough to Be Called a City

Extensive villages of the **Arikara** and **Mandan** Indians **stretched** along the **Missouri River,** in what is now **South** and **North Dakota.**

W hile the French probed the Mississippi Valley in the 1680s, the combined population of Boston, New York, Philadelphia, and Charlestown had not yet reached 12,000 people. Surprisingly, larger commercial centers existed in the distant interior, unseen by Europeans. Extensive villages of the Arikara and Mandan Indians stretched along the Missouri River, in what is now South and North Dakota. These prosperous agricultural communities exchanged abundant food supplies for meat, hides, and other goods brought long distances by hunting groups traveling from all directions.

La Salle's death in 1687 stirred younger French explorers, eager to venture west of the Mississippi and discover a trade route to the Pacific. One such adventurer, known as Baron Lahontan, had sailed to Canada in 1683, at age seventeen. The restless nobleman spent several winters with Algonquin Indians to learn their language, sending occasional reports home to France. After returning to Europe in 1694, Lahontan published these letters as **New Voyages to North America** (1703). His popular account appeared in several languages and went through numerous editions.

The most intriguing and controversial section, Letter XVI, described an expedition west of the Mississippi to a "Long River" in the winter of 1688–1689. There, Lahontan encountered densely populated Native American trading towns. However, **New Voyages** belittled Jesuit efforts to convert Canada's Indians, so Catholic officials denounced the author and his book. Specifically, they attacked Letter XVI, asserting the writer had fabricated an impossible journey to imaginary places. Lahontan's reputation never recovered—although his positive account of Indian life influenced Jean-Jacques Rousseau's Enlightenment ideas about the "noble savage."

Today, some scholars suspect Letter XVI may actually document the first European encounter with populous trading

Artist George Catlin sketched large Arikara and Mandan villages when he went up the Missouri River in the 1830s. If Lahontan visited the same towns in 1688, he was justified in saying that the beehive shape of their numerous earthen lodges reminded him of traditional French outdoor baking ovens. Why would historians be inclined to think that Lahontan's account of his journey into the interior of the continent lacked veracity?

SOURCE: Smithsonian American Art Museum, Washington DC/Art Resource, NY

towns on the Upper Missouri, 116 years before the expedition of Lewis and Clark. Lahontan claimed to have set out by canoe in September 1688 from Michilimackinac in Lake Huron, heading a small group of Frenchmen and Ottawa Indians. Near Green Bay, Wisconsin, Lahontan engaged ten Outagami (Fox) men who knew the language and country of "the Eokoros" (the Arikara on the Missouri River?) through decades of peaceful contact. These knowledgeable Indians led Lahontan's party westward, reaching the trading centers on the "Long River" in early November. Near the first village, Lahontan relates, a band of Eokoros hunters recognized the friendly shouts of his Outagami guides.

As soon as the hunters heard the voices of the Outagamis, they threw down their weapons. [After offering venison and receiving gifts of knives and tobacco in return,] they hurried back to their villages and informed their associates what a good sort of people they had encountered. The next day towards evening, there appeared upon the river bank more than two thousand Indians, who started to dance as soon as they spotted us. Thereupon, our Outagamis went ashore and, after a short conference, we all steered to the chief village.

Next day, I went myself to visit the grandees of this nation, to whom I gave presents of knives, scissors, needles, and tobacco. They led me to understand that they were extremely pleased with our arrival in their country, for they had heard other nations speak very honorably of the French. I took leave of them on the 12th and set out with a convoy of five or six hundred Indians, who marched along the shore, keeping pace with our canoes. The commanders of this nation acquainted me that they had twelve villages peopled by 20,000 warriors.

Numbers were equally large upstream, where Lahontan's party received "a very honorable reception" at the towns of the Essanapes (Mandan?).

Upon our first appearance, three or four hundred Essanapes came running to the shore, and, after dancing, invited us ashore. The large extent of this town might justly entitle it to be called a city. The houses are built almost like [traditional French] ovens, but they are large and high.

Questions for Discussion

1. What motives might Lahontan have had to invent a false journey or to disguise details of an actual trip?
2. If Letter XVI proves to be a real account of large Arikara and Mandan villages in 1688, could it have any implications for traditional notions of early American history?

laid out a garrison where Lake Huron joins Lake Michigan. In 1701, they created a lasting town on the strait (*le détroit* in French) connecting Lake Erie to Lake Huron. The founder of Detroit, Antoine de La Mothe Cadillac, foresaw a prosperous future for this trading post, since the new village would be accessible "to the most distant tribes which surround these vast sweet water seas."

In 1712, the French crown, its resources depleted by a decade of warfare in Europe, granted control over Louisiana to a powerful Paris merchant, Antoine Crozat. Drawing Cadillac from Detroit to serve as Louisiana's governor general, Crozat hoped to develop connections to mineral-rich Mexico and to discover precious metals in the Mississippi watershed. But probes on the upper Mississippi, the Missouri, and the Red rivers yielded no easy bonanza. Instead, explorers established three new trading posts among the Indians: Natchitoches on the Red River, Fort Rosalie (at Natchez), and Fort Toulouse (near modern Montgomery, Alabama).

When Louis XIV died in 1715, the colonial population of Lower Louisiana stood at scarcely 300 people. But over two generations, the French had established a solid claim on the American interior. Their position was an ongoing challenge to English and Spanish competitors. The crescent of wilderness outposts arcing north and then east from the Gulf Coast offered a useful network for additional exploration, Indian trade, and military conquest. French control of the Mississippi Valley remained a real possibility until the era of Thomas Jefferson and Napoleon Bonaparte nearly a century later.

The Spanish Empire on the Defensive *Here.*

Did Indian experiences with Spanish colonization vary widely in Arizona, New Mexico, and Florida?

Whereas France's power expanded during Louis XIV's reign, Spain's overextended empire continued to weaken. This decline opened the door for Louis to maneuver his own grandson onto the Spanish throne in 1700 as Philip V. Meanwhile, Spanish colonizers struggled to defend vast territorial claims in North America that spread—on paper—from the Gulf of California to the Florida peninsula.

In Spain's remote colonies of New Mexico and Florida, local administration often proved corrupt, and links to imperial officials at home remained weak and cumbersome. For several generations, the Indian majority had resented the harsh treatment and strange diseases that came with colonial contact. Now, cultural disruptions and pressures from hostile Indian neighbors fanned the flames of discontent. In the late seventeenth century, a wave of Native American rebellions swept the northern frontier of New Spain.

The Pueblo Revolt in New Mexico

The largest and most successful revolt took place along the upper Rio Grande. There, Pueblo Indians from dozens of separate communities (or pueblos) united in a major upheaval in August 1680. They murdered twenty-one of the forty friars serving in New Mexico, ransacked their churches, and killed more than 350 settlers. After laying siege to Santa Fe, the rebels drove the remaining Spanish colonists and their Christian Indian allies south out of the province and kept them away for more than a decade. Several thousand stunned survivors took refuge at what is now El Paso. When they began questioning Indian informants to learn causes for the revolt, explanations for the fearsome uprising quickly emerged.

Diverse pressures had combined to ignite the Pueblo Revolt of 1680. First, a five-year drought beginning in 1666 had inflicted a prolonged famine upon the peoples of New Mexico. Second, neighboring Apache and Navajo communities were embittered by colonial slave raids that took Indian captives to work in Mexican silver mines. In

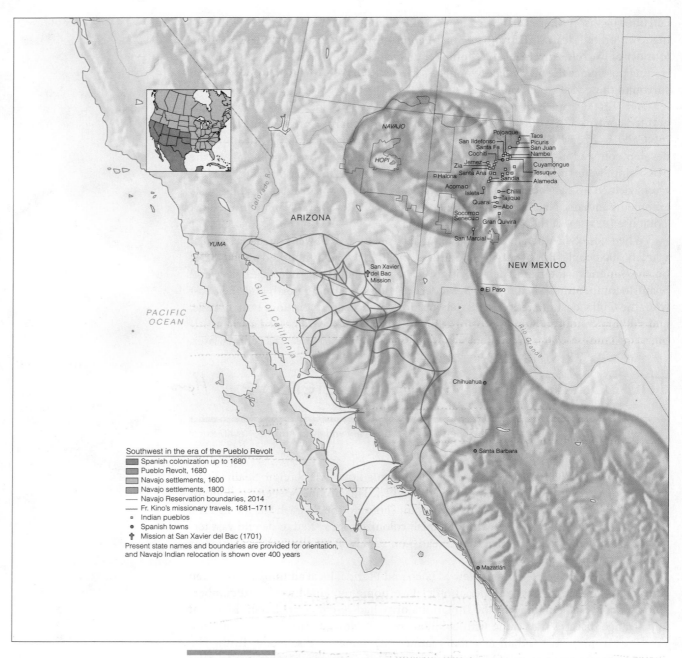

MAP 3.2 CHANGES IN THE SOUTHWEST The 1680 Pueblo Revolt (green) overwhelmed Spain's small New Mexico colony. In the next three decades, Father Eusebio Kino (blue lines) and other Jesuits moved the mission frontier north into what is now Arizona. Over time, the Navajo relocated their homelands; they remain an important presence in the region.

retaliation, they stepped up their hostilities against the small colonial population and the numerous Pueblo Indians who had been linked with the Spanish over several generations. These raiding parties, riding stolen Spanish horses, killed livestock and seized scarce food. When colonial soldiers proved unable to fend off the hit-and-run attacks, their credibility among local Pueblo Indians weakened.

Third, a smoldering controversy over religion flared during the 1670s. When an epidemic struck in 1671, Spanish missionaries could not stem the sickness with Christian prayers. In response, traditionalist Indian priests revived age-old Pueblo religious customs. Horrified, the Spanish friars and government officials punished what they saw as backsliding away from Catholicism within the Pueblo population. At Santa Fe in 1675, they hanged three respected Indians for idolatry and whipped and imprisoned forty-three others—including a militant leader from San Juan pueblo named Popé. Before the captives could be sold into slavery, armed Indians successfully demanded the release of Popé and the other prisoners.

Popé withdrew to Taos, the northernmost pueblo in New Mexico. From there, he negotiated secretly with like-minded factions in other pueblos, unifying resistance to Spanish domination and forging an underground movement. In part, he built support around widespread resentment of the Spanish *encomienda* system (requiring Indian communities to supply labor or pay tribute) and the Catholic Church (which forbade traditional Indian religious ceremonies). Indian women whom Spanish priests or soldiers had abused took Popé's side in this cultural clash. The movement also received covert support from numerous **mestizos** and **mulattos**, mixed-race people whose lack of "pure" Spanish blood cost them any chance for advancement. Popé sent runners to each conspiring pueblo, fixing the date for the rebellion. When the time came, his Pueblo warriors swiftly routed their adversaries. Unified in triumph, the zealous victors smeared excrement on Christian altars and bathed themselves to remove the stigma of baptism.

But initial cohesion gave way to friction. The successful rebels soon quarreled over who should hold power and how best to return to ancient ways. Kivas would replace churches, and the cross would give way to the **kachina.** But what other parts of the imported culture should the Indians abandon? Various Pueblo groups could not agree on which Spanish words, tools, and customs to discard or which foreign crops and animals to retain.

In 1681, the Pueblo fended off a Spanish attempt at reconquest. But they remained divided among themselves and more vulnerable than ever to Apache raids. Within a decade, rival factions had deposed Popé, and another Spanish colonial army, under Governor Diego de Vargas, had entered New Mexico. It took the new governor several years to subdue the province, and the Pueblo managed another full-scale rebellion in 1696. But Vargas anticipated the revolt and crushed the opposition, as Oñate had done a century earlier. In 1706, several soldiers and their families established the town of Albuquerque. Learning from prior mistakes, Spanish officials did not reimpose the hated *encomienda* system. A new generation of Franciscan missionaries tolerated indigenous Pueblo traditions as long as the Indians also attended Catholic mass.

Navajo and Spanish on the Southwestern Frontier

The repercussions of rebellion and reconquest along the upper Rio Grande echoed through the Southwest. To the north, Pueblo refugees joined the Navajo and brought valuable experience as corn farmers. Corn, already known to the Navajo, now became an increasingly important food and sacred symbol for them.

Moreover, these Pueblo refugees shared knowledge learned from the Spanish about planting peach orchards and raising sheep. Navajo women—the weavers in their society—soon owned large flocks and created wool blankets on their traditional portable looms. The Pueblo also brought more Spanish horses, a key asset that let the Navajo spread their domain west into fine grazing country in what is now northeast Arizona.

Despite limited resources, authorities in Mexico City sent missionaries north to spread Christianity to hostile Indians near the Gulf of California. Year by year, these friar-explorers edged toward what is now southern Arizona, reaching the cactus-studded landscape of the Sonoran Desert by the 1690s.

Eusebio Kino, a tireless Jesuit missionary born in Italy and educated in Germany, spearheaded the early exploration of the Arizona region. In 1701, this padre on horseback established a mission at San Xavier del Bac, below modern Tucson. But Father Kino's missions languished after his death in 1711. Twenty-five years later, a silver strike at "Arizonac," near present-day Nogales on the U.S.-Mexican border, provided a new name for the region, which would eventually become the state called Arizona.

Encomienda The Spanish *encomienda* system, imposed in Spain's American empire, requiring Indian communities to supply labor or pay tribute to a local colonial overlord (identified as an *encomendero*).

Mestizo A person of mixed European and American Indian ancestry.

Mulatto A person of mixed European and African ancestry; the first-generation offspring of a Caucasian and a Negroid parent.

Kachina An Indian religious system, inspired by Mesoamerican traditions, and present in the American Southwest for more than 800 years; the kachina cult used masks for group performances associated with rain, curing, fertility, warfare, and the ancestors. Among many Pueblo and Hopi Indians, this tradition was epitomized by kachina (or katsina) dolls.

Borderland Conflict in Texas and Florida

The encounters on Spain's other North American frontiers took different forms, in part because European rivals appeared on the scene. Conflict with the French led the Spanish to found missions in Texas, a land they named after the local Tejas Indians. At first, responding to news about La Salle's ill-fated French colony, the Spanish made a brief attempt to establish a Texas mission in 1690, departing again in 1693. They renewed their effort two decades later, after Governor Cadillac sent explorers from Louisiana across eastern Texas to forge ties with Spanish communities south of the Rio Grande. Eager to open trade with the Spanish, these French visitors reached San Juan Bautista, below the modern U.S.-Mexican border, in 1714.

Spanish authorities, taken by surprise, dusted off plans for colonizing Texas. By 1717, they had established half a dozen small missions near the Sabine River, the boundary between modern Texas and Louisiana. The next year, to expand their missionary activities and secure the supply route from San Juan Bautista to these distant outposts in east Texas, the Spanish built a cluster of settlements beside the San Antonio River, at a midpoint in the trail. Within two decades, a string of missions stretched along the river. Indian converts tended herds of cattle and sheep and constructed aqueducts to irrigate new fields of wheat and corn. The earliest mission, San Antonio de Valero (1718), provided a nucleus for the town of San Antonio. Later known as the Alamo, the mission also strengthened Spanish claims to Texas against threats of French intrusion.

During the second half of the seventeenth century, the Indians of Florida, like the Pueblo in New Mexico, debated whether to reject generations of Spanish rule. The Columbian Exchange had altered their lives in dramatic ways. They ate new foods such as figs, oranges, peas, and cabbages. They used Spanish words—*azucár* (sugar), *botija* (jar), *caballo* (horse)—and metal hoes from Europe allowed them to produce more corn. But expanding contact with missionaries created major problems as well. By 1660, devastating epidemics had whittled away at Florida's Native American towns. The Indians still outnumbered the newcomers more than ten to one, but they had to expend enormous energy raising, processing, and hauling food for the Spanish. When colonists grew fearful of French and English attacks after 1670, they forced hundreds of Indians to perform even more grueling labor: constructing the stone fortress of San Marcos at St. Augustine.

Nothing proved more troubling to Florida's Indians than the spread of livestock farming. St. Augustine's elite had established profitable cattle ranches on the depopulated savannas of Timucua, near present-day Gainesville in north-central Florida. These entrepreneurs ignored requirements to keep cows away from unfenced Indian gardens, and they enforced harsh laws to protect their stock. Any Florida Indian who killed cattle faced four months of servitude; people caught raiding Spanish herds had their ears cut off.

Resentment grew in Florida's scattered mission villages. Restless Indian converts wondered whether the English, who had founded their Carolina colony in 1670, might make viable allies. The English seemed eager to trade for deerskins, and they offered the Native Americans a steadier supply of desirable goods than the Spanish could provide. Several Indian communities moved closer to Carolina to test this new alternative for trade. But when France and Spain joined forces against the English after 1700, Florida's Indians found themselves caught up in a struggle far larger than they had bargained for.

Ever since the days of Francis Drake, the English had schemed to oust the Spanish from St. Augustine. In 1702, led by South Carolina Governor James Moore, English raiders and their Indian allies rampaged through the Florida town. Yet the new stone fortress of San Marcos held firm, protecting the inhabitants. Two years later, Moore invaded Apalachee (near modern Tallahassee). His troops crushed the mission towns, killing hundreds and carrying away more than 4,000 Indian captives. Most of them were women and children, whom the English sold as slaves. By 1706, the mission villages in Apalachee and Timucua lay in ruins. "In all these extensive dominions," lamented a Spanish official from St. Augustine, "the law of God and the preaching of the Holy Gospel have now ceased."

Explore Changes in the Southwest on MyHistoryLab

HOW DID THE SPANISH IMPACT THE SOUTHWEST?

By the early 1600s, the claims of the Spanish Empire in the Americas had extended into what would become the Southwest of the United States. These lands had long been inhabited and controlled by a number of distinct Native American peoples, including the Pueblo, Hopi, and Zuni. Spanish colonizers and rival Indian groups—Apache, and later, Comanche—contested for dominance. The Spanish attempted to consolidate their power and influence by sending missionaries through the region. Pueblo tribes responded in 1680 with the Pueblo Revolt in which they destroyed missions and drove the Spanish out of their territory. The Spanish returned, however, and their numbers grew as those of the Native Americans began to decline.

Mission San Juan Capistrano in present-day San Antonio, Texas, was a Spanish missionary community established in 1716 and was part of Spain's colonization system, which stretched across the American Southwest in the seventeenth, eighteenth, and early nineteenth centuries.

THE SHIFTING POPULATION OF THE SPANISH PROVINCE OF NEW MEXICO (NUEVO MEXICO), 1600–1800

Year	Native American	Spanish	Total	Native American (%)	Spanish (%)
1600	80,000	0	80,000	100	0
1640	40,000	800	40,800	98	2
1680	17,000	1,500	18,500	92	8
1750	11,000	15,000	26,000	42	58
1780	8,600	19,000	27,600	31	69
1800	9,700	29,000	38,700	25	75

SOURCE: Population data for the Province of Nuevo Mexico comes from Ramon A. Gutierrez, *When Jesus Came the Corn Mothers Went Away: Marriage, Sexuality, and Power in New Mexico, 1500–1846* (Stanford, CA: Stanford University Press, 1991)

KEY QUESTIONS   Use **MyHistoryLab** *Explorer* to **answer** these **questions:**

Comparison ▶▶▶ *How did Spanish land claims contrast to those of Native American tribes?*

Map these territories to see potential conflicts.

Response ▶▶▶ *Where did the Spanish set up missions?*

Use the locations of these outposts to conjecture what logistical problems the Spanish might have faced.

Analysis ▶▶▶ *What is the best way to explain the rapid decline in the Native American population of the Southwest?*

Understand the reasons behind this dramatic shift.

England's American Empire Takes Shape

3.3 Why did England's varied new Restoration-Era American colonies present so many contrasts?

I n 1660, as Louis XIV began his long reign in France and Spanish missionaries labored in obscurity in New Mexico and Florida, England experienced a counter-revolutionary upheaval that dramatically influenced American colonial affairs.

Earlier, during years of violent civil war, English rebels supporting Puritans and Parliament had defeated the royal army and overthrown the ruling Stuart family. In 1649, they tried and executed King Charles I, and then abolished hereditary monarchy altogether. For a brief period, England became a republican commonwealth without a king. But Oliver Cromwell, the movement's dictatorial leader, became the country's self-styled Lord Protector. When Cromwell died in 1658, pressures quickly mounted to undo the radical Puritan Revolution and return to monarchical government. In May 1660, a strong coalition of conservative interests welcomed the late king's son back from exile and restored him to the throne as King Charles II. The renewed Stuart dynasty ruled from 1660 to 1688, a period remembered in English politics and culture as the **Restoration Era.**

The shift in London's political winds could hardly have been more sudden. Charles II moved swiftly in 1660 to underscore the end of England's Puritan experiment. He ordered the execution of those who had beheaded his father. Others who had fought to end monarchy and strengthen Parliament abruptly fell out of favor for their religious and political beliefs, and some found refuge across the Atlantic, where English colonies were expanding more rapidly than their French and Spanish counterparts. All along North America's Atlantic coast, positive demographic patterns—rising immigration, early marriage, high birth rates, and a lowering level of child mortality—were contributing to population expansion.

Restoration Era Royalist supporters restored the English monarchy in 1660. Charles II became king and the Stuart dynasty resumed its rule of England until Charles's successor, the pro-Catholic James II, was forced into exile in 1688.

Monarchy Restored and Navigation Controlled

Because most English colonists still lived within fifty miles of the Atlantic, an increase in people steadily broadened the opportunities for seaborne trade. Growing ship traffic, in turn, sparked government desires to regulate colonial navigation to benefit the restored monarchy. In 1660, Parliament passed a major new law, based on mercantilism, designed to promote English shipping and trade.

The Navigation Act of 1660 laid out important conditions that shaped England's colonial commerce for generations. First, merchants could not conduct trade to or from the English colonies in foreign-owned ships. Second, key non-English products imported from foreign lands—salt, wine, oil, and naval stores (the tar, pitch, masts, and other materials used to furnish boats)—had to be carried in English ships or in ships with mostly English crews. Third, the law contained a list of **enumerated articles** produced overseas—tobacco, cotton, sugar, ginger, indigo, and dyewoods—that could no longer be sent directly from a colony to a foreign European port. Instead, merchants had to ship them to England first and then reexport them, a step that directly boosted England's domestic economy. Another Navigation Act (1663) required that goods moving from the European continent to England's overseas colonies must pass through England, arriving and departing on English ships.

Enumerated articles Colonial products listed (enumerated) in the Navigation Act of 1660, such as tobacco, sugar, and indigo, had to pass through an English port before reexport to Europe, to aid the domestic economy.

A later measure—the Plantation Duty Act of 1673—tried to close loopholes regarding enumerated articles. The new act required captains to pay a "plantation duty" before they sailed between colonial ports with enumerated goods. Otherwise, colonial vessels carrying such goods had to post bond before leaving harbor to ensure that they would sail directly to England. To enforce these rules, the government sent customs officers to the colonies for the first time. Backed by the Navigation Acts, England's fleets grew and colonial trade became a major sector in England's economy.

Even the Great Plague, which swept England in 1665, could not blunt this mercantile growth. And when a catastrophic fire destroyed most of London the next year, planners redesigned the city with the broad streets and impressive buildings that suited the prosperous hub of an expanding empire. The fashionable coffee shops that sprang up as a novelty in late-seventeenth-century London became common meeting places for exchanging news and views about England's increasingly profitable activities overseas.

Dutch New Netherland Becomes New York

At the beginning of his reign, Charles II knew he had to build loyalty and strengthen an economy weakened by civil war. The king, with expensive tastes and a depleted treasury, found that he could reward loyal family members and supporters, at no cost to the crown, by granting them control over pieces of England's North American domain. With this prospect in hand, the king and his ministers sought to bolster foreign trade, strengthen the royal navy, and outstrip England's commercial rivals. They focused first on the Dutch.

As London stepped up its search for new profits, English officials moved to strengthen control over existing colonies and establish (or seize) new ones wherever possible. The Navigation Acts cut sharply into the Dutch carrying trade and spurred a decade of renewed warfare between England and Holland. For the most part, these intermittent Anglo-Dutch Wars ended in stalemate. But at the final Peace of Westminster in 1674, the English emerged with several important gains in Africa and America.

In West Africa, the English captured and held several key coastal outposts: an island at the mouth of the river Gambia (renamed James Fort for the Duke of York) and Cape Coast Castle on the Gold Coast (near Elmina, the African headquarters of the Dutch West India Company). This encroachment challenged Dutch dominance in the commerce for African gold and ivory. It also gave England the footholds it needed to force its way into the Atlantic slave trade. Charles II granted a monopoly to the Royal Adventurers into Africa (1663) and then the Royal African Company (1672) to exploit the grim but profitable slave traffic. Within several generations, this ruthless initiative reshaped England's American colonies at enormous human cost.

Across the Atlantic, the English had seized the Dutch colony of New Netherland and its poorly defended port of New Amsterdam. Charles II claimed that the land had belonged to England from the time his grandfather endorsed the Virginia Company in 1606. In 1664, the king used his royal prerogative to regain control of this domain. He put the entire disputed region between the Delaware and Connecticut rivers under the personal control of his brother James, Duke of York. That same year, James sent a fleet to claim his prize. When Governor Peter Stuyvesant surrendered the Dutch colony without a fight, the province and its capital on Manhattan Island each received the name New York. Fort Orange on the Hudson became Albany, because *Albion* had been an ancient name for Britain.

James never visited New York, but as proprietor of his new dukedom (including the Dutch and English settlements on Long Island) he wielded enormous powers. He chose the colony's governor, who ruled with an appointed council and enforced "the Duke's Laws" without constraint by any assembly. English newcomers to the colony resented the absence of an elected legislature, and the governor finally authorized an elected body in 1683. But when the new assemblymen approved a Charter of Liberties endorsing government by consent of the governed, the Duke of York disallowed the legislature.

Married women living in New Netherland lost ground in the transition to English rule. Dutch law codes had ensured their full legal status, whereas English common law assigned wives to an inferior status known as **coverture.** They could not own property or keep control over money they earned, and they lacked any independent standing before the law.

As the English asserted political control over New York, the Dutch presence remained evident everywhere. Many English married into Dutch families and worshipped in the Dutch Reformed Church. The village of Harlem built a proper road to lower Manhattan in 1669, but an effort to change the town's Dutch name to Lancaster

Coverture French term for the dependent and legal status of a woman during marriage. Under English law, the male family head received legal rights, and his wife lost independent status, becoming, in legal terms, a *femme covert*.

failed. English-speaking New Yorkers borrowed such Dutch words as *waffle*, *cookie*, *coleslaw*, and *baas* (boss). Anyone who was bilingual, such as Albany merchant Robert Livingston, had a special advantage. Livingston, an immigrant from Scotland, had learned to speak Dutch in Holland in his youth. His marriage linked him to powerful Dutch families in the Hudson Valley, and much of his early wealth came from his ability to translate commercial documents between English and Dutch.

The New Restoration Colonies

Charles II had spurred England's seizure of New Netherland by issuing a charter for control of the contested region to his brother, the Duke of York. To reward supporters, the king continued to issue royal charters for American land, hoping to expand colonization at no cost to the crown. In 1670, for example, he granted a charter to the Hudson's Bay Company. The deal gave the company's proprietors a monopoly on trade, minerals, and land across northern Canada. Farther south, Charles used charters to redistribute control along major portions of the Atlantic coast. His actions prompted an unprecedented scramble for colonial property and profits. Within decades, the English launched important settlement clusters along the Delaware River valley and the Carolina coast. Each depended upon lucrative charters for a small network of friends.

Most of these well-placed people belonged to the Councils for Trade and Plantations in London. Created in 1660, these advisory groups linked England's powerful merchants with crown officials. When Charles II issued a charter for Carolina in 1663, five of its eight initial proprietors served on those councils. And the interlocking network extended further. In 1665, two of these same eight men became the proprietors of New Jersey. In addition, three of the eight played an active role in the Royal African Company, four became founders of the Hudson's Bay Company, and five became initial proprietors of the Bahamas.

Occasionally, Charles reached beyond this small group of friends. In 1679, he made New Hampshire a proprietorship (an ill-fated experiment that lasted to 1708).

📖 Read the Document   **The Pennsylvania Charter of Privileges (October 28, 1701)**

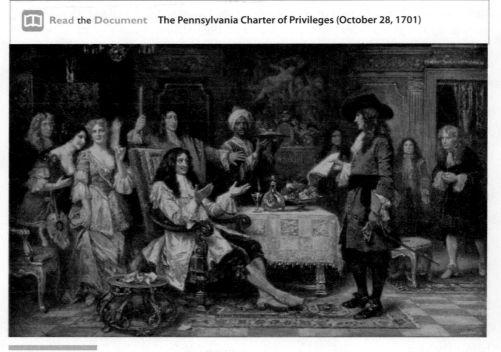

In 1681, after the death of Sir William Penn, King Charles II repaid a debt owed to the famous English admiral by bestowing a vast land grant in America upon his son. The younger William Penn—to the dismay of his upper-class Anglican family—had become a convert to Quakerism at age 22, so he used the gift to found a settlement in the New World for harassed followers of the controversial new pacifist sect. This painting imagines Penn receiving his first word of the royal favor from the flamboyant Restoration monarch in 1680 in the king's breakfast chamber at Whitehall. How did both Charles II and William Penn benefit from the creation of Pennsylvania?

In 1681, he paid off a debt owed to a deceased admiral by granting a charter for an enormous New World tract of land to the officer's son and namesake: the aristocratic Quaker, William Penn. (The huge expanse, called Pennsylvania in honor of the admiral, included the "Lower Counties" that became Delaware in 1704.)

Penn's "holy experiment" to create a Quaker refuge benefited from earlier colonization south of New York. Dutch and Swedish settlers had inhabited the lower Delaware Valley for more than a generation. In 1665, the Duke of York carved off a portion of his vast proprietorship, granting the area between the Delaware and the Hudson to two friends: Lord John Berkeley and Sir George Carteret. They named the area New Jersey because Carteret had been born on the Isle of Jersey in the English Channel. Berkeley and Carteret promptly announced liberal "Concessions"—a representative assembly and freedom of worship—to attract rent-paying newcomers from England and the existing colonies. But their plans for profit made little headway.

In 1674, the proprietors divided these fertile lands into two separate provinces. East Jersey—where Newark was established in 1666—attracted Puritan families from New England, Dutch farmers from New York, and failed planters from Barbados. West Jersey was sold to William Penn and other members of the Quaker sect, also known as the Society of Friends. Filled with egalitarian beliefs, the Quakers inaugurated a political experiment along the Delaware River. They created a one-house unicameral legislature, used secret ballots, and gave more power to juries than to judges. Their forward-looking "Concessions and Agreements" of 1677 barred taxation without the consent of the governed, made all public records open and available, and aimed to keep all inhabitants "free from oppression and slavery." West Jersey's idealistic effort foundered within decades, and by 1702, all New Jersey came under crown control as a single royal colony. But by then, the Quakers had established a foothold in the neighboring colony of Pennsylvania.

Unicameral A legislative body that has only one chamber, or house.

Contrasting Worlds: Pennsylvania and Carolina

Proprietor William Penn laid out his capital for the Pennsylvania colony in 1682, naming it Philadelphia. Within two decades, this market center had more than 2,000 inhabitants. An earnest Quaker, Penn professed pacifism. He made it a point to deal fairly with the Lenni-Lenape (Delaware) Indians. After purchasing their land, he resold it on generous terms to English, Dutch, and Welsh Quakers who agreed to pay him an annual premium, called a **quitrent**. He also emphasized religious tolerance. A growing stream of German Protestants and others facing persecution in Europe began to flow into Pennsylvania after 1700.

Penn drew inspiration from James Harrington, the English political philosopher. Harrington's book *Oceana* (1656) argued that the best way to create an enduring republic was for one person to draft and implement its constitution. After endless tinkering, Penn devised a progressive "Frame of Government" that allowed for trial by jury, limited terms of office, and no use of capital punishment except in cases of treason and murder. But he remained ambivalent about legislative democracy. Settlers resented his scheme for a lower house that could approve acts drafted by the governor but could not initiate laws. In a new Charter of Privileges in 1701, Penn agreed to the creation of a unicameral legislature with full lawmaking powers. Penn's expansive proprietorship belonged to his descendants until colonial rule ended in 1776.

In contrast to William Penn, the proprietors of the new Carolina colony—which split into North and South Carolina a generation later—aspired to establish a stable aristocratic system. Their leader, Anthony Ashley-Cooper, also drew inspiration from Harrington, since *Oceana* stressed that land distribution determined the nature of any commonwealth. Ashley-Cooper (later the first Earl of Shaftesbury) worked in 1669 with his young secretary, John Locke (later an influential political philosopher), to prepare a set of "Fundamental Constitutions." They proposed a stratified society in which hereditary nobles controlled much of the land and wealthy manor lords employed a lowly servant class of "leetmen." Their unrealistic document tried to revive the elaborate feudal hierarchy of medieval times.

Quitrent A fixed annual tax, included in many colonial land grants, paid by the recipient to the donor.

The new government framework also endorsed racial slavery, declaring that "Every Freeman of Carolina shall have absolute Power and Authority over his Negro Slaves." This endorsement was not surprising, given the proprietors' involvement with England's new slave-trading monopoly in Africa and their initial recruitment of settlers in 1670 from the Caribbean sugar island of Barbados. When Carolina colonists relocated Charlestown (later Charleston) between the Ashley and Cooper rivers in 1680, the proprietors had already modified aspects of their complicated scheme, setting aside feudalism to encourage greater immigration. Nevertheless, their endorsement of slavery shaped the region's society for hundreds of years.

Bloodshed in the English Colonies: 1670–1690

3.4 To what degree was colonial violence after 1670 sparked by internal tensions or by affairs in England?

The appearance of English settlements along the Atlantic coast did little, in most places, to alter the traditional rhythms of life. Year after year, the daily challenges of subsistence dominated American life for Indians and colonists alike. The demanding seasonal tasks of clearing fields, planting seeds, and harvesting crops remained interwoven with the incessant chores of providing clothing, securing shelter, and sustaining community.

Over time, however, changing circumstances in America and Europe introduced new pressures up and down the Atlantic seaboard. On occasion after 1670, familiar routines gave way to episodes of bloodshed that threatened to tear whole colonies apart. Elsewhere in North America, Pueblo rebels were resisting the Spanish in New Mexico, and Iroquois warriors were challenging the French in Illinois country. The English, with their larger numbers, posed an even greater cultural and economic problem for Native American inhabitants.

In 1675, embittered Indians rose up across southern New England in Metacom's War (or King Philip's War). The next year, frontier tensions in Virginia sparked the upheaval known as Bacon's Rebellion. A decade later, events in England prompted further tremors. In London, mounting opposition forced the unpopular James II to surrender the English throne to William of Orange. Parliament emerged from this "Glorious Revolution" with enhanced powers. In America, the end of rule by the Stuart dynasty was punctuated by controversy and violence in one colony after another.

Metacom's War in New England

By 1675, the Indians of southern New England, like the Pueblo in New Mexico, had endured several generations of colonization. Yet, they disagreed over how much English culture they should adopt. Many used English words for trading, English pots for cooking, and English weapons for hunting. Some had converted to Christianity, living in protected "praying towns." Several young men had enrolled in Harvard's Indian College, where they learned to write English and Latin with an eye toward entering the ministry.

Massasoit, the Wampanoag **sachem** (leader) who had assisted the Pilgrims at Plymouth, made sure that his sons, Wamsutta and Metacom, learned English ways. The two men raised pigs and fired guns, and the colonists called them Alexander and Philip, after the kings of ancient Macedon. But when Wamsutta died in the 1660s, shortly after succeeding his father, Metacom (now called King Philip) suspected foul play by the English. And Metacom had other grievances. Colonial traders made the Indians drunk and then cheated them. English livestock trampled Wampanoag corn, and if Indians shot the cattle, colonial courts imposed punishments. Worst of all, colonists now outnumbered the remaining 20,000 Indians in southern New England by more than two to one.

Sachem Algonquin Indian term for a Native American leader or chief.

When a white man shot and wounded a Native American in 1675, it triggered a long-expected conflict. Metacom's warriors ravaged towns along the Connecticut River valley and closer to the coast, using the victories to recruit additional Indian allies. The colonists, unprepared after forty years of peace and unchallenged dominance, were caught off guard. Distrusting even the Christian Indians, Massachusetts officials relocated whole praying towns of Indian converts to windswept Deer Island in Boston Harbor.

By December, the Connecticut and Rhode Island colonies, terrified of being wiped out, united with Plymouth and Massachusetts Bay to create a force of more than 1,000 men. An Indian captive led them to a stronghold of the still-neutral Narragansett in a swamp a dozen miles west of Newport, Rhode Island. The colonists surprised and overwhelmed the fortified village, setting it ablaze during the fierce fighting. Indian survivors fled, leaving behind more than 600 dead. Many of the men, women, and children were "terribly Barbikew'd," minister Cotton Mather later recorded.

This "Great Swamp Fight," reminiscent of an earlier battle in the Pequot War, infuriated the Narragansett survivors, who joined Metacom's growing alliance. But as spring arrived in 1676, the coalition weakened and the tide turned. Sickness broke out among the fighters, who lacked food and gunpowder. The powerful Mohawk of the Iroquois Confederacy opposed Metacom from the west. Numerous Christian Indians joined the colonial forces, despite their painful internment at Boston's Deer Island.

With Metacom facing defeat, defections increased. In August, a former ally betrayed the resistance leader, shot him, and delivered his head to the English. As the struggle ground to a close, the colonists captured Metacom's wife and child, selling them into slavery in the West Indies along with hundreds of other prisoners of war. New England's remaining Indians became second-class inhabitants, confined to reservation-like enclaves, while the colonists soon rebuilt and extended their domain.

Bacon's Rebellion in Virginia

While smoke still billowed over New England, new flames broke out in Virginia. Social unrest had been growing under the stern governorship of Sir William Berkeley. England's wars with the Dutch cut into the tobacco trade, and unfree tobacco workers—more than 6,000 indentured Europeans and nearly 2,000 enslaved Africans—chafed against their harsh treatment. On the frontier, colonists resented the dependent Indians (Occaneechi, Pamunkey, and others) who traded furs in exchange for protection from enemy tribes. Settlers also feared the well-armed Susquehannock living near the Potomac River. "Consider us," Berkeley wrote to the king in 1667, "as a people press'd at our backes with Indians, in our Bowills with our Servants . . . and invaded from without by the Dutch."

By 1676, tensions in Virginia reached the breaking point. Officials had increased taxes to pay for fortifications, servant plots and mutinies abounded, and corruption ran rampant among Berkeley's close associates. The aging governor ruled from Green Spring, his huge estate near the capital, Jamestown. Fearing the hostile views of free men who did not own property, Berkeley had revoked their right to vote. He had not dared to call an election in fourteen years. He also dreaded outspoken preachers, free schools, and printing presses. "How miserable that man is," he wrote, "that Governes a People where six parts of seaven at least are Poore Endebted Discontented and Armed."

Even wealthy newcomers such as Nathaniel Bacon had trouble gaining access to Berkeley's inner circle. When Bacon arrived from England in 1674 at age twenty-seven, he received a council seat because of his connections. But rivals denied the ambitious gentleman a license to engage in the fur trade. Impatient, Bacon condemned Berkeley's ruling Green Spring faction as sponges who "have sukt up the Publique Treasure." When frontier tensions erupted into racial violence, Bacon threw himself into the conflict, challenging Berkeley's leadership and launching aggressive campaigns. His frontier followers, eager for Indian land, killed friendly Occaneechi as well as hostile Susquehannock.

Killed Indians for land

Bacon's army continued to grow, as backcountry leaders joined landless poor and runaway workers—both black and white—to support his anti-Indian cause. When Berkeley called for a rare election to assert his strength, Bacon's supporters dominated the new House of Burgesses. The desperate governor retreated across Chesapeake Bay and hid on Virginia's eastern shore.

Throughout the summer of 1676, rumors swirled that Bacon might join malcontents in Maryland and in the Albemarle region south of Virginia to carve out an independent enclave and seek aid from the Dutch or the French. The new assembly quickly restored the vote to propertyless men and forbade excessive fees. It limited sheriffs to one year in office and passed other measures to halt corruption and expand participation in government. As an incentive for enlistment in the frontier war, the assembly granted Bacon's recruits the right to sell into slavery any Indians they captured.

For their part, slaves and indentured servants took advantage of the breakdown in public controls to leave their masters and join Bacon. Networks of news wives (women who used facts and rumors to fan worker discontent) spread stories of oppressive conditions. In June, rebel soldiers talked openly of sharing estates among themselves, and in August, they took over Green Spring Plantation, where Berkeley kept sixty horses and 400 head of cattle. A month later, Bacon's army burned Jamestown to the ground.

But by October, the tide had turned. Bacon was dead, struck down by dysentery, and reinforcements for Berkeley were on the way from England. With armed vessels patrolling the rivers, Berkeley dared to return from the eastern shore. Soon propertied men who had joined with Bacon were changing sides again and receiving amnesty from the governor.

The revolt had been crushed, but its impact proved huge. On the frontier, Bacon's violent campaign against the Indians had killed or enslaved hundreds and fostered bitter hatreds. In the Tidewater, the uprising had raised a frightening prospect for wealthy tobacco planters: a unified and defiant underclass of white and black workers. From then on, Virginia's gentry applied themselves to dividing the races and creating a labor force made up of African slaves. In London, the new Royal African Company stood ready to further such a design.

The "Glorious Revolution" in England

No sooner had peace returned to New England and Virginia than Stuart policies brought a new round of turmoil on both sides of the Atlantic. In England, debate revived over who would succeed Charles II on the throne. The irreligious Charles, an Anglican in name only, had no legitimate children. Therefore, his brother James, a convert to Catholicism, was first in line to inherit the crown.

In 1678, rumors spread regarding a "Popish Plot" by Catholics to kill the king so that James could take power. The House of Commons, fearful of rule by a Catholic king, urged that James be excluded from the line of succession. Instead of James, House members argued, why not consider James's Protestant daughters by his first marriage: either Mary (recently wedded to her Dutch cousin, William of Orange) or Anne? Angered by such interference, Charles II dissolved Parliament in 1681 and ruled on his own for the last four years of his life.

When Charles II died in 1685, the traditional rule of succession prevailed: James II took over the English throne. In France that same year, Louis XIV revoked the Edict of Nantes, which had protected French Protestants. Fear spread among England's Protestant majority that their country's new Catholic ruler, James II, might also sanction persecution of non-Catholics. These concerns mounted when James disbanded Parliament, raised a standing army, and placed a Catholic in command of the navy. Then in 1688, James's queen gave birth to a male heir. Protestant anxieties about a pending Catholic dynasty erupted into open resistance.

United by their fear of Catholicism, rival factions among England's political elite (known for the first time as "Whigs" and "Tories") temporarily papered over their differences. They invited the Protestant William of Orange, James's Dutch son-in-law, to

The Dutch painter Jan Wyck portrayed William of Orange as a dashing savior on a white horse, leading his army ashore at Torbay on England's south coast in November 1688. Protestants in England and America who had opposed James II welcomed news that the king's son-in-law had arrived from Holland to take over the English throne as King William III, alongside his English wife, Queen Mary. Could you argue that this painter (like the artist of the previous history painting of Charles II) transforms royal portraiture into subtle propaganda? If so, how?

lead an army from Holland and take the English crown. In November 1688, he crossed the English Channel with 15,000 men, prompting James to abdicate the throne and escape into exile. William and Mary were proclaimed joint sovereigns in 1689, accepting a Bill of Rights that limited royal power.

Its position now enhanced, Parliament moved to grant toleration to Protestant dissenters, establish limited freedom of the press, and ensure regular parliamentary sessions. It also imposed limits on any permanent, paid military forces, known as standing armies, because they could accrue their own power and jeopardize civil authority. The English had thus preserved Protestantism and curtailed royal absolutism, all without bloodshed. Parliament hailed King William III as "our great Deliverer from Popery and Slavery." The propertied classes, who benefited most from the peaceful transition, hailed it as the "Glorious Revolution."

The "Glorious Revolution" in America

Following the death of Charles II in 1685, the succession of his brother to the throne did not augur well for England's Protestant colonies in America. James II not only professed the Catholic faith but also cherished absolute monarchy and distrusted elected assemblies. In colonial affairs, James favored revenue-generating reforms and direct obedience to the crown. He detested the powerful leaders in Massachusetts since, as Congregationalists, they believed in a decentralized Protestant church. James also resented the fact that they disobeyed the Navigation Acts and asserted their right to self-rule, even after the crown revoked their charter in 1684. Moreover, he rejected the notion that colonists possessed the precious right claimed by the English at home: not to be taxed without giving their consent. The king envisioned an extensive reorganization of the American colonies.

When James assumed the throne, his own colony of New York automatically became a royal province. Convinced of his divine right to set policy, the king nullified the charters of certain colonies in order to bring them under his control. As the cornerstone of his reorganization plan, James linked the New England colonies (plus New York and New Jersey in 1688) into one huge *Dominion of New England*. This consolidation, under an appointed governor general, would make it easier for England to suppress dissent, enforce shipping regulations, and defend the Dominion's frontiers—at least in theory.

In practice, the effort to forge a Dominion of New England proved a disaster. Control of the Dominion went to a military officer, Sir Edmund Andros, who met stiff resistance from the start. The heavy-handed Andros attempted to rule from Boston through a council he appointed, made up of loyal associates, without aid or interference from any elected legislature. He asserted the crown's right to question existing land patents, and he requisitioned a Congregational church for Anglican services. Worse, he offended local leaders by strictly enforcing the Navigation Acts to collect revenue. When participants in democratic town meetings raised objections, he jailed the leaders.

Colonists resented this revival of Stuart absolutism, which claimed total obedience to the king and his officers as a divine right for the Stuart monarchy. Rumors of French invasions and Catholic plots swirled among staunch Protestants. In April 1689, welcome news that the Protestant William of Orange had invaded England inspired a revolt in Boston. Mobs showed public support for overthrowing the Stuart regime, and local leaders locked Governor Andros in jail.

The success of William and the demise of the Dominion of New England did not end royal efforts to tighten imperial control over New England. The new Massachusetts charter of 1691 consolidated neighboring Plymouth and Maine into the Massachusetts Bay colony. Moreover, it proclaimed that future governors would be appointed by the monarchy, as in other colonies. The men of Massachusetts, who had elected their own governor since the days of John Winthrop, would no longer have that right.

Emboldened by Boston's actions in 1689, New Yorkers ousted their own Dominion officials and set up a temporary government headed by Jacob Leisler. This German-born militia captain was a staunch Calvinist and hostile to the town's growing English elite. In Leisler's Rebellion, long-standing ethnic and religious rivalries merged with vague class hostilities: Leisler's supporters resented their treatment at the hands of the rich. They freed imprisoned debtors and attacked the houses of leading merchants. After a new governor arrived to take charge in 1691, the elite fought back. They lowered artisan wages and pressured the governor into hanging Leisler, on the grounds that his rebel followers were "growing dayly very high and Insolentt."

Similar tremors shook the Chesapeake region. In Maryland, where the Catholic proprietor ruled over a large and restive Protestant population, the governing Calvert family waited too long to proclaim its loyalty to King William. Fearing a "Popish" plot, assemblyman John Coode and a force of 250 armed Protestants marched on St. Mary's City and seized the government by force. The "happy Change in England" had replaced divine right rule with a more balanced constitutional monarchy, and Maryland settlers were determined to show their support.

Consequences of War and Growth: 1690–1715 ✗

3.5 How did worldly success and wartime profits contribute to colonial unrest after 1690?

The success of the Glorious Revolution hardly brought peace to England or its empire. On the contrary, warfare marked the reign of William and Mary and also that of Mary's sister, Queen Anne, who ruled from 1702 until her death in 1714. English involvement against France in two protracted wars on the European continent had implications for colonists and Indians living in eastern North America. The War of the League of Augsburg in Europe became known to English colonists in America as King William's War (1689–1697), and the protracted War of Spanish Succession was experienced in America as Queen Anne's War (1702–1713).

Nowhere was the impact of these imperial wars more evident than in the rapidly growing colonies of the Northeast. Indeed, the earlier bloodshed of Metacom's War, starting in 1675, had already aroused consternation and soul-searching. Bible-reading New Englanders viewed the violent decades that followed as a harsh test, or a deserved punishment, sent from the Almighty. They believed that God had watched closely over the initial Puritan "errand into the wilderness." Could it be, ministers now asked from the pulpit, that the Lord had some special controversy with the current generation? As communities grew more prosperous and became caught up in the pursuit of worldly success, were church members forgetting their religious roots and leading less pious lives? Invoking the Old Testament prophet Jeremiah, clerics interpreted personal and collective troubles as God's punishment for the region's spiritual decline.

But such a sweeping explanation of misfortune only raised deeper questions. New Englanders could see clearly that the consequences of rapid change were not spread equally among all towns, congregations, and families. As in most war eras, some people and localities suffered more than others. Certain individuals and groups seemed to benefit economically while others fell behind. Some anxious believers saw the hand of Satan in the day-to-day struggles of village life. Others argued that the worldly success and wartime profits of an expanding elite had undermined the community ideals of earlier generations. While flames engulfed isolated Massachusetts communities such as Deerfield and portions of the Maine frontier, fiery passions were also being aroused in older settlements, such as Salem and Boston.

Salem's Wartime Witch Hunt

One of the most memorable disruptions, the Salem witch hunt, occurred in Essex County, Massachusetts, a two-day ride on horseback from the embattled Maine frontier. In 1692, an outburst of witchcraft accusations engulfed the farm community of Salem Village. The strange episode remains one of the most troubling in early American history.

Among European Christians, a belief in witches with a supernatural power to inflict harm stretched back for centuries. In the 1600s, witchcraft trials abounded in Europe, and in New England, zealous believers had executed several dozen supposed witches in isolated cases. Three-fourths of those accused (and even more of those executed) were women. Most were beyond childbearing age, often poor or widowed, with limited power to protect themselves in the community. But Salem's hysteria went far beyond other colonial incidents, with more than 200 people accused and twenty put to death.

Early in 1692, more than half a dozen young women in Salem Village, ranging in age from nine to twenty, began to suffer violent convulsive fits. With reduced appetites and temporary loss of hearing, sight, and memory, they also experienced choking sensations that curtailed their speech. Vivid hallucinations followed. By April, the adolescents had accused ten people of being witches. Then some of the ten named others in their elaborate confessions, and the hysteria snowballed.

In a world where people considered satanic influence very real, frightened authorities seriously weighed the young women's stories of people appearing to them as devilish specters and apparitions. Overriding tradition, jurists allowed such "spectral evidence" in court, and convictions mounted. The court ordered public hangings on Gallows Hill that continued through September. Only when accusations reached too high in the social hierarchy and when several accusers recanted their stories did the new governor finally intervene. He emptied the jails, forbade further imprisonments, and pardoned the surviving accused until the tremor could subside.

Why this terrible outburst? Some historians argue that strained relations between farm families and more prosperous urban residents nearby may have influenced the craze. Others emphasize the zeal and gullibility of those first assigned to investigate. Still others speculate that the absence of central authority, until Governor Phips arrived in the colony in May, allowed a troubled situation to spin out of control. Could a local wave of mass hysteria, what some modern doctors diagnose as "conversion disorder," have produced real shared symptoms, even without any physical causes? Finally, commentators stress a perverse psychological dynamic that arises in any witch hunt, ancient or modern. In such cases, accused suspects often can save their own lives by supplying damaging and vivid confessions implicating others rather than by offering heartfelt denials of guilt. One or more of these factors surely came into play.

Yet devastation on the Maine frontier also contributed to what happened in Salem Village. Traumatized survivors from King William's War—the current conflict against the Abenaki and French—had trickled into the Massachusetts community. Significantly, more than half the young women who leveled witchcraft accusations had lost one or both parents in the brutal Indian wars. On February 5, just weeks before the first accusations, attackers had burned the Maine village of York 80 miles north of Salem, killing forty-eight people, and taking seventy-three captives. Word of the raid no doubt triggered shocking memories among Salem's war refugees, especially the orphans who worked as servants in local households.

Fears deepened in April when one of the accused testified that the Devil had tempted her while she had been living in Maine. Then a servant named Mercy Short, who had been captured and orphaned by Indians, recalled disturbing dreams of the Devil. She told minister Cotton Mather that in her dreams Satan and his minions (who had "an Indian colour") had made "hideous assaults" upon her. Much of what Mather and others recorded as the work of Satan may actually have been posttraumatic stress in a frayed community during wartime.

The Uneven Costs of War

Throughout the 1690s and beyond, King William's War and then Queen Anne's War made conflict a constant element of colonial life, but the burdens fell unevenly. For many colonial families, incessant warfare brought only death and dislocation. But for others, it offered new opportunities as the colonial economies expanded. Farmers with access to port towns shifted away from subsistence agriculture and grew crops for commercial sale. In doing so, they exposed themselves to greater financial risks, given transportation costs and market fluctuations. But they hoped to reap large profits.

Overseas trade and wartime smuggling offered investors even higher gains and larger risks. The crews of **privateers** (boats licensed to harass enemy shipping in wartime) made money if they captured a foreign vessel as a prize. Profits for outright pirates were greater still. Therefore, some colonial mariners chose to become buccaneers who operated for their own gain while avoiding the arm of the law. Englishman Edward Teach, known as Blackbeard, won notoriety as a privateer-turned-pirate, haunting the Carolina coast until his death in 1718.

Everywhere, poorer families were most likely to sink under the burdens of war. Regressive taxes, requiring the same amount from a poor carpenter as from a rich

Privateers Ships (and their crew members) licensed to harass enemy shipping in wartime.

 **Read** the Document   The Parliament of England, Navigation Act (1660)

3.1

3.2

3.3

3.4

3.5

After 1660, when Parliament imposed a series of Navigation Acts intended to control and profit from expanding colonial commerce, one unintended result was an increase in Atlantic piracy. For protection from the Royal Navy, the pirate Blackbeard often brought his ship into the shallow waters behind the barrier islands that form North Carolina's Atlantic coast. There, his crew bartered stolen goods at Ocracoke Island and reveled on the beach with local inhabitants. Why did some remote North Carolina colonists identify more readily with Blackbeard and other pirates than with the naval authorities enforcing the Navigation Acts?

merchant, obviously hurt impoverished people the most. So did high wartime prices for food and other basic necessities. Furthermore, many of the poor men recruited by the military became casualties of combat or disease, increasing the number of widows living in poverty. As New England towns expanded, the growing distance between rich and poor struck local residents. The moral ties and community obligations—known as the social covenant—that Puritan elders had emphasized two generations earlier were loosening. In their place emerged a focus on secular priorities and a new, individualistic spirit.

In Boston, troubled ministers decried the hunger and poverty that they saw deepening in their parishes alongside unprecedented displays of wealth. Between 1685 and 1715, the share of all personal wealth in the town controlled by the richest 5 percent climbed from 26 percent to 40 percent. Angry writers published irate pamphlets encouraging working people to take political action. They charged once-respected elites with studying "how to oppress, cheat, and overreach their neighbours." Predictably, when an English fleet of sixty warships carrying 5,000 men docked at Boston in 1711, powerful merchants who controlled the flow of provisions reaped huge rewards from this windfall.

Storm Clouds in the South

Peace returned to New England's frontier villages and port towns in 1711, as negotiations began for ending Queen Anne's War in America and the related War of Spanish Succession in Europe. British diplomats gained favorable terms from France and Spain when they signed a treaty at Utrecht two years later. (The formal union of England and Scotland in 1707 under the name *Great Britain* had transformed the *English* empire into the *British* empire.) But London officials could not prevent fresh violence in North America, given the expansion of their British colonies. The Wampanoag, Narragansett, and Abenaki Indians had attempted to roll back the advancement of northeastern settlers into Connecticut, Massachusetts, and Maine. Now Native Americans in the Southeast sought to counter the encroachments of newcomers along the Carolina coast.

By the 1660s, settlers drifted into what would become the colony of North Carolina. Some were English radicals fleeing the Restoration. Others, such as John Culpeper, had moved north from the Carolina settlement on the Ashley River, resentful that Shaftesbury and Locke had given Carolina proprietors firm control over the new colony. Still others were runaway servants from Virginia, and later came refugees escaping after Bacon's uprising. In 1677, these newcomers, led by Culpeper, seized control in the Albemarle region. The proprietors suppressed "Culpeper's Rebellion," but in 1689, they agreed to name a separate governor for the portion of Carolina "That Lies north and east of Cape Feare." Another disturbance, "Cary's Rebellion" in 1710, led to official recognition of "North Carolina, independent of Carolina," the next year. (Surveyors marked off the dividing line with Virginia in 1728.)

In 1680, Native Americans still outnumbered newcomers in eastern North Carolina by two to one, but within thirty years, that ratio had been reversed. The Naval Stores Act of 1705, passed by Parliament to promote colonial production of tar and pitch for shipbuilding, drew a stream of settlers to the pine forests of eastern North Carolina. By 1710, English communities existed on Albemarle Sound, at what is now Edenton, and on Pamlico Sound, at Bath (where Blackbeard and other pirates were frequent visitors). Farther south, Protestant immigrants from Bern, Switzerland, had staked out the town of New Bern on the site of a Native American village. John Lawson, who had explored the Carolinas before helping to lay out Bath and New Bern, conceded that the Indians had been "better to us than we are to them."

Eventually, the Tuscarora Indians struck back. Frustrated by corrupt traders and land encroachment, they killed Lawson and launched a war in 1711 to drive out the intruders. But they had waited too long. Within two years, the settlers—aided by a South Carolina force of several dozen whites and nearly 500 Yamasee Indians—had crushed the Tuscarora resistance. Most of the Tuscarora survivors migrated north, where they became the sixth nation within the powerful Iroquois Confederacy.

Explore the Topic   Population Pressure in the Coastal Southeast

The loblolly pine is native to the Carolinas. The Naval Stores Act of 1705, passed by Parliament to promote colonial production of tar and pitch for shipbuilding, drew a stream of settlers to the pine forests of eastern North Carolina. Why would England encourage the development of a naval stores industry in its American colonies?

Yamasee warriors from the Savannah River region helped British colonists quell the Tuscarora uprising. But, in 1715, they led their own rebellion against advancing settlers and corrupt traders linked to Charleston. They received support from Creek Indians, Spanish settlers in Florida, and French traders at the new Alabama outpost of Fort Toulouse. The still-powerful Cherokee in southern Appalachia opted not to join in the Yamasee War. Otherwise, the Indians might have overwhelmed the South Carolina colony.

Conclusion

Inspired by the exploits of La Salle and a generation of voyageurs and missionaries, the French had made inroads into the huge Mississippi Valley. But most European intrusions remained confined to the fringes of the vast continent. The French established themselves in Louisiana, and small numbers of Spanish held onto footholds in New Mexico and Florida, while venturing into parts of Arizona and Texas. The English newcomers, far more numerous, remained clustered along the Atlantic seaboard.

When English colonists penetrated up eastern rivers, warfare with traditional inhabitants ensued. Along the length of eastern North America, from the Kennebec River to the Savannah, hundreds of settlers and Indians died violently during the half-century before 1715. Often, the frontier struggles became entwined with wider conflicts between the rival European empires. These wilderness skirmishes seem minute compared with the battles raging in Europe at the same time. Despite the small scale of the conflicts in North America, however, Europe's imperial wars had started to influence developments in the English colonies.

Another element of Europe's expansion overseas—the transatlantic slave trade—had also begun to alter the shape of England's North American colonies. What had seemed only a small cloud on the horizon in the early seventeenth century had grown into an ominous force, with a momentum of its own, by the early eighteenth century. The storm hit hardest along the southeast coast, where the forced importation of thousands of Africans soon shaped a distinctive and repressive world of enslavement and exploitation that endured for generations. No sooner had the English gained control along the Atlantic edge of North America than they orchestrated this fateful transition—historians often call it "the terrible transformation"—placing thousands in bondage and altering the shape of American history for centuries.

Chapter Review

France and the American Interior

3.1 Why did France gain access to North America's interior before other European powers? p. 53

The French, lured inland via the St. Lawrence in pursuit of furs and a Northwest Passage, explored the Great Lakes and large parts of the Mississippi River Basin before 1690. Added geographical knowledge and Indian contacts soon allowed Canadian towns to connect to new French outposts in Illinois and Louisiana.

The Spanish Empire on the Defensive

3.2 Did Indian experiences with Spanish colonization vary widely in Arizona, New Mexico, and Florida? p. 59

Novel Spanish introductions, such as sheep, horses, and oranges, varied to suit the environment. But devastating new diseases, the incursion of a foreign religion, and exploitation of Indian labor materialized all along the northern edge of Spain's American empire. As a result, Spanish colonization efforts confronted widespread Native American resistance.

England's American Empire Takes Shape

3.3 Why did England's varied new Restoration-Era American colonies present so many contrasts? p. 64

Some differences derived from climate, but the largest contrasts between England's new colonies stemmed from differing origins. New York took over a prosperous Dutch colony, while Carolina represented a royal gift to proprietors who shared the king's hierarchical views. In contrast, West Jersey and Pennsylvania became havens for egalitarian Quakers.

Bloodshed in the English Colonies: 1670–1690

3.4 To what degree was colonial violence after 1670 sparked by internal tensions or by affairs in England? p. 68

Disputes with neighboring Indians, competition for land, intercolonial rivalries, and growing class antagonisms all served to foster warfare in English colonies after 1670. But tensions which originated in Europe—between Protestants and Catholics, Puritans and Royalists, Whigs and Tories, English and non-English—also contributed to colonial violence in these decades.

Consequences of War and Growth: 1690–1715

3.5 How did worldly success and wartime profits contribute to colonial unrest after 1690? p. 73

Economic prosperity fed a focus on worldly matters and prompted a decline in religious commitment. Increasing individualism and demographic growth weakened community bonds. Settlers caught up in frontier warfare paid a heavy price and came to resent local merchants and politicians who managed to reap unusual profits during such disturbances.

Timeline

1660
England's American Empire—Restoration of monarchy in England under Charles II
— 1660

1664
England's American Empire—Charles II grants a charter to his brother James, Duke of York, sanctioning the takeover of the Dutch New Netherland colony and the creation of New York
— 1664

1675 to 1676
Bloodshed—Metacom's War in New England
— 1675 to 1676

1676
Bloodshed—Bacon's Rebellion in Virginia
— 1676

1680
Spanish Empire on the Defensive—Pueblo Revolt in New Mexico
— 1680

1681
England's American Empire—Quaker William Penn receives charter for Pennsylvania
— 1681

1682
France and the American Interior—La Salle explores the Mississippi River and claims Louisiana for France
— 1682

1689
England's American Empire—Dutch leader William of Orange and his wife Mary become joint English sovereigns in the Glorious Revolution, replacing King James II
— 1689

1692
Consequences of War and Growth—Accusations of witchcraft followed by trials in Salem, Massachusetts
— 1692

1699
France and the American Interior—Iberville begins colony in French Louisiana
— 1699

1711 to 1715
Consequences of War and Growth—Tuscarora Indians in North Carolina, and then the Yamasee in South Carolina, resist English colonial expansion
— 1711 to 1715

4 African Enslavement: The Terrible Transformation

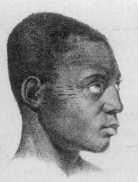

CABINDA

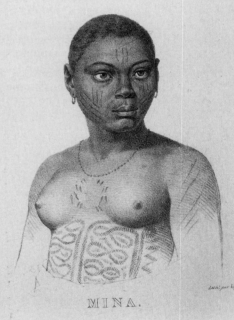

QUILOA.

How could an enslaved **young** woman obtain her freedom? Elizabeth Key felt she had been wronged, and in 1656 she wanted her day in court. But how would the magistrates in Northumberland County, Virginia, view her high-stakes case against the executors of a will? The twenty-five-year-old mulatto servant was suing for her freedom and back pay, and the will belonged to the late Colonel John Mottrom, a respected justice of the peace.

Born in 1631, Elizabeth (Bess) was the daughter of Thomas Key, a member of the Virginia Assembly, and the "Negro woman" with whom he had lived openly. Five years later, not long before he died, Key had bound the little girl to Humphrey Higginson, a member of the Council of State, until she reached age fourteen. Higginson, who stood as Bess's godfather when she was christened, promised to treat her "as well as if shee were his own Child . . . more Respectfully than a Comon servant or slave." He assured Key that he would not sell Bess to anyone else, and that when her nine-year term of service expired, he would give her the usual "freedom portion" of corn and clothes "and lett her shift for her selfe," either in England or Virginia. Instead, he later sold her to Mottrom, who had kept the young woman as a slave in perpetual bondage.

MINA.

LEARNING OBJECTIVES

4.1	4.2	4.3	4.4	4.5
How important was precedent in the English shift to impose hereditary enslavement on Africans deported to North America? p. 81	What factors created a vicious circle that sealed the fate of African workers in Virginia? p. 85	Why did England, once suspicious of the trade, become a leader in transporting enslaved Africans? p. 87	How did diverse Africans, enslaved in America, find common ground for resistance? p. 93	What prevented antislavery ideas from gaining a stronger foothold in the American colonies? p. 96

((Listen to **Chapter 4** on MyHistoryLab

As dark-skinned non-Christians, early Africans in North America differed from European colonists in their beliefs and their appearances. At first, religious differences served as a rationale for exploiting African labor. But when conversions undermined that argument, planters made black skin the grounds for permanent enslavement. Why did this shift play a key part in the Terrible Transformation?

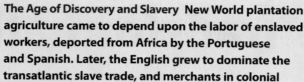 Watch the Video Series on MyHistoryLab

Learn about some key topics related to this chapter with the *MyHistoryLab Video Series: Key Topics in U.S. History.*

1 **The Age of Discovery and Slavery** New World plantation agriculture came to depend upon the labor of enslaved workers, deported from Africa by the Portuguese and Spanish. Later, the English grew to dominate the transatlantic slave trade, and merchants in colonial North America took part as well. This video introduces the European origins of Atlantic chattel slavery during the Age of Discovery, and it examines the slave economy that developed in the American colonies.

 Watch on MyHistoryLab

Race Slavery Profits and the economic considerations that drove slavery in the Americas are discussed in this video. Slave traders and owners, eager for the wealth generated by forced labor in a system of hereditary slavery, rationalized their brutal treatment of non-Christians and non-Europeans. Harsh practices aimed at maximizing profits, often at the expense of the health, safety, and humanity of the enslaved workers themselves. **2**

Watch on MyHistoryLab

3 **The Evolution of Slavery in North America** At first, African workers on Virginia's early plantations were treated in a manner similar to North America's white indentured servants. This video surveys a gradual descent into the system of hereditary, race-based enslavement that typified Britain's American colonies after the Terrible Transformation of the late seventeenth century.

 Watch on MyHistoryLab

Slavery in the Colonies Most Africans who were brought to the Americas stayed in the Caribbean. Others, after a period of "seasoning," were deported to North America and sold throughout the British colonies. This video examines how slavery differed from colony to colony and the ways, although severely limited, that enslaved men and women devised to shape their own lives and destinies in the New World. **4**

Watch on MyHistoryLab

Bess and her white attorney presented a threefold argument. First, as the daughter of a free man, she should inherit her father's legal status according to English law. Second, as a baptized Christian, she should not be enslaved. (In court, Bess gave "a very good account of her faith"—no small matter at a time when Europeans viewed enslavement as a status reserved for non-Christians captured in wars.) And third, she could produce a document showing that as a small child she had been "put out" to work for a fixed number of years, following local custom. Such contracts for apprenticing a child were common in America, where labor was in short supply. But her term of work had expired long ago.

After much debate and several appeals, Key finally prevailed. Virginia's Assembly approved her liberty, an overdue "freedom portion," and back pay. She went on to marry her attorney and raise a family. But several decades later, Virginia courts would have decided the case differently, forcing Elizabeth to remain enslaved for life, with her children inheriting slavery status as well.

By the 1660s, a Terrible Transformation was under way in English colonial culture that would warp American society for centuries. It spread gradually, like a cancer, revealing a different pace and pattern in each colony. Earlier, a few African servants were working alongside European servants. But before the end of the century, the grandchildren of those workers had been separated according to emerging notions of "race." Free blacks persisted in the English colonies, but the tide was flowing against them. From now on, people of African ancestry were to be legally enslaved for life, generation after generation.

The Descent into Race Slavery

> **4.1** How important was precedent in the English shift to impose hereditary enslavement on Africans deported to North America?

Some major transitions in human affairs evolve slowly, even imperceptibly. Nothing shaped colonial cultures more forcefully than the European colonists' gradual commitment to the legalized enslavement of hundreds of thousands of people and their descendants. It is important to examine the slippery slope that led to perpetual servitude based on race.

The Caribbean Precedent

The roots of race slavery in the Americas extend back to the era of Columbus, when warfare, sickness, and exploitation quickly decimated the native populations of the Caribbean after 1492. Hungry for human labor, the Spanish intruders began to import people from Africa to grow crops and dig for gold in the Caribbean islands. As the native population declined sharply through epidemics, the traffic in black newcomers expanded.

Spanish pressure for labor in the New World intensified further with the discovery of additional mines for precious metals in Mexico and Peru. To meet the growing demand, Spain's king even issued a contract called the **asiento** that allowed other European powers—such as Portugal, France, or the Netherlands—to import African slaves to the Spanish colonies. High profits drew eager participation. In the half-century between 1590 and 1640, more than 220,000 people arrived in chains from Africa at the Spanish colonial ports in Central and South America.

Meanwhile, the Portuguese purchased enslaved Africans to work their own expanding sugar plantations. They imported more than 75,000 slaves, mostly from the Congo River region of West Central Africa, to the Atlantic island of São Tomé in the sixteenth century. When Portuguese sugar production spread to coastal Brazil, so did the exploitation of African labor. By 1625, Brazil imported the majority of slaves crossing the Atlantic each year and exported most of the sugar consumed in Europe.

Long before the 1660s, therefore, Europeans had set a precedent for exploiting African workers in New World colonies. Religious and secular authorities frowned on actively enslaving people, especially if they were fellow Christians, but purchasing so-called infidels (those who followed other religions) could be tolerated, particularly if slavery had already been imposed on them by someone else. These West African victims were non-Christians, and most had already been enslaved by others, captured by fellow Africans in war.

Confident in this rationale, the Spanish and Portuguese adapted their laws to accept the enslavement of Africans. Moreover, the condition would be hereditary, with children inheriting at birth their mother's legal status. The Catholic Church backed the new labor system, though priests occasionally worked to alleviate suffering among Africans in the Americas. The pope did nothing to condemn the growing traffic, nor did the Protestant Reformation have a dampening effect. On the contrary, the rising Protestant sea powers of northern Europe proved willing to assist in the slave trade and take part in the dramatic "sugar revolution," growing sugar on a massive scale for expanding Atlantic markets.

The Dutch, for example, ruled Brazil for a generation in the first half of the seventeenth century, importing slaves to South America and exporting sugar. When the Portuguese regained control of Brazil at midcentury, they pushed out Dutch settlers. These outcasts took their knowledge about managing sugar plantations to the islands of the Caribbean. Some appeared in the new English possessions of Barbados and Jamaica, and soon they were directing African slaves in cutting, pressing, and boiling sugar cane to make molasses. The thick molasses could then be processed further to make rum

Asiento A contract negotiated by the Spanish crown (between 1595 and 1789) with other European powers such as Portugal, France, England, and the Netherlands to provide a fixed number of slaves annually to Spain's American colonies for a set payment.

and refined sugar for export. By the 1650s, slavery and sugar production were engulfing England's West Indian possessions, just as these twin features had already become central to the New World colonies controlled by Spain and Portugal. A looming precedent had been set. But as late as 1660, it was not at all clear that African slavery would gain a prominent place, or even a lasting foothold, in any North American colonies.

Ominous Beginnings

As far back as the sixteenth century, African men had participated in Spanish explorers' forays into the Southeast, and some had remained, fathering children with Indian women. African slaves had helped to establish the small Spanish outpost at St. Augustine in 1565, but a century later no additional coastal colonies had yet appeared on the mainland anywhere south of Chesapeake Bay.

Granted, Africans were present farther north in the fledgling settlements of the French, Dutch, and English. But their numbers remained small—several thousand at most—and few of these newcomers had come directly from Africa. Most had lived for years in the Caribbean or on the mainland, absorbing colonial languages and beliefs. So they and their children, like Bess Key, were not viewed as complete outsiders by the European colonists. The legal and social standing of these early African Americans remained vague before the 1660s. Everywhere, workers were in demand, and most black newcomers found themselves laboring alongside European servants.

In the Massachusetts Bay colony, early Puritan settlers, seeking viable markets and new sources of labor, exchanged goods for slaves in the Caribbean. In 1644, seafaring New Englanders even attempted direct trade with Africa. But the following year, Massachusetts authorities ordered a New Hampshire resident to surrender a black worker he had purchased in Boston. They argued that the man had been stolen from Africa, not captured in war, and should be returned to his home. In 1652, Rhode Island passed a law limiting all involuntary service—for Europeans or Africans—to no more than ten years.

Along the Hudson River, the Dutch colonists had close ties with the sugar islands of the West Indies, where race slavery was already an accepted system. In New Netherland, therefore, the laws discriminated against black workers and limited their rights. But the statutes also provided loopholes that permitted social and economic advancement to the community's Africans, most of whom spoke Dutch.

Chesapeake Bay lay even closer to the main routes of the Atlantic slave traffic. In 1619, a Dutch warship brought to Virginia more than twenty African men and women acquired as slaves in the Caribbean. Like people deported from England to the Chesapeake, they were sold as servants. Terms of service varied, and some black newcomers earned their freedom quickly and kept it. But others saw their terms extended arbitrarily. In 1640, Virginia's General Court considered punishment for "a negro named John Punch" and two European servants who had escaped to Maryland. When apprehended, the Dutchman and the Scotsman each received four additional years of service, but the African was sentenced to unending servitude "for the time of his natural life." That same year, Virginia passed a law that prevented blacks from bearing arms. A 1643 law taxing productive field hands included African American women but not white women.

These early efforts to separate Africans from Europeans by law set an ominous precedent in the use of skin color as a distinguishing marker. Still, rules governing the lives of people of color and their offspring remained ambiguous for several decades, and (as the case of Bess Key makes clear) efforts at exploitation could often be undone in court. But new forces would come into play in the mainland American colonies after 1660, consolidating the transition to hereditary enslavement of Africans.

Alternative Sources of Labor

The legal status of African newcomers to English North America became distinctly clearer and less hopeful in the decades after 1660. The transatlantic slave trade, already more than a century old, provided certain English colonies with a ready source of

African workers at a time when more obvious streams of inexpensive labor—captured Native Americans and impoverished Europeans—were dwindling.

For labor-hungry colonists, Native Americans were close at hand and knew the country well. They took captives when fighting one another, so colonists could buy Indian prisoners or seize them in frontier warfare. Europeans felt they could enslave such people in good conscience, since they were non-Christians who had been taken captive in war. But Native American numbers were declining steadily, owing to epidemics. And those who did become enslaved knew the countryside well enough to escape. Besides, traffic in Indian slaves disrupted the profitable deerskin trade, undermined wilderness diplomacy, and sparked conflict on the frontier.

Efforts to maintain a steady flow of cheap labor from Europe ran into different problems. The Great Plague of 1665 devastated the English population, and the London Fire the following year created a new need for workers of all kinds to rebuild the capital. England's labor surplus, which had been a boon to the first colonies half a century earlier, rapidly disappeared. The use of **indentures** persisted, whereby people too poor to buy their own passage would agree to sell their labor for a fixed period. When these indentured workers reached America, they served a set term for room and board; then their employer needed to find replacements.

Equally important, when indentured servants were mistreated, they had little difficulty in relaying their complaints home to other potential workers. The flow of ships back and forth between Europe and North America grew steadily in the century after 1660, so word of places where indentured servants were regularly abused or swindled quickly reached the other side of the Atlantic. In contrast, the African slave trade lacked any similar "feedback loop." As a result, the brutal treatment of black workers never had a chance, through accurate feedback across the Atlantic, to influence the future flow of captives from Africa.

Indenture A document binding one person to work for another for a given period of time. Indentured servants received food, shelter, and clothing, plus "freedom dues" when their terms of service ended to help them get started independently.

The Fateful Transition

In general, powerful Chesapeake tobacco planters were encouraged in 1660 by news of the Restoration of Charles II, since England's new king was likely to support their interests and reward their loyalty. These men had noticed the rising profits that sugar growers were making by using slaves in the Caribbean. In Virginia and Maryland, therefore, planters passed a series of laws that sharpened distinctions between servants working for a fixed period and slaves consigned to labor for life.

In shaping new legislation, local leaders even challenged long-standing English legal traditions, such as the right of children to inherit their father's status. In 1662, Virginia's General Assembly considered whether any child fathered "by an Englishman upon a negro woman should be slave or Free." In a crucial reversal of precedent, the legislature said that in such cases children shall be "bond or free *only according to the condition of the mother.*" From now on, the infant of any female slave would be enslaved from birth. Slavery was becoming a hereditary condition.

Could enslaved persons receive their freedom if they accepted Christianity, as sometimes happened in Spanish colonies? A 1664 Maryland law closed off that prospect. The act made clear that the legal status of non-Christian slaves did not change if they experienced religious conversion. Three years later, Virginia's government agreed that "the conferring of baptisme doth not alter the condition of the person as to his bondage." By removing religion as a determining factor, legislators shifted the definition of who could be enslaved from someone who was not Christian to someone who did not look European.

In scarcely a generation, black bondage had become a hereditary institution, and the conditions of life had grown markedly worse for African Americans. Increasingly, they faced corporal punishments: whippings and mutilation. Black slaves—and often free blacks—lost their right to accuse, or even testify against, a white person in court. "And further," stated Virginia's formative slave law of 1680, "if any Negro" raises a hand, even in self-defense, "against any Christian, he shall receive thirty lashes, and if he absent himself . . . from his master's service and resist lawful apprehension, he may be killed."

✳ Explore the Transatlantic Slave Trade on MyHistoryLab

IN WHAT WAYS WAS BRITISH NORTH AMERICA INVOLVED IN THE TRANSATLANTIC SLAVE TRADE?

For some three centuries, the transatlantic slave trade brought a total of more than 10 million Africans to the Americas, but scarcely 5 percent came to North America. These unpaid bondservants found themselves enslaved up and down the Eastern Seaboard, but the vast majority lived in the southern colonies, toiling as an agricultural labor force. Besides the white planters who purchased and exploited African workers, other colonists participated in the slave trade as shipbuilders, sailors, captains, and financiers. Still others ran slave markets, enforced slave laws, or put enslaved Africans to work in shops, homes, fields, and forests. In lasting and disturbing ways, race-based slavery shaped the economy and society that would become the United States.

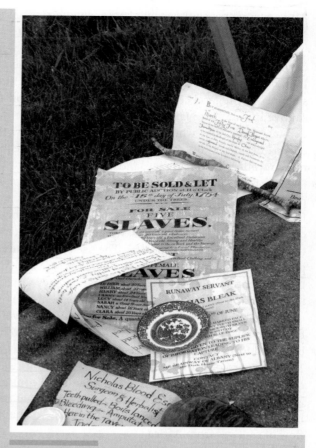

Handbills such as these alerted buyers when and where they could purchase chattel slaves, who were sold as commodities. Ads offering a reward for the capture and return of an escaped worker became commonplace.

ORIGINS OF AFRICANS IN NORTH AMERICA, 1700–1800

Regions of Origin Along Africa's Atlantic Coast*
Senegambia
Sierra Leone
Gold Coast
Bight of Benin
Bight of Biafra
Angola

*Listed geographically, from north to south

ECONOMIES TAKING PART IN THE SLAVE TRADE, 1700–1800

North Atlantic Economies Engaged in Slave Trading*
Britain
Portugal
France
The Netherlands
Denmark
British Colonies/North America

*In order of most to fewest number of slaves traded

KEY QUESTIONS   Use **MyHistoryLab** *Explorer* to **answer** these **questions:**

Comparison ▶▶▶ *Which colonies, later states, imported the most slaves?*

Map the differences, with regard to the importation of enslaved Africans, among the regions of Atlantic North America.

Analysis ▶▶▶ *How did the ratio of male to female slaves differ across the Thirteen Colonies?*
Hypothesize the explanations for this distribution.

Consequence ▶▶▶ *What were the major economic activities for different regions of mainland British America and the early United States?*

Consider the connections between slavery and regional economic production.

The Growth of Slave Labor Camps

4.2 What factors created a vicious circle that sealed the fate of African workers in Virginia?

South Carolina = Racist AF

Over two generations, beginning in the late seventeenth century, tobacco growers in the Chesapeake and rice producers in the new colony of South Carolina embraced the system of hereditary race slavery that had developed in the Caribbean. For those forced to cut the trees, drain the swamps, and harvest the crops, the shift in production strategy represented—in modern terminology—the emergence of slave labor camps. These people received no wages, had no legal rights, and were denied freedom to marry or move about. This deterioration in conditions occurred first, and most dramatically, in Virginia, where several thousand African Americans lived and labored by the 1670s.

First in Virginia.

Read the Document   *South Carolina Gazette,* Runaway Slave Notices (1732, 1737)

Rice plantations that emerged in coastal South Carolina around 1700 became labor camps where enslaved blacks were confined for generations, without wages or legal rights. In the 1850s, distant descendants of the region's first African workers were still being forced to plant, harvest, and process the huge rice crops that made their masters rich. How might mass enslavement over numerous generations differ in its impact from harsh exploitation during a single lifetime?

Black Involvement in Bacon's Rebellion

Nothing did more to consolidate Virginia's slide toward race slavery than Bacon's Rebellion, the major uprising that shook the Chesapeake region in 1676 (see Chapter 3). The episode pitted aspiring gentry, led by Nathaniel Bacon, against hard-pressed Indian groups on the frontier and an entrenched elite in Jamestown.

Free men, would-be farmers in search of land, made up part of Bacon's following, but diverse unfree workers also proved eager recruits. Such ill-treated people remained legally indentured to large landholders for varying terms, and many of the Africans were undoubtedly bound for life. Together, they raised the colony's annual tobacco crop, and the backbreaking labor prompted frequent unrest. These ragged workers, however long their term of service might be, had the most to gain and the least to lose from Bacon's revolt. According to the Virginia Assembly, "many evill disposed servants . . . taking advantage of the loosenes of the tymes . . . followed the rebells in rebellion." When Bacon died in October 1676, many of his wealthier supporters gave up, renewing their loyalty to the colonial government. But bound workers who had escaped from their masters continued the fight.

A letter reaching London that fall suggested that at the height of the rebellion Bacon had "proclam'd liberty to all Servants and Negroes." Clearly, the widespread unrest had given hope to downtrodden tobacco pickers, about a quarter of whom were black. When military reinforcements arrived in Chesapeake Bay from England in November, the commander, Captain Thomas Grantham, found hundreds of laborers still in active revolt.

Impressed by their strength, Grantham chose to use deceit when he met with 800 heavily armed rebels, both white and black, at their headquarters near the York River. Making vague promises regarding pardons and freedom, he persuaded most of the white men to surrender and return home. Only about "Eighty Negroes and Twenty English" demanded "their hoped for liberty and would not quietly laye downe their armes." But when these last holdouts boarded a sloop, Grantham disarmed the rebels and chained them below decks for return to their masters.

The Rise of a Slaveholding Elite in the Chesapeake Tidewater

With Bacon's death and the arrival of British ships, propertied Virginians had narrowly averted a successful multiracial revolution, fueled from below by workers who resented their distressed condition. But clearly some future revolt might succeed, so the great planters of the Chesapeake Tidewater region moved to tighten their hold on political and economic power. After Bacon's Rebellion, a strategy of divide and conquer seemed in order. They moved to improve conditions for poor whites in ways that would ensure class deference and racial solidarity among Europeans. At the same time, they further reduced the legal status of blacks and solidified their enslavement for life.

For precedent, planters had the model provided by slavery-based colonial societies in the West Indies, including the English sugar island of Barbados. Their uneasiness continued over importing non-Christian strangers who spoke little, if any, English. But such doubts were more than offset by the prospect of laying claim to the children of slaves and to the lives and labor of all generations to come. Increasing life expectancy in the Chesapeake region meant that Africans enslaved for life would yield profitable service for an increasingly long time. Besides, all their healthy offspring who survived childhood could then be forced to clear more land to grow additional crops.

Seizing the moment, a circle of aggressive entrepreneurs established themselves as the leading families of Virginia. These ambitious merchant-planters expected that the English-speaking Africans already present could assist in teaching newcomers to receive orders. They also assumed that slave laborers from diverse African societies could not communicate well enough with one another to cause dangerous disturbances. And of course, having now made skin color a determining feature of social order, they knew that black runaways could be spotted and apprehended readily. As the profitability of the slavery option increased, so did its appeal. By 1700, some 4,500 people were enslaved in Maryland in a total population of 35,000. And the colony's assembly was actively encouraging the importation of slaves. Growing demand meant that merchants and sea captains now devoted more time and larger ships to slave-trading, making African workers more available and affordable.

As the supply of enslaved black newcomers grew larger, planters eager to strengthen their position manipulated the established headright system. Traditionally, under this system, the colonial government granted to any arriving head of household 50 acres for every family member or hired hand he brought into the colony. The incentive was intended to spur migration from Europe, expand the free population, and develop the land through the establishment of family farms. But the wealthy planters who saw African slavery as a profitable labor source also controlled Virginia's legal system. For their own benefit, therefore, they extended the headright system so that a land bonus also went to anyone who purchased an African arrival as a lifelong slave. Thus, before the seventeenth century closed, a Virginia investor buying twenty slaves could also lay claim to headrights worth 1,000 acres of land.

To consolidate their new regime, planters worked through the church and the legislature to separate whites from blacks socially and legally. They undermined the position of free blacks and stigmatized interracial ties. A 1691 Virginia statute decried the "abominable mixture and spurious issue" that resulted from "Negroes, mulattoes and Indians intermarrying" with English or other white people. All such couples were "banished from this dominion forever." It also prohibited masters from freeing any black or mulatto unless they paid to transport that person out of the colony within six months.

Virginia's Negro Act of 1705 further underscored the stark new boundaries. It mandated that white servants who were mistreated had the right to sue their masters in county court. Slaves, in contrast, had no such right. Any enslaved person who tried to escape could be tortured and even dismembered in hopes of "terrifying others" from seeking freedom. When masters or overseers killed a slave while inflicting punishment, they were automatically free of any felony charge. If slaves were killed or put to death by law, the owners would be paid public funds for the loss of their "property." In scarcely forty years, prominent whites had used the law to transform the labor system of the Chesapeake, entrapping Africans and their descendants in perpetual slavery.

England Enters the Atlantic Slave Trade

4.3 Why did England, once suspicious of the trade, become a leader in transporting enslaved Africans?

The Atlantic slave trade remains the largest and longest-lasting deportation in human history. In nearly four centuries, more than 10 million people were torn from their homelands against their will and transported to the Caribbean and to Central, South, and North America. Several million more perished in transit. By 1700, more Africans than Europeans had already crossed the Atlantic to the Western Hemisphere. Their numbers grew over the following century as the traffic reached its height. The importation of Africans to North America expanded after 1700, but it remained a small proportion of the overall Atlantic slave trade.

England took little part in the trade at first. However, the development of Barbados as a lucrative sugar colony and the expansion of English overseas ambitions changed matters quickly after 1640. With the restoration of the English monarchy in 1660, Charles II immediately granted a monopoly on African trade to a small group of adventurers, and in 1672 he chartered the powerful new Royal African Company (RAC).

The RAC dispatched from England a steady flow of merchant ships along a triangular trade route. The first leg took captains to English outposts along the coast of

Middle passage For European slave ships, the middle passage was the second of three legs in the triangular round-trip voyage from Europe to Africa to America and back to Europe. For enslaved Africans, the middle passage came to mean not only the transatlantic journey itself, but the entire process of removal from an African homeland and ultimate sale to an American master.

Trading factory The overseas trading outposts built by competing European empires became known as factories, since each was run by a *factor*, or manager. Along the west coast of Africa, from Senegal to Angola, such posts played a central role in the Atlantic slave trade.

Coffle A procession or train of enslaved prisoners, bound together for travel (from the Arabic word for "caravan").

West Africa, where they exchanged textiles, guns, and iron bars for gold, ivory, and enslaved Africans. After a transatlantic **middle passage** of one to three months, the captains sold slaves and took on sugar in the West Indies before returning to England on the final leg of the triangle. Of course, weather, warfare, shifting prices, and changing market opportunities meant that many voyages strayed from this basic pattern. The scope of English slave trading expanded when the RAC's monopoly ended officially in 1698, allowing more competition. Britain's slave trade ballooned further after 1713 when it obtained the lucrative *asiento*, or contract, from Spain to deliver Africans to the Spanish colonies in America. By the 1730s, ships under the British flag controlled the largest share of the Atlantic slave trade. (This fleet included vessels built and based in New England that carried on a triangular trade of their own, shipping rum to West Africa, transporting slaves to the Caribbean, and bringing molasses back to colonial distilleries in the Northeast to be made into more rum.) They continued to dominate the traffic for the next seventy years.

The Slave Trade on the African Coast

By the 1680s, Africa's western sub-Saharan coastline contained dozens of trading depots, each controlled by some rival European power. (The depot manager was called the *factor*, so these imperial posts became known as **trading factories**.) This string of European outposts began at the mouth of the Senegal River, just above Cape Verde, the continent's westernmost point; it ended below the mouth of the Congo River, in present-day Angola. In between, the coastline curved some 5,000 miles. It embraced diverse geographic environments—from open savannas to thick forests—and scores of distinctive cultures. All along this coastline, villagers caught fish and gathered salt for trade with herders and farmers living farther inland.

Generations of contact with oceangoing ships brought new pressures and opportunities to African coastal communities. Local merchants, who traded gold and ivory to sea captains for imported textiles and alcohol, formed alliances with European trading partners in response to the growing demand for human labor. They consolidated their positions near suitable harbors and navigable rivers. From there, they bartered local servants and war captives to white agents for linen, beads, metalwares, and muskets.

Inland traders, alert to the rising demand for slaves in the port towns, annually brought thousands of captives from the backcountry to the coast. The traders traveled by land and water, binding their prisoners together in small groups to form a **coffle** (from the Arabic word for "caravan"). The overseas goods they received as payment

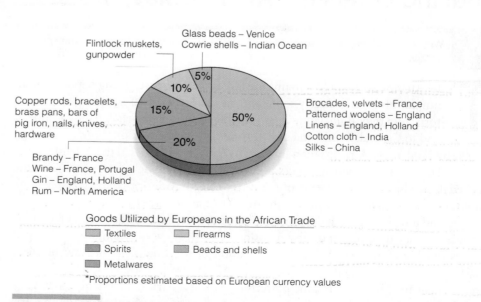

Glass beads – Venice
Cowrie shells – Indian Ocean

Flintlock muskets, gunpowder

Copper rods, bracelets, brass pans, bars of pig iron, nails, knives, hardware

Brocades, velvets – France
Patterned woolens – England
Linens – England, Holland
Cotton cloth – India
Silks – China

Brandy – France
Wine – France, Portugal
Gin – England, Holland
Rum – North America

5%
10%
15%
50%
20%

Goods Utilized by Europeans in the African Trade

☐ Textiles   ☐ Firearms
☐ Spirits   ☐ Beads and shells
☐ Metalwares

*Proportions estimated based on European currency values

FIGURE 4.1 GOODS TRADED IN AFRICA As European ship captains expanded trade along the African coast, they tailored their cargoes to suit the demands of local markets.

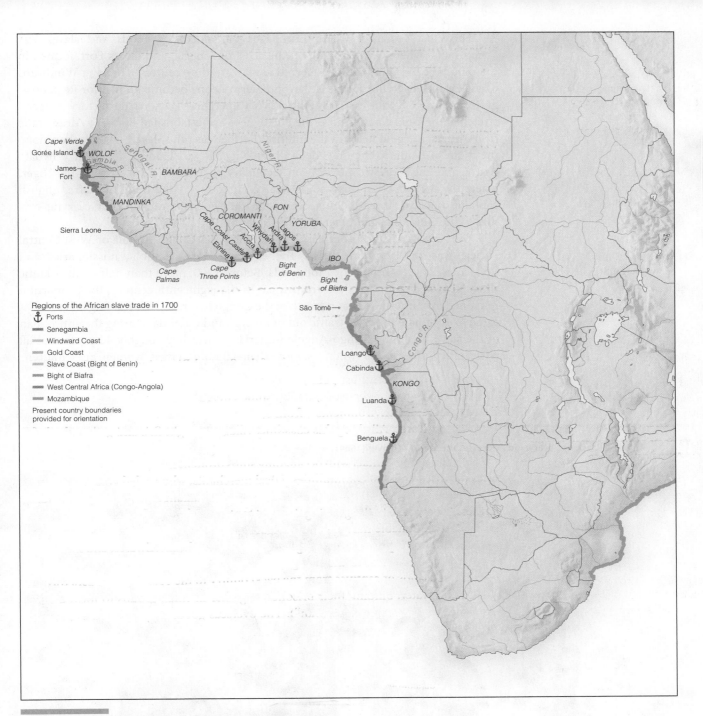

Regions of the African slave trade in 1700
⚓ Ports
▬ Senegambia
▬ Windward Coast
▬ Gold Coast
▬ Slave Coast (Bight of Benin)
▬ Bight of Biafra
▬ West Central Africa (Congo-Angola)
▬ Mozambique
Present country boundaries
provided for orientation

MAP 4.1 REGIONS OF THE AFRICAN SLAVE TRADE IN 1700

included firearms, gunpowder, and knives, which they used in additional wars to secure more captives.

By the 1670s, the pace of African deportation to the Western Hemisphere had reached an average rate of nearly 15,000 people each year. That average rose steadily to a high of almost 100,000 people per year by the 1780s. As the traffic grew, it became increasingly organized, competitive, and routine. Shrewd African traders played one European vessel against another for the best deals. Hardened European agents learned to curry favor with local officials and to quell unrest among captives, confined in the holding pens known as **barracoons**. Experienced captains timed their ventures to avoid the months when sickness was most rampant in the tropics. Through repeated voyages, improved charts, and accumulated lore, they came to differentiate and exploit half a dozen major slaving regions along Africa's Atlantic coast. On occasion, they even ventured to Mozambique in southeast Africa and the nearby island of Madagascar.

Barracoon An enclosure or barrack used for the confinement of slaves before their forced deportation from the African coast.

The closest market where Europeans bargained for goods and slaves was Senegambia, where Gorée Island, off the coast of Senegal, and James Fort, located in the mouth of the Gambia River, served as slave-trading centers. The long Windward Coast extending to the southeast beyond Sierra Leone became known for its pepper, grain, and ivory. To the east, from the area of Cape Three Points to the factory at Accra, stretched the Gold Coast. There, the Portuguese had established Elmina to draw trade from the Asante gold fields in the interior. Farther east, the Slave Coast reached along the Bight of Benin to the huge delta of the Niger River. Trading depots at Whydah, Ardra, and Lagos drew captives from secondary ports in between. Beyond the Niger, where the African coast turns south near Cameroon, lay the Bight of Biafra. English captains quickly learned the preferences for trade goods in each district, carrying textiles to the Gold Coast and metals to the Bight of Biafra.

The largest and most southerly region, known as Congo-Angola or West Central Africa, was the only one below the equator. Here, Catholic missionaries and Portuguese traders established footholds. Before 1700, more than half of all Atlantic slaves departed from West Central Africa. In the eighteenth century, the proportion remained over one-third. Later, north of the Congo River, French and English interests came to dominate the slave traffic out of Loango and Cabinda. During the entire span of the slave trade, the Congo-Angola hinterland furnished roughly 40 percent of all African deportees to the Americas: more than 4.5 million men, women, and children.

Read the Document   Maryland Addresses the Status of Slaves (1664)

In Africa, captives taken in war and enslaved by a rival group were eventually allowed to assimilate into their new community. When European trading ships tapped into this West African slave traffic, persons captured in the African interior were marched to the coast in shackles, in groups known as coffles. From coastal prisons, they were sold to competing European captains and deported overseas, where they became slave laborers with little prospect of assimilation. Why is the contrast between assimilating and nonassimilating slave societies a significant one?

The Middle Passage Experience

The grim transatlantic exodus was different for every person. Nevertheless, the long nightmare of deportation contained similar elements for all. The entire journey, from normal village life to enslavement beyond the ocean, could last a year or two. It unfolded in at least five stages, beginning with capture and deportation to the African coast. The initial loss of freedom—the first experience of bound hands, harsh treatment, and forced marches—was made worse by the encounters with strange landscapes and unfamiliar languages. Hunger, fatigue, and anxiety took a steady toll as coffles of young and old were conveyed slowly toward the coast through a network of traders.

The next phase, sale and imprisonment, began when a contingent reached the sea, and African traders transferred "ownership" of the captives. European buyers subjected their new property to demeaning inspections and burned brands into their skin. Then they were put in irons alongside hundreds of other captives and guarded in a secure spot to prevent escape. After several months, canoes transported the captives through the surf to a waiting vessel. (Their hands were bound, so if a canoe capsized, it meant certain drowning.) Once aboard, they might languish in the sweltering hold for weeks while the captain cruised the coast in search of additional human cargo. Crew members sometimes raised nets surrounding the deck to prevent attempts at escape or suicide.

The ship's captain decided when to begin crossing the Atlantic, the harrowing third phase that constituted the middle passage. The Africans below deck now faced an utterly alien plight, trapped in a strange wooden hull. When the crew unfurled the vessel's huge sails, the captives could only anticipate the worst. The dark crowded hold became increasingly fetid and foul. The rolling of the ship on ocean swells brought seasickness and painful chafing from lying on the bare planks. Alexander Falconbridge, who sailed as a surgeon on several slave ships, recorded that "those who are emaciated frequently have their skin and even their flesh entirely rubbed off, by the motion of the ship, from the . . . shoulders, elbows and hips so as to render the bones quite bare."

Historians have documented more than 27,000 slave voyages from Africa to the Americas, and in each one an array of variables came into play to shape the Atlantic crossing. These included the route, the season, the adequacy of supplies, the crew's navigational

England's Royal African Company maintained more than a dozen small posts along the Gold Coast. Each outpost funneled slaves to this strong seventy-four-gun fortress known as Cape Coast Castle. Cut into rock beneath the parade ground, the vaulted dungeon inside could "conveniently contain a thousand Blacks . . . against any insurrection." In what ways was it significant for President Barack Obama and his family to visit this site in Ghana in 2009?

((•	Read the Document	Olaudah Equiano, "The Middle Passage" (1788)

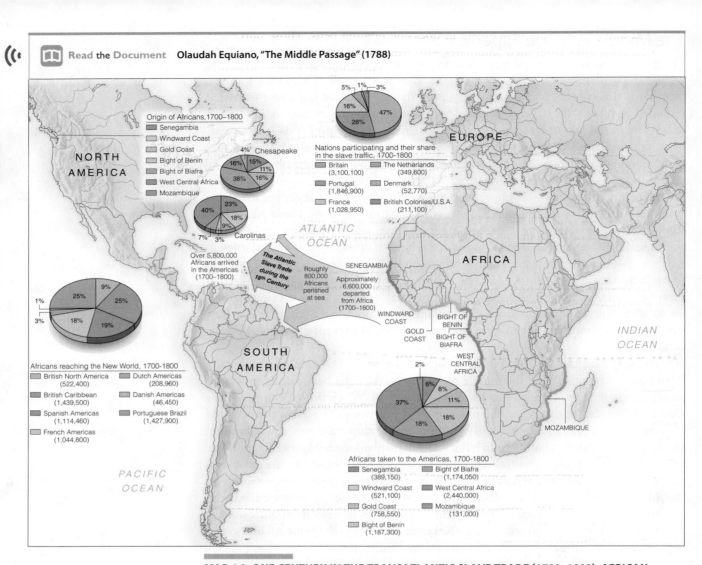

MAP 4.2 ONE CENTURY IN THE TRANSATLANTIC SLAVE TRADE (1700–1800): AFRICAN ORIGINS, EUROPEAN CARRIERS, AMERICAN DESTINATIONS The Atlantic slave trade reached its greatest size in the eighteenth century, and Britain replaced Portugal as the largest transporter. Between 1700 and 1800, ship captains purchased more than 6.6 million Africans. Of these, nearly 800,000, or 12 percent, died during the middle passage. Therefore, just over 5.8 million captives survived the Atlantic crossing during the century. Of these middle passage survivors, only about 9 percent (over half a million Africans) were sent to North America during the eighteenth century. Their ethnic backgrounds varied from colony to colony. In South Carolina, people from Senegambia and West Central Africa made up nearly two-thirds of the new black population; in the Chesapeake region, 38 percent of African arrivals came from the Bight of Biafra.

skills, and the vessel's condition. The resolve of the prisoners, the vagaries of piracy and ocean warfare, and the ravages of disease also became factors. A change in weather conditions or in the captain's mood could mean the difference between life and death.

While the grim details varied, the overall pattern remained the same. The constant rolling of the vessel; the sharp changes in temperature; the crowded, filthy conditions; and the relentless physical pain and mental anguish took a heavy toll. Pregnant mothers gave birth or miscarried; women were subjected to abuse and rape by the crew. Sailors threw the deceased to the sharks and even used corpses as bait, catching sharks that they fed to the captives.

Saltwater Slaves Arrive in America

For the emaciated survivors of the Atlantic ordeal, two further stages remained in their descent into slavery: the selling process and the time called "seasoning." The selling process on American soil could drag on for weeks or months, as prospective owners examined and prodded the newcomers in dockside holding pens. Those purchased were wrenched away from their shipmates with whom they had formed strong links during their miseries at sea. Slaves often were auctioned in groups, or parcels, to ensure sale of the weak along with the strong. A final journey brought them to the particular plantation where many would work until they died.

Most Africans did not begin their forced labor immediately. Instead, they entered a final stage, known as seasoning, which lasted several months or longer. The newcomers were distinguished as "**saltwater slaves**"—in contrast to "country-born slaves" who had grown up in America from birth. Seasoning gave newcomers time to mend physically and begin absorbing a new language. Inevitably, many suffered from what we call posttraumatic stress disorder.

As adults and children recovered from the trauma of the middle passage, they faced a series of additional shocks. They confronted foreign landscapes, strange foods, unfamiliar tasks, and even new names. Worst of all, fresh arrivals encountered a master or overseer determined to turn them into compliant bondservants. Repeatedly, the powerful stranger used arbitrary force to demand the slaves' obedience, destroy their hope, and crush any thoughts of resistance.

Saltwater slaves This term applied to Africans in America who had personally endured the transatlantic middle passage. It distinguished them from their descendants, the "country-born slaves" who had grown up in America from birth.

Survival in a Strange New Land

4.4 How did diverse Africans, enslaved in America, find common ground for resistance?

By 1700, race slavery was accepted throughout the mainland colonies. Africans found themselves scattered from New England to Louisiana, but their distribution was far from even. Among roughly 247,000 slaves in the North American colonies in 1750, only 30,000 (or 12 percent) resided in the North, where they made up just 5 percent of the overall population from Pennsylvania to New Hampshire. More than one-third of these northerners (11,000) lived in the colony of New York, where they constituted 14 percent of the colonial inhabitants. All the rest of the people of African descent in North America—some 217,000 men, women, and children by the mid-eighteenth century—lived and worked in the Chesapeake region and the lower South. Fewer than 500 of these black southerners were in Spanish Florida, and fewer than 5,000 resided in French Louisiana.

African Rice Growers in South Carolina

In eighteenth-century North America, by far the greatest number of enslaved workers lived in Virginia or Maryland: 150,000 by 1750. But South Carolina had the highest *proportion* of slaves; there Africans began outnumbering Europeans by 1708. By 1750, South Carolina's black majority (over 40,000 people) constituted more than 60 percent of the colony's population. Almost all had arrived through the deepwater port of Charleston. Sullivan's Island, near the entrance to the harbor, with its so-called **pest house** to quarantine incoming slaves and reduce the spread of shipborne disease, has been called the Ellis Island of black America.

What explains the emergence of South Carolina's slave concentration? For one thing, the colony was closer than Virginia to Africa and to the Caribbean. Moreover, it had been founded in 1670, just as aggressive English capitalists were embracing plantation slavery and the African trade. Indeed, some of the colony's original wealthy proprietors owned stakes in the Royal African Company. Also, some of Carolina's influential early settlers came directly from Barbados, bringing enslaved Africans and planter ambitions with them.

In the earliest days, South Carolina colonists lacked sufficient labor to clear coastal forests and plant crops. Instead, newcomers let their cattle and pigs run wild. With

Pest house In colonial times, a shelter to quarantine those possibly infected with contagious diseases (such as newcomers arriving in American ports from Africa or Europe) to prevent the spread of shipborne pestilence.

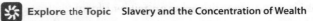

Explore the Topic Slavery and the Concentration of Wealth

Drayton Hall on the Ashley River near Charleston, completed in 1742 with profits from the rice trade, was one of many massive estates reflecting the remarkable concentration of wealth in the South Carolina low country. "The Planters in General have throve and grown Rich," Richard Hill observed a year later, "by the help and Labour of their Slaves (for their Lands tho' ever so Fertile are of no use or Profitt without them)." Why, by the 1740s, were social and economic inequalities more extreme in South Carolina than in Massachusetts?

easy foraging and warm winters, the animals reproduced rapidly. Settlers slaughtered them and shipped quantities of meat to the Caribbean, where forests and grazing habitat were giving way to cane fields. Early Carolinians, clearing dense woodlands, made money exporting to the islands firewood for boiling sugar cane and wooden barrels for transporting sugar. Ship captains also carried enslaved Native Americans to the West Indies and brought back African slaves.

The arriving Africans understood South Carolina's subtropical climate, with its alligators and palmetto trees, better than their European owners did. Many of these enslaved newcomers were already familiar with keeping cattle. Others, obliged to feed themselves, began growing rice in the fertile swamplands just as they had in West Africa. Slave owners quickly realized that this plant, unfamiliar to much of northern Europe, held the answer to their search for a profitable staple crop. Soon, people who had tended their own irrigated rice crops near the Gambia River were clearing cypress swamps along the Ashley and Cooper rivers to grow rice for someone else. They planted and harvested the crop, pounding the grain by hand. They made the fanner baskets used to winnow the rice and wooden barrels needed to export it.

Before long, Carolina entrepreneurs were shipping tons of rice to Europe, where it proved a cheap grain for feeding soldiers, orphans, and peasants. By the middle of the eighteenth century, their fortunes improved even more when indigo, another African crop, joined rice as a profitable export commodity. Outnumbered by their enslaved workers, South Carolina's white landowners passed strict Negro Acts that prohibited slaves from carrying guns, meeting in groups, raising livestock, or traveling without a pass. Everywhere, mounted patrols enforced the regulations with brutal severity.

Patterns of Resistance

In South Carolina and elsewhere, enslaved African Americans pressed to relieve their condition in any possible way. Like any other imprisoned population, they spread rumors, refused to work, broke tools, feigned illness, or threatened violence. In response, their owners tried to divide them in order to control them. Masters rewarded workers who were obedient and diligent or who informed on fellow slaves. They imposed harsh punishments—whipping, mutilation, sale, or death—on those suspected of taking food, sowing dissent, or plotting revolt. And they encouraged the formation of black families, not only to gain another generation of laborers at no cost but also to create the emotional ties that they knew would hold individuals in check for fear of reprisals against loved ones.

Owners confined residents in the slave labor camps with curfews and pass systems, denying them literacy and limiting communication with neighbors and relatives. Enslaved families had no viable system for expressing grievances or appealing arbitrary punishments. Faced with such steep odds, many slaves submitted to the deadening routine of the prison camp to survive. But others resorted to diverse strategies to improve their situation or undermine their masters' dominance. Running away, even for a brief period, provided relief from forced work and deprived owners of the labor they depended on. Because arson created serious damage and was difficult to detect, some slaves burned down barns at harvest time. Others succeeded in killing their masters or overseers. Such acts of pent-up rage usually proved suicidal, but they also confirmed slave owners' worst fears.

Above all, the prospect of open rebellion burned in the minds of prisoners and jailers alike. Often, therefore, it is hard to untangle episodes of white paranoia from incidents of actual revolt. Many innocent slaves were falsely accused. But countless others did discuss plans for resistance, and a few freedom fighters avoided detection or betrayal long enough to launch serious uprisings. Word of one upheaval, real or imagined, could spark others.

An early wave of slave unrest erupted in the dozen years after 1710, highlighted by violence in New York City in the spring of 1712. The leaders of the conspiracy were "Coromantee," or Akan people from Africa's Gold Coast region. Several dozen enslaved Africans and Indians, bent on obtaining their freedom and killing their white oppressors, set fire to a building. As citizens rushed to put out the blaze, the rebels attacked them, killing eight and wounding more. When the militia prevailed, six of the insurgents committed suicide. Authorities executed eighteen, burning some at the stake, hanging others and leaving their bodies on display.

A Wave of Rebellion

A second wave of black resistance swept the mainland colonies after 1730, fueled by the largest influx of Africans to date. In Louisiana, as French landowners staked out riverfront plantations, they also imported African slaves. The several thousand black workers soon outnumbered European settlers, and in 1731 fearful whites broke up two presumed slave plots. One involved a scheme to rebel on Christmas while Catholic colonists attended a midnight mass. Another apparent plot was revealed by the careless boast of a black servant woman. It included several hundred Bambara newcomers from Senegal who aspired to massacre whites, enslave other Africans, and take control of the region. When torture by fire failed to force confessions from key suspects, officials hanged the servant woman. Then the leader and half a dozen other men were "broken on the wheel" (put to death slowly by being tied to wagon wheels and having their bones broken).

The largest slave uprising in colonial North America broke out in 1739 near the Stono River, twenty miles southwest of Charleston. Several factors fueled the Stono Rebellion. By 1739, blacks exceeded whites nearly two to one among South Carolina's 56,000 people. The proportion of recently imported slaves had reached an all-time high. In addition, working conditions had worsened steadily as rice production expanded. Moreover, for several decades the Spanish in Florida had been luring slaves from South Carolina, knowing that the promise of freedom might destabilize Carolina's profitable slave regime. More than a hundred fugitives had escaped to Florida by 1738, when Florida's governor formed them into a free black militia company at St. Augustine.

Hoping to win more defections, he allowed thirty-eight African American households to settle north of the town and build a small fortress—Fort Mose.

Meanwhile, the wide commercial rivalries of Spain and Britain led to open warfare in 1739. The slave uprising at Stono erupted just after word reached Charleston that war had broken out between the two Atlantic empires. Other factors may also have influenced the rebels' timing. An epidemic in Charleston had disrupted public activities, and a new Security Act requiring all white men to carry arms to church was to take effect before the end of September.

Early on Sunday, September 9, 1739, twenty slaves from a work crew near the Stono River broke into a local store. There they seized weapons and executed the owners, then raised a banner and marched south, beating drums and shouting "Liberty!" The insurgents burned selected plantations, killed a score of whites, and gathered more than fifty new recruits. But armed colonists overtook them and blocked their escape to St. Augustine. Dozens of rebels died in the ensuing battle. In the next two days, militia and hired Indians killed twenty more and captured an additional forty people, whom they immediately shot or hanged.

Yet even fierce reprisals and a harsh new Negro Law could not quell black hopes. In June 1740, several hundred slaves plotted to storm Charleston and take arms from a warehouse. However, a comrade revealed the plan. According to a report, "The next day fifty of them were seized, and these were hanged, ten a day, to intimidate the other negroes." In November, a great fire of suspicious origin destroyed much of Charleston.

Fire also played a role in hysteria that broke out in New York City in 1741. In March, a blaze consumed the residence of New York's governor and a local fort. Other fires soon focused suspicions on a white couple, John and Sarah Hughson, who had often entertained blacks at their alehouse. The Hughsons—thought to fence stolen goods for a black crime ring—were accused of inciting working-class unrest. In exchange for her freedom, a sixteen-year-old Irish indentured servant at the Hughsons' tavern testified that she had overheard the planning of an elaborate plot.

In a gruesome spiral of arrests and executions, New York authorities put to death thirty-four people, including four whites, and banished seventy-two blacks. On one hand, the debacle recalled the Salem witch trials, as a fearful community engaged in judicial proceedings and killings on the basis of rumors and accusations. On the other hand, the New York Slave Plot recalled Bacon's Rebellion, for evidence emerged of cooperation between impoverished blacks and poor whites eager to see a redistribution of property. According to his accusers, a slave named Cuffee had often observed that "a great many people had too much, and others too little." He predicted that soon his master "should have less, and that he (Cuffee) should have more." Instead, he was burned at the stake.

The Transformation Completed

4.5 What prevented antislavery ideas from gaining a stronger foothold in the American colonies?

The mechanisms for extorting labor from tens of thousands of people were firmly in place. But to maintain the slave labor system, local governments had to be vigilant and repressive, prompting debates within the white population. Some colonists saw slavery as too morally degrading and physically dangerous to maintain. Powerful supporters of the institution, however, found it too rewarding to give up and suggested modifications instead.

Debating Racial Status in the South and the North

Stakes were highest in the South, where most African Americans lived. As race-based slavery expanded, white colonists treated the continuing presence of free blacks as a contradiction and a threat. As early as 1691, the Virginia assembly passed an act restricting **manumissions** (grants of individual freedom by masters) because "great inconvenience may happen to this country by setting of negroes and mulattoes free." According to the act, such people fanned hopes of freedom among enslaved blacks. Besides, when they grew old and infirm, their care at public expense could constitute "a charge upon the country." By 1723, additional Virginia statutes prevented free people of color from voting, taxed them unfairly, and prevented them from owning or carrying firearms. Lawmakers went on to prohibit all manumissions, except when the governor rewarded "meritorious service," such as informing against other enslaved workers.

Following the Stono uprising, whites in South Carolina conducted their own debate. Leaders imposed a heavy import duty on new African arrivals for several years, hoping to increase the colony's ratio of whites to enslaved blacks. At a time of growing humanitarian concerns in Enlightenment Europe, it took great effort to maintain the rationale for building slavery-based societies in the South. But free people who questioned the institution met stiff resistance from those with vested interests.

While the southern planters labored to intimidate enslaved populations and weaken or contain free black communities, African Americans in the North, both enslaved and free, faced related challenges. Northern slave populations, though far smaller than those in the South, were growing steadily. As the North's involvement in the Atlantic slave trade expanded, its economic and legal commitment to race slavery increased. Rhode Island's slave ranks jumped from 500 in 1720 to more than 3,000 in 1750. Everywhere, new laws made manumission more difficult, and those African Americans already free faced growing discrimination when attempting to hold jobs, buy land, obtain credit, move about safely, and take part in civic life. Only in the century after 1760 did northern free black communities gain the numerical and social strength to offer effective opposition to enslavement.

Whereas free blacks lacked the means to oppose slavery, prominent white Christians lacked the will. Even in Massachusetts, where religion remained a dominant force in 1700 and the number of slaves had scarcely reached 1,000 people, many leaders already owned black servants, and most ministers defended the practice.

The protests that did appear were ambivalent at best. Judge Samuel Sewell questioned African enslavement in *The Selling of Joseph* (1700). But the tract revealed Sewell's sense of superiority and his skepticism that blacks could play a part in "the Peopling of the Land." African Americans, the judge commented, "can seldom use their freedom well; yet their continual aspiring after their forbidden Liberty, renders them unwilling servants." Reverend Cotton Mather, a slave owner who once berated Sewell as one who "pleaded much for Negroes," was even more ambivalent. In *The Negro Christianized* (1706), the influential Puritan stressed that conversion and Christian instruction, far from earning African slaves their freedom, would make them into "better servants."

Is This Consistent with Christianity or Common Justice?

The conversion and instruction of slaves, rather than the abolition of slavery, became a mission for earnest whites such as Thomas Bray. This well-to-do English philanthropist was committed to spreading the Anglican faith in America among Europeans, Indians, and Africans. In 1701, Bray established the Society for the Propagation of the Gospel in Foreign Parts (SPG). The SPG strengthened the Church of England abroad in the eighteenth century by providing dozens of ministers to serve in the colonies.

But this Anglican foothold came at a steep price. Southern planters made SPG ministers agree that any hopes they offered to slaves regarding heavenly salvation would not include hints of earthly freedom. With few exceptions, the Anglican clergy gave in, strengthening religious support of race slavery. In 1723, a heartfelt petition from a mulatto slave to the Bishop of London, in which the author protested "Cruell Bondegg" in Virginia, went unanswered. That same year, Bray set up a trust of "Associates" to carry on his work. With limited success, they focused on converting blacks in the British plantation colonies.

By the 1730s, only a few whites in Europe or America dared to press publicly for an end to slavery. Christian Priber, who arrived in the South in 1735, was one such activist.

Manumission A formal emancipation from slavery; the act (by an individual owner or government authority) of granting freedom to an enslaved person or persons.

The idealistic German hoped to start a utopian community in southern Appalachia. But his radical proposal for a multiracial "Paradise" uniting Indians, Africans, and Europeans posed a huge threat to South Carolina authorities. "He enumerates many whimsical Privileges and natural Rights, as he calls them, which his Citizens are to be entitled to," wrote a scornful detractor, fearful that this egalitarian haven "at the Foot of the Mountains among the Cherokees" was to be "a City of Refuge for all Criminals, Debtors, and Slaves who would fly thither from Justice or their Masters." Priber's brief career as a social agitator challenging the status quo ended in 1743, when he was arrested and brought to jail in Charleston. He died—or was killed—before his case could be heard in court.

At the same time, a New Jersey tailor and bookkeeper named John Woolman posed a less defiant but more enduring threat to race slavery. In 1743, at age twenty-three, this shy Quaker began to question his role in writing out bills of sale when his fellow Quakers purchased slaves. It struck him forcefully that "to live in ease and plenty by the toil of those whom violence and cruelty have put in our power" was clearly not "consistent with Christianity or common justice." Woolman traveled widely to Quaker meetings, north and south, pressing an issue that most Quakers preferred to ignore. When he drafted *Some Considerations on the Keeping of Negroes* (1754), members of the Quaker Yearly Meeting in Philadelphia published his booklet and circulated it widely. Four years later, led by Anthony Benezet, this group outlawed slaveholding among its local members. They set a precedent that many Quakers followed in the next generation, and they challenged other denominations to do the same.

Oglethorpe's Antislavery Experiment

The most sustained early challenge to the slavery system in the American South came in the Georgia colony. In 1732, a group of well-connected London proprietors (known as trustees) obtained a twenty-year charter for the region between English South Carolina and Spanish Florida. Ten of the twenty-one initial trustees were members of Parliament. They included James Oglethorpe, who had recently organized and chaired a "committee on jails" to investigate the condition of debtors in English prisons.

The trustees foresaw three related purposes—charitable, commercial, and military—for their experimental colony, which they named after King George II. Georgia would provide a haven for England's worthy poor, selected members of the neediest classes who could be transported across the Atlantic and settled on small farms. These grateful newcomers would then produce warm-weather commodities—olives, grapes, silk—to support the empire. Their prosperity would create a growing market for English goods. Finally, their presence would provide a military buffer to protect South Carolina from further warfare with the Yamasee and Creek Indians and from possible invasion by the Spanish in St. Augustine.

With Oglethorpe as their governor, an initial boatload of 114 settlers arrived in 1733 and began building a capital at Savannah. By 1741, the town, located on a bluff 15 miles up the Savannah River, boasted more than 140 houses. By then, more than 1,000 needy English, plus 800 German, Swiss, and Austrian Protestants, had journeyed to Georgia at the trustees' expense. Another thousand immigrants had paid their own way. Like earlier colonizers, Georgia's first arrivals had trouble adjusting to a strange environment. Alligators, rattlesnakes, and hurricanes tested their resolve. Tension over governance only deepened their discouragement.

The idealistic trustees in London declined to accumulate property and profits for themselves in the colony, but they felt justified in controlling every aspect of Georgia's development. For example, they knew that gin was becoming a source of debt and disruption in Europe and that rum and brandy sold by traders was poisoning colonial relations with southeastern Indians. So, in 1735, they outlawed the use of every "kind of Spirits," while still allowing consumption of wine and beer. Georgia's early experiment with prohibition of hard liquor proved difficult to implement, and officials quietly stopped enforcing the law in 1742.

Read the Document   James Oglethorpe, "Establishing the Colony of Georgia" (1733)

4.1

4.2

4.3

4.4

4.5

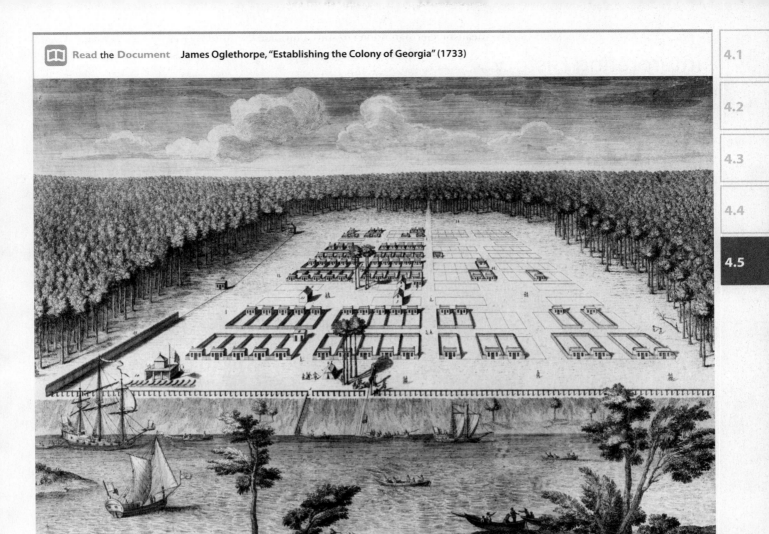

Savannah, the capital of Oglethorpe's Georgia, was a year old when this view was sketched in 1734. As the founder of Georgia, Oglethorpe convinced Georgia's trustees to outlaw slavery in the new colony in 1735, creating a sharp contrast with other British colonies in North America, especially neighboring South Carolina on the opposite bank of the Savannah River. The ban on enslavement in Georgia was overturned fifteen years later, due partly to pressure from ambitious planters in South Carolina, already active in slave trading and rice production. Why did South Carolina rice planters work hard to ensure race slavery was legalized in Georgia?

Other efforts at control from above went further. The trustees refused to set up a legislature or to let settlers buy and sell land. Instead, they gave 50 acres of farm land to each family they sent over, plus a house lot in a local village, so all new towns could be well defended. But they parceled out land with little regard for variations in soil fertility. They also stipulated that owners could pass land on to sons only. To prevent the concentrations of wealth that they saw developing in other colonies, the trustees said that no one could own more than 500 acres. Prohibiting massive estates would allow for thicker settlement and therefore greater manpower to defend the colony militarily.

But the most important prohibition, by far, involved slavery. Oglethorpe began his career as a deputy governor of the Royal African Company, but he died in 1785 opposing the slave trade. His sojourn in Georgia turned him against slavery. In neighboring South Carolina, he saw firsthand how the practice degraded African lives, undermined the morals of Europeans, and laid that colony open to threats of revolt and invasion. So Oglethorpe persuaded the trustees to create a free white colony, convincing them to enact a law in 1735 that prohibited slavery and also excluded free blacks. He believed that this mandate would protect Georgia from the corruptions of enslavement while also making it easier to apprehend black runaways heading to Florida from South Carolina.

Interpreting History
"Releese Us Out of This Cruell Bondegg"

"and to be **plain** they doo **Look no more** upon us **then** if **wee** ware **dogs**"

T he Terrible Transformation had done its work by 1723, when a mulatto slave drafted this halting appeal on behalf of numerous enslaved Virginians. Christian belief no longer protected individuals from enslavement, as it had a century earlier, and many mixed-race Virginians found themselves owned by their own white relatives. Recently rediscovered in a London archive, "these Strange lines" are addressed to Edward Gibson, the Bishop of London, whose position gave him religious oversight for all the Anglican parishes in England's American colonies. Gibson had voiced concern for the Christianization of enslaved Africans, but he showed less interest in the liberation of slaves. This heartfelt document, prepared and sent at enormous risk, never received a response or prompted any inquiry into conditions in Virginia.

August the forth 1723
to the Right Raverrand father in god my Lord arch Bishop of Lonnd....

this coms to sattesfie your honour that there is in this Land of verJennia a Sort of people that is Calld molatters which are Baptised and brouaht up in the way of the Christian faith and followes the ways and Rulles of the Chrch of England and sum of them has white fathars and sum white mothers and there is in this Land a Law or act which keeps and makes them and there seed Slaves forever....

wee your humbell and poore partishinners doo begg Sir your aid and assisttancce in this one thing ... which is that

your honour will by the help of our Sufvering [i.e., sovereign] Lord King George and the Rest of the Rullers will Releese us out of this Cruell Bondegg. . . . and here it is to bee notd that one brother is a Slave to another and one Sister to an othe which is quite out of the way and as for mee my selfe I am my brothers Slave but my name is Secrett

wee are commandded to keep holey the Sabbath day and wee doo hardly know when it comes for our task mastrs are has hard with us as the Egypttions was with the Chilldann of Issarall. . . . wee are kept out of the Church and matrimony is deenied us and to be plain they doo Look no more upon us then if wee ware dogs which I hope when these Strange lines comes to your Lord Ships hands will be Looket in to. . . .

And Sir wee your humble perticners do humblly beg . . . that our childarn may be broatt up in the way of the Christtian faith and our desire is that they may be Larnd the Lords prayer the creed and the ten commandements and that they may appeare Every Lord's day att Church before the Curatt to bee Exammond for our desire is that godllines Shoulld abbound amongs us and wee desire that our Childarn be putt to Scool and Larnd to Reed through the Bybell

My Riting is vary bad. . . . I am but a poore Slave that writt itt and has no other time butt Sunday and hardly that att Sumtimes. . . . wee dare nott Subscribe any mans name to this for feare of our masters for if they knew that wee have Sent home to your honour wee Should goo neare to Swing upon the gallass tree.

When abolition of the slave trade finally became a public issue in England in the 1780s, British artists painted scenes criticizing the traffic. But two generations earlier, pleas from New World slaves aroused no response, even from the Bishop of London, who supervised the Church of England in the American colonies. What had changed, in the intervening years, that might account for the differing responses?

SOURCE: Thomas N. Ingersoll, "'Releese Us out of This Cruell Bondegg': An Appeal from Virginia in 1723." *William and Mary Quarterly*, Third Series, 51 (October 1994): 776–782.

Questions for Discussion

1. In 1723, do these mulatto petitioners identify more closely with their African and non-Christian relatives who are enslaved or with their European and Anglican relations who are free? Explain.
2. If you were the clerk who opened the bishop's mail and suggested possible replies, what memo would you attach to this letter that might gain his attention and prompt a serious response?

In 1739, the Stono Rebellion and the outbreak of war between England and Spain strengthened Oglethorpe's belief that slavery undermined security by creating internal enemies who would support foreign attackers. He saw further evidence in 1740, when he failed in a wartime attempt to capture St. Augustine from Spain. Unable to take the Florida stronghold, the governor seized neighboring Fort Mose, the bastion erected by anti-English slaves who had escaped from Carolina. Later, a Spanish force relying heavily on Indian and African American fighters retook Fort Mose, showing Oglethorpe the intensity with which ex-slaves would fight the English, their former masters.

The next year, fearing a counterattack, Oglethorpe issued a warning to imperial officials. He predicted that if Spanish soldiers captured Georgia, a colony inhabited by "white Protestants and no Negroes," they would then send agents to infiltrate the vulnerable colonies farther north and stir black rebellion.

The End of Equality in Georgia

As Britain's war with Spain continued, few whites could deny the Georgia governor's assertion that slavery elsewhere in British America was a source of internal weakness and strategic danger. Just as Oglethorpe had predicted, Spain pushed from Florida into Georgia with an eye toward destabilizing the colonies farther north. In 1742, Oglethorpe's troops repulsed the invading Spanish force in the crucial Battle at Bloody Marsh on St. Simon's Island.

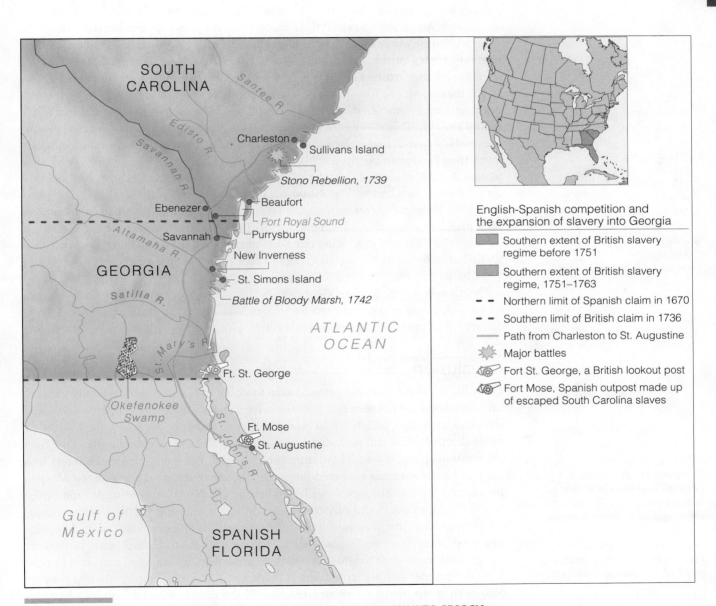

English-Spanish competition and the expansion of slavery into Georgia

■ Southern extent of British slavery regime before 1751

■ Southern extent of British slavery regime, 1751–1763

- - Northern limit of Spanish claim in 1670

- - Southern limit of British claim in 1736

— Path from Charleston to St. Augustine

✴ Major battles

Fort St. George, a British lookout post

Fort Mose, Spanish outpost made up of escaped South Carolina slaves

MAP 4.3 ENGLISH-SPANISH COMPETITION AND THE EXPANSION OF SLAVERY INTO GEORGIA
The Spanish and the British had competing land claims along the southeast coast after 1670. Creation of the Georgia colony in 1732 intensified the rivalry. The Spanish in Florida offered freedom to any slaves who escaped from South Carolina to St. Augustine, sparking the Stono Revolt in 1739. During the war between Britain and Spain (1739–1743), Georgians defeated the Spanish at Bloody Marsh and secured the disputed "Sea Island" region for the British. Within a decade, slavery became legal in Georgia, and scores of new labor camps appeared between the Savannah and the St. Mary's River, producing rice for export.

The victory at Bloody Marsh reduced the immediate threat to Britain's North American colonies, especially neighboring South Carolina, where Oglethorpe and his idealistic policies had numerous powerful opponents. These opponents now joined a group of so-called Malcontents in Savannah to question Georgia's continued prohibition against slavery. By challenging the trustees' antislavery stance, this self-interested coalition prompted the first protracted North American debate about enslavement.

Given Georgia's numerous drawbacks—including a sickly climate, poor soil, restrictive land policies, and lack of representative government—a well-organized faction argued that the colony needed slavery in order to prosper. But not everyone agreed. In 1739, Scottish Highlanders living at Darien on the Altamaha River had contacted Oglethorpe to lay out their practical arguments against importing Africans. Their petition expressed shock "that any Race of Mankind, and their Posterity, Should be sentenced to perpetual slavery." Immigrants from Salzburg, Germany, residing at Ebenezer on the Savannah River drafted a similar statement. But Georgia's Malcontents pushed back, demanding the right to import slaves. They drew encouragement and support from powerful merchant-planters in South Carolina, eager to expand their trade in slaves from Africa and to extend their successful rice operations into coastal Georgia.

Oglethorpe warned that the proslavery lobby, hungry to create large estates, seemed bent on "destroying the Agrarian Equality" envisioned in Georgia's initial plan. But over time, the colony's trustees in London grew less unified, committed, and informed. Eventually, the persistent efforts of the proslavery pamphleteers bore fruit. In 1750, the trustees gave in on the matter of land titles. They allowed acreage to be bought and sold freely in any amount. This invited the creation of large plantations, and that pointed toward the drastic step to allowing slavery. The trustees finally caved in on the question of bondage, letting Georgians purchase enslaved workers. The 1750 law permitting slavery after January 1, 1751, made futile gestures to ensure kind treatment and Christian education for slaves. But the dam had broken. Hundreds of slave-owning South Carolinians streamed across the Savannah River to invest in Georgia land. In 1752, the trustees disbanded, their patent expiring, their vision undone. By 1754, Georgia had become a royal colony.

Slave labor camps producing rice and indigo for export soon dotted the low country on both sides of the Savannah River. Georgia's assembly passed a harsh slave code in 1755, based on South Carolina's. Two years later, it legislated a system of patrols to keep the brutal new regime in place. Georgia's effort to counter race slavery in North America had failed, a case of too little, too late. After holding out for nearly two decades, the colony fell victim to the same divisive institution that had already taken root elsewhere.

Conclusion

Bit by bit, the slavery system gained a firm foothold in North America during the century after 1660. In southern colonies, the system shaped the entire economy and social structure, creating a society based on race slavery. Farther north, where the institution never dominated, it still persisted as a disturbing element of colonial life. Two final observations provide a wider Atlantic context. First, the influx of African slaves into English North America occurred long after the **diaspora**, or dispersion, to Mexico, Brazil, and the Caribbean was well established. The North American portion of the gigantic African traffic did not expand steadily until after the 1670s. A century later, on the eve of the American Revolution, the proportion of blacks in the colonial population (over 20 percent) was higher than it has ever been in the United States since then.

Second, even at its height, the North American trade remained marginal in relation to the wider Atlantic commerce in African labor. For example, whereas roughly 50,000 enslaved men and women reached all the docks of North America between 1721 and 1740, the small West Indian islands of English Barbados and French Guadeloupe *each* received more than 53,000 Africans during the same period. In the next two decades, while Britain's mainland colonies purchased just over 100,000 Africans, Caribbean Islands such as English Jamaica (120,000) and French Saint Domingue (159,000) absorbed many more slaves.

Diaspora The dispersion of a population abroad, whether forced or voluntary. The term is often applied to Jewish settlement outside the eastern Mediterranean region, and to the spread of Africans across the Americas, as a result of the Atlantic slave trade.

During this single forty-year span (1721–1760), Brazil bought 667,000 African workers—more than would reach North America during the entire slave trade. All told, scholars currently estimate that some 650,000 Africans were brought to North America over several centuries. They represented roughly 6 percent of the total Atlantic commerce in enslaved people. Still, the number of mainland slaves expanded from scarcely 7,000 in 1680 to nearly 29,000 in 1700 and to more than 70,000 in 1720. Half a century later in 1770, because of importation and natural increase, an estimated 470,000 individuals were enslaved in all the diverse colonies from New Hampshire to French Louisiana.

A century had passed since Elizabeth Key's generation saw the Terrible Transformation begin. Relative openness had given way to systematic oppression, and slavery's corrosive effects were felt at every level of society. An English visitor to the South in 1759 found provincial planters "vain and imperious," subject "to many errors and prejudices, especially in regard to Indians and Negroes, whom they scarcely consider as of the human species." It took another century before pressures developed that could unseat race slavery, sanctioned by law, as a dominant institution in the land.

Chapter Review

The Descent into Race Slavery

4.1 How important was precedent in the English shift to impose hereditary enslavement on Africans deported to North America? p. 81

At first, Protestant England opposed the exploitation of Africans shipped to the Americas by the Catholic Spanish. But righteousness gave way to envy, as English colonists adopted both race slavery and sugar production in the Caribbean. Once enslavement gained acceptance in North America, court cases added precedents for its expansion.

The Growth of Slave Labor Camps

4.2 What factors created a vicious circle that sealed the fate of African workers in Virginia? p. 85

The rise of racism allowed Tidewater planters to divide black and white tobacco workers. Victimized white servants could warn European relatives to migrate to other colonies. But black Virginians, forced into lifetime servitude, had no way to provide negative feedback to Africa that would stop the flow of additional slaves.

England Enters the Atlantic Slave Trade

4.3 Why did England, once suspicious of the trade, become a leader in transporting enslaved Africans? p. 87

After 1660, the restored English monarchy entered into a new phase of Atlantic competition with European rivals. Seeking profits, and taking advantage of his realm's growing maritime power, King Charles II chartered the Royal Africa Company in 1672, which rapidly captured a large portion of the growing transatlantic slave trade.

Survival in a Strange New Land

4.4 How did diverse Africans, enslaved in America, find common ground for resistance? p. 93

As slavery grew, North America's diverse African newcomers gave birth to several generations of African Americans who spoke English and lacked first-hand knowledge of Africa. Their circumstances varied widely, but most experienced legally sanctioned exploitation and socially endorsed discrimination. Sharing a grave situation forced them to find strength in community.

The Transformation Completed

4.5 What prevented antislavery ideas from gaining a stronger foothold in the American colonies? p. 96

Slave importation and the exploitation of unpaid African labor yielded massive wealth to colonial merchants and slave owners, who then grew in political power. Churches and schools offered little opposition, so slave interests on both sides of the Atlantic managed to crush promising alternatives, such as Oglethorpe's anti-slavery experiment in Georgia.

Timeline

1672 **England Enters Slave Trade**—Royal African Company (RAC) formed in London

1676 **Survival**—Virginia and Maryland slaves join in Bacon's Rebellion

1705 **Race Slavery**—Virginia approves Negro Act

1712 **Survival**—New York City slave revolt

1713 **England Enters Slave Trade**—British receive the contract (asiento) to supply African slaves to Spanish colonies

1732 **Transformation Completed**—James Oglethorpe gains charter to launch Georgia as a non-slave colony

1739 **Survival**—Slave revolt in Stono, South Carolina

1741 **Survival**—Alleged slave plot in New York City

1751 **Transformation Completed**—Slavery is legalized in Georgia

5 Colonial **Diversity,**
1713–1763

What would drive a **German newcomer** to seek a life of seclusion in backwoods Pennsylvania? And why would dozens of fellow immigrants join Conrad Beissel in 1732 to establish an isolated Christian community that they called Ephrata? The jarring new diversity of colonial life may have had something to do with the creation of such a cloistered retreat from the secular world.

In 1720, Beissel had joined a wave of German immigrants arriving in Philadelphia, drawn by Pennsylvania's commitment to freedom of conscience. Intent upon leading a simple and pious life, the former baker sought seclusion near modern-day Lancaster. His charismatic leadership drew others to join him at Ephrata Cloister, the earliest of many utopian communities in North America. Nearly 80 devout men and women lived in celibate harmony, taking in occasional novices to maintain their ranks. For more than a generation, they prayed daily and operated a paper mill and printing press, gathering regularly at midnight for a two-hour religious vigil.

Only such separation and discipline could resist the culture shock that came to characterize America as the eighteenth century unfolded. Most newcomers were far less willing or able to remove themselves from the swirling currents of colonial life. Everywhere,

LEARNING OBJECTIVES

5.1 ((	5.2 ((	5.3 ((	5.4 ((	5.5 ((
How and why did life change dramatically for the Comanche and Sioux Indians after 1700? p. 107	In what ways did Britain's North American colonies become "less English" after 1700? p. 111	What role did geography play in shaping the emerging regional colonial economies? p. 115	What prompted increased toleration at a time of fresh religious intensity after 1730? p. 121	What key factors undermined the French position in America in the decades after 1740? p. 126

This modern photograph shows historic Ephrata Cloister in Pennsylvania, where Conrad Beissel founded a semi-monastic community in the 1730s. His followers were to remain celibate, sleep on benches, eat only one vegetarian meal per day, and gather each midnight to "watch" for the coming of Christ. Such communal discipline and isolation proved exceptional. What was Ephrata's possible appeal, as diversity and contentious interaction became the norm in eighteenth-century America?

((• Listen to Chapter 5 on MyHistoryLab

◉ Watch the Video Series on MyHistoryLab

Learn about some key topics related to this chapter with the *MyHistoryLab Video Series: Key Topics in U.S. History.*

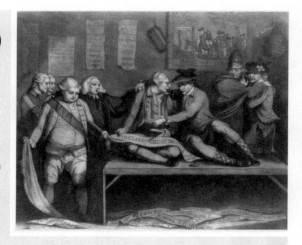

1 **Great Britain's Empire in North America: 1713–1763** During the first half of the eighteenth century, British North America experienced an increase in its population largely driven by the arrival of new colonists, indentured servants, and slaves. This video surveys the second wave of immigrants who came from Ireland, Scotland, and German states, especially those ruled by Great Britain's monarchs. The newcomers contributed to the commercial growth of the British colonies. By the 1750s, this success intensified the long-standing rivalry between Britain and France, helping to spark the Seven Years' War between these competing colonial powers.

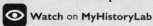 Watch on MyHistoryLab

Scots-Irish Migration English migration to North America slowed in the late seventeenth century, and it was followed by a more diverse wave of immigrants, including streams of Scots-Irish and German settlers. Those too poor to pay their own way came as indentured servants, accepting voluntary servitude for several years, while using their labor to pay off their debts. As this video suggests, new arrivals and those completing their indentures often settled inland, claiming uncleared land near Native Americans. Non-English settlers brought their own cultures and languages, and many, such as the Scots-Irish, felt indifferent or hostile to the mother country, a sentiment that would fuel desires for independence from England.

Watch on MyHistoryLab **2**

3 **The First Great Awakening** This video discusses the heightened religious and evangelical activity in the American colonies in the second quarter of the eighteenth century. This period of spiritual questioning later became known as the First Great Awakening. Religious leaders such as Jonathan Edwards and George Whitefield pressed for renewed emphasis on emotional and personal commitment, rather than rites and doctrine. Their theology had a lasting impact on religion in America.

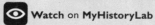 Watch on MyHistoryLab

Seven Years' War The expanding empires of France and Britain competed for trade and territory around the world, especially in North America, where war broke out in 1754. The French, despite strong alliances with Native American tribes, could not overcome British naval superiority. In the Treaty of Paris in 1763, France gave up its colonial possessions in North America, while Great Britain expanded its control westward to the Mississippi River. But when Britain subsequently taxed its American colonies to help cover the war's huge expenses, it sparked an independence movement that cost the British most of their recent territorial gains.

Watch on MyHistoryLab **4**

different languages and ideologies collided, local populations multiplied, and expanding economies diversified. Once-isolated regions competed for trade, and European empires clashed to gain dominance over the distant continent, even though its full nature and scope still eluded them.

> **T**he years between 1713 and 1763 constituted a half century of dramatic population growth that brought surprising new contacts all across the continent. Spanish missionaries lived among Tejas Indians in eastern Texas. French intruders laid claim to, and then lost control over, the Mississippi Valley. In Florida, English militia invading from Georgia fought escaped African slaves on the outskirts of Spanish St. Augustine. Often, the power imbalance in such encounters was stark, as in the slave markets of

Williamsburg, Charleston, and New Orleans. At other times, an uneasy equilibrium prevailed, as when Europeans and Native Americans met to parley and trade at Detroit, Albany, Savannah, Mobile, or San Antonio.

Colonial expansion brought novel confrontations between Europeans, Africans, and Native Americans. It also forced different peoples *within* each of these three categories to rub shoulders in unprecedented ways. Some day-to-day meetings proved rewarding—a sound bargain, a helpful remedy, or a happy marriage. But other mixing was strained and uneasy—full of verbal misunderstandings, competing claims, harsh commands, or open violence. Everywhere, motives differed, accents jarred, and cultures clashed—perhaps reminding some Christians of **Babel** in the Old Testament.

The strand of idealism and religious zeal that characterized Ephrata persisted, especially during the great religious awakening of the 1740s, when the prospect of building something new and transcendent seemed close at hand. But such utopian dreams were not to be. Instead, the bustling colonies carved out distinctive regional economies, and rising port towns showed increasing social stratification. Yet even as greater numbers brought more diversity, the elements of a shared and recognizable Anglo-American culture began to emerge throughout the Atlantic colonies.

Babel A city described in the Old Testament where constructing a tower was made impossible by the confusion of varied languages. This term from the Book of Genesis is used to describe any scene of clamor and confusion.

New Cultures on the Western Plains

5.1 How and why did life change dramatically for the Comanche and Sioux Indians after 1700?

North America's new diversity hinged on increasing oceanic traffic that brought a growing stream of newcomers—both free and enslaved. Conrad Beissel was only one arrival among thousands, as movement across the Atlantic from Europe and Africa intensified. The ripple effects from such human movements reached far beyond the Atlantic coast and often involved nonhuman surprises. Nowhere were such transformations more evident than on the western plains, where the advent of horses and guns brought sweeping changes to numerous Native American cultures.

For two centuries, the "Columbian Exchange" of plants, animals, and microbes— as well as people—had been reshaping New Spain. Spanish intrusions north into New Mexico and Arizona in the sixteenth and seventeenth centuries brought unfamiliar people, ideas, foods, diseases, and livestock into the American Southwest. While local Indians adopted some novelties and struggled to avoid others, one new technology—the gun—remained mostly out of reach. From the time of Spain's arrival in the New World, official Spanish policy had forbidden the sale of firearms to Native Americans.

In contrast, the French, Dutch, and English desired trade at almost any cost. They showed less hesitation about supplying Indians with guns in return for furs, so firearms had become familiar to many eastern Indians in the seventeenth century. In the eighteenth century, guns began to spread west across the Mississippi River. Combined with the movement of horses from the south, this development had enormous consequences. New patterns of warfare altered Indian cultures, and more powerful hunting techniques affected the regional economies and ecologies of the Native American West.

The Spread of the Horse

Although small horses once roamed the ancient West, they migrated into Asia thousands of years ago and became extinct in America. Horses returned with the early Spanish explorers. Around 1600, when New Mexico's early colonists brought mares north for breeding, horse herds developed in the Rio Grande valley. After the Pueblo Revolt in 1680, Spanish horses taken by the Indians were rapidly traded northward from one culture to another.

By 1690, the Ute had obtained horses and traded them to the Shoshone. Before the mid-eighteenth century, horses had moved west of the Rocky Mountains to the Nez Perce and north to the Blackfoot. The Apache brought horses east to the Caddoan cultures near the Red River and then north to the Pawnee, Arikara, and Hidatsa. Even

After the Pueblo Revolt of 1680, Native Americans traded horses northward, marking the appearance of a powerful new animal on the western landscape. Tribes that had once tracked buffalo on foot at the edge of the Great Plains could now ride horseback to pursue buffalo herds across miles of open grassland. The Cheyenne, living in fixed villages in what is now South Dakota, got their first horses in the early eighteenth century. John Stands-in-Timber recalled that when "they learned there were more of them in the South . . . they went there after them." Why did the acquisition of Spanish horses represent a revolutionary shift for Native Americans in the Great Plains region?

tribes in the Southeast acquired Spanish horses from the West before they obtained English horses from the Atlantic coast. When a Chickasaw leader drew a regional map on deerskin in 1723, he showed a Native American leading a horse east of the Mississippi River.

The first horses seemed utterly strange to the Indians. "The people did not know what they fed on. They would offer the animals pieces of dried meat," one elder recalled. "He put us on mind of a Stag that had lost his horns," another remembered, "and we did not know what name to give him. But as he was a slave to Man, like the dog, which carried our things, he was named the Big Dog." For generations, Native Americans had used dogs to pull provisions and bedding on a *travois,* an A-frame device made with tent poles. A larger animal could haul bigger loads, including longer tent poles that allowed for more spacious tipis.

Whether or not a tribe used tipis as dwellings, it could readily use the horse as a new source of meat and as an aid in hunting. As herds expanded and horsemanship improved, warriors rode into battle. On horses, they could conduct lightning raids over long distances. Soon raising, trading, and stealing horses became important activities, and a family's wealth and status depended partly on the number of horses at its command.

The Rise of the Comanche

By the 1770s, mounted Comanche warriors commanded respect and fear across a vast domain. Their territory stretched south nearly 600 miles from western Kansas to central Texas, and it spanned 400 miles from eastern New Mexico to what is now eastern Oklahoma. This area, known as the **Comanchería**, roughly equaled all the

Comanchería The area dominated by the Comanche Indians during the second half of the eighteenth century, after they acquired the horse and conquered the Plains Apache. This vast domain, shown on Map 5.1, covered much of the southern plains and embraced large parts of five modern western states.

English settlements on the Atlantic coast in size, but its origins were recent and humble. The Comanche's Shoshone-speaking ancestors had been hunter-gatherers on the high plains of Wyoming, living on small game, roots, and berries. The arrival of the horse around 1690 changed everything, allowing family bands to migrate southeast from the Rockies to the western edges of the Great Plains. There, they could hunt buffalo and then ride south annually to trade hides for additional horses at Taos and Santa Fe.

The Comanche were not the first to make their homes in what is now eastern Colorado. For generations, groups of Apache had settled in the region near the upper reaches of the Platte and Arkansas rivers. The Apache settlements—with their irrigated gardens and herds of horses—provided easy targets for Comanche newcomers. Within two decades, the Comanche had hammered their enemies south through one river valley after another. By 1720, the first Apache bands reached south-central Texas and the new Spanish town of San Antonio, founded just two years earlier. They killed several settlers and stole Spanish livestock to survive. But in 1749, still threatened by the Comanche, the hard-pressed Apache sealed a peace pact with the Spanish at San Antonio.

The Spanish soon began building a mission and presidio among their new Apache allies. But the outpost, 150 miles northwest of San Antonio on the San Saba River, had been established for less than a year when the Comanche attacked it in 1758. They returned the next year, capturing 700 horses. "The heathen of the north are innumerable and rich," exclaimed a Spanish officer at San Saba. "They dress well, breed horses, [and] handle firearms with the greatest skill." The Comanche onslaught continued, and the attacks finally forced the Spanish to withdraw from San Saba in 1767.

In less than two decades, the Comanche had overrun most of Texas. They continued to absorb smaller Native American groups and swell in numbers. By 1780, they had grown into a proud Indian nation of more than 20,000 people. Their domain, the Comanchería, remained a powerful entity in the Southwest for decades.

The Expansion of the Sioux

Comanche strength depended not only on mounted warfare but also on using the horse as a trade commodity to obtain guns. Because Spanish policy prohibited the sale of firearms to Native Americans, the Comanche looked east for weapons. They discovered that by selling horses to their eastern allies, such as the Wichita Indians, they could receive French muskets from Louisiana in return. But the Comanche were not alone; the Sioux also took advantage of the gun frontier as it inched steadily west.

By 1720, the French had established settlements at Peoria, Cahokia, and Kaskaskia in Illinois and at New Orleans, Natchez, and Natchitoches in Louisiana. French traders at these sites provided guns and other metal goods to Indians in exchange for salt, deerskins, beaver pelts, horses, and war captives. Native American groups that took advantage of this trade included the Tunica beside the Mississippi, the Caddo and Wichita along the Red and Arkansas rivers, and the Osage, Pawnee, and Omaha tribes near the Missouri.

Farther north, muskets carried west from French posts on the Great Lakes and south from English bases on Hudson Bay proved especially important among the Sioux peoples, who trapped game and gathered wild rice by the lakes of their Minnesota homeland. When the Sioux first encountered a gun from French voyageurs in the mid-seventeenth century, they called it *mazawakan*, meaning "mysterious or sacred iron." Initially, they used the few muskets they could obtain to fight their less well-armed Indian neighbors. By 1700, French traders, moving from the east, had established direct trade with the Sioux, offering a steady supply of guns and powder in exchange for furs.

For a generation, several Sioux bands (the Teton and Yanktonai) walked between two worlds. In the summers, they followed the buffalo onto the prairies, with dogs pulling travois and women carrying heavy burdens. As cold weather approached, they retreated to the edge of the woodlands to gather firewood and seek beaver. In

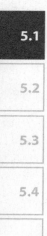

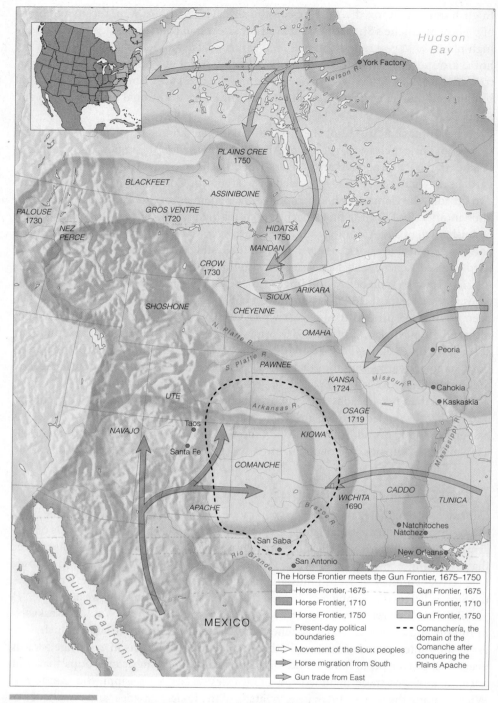

MAP 5.1 THE HORSE FRONTIER MEETS THE GUN FRONTIER, 1675–1750

the spring, after trading meat and pelts to the French for guns and ammunition, they returned to the edge of the plains. They glimpsed their first horses not long after 1700. But it was several generations before the western Sioux had acquired enough mounts to drop their old customs and adopt a horse-centered way of life.

By midcentury, the horse frontier on the northern Great Plains had met the gun frontier. Saukamappee, a Cree Indian living with the Blackfoot, remembered vividly the surprise of the initial encounter. When he was a young man, his war party—well-armed and on foot—had gone into battle against the Shoshone. "We had more guns and iron headed arrows than [ever] before," he recalled years later. "But our enemies . . . had Misstutim [Big Dogs, that is, Horses] on which they rode, swift as the Deer."

110

As the overlap of horse and gun proceeded after 1750, Sioux women assumed the burdensome task of processing slain buffalo. Sioux men, meanwhile, used muskets to acquire more mounts and dominate the buffalo grounds. Their competitors now had guns and horses as well, but within several decades, the Sioux pushed their domain west to the Missouri River. Like the Comanche farther south, they emerged as a dominant power on the Great Plains.

Britain's Mainland Colonies: A New Abundance of People

5.2 In what ways did Britain's North American colonies become "less English" after 1700?

West of the Mississippi, horses and guns brought dramatic shifts in the balance of power between Indian groups as the eighteenth century progressed. But east of the Appalachian Mountains, a different force prompted striking change: population growth. Several factors came together to push the demographic curve upward at an unprecedented rate after 1700. From our vantage point in the twenty-first century, the colonial seaports and villages appear tiny, and rural settlement seems sparse. But by the mid-eighteenth century, the coastal colonies represented the largest concentration of people that had ever occupied any portion of the continent.

On both sides of the North Atlantic, population growth characterized eighteenth-century life. But in Europe numbers rose at a gradual pace, while the population along the eastern seaboard of North America surged at an astounding rate. England in 1700 had 5.1 million people. By 1750, that figure had increased only 14 percent, to 5.8 million. In contrast, during the same half-century, the colonial population in British North America more than quadrupled, from 260,000 to nearly 1.2 million. Also, these Atlantic seaboard colonies made a permanent and dramatic shift away from a population that was mostly of English origin. Instead, numerous cultures and languages from Europe, Africa, and eastern North America mixed and mingled.

Population Growth on the Home Front

Natural increase—more births per year than deaths—played an important role in colonial population growth. Marriages occurred early, and the need for labor created an incentive for couples to have large families. Benjamin Franklin, who rose to become the best-known colonist of his generation, was born in Boston in 1706. He grew up in a household of seventeen children. Large families had long been commonplace, to compensate for frequent infant deaths. What made the Franklin children unusual was that all survived to adulthood and started families of their own.

Although a high birth rate typified most preindustrial cultures, it was the low death rate and long average life span that pushed up American population numbers. The colonies had no huge urban centers, so epidemic diseases proved less devastating than in Europe. Food was plentiful, and housing improved steadily. Newborns who survived infancy could live a long life. (Franklin himself lived eighty-four years.) Moreover, the 1720s and 1730s proved peaceful compared to earlier decades, so soldiering did not endanger lives among men of military age. For women, death related to pregnancy and childbirth still loomed as a constant threat. (Franklin's own mother was his father's second spouse; the first wife died after bearing seven children.) Yet women still outnumbered men among people living into their seventies and eighties.

Although grandparents often endured far into old age, the average age for the total population stayed remarkably young. The reasons seem clear. The ratio between men and women was becoming more even over time, the marriage rates for women

5.1

5.2

5.3

5.4

5.5

⚙ **Explore the Topic**　Age Distribution and Its Implications

In 1729, Maryland planters founded Baltimore, at the head of the Patapsco River estuary, to provide a port on Chesapeake Bay for shipping tobacco. The community had only 50 homes and 200 inhabitants when this early sketch was made in 1752, but the town grew rapidly after that, along with other colonial seaports, where frequent births, improving survival rates, and immigration fueled population growth. What similarities and differences do you see between this English colonial town site and French-built New Orleans, pictured later in the chapter?

remained extremely high, and there was no effective means of contraception. Women could resort to sexual abstinence to avoid pregnancy, and mothers could extend the time between births by nursing their infants for a long period (since lactation reduces the chances of conception). Not surprisingly, children abounded.

"Packed Like Herrings": Arrivals from Abroad

Frequent births and improving survival rates were only part of the population story. Immigration—both forced and free—also contributed mightily to the colonies' growth. Unfree newcomers arrived in two different streams from separate continents, and they faced very different prospects. The largest flow of unfree arrivals came from Africa. By the 1730s, the expanding African slave trade brought at least 4,000 people to the mainland colonies every year, and the rate increased steadily. These forced migrants to a strange land faced a bleak new life with few options for improvement.

A separate stream of unfree laborers came to the colonies from Europe. Compared with enslaved Africans, these European migrants faced long-term prospects that were far more promising. Every year, hundreds of detainees in British jails were offered transportation to the colonies and a term of service laboring in America as an alternative to prison time or execution. Deported felons joined the larger flow of unfree migrants drawn from Europe's poor. Unable to pay for their own passage, these people accepted transportation to America as indentured servants. All were sold to employers to serve as workers, with scant legal rights, until their indenture expired, usually after three to six years.

In the 1720s, Philadelphia shippers devised a variation on indentures known as the redemption contract. Under this **redemption system**, agents in Europe recruited migrants by contracting to loan them money for passage and provisions. On arrival in America, the recruits could then sign a pact with an employer of their own choosing. That person agreed to pay back the shipper, "redeeming" the original loan that had been made to the immigrant. In exchange, the newcomer (called a redemptioner) promised to work for the employer for several years, receiving no more than room and board. After that, the redemptioners were on their own, and in a growing local economy, their prospects usually improved.

Besides Africans who remained unfree for life and Europeans who gained freedom after a period of service, a smaller stream of newcomers involved free families arriving from Europe who could pay their own way. Poor conditions at home pushed these risk-takers to try their luck in the New World, and glowing descriptions of abundant land at bargain rates caught their attention. American land speculators hoped to rent forest tracts to immigrant farmers who would improve the value of the land by clearing trees and building homes. Britain's imperial administrators also sought to recruit non-English families from the European continent. Their immigrant settlements near the American frontier could bolster colonial defenses against foreign rivals and provide a buffer to ward off Indian attacks.

Even for those newcomers who paid for their own crossing, the Atlantic passage was a life-threatening ordeal. "The people are packed densely, like herrings," Lutheran minister Gottlieb Mittelberger recorded after a voyage to Pennsylvania. "During the journey the ship is full of pitiful signs of distress—smells, fumes, horrors, vomiting, various kinds of sea sickness, fever, dysentery, headaches, heat, constipation, boils, scurvy, cancer, mouth-rot, and similar afflictions." Despite such hardships, economic opportunities awaited most arriving Europeans, and literate newcomers often sent home glowing accounts of life in America. Their positive letters drew more new recruits for the rising colonial population.

Non-English Newcomers in the British Colonies

Colonies that were thoroughly English at their origin became decidedly more varied after 1700. By far the largest change came from North America's increasing involvement in the Atlantic slave trade. By 1750, 240,000 African Americans made up nearly 20 percent of the population of the British colonies. Native Americans had been drawn into the mix in small numbers as slaves, servants, spouses, and Christian converts. But roughly four out of five colonists were of European descent. Among them, as among the Africans and Indians, many spoke English with a different accent, or as a second language, or not at all.

The New England colonies remained the most homogenous, but even there, 30 percent of the residents had non-English roots by 1760. The new diversity was most visible in New York because of the colony's non-English origins. A 1703 census of New York City shows that the town remained 42 percent Dutch, with English (30 percent) and Africans (18 percent) making up nearly half the population. The remainder included a nascent Jewish community (1 percent) and a growing number of French Protestants (9 percent).

The French New Yorkers had fled to America after 1685, when Louis XIV decided to end protection for the Protestant minority of France by revoking the long-standing Edict of Nantes. In addition, the king prohibited **Huguenot** emigration, but several thousand of these French Protestants escaped illegally and sought refuge in America. They established small communities, such as New Rochelle in New York. Everywhere, they intermarried with the English and prospered in commerce. By the 1760s, several families with humble Huguenot origins, such as the Faneuils in Boston and the Laurenses and Manigaults in Charleston, had amassed enormous fortunes.

At a time when France and Great Britain were at war, another infusion of French-speaking refugees, the Acadians, fared less well. In 1755, authorities evicted French

Redemption system An eighteenth-century arrangement in which potential migrants in Europe signed up with an agent who agreed to pay for their Atlantic passage. Reaching America, the newcomer signed a pact to work for several years for an employer. In exchange for much-needed labor, the employer agreed to pay back the shipper, "redeeming" the original loan that had been made to the immigrant "redemptioner."

Huguenots The term applied to Protestants living in Catholic France. In 1685, King Louis XIV revoked the Edict of Nantes, which had assured protection to this minority. Despite a royal ban on Huguenot emigration, thousands fled to other parts of Europe and many families migrated to North America.

Life in colonial New York City was already a cultural melting pot, as illustrated by the unique portraits and letters of the family of Moses Raphael Levy. Born in Germany in 1665, this Jewish merchant moved from London to Manhattan near the turn of the century and used his Atlantic contacts to build a successful import-export business, using his own ships. After his first wife died, Levy remarried in 1718 to Grace Mears (1694–1740), a young Sephardic Jewish woman from Spanish Town, Jamaica, three decades his junior, who bore him seven children before he died in 1728. Their prominent descendants include poet Emma Lazarus, whose famous verses—"Give me your tired, your poor,/ Your huddled masses yearning to breathe free"—are inscribed on the Statue of Liberty. What do you make of the fact that the Levys were leading members of Shearith Israel, the oldest Jewish congregation in the colonies, while they also courted Christian leaders, even helping to fund a new spire for Trinity Church on Wall Street?

SOURCE: Mrs. Moses Levy (Grace Mears), 1720-28, attributed to Gerardus Duyckinck 1(l695-cl746), Museum of the City of New York, New York, NY, U.S.A..

Cajuns The Louisiana word for French-speaking people from Acadia (Nova Scotia) who were forced to migrate south in 1755 during the French and Indian War. Many of these refugees eventually moved to French Louisiana, where they have had a lasting impact on the culture.

Catholics from Acadia in British Nova Scotia, fearing they might take up arms for France. Officials burned their homes and deported more than 6,000 to various English-speaking colonies farther south. These unwelcome Acadian strangers, struggling to get by, found themselves resented for their Catholicism and feared as enemies during wartime. Many moved on to French Louisiana where, known as **Cajuns**, they became a lasting cultural force.

Scotland provided a much larger flow of migrants than France, stemming from two different sources. A growing stream of families, at least 30,000 people by 1770, came from Scotland itself. They were pushed by poverty, land scarcity, famines, and a failed political rebellion in 1745. In addition, a larger group known as the Scots-Irish came from Ulster in Northern Ireland. The British had encouraged these Scottish Presbyterians to settle in Ireland in the seventeenth century, displacing rebellious Irish Catholics. In Ulster, the Scottish newcomers soon faced restrictions from Parliament and the Anglican Church. By 1770, nearly 60,000 Scots-Irish had opted to leave Ireland for America.

Another stream, German-speaking immigrants, nearly equaled the combined flow of Scots and Scots-Irish settlers. They began to arrive shortly after 1700, as religious persecution, chronic land shortages, and generations of warfare pushed whole communities out of southern Germany and neighboring Switzerland. By 1770, the total had reached 85,000. These refugees generally came as whole families, taking up farmland on the fringes of the colonies. Germans occupied New York's Mohawk Valley and Virginia's Shenandoah Valley, and they fanned out from Germantown across the rich farmland of Pennsylvania. Swiss founded New Bern, North Carolina, in 1710; German-speaking Protestants who had been expelled from Catholic Salzburg in 1731 laid out Ebenezer, Georgia, in 1734.

Almost all of the white, non-English newcomers, including several thousand migrants from Wales, were Protestant Christians. Many clung to their language and traditions. But most arrivals learned English, and their children intermarried with English settlers. A French visitor described a typical American "whose grandfather was an Englishman, whose wife is Dutch, whose son married a French woman, and whose present four sons have now four wives of different nations."

If relative religious and ethnic tolerance attracted many European newcomers, the promise of economic opportunity increased the flow of immigrants even more. A prior century of colonization had made the bounty of North America's long Atlantic coast abundantly clear. Scores of inviting rivers gave access to the hinterland and provided cheap power for gristmills and sawmills. Everywhere, supplies of timber, game, and fish proved plentiful, and the coast's snug harbors and wide bays offered opportunities for Atlantic trade. But the local flora and fauna—somewhat familiar to Europeans—varied widely with latitude, as did the seasonal temperatures and agricultural soils. As new generations adapted to different portions of this bountiful coastline, five distinctive economic regions took shape.

The Varied Economic Landscape

5.3 What role did geography play in shaping the emerging regional colonial economies?

Population growth had consequences, and the changes began at the water's edge. The seaports of Boston, New York, Philadelphia, and Charleston each grew from a village to a commercial hub, absorbing manufactured goods from Britain and shipping colonial produce abroad. All four towns developed an active coastal trade with secondary ports located on nearby rivers. In contrast, Chesapeake Bay had no single dominant port. There, Annapolis, Alexandria, and Norfolk all expanded, and two additional towns were founded farther north. Chestertown began in 1705 and Baltimore appeared in 1729 to give Maryland planters new ports for shipping tobacco. Still, given the bay's many rivers, Atlantic ships often stopped at riverside plantations and villages to conduct business.

In Chesapeake Bay and elsewhere, inland commerce was conducted by boat wherever possible. Hartford on the Connecticut River, Albany on the Hudson, Trenton on the Delaware, and Augusta on the Savannah all become interior trading centers. Richmond, Virginia, which began as a trading post at the falls of the James River, already had 250 inhabitants when it incorporated as a town in 1742. Rough trails and former Indian paths connected these river-based communities for travelers in the hinterland. By the 1740s, a path known as the Great Wagon Road headed southwest from Philadelphia to Winchester in Virginia's Shenandoah Valley and then south through gaps in the Blue Ridge Mountains to the Piedmont region of Carolina.

Widening networks of contact, using boats and wagons, extended inland from the primary seaports. And expanding fleets of ships tied each major hub to distant Atlantic ports. As a result, farmsteads and villages that had been largely self-sufficient before 1710 gradually became linked to wider markets. Local production still met most needs. But increasingly, the opportunity existed to obtain a needed tool, a piece of cloth, or a printed almanac from far away. The new possibility of purchasing such goods lured farmers to grow crops for market rather than plant only for home consumption.

As local commercial systems gained coherence and strength, a string of regional economies developed along the Atlantic seaboard. Coastal vessels and a few muddy roads linked them tenuously to one another. But geographical and human differences caused each to take on a character of its own. Migration patterns reinforced this diversity, since arrivals from Europe often sought out areas where others spoke their language or shared their form of worship. The influx of German farmers through Philadelphia, for example, gave unique traits to Pennsylvania. (The newcomers spoke German, or *Deutsch*, so they became known as Pennsylvania Dutch.) Likewise, the rising importation of Africans helped shape the economy and culture of Chesapeake Bay and of coastal South Carolina. Besides the diversity among arriving peoples, ecological variations in land and climate also helped to shape five different economic regions.

Sources of Gain in the Carolinas and Georgia

In the Southeast, two related but distinctive regions emerged, linked respectively to the two Carolina colonies. The larger one centered on the low country of coastal South Carolina and Georgia. There, the Atlantic's warm Gulf Stream current provided a long growing season. It also assured mild winters, meaning that cattle and hogs could forage unattended for most of the year. As livestock multiplied, settlers sold meat, barrel staves, and firewood to the sugar islands of the West Indies, purchasing African slave labor in return.

Some of the newcomers had grown rice in Africa before their enslavement. Planting rice for their own use, they soon showed that the crop could thrive in Carolina. Once African know-how made clear the potential for rice cultivation, a system of plantation agriculture, imported from Barbados, took hold quickly after 1700. Rice production spread to Georgia after that colony legalized slavery in 1751. Another African plant, indigo, also took root as a money-making staple crop. For several generations after 1740, indigo from South Carolina provided the blue dye for England's rising textile industry. Beside the barrels of rice and indigo that piled up on Charleston's docks, casks also appeared containing deerskins from the interior. At the height of that trade before 1750, Creek and Cherokee hunters provided more than a million deerskins per year.

In North Carolina, a second regional economy evolved behind the Outer Banks. These sandy barrier islands edging the Atlantic prevented easy access for oceangoing vessels and hindered efforts to promote staple crop agriculture. So colonists turned to the pine forest to make a living. An extensive band of longleaf pine stretched inland for a hundred miles. With labor, this pine forest yielded naval stores: the tar and pitch used by sailors to protect their ships and rigging. Workers hauled the finished products to Wilmington on the Cape Fear River, the colony's best outlet to the sea. By the 1770s, the port was well known for exporting naval stores, and a dozen sawmills dotted the river.

Farther inland, Scots-Irish and German families moved down the Great Wagon Road after 1740 to carve out farms across the Carolina Piedmont on lands controlled largely by several absentee owners in Britain. By 1763, Ben Franklin estimated that Pennsylvania had lost 10,000 families to North Carolina. Typical of this migration were the Moravians, who established towns at Nazareth and Bethlehem, Pennsylvania, in the 1740s. In 1753, members of this German-speaking religious group bought a tract near modern-day Winston-Salem, North Carolina. They named it Wachovia, meaning "Peaceful Valley." Within several years, they had developed prosperous farms, a pottery shop, and a tannery around their initial settlement, called Bethabara. The newcomers bartered seeds and tools with one another and shipped extra produce overland to South Carolina and Virginia.

Chesapeake Bay's Tobacco Economy

North of the Carolinas, farmers in the colonies bordering Chesapeake Bay committed to tobacco production in the seventeenth century. They clung to that staple crop despite a long decline in its market price. After 1710, demand for tobacco revived and prices rose again, in part because snuff (pulverized tobacco inhaled through the nostrils) became popular among Europeans. Tobacco continued to dominate the Chesapeake economy.

However, local conditions in parts of Virginia and Maryland prompted crop diversification as the century progressed. Constant tobacco planting depleted the soil. Moreover, most farms lay far from any navigable river, and rolling huge casks of tobacco many miles to market proved expensive. Wheat and corn thus became important secondary staples. These new crops, along with flax, hemp, and apples for making cider, provided a buffer against poor tobacco harvests and spurred related activities such as building wagons, making barrels, and constructing mills. These trades, in turn, produced widening networks of local exchange and prosperity for white yeoman families, with or without slaves.

Before 1700, all the mainland colonies could be described as *societies with slaves*. After that, the northern colonies continued to allow enslavement, but they never relied on it. In contrast, the southern colonies, except for certain inland farmlands settled from the north, shifted early in the eighteenth century to become something different: full-fledged *slave societies*, tied economically and culturally to slavery. By midcentury, plantation owners remained less wealthy than their counterparts in the West Indies who lived off the profits of slave-grown sugar. But on average, members of the southern elite controlled far more wealth than their counterparts in the North. The profits of the plantation system spread widely, though unevenly, through the rest of the European American community. By the 1770s, whites in the South averaged more than twice as much wealth per person as whites in the North. An estimate for 1774 puts the average net worth among white Southerners at £93, a sharp contrast to their counterparts in the middle colonies (£46) and New England (£38).

New England Takes to the Sea

North of Chesapeake Bay, two overlapping economic regions emerged: the long-established New England colonies and the somewhat newer and more prosperous middle colonies. New England faced peculiar disadvantages, beginning with the rocky soil. As imports from London increased, New Englanders found no staple crop that could be sold back directly to Britain to create a balance of trade. All the beaver had been hunted, and much of the best land had been occupied. The region's farm families had adapted well to the challenging environment and short growing seasons. Both men and women worked on handicrafts during the long, hard winters, and networks of community exchange yielded commercial prosperity in many towns. But with a rapidly growing population, successive generations had less land to divide among their children.

Increasingly, young men with little prospect of inheriting prime farmland turned to the sea for a living. In timber-rich New England, shipbuilding prospered. Colonists established shipyards at the mouth of nearly every river, drawing skilled carpenters and willing deckhands to the coast. Providence, Rhode Island, opened its first shipyard in 1711. By 1763, Marblehead, Massachusetts, had a fleet of a hundred ships and a population of 5,000, making it the sixth largest town in the thirteen colonies, behind only Philadelphia, New York, Boston, Charleston, and Newport, Rhode Island.

On Nantucket Island off Cape Cod, whaling became a new source of income. For generations, the islanders had cooked the blubber of beached whales to extract oil for lamps. In 1715, they outfitted several vessels to harpoon sperm whales at sea and then return with the whale blubber in casks to be rendered into oil. In the 1750s, they installed brick ovens on deck and began cooking the smelly blubber at sea in huge iron vats. This change turned the whaling vessel into a floating factory, and it allowed longer voyages in larger ships. By the 1760s, Nantucket whalers were cruising the Atlantic for four or five months at a time and returning loaded with barrels of oil.

Read the Document Benjamin Franklin, "Advice to a Young Tradesman" (1748)

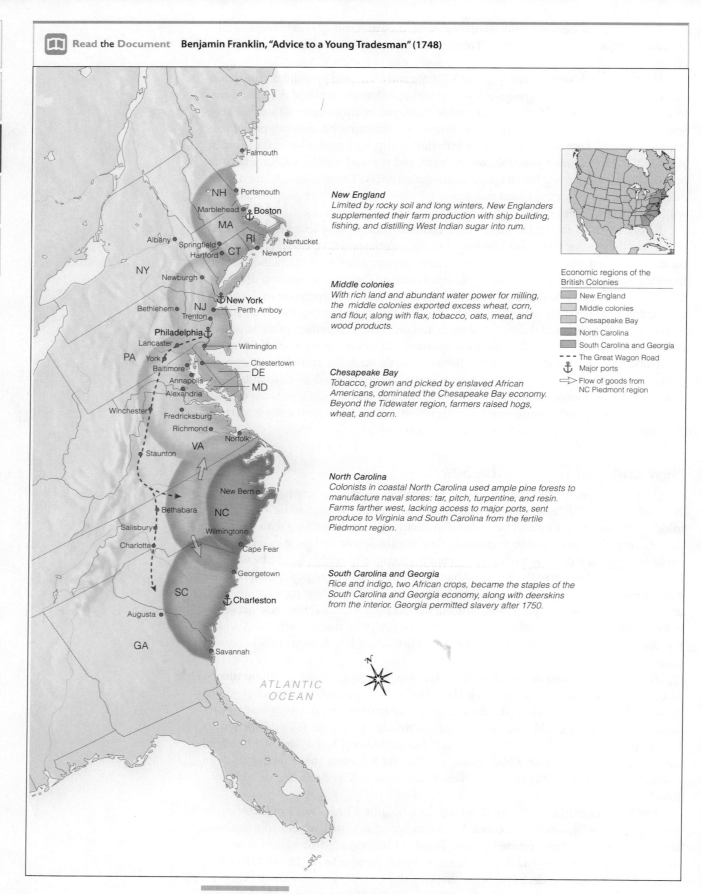

New England
Limited by rocky soil and long winters, New Englanders supplemented their farm production with ship building, fishing, and distilling West Indian sugar into rum.

Middle colonies
With rich land and abundant water power for milling, the middle colonies exported excess wheat, corn, and flour, along with flax, tobacco, oats, meat, and wood products.

Chesapeake Bay
Tobacco, grown and picked by enslaved African Americans, dominated the Chesapeake Bay economy. Beyond the Tidewater region, farmers raised hogs, wheat, and corn.

North Carolina
Colonists in coastal North Carolina used ample pine forests to manufacture naval stores: tar, pitch, turpentine, and resin. Farms farther west, lacking access to major ports, sent produce to Virginia and South Carolina from the fertile Piedmont region.

South Carolina and Georgia
Rice and indigo, two African crops, became the staples of the South Carolina and Georgia economy, along with deerskins from the interior. Georgia permitted slavery after 1750.

Economic regions of the British Colonies

- New England
- Middle colonies
- Chesapeake Bay
- North Carolina
- South Carolina and Georgia
- - - The Great Wagon Road
- ⚓ Major ports
- ⇨ Flow of goods from NC Piedmont region

MAP 5.2 ECONOMIC REGIONS OF THE BRITISH COLONIES

The fishing industry also prospered. All along the coast, villagers dispatched boats to the Grand Banks, the fishing grounds off Newfoundland. When the vessels returned, laden with fish, townspeople graded, dried, and salted the catch. The colonists sent the best cod to Europe in exchange for wine and dry goods. They shipped the lowest grade to the Caribbean, where sugar planters bought "refuse fish" as food for their slaves. In return, the Yankee captains brought back kegs of molasses to be distilled into rum. By 1770, 140 American distilleries, most of them in New England, produced 5 million gallons of rum annually. Much of it went to colonial taverns and Indian trading posts. But some also went to Africa, aboard ships from Britain and New England. American rum, along with various wines and spirits from Europe, made up one-fifth of the total value of goods used to purchase African slaves.

As the New England economy stabilized, it became a mixed blessing for women. On the farm, their domestic labors aided the household economy and helped to offset bad harvests. Mothers taught their daughters to spin yarn, weave cloth, sew clothes, plant gardens, raise chickens, tend livestock, and churn butter. The products from these chores could be used at home or sold in a nearby village to buy consumer goods. While the husband held legal authority over the home, a good wife served as a "deputy husband," managing numerous household affairs, or perhaps earning money as a midwife to help make ends meet. She took charge entirely if her husband passed away or went to sea.

But for all their labors, women seemed to lose economic and legal standing to men as New England towns became larger and more orderly. Networks of local officials, consisting entirely of men, drafted statutes and legal codes that reinforced male privileges. Women found it difficult to obtain credit or receive a business license, and the law barred married women from making contracts, limiting their chance for activities outside the home. Gradually, male apothecaries and physicians with a smattering of formal training pushed traditional midwives away from the bedside. Overseers of the poor had the power to remove children from a widowed mother and place them in the **almshouse**.

Economic Expansion in the Middle Colonies

The fifth regional economy, the one that flourished in the middle colonies between New England and Chesapeake Bay, improved upon these two neighboring worlds. The Europeans who resettled Indian lands in Delaware, Pennsylvania, New Jersey, and New York found a favorable climate, rich soil, and numerous millstreams. Unlike New Englanders, they developed a reliable staple by growing an abundance of grain. They exported excess wheat, flour, and bread as effectively as Southerners shipped tobacco and rice. But unlike the planters in Virginia and South Carolina, middle-colony farmers did not become locked in the vicious cycle of making large investments in enslaved workers and exporting a single agricultural staple. Instead, they developed a more balanced economy, using mostly free labor. Besides grain products, they also exported flaxseed, barrel staves, livestock, and pig iron (the oblong ingots of crude iron extracted from a smelting furnace). Large infusions of money from Britain during its long war against France in the 1750s further boosted this prosperous economy.

Whereas the Chesapeake had no dominant seaport, the middle colonies boasted two major ports of entry. European craftsmen, unwilling to compete with unpaid slave artisans in the South, migrated to the middle-colony seaports instead. Both Philadelphia and New York grew faster than rival ports in the mid-eighteenth century, passing Boston in size in the 1750s. By 1763, Philadelphia had more than 20,000 people, New York had nearly as many, and both cities faced a set of urban problems that had already hit Boston.

As the port towns grew, so did economic and social distance between rich and poor. Large homes and expensive imports characterized life among the urban elite. In contrast, the poorest city dwellers lacked property and the means to subsist. By the

Almshouse Such establishments to care for the indigent of a locality had existed in Europe since the Middle Ages. They appeared in the British colonies in the eighteenth century, as towns grew larger and society became more stratified. In Christian tradition, *alms* constituted money or services donated to care for the poor.

1760s, Philadelphia's almshouse and the new Pennsylvania Hospital for the Sick Poor were overflowing. In response, Quaker leaders established a voluntary Committee to Alleviate the Miseries of the Poor, handing out firewood and blankets to the city's needy. They also built a "Bettering House," patterned on Boston's workhouse, that provided poor Philadelphians with food and shelter in exchange for work. To limit urban poverty, New York and Philadelphia authorities moved newcomers to the countryside, where Dutch and German settlers had already established an efficient farming tradition. As immigration rose, the region slowly expanded its economy far up the Hudson Valley, east into Connecticut and Long Island, and south toward Maryland.

The farm frontier pushed west as well. The acquisitive Thomas Penn had inherited control of Pennsylvania from his more idealistic father, founder William Penn. In 1737, the young proprietor defrauded the Lenape, or Delaware, Indians out of 1,200 square miles of potential farmland west of the Delaware River. In the infamous Walking Purchase, Penn claimed a tract based on one boundary side that could be walked in a

In 1735, Gustavus Hesselius, an immigrant artist and organ builder from Sweden, painted this portrait of a Delaware chief with his clay pipe and squirrel-skin tobacco pouch. Two years later, Tishcohan's people lost valuable land through Pennsylvania's notorious Walking Purchase. What options did Native American leaders have in resisting the pressure for farmland exerted by British colonists?

SOURCE: Tishcohan, 1735, by Gustavus Hesselius, Courtesy of the Philadelphia History Museum at the Atwater Kent, The Historical Society of Pennsylvania Collection

day and a half. Then he hired three fast runners to mark the distance, and one managed to cover more than 55 miles in thirty-six hours. This ruse gave Penn title to more than 1 million choice acres. Land-hungry settlers pressed the reluctant Delaware west toward the Allegheny Mountains and occupied the rich river valleys of eastern Pennsylvania. Land agents and immigrant farmers called the fertile region "the best poor man's country."

Matters of Faith:
The Great Awakening

5.4   What prompted increased toleration at a time of fresh religious intensity after 1730?

Philadelphia epitomized the commercial dynamism of the eighteenth-century British colonies. The city was a hub in the fastest-growing economic region on the Atlantic seaboard. Ben Franklin, arriving there in 1723 at age 17, achieved particular success. Within seven years, he owned a printing business. Within twenty-five years, he was wealthy enough to retire, devoting himself to science, politics, and social improvement. He created a lending library, developed an efficient stove, promoted schools and hospitals, supported scientific and philosophical organizations, and won fame experimenting with electricity.

The outburst of scientific inquiry and religious skepticism spreading through the Atlantic world at the time became known as the Enlightenment, and its spirit of rational questioning and reason was greatly aided by the printing press. In America, Franklin and his fellow printers personified the new **Age of Enlightenment**. By 1760, the British mainland colonies had twenty-nine printing establishments, more presses per capita than in any country in Europe. These presses squeezed out eighteen weekly newspapers and countless public notices, fostering political and business communication throughout the colonies. But American printers also published an array of religious material, for the colonial spirit of worldly enterprise existed uneasily beside a longing for spiritual community and social perfection.

In the first half of the eighteenth century, colonists witnessed breakthroughs in religious toleration and controversies within the ministry. They also experienced a revivalist outpouring with roots in Europe and America, later known as the **Great Awakening**. This stirring began in the 1730s, and it gained momentum through the visits from England of a charismatic preacher named George Whitefield (pronounced "Whitfield"). The Awakening, with its wide popular appeal, had a profound equalizing effect, within and among Protestant congregations. Its aftershocks persisted for a full generation, helping to lay the groundwork for the American Revolution.

Seeds of Religious Toleration

The same population shifts that made Britain's mainland colonies more diverse in the eighteenth century also introduced competing religious voices that included many non-Christians. Africans, the largest of all the new contingents, brought their own varied beliefs across the Atlantic. Some slaves from Portuguese Angola had been exposed to Catholicism in their homeland. But most Africans retained much of their traditional cultures and showed skepticism toward Christianity. Efforts to convert Native Americans also brought mixed results. A minister living near the Iroquois reported that Indians would beat a drum to disrupt his services and then "go away Laughing."

Age of Enlightenment This term is applied to the century stretching from the late seventeenth to the late eighteenth century, when generations of European writers, scientists and philosophers began to question the predominance of organized religion and elevate the use of rational argument and scientific investigation. In the American colonies, the practical experimenter Benjamin Franklin came to epitomize this new Age of Reason.

Great Awakening The title that was applied, in retrospect, to the interdenominational Christian revival that swept Britain's North American colonies between the 1730s and the 1750s, inspired at first by the preaching of Jonathan Edwards and George Whitefield. (A religious revival in the early nineteenth century became known as the Second Great Awakening.)

Another non-Christian contingent, Jewish immigrants, remained few in number, with only several hundred families by 1770. Merchants rather than farmers, they established communities in several Atlantic ports, beginning in Dutch New Amsterdam (1654) and in Newport (1658). Most were Sephardic Jews; that is, their ancestral roots were in Spain and Portugal. They came by way of the Caribbean, reaching Charleston in 1697, Philadelphia after 1706, and Savannah in 1733. A few of their children married into the Protestant culture, but more than 80 percent of Jewish young people found partners within their own small communities.

The majority of eighteenth-century newcomers to the British colonies were Christians. A few, such as the Acadians, were Catholics, but the rest had some Protestant affiliation. In the two centuries since the Reformation, numerous competing Protestant denominations had sprung up across Europe. Now this wide array made itself felt in America, as Presbyterians, Quakers, Lutherans, Baptists, Methodists, and smaller sects all increased in numbers. To attract immigrant families, most colonies abolished laws that favored a single "established" denomination. Nevertheless, New England remained firmly Congregational, while the southern gentry (plus merchant elite everywhere) concentrated increasingly within the Anglican Church.

Rhode Island had emphasized the separation of church and state from the start, and Pennsylvania had likewise favored toleration, both as a matter of principle and as a practical recruitment device to attract new settlers. Since migration from Europe was a demanding ordeal, those who took the risk were often people with strong religious convictions. Such newcomers looked for assurances that they could practice their religion freely, and colonies competed to accommodate them. In many places, religious tests still limited who could hold public office, but tolerance for competing beliefs was expanding.

Many felt that if any institution threatened the growing religious toleration in the colonies, it was, ironically, the British king's own denomination. The monarch headed the Anglican Church, and it had influential American members, including almost every colonial governor. Therefore, repeated talk by the Church of England about installing a resident bishop in America aroused suspicions among colonists who worshipped in other denominations. This was especially true in New England, where Congregationalists had long opposed ideas of religious hierarchy. In 1750, Boston, which had eighteen churches, rose up against a plan for an Anglican bishop. In a passionate sermon, Reverend Jonathan Mayhew preached that the town must keep "all imperious bishops, and other clergymen who love to lord it over God's heritage, from getting their feet into the stirrup."

The Onset of the Great Awakening: Pietism and George Whitefield

As relative toleration became a hallmark of the British colonies, no one benefited more than German-speaking Protestant groups. Numerous religious sects, such as the Moravians, Mennonites, Schwenkfelders, and Dunkers, were escaping from persecution as well as poverty at home. Their numbers multiplied after 1730, and hymns in German became a common sound on Sabbath day. In 1743, before any American printer produced an English-language Bible, a press in Pennsylvania put out a complete German edition of Luther's Bible, using type brought from Frankfurt.

Collectively, these newcomers were part of a European reform movement to renew piety and spiritual vitality among Protestant churchgoers in an age of increasing rationalism and worldliness. Pietism, as this "Second Reformation" was called, had roots in eastern Germany and stressed the need to restore emotion and intensity to worship that had become too rational and detached. The German pietists reached out after 1700 to inspire Huguenots in France and Presbyterians in Scotland. They influenced reformers in the Church of England such as John Wesley, the founder of Methodism and a teacher at Oxford University. Through Wesley, pietist ideas touched George Whitefield, a preaching prodigy in Oxford's class of 1736. Over the next decade, "the boy parson" sparked a widespread religious awakening in the American colonies.

Whitefield's mentor, Wesley, had preached briefly in Georgia. So in 1738, at age 23, Whitefield spent several months in the new colony, where he laid plans for an orphanage near Savannah. Arriving back in England, Whitefield quickly achieved celebrity status, drawing large crowds with fiery sermons that criticized the Anglican Church. His popularity preceded him in 1739 when he returned to America for an extended tour, the second of seven transatlantic journeys during his career. Building on religious stirrings already present in the colonies, Whitefield preached to huge and emotional crowds nearly 350 times in 15 months. He made appearances from Savannah to Boston, something no public figure had ever done. "God shews me," he wrote in his journal, "that America must be my place for action."

The timing was perfect. Whitefield's brother was a wine merchant who understood the expanding networks of communication and consumption in the British Atlantic world. So Whitefield realized that in America, as newspapers multiplied and roads improved, he could advertise widely and travel extensively. He had little taste for Protestant debates over church organization and sectarian differences. Instead, he believed that an evangelical minister should simply preach the Bible fervently to a wide array of avid listeners. Everywhere he went, Whitefield served as a catalyst for religious activity.

"The Danger of an Unconverted Ministry"

The heightened commotion in American churches had local origins as well. The same tension felt in European parishes—between worldly, rational pursuits and an emotional quest for grace and salvation—also troubled colonial congregations. Occasional local revivals had taken place in America for decades. The most dramatic one occurred in Northampton, Massachusetts, in 1734–1735, spurred by a talented minister named Jonathan Edwards. As the colonies' most gifted theologian, Edwards anticipated Whitefield's argument that dry, rote "head-knowledge" made a poor substitute for "a true living faith in Jesus Christ." "Our people do not so much need to have their heads stored," Edwards observed, "as to have their hearts touched."

In a fast-growing society, who would prepare suitable church leaders for the next generation? Candidates for the ministry could train at Harvard College (founded 1636), William and Mary (1693), Yale (1707), or one of several small academies. But these institutions could not instruct sufficient numbers. The shortage of educated ministers, combined with geographic expansion, meant that one preacher might oversee several parishes. Even if he tended only a single parish, the great distances separating parishioners made it hard for any pastor to travel widely enough to address their needs.

Problems in the pulpit included quality as well as quantity. Many college graduates had too much "head-knowledge." Their fluency in Latin and Greek often earned them more disdain than respect from down-to-earth congregations. Most foreign-born ministers, such as Anglicans sent from England and Presbyterians from Scotland, had failed to find good positions at home. Too often, they showed limited appreciation for the local church members who paid their salaries, and they resented those who criticized their ministries.

One such critic was William Tennent, a Scots-Irish immigrant who arrived in Pennsylvania with his family in 1716. Dismayed by the cold, unemotional outlook of Presbyterian ministers, Tennent opened a one-room academy in a log house to train his four sons and other young men for the ministry. But local Presbyterian authorities challenged his credentials and disparaged the teachings of his "Log College."

Eventually, the school moved and grew, becoming linked in 1746 to the new College of New Jersey, which later evolved into Princeton University. But before this happened, Tennent's preacher sons allied themselves with Whitefield and managed to shake the colonial religious establishment to its roots.

One of Tennent's sons, Gilbert, eventually led a Presbyterian church in Philadelphia created by Whitefield's supporters. In 1740, at the time of Whitefield's triumphal tour, young Gilbert Tennent delivered a blistering sermon entitled "The Danger of an Unconverted Ministry" that cut to the heart of the matter. He condemned the "sad security" offered by incompetent, uncaring, and greedy ministers, condemning their followers for being "as blind as Moles, and as dead as Stones, without any spiritual Taste and Relish." He argued that congregations should turn away from these "Letter-learned . . . Old Pharisee-Teachers" and listen to more inspirational traveling preachers instead.

The Consequences of the Great Awakening

Whitefield hailed the Tennents as "burning and shining lights" of a new kind. All the ministers and worshipers who joined in the movement began to call themselves "New Lights." Opponents, whom they dismissed as "Old Lights," continued to defend a learned clergy and emphasized head-knowledge and the role of rational enlightenment on the difficult road to salvation. The Old Lights opposed the disruptions caused by so-called **itinerant ministers** who moved freely from parish to parish without invitation. These New Light ministers, in contrast, appealed to people's emotions and stressed the prospect of a more democratic salvation open to all. They defended their wanderings, which made them more accessible to a broader public and less likely to become set in their ways. "Our Blessed Saviour was an Itinerant Preacher," they reminded their critics; "he Preach'd in no other Way."

Itinerant minister During the era of the Great Awakening, some Protestant ministers practiced itinerancy; that is, they traveled widely and spoke to diverse communities, rather than being committed to one particular geographical parish or Protestant denomination.

Just as New Light preachers moved readily across traditional parish boundaries, they also transcended the lines between different Protestant sects. Their simple evangelical message reached across a wide social spectrum to diverse audiences of every denomination. Moreover, their stress on communal singing, expressive emotion, and the prospects for personal salvation drew special attention from those on the fringes of the culture, such as young people, women, and the poor. Not surprisingly, New Light ministers also made headway in spreading Christianity within various African American and Native American communities.

Members of the religious establishment, once secure as unchallenged leaders in their communities, now confronted a stark choice. Some powerful churchmen acknowledged their New Light critics and reluctantly welcomed the popular renegades into the local pulpits. Such a strategy might blunt the thrust of the revival, and it would surely raise church attendance. Other Old Lights, however, took the opposite approach; they clung to tradition and stability, challenging their new rivals openly. They condemned itinerancy and disputed the interlopers' right to preach. They mocked the faddish popularity of these overemotional zealots and even banned the New Light itinerants from local districts for the good of their parishioners.

In the end, neither tactic stemmed the upheaval, which peaked in the North in the 1740s and in the South during the 1750s and 1760s. But the long-term consequences of the Great Awakening were mixed. Zealous New Light men and women tried to transcend the competing denominations and create a broad community of Protestant believers. But the reformers could never create such unity, and they left behind no new set of doctrines or institutional structures. Nevertheless, they created an important legacy. First, they infused a new spirit of piety and optimism into American Christianity that countered older and darker Calvinist traditions. Second, they established a manner of fiery evangelical preaching that found a permanent place in American life. Finally, and most important, they underscored democratic tendencies in the New Testament gospels that many invoked in later years when faced with other apparent infringements of their liberties.

Interpreting History

"Is a Dead Man FIT TO BRING OTHERS TO LIFE?"

"While **some are** sincere **Servants of God,** are not many **Servants** of Satan, under a religious Mask?"

W hen the charismatic English minister George Whitefield preached before thousands of sympathetic listeners in Philadelphia late in 1739, he praised William Tennent and his son Gilbert as "the burning and shining lights of this part of America." If the threat of "darkness" had once lurked in wilderness forests, a new generation of town-dwelling colonists now sensed a suffocating lack of light within their own religious lives. Dissatisfied parishioners looked with increasing skepticism at once-respected clergymen. These "Old Light" leaders appeared overeducated and uninspiring; they seemed too worldly, secure, and self-important. As many Protestant colonists began questioning, and even blaming, their local ministers, they became receptive to the more emotional sermons of "New Light" preachers. Emboldened by Whitefield's tour, the Tennents began expanding their "itinerant" ways, sending evangelists into distant parishes and posing a challenge to local clergy.

On March 8, 1740, Gilbert Tennent ventured to tiny Nottingham, Pennsylvania, near the Maryland border, and preached a scathing sermon against complacent and "unconverted" ministers. His published text circulated widely and became a manifesto for the revival. Tennent chose Mark 6:34 as his New Testament text: "And Jesus, when he came out, saw much People and was moved with Compassion towards them, because they were as Sheep not having a Shepherd." He then compared the established colonial ministers to the proud, wily, and overeducated leaders who disparaged Jesus in Biblical times. Though "masterly and positive in their Assertions," they failed to guide their flocks and treated "common People with an Air of Disdain." Such "Pharisee-Shepherds, or unconverted Teachers," Tennent thundered, "are like whited Sepulchres, which indeed appear beautiful outward, but are within full of dead Bones."

As a faithful Ministry is a great Ornament, Blessing and Comfort, to the Church of GOD. . . . So on the contrary, an ungodly Ministry is a great Curse and Judgment: These Caterpillars labour to devour every green Thing. . . .

📖 Read the Document Benjamin Franklin, On George Whitefield (1771)

George Whitefield (d. 1770), shown here at the end of his long career, visited America seven times. In 1739, at age 24, his preaching as "the boy parson" spurred the Great Awakening. Why did some settled ministers object to such itinerant preaching?

SOURCE: Courtesy, Winterthur Museum (63.639)

The old Pharisee-Shepherds were as crafty as Foxes; they tried by all Means to ensnare our Lord by their captious Questions, and to expose him to the Displeasure of the State; while in the mean Time, by sly and sneaking Methods, they tried to secure for themselves the Favour of the Grandees. . . . They must keep the People in their Interests: Ay, that was the main Chance, the Compass that directed all their Proceedings. . . .

Is a blind Man fit to be a Guide in a very dangerous Way? Is a dead Man fit to bring others to Life? . . . Isn't an unconverted Minister like a Man who would learn others to swim, before he has learn'd it himself, and so is drowned in the Act, and dies like a Fool? . . . Look into the Congregations of unconverted Ministers, and see what a sad Security reigns there; not a Soul convinced that can be heard of, for many Years together; and yet the Ministers are easy; for they say they do their Duty! . . . Swarms of Locusts [have] crept into the Ministry, in this adulterous Generation! who as nearly resemble the Character given of the old Pharisees . . . as one Crow's Egg does another. . . . They are blind who see not this to be the Case of the Body of the Clergy, of this Generation. . . .

From what has been said, we may learn, That such who are contented under a dead Ministry, have not in them the Temper of that Saviour they profess. It's an awful Sign, that they are as blind as Moles, and as dead as Stones, without any spiritual Taste and Relish. And alas! isn't this the Case of Multitudes? If they can get one, that has the Name of a Minister, with a Band, and a black Coat or Gown . . . ; if he is free from gross Crimes in Practice, and takes good Care to keep at a due Distance from their Consciences. . . . O! think the poor Fools, that is a fine Man indeed. . . . Poor silly Souls!

Given the weakness of current ministers, Tennent concluded ominously:

It is both lawful and expedient to go from them to hear Godly Persons. . . . Is not the visible Church composed of Persons of the most contrary Characters? While some are sincere Servants of God, are not many Servants of Satan, under a religious Mask? . . . How is it then possible, that a Harmony should subsist between such, till their Nature be changed? Can Light dwell with Darkness?

Questions for Discussion

1. What are the most effective rhetorical flourishes and literary devices that Tennent uses to rouse his listeners and readers?

2. Strategically, as a local minister faced with such scathing criticism, would you be inclined be to accept it gracefully, or to reject Tennent's sermon entirely as a divisive polemic?

SOURCE: Gilbert Tennent, *The Danger of an Unconverted Ministry* (2nd ed., Boston, 1742).

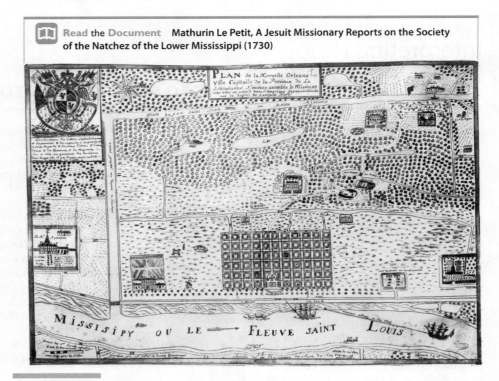

Read the Document   Mathurin Le Petit, A Jesuit Missionary Reports on the Society of the Natchez of the Lower Mississippi (1730)

New Orleans, laid out along the Mississippi River in 1718, became the capital of French Louisiana in 1722, the year of a devastating hurricane. Inhabitants quickly expanded the levees along the waterfront, but flooding remains a threat to the low-lying city even today, as the devastation of Hurricane Katrina in 2005 made clear. Would boats leaving the town, taking French trade goods upriver to the interior, first head south as shown here? Why?

The French Lose a North American Empire

5.5   What key factors undermined the French position in America in the decades after 1740?

In 1739, while George Whitefield launched his tour of the English colonies and the Stono slave rebellion erupted in South Carolina, the French dreamed of expanding their American empire. When Pierre and Paul Mallet paddled up the Mississippi River from New Orleans that year, the two French Canadians suspected that the Missouri River, the Mississippi's mightiest tributary, stretched to New Mexico. If so, they hoped to claim a new trading route for France. Pausing in Illinois to gather seven French Canadian recruits, the Mallet brothers pushed up the Missouri, hoping it flowed from the southwest.

But the river flowed from the northwest instead. Disappointed, the party left the river in Nebraska, purchased horses at an Omaha Indian village, and set off across the plains, reaching Santa Fe in July. After a nine-month stay, most of them returned east across the southern plains the next year. When the Mallets completed their enormous circuit and returned to New Orleans, they brought word from the West of Indian and Spanish eagerness to engage in greater trade. From their perspective, the future of France in America looked bright indeed. But the promise disappeared entirely—within their lifetimes.

Prospects and Problems Facing French Colonists

In 1740, French colonists had grounds for cautious optimism. France already claimed a huge expanse of North America, and its wilderness empire ran strategically through the center of the continent. The potential for mineral resources and rich farmland seemed boundless. Moreover, no Europeans had shown greater skill in forging stable and respectful relations with Native Americans. French forts stretched up the Mississippi River and then east to the lower Great Lakes and the St. Lawrence Valley. These posts facilitated trade with Native Americans and secured ties between Canada and Louisiana.

With Indian support, more outposts could be built farther east near the Appalachian Mountains to contain the English settlers and perhaps one day to conquer them.

At least three problems marred this scenario. First, the French population in America paled in comparison to the large number of English settlers. Canada still had fewer than 50,000 colonial inhabitants in 1740, whereas Britain's mainland colonies were rapidly approaching 1 million. Louisiana contained only 3,000 French people, living among nearly 4,000 enslaved Africans and 6,000 Native Americans. Second, French colonists lacked sufficient support from Paris to develop thriving communities and expand their Indian trade. The importation of goods from France was still meager and unpredictable. Finally, an ominous trickle of British hunters and settlers was beginning to cross the Appalachian chain. Carolina traders already had strong ties with the Chickasaw Indians living near the Mississippi River, and Virginia land speculators were eyeing lands in the Ohio Valley.

What seemed a promising situation for the French in 1740 was soon put to the test. Britain and France had long been on a collision course in North America. Colonial subjects of the two European superpowers had already clashed in a series of wars. After several decades of peace, warfare was about to resume. King George's War (1744–1748) and the French and Indian War (1754–1763) preoccupied colonists and Native Americans alike over the next two decades. In 1763, the Treaty of Paris ended the French and Indian War, part of a far broader conflict known in Europe as the Seven Years' War. At that point, less than a quarter century after the Mallet brothers' optimistic journey through the heartlands, the British gained the upper hand. The expansive French empire in North America suddenly vanished.

British Settlers Confront the Threat from France

These colonial conflicts of the mid-eighteenth century, generally linked to wider warfare in Europe, had a significant impact on everyone living in the British mainland colonies. A few people took advantage of the disturbances to become rich. They provisioned troops, sold scarce wartime goods, sponsored profitable privateering ventures, or conducted forbidden trade with the enemy in the Caribbean. But many more people paid a heavy price because of war: a farm burned, a job lost, a limb amputated, a husband or father shot in battle or cut down by disease. From London's perspective, the Americans made ill-disciplined and reluctant soldiers. From the colonists' viewpoint, the British offered them little respect and less assistance.

Adding insult to injury, a hard-won victory in North America could be canceled out at the peace table in Europe. In 1745, during King George's War, Massachusetts called for an attack on Louisburg, the recently completed French fortress on Cape Breton Island that controlled access to the St. Lawrence River and nearby fishing grounds. After a long siege, New England's forces prevailed. But British diplomats rescinded the colonial victory, handing Louisburg back to France in 1748 in exchange for Madras in India.

Whatever their differences, the American colonists and the British government saw potential in the land west of the Appalachian Mountains, and both were eager to challenge French claims there. In 1747, colonial speculators formed the Ohio Company of Virginia to develop western lands. Two years later, the crown granted them 200,000 acres south of the Ohio River, if they would construct a fort in the area. Moving west and north, the Virginians hoped to occupy a valuable spot (modern-day Pittsburgh, Pennsylvania) where the Monongahela and Allegheny rivers come together to form the Ohio River. But the French had designs on the same strategic location.

In 1753, the Virginia governor sent an untested young major in the colonial militia named George Washington—at age 21 already regarded as a promising officer—to warn the French to leave the area. The next spring, Virginia workers began erecting a fort at the Fork of the Ohio, but a larger French force drove them off and constructed Fort Duquesne on the coveted site. When Major Washington returned to the area with troops, he probed for enemy forces. In a skirmish on May 28, 1754, near modern Uniontown, Pennsylvania, his men killed ten French soldiers, the initial casualties in what soon became the world's first truly global war. With 450 men and meager supplies, Washington fortified his camp, calling it Fort Necessity, and dug in to prepare for a counterattack.

Throughout the British colonies in the early summer of 1754, fears spread about the dangers of the French offensive and the loyalties of Native American allies. Officials in London requested that all the colonies involved in relations with the Iroquois send delegates to a special congress in Albany, New York, to improve that Indian alliance. Seven colonies sent twenty-three representatives, who hoped to strengthen friendship with the Iroquois nations and also discuss a design for a union of the colonies. The delegates to the Albany Congress adopted Benjamin Franklin's proposal for a colonial confederation that would unify the colonies through an elected Grand Council and a president general appointed by the crown. But no colonial legislature ever ratified Franklin's far-sighted Albany Plan. "Everyone cries, a union is necessary," Franklin wrote, "but when they come to the manner and form of the union, their weak noodles are perfectly distracted."

The main distraction for delegates came when word reached Albany that the French, on July 3, had defeated Major Washington's force at Fort Necessity. But the British were not willing to give up their claims to the Ohio Valley without a fight. The crown responded by dispatching General Edward Braddock and two regiments of Irish troops to America. Early in 1755, his force arrived in Virginia, where preparations were already under way

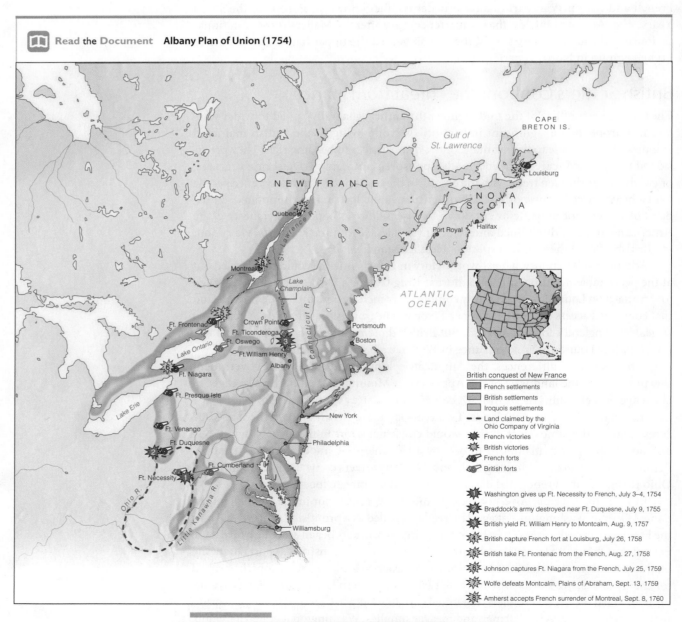

Read the Document Albany Plan of Union (1754)

British conquest of New France
French settlements
British settlements
Iroquois settlements
Land claimed by the Ohio Company of Virginia
French victories
British victories
French forts
British forts

1 Washington gives up Ft. Necessity to French, July 3–4, 1754
2 Braddock's army destroyed near Ft. Duquesne, July 9, 1755
3 British yield Ft. William Henry to Montcalm, Aug. 9, 1757
4 British capture French fort at Louisburg, July 26, 1758
5 British take Ft. Frontenac from the French, Aug. 27, 1758
6 Johnson captures Ft. Niagara from the French, July 25, 1759
7 Wolfe defeats Montcalm, Plains of Abraham, Sept. 13, 1759
8 Amherst accepts French surrender of Montreal, Sept. 8, 1760

MAP 5.3 THE BRITISH CONQUEST OF NEW FRANCE, 1754–1760

for a campaign to conquer Fort Duquesne. In June, Braddock's combined British and colonial army of 2,500 began a laborious march west to face the French.

An American Fight Becomes a Global Conflict

The early stages of the war in America could hardly have been more disastrous for Britain or more encouraging for France. A French and Indian force ambushed Braddock's column in the forest near Fort Duquesne, cutting it to pieces in the most thorough defeat of the century for a British army unit. Elsewhere, Indian raids battered the frontiers, spreading panic in the northern colonies. With the local militia away at war, fears of possible slave uprisings swept through the South. The French commander, the Marquis de Montcalm, struck into New York's Mohawk Valley from Lake Ontario in 1756, then pushed south down Lake Champlain and Lake George in 1757. After a seven-day siege, he took 2,000 prisoners at Fort William Henry. In an episode made famous in *The Last of the Mohicans*, France's Huron Indian allies killed more than 150 men and women after their release from the fort.

The change in British fortunes came with the new ministry of William Pitt, a vain but talented member of the House of Commons. Pitt was an expansionist committed to the growth of the British Empire at the expense of France. He brought a daring new strategy to the war effort, and he had the determination and bureaucratic skill to carry it out. Stymied in Europe by the military might of the French army, the British would now concentrate their forces instead on France's vulnerable and sparsely populated overseas colonies. Under Pitt, the British broadened the war into a global conflict, taking advantage of their superior naval power to fight on the coasts of Asia and Africa and in North America as well. By 1758, Britain had undertaken a costly military buildup in America, with nearly 50,000 troops.

To win colonial support for his plan, Pitt promised to reimburse the colonies generously for their expenses. In the South, guns, ammunition, and trade goods flowed freely to Britain's Native American allies. In the North, France lost Louisburg again in July 1758. Fort Frontenac on Lake Ontario fell in August. In November, the French destroyed and abandoned Fort Duquesne at the Fork of the Ohio. The British seized the strategic site and erected a new post (aptly named Fort Pitt), laying out the village of Pittsburgh beside it. In Canada, autumn brought a poor harvest, followed by the harshest winter in memory. Ice in the St. Lawrence River, plus a British naval blockade, cut off overseas support from France. The Marquis de Montcalm huddled in Quebec with his ill-equipped army.

In the spring of 1759, the British pressed their advantage, moving against Canada from several directions. Britain's superintendent of Indian affairs in the region, Sir William Johnson, sensed that many Native Americans were eager to support the winning side. Johnson successfully recruited 1,000 formerly neutral Iroquois to join 2,000 British regulars on the shores of Lake Ontario to lay siege to Fort Niagara. The fort fell in July, a British victory that effectively isolated enemy posts farther west and obliged the French to abandon them. In August, a British force under Jeffery Amherst captured Ticonderoga and Crown Point on Lake Champlain. The stage was set for an assault on Quebec.

Quebec Taken and North America Refashioned

In London, William Pitt knew that capturing Quebec would conquer Canada. Months earlier, he had ordered James Wolfe "to make an attack upon Quebeck, by the River St. Lawrence." Wolfe's **flotilla**, with 8,500 troops, anchored near the walled city in late June. But the French held their citadel despite weeks of heavy shelling. Desperate and sick, Wolfe resorted to a ruthless campaign against the countryside that left 1,400 farms in ruins. Even this strategy failed to draw Montcalm's forces out to fight.

As a last resort, Wolfe adopted a risky plan to climb a steep bluff and attack the vulnerable west side of the city. On the night of September 12, 1759, he dispatched troops to float quietly past French sentries and scale the formidable cliffs. At daybreak, twelve British battalions emerged on a level expanse known as the Plains of Abraham. The future of the continent and its inhabitants hinged on a pitched battle between

Flotilla Any sizeable fleet of ships, or, more specifically, a naval term for a unit consisting of two or more squadrons of small warships.

129

✺ Explore the Seven Years' War on MyHistoryLab

WHAT DID THE GLOBAL SEVEN YEARS' WAR MEAN FOR NORTH AMERICA?

The period of the Seven Years' War, ending in 1763, marked a "world war" that tested the security of the thirteen British mainland colonies in North America during an intense period of imperial European—and global—rivalries. The war began in North America in 1754 as a frontier conflict between Virginia and New France. Two years later it reached across the Atlantic to embroil many European powers, eventually spreading all the way to India. The conflict pitted Great Britain and its allies against France and its allies while both sides used alliances with Native Americans to bolster their positions. The British emerged victorious in 1763, which dramatically changed the situation in North America: the British gained Canada from the French and Florida

This political allegory shows two opponents in Seven Years' War (1756–1763), Empress Maria Theresa of Austria and King Fredrick II of Prussia, playing chess with Mars, the Roman god of war.

from Spain. Native American nations could no longer play the French and the British off against one another in trade and diplomacy. For their part, British colonists in North America suddenly found they were no longer surrounded by competing colonial powers.

THE OPPOSING SIDES OF THE SEVEN YEARS' WAR

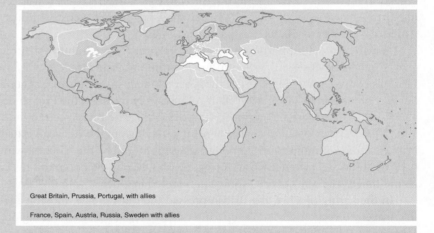

Great Britain, Prussia, Portugal, with allies

France, Spain, Austria, Russia, Sweden with allies

KEY QUESTIONS   Use **MyHistoryLab** *Explorer* to **answer** these **questions:**

Response ▶▶▶ *How did other colonial claims in North America create instability for the thirteen British mainland colonies?*

Situate the location of these British colonies in relation to competing colonial claims.

Analysis ▶▶▶ *What made this eighteenth-century war a "world war"?*

Map the main battles in various parts of the world.

Consequences ▶▶▶ *In what ways did the territorial results of the war impact British mainland colonies?*

Conceptualize what these changes, especially the Proclamation Line of 1763, meant for the British colonialists.

opposing European armies. Montcalm and Wolfe staked everything in the clash, and both lost their lives in the encounter. By nightfall, the British had won a decisive victory, and four days later the surviving French garrison surrendered the city of Quebec.

Montreal fell to Britain the following year, and fighting subsided in America. But Pitt continued to pour public money into the global war, and one military triumph followed another. The British conquered French posts in India, took French Senegal on the West African coast, and seized the valuable sugar islands of Martinique and Guadeloupe in the French West Indies. When Spain came to France's aid in 1762, British forces captured the Philippines and the Cuban city of Havana. But British taxpayers resented the huge costs of the war. Many also worried that the effort to humiliate France and Spain could spark retaliation. Rising criticism pushed Pitt from office, and peace negotiations began.

In a matter of months, the European powers redrew the imperial map of North America. Their complex swaps constituted the largest rearrangement of territorial claims in the history of the continent. First, France ceded to Spain the port of New Orleans and all of the Louisiana territory west of the Mississippi River. Then, in the 1763 Treaty of Paris, Spain turned over East Florida to Britain, receiving back Havana and the Philippines in return. France gave Britain its holdings between the Appalachians and the Mississippi River as well as the parts of Canada not already claimed by the Hudson's Bay Company. For this vast acquisition, the British returned the French sugar islands of Martinique and Guadeloupe, and they allowed France to retain fishing rights off Newfoundland.

Those negotiating the peace agreed that French Canadians could choose between leaving Canada or becoming British subjects. But the Paris treaty made no mention of the thousands of Native Americans whose homelands were being reassigned. The final results were striking. Britain emerged as the world's leading colonial power, and after two centuries, the empire of France in North America abruptly disappeared.

Conclusion

The half century before 1763 brought unprecedented changes to the North American continent. On the western plains, the spread of horses and guns reshaped competing Native American cultures. In the East, Britain's seaboard colonies became more diverse, evolving into distinctive economic and cultural areas. Moreover, the number of inhabitants soared throughout these Atlantic colonies, reaching 1.6 million people by 1763. No other region of the continent had ever experienced such population growth. Between 1750 and 1763, the British mainland colonies added more than 400,000 people through natural increase, European immigration, and the slave trade. Amazingly, the sum of these additions over just thirteen years exceeded the entire population of those same British colonies five decades earlier, in 1713.

Fifty years of population growth brought dramatic alterations in the fabric of colonial society. As settlements expanded, dependence on friends and relations gave way to regular interactions with strangers, many of whom spoke broken English and showed limited loyalty toward the British crown. Expansion brought more than cultural diversity; it also brought greater social inequality. In the South, the consolidation of slavery created a stark separation between extremes of wealth and poverty, with political and economic power concentrated in the hands of the white gentry. In the northern ports of Philadelphia, New York, and Boston, successful merchants created educated elites that developed their own gracious lifestyle, attentive to European politics and fashions.

These influential elites, though bound together by strategic marriages and business alliances, were hardly unified. Ship owners vied with one another for trade; ministers competed to fill rival congregations, and men of property contended for public office and posts in the colonial government. In all these endeavors, the colonial gentry courted public approval, while also expecting deference from those below them in the social hierarchy. After 1763, with French power removed from the continent, local leaders suddenly faced a difficult question: Did their best interests lie with the diverse colonists around them in America, or with the British crown and parliament in London that was asserting increasing control over colonial affairs?

On MyHistoryLab

☑ **Study and Review** on MyHistoryLab

Chapter Review

New Cultures on the Western Plains

5.1 How and why did life change dramatically for the Comanche and Sioux Indians after 1700? p. 107

For centuries, Native Americans near the Great Plains had eaten domestic dogs and used them to pull small travois. The arrival of Spanish horses provided a larger animal to haul loads and provide meat. Riding skills gave hunters greater mobility, and horse herds provided a new way of measuring wealth.

Britain's Mainland Colonies: A New Abundance of People

5.2 In what ways did Britain's North American colonies become "less English" after 1700? p. 111

Migration from England slowed after 1700, and the trade in enslaved Africans expanded. An influx of French Huguenots and German pietists sought religious freedom and economic opportunities, joining Scots-Irish indentured servants. After 1755, French Acadians expelled from British Nova Scotia entered colonies further south. Few colonists had ever seen Britain.

The Varied Economic Landscape

5.3 What role did geography play in shaping the emerging regional colonial economies? p. 115

Access to water was crucial everywhere, since coastal fisheries yielded wealth, swift streams provided mill power, and rivers afforded cheap transportation for goods. But colonies east of the Appalachian Mountains varied greatly with regard to climate extremes, soil fertility, hardwood forests, furbearing animals, and marketable crops that would grow successfully.

Matters of Faith: The Great Awakening

5.4 What prompted increased toleration at a time of fresh religious intensity after 1730? p. 121

Even as George Whitefield sparked a religious revival among colonial Protestants, growing diversity among American immigrants fostered a variety of religious beliefs. Colonial governments, competing for the labor of these newcomers, ended commitments to an "established" church and stressed relative toleration, encouraged by the spreading doctrines of the rational Enlightenment.

The French Lose a North American Empire

5.5 What key factors undermined the French position in America in the decades after 1740? p. 126

In 1740, France's prospects for expansion in the North American interior seemed promising. But the French colonial population remained small, giving British colonists an increasing demographic advantage. The commitment of Paris bureaucrats to colonial enterprise proved weak. Britain's naval strength and colonial encroachments westward increased the French dilemma in America.

Timeline

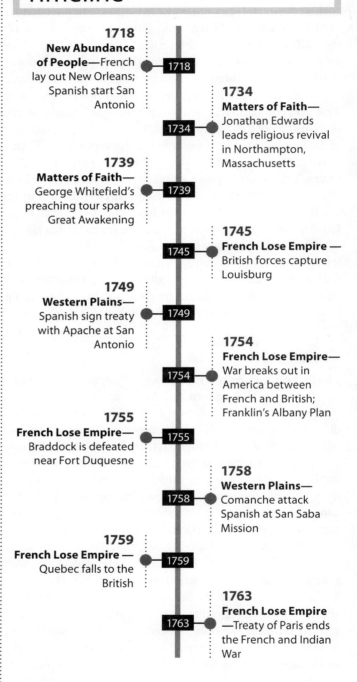

1718
New Abundance of People—French lay out New Orleans; Spanish start San Antonio

1734
Matters of Faith—Jonathan Edwards leads religious revival in Northampton, Massachusetts

1739
Matters of Faith—George Whitefield's preaching tour sparks Great Awakening

1745
French Lose Empire—British forces capture Louisburg

1749
Western Plains—Spanish sign treaty with Apache at San Antonio

1754
French Lose Empire—War breaks out in America between French and British; Franklin's Albany Plan

1755
French Lose Empire—Braddock is defeated near Fort Duquesne

1758
Western Plains—Comanche attack Spanish at San Saba Mission

1759
French Lose Empire—Quebec falls to the British

1763
French Lose Empire—Treaty of Paris ends the French and Indian War

132

6 The **Limits** of **Imperial** Control, 1763–1775

With French power vanishing from Canada and Louisiana after 1763, what could prevent British ascendancy in North America for the foreseeable future? Granted, other imperial rivals, new and old, still posed a threat. Russian investors and fur traders were eyeing Alaska; Spanish sailors and missionaries were exploring the coast of California. But in London, these adventures along the Pacific Coast appeared as tiny clouds on a distant horizon. Instead, the empire's greatest challenge would arise within the English-speaking colonies along the Atlantic Coast. The insurgency's unity and success would hinge on an unlikely alliance between portions of the colonial elite and a spectrum of working people that evolved gradually between 1763 and 1775.

Relations between a prominent business magnate and a struggling New England cobbler illustrate this evolving alliance. Both lived in Boston, a busy seaport of 16,000 people,

Angry colonists from different social classes united in December 1773 to throw East India Company Tea into Boston Harbor. These activists, disguised as Indians, galvanized opposition to British taxation. Parliament's harsh reprisals against Massachusetts pushed Britain's North American colonies closer to revolution. How did the symbolic use of Mohawk Indian garb aid colonists from all social classes in unifying and expanding their opposition movement?

LEARNING OBJECTIVES

6.1 ((·	6.2 ((·	6.3 ((·	6.4 ((·	6.5 ((·
How did French, British, and Russian explorers in the Pacific threaten Spain's American empire? p. 135	Why did the removal of French and Spanish interests pose new problems for Britain's North American empire? p. 138	How did events in America and Britain in the 1760s confirm the skeptical worldview of "Real Whigs"? p. 145	Did the Boston Massacre highlight justifiable colonial grievances, or was it a provoked attack, exploited by dissidents? p. 149	Could the British, through a more creative response to the Boston Tea Party, have averted the ensuing escalation toward violence? p. 152

((· Listen to Chapter 6 on MyHistoryLab

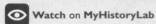 Watch the Video Series on MyHistoryLab

Learn about some key topics related to this chapter with the *MyHistoryLab Video Series: Key Topics in U.S. History.*

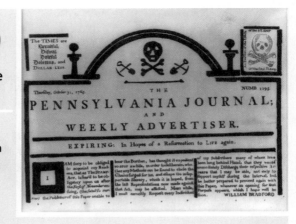

1 **The Burdens of an Empire: 1763–1775** Following the Seven Years' War, the American colonies chafed under an increased tax burden, military occupation, and a lack of influence in Great Britain's political system. This video surveys the economic and self-rule issues that led to a formal break with the mother country and revolution.

Watch on MyHistoryLab

The Stamp Act The British government's efforts to pay off debts incurred during the Seven Years' War directly affected colonists in various ways. One key attempt involved the controversial Stamp Act of 1765. This video discusses the origins of the act, colonial resistance to it, and the way it was rescinded. The Stamp Act controversy severely strained relations between the British crown and its colonies in North America. **2**

Watch on MyHistoryLab

3 **Boston Massacre** After Britain obliged colonists to pay customs duties on imported items (Townshend Revenue Act) and stationed soldiers in American cities, tensions boiled over in the "Boston Massacre" of 1770. This video explores the background for that watershed event, as heavy-handed British measures further alienated American colonists from Parliament and the monarchy of King George III.

Watch on MyHistoryLab

Boston Tea Party Parliament's Tea Act of 1773 imposed a tax on imported tea, provoking anger in colonial ports. Massachusetts activists, dressed as Native Americans, dumped a valuable tea shipment into Boston Harbor to prevent its sale. Outraged by this resistance, Parliament passed four "Coercive Acts," which further unified colonial opposition and galvanized the push for independence from Great Britain. **4**

Watch on MyHistoryLab

where the wealth gap had widened sharply in the 1750s as merchants reaped profits during the Seven Years' War. In 1764, at age twenty-seven, John Hancock inherited a vast fortune of £80,000 from his uncle's shipping business. But most Bostonians lived in a very different world. Half the townspeople had property and savings worth less than £40, and many, such as the young cordwainer George Hewes, possessed even less.

Hewes, who repaired Hancock's expensive shoes, remembered being scared "almost to death" in 1763, when he attended a New Year's open house at the merchant's impressive mansion. Yet the two men met again on far less deferential terms a decade later. In December 1773, the shoemaker joined other activists, disguised as Indians, to empty chests of British tea into Boston Harbor. Hewes, who recalled that night as an old man, was one of the first to refer to the event as a "tea party." He swore that in the darkness he had rubbed elbows with Hancock himself and had joined him in smashing a crate of tea. Symbolically, the two men were now working shoulder to shoulder, on an equal footing.

Secure after its victory over France, Britain could scarcely imagine that it would soon be battling to retain the parts of North America that it confidently claimed to control. Even less conceivable for London's self-assured leaders was the idea that Britain could lose any such struggle. After all, throughout British North America, class and regional interests still divided colonists on most occasions. Prosperous merchants, urban artisans, rural farmers, enslaved African Americans, and numerous wives and widows did not necessarily share common views and concerns. Indeed, they were frequently at odds.

During the dozen years after 1763, however, all that would change, as rifts emerged within the provincial ruling class. Throughout the colonies, British officials and other people who supported the crown's policies became known as Loyalists, or Tories. The wealthy among them saw social and economic dominance as their birthright and scorned their rivals for courting favor with the poor. In contrast, leaders of the emerging opposition (known as Whigs or Patriots) consisted of less conservative—often young and ambitious—members of the educated and professional classes. These people downplayed their rank and privilege to win popular support from those beneath them on the social scale.

Elsewhere, the years after 1763 brought change as well. In the Midwest, thousands of Native Americans under the leadership of Pontiac rose up to assert their own independence from British encroachment. On the Great Plains, the Comanche and Sioux contended for new territories. Still farther west, other peoples experienced the initial shocks of colonial contact. Suddenly, inhabitants of the Hawaiian Islands and the Alaskan coast were encountering European intruders for the first time.

New Challenges to Spain's Expanded Empire

6.1 How did French, British, and Russian explorers in the Pacific threaten Spain's American empire?

With Spain's acquisition of Louisiana from France in 1763, the Spanish held nominal title to the entire West, from the Mississippi to the Pacific, populated by more than 1 million Native Americans. But whether Spain could explore and defend this vast domain, stretching north toward Alaska, remained an open question. After all, envious rivals were already probing North America's Pacific coast. French and British exploration voyages challenged Spain's dominance in the Pacific, and Russian colonization in Alaska spurred the Spanish to establish posts along the coast of California. These rivalries, in turn, brought new pressures to bear on the West's diverse Indian peoples, even before the United States emerged as a separate entity with expansionist ambitions of its own.

Pacific Exploration, Hawaiian Contact

Removed from North America in 1763 and burdened with heavy debts from the Seven Years' War, the French sought fresh prospects in the unexplored South Pacific. Not to be outdone, British captains pressed their own Pacific explorations. The most skilled and successful was James Cook, who ranged from the Arctic Circle to Antarctica during three momentous voyages beginning in 1768. In January 1778, during Cook's final voyage, his two vessels happened upon the Hawaiian Islands, eight major volcanic islands, plus 114 minor isles, stretching over 300 miles. More than thirteen centuries earlier (300–500 C.E.), seafaring Polynesians had migrated here in ocean-sailing **outrigger canoes**. They had arrived from the Marquesas Islands far to the south, and their descendants, perhaps as many as 300,000 people, lived in agricultural and fishing communities dominated by powerful chiefs.

The Hawaiians treated Cook with hospitality and respect. "No people could trade with more honisty," the captain observed. During the next twelve months, Cook cruised up the west coast of North America. Two centuries after Francis Drake's visit, English mariners still hoped to find a sea passage through North America to shorten voyages from the Atlantic to Asia. But Cook encountered a solid coastline stretching all the way to Alaska. Along the way, he traded with Northwest Coast Indians for sea otter pelts.

Outrigger canoe Polynesian mariners in Southeast Asia developed large canoes with one or more lateral support floats, known as outriggers, that gave stability for ocean sailing. They used such canoes to reach Hawaii.

English explorers like James Cook challenged Spanish dominance in the Pacific Ocean. When Captain Cook anchored at Hawaii's Kealakekua Bay in 1779, he wrote in his journal that the islanders crowded aboard his two vessels and paddled around them in "a multitude of Canoes." Hundreds of others swam about the ships, along with "a number of men upon pieces of Plank." One such surfboarder is visible in the foreground. How does this painting by a member of Cook's crew suggest the mixed emotions and nervous excitement of initial contact?

Cook's vessels returned south in 1779, making their first visit to the big island of Hawaii, and once again they were greeted with fanfare. But admiration turned to resentment as the English outstayed their welcome, and an angry crowd of Hawaiians killed Cook and four of his mariners. After the captain's death, his two sloops stopped at Macao in China, where the crew sold their furs at a huge profit. They then sailed back to England in 1780 with word of money to be made selling North American sea-otter pelts in China. The voyagers also confirmed a disturbing rumor: Russia already had a foothold in this lucrative Pacific traffic.

The Russians Lay Claim to Alaska

Half a century before Cook visited Hawaii, a Danish captain in the Russian naval service trekked across Siberia. Vitus Bering reached the Kamchatka peninsula on the Pacific Ocean in 1728. From there, he built a boat and sailed north through the strait that bears his name. The journey ended European speculation that Asia was linked to North America. On a second expedition in 1741, Bering visited the Alaskan mainland and claimed it for Russia. He died during the return voyage, after a winter shipwreck on a frozen island.

Bering's crew finally returned to Kamchatka with valuable pelts. Over the next generation, Russian merchants sent several expeditions to Alaska each year, bringing back furs that they traded with the powerful Chinese Empire. In Alaskan waters, the Russian trappers lacked the numbers and the skill to collect furs on their own. So they captured native women and children as hostages, then ransomed them back to their men in exchange for a fixed number of furs. Native Alaskans resisted these rough intruders, but many eventually submitted in a desperate effort to survive.

In the quarter-century before 1780, thirty different Russian companies sponsored expeditions to Alaskan waters. The competing newcomers, bringing diseases, firearms, and their brutal hostage-taking system, reduced the population of the Aleutian Islands. As the number of humans and animals on the Aleutian Islands declined, the Russians pushed farther east in search of new hunters and hunting grounds. The Russian voyages from Kamchatka grew longer and more expensive.

To facilitate operations, Grigorii Shelikov and a partner formed a new company in 1781 and planned an Alaskan base. In 1784, they founded a permanent colonial settlement on Kodiak Island east of the Aleutians, despite fierce opposition from the island's native residents. By 1799, the firm had absorbed smaller competitors to become the Russian American Company, with a monopoly from the **czar**.

In 1790, with the Kodiak base secure, Russians forced more than 7,000 island inhabitants to embark on vast fur hunts in their versatile two-seat **kayaks**. That same year, Shelikov hired Alexander Baranov to oversee the Kodiak post and expand operations down the Alaskan coast. In 1799, Baranov established an additional outpost at Sitka in southeast Alaska. Called New Archangel at the time, the post became the capital of Russian America in 1808. From here, Baranov eventually extended the company's reach south toward California, seeking new hunting grounds and a longer growing season.

Spain Colonizes the California Coast

The Seven Years' War had left Spain's king, Carlos III, with vast new land claims in western North America. His bureaucrats in Spanish America struggled to control the huge domain. Across the Southwest, many Native Americans resisted military suppression and slave raids. In addition, clerics offered their own resistance to government designs. The powerful Jesuits opposed administrative reform in the colonies, and in 1767, Carlos III expelled them from the Spanish realm. Unruly colonists posed a threat of their own. French inhabitants of New Orleans led a brief rebellion against Spanish rule in 1768. Finally, officials feared challenges in the Pacific from the British and the Russians. As early as 1759, a Spanish Franciscan had published *Muscovites in California*, warning of Russian settlements.

Mindful of the Russian threat, Spanish leaders in Mexico City moved to establish a token presence along the California coast. In 1769, Gaspar de Portolá and Franciscan friar Junípero Serra led a small vanguard north to establish an initial outpost at San Diego Bay. Portolá then pressed farther up the coast, building a presidio (or military garrison) at Monterey in 1770 to "defend us from attacks by the Russians, who," he believed, "were about to invade us."

After Carlos III removed all Jesuits from Spanish America in 1767, members of the competing Franciscan order expanded their work and took on new responsibilities. Following the lead of Father Serra, other Franciscans soon planted several missions between San Diego and Monterey. These included the San Gabriel mission in 1771, where colonists established the town of Los Angeles ten years later. In 1775, a Spanish captain sailed into San Francisco Bay, and the next year, a land expedition laid out the presidio and mission of San Francisco. A town sprang up at nearby San José the following year. As Franciscan fathers labored to convert the coast's diverse Indians, Spanish vessels pushed far up the Pacific shoreline. Captain Ignacio de Arteaga reached the Gulf of Alaska in 1779, fourteen months after Captain Cook had been there.

Since Spanish ships had difficulty supplying the few dozen settlers in California, authorities looked for an overland supply route. In 1774, Juan Bautista de Anza set out in search of a land route to California from the presidio he commanded at Tubac, south of Tucson. Accompanied by a Franciscan named Father Garcés, he forded the Colorado River and then crossed desert and mountains to reach the coast at San Gabriel. The next year, Anza led 240 reinforcements—mostly Spanish women and children—along a similar route, pausing at San Gabriel and heading north to San Francisco Bay.

Further explorations proved less successful. In July 1776, Fathers Domínguez and Escalante left Santa Fe on horseback. The Franciscans headed northwest across Colorado and Utah in search of a more northern route to Monterey on the Pacific coast. But no such trail existed. Instead, their 1,800-mile trek revealed the huge expanse of the Great Basin. Moreover, the path to California that Anza had established proved short-lived. The Yuma Indians, near the Colorado River, soon grew to resent Spanish trespassers, and they rebelled in the summer of 1781. Hopes for a rapid expansion of the Spanish colony in California died in the bloody Yuma Revolt.

Despite these problems, Spain managed to retain control over its recently expanded North American empire. The same could not be said for the British in their

Czar The title for a male ruler, or king, of Russia during the centuries before the Russian Revolution of 1917.

Kayak A highly maneuverable, decked-in canoe used by Native Alaskans for travel and hunting. The light frame is covered with skins, and the paddle has a blade at each end. Popular modern versions of this traditional boat are made with canvas or fiberglass.

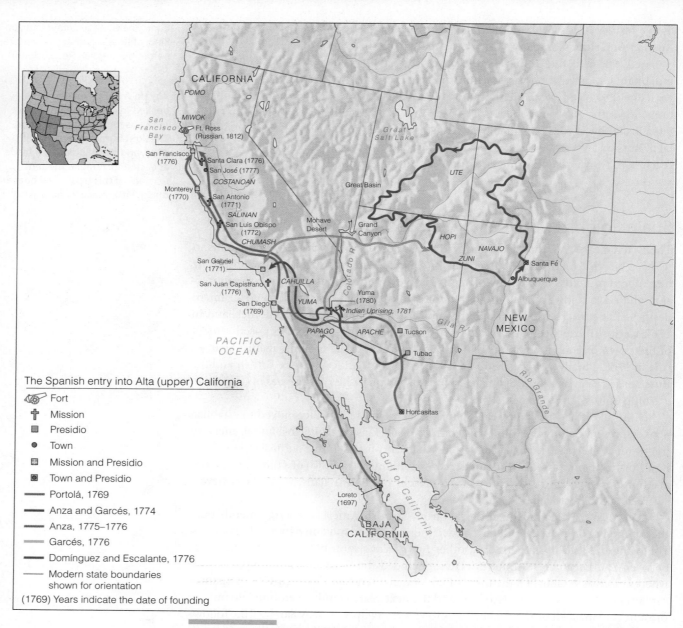

The Spanish entry into Alta (upper) California

- Fort
- Mission
- Presidio
- Town
- Mission and Presidio
- Town and Presidio
- Portolá, 1769
- Anza and Garcés, 1774
- Anza, 1775–1776
- Garcés, 1776
- Domínguez and Escalante, 1776
- Modern state boundaries shown for orientation

(1769) Years indicate the date of founding

MAP 6.1 SPANISH EXPLORATION AFTER 1760 AND THE FOUNDING OF THE CALIFORNIA MISSIONS

own newly enlarged empire farther east. They had taken French Canada, and their military might dominated the Atlantic world. But their fortunes in North America were about to change.

New Challenges to Britain's Expanded Empire

6.2 Why did the removal of French and Spanish interests pose new problems for Britain's North American empire?

n September 1760, French forces at Montreal submitted to British commander Jeffery Amherst. For Native Americans living east of the Mississippi, the French defeat in Canada had an immediate impact. General Amherst, who despised Indians as "contemptible," intended to alter Native American relations in the interior to reflect the new balance of power. He promptly sent James Grant to South Carolina with

138

instructions "to chastise the Cherokees," who had taken up arms against the growing number of English traders and settlers in western Carolina. Grant invaded Cherokee country in 1761, burning fifteen villages.

With the Cherokee chastened in the South, Amherst turned his attention to the Indians north of the Ohio River. Here, his harsh policies brought a sudden retaliation from the Native Americans; their actions took many lives and cost Amherst his command. And if Indians in the Midwest posed fresh challenges to Britain, so did the colonists themselves.

Midwestern Lands and Pontiac's War for Indian Independence

As soon as the British unseated their French competitors in the Ohio River valley, they prohibited traffic with Indians in such goods as knives, tomahawks, muskets, powder, and lead. As French traders withdrew, the British took over their strategic posts at Detroit and Michilimackinac. English settlers built new forts in the Ohio Valley and erected Fort Pitt over the ruins of Fort Duquesne. Then, early in 1763, word spread among Indians that France would cede Louisiana to Spain and give up Canada and the entire Midwest to Great Britain. This shocking news undercut moderate Native American leaders and strengthened the hand of pro-war factions.

Word that a treaty in far-off Paris might disrupt the entire region drew attention to Neolin, a Delaware Indian prophet urging a return to ancient ways and a sharp separation from the corrupting Europeans. Neolin's popular vision of renewing Native American independence by driving out the British appealed to Pontiac, a militant Ottawa warrior. In April, Pontiac addressed a secret council of more than 400 Ottawa, Potawatomie, and Huron, meeting within ten miles of Fort Detroit. Invoking the Delaware Prophet's vision, he announced that the Master of Life resented the British and wanted them removed: "Send them back to the lands which I have created for them and let them stay there." By May, Pontiac had mobilized a coalition and laid siege to Detroit.

Soon, Indians from eighteen nations had joined in Pontiac's widespread uprising. By mid-June 1763, both Detroit and Fort Pitt were under siege, and the British had lost every other Ohio Valley and Great Lakes outpost. As Indian raiding parties ravaged white communities in western Virginia and Pennsylvania, embittered settlers responded with racial killing. In December, white men from Paxton Creek descended on Christian families of Conestoga Indians near Lancaster, Pennsylvania, executing more than thirty peaceful converts. When Easterners protested this outrage, the "Paxton Boys" marched on Philadelphia to demand increased protection on the frontier. General Amherst ordered his officers to spread smallpox if possible, and to take no prisoners. The Indians deserved extermination, he ranted, "for the good of mankind."

The violence ended in a stalemate. Without French support, Native American munitions ran short, and Detroit and Fort Pitt endured. Indian militancy waned, and Pontiac was killed by a Peoria Indian in 1765. Still, the uprising proved costly for the British and prompted a shift in policy. To avoid further expensive warfare, officials moved to restore the Indian trade, keep squatters and debt evaders out of Indian country, and prevent colonial speculation in western lands. In October 1763, Major General Thomas Gage replaced Amherst in command of British forces.

In England, the crown went further. Late in 1763, it issued a proclamation forbidding colonial settlers from moving west across the Appalachian summit. Beyond that dividing line, all the land east of the Mississippi River would be reserved for Indians and a few authorized British soldiers and traders. While the Proclamation Line of 1763, drawn along the crest of the Appalachians, had only limited success, it frustrated Virginia's gentry. Such prominent men as George Washington and Thomas Jefferson were investors in land companies that speculated in large western tracts, hoping to obtain property cheaply from Native Americans and sell small parcels to eager settlers at a steady profit. But the British government, fearful of sparking unified Indian opposition and additional warfare, denied the Virginians' wishes and aroused their resentment.

Grenville's Effort at Reform

In 1763, King George III appointed George Grenville to head a new government in London. Grenville's ministry immediately faced a series of intertwined problems. Britain's victory over the French in the Seven Years' War had proved costly, nearly doubling the national debt to a staggering £146 million. As England's postwar depression deepened, returning soldiers swelled the ranks of the unemployed. In addition, rural mobs protested a new tax on domestic cider, imposed to help whittle away at the war debt.

No one promoted opposition to the government more than John Wilkes, a flamboyant member of Parliament (MP). Wilkes published the *North Briton*, an outspoken periodical that attacked the king's peace settlement with France and the king himself. Grenville reacted by arresting the publisher, despite his status as an MP. Angered by government suppression of dissent, protesters made "Wilkes and Liberty!" a popular rallying cry.

Pressured at home, Grenville set out to impose order on Britain's growing American colonies through a series of reforms. The first step was to maintain a military presence of nearly 7,000 troops in North America. The move would protect newly acquired territories while keeping young British men employed overseas rather than jobless at home. Strapped for funds, Grenville hoped to pay for the transatlantic forces with money drawn from the American colonies, reminding them of their subordination to the British Parliament.

A second step involved raising revenue by strengthening customs enforcement in colonial ports. Grenville dispatched forty-four navy ships to America to assist customs officials in nabbing smugglers, and he convinced Parliament to pass the American Duties Act of 1764. This new revenue law, also known as the Sugar Act, increased the duty on sugar and various other products entering the empire from non-British ports. Most importantly, it cut in half the import duty of sixpence per gallon on foreign molasses. Officials hoped that New England rum distillers, who had been secretly importing cheap molasses from the French West Indies without paying customs, would be willing to pay threepence per gallon. If enforced, the act would reduce smuggling and boost revenues.

To ensure compliance, the Sugar Act established the first of several vice-admiralty courts. The court sat at Halifax, Nova Scotia, so defendants had large travel expenses, and they faced a single appointed judge instead of a favorable hometown jury. "What has America done," protested critics, "to be stripped of so invaluable a privilege as the trial by jury?"

Colonists found Grenville's next statutes equally dismaying. The Currency Act of 1764 prohibited colonial assemblies from issuing paper money or bills of credit to be used as legal tender to pay off debts. The move worsened the money shortage in British America, where a lopsided trade balance was already draining gold and silver from the colonies to England. The next year, Parliament passed a Quartering Act that obliged colonists to assist the army by allowing soldiers to use vacant barns and other buildings as temporary quarters. The local governor was to supply the soldiers, at colonial expense, with such basic necessities as firewood, candles, bedding, salt, vinegar, utensils, and beer. Colonial assemblies had willingly voted such support during colonial wars. However, these peacetime requisitions, ordered by a distant Parliament, challenged their authority and smacked of indirect taxation.

The Stamp Act Imposed

There was nothing indirect about Grenville's most important reform: the Stamp Act. Early in 1765, Parliament approved the new statute "for raising a further revenue" to pay for "defending, protecting, and securing" the British colonies in America. The new act was patterned on a similar law in England, and it required stamps (like those on modern packs of cigarettes) to appear on a variety of articles in America after November 1, 1765. The list included legal contracts, land deeds, liquor licenses,

📖 **Read** the Document   Benjamin Franklin, Testimony Against the Stamp Act (1766)

6.1

6.2

6.3

6.4

6.5

Lawyers and artisans in the Sons of Liberty encouraged demonstrations against the Stamp Act. But they ran the risk, suggested here, that poor workers, black slaves, and women in the crowds might give their own meanings to the shouts of "Liberty!" Would calls for political freedom become inevitably linked to much broader calls for social equality?

indentures, newspapers, almanacs, and playing cards. Colonial lawyers and printers were to purchase these stamps from designated agents; the official stamp distributor in each colony would receive a handsome fee from all stamp sales. The British treasury anticipated taking in £100,000 per year, to be spent only for government operations in America.

Grenville's stamp bill generated little debate in England. Granted, colonists had no actual representation in the Parliament, but neither did the majority of subjects in England. Most of them did not have the right to vote in Parliamentary elections, yet all were said to be "virtually" represented by MPs, who supposedly had the interests of the entire country at heart. If MPs looked out for nonvoting subjects at home, surely they could provide the same sort of "virtual representation" for British subjects throughout the empire.

Most MPs viewed Grenville's stamp measure as appropriate and well conceived. They saw no legal distinction between external duties used to regulate trade and internal taxes imposed by Parliament within the colonies themselves to raise revenue. Because the stamp tax applied to daily articles used throughout the colonies, its mild burden would be widely distributed. Even better, revenues would grow steadily as colonial economic activity continued to expand.

So as not to cause alarm in the colonies, Parliament set initial stamp prices in America lower than those charged in England, although it could always raise the rates as colonists grew accustomed to the tax. Moreover, the tax was to be gathered quietly by Americans themselves in the course of doing business rather than extracted from citizens by tax collectors. Prominent colonists were eager to accept the lucrative stamp distributorships, and no one predicted an upheaval in ports where the stamps were to be sold. But the Stamp Act soon unleashed a storm of organized resistance.

The Stamp Act Resisted

At first, colonial assemblies had mixed responses to the new tax. But in late May, the youngest member of the Virginia House of Burgesses—a rising attorney named Patrick Henry—galvanized American resistance to the Stamp Act. As the House session was winding down, Henry introduced a series of fiery resolves challenging Parliament's right to impose taxes. The twenty-eight-year-old orator gained narrow passage of five separate resolutions.

Henry's fifth and most provocative resolve asserted that Virginia's assembly had the "sole exclusive right and power to lay taxes" on the colony's inhabitants. The resolution passed by just one vote. In fact, opponents reintroduced it the next day, after Henry left town, and voted it down. But the spark had been struck. Distant newspapers were soon reprinting Henry's "Virginia Resolves," including the resolution that had been voted down plus two that had been drawn up but never introduced for a vote. These provocative draft resolutions said that Virginians were "not bound to yield obedience" to such a tax, and anyone arguing otherwise must "be deemed an enemy" to the colony.

In Massachusetts, the assembly took a different approach. It issued a call for each colony to send delegates to a Stamp Act Congress in New York in October 1765 to "implore relief" from Parliament. Local citizens, inflamed by Virginia's resolutions and squeezed by an economic depression, prepared to take more direct action. In Boston, a small group of artisans and merchants known as the Loyal Nine mobilized to force the designated stamp distributor, Andrew Oliver, to resign before the stamps arrived from England. On August 16, a crowd of several thousand hanged an effigy of Oliver and tore down his Stamp Office. The protesters ransacked Oliver's elegant house, drinking his wine and smashing his furniture. The next day, Oliver resigned his appointment.

As word of the protest spread, crowds took to the streets in scores of towns. Often the mobs were encouraged by local leaders who opposed the Stamp Act. These prominent citizens had started to organize themselves in secret groups, which they called the Sons of Liberty. The crowds forced the resignation of potential stamp distributors in ports from New Hampshire to the Carolinas. When a shipment of stamps finally arrived in New York City, nearly 5,000 people risked open warfare to confiscate the hated cargo.

Throughout the second half of 1765, the Sons of Liberty promoted street violence against specific targets. But they could not always control the demonstrations, since the debtors, sailors, blacks, and women drawn to such crowds all had separate grievances of their own. For example, on August 26 in Boston, just ten days after the raid on Oliver's house, a second mob launched a broader assault. Without sanction from the Loyal Nine or the Sons of Liberty, the crowd went after the homes of several wealthy office holders, including the house of Lieutenant Governor Thomas Hutchinson. Because he also

✳ Explore the Imperial Crisis on MyHistoryLab

WHY DID WIDESPREAD UNREST REACH THE THIRTEEN COLONIES BY THE 1760S?

At the end of the Seven Years' War in 1763, colonists in British North America were proud to be part of the world's largest empire. Soon, though, allegiance to the empire started to fade as Parliament in London sought ways to pay for the costly war by imposing various revenue taxes on American colonists across the Atlantic. Colonists began to protest that Parliament's actions violated their rights as British subjects, and the famous cry "No Taxation without Representation!" echoed up and down the thirteen colonies. Taxation schemes sparked demonstrations in the American colonies, and some subjects even turned to violence.

The Boston Massacre occurred when British soldiers fired on a mob in Boston on March 5, 1770, and killed five civilians. This propaganda illustration depicts the event as an unprovoked atrocity. *Library of Congress.*

RIOTS OF THE 1760s

Year	Colony	Location	Year	Colony	Location
1760	New York	New York City	1766	Connecticut	New Haven, New London
1763–1764	Pennsylvania	Lancaster, Millerstown, Philadelphia		Massachusetts (Maine)	Falmouth
1764	Massachusetts	Dighton		New York	Dutchess County
	New York	New York City		Virginia	Norfolk
	Rhode Island	Newport	1767	Virginia	Norfolk
1765	Massachusetts	Boston, Northampton	1767–1769	South Carolina	Western frontier
	New York	New York City	1768	Massachusetts	Boston
	North Carolina	Mecklenburg County		North Carolina	Hillsborough
	Pennsylvania	Cumberland County		Virginia	Norfolk
	Rhode Island	Newport	1769	Connecticut	New Haven, New London
1765 and 1769	Pennsylvania	Conococheague Valley		Pennsylvania	Philadelphia
1765–1771	North Carolina	Anson, Cumberland, Granville, Orange, and Rowan counties		Rhode Island	Newport
			Late 1760s	New York	New York City
				Rhode Island	Newport, Providence

KEY QUESTIONS Use **MyHistoryLab** *Explorer* to answer these **questions:**

Consequence ▶▶▶ *How did differences in regional agricultural production influence colonists' reactions to revenue acts?*

Map the various crops grown in the colonies to see this connection.

Cause ▶▶▶ *What sorts of mob actions were launched by the colonists?*

Chart the riotous manifestations to understand the range of grievances of colonists.

Analysis ▶▶▶ *Where did crowds of colonists take action against Parliament's new regulations?*

Consider the factors that may have affected the geographical distribution of these actions.

📖 **Read** the **Document**   The Closing of the Frontier (1763)

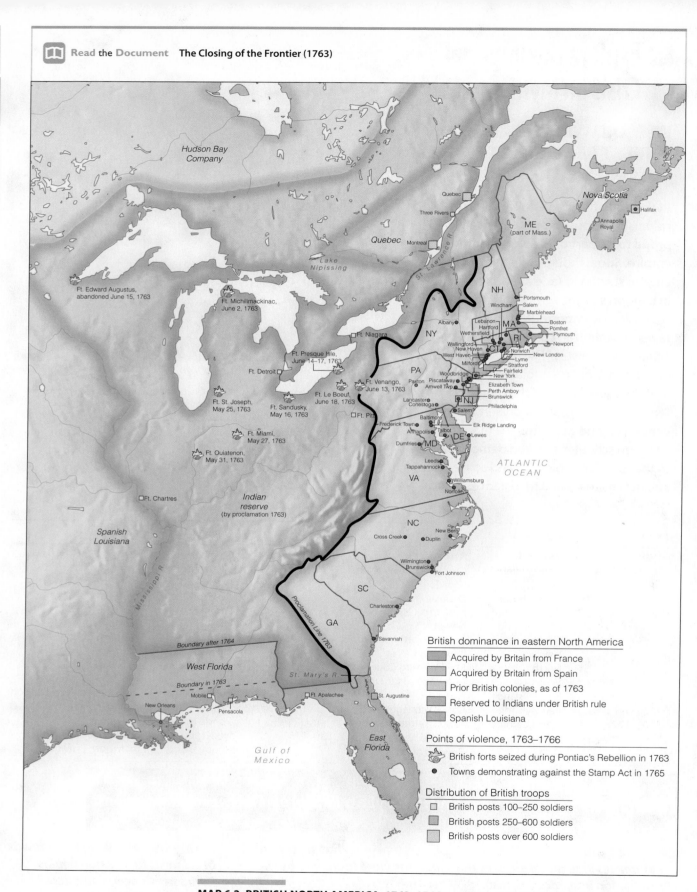

Hudson Bay
Company

Quebec

Three Rivers

Nova Scotia

Halifax

Annapolis
Royal

ME
(part of Mass.)

Quebec

Montreal

Lake
Nipissing

Ft. Edward Augustus,
abandoned June 15, 1763

Ft. Michilimackinac,
June 2, 1763

NH

Portsmouth
Windham   Salem
Marblehead

Albany
Lebanon
Hartford   MA   Boston
Pomfret
Plymouth
Wethersfield   RI
Wallingford   Norwich
New Haven   Newport
West Haven   New London
Milford   Lyme
Stratford
Woodbridge   Fairfield
New York

Ft. Niagara

NY

Ft. Presque Isle,
June 14–17, 1763

Ft. Detroit

PA

Paxton
Ft. Venango,
June 13, 1763

Amwell Twp.
Piscataway
Elizabeth Town
Perth Amboy
Brunswick
NJ

Ft. St. Joseph,
May 25, 1763

Ft. Sandusky,
May 16, 1763

Ft. Le Boeuf,
June 18, 1763

Lancaster
Conestoga
Salem
Philadelphia

Ft. Pitt

Ft. Miami,
May 27, 1763

Frederick Town
Baltimore
Talbot   Elk Ridge Landing
DE
Annapolis   Lewes
Dumfries   MD

Ft. Ouiatenon,
May 31, 1763

Leeds
Tappahannock

Ft. Chartres

Indian
reserve
(by proclamation 1763)

VA

Williamsburg

Norfolk

ATLANTIC
OCEAN

Spanish
Louisiana

NC

New Bern

Cross Creek   Duplin

Wilmington
Brunswick
Fort Johnson

SC

Charleston

Boundary after 1764

GA

West Florida

Boundary in 1763

Mobile

New Orleans

Pensacola

Savannah

Proclamation Line 1763

St. Mary's R.

Ft. Apalachee

St. Augustine

Gulf of
Mexico

East
Florida

British dominance in eastern North America

- Acquired by Britain from France
- Acquired by Britain from Spain
- Prior British colonies, as of 1763
- Reserved to Indians under British rule
- Spanish Louisiana

Points of violence, 1763–1766

- British forts seized during Pontiac's Rebellion in 1763
- Towns demonstrating against the Stamp Act in 1765

Distribution of British troops

- British posts 100–250 soldiers
- British posts 250–600 soldiers
- British posts over 600 soldiers

MAP 6.2 BRITISH NORTH AMERICA, 1763–1766 In 1763, the British worked to govern their new
provinces in Canada and Florida while suppressing an Indian uprising in the Midwest. With widely dispersed
troops, they also tried to keep colonists out of the Mississippi Valley and halt opposition to the 1765 Stamp Act.

served as chief justice of the Superior Court, Hutchinson had offended townspeople by issuing numerous warrants for debtors and collecting large fees for administering bankruptcies. Hutchinson recounted how he fled when "the hellish crew fell upon my house with the Rage of devils and . . . with axes split down the doors."

In South Carolina, the spirit of insurrection also went well beyond the careful boundaries intended by the Sons of Liberty. They were pleased when Charleston artisans hanged a stamp distributor in effigy, with a sign reading, "Liberty and no Stamp Act." And they gave tacit approval when white workers harassed the wealthy slave trader and potential stamp distributor Henry Laurens with chants of "Liberty, Liberty!" Soon, however, enslaved African Americans also took to the streets, raising their own defiant cry of "Liberty, Liberty!" Fearing an insurrection by South Carolina's black majority, the same people who had sanctioned earlier street demonstrations quickly shifted their focus, believing that ideas of freedom had spread too far. The colonial assembly temporarily banned further importation of Africans. Local leaders expanded slave patrols and placed Charleston briefly under martial law.

Elsewhere, too, the colonial elites took steps to contain the turbulence. Many moved—often reluctantly—toward more radical positions, joining the Sons of Liberty and ridiculing the British concept of virtual representation. Colonial assemblies condemned Grenville's intrusive reforms. The Stamp Act Congress passed resolutions vehemently protesting both the Sugar and Stamp Acts. But even as they challenged Parliament, these same local leaders stressed their loyalty to the crown and moved to control the violence, some of which was directed at them. Such moderation appealed to cautious merchants in Atlantic seaports, who reluctantly agreed to stop ordering Britain goods. They hoped that exporters in Britain, feeling the economic pinch of a colonial boycott, might use their political strength to force a repeal of the Stamp Act and defuse the tense situation.

When politics in London prompted Grenville's sudden removal from office, hopes rose in America for a possible compromise resolving the Stamp Act crisis. In March 1766, these hopes were nearly fulfilled. The new ministry of Lord Rockingham, responding to merchant pressure as predicted, and also to the compelling rhetoric of William Pitt, persuaded Parliament to repeal the Stamp Act. But colonial victory seemed hollow, for the repeal bill was accompanied by a blunt Declaratory Act. In it, Parliament declared its power "to make Laws . . . to bind the Colonists and People of America . . . in all Cases whatsoever."

"The Unconquerable Rage of the People"

6.3 How did events in America and Britain in the 1760s confirm the skeptical worldview of "Real Whigs"?

As news of the Stamp Act repeal spread, the Sons of Liberty organized elaborate celebrations in British America. But word of the Declaratory Act had a sobering effect. Clearly, the problems surrounding colonial taxation and representation remained unresolved. The atmosphere of mutual suspicion that had erupted during the Stamp Act crisis divided colonists further in the years ahead. A flurry of pamphlets from colonial presses broadened awareness of the issues and inspired new coalitions in a time of economic recession. As colonial leaders collaborated, they discovered a shared viewpoint that gave added meaning and importance to each new event. This emerging ideology had deep roots stretching back into English history.

Power Corrupts: An English Framework for Revolution

The radical ideas that had appeared during England's Civil War in the 1640s, when English subjects briefly overthrew their monarchy and proclaimed a Puritan Commonwealth, lived on long after the Restoration in 1660. English Whigs who led the Glorious Revolution in 1688 invoked some of these principles when they limited the monarchy's power and strengthened Parliament's authority. Succeeding generations hailed the rights of English subjects and congratulated themselves that Great Britain (as England and Scotland became known in 1707) had achieved a truly **balanced government**. They drew on the ancient Greek philosopher Aristotle to explain their accomplishment.

Aristotle, his modern readers noted, had observed a cycle in politics. He believed that too much power vested in a king could eventually corrupt the monarchical form of government. Unbounded royal power led to a tyranny, misrule by a despot wielding absolute control. When nobles then asserted themselves against the tyrant (as English barons had done when they forced King John to sign the Magna Carta in 1215), the resulting aristocracy could easily turn corrupt. Abuse of power by such an oligarchy of self-serving nobles could then prompt the common people, known as the commons, to rise up. If the commons gained sway, they might build a democracy, but it too could degenerate, leaving only anarchy. Such a "mobocracy" paved the way for an opportunistic leader to once more seize the scepter of royal power and start the cycle over again.

Confident Whigs claimed that England had halted this vicious cycle by balancing the power of the nation's three estates: the king epitomized the legitimate interests of monarchy, the House of Lords represented the aristocracy, and the House of Commons represented the rest of the population. However, a few of the more radical Whig theorists continued to oppose this consensus view long after 1700. Calling themselves the "Real Whigs," these skeptics charged that Britain's mixed government—which claimed an ideal and lasting mixture between monarchy, aristocracy, and commons—was actually less perfect and more vulnerable than most people suspected.

A truly balanced government, they argued, is hard to achieve and difficult to maintain, for power inevitably corrupts. Schemers who obtain public office can readily disrupt such a fragile system, so its protection, these critics stressed, demanded constant vigilance. They urged citizens to watch for the two surest signs of decay: the concentration of wealth in a few hands and the political and social corruption that inevitably follows. Where others saw stability in England's exuberant growth, these Real Whigs perceived clear signs of danger in the powerful new Bank of England, the expanding stock market, and the rise in public debt.

No Real Whigs proved more vigilant than John Trenchard and Thomas Gordon. The two men sensed around them the same luxury and greed that had undermined the Roman Republic. They pored over the works of ancient writers such as the Roman statesman Cato, who described and challenged corrupt behavior. In 1721, they published *Cato's Letters: Essays on Liberty*, offering their own cautions against "the Natural Encroachments of Power" and warning that "public corruptions and abuses have grown upon us."

Trenchard and Gordon took particular offense at Britain's corrupt **patronage system**. Too many people gained public positions through political ties rather than through skill or training. The authors of *Cato's Letters* felt each new act of corruption set a dangerous precedent, if unopposed. They reminded readers that tyranny is usually imposed through small, subtle steps, for "if it is suffered once, it is apt to be repeated often; a few repetitions create a habit." Before citizens realize that they are losing their liberties, the permanent "Yoke of Servitude" is in place, supported by military force. All hope of successful protest has disappeared. The encroachment of power over liberty, Trenchard and Gordon concluded, is "much easier to prevent than to cure."

Americans Practice Vigilance and Restraint

Cato's Letters earned a wide American following during the 1760s, for colonists saw disturbing parallels between the warnings of Real Whig authors and current events in America. Now, as throughout history, a government tainted by corruption might deny adequate representation, initiate unjust taxes, or replace jury trials with arbitrary courts. Officials might curtail freedoms of press or religion to consolidate their power. Moreover, weak ministers might advise the king poorly or keep citizens' pleas from reaching his ears. If the populace relaxed its guard, these ministers might even sanction a standing army in peacetime to impose arbitrary rule over their own population.

Balanced government This idealized form of governance (based on the ideas of Aristotle) was supposed to avoid the pitfalls created by monarchy ("tyranny"), aristocracy ("oligarchy"), and democracy ("mobocracy").

Patronage system Any structure where individuals—in order to obtain a post, retain it, or advance—must rely more on inside connections and networks of friends than upon superior competence, effort, or dedication.

According to Real Whig doctrine, ordinary people must be alert but circumspect; a measured response to these threats was all-important. One stubborn or mistaken act by officials did not prove a pattern of conspiracy, and it could be counterproductive to raise alarms too often. So prudent citizens should turn first to legal methods of **redress**. If the system was functioning properly, claims of real abuses would bring forth proper corrections. Even if forced to take to the streets as a last resort, crowds should be organized, not uncontrolled. They should threaten property before people and hang effigies, not actual office holders.

Redress A remedy for a wrong; a correction or reparation. As a verb, to redress means to correct, to set right, or to remove the cause of a grievance.

For the most part, the Stamp Act demonstrations had followed this logic of restraint and had gained the desired effect. "In every Colony," wrote John Adams, "the Stamp Distributors and Inspectors have been compelled, by the unconquerable Rage of the People, to renounce their offices." But did individual demands for liberty have limits? Could slaves seek liberty from their masters? What about wives from husbands? Could tenants press for redress from rich landlords, or debtors from powerful creditors? Such questions generated widespread, heated debate in the turbulent quarter-century ahead.

Rural Unrest: Tenant Farmers and Regulators

In local controversies, both large and small, the "Rage of the People" frequently boiled up from below. "The People, even to the lowest Ranks, have become more attentive to their Liberties," John Adams observed, "and more determined to defend them." While stamp protesters demonstrated in New York City, aggrieved tenant farmers staged a violent revolt against powerful landholders in the Hudson River valley. They chose an Irish immigrant as their leader, established a council, organized militia companies with elected captains, and broke open jails to free debtors. They even set up their own people's courts to try captured Hudson Valley gentry, before British troops finally suppressed the revolt.

Unrest also shook the Carolinas in the interior region known to colonists as the backcountry, or the Piedmont. In South Carolina, the absence of civil government beyond the coastal parishes fostered lawlessness among white settlers until the governor extended circuit courts into the interior in 1769. In North Carolina, migrants seeking fertile land moved south from Virginia and Pennsylvania in a steady stream. When they arrived in the Piedmont, they found a local elite already appointed to county posts by the governor. The newcomers disliked these grasping office holders who possessed strong family and financial ties to powerful planters and merchants farther east. They seemed to epitomize, at the local level, the sorts of corruption that had long troubled Real Whig pamphleteers.

As backcountry settlers grew in numbers, they protested against their inadequate representation in North Carolina's assembly. They began organizing into local groups to better "regulate" their own affairs, and they soon became known as Regulators. These small farmers, many in debt, protested loudly against regressive taxes that imposed the same burden on all colonists, regardless of their wealth. The Regulators' discontent turned into outrage when coastal planters who dominated the assembly voted public funds to build a stately mansion in New Bern for William Tryon, the colonial governor. By this act, the eastern slaveholding elite hoped to establish North Carolina's permanent capitol building on the coast, and yet Piedmont farmers would bear most of the cost of constructing the mansion.

The decision to erect "Tryon's Palace" at public expense confirmed backcountry suspicions that leading officials were looking out for their own interests at the expense of the public. Both sides dug in their heels. In 1771, Governor Tryon finally called out the militia and marched into the Piedmont. After defeating several thousand angry farmers at the battle of Alamance in May 1771, Tryon hanged six Regulator leaders in Hillsborough and forced the farmers to swear an oath of loyalty. Many refused, migrating farther south to Georgia or west to the Appalachian Mountains. Their leader, a Quaker named Herman Husband, barely escaped with his life. In North Carolina, just as in the Hudson Valley, well-to-do members of the Sons of Liberty dismissed the organized and militant farmers as misguided rabble.

Interpreting History
"Squez'd and Oppressed": A 1768 PETITION BY THIRTY REGULATORS

"To **Gentlemen** Rowling in *affluence*, a few **shillings** per man may seem *trifling*."

In the 1760s, corruption prevailed among appointed officials in central North Carolina. Often holding numerous offices at once, these men managed elections, controlled courts, and gathered taxes. Apparently not all the tax money they collected made it to the public treasury. Nevertheless, any farmer who resisted paying might lose the plow horse or the milk cow that sustained the family. It could be "seized and sold" to cover a small tax payment or minor debt, with "no Part being ever Return'd" from the proceeds.

Banding together to better regulate their own affairs, these farmers sought relief through every possible legal means. By 1768, these organized Regulators had exhausted most avenues of peaceful protest. The western counties where they resided were badly underrepresented in the colonial assembly. As a new session prepared to convene, they fired off a final round of petitions, assuring legislators that they were law-abiding citizens willing to pay their legal share of taxes. In this message of October 4, 1768, thirty Regulators begged for the appointment of honest public officials.

In 1768, the creation of Tryon's Palace, a mansion for the North Carolina governor at New Bern, prompted backcountry protests. Irate farm families, feeling heavily taxed and poorly represented, joined the Regulator Movement. They filed petitions, withheld taxes, closed courts, and harassed corrupt officials, What justifications did they have for protesting the "unequal chances the poor and weak have in contentions with the rich and powerful"?

To the Worshipful House of Representatives of North Carolina

Your Poor Petitioners [have] been Continually Squez'd and oppressed by our Publick Officers both with Regard to their fees as also in the Laying on of Taxes as well as in Collecting. . . . Being Grieved thus to have our substance torn from us [by] . . . such Illegal practices, we applied to our public officers to give us some satisfaction . . . which they Repeatedly denied us.

With Regard to the Taxes, . . . we labour under Extreem hardships. . . . Money is very scarce . . . & we exceeding Poor & lie at a great distance from Trade which renders it almost Impossible to gain sustenance by our utmost Endeavours. . . .

To Gentlemen Rowling in affluence, a few shillings per man may seem triffling. Yet to Poor People who must have their Bed and Bedclothes, yea their Wives Petticoats, taken and sold to Defray, how Tremenious [tremendous] . . . must be the Consequences. . . . Therefore, dear Gentlemen, to your selves, to your Country, and in Pity to your Poor Petitioners, do not let it stand any longer to Drink up the Blood and vitals of the Poor Distressed.

After seeking relief from existing taxes, the petitioners went on to question new burdens, such as the law imposing an additional tax "to Erect a Publick Edifice" for Governor William Tryon in New Bern.

Good God, Gentlemen, what will become of us when these Demands come against us? Paper Money we have none & gold or silver we can Purchase none of. The Contingencies of Government Must be Paid, and . . . we are Willing to Pay, [even] if we [must] sell our Beds from under us. And [yet] in this Time of Distress, it is as much as we can support. . . . If, therefore, the Law for that Purpose can be happily Repealed, . . . May the God of Heaven Inspire you with sentiments to that Purpose.

We humble Begg you would . . . Use your Influence with our Worthy, Virtuous Governor to discontinue . . . such Officers as would be found to be ye Bane of Society, and [instead to] Put in the Common Wealth [officials willing] to Encourage the Poor and . . . to stand [up] for them. This would Cause Joy and Gladness to Spring from every Heart. This would cause Labour and Industry to prevail over Murmuring Discontent. This would Raise your poor Petitioners . . . to a flourishing Opulent and Hoping People. Otherwise . . . disatisfaction and Melancholy must Prevail over such as Remain, and Numbers must Defect the Province and seek elsewhere an Asylum from Tyranny and Oppression. . . .

We leave it to you . . . in your great Wisdom . . . to pass such Act or Acts, as shall be Conducive to the welbeing of a whole People over Whose welfare ye are plac'd as Guardians. . . . For the Lords Sake, Gentlemen, Exert your selves this once in our favour.

Questions for Discussion

1. How, specifically, do the tone and content of this petition reflect the widespread political outlook, combining vigilance and restraint, described in *Cato's Letters*?
2. Pick some current issue that concerns you deeply and draft a brief, impassioned petition to your legislators. In compelling language, lay out your best arguments for action. Then see if 30 people will sign your petition.

SOURCE: William S. Powell, James K. Huhta, and Thomas J. Farnham, eds., *The Regulators of North Carolina: A Documentary History, 1759–1776* (Raleigh: State Department of Archives and History, 1971), pp. 187–189.

A Conspiracy of Corrupt Ministers?

6.4 Did the Boston Massacre highlight justifiable colonial grievances, or was it a provoked attack, exploited by dissidents?

Numerous sharp divisions—some leading to armed conflict—continued to separate colonists of different classes and regions. But ill-timed steps by successive administrations in London attracted widening attention throughout British America, prompting uneasy new alliances. Colonists familiar with the dire warnings of Real Whig pamphleteers asked themselves a question: in the weak and short-lived ministries that succeeded Grenville's, were the leaders simply ill-informed, or were they actively corrupt? Colonists wondered whether some official conspiracy existed to chip away at American liberties. Even loyal defenders of the crown expressed frustration with new policies that appeared too harsh to calm irate colonists, yet too weak to force them into line.

Parliament's first new imposition after repeal of the Stamp Act was the Revenue Act of 1766. The act further reduced the molasses duty, from threepence per gallon to a single penny, to discourage smuggling and raise revenue. Colonial merchants accepted this measure as an external tax designed to regulate imperial trade. Most paid the new duty, and customs revenues rose. But the Real Whigs' warnings reminded colonists that compliance with seemingly innocuous legislation could set a dangerous precedent.

The skeptics had a point, for Parliament soon imposed new hard-line measures. Before his sudden death in 1767, Charles Townshend, the Chancellor of the Exchequer (or chief finance minister) put these distasteful statutes in motion. Townshend's new duties sparked angry reactions from colonists. The most telling reply came from John Dickinson, a moderate Philadelphia lawyer. He drafted a series of widely circulated "Letters from a Farmer in Pennsylvania," urging colonists to respond "peaceably—prudently—firmly—jointly." He dismissed any distinction between external and internal taxation, and he also rejected the idea that Americans had virtual representation in Parliament. "We are taxed without our own consent," Dickinson proclaimed to his readers. "We are therefore—SLAVES."

The Townshend Duties Prompt an American Boycott

In search of funds, Parliament passed the Townshend Revenue Act of 1767. It obliged colonists to pay duties on imported glass, paint, lead, paper, and tea. Proceeds were to be spent in the colonies for "the administration of justice, and the support of civil government," a seemingly benevolent gesture. But Dickinson and other colonists pointed out what these two phrases actually meant. "The administration of justice" cloaked expanded searches of American homes and shops in which customs officers used hated "writs of assistance" to ferret out smuggled goods. "The support of civil government" ensured that governors and appointed office holders could draw their pay directly from the new duties instead of depending on an annual salary grant from the local assembly. In short, the new act removed from colonial legislatures one of their strongest bargaining tools in dealing with the crown: the power to pay or withhold yearly salaries for key officials sent from Britain.

Similar acts and instructions followed. Asserting its sovereignty, Parliament disciplined the New York Assembly for defying the Quartering Act of 1765. The crown instructed governors in America, now less dependent for their salaries on colonial lower houses, to disapprove any measures from legislatures asserting their traditional control over how members were chosen, what their numbers should be, and when they would meet. Equally galling, the Customs Act of 1767 established a separate Board of Customs for British North America. Ominously, the commissioners would live in Boston rather than London. To strengthen the board's hand, in 1768, Britain expanded the number of vice-admiralty courts in North America from one to four, adding new courts in Boston, Philadelphia, and Charleston. Furthermore, to look after its trouble-some mainland colonies, the British government created a new American Department, overseen by Lord Hillsborough. It also began to move British troops in America from remote frontier outposts to major Atlantic ports, both as a cost-cutting measure and as a show of force.

Americans found these measures threatening, especially when considered as a whole. In February 1768, the Massachusetts legislature, led by forty-six-year-old Samuel Adams, petitioned the king for redress. The legislators circulated a call to other colonial assemblies for similar protests. Condemning the Townshend Revenue Act as uncon-stitutional, they argued that it imposed taxation without representation. By removing control of the governors' salaries from colonial legislatures, they said, Parliament set the dangerous precedent of making royal officials "independent of the people." Lord Hillsborough demanded an immediate retraction of this provocative "Circular Letter" and ordered the dissolution of any assembly that took up the matter.

In June, events in Boston took a more radical turn. Defying Hillsborough, the Massachusetts assembly voted against rescinding its circular letter. On June 5, a dockside crowd faced down a "press-gang" from a British warship and protected local sailors from being forced (or "pressed") into naval service. Five days later, customs officials seized John Hancock's sloop, *Liberty*, and demanded that he pay import duties for a cargo of Madeira wine. This move sparked a huge demonstration as citizens dragged a small customs boat through the streets and then burned it on Boston Common. Impa-tient Sam Adams was heard to say, "Let us take up arms immediately and be free."

Emotions ran high. But most leaders sensed that any escalation of the violence would be premature and perhaps suicidal. They reined in demonstrations and instead initiated a boycott of British goods. Nonimportation plans called upon colonists to refrain from imported luxuries and opt instead for virtuous self-sufficiency. The pros-pect of nonviolent resistance held broad appeal. As the nonimportation movement expanded, women of all ranks, self-proclaimed Daughters of Liberty, turned to mak-ing and selling homespun garments. Local associations sprang up, pledging to forgo imported tea and London fashions. A dozen colonial assemblies voted to halt importa-tion of selected goods. In New York, the value of imports from Britain shrank from £491,000 to just £76,000 in a single year.

The damage to English shipping proved substantial. Britain was losing far more revenue in colonial trade than it was gaining through the expanded customs duties. Soon, influential British exporters were pressing their government for relief. Baron Frederick North had succeeded Townshend as Chancellor of the Exchequer in 1767. When he became Prime Minister in January 1770, he received the king's consent to work toward a better arrangement with the colonies. Lord North quickly persuaded Parliament to repeal all the Townshend Duties except the one on tea. The move defused the colonial boycott, but it offered too little, too late. Like the earlier Declaratory Act, this measure reaffirmed Parliament's disputed right to tax the colonists at will. More-over, the repeal came on March 5, 1770, the exact day that violence escalated in Boston.

The Boston Massacre

After the *Liberty* riot in June 1768, tensions had mounted in Boston, especially with the arrival in October of two regiments of British soldiers, well armed and dressed in their traditional red coats. According to Real Whig beliefs, any appearance by a stand-ing army in peacetime constituted danger. Artisans in a sluggish economy welcomed the increased business that the men in uniform generated, but numerous unemployed workers resented the soldiers' "moonlighting," trying to earn extra pay by applying for local jobs. With 4,000 armed men encamped in a seaport of scarcely 16,000, confronta-tion seemed inevitable. Affairs "cannot long remain in the state they are now in," wrote one observer late in 1769; "they are hastening to a crisis. What will be the event, God knows."

📖 **Read** the Document   *Boston Gazette,* Description of the Boston Massacre (1770)

6.1

6.2

6.3

6.4

6.5

In Paul Revere's image of the 1770 Boston Massacre, soldiers defend the hated customs house by moonlight, while a sniper fires from a window clearly labeled "Butcher's Hall." How might Revere's partisan engraving of the uneven fight help to spread an anti-British view of the bloody event?

In March 1770, protesters took to the streets after a run-in between local workers and job-seeking soldiers. Rumors spread about a larger confrontation, and on March 5, around 9 P.M., a crowd gathered outside the customs house. When a harassed sentry struck a boy with his rifle butt, angry witnesses pelted the guard with snowballs. As fellow soldiers pushed through the mob to assist him, firebells summoned more townspeople to the scene. The British fixed their bayonets, loaded their rifles, and aimed at the crowd.

Into this tense standoff marched several dozen sailors, waving banners and brandishing clubs. Their leader was Crispus Attucks, an imposing ex-slave who stood 6 feet 2 inches. The son of a black man and an Indian woman, he had run away from his master and then taken up a life at sea. Damning the soldiers and daring them to fire, Attucks pressed his band of colonial sailors to the front, waving a long stick in the moonlight. In the mayhem, a British gun went off, prompting a volley of fire from the other soldiers. The crowd recoiled in disbelief at the sight of dead and wounded Americans lying in the street. According to a printed report, Attucks and four others had been "killed on the Spot." The anti-British cause had its first martyrs.

By grim coincidence, the bloody episode in New England occurred only hours after Lord North addressed the House of Commons to urge removal of most Townshend Duties. His effort at reconciliation immediately became lost in a wave of hostile publicity. Paul Revere, a Boston silversmith, captured the incident in an inflammatory engraving that circulated widely. The Sons of Liberty quickly named the event of March 5 the Boston Massacre. "On that night," John Adams remarked, "the foundation of American independence was laid."

Creating Committees of Correspondence

Everywhere, crown officials who appeared overzealous aroused further resentment and distrust. After customs officers confiscated John Hancock's sloop, the *Liberty*, and refitted it as an armed cruiser to patrol for customs violators, angry Rhode Island citizens attacked and scuttled the vessel in 1769. In the Delaware River region, residents jailed a customs collector in 1770, and the next year, local protesters stormed a customs schooner and beat up the crew. In June 1772, the *Gaspée*, another customs boat said to harass local shipping, ran aground near Pawtuxet, Rhode Island. In a midnight attack, more than a hundred local raiders descended on the stranded schooner and set fire to the vessel.

The destruction of the *Gaspée* renewed sharp antagonisms. The irate Earl of Hillsborough, secretary of state for the American colonies, sent a royal commission from London to investigate and to transport suspects to England for trial. But many of the attackers, such as John Brown of Providence, came from important Rhode Island families. Even a £500 reward could not induce local inhabitants to name participants. Besides, many viewed the order to deport accused citizens to England as a denial of their fundamental right to trial by a jury of their peers.

When the colonists took action, Virginia's House of Burgesses again led the way, as it had in the Stamp Act crisis. In March 1773, Patrick Henry, Thomas Jefferson, and Richard Henry Lee pushed through a resolution establishing a standing committee to look into the *Gaspée* affair and to keep up "Correspondence and Communication with our sister colonies" regarding the protection of rights. Following Virginia's example, ten other colonial legislatures promptly established their own Committees of Correspondence. In Massachusetts, local communities formed similar committees, linking individual towns. Within months, a new act of Parliament, designed to rescue the powerful East India Company from bankruptcy, gave these emerging communication networks their first test.

Launching a Revolution

6.5 Could the British, through a more creative response to the Boston Tea Party, have averted the ensuing escalation toward violence?

I n 1767, before Parliament imposed the Townshend Duties, Americans annually imported nearly 870,000 pounds of tea from England. But the boycott movement cut that amount to less than 110,000 pounds by 1770; colonists turned to smuggling Dutch blends and brewing homemade root teas. When nonimportation schemes lapsed in the early 1770s, purchase of English tea resumed, though a duty remained in effect. Encouraged by this apparent acceptance of parliamentary taxation, Lord North addressed the problem facing the British East India Company, which owed a huge debt to the Bank of England and had 18 million pounds of unsold tea rotting in London warehouses. Many MPs held stock in the East India Company, so Parliament passed a law to assist the ailing establishment.

The Tempest over Tea

The Tea Act of 1773 let the struggling East India Company bypass the expensive requirement that merchants ship Asian tea through England on its way to colonial ports. Now they could send the product directly to the colonies or to foreign ports, without paying to unload, store, auction, and reload the heavy chests. Any warehouse tea destined for the colonies would have its English duty refunded. These steps would reduce retail prices and expand the tea market. They would also quietly confirm the right of Parliament to collect a tea tax of threepence per pound.

The company promptly chose prominent colonial merchants to receive and distribute more than 600,000 pounds of tea. These consignees would earn a hefty 6 percent commission. But wary colonists in port towns, sensing a repetition of 1765, renewed the tactics that had succeeded against the Stamp Act. Sons of Liberty vowed to prevent tea-laden ships from docking, and crowds pressured local distributors to renounce participation in the scheme. "If they succeed in the sale of that tea," proclaimed New York's Sons of Liberty, "then we may bid adieu to American liberty."

In Boston, where tea worth nearly £10,000 arrived aboard three ships in November, tension ran especially high. The credibility of Governor Thomas Hutchinson, who had taken a hard line toward imperial dissent, had suffered in June when Benjamin Franklin published private correspondence suggesting the governor's willingness to trim colonial rights. When Hutchinson's sons were named tea consignees, the appointments reinforced townspeople's suspicions. The governor could have signed papers letting the three vessels depart. But instead he decided to unload and distribute the tea, by force if necessary.

On December 16, the largest mass meeting of the decade took place at Boston's Old South Church. A crowd of 5,000, including many from other towns, waited in a cold rain to hear whether Hutchinson would relent. When word came that the governor had refused, the cry went up, "Boston Harbor a teapot tonight!" A band of 150 men, disguised as Mohawk Indians and carrying hatchets, marched to the docks and boarded the ships.

As several thousand supporters looked on, this disciplined crew spent three hours methodically breaking open chests of tea and dumping the contents overboard. The well-organized operation united participants representing all levels of society—from merchants such as John Hancock to artisans such as George Hewes—and news of the event spurred similar acts of defiance in other ports. Sixty years later, as one of the oldest veterans of the Revolution, Hewes still recalled with special pride his role in "the destruction of the tea."

The Intolerable Acts

"The crisis is come," wrote General Thomas Gage, commander of British forces in America, responding to the costly Tea Party in Boston Harbor; "the provinces must be either British colonies, or independent and separate states." Underestimating the strength of American resolve, Parliament agreed with King George III that only stern measures would reestablish "the obedience which a colony owes to its mother country." Between March and June 1774, it passed four so-called Coercive Acts to isolate and punish Massachusetts.

The first of the Coercive Acts, the Boston Port Act, used British naval strength to cut off the offending town's sea commerce—except for shipments of food and firewood—until the colonists paid for the ruined tea. By the Administration of Justice Act, revenue officials or soldiers charged with murder in Massachusetts (as in the Boston Massacre) could have their trials moved to another colony or to Great Britain. The Quartering Act gave officers more power to requisition living quarters and supplies for their troops in the colonies. Most important, the Massachusetts Government Act removed democratic elements from the longstanding Massachusetts Charter of 1691. From now on, the assembly could no longer elect the colony's Upper House, or Council. Instead, the governor would appoint council members, and any locality would need his written permission to hold a town meeting.

Nº X   Engraved for Royal American Magazine.   Vol. I.

The able Doctor or America Swallowing the Bitter Draught.

Four years after Paul Revere made his powerful engraving of the Boston Massacre, the silversmith made an even angrier cartoon to protest the Coercive Acts of 1774. In retaliation for the Boston Tea Party, Parliament has closed the port of Boston to shipping, and British troops are imposing "Military Law." Petitions for relief have been cast aside, and "able Doctor" North is imposing a "bitter draught" of tea on prostrate America, aided by violent and lascivious British officials. What message is conveyed by Mother Britain, who turns away and hides her eyes, instead of using her spear and shield to protect her colonial "daughter" from abuse?

Lord North's government went even further. It replaced Hutchinson with Gage, installing the general as the governor of Massachusetts and granting him special powers and three additional regiments. It also secured passage of the Quebec Act, new legislation to address nagging problems of governance in Canada after a decade of English rule. The act accommodated the Catholic faith and French legal traditions of Quebec's inhabitants. Moreover, it greatly expanded the size of the colony to draw scattered French settlers and traders under colonial government. Suddenly, Quebec took in the entire Great Lakes region and all the lands north of the Ohio River and east of the upper Mississippi River.

Expanding the province of Quebec to the Ohio River might extend British government to French wilderness outposts and help to regulate the Indian trade. But the move also challenged the western land claims of other American colonies. The Quebec Act appeared to favor French Catholics and Ohio Valley Indians—both recent enemies of the crown—over loyal English colonists. Resentment ran especially high in New England, where Protestants had long associated Catholicism with despotism. The Quebec Act, which denied the former French province a representative assembly and jury trials in civil cases, set an ominous precedent for neighboring colonies.

The Coercive Acts and the Quebec Act—lumped together by colonial propagandists as the Intolerable Acts—brought on open rebellion against crown rule. Competing pamphlets debated the proper limits of dissent. *A Summary View of the Rights of British America*, a tract written by Thomas Jefferson in 1774, went beyond criticisms of Parliament to question the king's right to dispense land, control trade, and impose troops in America. Within months, Massachusetts called for a congress of all the colonies and established its own Provincial Congress at Concord, a village 17 miles west of Boston. Out of reach of British naval power, this **de facto** Massachusetts government

De facto Latin phrase meaning "in reality," sometimes applied to a government that is exercising real power, though it has not been legally constituted.

reorganized the militia into units loyal to its own Committee of Public Safety. These farmer-soldiers became known as Minutemen for their quick response to Gage's repeated efforts to capture patriot gunpowder supplies.

From Words to Action

While Massachusetts chafed under new restrictions, shifting coalitions in each colony, ranging from conservative to radical, vied for local political control. Extralegal committees, existing outside the authorized structure of colonial government, took power in hundreds of hamlets. In Edenton, North Carolina, fifty-one women signed a pact to abstain from using imported products for the "publick good." London cartoonists mocked the action as the "Edenton Ladies' Tea Party," but women in other colonies made similar agreements to boycott British tea and textiles. During the summer, all colonies except Georgia selected representatives to the First Continental Congress.

In September 1774, fifty-six delegates convened at Carpenters Hall in Philadelphia. Most had never met before, and they disagreed sharply over how to respond to the Intolerable Acts. Joseph Galloway, a wealthy lawyer and land speculator from Pennsylvania, urged a compromise with Britain modeled on the Albany Congress of 1754. His plan called for the creation of a separate American parliament, a grand council with delegates elected by the colonial legislatures. The less conservative delegates opposed this idea for a colonial federation, under a president-general appointed by the king. Led by Patrick Henry of Virginia, they managed to table the Galloway Plan by a narrow vote.

When Paul Revere arrived from Boston on October 6, bearing a set of militant resolves passed in his own Suffolk County, further rifts appeared. Moderates from the South expressed sympathy for Massachusetts but still resisted calls for a non-exportation scheme that would withhold southern tobacco, rice, and indigo from Great Britain. By the time the Congress adjourned in late October, it had issued a Declaration of Rights and passed a range of measures that seemed to balance competing views. On one hand, the Congress endorsed the fiery Suffolk Resolves, which condemned Parliament's Coercive Acts as unconstitutional and spoke of preparation for war. On the other, it humbly petitioned the king for relief from the crisis and professed continued loyalty. But in practical terms, Galloway and the more conservative members had suffered defeat. Most importantly, the delegates signed an agreement to prohibit British imports and halt all exports to Britain except rice. They called for local committees to enforce this so-called Association, and they set a date—May 10, 1775—for a Second Congress.

Before delegates could meet again in Philadelphia, the controversy that had smoldered for more than a decade on both sides of the Atlantic erupted into open combat. Predictably, the explosion took place in Massachusetts, where General Gage had received secret orders to arrest the leaders of the Massachusetts Provincial Congress and regain the upper hand before the strained situation grew worse. He was to use force, even if it meant the outbreak of warfare.

On April 18, Gage ordered 700 elite troops from Boston to row across the Charles River at night, march ten miles to Lexington, and seize John Hancock and Sam Adams. Next, the soldiers were to proceed seven miles to Concord to capture a stockpile of military supplies. Alerted by signal lanterns, express riders Paul Revere and William Dawes eluded British patrols and spurred their horses toward Lexington along separate routes to warn Hancock and Adams. Bells and alarm guns spread the word that the British were coming. By the time the British soldiers reached Lexington, shortly before sunrise, some seventy militiamen had assembled on the town green. When the villagers refused to lay down their arms, the redcoats dispersed them in a brief skirmish that left eight militiamen dead.

Rising colonial unrest brought on strong countermeasures. The British government organized regional vice-admiralty courts to punish smugglers; it greatly expanded Quebec in 1774; and it imposed a military governor on Massachusetts, reinforced with

✳ **Explore the Topic**   Challenges to British Power, 1763–1775

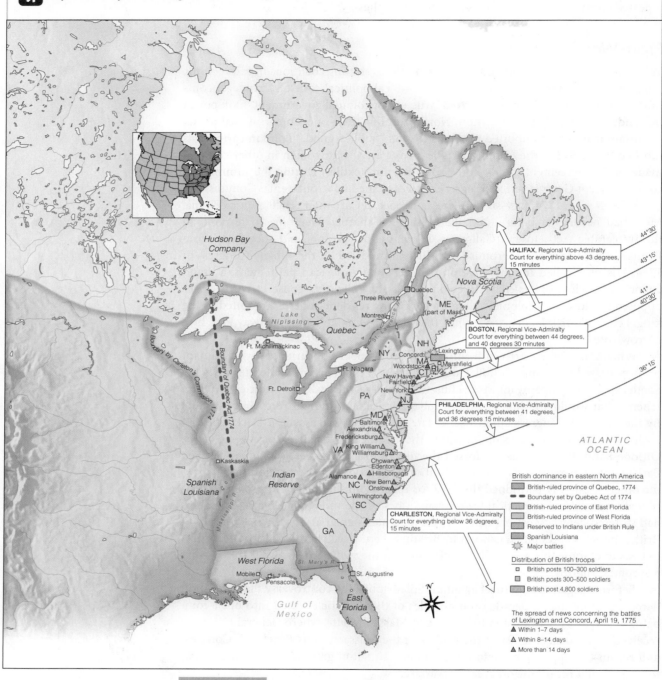

MAP 6.3 BRITISH NORTH AMERICA, APRIL 1775 The Paris Peace Treaty of 1763 redrew the political map of North America. Britain's triumph over France and Spain disrupted diverse power balances, so tensions ran high. Over the next dozen years, American subjects of the crown, old and new, eyed neighbors warily and prepared to defend their rights. This generated fresh problems for London.

special powers and additional regiments. When warfare erupted near Boston in April 1775, the news spread throughout the colonies within weeks.

The British column trudged west to Concord and searched the town for munitions. Four hundred Minutemen who had streamed in from neighboring communities advanced on the town in double file, with orders not to shoot unless the British fired first. At the small bridge over the Concord River, British regulars opened fire. "The shot heard 'round the world" killed two men. The Americans loosed a volley in return, killing three. By noon, exhausted British forces were retreating toward Boston in disarray.

More than a thousand Minutemen, shooting from behind stone walls along the route, found the redcoats made easy targets. A relief party prevented annihilation, but the British suffered severe losses: 73 killed and 200 wounded or missing. The Americans, with only 49 dead, had turned the tables on General Gage, transforming an aggressive raid into a punishing defeat.

Conclusion

For Britain, festering administrative problems in America had suddenly become a military emergency. A decade of assertive but inconsistent British policies had transformed the colonists' sense of good will toward London into angry feelings of persecution and betrayal. The years of incessant argument and misunderstanding reminded many, on both sides of the Atlantic, of watching a stable household unravel into mutual parent-child recrimination. They saw a once-healthy family becoming increasingly dysfunctional and troubled. The colonies, like assertive children, grew steadily in strength, while British officials chafed like aging parents, receiving diminished respect. Predictably, authorities in London found the once-dependent colonists to be ungrateful, intemperate, and occasionally paranoid. With equal assurance, the American subjects saw Parliament, government ministers, and eventually the king himself as uninformed, selfish, and even deceitful.

Britain's overseas empire, which had expanded steadily for two centuries, now seemed on the verge of splitting apart. As the limits of imperial control in North America became more evident, colonists worked to overcome the various differences that had long been part of their eighteenth-century world. Political independence no longer seemed implausible. With effort, class and ethnic hostilities, regional and religious rivalries, and urban–rural divisions might all be curtailed or contained. Redirecting old local resentments toward the British crown could increase a sense of unity among people with different personal backgrounds and resources.

Nor would British colonists be alone if they mounted a rebellion. On one hand, they could make the unlikely choice of liberating half a million slaves, empowering colonial women, and embracing the anti-British cause of Pontiac and numerous Native Americans. Such revolutionary moves would increase their strength dramatically in one direction. On the other hand, they could also take a more cautious and less democratic route. If men of substance could gain control of the forces that were being unleashed, they might curb potential idealism among slaves, women, tenant farmers, and the urban poor, giving precedence instead to policies that would win vital support from the continent of Europe in an American fight for independence. France, recently evicted from North America, and Spain, anxious about British designs in the Pacific, might both be willing allies, despite their commitment to monarchy. Such an alliance, if it ever came about, could push the limits of British imperial control to the breaking point.

Chapter Review

New Challenges to Spain's Expanded Empire

6.1 How did French, British, and Russian explorers in the Pacific threaten Spain's American empire? p. 135

In the mid-eighteenth century, European powers that had once vied to explore and dominate the Atlantic competed for control of the more distant Pacific. Aided by navigational improvements, French, British, and Dutch rivals challenged Spain's weakening claims to Pacific supremacy, while Russian traders seized hold of the fur-rich Alaskan coast.

New Challenges to Britain's Expanded Empire

6.2 Why did the removal of French and Spanish interests pose new problems for Britain's North American empire? p. 138

British victory in the Seven Years' War created the challenge of ruling what had been French Canada. It also disrupted the balance of power in the Mississippi Valley, as English traders and colonists threatened Native American homelands. Moreover, the war's high costs prompted Britain's Parliament to assess onerous new taxes.

"The Unconquerable Rage of the People"

6.3 How did events in America and Britain in the 1760s confirm the skeptical worldview of "Real Whigs"? p. 145

Colonial demonstrations underscored the inequities of the Stamp Act and won its repeal, affirming the Real Whig principle that restrained protest can win relief from a reasonable government. But suspicious colonists saw evidence that imperial patronage bred widespread corruption and that loss of freedom could begin with small, innocuous steps.

A Conspiracy of Corrupt Ministers?

6.4 Did the Boston Massacre highlight justifiable colonial grievances, or was it a provoked attack, exploited by dissidents? p. 149

London's show of strength—moving 4,000 British troops to Boston—was viewed in Massachusetts as a peacetime provocation. Inevitably, tensions between bored soldiers and Boston workers erupted into bloodshed. While both sides were to blame, colonists won the ensuing propaganda war, labeling the event a "massacre" and glorifying the fallen martyrs.

Launching a Revolution

6.5 Could the British, through a more creative response to the Boston Tea Party, have averted the ensuing escalation toward violence? p. 152

British politicians, reacting like irate parents, did not realize how much colonial disaffection and resolve had grown by 1773. Colonists took affront at the "intolerable" Coercive Acts of 1774. Eventually, Britain conceived a global commonwealth, making colonies into independent partners loyal to the crown, but this major shift took generations.

Timeline

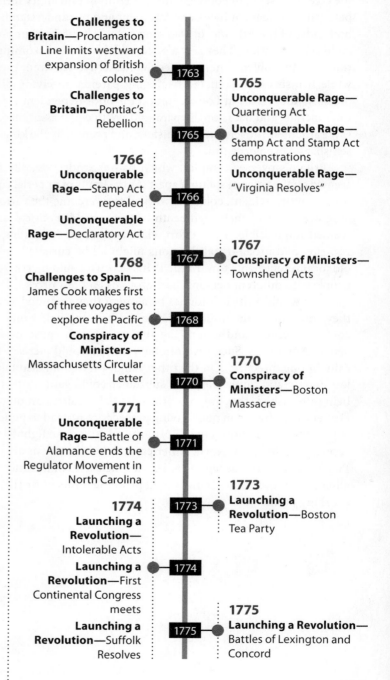

Challenges to Britain—Proclamation Line limits westward expansion of British colonies — 1763

Challenges to Britain—Pontiac's Rebellion — 1765

1765 Unconquerable Rage—Quartering Act

Unconquerable Rage—Stamp Act and Stamp Act demonstrations

Unconquerable Rage—"Virginia Resolves"

1766 Unconquerable Rage—Stamp Act repealed — 1766

Unconquerable Rage—Declaratory Act

1767 Conspiracy of Ministers—Townshend Acts

1768 Challenges to Spain—James Cook makes first of three voyages to explore the Pacific — 1768

Conspiracy of Ministers—Massachusetts Circular Letter

1770 Conspiracy of Ministers—Boston Massacre

1771 Unconquerable Rage—Battle of Alamance ends the Regulator Movement in North Carolina — 1771

1773 Launching a Revolution—Boston Tea Party

1774 Launching a Revolution—Intolerable Acts

Launching a Revolution—First Continental Congress meets — 1774

1775 Launching a Revolution—Battles of Lexington and Concord

Launching a Revolution—Suffolk Resolves — 1775

7 Revolutionaries at War, 1775–1783

Would you risk your life in a rebellion? After the shots at Concord Bridge, farmers and artisans who joined the army heard this question often, from anxious family members and cautious ministers. If captured, they heard it from British officers as well. Replies differed from soldier to soldier, and from one campaign to the next. But the collective answer over long years of war would determine the outcome of the American Revolution.

"I was a Shoemaker, & got my Living by my Labor," recalled William "Long Bill" Scott of Peterborough, New Hampshire. The 33-year-old husband and father joined the local militia company as a lieutenant in April 1775, and two months later he was wounded at Bunker Hill. Taken captive and questioned, he hid his convictions from the British, claiming that he had only risked his life for personal advancement: "If my Captain was killed," he explained, "I should rise in Rank." Regarding the "Dispute

In April 1775, riders spread word across New England that violence had erupted near Boston. William Ranney's history painting, *First News of the Battle of Lexington* (1847), imagined a small town preparing to send reinforcements. What visual cue has the artist used to suggest impending war?

SOURCE: William Tylee Ranney, First News of the Battle of Lexington, 1847. Oil on canvas. North Carolina Museum of Art, Purchased with funds from the State of North Carolina, 52.9.25

LEARNING OBJECTIVES

7.1 ((•
How were the Americans able to drive British forces out of Boston in March 1776, less than a year after the Battle of Lexington? p. 161

7.2 ((•
In the context of the entire year 1776, why was Washington's successful crossing of the Delaware River on December 25 so significant? p. 164

7.3 ((•
If the rebellious Americans opposed monarchy, why did the French crown decide to back their cause? p. 169

7.4 ((•
If Americans were so fearful of centralized authority, how did they coordinate a successful political and military revolt against the powerful British Empire? p. 173

7.5 ((•
What conditions and events in America and Europe led to final American success in the War for Independence? p. 177

((• Listen to Chapter 7 on MyHistoryLab

Watch the Video Series on MyHistoryLab

Learn about some key topics related to this chapter with the *MyHistoryLab Video Series: Key Topics in U.S. History.*

1 **The American Revolution: 1763–1783** The roots, progress, and results of the American Revolution are discussed in this video. A mounting list of colonial grievances sparked confrontations with the London government and eventually prompted an American bid for independence from the British Empire. After eight years of warfare, the thirteen former colonies gained victory and went on to establish a politically unified nation.

 Watch on MyHistoryLab

The Second Continental Congress This video describes how the Second Continental Congress created an American army, named George Washington its commander, and debated the goals of the struggle. Its supreme achievement was the creation of the Declaration of Independence. That document summarized colonial grievances and justified an unprecedented anti-imperial revolution to fellow Americans and to the world. **2**

Watch on MyHistoryLab

3 **Declaring Independence** This video examines the background and implications of the decision by the Second Continental Congress to issue, at last, an official Declaration of Independence. It discusses various earlier declarations of independence approved by separate colonies, and it explores the foundational draft of the Declaration, authored by a young delegate from Virginia: Thomas Jefferson.

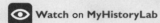 Watch on MyHistoryLab

Battle of Saratoga British defeat at the Battle of Saratoga in 1777 foiled their plan to divide the colonies and isolate New England. This video focuses on that crucial American victory, showing how it prompted vital support from France and other European powers, broadening the scope of the war and helping to bring about Great Britain's eventual defeat. **4**

Watch on MyHistoryLab

between Great Britain and the Colonies," Scott told his captors, "I know nothing of it; neither am I capable of judging whether it is right or wrong."

Perhaps, but in contrast to many whose initial zeal seemed stronger, Long Bill Scott stayed the course. When the British evacuated Boston, they deported him to Nova Scotia. But he escaped and fought at New York, only to be captured again. In his next dramatic escape, he tied his sword around his neck, pinned his watch to his hat, and swam across the Hudson River at night. Scott returned to Peterborough in 1777 to recruit a company of his own, serving for several more years before old wounds made marching difficult. He finished the war as a volunteer on a navy frigate. In all, Long Bill sustained nine wounds and was captured twice, but his rewards proved slim—in fact, he was destitute when he died in 1796 at age fifty-four.

B ut for most, the War of American Independence was not a clear, two-sided struggle. Instead, alliances often proved the old adage that "My enemy's enemy is my friend." Numerous powerful merchants and planters threw in their lot with the people in part because they had grown disillusioned with Parliament's political and commercial controls. Many enslaved blacks, eager for liberty from their masters, escaped to join the British. On the international scale, the monarchies of France and Spain swallowed their dislike for America's republican rhetoric and joined in a war that allowed them an opportunity to attack their long-standing rival, Britain. On the other hand, many Cherokee and Iroquois Indians, disillusioned by contact with land-hungry settlers, cast their lot with the British forces from overseas.

Not all Indian warriors or enslaved Africans sided with the British, and by no means did all New England farmers or Virginia planters embrace the Patriot cause. Large numbers of people at all levels of society opted for cautious neutrality as long as they could, while others shifted their allegiance as the winds changed. The final outcome of the conflict, therefore, remained a source of constant doubt. Looking back, Americans often view the results of the Revolutionary War as inevitable, perhaps even foreordained. In fact, the end result—and thus independence itself—hung in the balance for years.

"Things Are Now Come to That Crisis"

7.1 How were the Americans able to drive British forces out of Boston in March 1776, less than a year after the Battle of Lexington?

New England's Minutemen had rallied swiftly at Lexington. In the ensuing months, Congress took the initial steps to form a Continental Army. It also launched efforts to force the British out of Boston and to pull Canada into the rebellion. If these predominantly Protestant rebels hoped to draw the French Catholics of Quebec into their revolt, would free whites also be eager to include the blacks of Boston, Williamsburg, and Charleston in the struggle for liberty? Or would it be the British who recruited African Americans and furnished them with arms? The answers to such questions became clear in the fifteen months between the skirmish at Lexington and the decision of Congress to declare political independence from Britain in July 1776.

The Second Continental Congress Takes Control

Enthusiasm ran high in Philadelphia in May 1775 as the Second Continental Congress assembled, and the delegates moved quickly to put the colonies on a wartime footing. They instructed New York to build fortifications, and they paid for a dozen companies of riflemen to be sent north to aid the Minutemen surrounding Boston. They created an Army Department under the command of a New York aristocrat, General Philip Schuyler, and approved an issue of $2 million in currency to fund the military buildup.

In late May, word arrived from Lake Champlain in New York of a victory for soldiers under Benedict Arnold of Connecticut and for the Green Mountain Boys (farmers from the area that became Vermont), led by Ethan Allen. They had captured Fort Ticonderoga, along with its cannons, just the sort of heavy arms needed by the new Army Department. This initiative not only secured the Hudson Valley against a British attack from the north; it also allowed Schuyler to propose a strike against Montreal and Quebec via Lake Champlain. Congress approved the assault, to be led by General Richard Montgomery. It also approved a daring scheme submitted by Arnold. He planned to lead separate forces up the Kennebec River. They would assist Montgomery in seizing Quebec and winning Canada before the region could become a staging ground for British armies.

No single action by Congress had greater implications than the one taken on June 15, 1775. That day, members voted unanimously to appoint George Washington, a forty-three-year-old delegate from Virginia, "to command all the continental forces." Colonel Washington already headed a committee drawing up regulations to run the new army, and he had notable military experience. But his strongest asset may have been his southern roots. Northern delegates sensed the need to foster colonial unity by placing a non–New Englander in charge of the army outside Boston. In military and political terms, the selection of Washington proved auspicious. The tall, imposing master of Mount Vernon emerged as a durable and respected leader in both war and peace. But putting a plantation owner in command reduced the prospect of freedom for slaves. It also signaled the beginning of an unlikely alliance between wealthy regional leaders of the North and South, contributing to the particular shape of the Federal Constitution a dozen years later.

"Liberty to Slaves"

The selection of Washington sent a strong message to half a million African Americans, spurring many of them to risk siding with the British. For their part, the British sensed an opportunity to undermine rebellious planters. In June 1775, the British commander in America, Thomas Gage, wrote to London: "Things are now come to that crisis, that we must avail ourselves of every resource, even to raise the Negros, in our cause."

In the South, rumors of liberation swept through the large African American community during 1775. Slaveholding rebel authorities countered with harsh measures to quell black unrest. In South Carolina that spring, attention focused on a prominent free black man named Thomas Jeremiah, a skilled pilot in the port of Charleston. In April, Jeremiah supposedly told an enslaved dockworker of a great war coming and urged slaves to seize the opportunity. Weeks later, nervous Patriot planters made the well-known free black into a scapegoat, accusing him of involvement in a plot to smuggle guns ashore from British ships to support a slave uprising. In August 1775, despite a lack of hard evidence against him, Jeremiah was publicly hanged and then burned, sending a fearsome message.

That September, a Georgia delegate to Congress made a startling comment. He said that if British troops were to land on the southern coast with a supply of food and guns, offering freedom to slaves who would join them, 20,000 blacks would respond. In November, the beleaguered royal governor of Virginia, Lord Dunmore, attempted just such a scheme. Dunmore issued a proclamation granting freedom to any slave, owned by a rebel, who agreed to take up arms on behalf of the king. Hundreds responded to Dunmore's proclamation. They formed the Ethiopian Regiment and wore sashes proclaiming "Liberty to Slaves."

The Struggle to Control Boston

In the North, British forces had been confined in Boston ever since the Battle of Lexington. They would remain isolated on the town's main peninsula for nearly a year, supported by the Royal Navy. In early July 1775, Washington arrived at nearby Cambridge to take up his command and oversee the siege of Boston. He quickly set out to improve order among his men, tightening discipline, calming regional jealousies, and removing incompetent officers. In addition, he wrote scores of letters to civilian political leaders and the president of Congress to muster support for his feeble army.

Washington made clear that nearly everything was in short supply, from tents and uniforms to muskets and cannons. He dispatched twenty-five-year-old Henry Knox, a former bookseller and future general, to retrieve the cannons captured at Ticonderoga. The Patriots' siege could not succeed without heavy fieldpieces to bombard the city from the heights at Dorchester and Charlestown that lay across the water from Boston.

Even before Washington's arrival, the British and the Americans had vied for control of these strategic heights. Indeed, General Gage drew up plans to secure Charlestown peninsula by seizing its highest point, Bunker Hill. But the Patriots learned of the scheme. On the night of June 16, 1775, they moved to fortify the area. The next afternoon, 1,500 Patriots confronted the full force of the British army in the Battle of Bunker Hill.

✳ Explore the Topic   War as an Opportunity for Escaping Slavery

7.1

7.2

7.3

7.4

7.5

By his Excellency the Right Honourable JOHN Earl of DUNMORE, his Majesty's Lieutenant and Governour-General of the Colony and Dominion of Virginia, and Vice-Admiral of the same:

A PROCLAMATION.

AS I have ever entertained Hopes that an Accommodation might have taken Place between *Great Britain* and this Colony, without being compelled, by my Duty, to this most disagreeable, but now absolutely necessary Step, rendered so by a Body of armed Men, unlawfully assembled, firing on his Majesty's Tenders, and the Formation of an Army, and that Army now on their March to attack his Majesty's Troops, and destroy the well-disposed Subjects of this Colony: To defeat such treasonable Purposes, and that all such Traitors, and their Abetters, may be brought to Justice, and that the Peace and good Order of this Colony may be again restored, which the ordinary Course of the civil Law is unable to effect, I have thought fit to issue this my Proclamation, hereby declaring, that until the aforesaid good Purposes can be obtained, I do, in Virtue of the Power and Authority to me given, by his Majesty, determine to execute martial Law, and cause the same to be executed throughout this Colony; and to the End that Peace and good Order may the sooner be restored, I do require every Person capable of bearing Arms to resort to his Majesty's S T A N-DARD, or be looked upon as Traitors to his Majesty's Crown and Government, and thereby become liable to the Penalty the Law inflicts upon such Offences, such as Forfeiture of Life, Confiscation of Lands, &c. &c. And I do hereby farther declare all indented Servants, Negroes, or others (appertaining to Rebels) free, that are able and willing to bear Arms, they joining his Majesty's Troops, as soon as may be, for the more speedily reducing this Colony to a proper Sense of their Duty, to his Majesty's Crown and Dignity. I do farther order, and require, all his Majesty's liege Subjects to retain their Quitrents, or any other Taxes due, or that may become due, in their own Custody, till such Time as Peace may be again restored to this at present most unhappy Country, or demanded of them for their former salutary Purposes, by Officers properly authorised to receive the same.

GIVEN under my Hand, on Board the Ship William, off Norfolk, the 7th Day of November, in the 16th Year of his Majesty's Reign.

D U N M O R E.

G O D   SAVE   THE   K I N G.

In 1775, Lord Dunmore, Governor of Virginia, issued a proclamation, declaring that the British would guarantee the freedom of slaves who fought for them. What diverse effects was Lord Dunmore's Proclamation likely to have on support in the American South for the British cause?

Gage might easily have sealed off Charlestown peninsula with his naval power. Instead, he used 2,500 British infantry to launch three frontal attacks from the shoreline. The first two uphill charges fell back, but a third assault finally dislodged the Americans. Although the Battle of Bunker Hill was technically a British victory, success came at a terrible price. The encounter left 42 percent of British troops (1,054 men) wounded or dead—the worst casualty figures of the war. Gage lost his command, replaced by General William Howe, and the Royal Army no longer appeared invincible.

With Washington and his army encamped outside Boston, Henry Knox worked to retrieve the British **ordnance** captured at Ticonderoga. Using oxen, sledges, and local

Ordnance Cannons, artillery, and by extension general military supplies, including weapons, ammunition, combat vehicles, and tools.

volunteers, he hauled forty-three heavy cannons east, across trails covered with snow and ice, from the Hudson Valley to the coast. His men delivered the guns in late winter. In March 1776, the Americans, in a surprise move, placed them on Dorchester Heights, where they could bombard the enemy huddled in Boston. Threatened, and unable to counterattack, General Howe evacuated his army, retreating by ship to Halifax, Nova Scotia. There, he made plans to attack the rebels again at New York, where Loyalist support was stronger.

Declaring Independence

7.2 In the context of the entire year 1776, why was Washington's successful crossing of the Delaware River on December 25 so significant?

As Washington laid siege to Boston, other Americans converged on British forces in Canada. General Montgomery's troops seized Montreal in November 1775. They then descended the St. Lawrence River to join Benedict Arnold's men, who had struggled north toward Quebec under brutal winter conditions. Their combined force attacked the walled city during a fierce snowstorm on the night of December 30. But their assault failed, and Montgomery perished in the fighting. When British reinforcements reached Quebec in May, the Americans retreated toward Lake Champlain. They left behind most of their baggage and hundreds of sick companions, dying from smallpox. Hundreds more died during the withdrawal or spread the deadly pox as they returned to New England towns. Everywhere, strained loyalty to the British was turning to explosive anger.

"Time to Part"

In January 1776, a brilliant pamphlet, *Common Sense*, captured the shifting mood and helped propel Americans toward independence. The author, a former corset-maker named Thomas Paine, had endured personal and economic failures in England before sailing to Philadelphia in 1774. At thirty-seven, the gifted writer found a fresh start in America and began to compose bold newspaper essays.

Common Sense sold an amazing 120,000 copies in three months. Paine promised to lay out "simple facts, plain arguments, and common sense" on the precarious American situation. He lambasted "the so much boasted constitution of England," attacking hereditary monarchy and the divine right of kings. "One honest man," Paine proclaimed, is worth more "than all the crowned ruffians that ever lived." He urged the creation of an independent constitutional republic that could become "an asylum for all mankind." "Reconciliation is now a fallacious dream," he argued: "'TIS TIME TO PART."

Paine's avid readers agreed. In the spring of 1776, one colony after another instructed its representatives to the Second Continental Congress to vote for independence. But many among the well-to-do held strong social and economic ties to London. They feared the loss of British imperial protection and the startling upsurge of democratic political activity among the lower orders. At first, Congress vacillated. Finally, with no sign of accommodation from England, most members agreed with Robert Livingston of New York that "they should yield to the torrent if they hoped to direct its course." In early June, young Livingston, age 30, joined the committee assigned to prepare a formal statement declaring independence from Great Britain. The Committee of Five also included Benjamin Franklin, John Adams, Roger Sherman, and the second youngest member of the Continental Congress, Thomas Jefferson.

The thirty-three-year-old Jefferson willingly took responsibility for crafting the document. He framed a stirring preamble, drawing on British philosopher John Locke's contract theory of government. Locke (1632–1702) believed that the sovereign power

📖 **Read** the **Document**   John Adams, Letter to Abigail Adams (July 3, 1776)

7.1

7.2

7.3

7.4

7.5

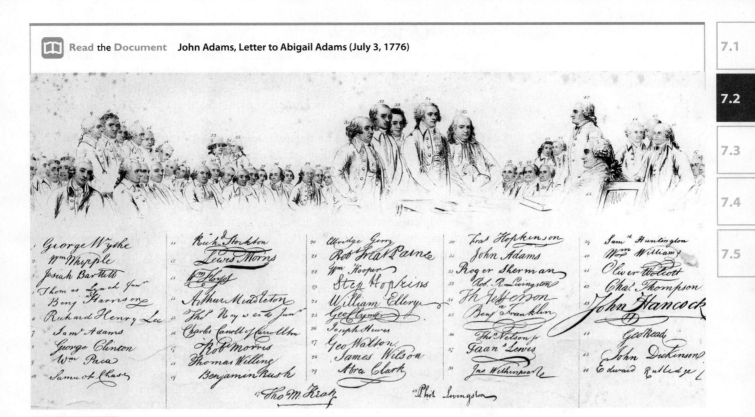

John Trumbull spent years gathering portraits for his famous painting *The Declaration of Independence*. This engraving identifies individuals in the painting with their signatures. Trumbull omitted signers for whom he had no likeness, and he included several nonsigners, such as John Dickinson. Why did the artist place the five-member Drafting Committee at the center of his idealized picture?

ultimately resided not in government but in the people themselves, who chose to submit voluntarily to civil law to protect property and preserve basic rights.

According to Locke, rulers possessed conditional, not absolute, authority over the people. Citizens therefore held the right to end their support and overthrow any government that did not fulfill its side of the contract. For any people facing "a long train of abuses," Jefferson wrote, "it is their right, it is their duty, to throw off such government and to provide new guards for their future security." He went on to catalogue the "repeated injuries and usurpations" committed by King George III. On July 2, when Congress voted on a statement affirming that "these United Colonies are, and of right, ought to be, Free and Independent States," twelve colonies approved, with the New York delegation abstaining. Having made the fundamental decision, the delegates then considered how to "declare the causes" behind their momentous choice to separate from Great Britain.

Over the next two days, Congress members edited the draft declaration submitted by the Committee of Five. They kept Jefferson's idealistic assertion that "all men are created equal." But they removed any reference to slavery, except for the charge that the king had "excited domestic insurrections amongst us," a veiled reference to the Thomas Jeremiah debacle in Charleston and to Lord Dunmore's proclamation. With other changes agreed upon, they finally voted to approve the revised Declaration of Independence on July 4, 1776.

John Hancock, the president of the Congress, signed the document with a flourish, and printers hastily turned it into a published broadside. The other signatures (contrary to folklore) came two weeks later, after New York had finally offered its approval. Then 56 delegates gathered to sign their names to "The unanimous declaration of the 13 United States of America." They did so at great risk, for signing the document exposed them to charges of treason, punishable by death.

The British Attack New York

While the Second Continental Congress debated independence, the British maneuvered to suppress the rebellion. Strangling the revolt with a naval blockade appeared impossible, given the length of the American coastline. But two other strategies emerged—one southern and one northern—that shaped British planning throughout the conflict.

The southern design rested on the assumption that loyalty to the crown remained strongest in the South. If the British could land forces below Chesapeake Bay, support from white loyalists and enslaved blacks might enable them to gain the upper hand and push north to reimpose colonial rule elsewhere. In June 1776, troops under General Henry Clinton arrived off the South Carolina coast with such a mission in mind. On June 28, British ships bombarded Sullivan's Island, at the mouth of Charleston harbor. But the Americans' log fortress withstood the cannon fire, and the attackers withdrew. The British did not renew their southern design for several years, concentrating instead on a separate northern strategy.

According to Britain's northern plan, troops would divide the rebellious colonies in two at the Hudson River valley, seizing New York City and advancing upriver while other forces pushed south from Canada. Then, having sealed off New England, they could finally crush the radicals in Massachusetts who had spearheaded the revolt while restoring the loyalties of inhabitants farther south. Lord George Germain, the aggressive new British cabinet minister in charge of American affairs, favored this plan. An overwhelming strike, he asserted, could "finish the rebellion in one campaign."

Early in 1776, Germain set out to generate a land and sea offensive of unprecedented scale, renting thousands of **mercenaries** from the German states. Eventually, 30,000 German troops traveled to America, so many of them from the state of Hesse-Cassel that onlookers called all of them Hessians. Canada, having already repulsed an American invasion, could provide a loyal staging ground in the north. "I have always thought Hudson's River the most proper part of the whole continent for opening vigorous operations," observed "Gentleman Johnny" Burgoyne, the dapper British general who arrived at Quebec with reinforcements in May 1776.

But plans for a strike south from Canada had to wait. Britain made its first thrust toward the mouth of the Hudson River by sea. In June, a convoy under General William Howe sailed from Halifax to Staten Island, New York, with 9,000 soldiers. By August, the general had received 20,000 reinforcements from across the Atlantic. His brother, Admiral Richard Howe, hovered nearby with 13,000 sailors aboard seventy naval vessels. On orders from Congress, General Washington moved south to defend New York City, a difficult task made harder by ardent Loyalist sentiment. Short on men and equipment, the general weakened his position further by dividing his troops between Manhattan and Brooklyn Heights on nearby Long Island.

A month after Congress members signed the Declaration of Independence, Washington nearly lost his entire force—and the cause itself. General Howe moved his troops by water from Staten Island to the Brooklyn area and then outflanked and scattered the poorly trained Americans in the Battle of Long Island on August 27. Remarkably, the British leader called off a direct attack that would have overrun the American batteries on Brooklyn Heights. Under cover of night, rebel troops slipped back across the East River to New York City in small boats.

"Victory or Death": A Desperate Gamble Pays Off

Washington's narrow escape from Long Island in August 1776 was the first of numerous retreats. His army left New York City on September 15. The rebels withdrew from upper Manhattan and Westchester in October and from Fort Washington and Fort Lee on the Hudson—with heavy losses—in November. The Americans "fled like

Mercenaries Soldiers (such as the German Hessians who served for the British in the Revolutionary War) who fight for pay rather than for any devotion to a specific cause.

scared rabbits," one Englishman wrote. With winter at hand, the Continental forces retreated southwest toward Philadelphia.

As the ragged American army withdrew across New Jersey late in 1776, General William Howe repeatedly failed to press his advantage. The British commander and his brother had received a commission from Lord North, who headed the government in London, permitting them to negotiate a peace settlement with the Americans whenever possible. They hoped that a strong show of force, without a vicious offensive that might alienate civilians, could bring the enemy to terms. Howe's troops offered pardons to rebels and encouraged desertions from Washington's army. In early December, the dwindling American force hurried through Princeton and slipped across the Delaware River into Pennsylvania. Confident of victory, the British failed to pursue them, instead making camp at Trenton. Washington realized that unless circumstances changed quickly, "the game will be pretty well up."

Distressed by civilian talk of surrender, Tom Paine again took up his pen. On December 19, he launched a new series of essays ("The American Crisis") that began, "These are the times that try men's souls." Paine mocked "the summer soldier and the sunshine patriot" who shrank from extreme trials. "Let it be told to the future world, that in the depth of winter, when nothing but hope and virtue could survive," vigilant citizens, "alarmed at one common danger, came forth to meet and to repulse it."

Action soon followed words. On Christmas Day 1776, Washington issued a new code phrase for sentinels: "Victory or Death." He ordered Paine's words read aloud to the troops. Then, after dark, his men recrossed the windswept Delaware River in

Read the Document   Thomas Rodney, Letter from a Revolutionary War Soldier (1776)

This picture depicts the noise and movement at the Battle of Princeton from the perspective of the victorious American forces. Does it deepen your understanding of the painting's emotional content to know that the artist, William Mercer, was a deaf mute from his birth in 1773, or that his father, Brigadier General Hugh Mercer, died in the battle?

SOURCE: Battle of Princeton, by Wm. Mercer, Courtesy of the Philadelphia History Museum at the Atwater Kent, The Historical Society of Pennsylvania Collection

Interpreting History

Thomas Paine ADDRESSES ADMIRAL RICHARD HOWE

"By what means, may I ask, do you expect to Conquer America?"

Weeks after Thomas Paine lifted American spirits with his first "American Crisis" essay, he was back in print with another installment. "American Crisis II" appeared in Philadelphia in January 1777, only eleven months after his publication of Common Sense. In it, the skilled propagandist rolled out a new phrase, "The United States of America." Paine's confident tone reflected the Patriots' improved situation after Washington's victories at Trenton and Princeton.

The short pamphlet took the form of a defiant public letter to Admiral Richard Howe. Besides stressing "the wickedness" of the British cause, the author reminded the commander of "the impossibility of conquering us." "Your experiment in the Jerseys," Paine chided, "is like robbing an orchard in the night before the fruit be ripe, and running away in the morning. . . . The mighty subduers of the continent are retreated into a nutshell." Though brash, Paine also proved astute. In this abridged excerpt, he warns Lord Howe why the British might not prevail in a drawn-out war.

TO LORD HOWE

Soon after your return to New York, you published a very illiberal and unmanly handbill against the Congress, "with their extravagant and inadmissible claim of independence." Why, God bless me! What have you to do with our independence? We ask no leave of yours to set it up; we ask no money of yours to support it; we can do better without your fleets and armies than with them.

By what means, may I ask, do you expect to conquer America? If you could not effect it in the summer, when our army was less than yours, nor in the winter, when we had none, how are you to do it? In point of generalship you have been outwitted, and in point of fortitude outdone; your advantages turn out to your loss, and we can always prevent a total defeat.

When Thomas Paine drafted a public letter to Admiral Howe in 1777, he mocked the British war effort and reminded readers that time, geography, and principle were all working in favor of the American cause. Was Paine justified in thinking the English people would "soon grow discontented" and become "clamorous for peace"?

You see that we have two to one the advantage of you, because we conquer by a drawn game, and you lose by it.

In all the wars which you have formerly been concerned in you had only armies to contend with; in this case you have both an army and a country to combat with. In former wars, the countries followed the fate of their capitals; Canada fell with Quebec. . . . Here it is otherwise; if you get possession of a city here, you are obliged to shut yourselves up in it, and can make no other use of it, than to spend your country's money in. This is all the advantage you have drawn from New York; and you would draw less from Philadelphia, because it requires more force to keep it, and is much further from the sea.

Were you to garrison the places you might march over, your army would be like a stream of water running to nothing. By the time you extended from New York to Virginia, you would be reduced to a string of drops not capable of hanging together; while we, by retreating from State to State, like a river turning back upon itself, would acquire strength in the same proportion as you lost it, and in the end be capable of overwhelming you. What we contend for is worthy the affliction we may go through. What are salt, sugar and finery, to the inestimable blessings of "Liberty and Safety!" Or what are the inconveniences of a few months to the tributary bondage of ages?

'Tis the unhappy temper of the English to be pleased with any war, right or wrong, be it but successful; but they soon grow discontented with ill fortune, and it is an even chance that they are as clamorous for peace next summer, as the king and his ministers were for war last winter. What lately appeared to us misfortunes, were only blessings in disguise; the more surface you spread over, the thinner you will be, and the easier wiped away. "We have put, sir, our hands to the plough, and cursed be he that looketh back."

Questions for Discussion

1. Why does Paine tell the British that if the war ends in a draw, the Americans win "and you lose by it"?
2. Was Paine correct to warn that "the possession of a city here" would not aid the British cause? If so, why?

SOURCE: Eric Foner, ed., *Thomas Paine: Collected Writings* (New York: Library of America, 1995), pp. 100–115.

a driving snowstorm and advanced on Trenton. Holiday festivities and foul weather had left the enemy unprepared. The Americans inflicted a startling defeat, killing several dozen and capturing more than 900 Hessian soldiers. As Washington advanced again on December 30, Howe sent fresh troops forward under Charles Cornwallis to confront the rebels, pinning them down near Trenton. But when the British paused before attacking, the Americans left their campfires burning and slipped out of reach. They then circled behind Cornwallis to defeat his reinforcements at Princeton on January 3. It was not the last time that Washington bested Cornwallis.

The Struggle to Win French Support

7.3 If the rebellious Americans opposed monarchy, why did the French crown decide to back their cause?

The success at Trenton and Princeton restored a glimmer of hope for the tattered Continental Army and its supporters. As American forces took up winter quarters at Morristown, Howe withdrew his army from much of New Jersey to await the spring campaigns. As a result, anxious civilians who had sworn their loyalty to the crown felt deserted. Public sentiment in the region again swung toward the rebels. More importantly, news of the victories spurred support overseas for the American cause. French officials, eager to see their European rival bogged down in a colonial war, dispatched secret shipments of munitions to aid the revolutionaries.

One young aristocrat, the idealistic Marquis de Lafayette, was already on his way from France to volunteer his services to General Washington. But drawing forth an official French commitment to the American cause would take a larger show of success. That triumph finally came at the end of the next campaign season, with the Americans' stunning victory at Saratoga, deep in the Hudson Valley, 185 miles above New York City.

Breakdown in British Planning

Among the Americans, two years of grim conflict had dampened the initial zeal that had prompted citizens to enlist. Washington felt armed resistance could not continue for long unless more men made longer commitments to fight. He insisted that soldiers needed tighter discipline and better pay. In response, Congress expanded his disciplinary powers and offered a bonus to those who enlisted for a three-year term.

In a slumping economy, numerous recruits answered the call, including immigrants and unemployed artisans who lacked training, supplies, and experience. Many rural recruits also lacked immunity to smallpox, since they had never been exposed to the disease. When smallpox broke out among the soldiers at Morristown, Washington ordered a mass inoculation, a risky but farsighted decision that left his recuperating army vulnerable for weeks.

Despite American vulnerability, the British were slow to move. Lord North's ministry had fallen victim to its own contradictions. By seeking a decisive blow *and* a negotiated settlement in 1776, the British had achieved neither objective. They had also underestimated the persistence of Washington's army. During the 1777 campaigns, they learned further lessons about the difficulty of their task and the need for coordinated plans.

General Burgoyne, returning to London for the winter, won government support for a major new offensive. He planned to lead a large force south from Canada, using the Hudson Valley to drive a wedge through the rebellious colonies. In support, a combined British and Indian force would strike east from Lake Ontario, capturing Fort Stanwix and descending eastward along the Mohawk River to meet Burgoyne at Albany. William Howe would push north from New York City to complete the design.

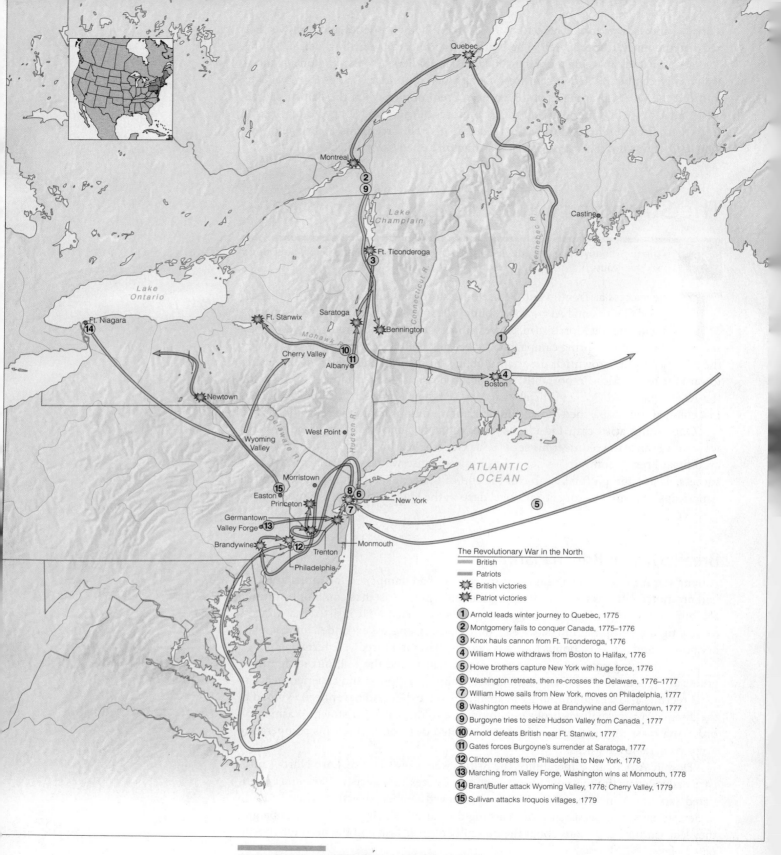

The Revolutionary War in the North

━━━ British
━━━ Patriots
✴ British victories
✴ Patriot victories

1 Arnold leads winter journey to Quebec, 1775
2 Montgomery fails to conquer Canada, 1775–1776
3 Knox hauls cannon from Ft. Ticonderoga, 1776
4 William Howe withdraws from Boston to Halifax, 1776
5 Howe brothers capture New York with huge force, 1776
6 Washington retreats, then re-crosses the Delaware, 1776–1777
7 William Howe sails from New York, moves on Philadelphia, 1777
8 Washington meets Howe at Brandywine and Germantown, 1777
9 Burgoyne tries to seize Hudson Valley from Canada , 1777
10 Arnold defeats British near Ft. Stanwix, 1777
11 Gates forces Burgoyne's surrender at Saratoga, 1777
12 Clinton retreats from Philadelphia to New York, 1778
13 Marching from Valley Forge, Washington wins at Monmouth, 1778
14 Brant/Butler attack Wyoming Valley, 1778; Cherry Valley, 1779
15 Sullivan attacks Iroquois villages, 1779

MAP 7.1 THE REVOLUTIONARY WAR IN THE NORTH

But General Howe had formed a different plan. Assuming Burgoyne would not need his help in the Hudson Valley, he intended to move south against Philadelphia. The two generals never integrated their separate operations, and the results were disastrous. In one six-month span, the British bungled their best chance for victory and handed their enemies an opening that permanently shifted the course of the war.

Saratoga Tips the Balance

The isolated operations of Burgoyne and Howe got off to slow starts in late June 1777. Howe took two months to move his troops by sea from New York harbor to the headwaters of Chesapeake Bay. This delay gave the Americans time to march south, but an engagement at Brandywine Creek on September 11, 1777, failed to check the British advance on Philadelphia. The British finally entered the city in late September only to find that the rebel Congress had retreated to York, Pennsylvania.

Just north of Philadelphia, Washington attacked the large Hessian garrison at Germantown on October 4. The surprise succeeded, but morning fog created so much confusion that the inexperienced Patriot troops allowed victory to slip away. Despite defeats at Brandywine and Germantown, the Americans had gained combat experience and had made Howe pay heavily for his hollow capture of Philadelphia. As Washington's battered army took up winter quarters at nearby Valley Forge, he looked expectantly northward, hoping "all New England" would "turn out and crush Burgoyne."

Moving south from Canada in late June, "Gentleman Johnny" saw little likelihood of being crushed. The British officers believed their huge army to be invincible. The worried Americans fell back from Crown Point and Ticonderoga on Lake Champlain. But as British supply lines lengthened, the crown's army grew less certain of victory. Burgoyne's soldiers expended valuable time cutting a roadway through the wilderness. Also, the reinforcements anticipated from the west had been turned back by Benedict Arnold's men at Fort Stanwix. Even worse, American militia near Bennington badly mauled a British unit of 600 sent to forage for corn and cattle. With cold weather approaching and supplies dwindling, Burgoyne pushed south toward Albany, unaware that Howe would not be sending help up the Hudson to meet him.

As Burgoyne's situation worsened, the American position improved. An arrogant British proclamation demanding submission from local residents only stiffened their resolve and drew out more rebel recruits. While Burgoyne's army crossed to the Hudson River's west bank at Saratoga, General Horatio Gates's American forces dug in on Bemis Heights, 10 miles downstream.

On September 19, 1777, Patriot units under two aggressive officers, Benedict Arnold and Daniel Morgan, confronted the enemy at Freeman's Farm, not far from Saratoga. In the grueling battle, British forces suffered 556 dead or wounded, nearly twice the American losses. Gates's refusal to commit reinforcements prevented the Patriots from achieving total victory. Nevertheless, the American ranks swelled with new recruits who sensed a chance to inflict losses on Burgoyne's forces. On October 7, the beleaguered British tried once more to smash southward, only to suffer defeat in a second battle at Freeman's Farm. Morgan and Arnold once again played key roles, though Arnold suffered a crippling leg wound. When Burgoyne's entire army of 5,800 surrendered at nearby Saratoga ten days later, Gates took full credit for the stunning triumph.

Forging an Alliance with France

Ever since declaring independence, Congress had maneuvered to win international recognition and aid for the new nation. Benjamin Franklin was sent to Paris as part of a commission seeking European support. Since the French government doubted the rebellion's chances for success, it moved cautiously at first, confining itself to covert assistance. Word of the American victory at Saratoga suddenly gave Franklin greater leverage. When he hinted that he might bargain directly with London for peace, the

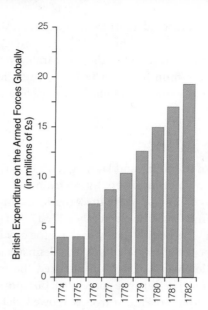

FIGURE 7.1 BRITISH GOVERNMENT EXPENSES ON ARMED FORCES THROUGHOUT THE WORLD (IN MILLIONS OF POUNDS), 1774–1782 Britain's war budget soared after France entered the conflict in 1778, but major resources flowed toward India and the Caribbean, limiting the share available for North America.

French foreign minister, Comte de Vergennes, moved immediately to recognize American independence.

In negotiating a vital alliance, France agreed to renounce forever any claim to English land in North America, and Franklin promised that the Americans would help defend French holdings in the Caribbean. Both parties pledged to defend the liberty of the new republic, and each agreed not to conclude a separate peace with Great Britain or to cease fighting until U.S. independence had been ensured by formal treaty. In May 1778, the Continental Congress approved this alliance. The next month, France entered the war, adding its enormous wealth and power to the American cause. A year later, Spain—unwilling to ally itself directly with the upstart republic but eager to protect its vast American assets from Great Britain—entered the war on the side of France.

For the British, what had been a colonial brushfire swiftly flared into a global conflict reminiscent of the Seven Years' War. Hostilities with France meant possible invasions at home and inevitable attacks on outposts of Britain's empire. French ships seized Senegal in West Africa, took Grenada in the West Indies, and burned trading posts on Hudson Bay in Canada. London's annual war expenditures climbed from £4 million in 1775 to £20 million in 1782.

As war costs mounted in Britain, domestic opposition to the American conflict intensified. Some members of Parliament pushed for a swift settlement. In 1778, a peace commission led by Lord Carlisle offered concessions to the Continental Congress, hoping to tear the French alliance apart. But the Carlisle Commission failed to win a reconciliation. Other Britons went further in opposing the war. Their diverse reasons included fear of French power, desire for American trade, disgust over war profiteering, ties to friends in America, and idealistic belief in the revolution's principles. Many drank toasts to General Washington and openly supported the American cause.

Faced with growing economic and political pressure, the king and his ministers briefly considered withdrawing all troops from the rebellious colonies and focusing on the French threat. Instead, when General Howe resigned as commander in chief in America, they instructed his successor, Sir Henry Clinton, to retreat from Philadelphia to New York and devote his main resources to attacking the French in the Caribbean. Within Britain, discontent over an uncertain war strategy continued to escalate, as the government failed to either pacify the Americans or crush their rebellion.

Legitimate States, a Respectable Military

7.4 If Americans were so fearful of centralized authority, how did they coordinate a successful political and military revolt against the powerful British Empire?

Even with the new French alliance, the rebellious American states faced serious challenges on both the civilian and military fronts. They had thrown out their colonial governors and embarked on a dangerous war, but two fundamental questions still confronted them. First, how would the once-dependent colonies now be governed? And second, how could they shape a military force strong enough to defend themselves but not so powerful and unchecked as to seize control from their new civil governments?

The Articles of Confederation

The Continental Congress had taken prompt initiative. Without clear authority, it had declared independence, raised an army, issued currency, borrowed money from abroad, and negotiated an alliance with France. Then it moved to bring greater stability and legitimacy to its work. In November 1777, one month after the victory at Saratoga, it approved the Articles of Confederation and presented this formal plan for a lasting and unifying government to the states for ratification. Citizens were already debating how much authority each new state government would have in relation to the larger federation. Who would have the power to levy taxes, for example, and who would control the distribution of land?

The Articles declared "The United States of America" to be a "firm league of friendship" between the thirteen former colonies. Each independent state in this weak alliance retained all rights and powers not "expressly delegated" to the Confederation Congress. Indeed, ties between the sovereign states seemed so loose that France considered sending thirteen separate ambassadors to America.

According to the Articles, Congress could not collect taxes or regulate trade; it could only requisition funds from the states. Shares would vary depending on each state's free population. Moreover, the Confederation had no separate executive branch; executive functions fell to various committees of the Confederation Congress. In addition, to the dismay of land speculators, the Congress would not control the western domains that several large states had claimed. Maryland, a small state without western claims, protested this arrangement and refused to ratify. To win the required approval from all thirteen states, drafters changed the plan and granted the Confederation control of western lands. After four years, the Articles finally won ratification in 1781.

Given the importance of the states, the task of designing new state governments became a top priority, even for members of the Continental Congress. In May 1776, for example, two of Jefferson's friends in the Virginia delegation in Philadelphia returned home to help implement this state-level process. They left their younger colleague behind, but they carried his written draft for a possible state constitution. Those already at work in Virginia accepted Jefferson's proposed preamble. On June 29, 1776, Virginia led the way, adopting the first republican state constitution.

Virginia had already pioneered in another respect. Two weeks earlier, Virginia representatives approved a Declaration of Rights drawn up by George Mason. He affirmed the revolutionary concepts that all power derives from the people and that magistrates are their servants. He went on to endorse trial by jury, praise religious freedom, and condemn hereditary privilege. Over the next eight years, many states adopted a similar bill of rights to enumerate the fundamental limits of government power.

Creating State Constitutions

Each of the thirteen states had removed a functioning colonial government, and each needed to reestablish the rule of law under some new system. Britain itself possessed no written constitution, but the colonies had been ruled under published charters, and Americans believed in the value of such clear and open arrangements. Thus, they readily envisioned an explicit controlling document, or constitution, for each new state. Besides, the novel idea that government flowed from the people—as an agreement based on the consent of the governed—called for some all-encompassing, written legal contract.

A new written constitution, whether for a state or a union of states, represented something more fundamental and enduring than a regular law. It needed to be above day-to-day legal statutes and political whims. Somehow the people, through chosen representatives, had to prepare a special document that citizens would affirm, or ratify, only one time. After the new government structure was in place, the constitution itself would be difficult, though not impossible, to change.

In 1779, Massachusetts legislators, under pressure from the public, fixed upon a method for providing the elevated status and popular endorsement for such a new document. Local voters in town meetings chose representatives for a specific constitution-drafting convention. These delegates, building on a model suggested by John Adams, crafted a suitable document. Their proposed constitution was then submitted to all the state's free men (regardless of race or property) for ratification. This widened constituency was intended to give special weight to the endorsement process.

Approval of the Massachusetts document was hotly debated. Many objected to the limits on popular power that were part of Adams's novel design. A reluctant revolutionary, Adams argued that "interests" (like-minded groups), rather than people, should receive equal representation. In addition, he proposed sharing legislative responsibilities between a house, a senate, and a chief executive. Property requirements for these offices were steep, so wealthy interests would have power far beyond their numbers. The Massachusetts state constitution, ratified by a narrow margin, implemented these ideas. They signaled a turn away from the strongest popular radicalism of 1776 and foreshadowed the more conservative balance of interests that James Madison championed in the federal Constitution drafted in 1787.

This extended experiment in constitution writing was unprecedented. Never before in history, John Adams observed, had several million people had numerous opportunities "to form and establish the wisest and happiest government that human wisdom could contrive." Initial state efforts yielded varied results as citizens debated novel approaches to self-government. By 1780, the desire of established elites to rein in democratic power was evident. Yet in comparison to the overseas monarchy Americans had rejected, even the most conservative new state constitutions seemed risky and bold. Several common threads ran through all these documents.

First, fearing executive might, drafters curtailed the power of state governors to dismiss assemblies, raise armies, declare war, fill offices, or grant privileges. Colonial governors had been appointed from above, by proprietors or the crown, and they could serve terms of any length. In contrast, state governors would now be elected annually (usually by the assembly) and would be subject to impeachment and term limits. In Pennsylvania, the most radical of the new constitutions did away with a single governor altogether, placing executive power in the hands of a twelve-member council elected by the people.

Second, drafters expanded the strength of legislatures and increased their responsiveness to the popular will. They made elections more frequent, and they enlarged the size of assemblies to allow greater local involvement. They also reduced property requirements for holding office and changed limits on the right to vote to allow wider participation.

Third, constitution-makers feared that corruption emerged when people held more than one office at a time. Having experienced these glaring conflicts of interest under imperial rule, they stressed the separation of executive, legislative, and judicial posts. Preventing members of the executive branch from also holding a legislative seat removed any prospect for a cabinet-style government along the lines of the British model.

Tensions in the Military Ranks

Any new republican order required a fighting force to defend itself. But the new state militias and Washington's national army, which was controlled and paid by the Continental Congress, prompted debate from the start. Discussions erupted as to what constituted equitable pay, appropriate discipline, suitable tactics, and a proper distribution of limited supplies. Citizens argued over whether wealth, popularity, vision, military experience, political savvy, European training, or influential ties should play a role in determining who received, or retained, the cherished right to command.

One heated topic involved the election of officers. Wealthy gentry assumed that they would command the state militias, while citizen soldiers demanded the right to choose their own leaders. Another topic concerned opting out of military service. Should a prosperous individual have the right to buy an exemption or to send a paid substitute? In 1776, as Washington's army had retreated into Pennsylvania, militia in Philadelphia had chastised "Gentlemen who formerly Paraded in our Company and now in the time of greatest danger have turn'd their backs." They asked whether state authorities meant "to force the poorer kind into the field and suffer the Rich & the Great to remain at home?"

Three years later, some of these same Philadelphia militia staged a bitter demonstration that became known as the "Fort Wilson" riot. In October 1779, spurred by soaring food prices, impoverished militiamen marched past the stately home of James Wilson, where wealthy Patriots had gathered. "The time is now arrived," the demonstrators' handbill proclaimed, "to prove whether the suffering friends of this country, are to be enslaved, ruined and starved, by a few overbearing Merchants, . . . Monopolizers and Speculators." Shots were exchanged, and six died in the melee at "Fort Wilson." (Wilson himself went on to become a leader of the 1787 Constitutional Convention.)

Subtle class divisions also beset the Continental Army, where jealousies over rank plagued the status-conscious officer corps. Congressional power to grant military commissions, often on regional and political grounds, only intensified disputes. Also, Americans representing Congress abroad were empowered to promise high military posts to attract European officers. Some of these recruits served the American cause well, such as Johann de Kalb and Friedrich von Steuben (both born in Germany) and Thaddeus Kosciusko and Casimir Pulaski from Poland. In France, at age nineteen, the Marquis de Lafayette secured a commission to be a major general in America, and he assisted Washington impressively throughout the war.

In contrast, other foreign officers displayed arrogance and spread dissension. Irish-born Thomas Conway, for example, courted congressional opponents of Washington and encouraged the desires of General Horatio Gates to assume top command. Whether or not a concerted "Conway **Cabal**" ever existed, Washington managed to defuse tensions from Valley Forge during the hard winter of 1777–1778. His numerous letters helped to consolidate his position with Congress and to patch frayed relations with Gates.

Cabal A close group or faction united in some plan or secret intrigue to foster their own interests and views.

Another rival for command of the army, English-born Charles Lee, met disfavor several months later, when Washington ordered him to attack the rear guard of Clinton's army as it withdrew from Philadelphia to New York. Lee mismanaged the encounter at Monmouth, New Jersey, on June 28, 1778, and only Washington's swift action stopped a premature retreat. The Battle of Monmouth ended in a draw, but American troops claimed victory and took pride in their swift recovery and hard fighting.

Shaping a Diverse Army

The army's improved effectiveness came in large part from the efforts of Friedrich von Steuben, a European officer recruited by Benjamin Franklin after charges of homosexuality disrupted his German military career. He had arrived at Valley Forge in February 1778, offering to serve without pay. There he found soldiers with poor food, scant clothing, and limited training. Many Americans still wanted to see a more democratic citizen army, with elected officers and limited hierarchy. But Washington hoped to mold long-term soldiers into a more "Europeanized" force, and Steuben suited his needs. The German worked energetically to drill soldiers who, in turn, trained others.

New discipline helped boost morale. Still, terms of service and wage levels remained sources of contention. So did the disparities in treatment and pay between officers and enlisted men. There were other grievances: inept congressional committees overseeing the war effort, incompetent officers filling political appointments, and a frustrating shortage of new recruits. Arguments also persisted over whether women or African Americans could serve in the army.

Women organized in diverse ways to assist the war effort, making uniforms and running farms and businesses for absent husbands. A few American women, such as Deborah Sampson of Massachusetts, disguised themselves as men and fought. Far more accompanied the troops of both armies, earning scant pay to do cooking and washing. They also carried water to the weary and wounded on the battlefield. As many as 20,000 women may have accompanied the American army during the war. Mary Hays, wife of a Pennsylvania soldier, endured the winter at Valley Forge and later hauled pitchers of water on the battlefield at Monmouth. When her husband was wounded, she is said to have set down her jug and joined his gun crew, earning folk legend status as the cannon-firing "Molly Pitcher."

After petitioning to fight, free blacks were allowed to join the revolutionary army. Rhode Island even formed an African American regiment. But repeated proposals to arm southern slaves met with defeat. South Carolina and Virginia even moved in the opposite direction, offering to give away slaves captured from Loyalist planters as a bonus to white recruits. Not surprisingly, thousands of enslaved people, especially in the South, risked their lives to escape to British lines.

The War at Sea

Even as the Americans' army grew into a respectable force, their lack of naval strength proved a constant disadvantage. As early as October 13, 1775, the Continental Congress had agreed to arm two vessels to prey on British supply ships. The vote marked the birth of the American navy. Despite objections, Congress promptly appointed a committee to acquire sailing craft, and most of the thirteen states built up their own small navies, adding to the confusion. The lack of central coordination proved deadly. When Massachusetts sent its ships along the Maine coast to challenge a Loyalist buildup at Castine in 1779, British vessels cornered the fleet at Penobscot Bay and crushed the enterprise.

Despite its strength, the British navy faced increasing challenges as more European powers joined the fray: France in 1778, Spain in 1779, and Holland in 1780. The English feared possible invasion, and French corsairs harassed Britain's coastline, joined by American captains. One such captain, a Scottish immigrant named John Paul Jones, arrived in European waters from America in early 1778. In April, Jones raided the port of Whitehaven in his native Scotland, and the propaganda triumph of an American success in British waters proved huge. The brazen young captain won an even greater victory the next year when his crew managed to board Britain's sleek new HMS *Serapis* and capture the frigate before their own vessel sank.

Privateers A term for private ships (and their owners) licensed by government to engage in warfare at sea and to keep the profits of their raids, easing the burden on the navy to build ships, train officers, and pay sailors.

Prize money The proceeds earned by privateers from the capture and sale of enemy cargo and vessels. This money was divided among the ship's investors, officers, and crew, providing an incentive to join the war effort.

In all, the Continental Navy equipped more than 50 vessels and captured nearly 200 British craft as prizes. But these numbers pale in comparison to the activities of American **privateers**. More than a thousand private shipowners obtained licenses from Congress to seize enemy ships and divide any **prize money** among themselves and their crew. With international commerce curtailed, shipowners and sailors were eager to try their luck. Their small, quick vessels swarmed the Atlantic like troublesome gnats, frustrating England's mighty navy. By war's end, the British had surrendered 2,000 ships, 12,000 men, and goods valued at £18 million. And privateering drew merchant investors into the Patriot war effort, helping to bind the coastal elite more firmly to the American cause.

The Long Road to Yorktown

7.5 What conditions and events in America and Europe led to final American success in the War for Independence?

By July 1778, Clinton's British forces had returned to New York City, and their situation had not improved. Frustrated in New England and the middle tier of states, Clinton revived the southern strategy discussed at the beginning of the war. The South supposedly contained numerous Loyalists, and its lengthy growing season would mean more fodder for military horses. Besides, the long southern coastline had little protection, and Washington's distant army would have trouble defending the region. Moreover, nearly 500,000 slaves posed a threat to Patriot planters and represented potential support for British invaders. Finally, the same whites who dreaded slave rebellion also feared war with Native Americans, so the possible use of Indian allies also entered Britain's strategic calculation.

Indian Warfare and Frontier Outposts

Most Native Americans in eastern North America remained loyal to the British. Exceptions existed, such as the Oneida, Tuscarora, and Catawba, but many Indians had long-standing grievances about white encroachments. In Appalachia, colonial land investors and frontier squatters had defied the king's Proclamation Line for more than a decade. When dissident Cherokee, led by a young war chief named Dragging Canoe, attacked intruders on the Watauga River in July 1776, whites struck back. In all, 6,000 troops pushed into the mountains, laying waste to Cherokee villages.

Daniel Boone had already led migrants through Cumberland Gap in western Virginia to establish a fort on the Kentucky River at Boonesborough in 1775. By 1777, these pioneer families faced constant warfare against Indian adversaries fighting for their homelands. The Native Americans were also being urged on by Henry Hamilton, the British commandant at far-off Detroit. In one six-month span, Hamilton, who became known as the Scalp Buyer, received 77 prisoners and 129 scalps from this frontier warfare. Along the upper Ohio, violence escalated in 1777, when Americans killed Shawnee leader Cornstalk and his son during a truce. The next year, they murdered the neutral Delaware leader, White Eyes. Four years later, at the village of Gnadenhutten (south of modern-day Canton, Ohio), militia from Pennsylvania massacred 100 peaceful Delaware men, women, and children who had been converted to Christianity by missionaries of the Moravian Church.

By then, conflict involving Native Americans had also flared farther north. Joseph Brant, a mixed-race Mohawk leader educated in New England and loyal to the British, pushed south from Fort Niagara on Lake Ontario, attacking poorly guarded frontier settlements. First in the Wyoming Valley of northeastern Pennsylvania and later in New York's Cherry Valley, the raiders killed hundreds of non-Indian settlers. In the summer of 1779, American General John Sullivan led a campaign to annihilate Indian towns in reprisal.

Sullivan's revenge-minded troops, numbering more than 4,000, destroyed forty villages of the four tribes in the Iroquois Confederacy most linked to the British cause: the Mohawk, Onondaga, Cayuga, and Seneca. They avoided towns of the two Iroquois groups sympathetic to the Americans—the Oneida and Tuscarora—but elsewhere they chopped down orchards, torched crops, and sent Indian refugees streaming to Fort Niagara. Hunger and retaliatory raids haunted the region until the end of the war.

While the British were passing arms and supplies to the divided Iroquois Confederacy through Fort Niagara, they were also using several western posts to arm other Indian allies and seek an advantage in the interior. Soldiers at Fort Michilimackinac recruited Sioux, Chippewa, and Sauk warriors for an unsuccessful attack on Spanish-held St. Louis in 1780. At Fort Detroit, Hamilton continued to equip war parties

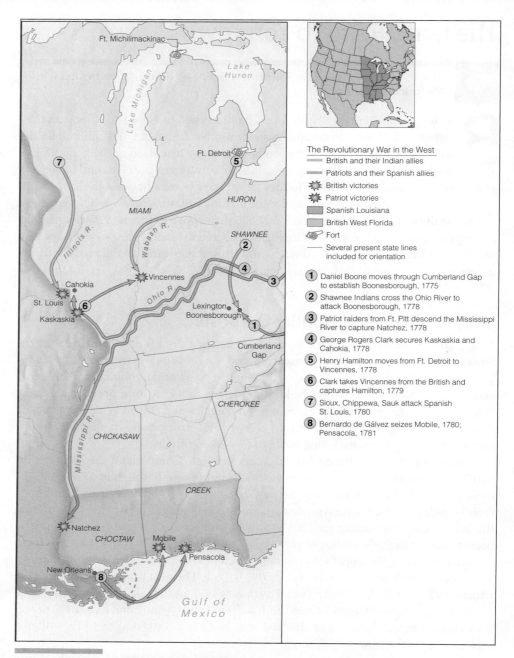

MAP 7.2 THE REVOLUTIONARY WAR IN THE WEST

of Ottawa, Fox, and Miami Indians to attack American newcomers migrating into the Ohio Valley.

In 1778, with support from his home state of Virginia, a young Patriot surveyor named George Rogers Clark organized a foray west to counter these raids and lend support to Spanish and French allies in the upper Mississippi Valley. He secured settlements on the Mississippi River, and in February 1779, he led a grueling winter march to surprise the fort at Vincennes, on the Wabash River in southern Indiana. Clark's men managed to capture Henry Hamilton, but they failed to seize Detroit.

The Unpredictable War in the South

The rebel war effort beyond the Appalachian Mountains expanded south in 1778, when Patriot raiders captured Natchez on the lower Mississippi and seized property in

The British used Fort Niagara (on the southwest edge of Lake Ontario, at the mouth of the Niagara River) to launch attacks on American settlements and to shelter Indian allies. During the harsh winter of 1779–1780, 5,000 Iroquois refugees, made homeless by the scorched-earth campaign of General John Sullivan, camped near the fort in 5 feet of snow. In what ways did British use of Native American allies strengthen, or undermine, the imperial cause?

British West Florida. But it was the energetic governor of Spanish Louisiana, Bernardo de Gálvez, whose actions proved decisive. Living in New Orleans, Gálvez maintained a careful neutrality between the Americans and their British rivals through 1778. But when Spain allied with France and declared war on Britain the next year, the governor acted quickly to keep the British from gaining ground on the Gulf Coast.

Moving from west to east, Governor Gálvez drove the British from the Mississippi River in 1779, seized their fort at Mobile in 1780, and conquered Pensacola, the capital of British West Florida, in 1781. The fall of Mobile and Pensacola cut British supply lines to the southeastern interior, hurting Creek and Cherokee warriors. Without additional guns, knives, and powder, the Indians could offer little assistance in Britain's ambitious plan to win back the South. It was support the British could ill afford to lose.

Still, the crown's forces regained control of most of Georgia from the rebels in 1778. The next year, they blocked American and French efforts to retake Savannah. Early in 1780, British generals Clinton and Cornwallis ferried troops by sea from New York to South Carolina, and by May they had isolated Charleston and forced the surrender of 5,500 American troops—the largest loss of American men and weapons during the entire war. A confident Clinton returned to New York, leaving Cornwallis in command in South Carolina as fierce fighting erupted across the state. Banastre Tarleton's British cavalry, along with Loyalist supporters, went head to head against the guerrilla bands led by Thomas Sumter, Andrew Pickens, and Francis Marion.

In June 1780, Congress appointed Horatio Gates to take command of southern operations, and he hurried to the Carolinas with fresh troops. On August 16, Gates's army confronted Cornwallis at Camden, South Carolina, 120 miles north of Charleston. The Americans, short on rest, food, and leadership, suffered a stinging defeat. Two days after the Camden disaster, as Gates fled north, Tarleton's cavalry landed another blow. They surprised Sumter's band of 800 partisans at Fishing Creek near the Catawba River and took 300 prisoners. Suffering almost no losses themselves, the cavalry inflicted 150 casualties and freed several hundred Loyalists and British regulars.

That September, as Washington absorbed word of the defeats at Camden and Fishing Creek, he received another rude shock. Benedict Arnold—in command of West Point, the key outpost controlling the Hudson River—had plotted to defect and

7.1

7.2

7.3

7.4

7.5

Read the Document   William Dobein James, The Rise of Partisan Warfare in the South (1778)

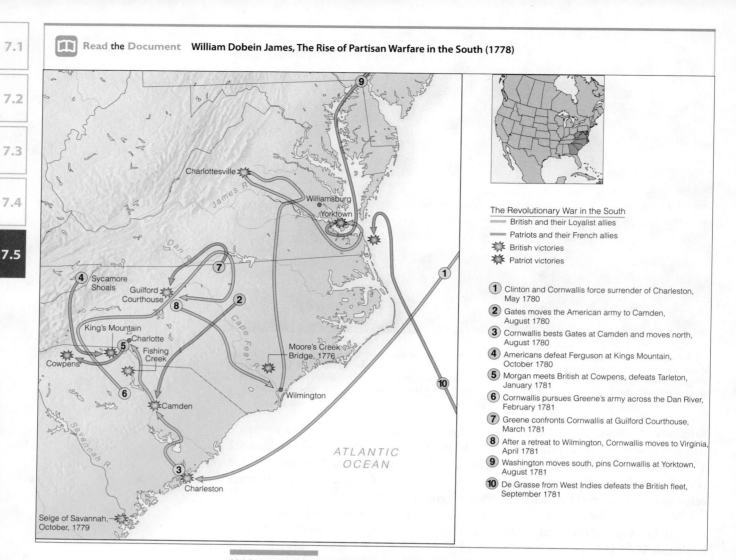

The Revolutionary War in the South
- British and their Loyalist allies
- Patriots and their French allies
- British victories
- Patriot victories

1. Clinton and Cornwallis force surrender of Charleston, May 1780
2. Gates moves the American army to Camden, August 1780
3. Cornwallis bests Gates at Camden and moves north, August 1780
4. Americans defeat Ferguson at Kings Mountain, October 1780
5. Morgan meets British at Cowpens, defeats Tarleton, January 1781
6. Cornwallis pursues Greene's army across the Dan River, February 1781
7. Greene confronts Cornwallis at Guilford Courthouse, March 1781
8. After a retreat to Wilmington, Cornwallis moves to Virginia, April 1781
9. Washington moves south, pins Cornwallis at Yorktown, August 1781
10. De Grasse from West Indies defeats the British fleet, September 1781

MAP 7.3 THE REVOLUTIONARY WAR IN THE SOUTH

yield the post to the British. When Congress failed to promote the self-centered officer, the admired leader became alienated from the Patriot cause. The capture of his British contact, Major John André, revealed General Arnold's scheme. Washington had Major André hanged as an enemy spy, but Arnold escaped and received command of British troops.

Five years of war left Washington and Congress facing severe problems: soaring inflation, scarce resources, sinking citizen morale, and mounting disobedience among enlisted men. Early in 1780, soldiers from Massachusetts, New York, and Connecticut had mutinied in separate incidents. Members of the Pennsylvania and New Jersey Lines soon staged similar strikes over disputed terms of enlistment. The British had reason for optimism as Cornwallis pressed into North Carolina in the fall of 1780. But the next 12 months saw a dramatic reversal in their fortunes.

That reversal began in October with a surprising Patriot victory in the southern backcountry, where Cornwallis had sent Major Patrick Ferguson with a troop of South Carolina Loyalists to guard the army's flank and harry rebel supporters. More than 800 frontiersmen rallied at Sycamore Shoals in the Watauga Valley and raced south to challenge the British at King's Mountain, just below North Carolina's southern border. On October 6, these sharpshooters surrounded and decimated the Loyalist troops. Ferguson died in the one-sided affair, and his force lost more than 1,000 men—killed, wounded, or captured.

The Final Campaign

A shrewd change in American leadership followed the victory at King's Mountain. Congress, on Washington's advice, replaced Gates in the southern command with General Nathanael Greene, an experienced Rhode Islander who had served as the army's quartermaster general. Greene arrived in Charlotte, North Carolina, in December 1780, taking charge of a tattered army of 1,600. Shocked by the violence of partisan warfare and conscious of the need to win public support, he urged restraint on such experienced guerrilla fighters as Sumter and Marion while weaving them into his overall plans to conduct an elusive "fugitive war." Greene decided to divide his small army and send half his men into South Carolina under the seasoned Daniel Morgan to harass the British flank. "It makes the most of my inferior force," he explained, "for it compels my adversary to divide his, and holds him in doubt as to his own line of conduct."

Cornwallis took the bait and dispatched Tarleton, who caught up with Morgan at Hannah's Cowpens, west of King's Mountain, on January 17, 1781. The outnumbered rebel militia lacked experience and discipline, but Morgan turned this weakness to an advantage at the Battle of Cowpens. He stationed the militia units in front of his Continental forces with orders to fire two rounds and fall back. The British force of 1,100, sensing an enemy retreat, advanced too far too fast, and Morgan's men promptly overwhelmed them. Tarleton managed to escape, but he left behind 100 dead, 800 prisoners, and most of his horses and ammunition. Morgan's victorious Patriot force suffered only 148 casualties. He rightly called the Battle of Cowpens "a devil of a whipping."

Though frustrated, Cornwallis clung to the belief that "a successful battle may give us America." He discarded all excess baggage and pursued the rebel army 200 miles across North Carolina. Greene, continuing his elusive "fugitive war," directed a speedy retreat over swollen rivers to the Virginia border. Then he doubled back to confront the weary British in the Battle of Guilford Courthouse on March 15. Although the American forces eventually withdrew from the field, Cornwallis sustained such heavy losses that he was forced to alter his plans.

The British retreated to the coast at Wilmington, North Carolina, and then marched north in early summer 1781 to Yorktown, Virginia. There, Cornwallis hoped to obtain reinforcements by sea, rally Loyalists in the Chesapeake region, and divide the rebelling colonies. The design's success hinged on naval superiority and timely support from General Clinton in New York. But Cornwallis could be assured of neither.

In August, the French fleet in the Caribbean set out for Chesapeake Bay. Admiral François De Grasse planned to spend eight weeks in North American waters. The move gave Washington (still in the north) brief access to impressive naval power, and he seized his chance. He sent word south to Lafayette in Virginia to keep Cornwallis contained at Yorktown. Then, to hold Clinton's forces in New York, he ordered his men to make a show as if preparing for a lengthy siege. But instead of besieging New York City, American soldiers and their French allies slipped away, secretly marching south to lay a trap for the British army.

Admiral De Grasse reached Chesapeake Bay with two dozen ships at the end of August. On September 5, he repulsed a British fleet off the mouth of the bay, dashing Cornwallis's hopes for relief by sea and allowing Washington to tighten the noose. When 9,000 Americans and 7,800 French converged on Yorktown in late September, they outnumbered their 8,000 opponents by more than two to one, and the siege proved brief. Plagued by sickness and shortages of food and munitions, the British surrendered on October 19, 1781. For Washington and his army, Yorktown was a stunning victory. Intermittent warfare continued for another year. But the Americans finally had powerful leverage to bargain for peace and force Britain to recognize their independence.

The joint American–French victory at the siege of Yorktown, Virginia, in October 1781 ended British hopes for preventing American independence. As Cornwallis's troops marched out to lay down their arms, a band played "The World Turned Upside Down." "Finally," Lafayette wrote proudly, "everything came together at once, and we had a sensational turn of events. . . . The play is over." How significant was the role of the French in bringing the American drama to a successful close?

Winning the Peace

After Yorktown, the final phase of the war played out in European courts. There, the diplomatic maneuvering proved complicated and risky, with Benjamin Franklin, John Adams, and John Jay as the key American players. Often at odds, the three men nevertheless managed to achieve a final triumph that proved as unlikely and momentous as Washington's victory in Virginia. They did it, wrote the immodest Adams, "in spite of the malice of enemies, the finesse of Allies, and the mistakes of Congress."

For the British, the road to the peace table had been long and unpleasant. Early feelers about a negotiated settlement—from the Howes in 1776 and the Carlisle Commission in 1778—had not mentioned independence. But conditions changed drastically after Yorktown. Domestic unrest in Britain had already boiled into riots, and the expanded war was going poorly in India and the West Indies. "O God, it is all over!" Lord North muttered when he received the news of Cornwallis's defeat in Virginia.

Within months, Sir Guy Carleton replaced Clinton in command of the remaining British forces in America, the hawkish Lord Germain stepped down from the Cabinet, and North resigned after 12 years as prime minister. Even the king spoke of abdicating. But instead, he approved a new ministry more suited to the rising antiwar sentiment in Parliament. The Earl of Shelburne became prime minister in July 1782. Even before he assumed office, he had authorized peace discussions with his old acquaintance, Benjamin Franklin.

Franklin was in a difficult position. The crucial alliance he had negotiated with France stated that the Americans would not sign a separate peace with Britain.

✳ Explore the American Revolution on MyHistoryLab

HOW DID THE AMERICAN REVOLUTION UNFOLD?

Between 1775, when fighting broke out near Boston, and 1783, when a treaty was finally concluded in Paris, the British fought a long and costly war against rebellious American colonists. In some sense, this anticolonial revolution was also a civil war, as some colonists remained loyal to the British Empire while their neighbors rebelled against imperial power. As the graph illustrates, the American army was heavily outnumbered by British troops (including Hessian mercenaries) and their Loyalist supporters. Inevitably, George Washington's forces lost more major battles than they won. But the Patriots eventually outlasted their adversaries, with the help of France. The British faced a widening global war, mounting military expenditures, and a growing loss of support at home. Finally, therefore, the thirteen colonies emerged as the independent United States of America.

This idealized later image of George Washington, the heroic wartime leader, depicts the victorious general bidding farewell to his officers on December 4, 1783. The scene occurred at Fraunces Tavern near Wall Street in Lower Manhattan, just nine days after the last British soldiers departed from the new American Confederation. *Library of Congress.*

HIGHEST LEVEL OF TROOP STRENGTH

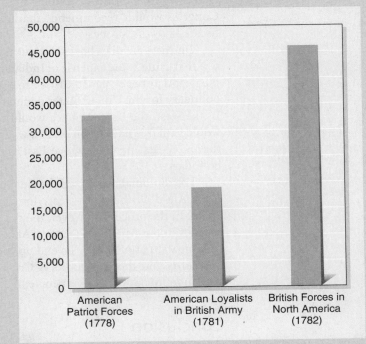

KEY QUESTIONS   Use **MyHistoryLab** *Explorer* to answer these **questions:**

Comparison ▶▶▶ *Where did the Americans have military successes?*

Map the losses and victories of the two sides in the Revolutionary War.

Analysis ▶▶▶ *Which regions were Loyalist and Patriot strongholds?*

Consider the roles of these two groups in the unfolding of the war.

Response ▶▶▶ *What position did the major cities play in the conflict?*

Understand the importance of urban areas for the two sides.

Moreover, Congress, grateful for vital French military and financial support, had instructed the American negotiators to defer to the wishes of Vergennes. The Americans did not realize that the French foreign minister had already entertained thoughts of a truce that would leave London in control of all the territory it currently held in America, including New York City and parts of the lower South. Vergennes opposed the Americans' republican principles, and he refused to treat the American diplomats as equal partners.

Still, the American peace commissioners fared surprisingly well in the treacherous waters of European diplomacy, starting with Franklin's first informal talks with the British. He laid out four "necessary" points, leading with the recognition of American independence. To this he added the removal of British troops, the right to fish in Newfoundland waters, and the revision of the Canadian border, which the Quebec Act of 1774 had pushed south to the Ohio River. Franklin then noted some "desirable" items for later bargaining. The British, he suggested, should consider paying an indemnity for war damages, an act that would officially acknowledge their own blame for the war. Perhaps they should cede Canada to the United States as well.

For its part, Britain sought compensation for roughly 70,000 American Loyalists who had been driven from their homes, plus the right to collect old debts that colonists had owed to British merchants before 1776. Hoping to disrupt the American–French alliance and to reestablish trade with their former colonies, the British negotiated preliminary peace terms with the Americans in November 1782. In return for independence, troop withdrawal, and fishing rights, the Americans agreed vaguely that their Congress would "recommend" that individual states approve compensation for confiscated Loyalist property.

On the Canadian boundary question, the Americans scored another success, but one that came at the expense of Indian nations. By giving up their bid for all of Canada, the negotiators persuaded Britain to relinquish the Ohio Valley and accept a northern boundary for the United States defined by the Great Lakes and the St. Lawrence River. In the west, the United States would reach to the Mississippi River, and Americans would gain free navigation on that waterway, despite Spanish opposition. In the South, the thirty-first parallel, above East and West Florida, would provide the American boundary.

The diplomats endorsed the final peace terms at Versailles, France, in September 1783. Amid all the other treaty terms, the British yielded East and West Florida to Spain. In the process, however, they made no mention of the Indians who had served as allies in the American conflict. Abandoned, the Native Americans had to confront their new situation alone. To end up "betrayed to our Enemies & divided between the Spaniards and the Americans is Cruel & Ungenerous," protested the Creek leader, Alexander McGillivray. His people had been "most Shamefully deserted."

Conclusion

The War for Independence that began at Lexington had lasted eight years. Like any lengthy armed struggle, it took a heavy toll on combatants and noncombatants alike. Personal survival was far from certain, as encounters with sickness and the enemy carried off enlisted men. American forces lost an estimated 25,000 soldiers, a huge number in proportion to the small overall population.

For those who avoided death, lesser dangers abounded. Uprooting from home became commonplace, losses of property were extensive, and indebtedness proved widespread. Despite constant uncertainties at the individual level, a makeshift revolutionary army, learning as it marched, had forced the British to concede American independence.

As in all wars, some of the most decisive action occurred far from the battlefield. In London, weakness in the chain of command, a lumbering bureaucracy, and divided public sentiment undermined the British war effort. Elsewhere in Europe, skillful American diplomats forged vital alliances needed to secure victory and won favorable peace terms. An unprecedented flurry of constitution writing had launched more than a dozen newly independent states, and the Articles of Confederation, approved after long delay, had knit them together into a formal league with a common Congress. The new and difficult art of republican self-government remained a work in progress, with some of the most difficult and contentious choices still to come. The fragile unity built on fighting a common enemy would be strained to the limit as new debates erupted over the meaning and direction of the unfinished revolution.

Chapter Review

"Things Are Now Come to That Crisis"

7.1 How were the Americans able to drive British forces out of Boston in March 1776, less than a year after the Battle of Lexington? p. 161

By seizing Bunker Hill in June 1775, the British Army, isolated in Boston, removed one location for shelling the town. But in March 1776, Washington's forces placed cannons hauled from distant Fort Ticonderoga on Dorchester Heights. Since these guns could bombard Boston, British troops finally elected to withdraw by ship.

Declaring Independence

7.2 In the context of the entire year 1776, why was Washington's successful crossing of the Delaware River on December 25 so significant? p. 164

In May 1776, Americans withdrew from Canada in disarray; in August, the Battle of Long Island nearly destroyed the Continental Army. As the Continentals withdrew from New York City and retreated to New Jersey, patriot support faltered badly; talk of American surrender increased. Washington's dramatic, unexpected move in late December reversed this trend.

The Struggle to Win French Support

7.3 If the rebellious Americans opposed monarchy, why did the French crown decide to back their cause? p. 169

Burgoyne's surrender at Saratoga demonstrated to France the staying power of the American rebels. French bureaucrats had little desire to see the fledgling republic succeed and grow strong. Still, to keep Britain bogged down in an expensive war on a remote continent, France recognized American independence and forged an alliance.

Legitimate States, a Respectable Military

7.4 If Americans were so fearful of centralized authority, how did they coordinate a successful political and military revolt against the powerful British Empire? p. 173

Jealous of their rights, Americans argued over effective ways to limit the powers of governors over their citizens and of officers over their soldiers. To assure winning the war, local elites conceded some of their traditional authority, but they also encouraged sufficient economic and military coordination to put victory within reach.

The Long Road to Yorktown

7.5 What conditions and events in America and Europe led to final American success in the War for Independence? p. 177

Rising war costs and sinking morale in Britain, success of the unlikely French–American alliance, and the global expansion of the conflict all aided the American cause. General Greene's shrewd

tactics in defeating Cornwallis's southern campaign ended Britain's last best hope, and the arrival of the French navy at Yorktown sealed the final victory.

Timeline

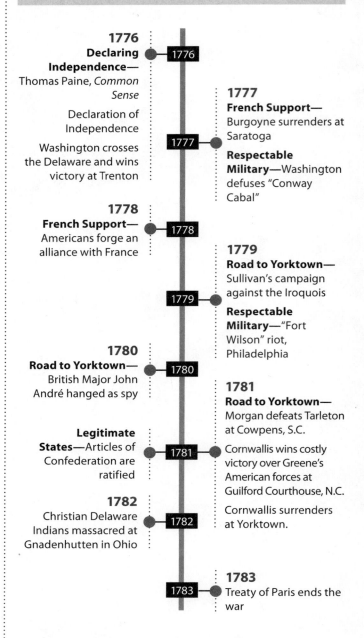

1776 Declaring Independence—Thomas Paine, *Common Sense*

Declaration of Independence

Washington crosses the Delaware and wins victory at Trenton

1777 French Support—Burgoyne surrenders at Saratoga

Respectable Military—Washington defuses "Conway Cabal"

1778 French Support—Americans forge an alliance with France

1779 Road to Yorktown—Sullivan's campaign against the Iroquois

Respectable Military—"Fort Wilson" riot, Philadelphia

1780 Road to Yorktown—British Major John André hanged as spy

1781 Road to Yorktown—Morgan defeats Tarleton at Cowpens, S.C.

Cornwallis wins costly victory over Greene's American forces at Guilford Courthouse, N.C.

Cornwallis surrenders at Yorktown.

Legitimate States—Articles of Confederation are ratified

1782 Christian Delaware Indians massacred at Gnadenhutten in Ohio

1783 Treaty of Paris ends the war

8 New Beginnings: The 1780s

How would the vast debt acquired in the course of the Revolutionary War be repaid? This burden loomed over the victorious American Confederation even before the Treaty of Paris had been signed. The struggle for answers spawned even more questions: Should the Confederation sell off western lands to speculators and settlers, even if Indians in the Mississippi Valley resisted fiercely? Should the new states issue paper currency to ease the tight money supply? Or should each legislature push the debt burden onto local residents by imposing steep new taxes, even though constituents felt strapped in the weak postwar economy? What if these citizens found it difficult or impossible to pay? And what if they petitioned for relief, and vowed, as irate New Jersey residents did, "to rise in opposition to authority by refusing to pay their taxes"?

On January 1, 1785, the constable of New Jersey's Mendham Township, who had confiscated property from local debtors unable to pay their taxes, attempted to sell off the debtors' goods in front of the Black Horse Tavern. Suddenly, as the public auction began, an organized party intervened, armed with "clubs &c." According to one observer, they "would not suffer anyone to make a bid for the articles set up or exposed to sale."

Again and again, similar scenes unfolded throughout the new American states during the 1780s, as beleaguered farmers, many of whom

In every new state, confrontations like this one took place outside taverns and courthouses during the 1780s. Angry debtors, many of them war veterans, confronted creditors and local officials who were determined to enforce the payment of small debts and steep new taxes, even in a tightened economy. Artist Howard Pyle (d. 1911) imagined this scene of angry farmers during Shays' Rebellion in Massachusetts in 1786. Enmeshed in debt and facing numerous foreclosures, were desperate citizens justified in disrupting public auctions, so no one could bid on family possessions put up for sale?

LEARNING OBJECTIVES

8.1	8.2	8.3	8.4	8.5
Why did the prospect of a Newburgh conspiracy and the creation of the Society of the Cincinnati upset many Americans? p. 190	Why did control of the Mississippi Valley matter so much to Americans after the revolution? p. 195	Why did large bondholders care so deeply about what forces were in control of the state and national governments? p. 200	How did nationalist leaders use their political skills to bring about the Constitutional Convention in Philadelphia? p. 204	Why was a bill of rights, expected by citizens, omitted by the drafters of the Constitution and later added? p. 209

Listen to **Chapter 8** on MyHistoryLab

Watch the Video Series on MyHistoryLab

Learn about some key topics related to this chapter with the
MyHistoryLab Video Series: Key Topics in U.S. History.

1 The Making of a New Nation: 1783–1789 The Articles of Confederation established a weak nation-state binding together thirteen very different former British colonies. Amid postwar depression and social unrest, well-to-do leaders felt the need for more centralized authority. This video reviews their decision to abandon, rather than revise, the Articles of Confederation. Their Philadelphia convention drafted a new constitution in 1787. When duly ratified, this document became the basis of the federal union we have today.

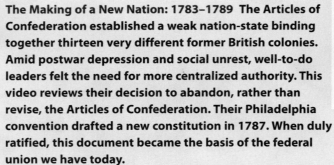 Watch on MyHistoryLab

Land Ordinances This video discusses a series of land ordinances instituted by Congress to establish American control over territory to the west, among them, the Northwest Ordinance, approved in 1787 by the Confederation Congress. It allowed new territories north of the Ohio River (no more than five in number) to enter the union on an equal footing with the original states. It prohibited slavery in these Northwest Territories, but it allowed for the deportation of fugitive slaves. **2**

Watch on MyHistoryLab

3 **Shays' Rebellion** Following the American Revolution, the primary problem for federal, state, and local government was a lack of hard currency. This money shortage, as well as economic depression, led to many rebellions over tax collection and debt payment. This video focuses on Shays' Rebellion (1786–1787) in Massachusetts. The determination of Daniel Shays and his associates generated fears among powerful creditors, who raised an army to suppress the rebellion. These anxieties helped fuel the push for a Constitutional Convention in 1787 that could shape a stronger federal government.

 Watch on MyHistoryLab

The Constitutional Convention From one perspective, the Constitutional Convention of 1787 has often been called the "Miracle in Philadelphia," as this video makes clear. While the delegates had much in common, they needed a series of compromises and deals to agree upon a viable constitution. When finished, they had shaped a stronger central government, but they had limited the democratic powers of the American people and had dodged the divisive issue of ending racial slavery. **4**

Watch on MyHistoryLab

had fallen into debt while fighting for independence, struggled against state and local officials protecting the rights of creditors. The unruly scuffle in Mendham, at the decade's midpoint, epitomizes the deepest dilemma of the immediate postwar period—but not the only one.

Historians now realize that a deadly smallpox epidemic had been ricocheting across North America since 1775. Like the Revolutionary War itself, the sickness had erupted first in Massachusetts, but its devastation spread far more widely than the war's destruction. It gained a foothold in New Orleans and Mexico City; it ravaged trading posts in Canada and Indian villages on the Northwest Coast. Even as Cornwallis surrendered at Yorktown, both armies witnessed the contagion's destructive force. By the time smallpox subsided in 1782, the fearsome virus had taken over 130,000 lives—many times the 25,000 American lives lost in service during the revolution.

A s the dual scourges of epidemic and war came to an end, the vast continent's political future remained uncertain. British power ruled Canada, Spanish authority claimed much of the West, and French officials still dreamed of regaining control over the Mississippi Valley. There, Native Americans whom Pontiac had rallied a generation earlier once again threatened fierce resistance to incursions into their ancestral lands. Were it not for the "hostile" demeanor of the Indians, lamented an eastern politician eager to solve the debt crisis in 1786, "7,000,000 acres of land belonging to the United States would now have been surveyed, and ready for sale."

On the eastern seaboard, the Confederation's Continental Congress in Philadelphia faced a host of problems. Members had a restless army to pay, a weak government to reform, and enormous war debts to confront. Moreover, despite the recent revolution's Enlightenment ideology of equality, half a million people remained legally enslaved—potential allies for any European power seeking to disrupt the fragile new **federation**. Acceptance of the Articles of Confederation in 1781 had not come easily, and all assumed that the basic structure of governance would demand further revision and adjustment. However, few could foresee that within eight years it would be set aside entirely for a more centralized federal design.

Federation An alliance or compact between political units that agree to surrender certain powers to a central authority while still retaining other powers.

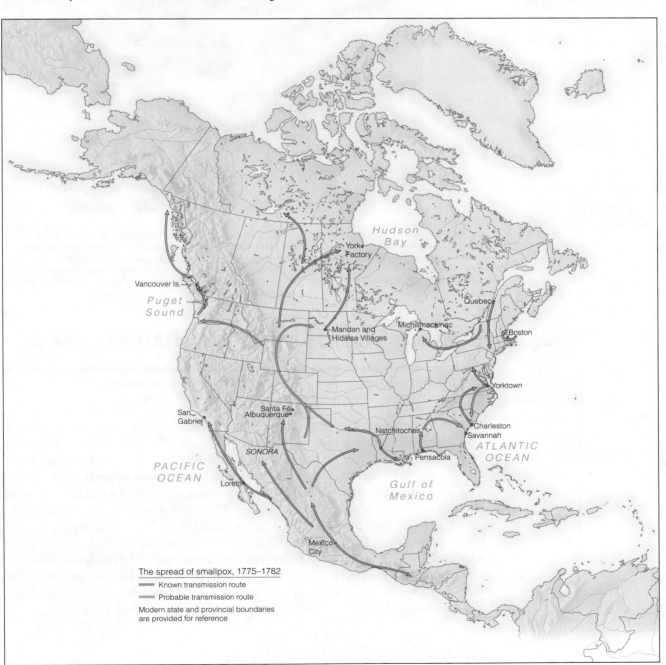

MAP 8.1 THE SPREAD OF SMALLPOX ACROSS NORTH AMERICA, 1775–1782 A great smallpox epidemic swept North America during the Revolutionary era. In 1781, it moved up the Baja Peninsula with settlers heading for San Gabriel, the Spanish mission that became Los Angeles, California.

Smallpox "spread like lightning through all the missions," wrote Father Luis Sales from Baja California in 1781. The sickness, he reported, caused "havoc which only those who have seen it can believe. The towns and missions were . . . deserted, and bodies were seen in the road." Time and again, "the poor little children, abandoned beside the dead, died without help." (This modern photo shows that smallpox persisted until its global eradication in the 1970s.) Why did it take American historians more than two centuries to comprehend the huge geographical scope and enormous human cost of this transcontinental epidemic at the time of the Revolutionary War?

Beating Swords into Plowshares

8.1 Why did the prospect of a Newburgh conspiracy and the creation of the Society of the Cincinnati upset many Americans?

Thanks to military victory and skillful diplomacy, the initial survival of the new United States seemed assured. The former colonies had banded together under the Articles of Confederation, finally ratified in 1781, which placed specific governmental powers in the hands of an elected national legislature, or Continental Congress. But deeper questions persisted regarding the republican experiment, now that peace was at hand. How would citizens transform their "swords into plowshares," as urged by the Biblical prophet Isaiah? Should power rest primarily with the victorious army, the wealthy merchants, or the artisans and farmers central to the revolutionary movement? Should authority be consolidated in the hands of a well-educated, new national elite, or should it be widely dispersed, with local communities and states empowered to manage their own affairs? Equally important, what cultural patterns would take hold within the fledgling society in these postwar years?

Will the Army Seize Control?

After their triumph at Yorktown, Washington's men had moved north to press British forces to evacuate New York City. More than 10,000 American troops and 500 officers encamped at Newburgh, on the Hudson River. Exhausted soldiers were eager to receive long-overdue pay and return home. Clearly, they could negotiate best for promised wages while they were still together and armed. Officers were especially reluctant to disband without certain assurances of money. In 1780, they had extracted from the Congress a promise of half pay for life. In December 1782, with no sign of compensation in sight, disgruntled officers sent a delegation to Philadelphia to press their claims.

Within Congress, the men around financier Robert Morris, including James Wilson and Alexander Hamilton, wanted to bolster and centralize the Confederation's finances. To that end, they sought a new duty of 5 percent on imported goods to raise money from the states. Revenue from this "continental impost" could make the Confederation solvent and allow it to assume responsibility for paying off war debts. In turn, this commitment would tie the interests of wealthy citizens to the Confederation government's success. Morris even threatened to resign his post if the "nationalists" did not get their way. Rumblings from the officer corps would help these politicians push through the impost measure, crucial to their long-term goals. So they quietly encouraged the military dissidents in Newburgh.

In March 1783, inflammatory petitions circulated among officers at Newburgh, hinting at a military takeover to impose stability after a turbulent revolution. These anonymous "addresses" urged officers to sit tight, neither fighting nor laying down their arms, until Congress guaranteed their payment. Without Washington's approval, the officers arranged a meeting to discuss their plight.

If the plotters at Newburgh hoped to draw Washington into the scheme, they were sorely disappointed. He did attend the officers' meeting on March 15, but he used his commanding presence to discredit the ill-advised plan. His eyes weakened by endless wartime correspondence, he drew a pair of spectacles from his pocket, a surprising gesture that underscored his years of dedication and sacrifice. He then read a letter from Congress containing assurances of support, and he urged his officers not to take any actions that would undermine the honor they had earned.

Within Congress, the frightening prospect of a coup dissolved resistance to certain demands from the officers. Chastised by Washington, the officers disavowed the "infamous propositions" and accepted a congressional offer of full pay for the next five years. In April 1783, as Congress passed a version of the 5 percent impost, momentous news arrived from Europe. Word spread that preliminary articles of peace had been signed in Paris. By June, most soldiers were headed home.

The Society of the Cincinnati

Washington's strong stance against the suspected Newburgh conspiracy reminded his admirers of the familiar story of Cincinnatus, a general in Rome's early republic. The Roman Senate called Cincinnatus from his farm to command an army against invaders. After defeating the enemy, he put down his sword and took up his plow again rather than seize power as a military ruler. His selfless act earned Cincinnatus the lasting respect of the Roman people. Similarly, at a crucial moment for the American republic, Washington urged fellow officers to respect the fragile principle of civilian control over the military. Your action, Thomas Jefferson told Washington, "has probably prevented this revolution from being closed as most others have been by a subversion of that liberty it was intended to establish."

Still, Jefferson and others had grounds to fear that some military officers might meddle in politics while hiding behind the noble name of Cincinnatus. In May 1783, General Henry Knox announced formation of the Society of the Cincinnati. The new organization invoked the name of the famous Roman, in a plural form, to put its members in the best light. But it was open only to officers in the Continental Army, their descendents, and invited honorary members, so some onlookers sensed that the "Cincinnati Club" had a sinister purpose. After all, members contributed to a charitable fund that resembled a political war chest, and they maintained contact with each other through newsletters concerning "the general union of the states." Critics feared a separate, self-perpetuating aristocracy of the very kind Americans had fought to erase.

Interpreting History

The Demobilization OF JOSEPH PLUMB MARTIN

"they were **turned** adrift like old **worn-out** horses"

J oseph Plumb Martin was born in western Massachusetts in 1760. He enlisted in the Continental Army before his sixteenth birthday and was encamped at West Point, New York, when peace finally arrived. Later, in a compelling narrative of his wartime experiences, he recalled the demobilization process from the perspective of a common soldier.

[On April 19, 1783,] we had general orders read which satisfied the most skeptical, that the war was over and the prize won [after] eight tedious years. But the soldiers said but little about it; their chief thoughts were closely fixed upon their situation. . . . Starved, ragged and meager, not a cent to help themselves with, and no means or method in view to remedy or alleviate their condition. This was appalling in the extreme. . . .

At length, the eleventh day of June 1783, arrived. "The old man," our captain, came into the room, with his hands full of papers. . . . He then handed us our discharges, or rather furloughs, . . . permission to return home, but to return to the army again if required. This was policy in government; to discharge us absolutely in our present pitiful, forlorn condition, it was feared, might cause some difficulties. . . .

Some of the soldiers went off for home the same day that their fetters were knocked off; others stayed and got their final settlement certificates, which they sold to procure decent clothing and money. . . . I was among those. . . . I now bid a final farewell to the service. I had obtained my settlement certificates and sold some of them and purchased some decent clothing, and then set off from West Point. . . .

When those who engaged to serve during the war enlisted, they were promised a hundred acres of land, each. . . . When the country had drained the last drop of service it could screw out of the poor soldiers, they were turned adrift like old worn-out horses, and nothing said about land to pasture them upon. . . . Congress did, indeed, appropriate lands, . . . but no care was taken that the soldiers should get them. [Instead,] a pack of speculators . . . were driving about the country like so many evil spirits, endeavoring to pluck the last feather from the soldiers. The soldiers were ignorant of the ways and means to obtain their bounty lands. . . . It was, soldiers, look to yourselves; we want no more of you.

We were, also, promised six dollars and two thirds a month. . . . And what was six dollars and sixty-seven cents of this "Continental currency," as it was called, worth? It was scarcely enough to procure a man a dinner. . . . I received one month's pay in specie while on the march to Virginia, in the year 1781, and except that, I never received any pay worth the name while I belonged to the army. . . . It is provoking to think of it. The country was rigorous in exacting my compliance to *my* engagements . . . but equally careless in performing her contracts with me, and why so? One reason was that she had all the power in her own hands and I had none. Such things ought not to be.

After the war, Martin settled on the Maine frontier, and a speculator bought his right to 100 acres of bounty land in Ohio. In 1818, as a disabled laborer with a large family, he successfully petitioned Congress for a small pension to support the household. He died poor in 1850.

William Ranney painted *Revolutionary War Veterans Returning Home* in 1848, when the United States was at war with Mexico. The image offered a positive reminder of earlier American military success. Does the artist suggest that some soldiers leaving the Continental Army in 1783 had clearly fared better than others?

SOURCE: William Ranney, *Veterans of 1776 Returning from the War*, c. 1848. Dallas Museum of Art, Museum League Fund, Special Contributors and General Acquisitions Fund

Questions for Discussion

1. Why did the government worry about discharging soldiers such as Martin in 1783, and why did many of them sell their final settlement certificates so swiftly?
2. Can you compare and contrast Martin's complaints with the situation of modern American combat veterans?

SOURCE: James Kirby Martin, ed., *Ordinary Courage: The Revolutionary War Adventures of Joseph Plumb Martin,* 2nd ed. (New York: Brandywine Press, 1999), pp. 159–164.

Washington was automatically a member of the society, but Jefferson and other friends urged the general not to accept a leadership position. Struck by this "formidable" opposition, Washington suggested changes in the society, including doing away with the hereditary and honorary memberships. However, he never played a central role in the organization, and Washington's well-publicized alterations were never implemented. The Society of the Cincinnati exerted influence as a pressure group before receding from politics in future generations.

Renaming the Landscape

The controversy over the Society of the Cincinnati represented part of a larger debate about the direction of postwar life. Many Americans—despite continuing disagreements—set out to build a national culture and a shared identity. Like the Puritans before them, they aspired to provide new models for the Atlantic world.

They began with names. Everywhere, people christened new towns, counties, streets, and schools and renamed old ones. They replaced numerous British names, such as those of hated prewar governors, so Virginia's Dunmore County received the Indian name *Shanando* (later spelled *Shenandoah*). Because most people found references to royalty distasteful, King Street in Boston quickly became State Street. Still, royal figures who had aided the revolution received their due. Newcomers on the Ohio River named their town Louisville, honoring America's wartime alliance with King Louis XVI of France.

Political leaders popularized Christopher Columbus as well. For generations, the English had downplayed the explorer's importance as they contested Spanish claims in the Western Hemisphere. Now, American writers coined the ringing term *Columbia* for their land to stress its separation from Britain. In South Carolina, citizens named their new capital Columbia in 1786. Five years later, the proposed national capital was christened the District of Columbia. In New York City, when King's College reopened in 1784 under local governance, it was called Columbia College (later Columbia University).

Exploring in Georgia, Philadelphian John Bartram and his botanist son William found a small unfamiliar tree. They named this "rare and elegant flowering shrub" *Franklinia* after their scientist friend Benjamin Franklin. William drew a watercolor of its blossom and saved seeds to protect the species from extinction. Novel American plants could become a source of national pride. How much history can be gleaned from the names of counties, towns, streets, and plants in a region?

SOURCE: Natural History Museum, London

Of all the new names, those honoring individual war heroes became the most popular. Citizens hailed foreign supporters of the revolution—such as Lafayette, Pulaski, and Steuben—by using their names on streets and towns. They saluted American officers the same way. Washington's name was used most often, but those of Montgomery, Wayne, Greene, Lincoln, Mercer, Marion, and others popped up as well. North Carolina named one of its trans-Appalachian forts on the Cumberland River Nashborough, after General Francis Nash, who had died at the battle of Germantown. Citizens changed the fort's name to Nashville in 1784. Two years later, inhabitants of a site on the Tennessee River named their new town Knoxville in honor of General Knox, who had become the Confederation's secretary of war the previous year.

An Independent Culture

New names were just part of the story. Many felt that the American language needed to be made more independent and accessible. Noah Webster, a schoolteacher who had fought against Burgoyne, believed that "as an independent nation, our honor requires us to have a system of our own, in language as well as government." In his *American Spelling Book* (1783), Webster championed a simple, uniform written language that rejected English conventions. Words such as *colour* and *labour* lost their silent *u*, *theatre* became *theater*, and *plough* was shortened to *plow*. The New Englander followed this success with an influential grammar book and a popular reader. Webster went on to produce *An American Dictionary of the English Language* (1828) that incorporated 5,000 new words, many of them reflecting Indian origins (*tomahawk*) and American nature (*rattlesnake*).

Webster also joined other reformers in lobbying state legislatures for copyright laws to protect the literary works that poured from the pens of ambitious writers. Philip Freneau, a classmate of James Madison at Princeton, drafted a poem titled "The British Prison Ship" (1781), about his war experiences. Authors living near Hartford, known as the Connecticut Wits, wrote similarly nationalistic poetry. Timothy Dwight, future president of Yale College, created "The Conquest of Canaan" (1785), and Joel Barlow composed an epic titled "The Vision of Columbus" (1787), heralding a bright future.

Increasingly, the land itself captured the imagination of Americans. In 1784, a Connecticut silversmith engraved the first map of the new United States. Jedidiah Morse, who published *Geography Made Easy* and *The American Geography* in the 1780s, became known as the "Father of American Geography." The Quaker naturalist William Bartram drafted a pioneering nature book about his travels throughout the Southeast, surprising readers with his detailed description of alligators. In Philadelphia, the versatile painter and patriot Charles Willson Peale launched a museum to promote interest in art and the natural world. At his Virginia estate, Monticello, Thomas Jefferson pursued his own fascination with the American landscape. He promoted exploration, tested new crops, and excavated ancient Indian mounds. In *Notes on the State of Virginia* (1785), Jefferson detailed his region's geography, society, and natural history.

In 1782, Hector St. John de Crèvecoeur, a Frenchman who made his home in America, published *Letters from an American Farmer*, posing the question "What is an American?" According to Crèvecoeur, free people flourished in America because "a new mode of living" nurtured community growth. Societies for bettering jails, assisting debtors, and building libraries had existed before independence, but after the war Crèvecoeur witnessed a burst in the creation of voluntary associations. Reformers launched more than thirty new benevolent organizations between 1783 and 1789, offering aid to the poor, the sick, and the disabled.

In 1785, prominent New Yorkers John Jay and Alexander Hamilton joined like-minded citizens to form a Society for the Promotion of the Manumission of Slaves. In Connecticut, citizens banded together in an early **temperance** organization to stop the abuse of liquor. Similar efforts to reform and improve the new nation sprang up everywhere. Amid such postwar cultural optimism, the former colonists of the British Empire began to speak of shaping an expansive empire of their own.

Temperance A social movement embracing either total opposition to alcohol consumption or support for its moderate use.

Competing for Control of the Mississippi Valley

8.2 Why did control of the Mississippi Valley matter so much to Americans after the revolution?

"It has ever been my hobby-horse," John Adams wrote in 1786, "to see rising in America an empire of liberty, and a prospect of two or three hundred millions of freemen, without one noble or one king among them. You say it is impossible. . . . I would still say, let us try the experiment." Westward expansion became a persistent American theme. But during the postwar decade, interest and activity centered mostly on the land just beyond the Appalachian Mountains, territory reserved for Indians until Britain ceded the region at the end of the revolution.

In the South in the 1780s, pioneer families searching for land pushed west through Cumberland Gap and spread out across parts of the lower Mississippi River valley, an area that eventually became known as the Old Southwest. These homesteaders promptly faced resistance from Native American inhabitants and their Spanish supporters. At the same time, north of the Ohio River, other American migrants were flocking to newly claimed woodlands later remembered as the Old Northwest. They, too, met stiff opposition from Native Americans and their British allies in neighboring Canada. By the time the Constitutional Convention met in Philadelphia in the summer of 1787, the Continental Congress of the existing Confederation government was busy revising an elaborate plan to draw this territory into the Union.

Disputed Territory: The Old Southwest

For a generation, Spain had been rebuilding its position north of the Gulf of Mexico and east of Texas in the Old Southwest. The Spanish had acquired Louisiana from France in 1763 and had conquered West Florida. In a 1783 treaty, Britain gave back East Florida to the Spanish and agreed that Spain would retain West Florida as well. The Spanish occupied St. Augustine, Pensacola, New Orleans, and Natchez, as well as St. Louis farther north.

Because Spain controlled both banks of the lower Mississippi, the Spanish determined who could use the huge river for trade. Since 1763, they had let British subjects navigate freely on the Mississippi, so trans-Appalachian fur traders had become accustomed to using this thoroughfare. Louisiana merchants paid for goods in Spanish silver, and settlers upriver needed the hard currency. During the Revolutionary War, Americans had retained access to the river, and the Spanish in New Orleans depended on produce from the north. Still, Spanish authorities feared American expansion into the Mississippi Valley. They debated whether to resist migrants pushing from the east, or to welcome newcomers and profit from their trade.

In 1783, Spain was shocked when Britain, through its separate treaty with the United States, granted the Americans a generous southern boundary: the thirty-first parallel. The treaty terms also included the right of Americans to navigate on the Mississippi. The Spanish believed that they alone should decide whose boats had access to the river. Moreover, Spain had good reason to claim that its West Florida province stretched north *above* 31 degrees, at least to the mouth of the Yazoo River and perhaps as far as the Tennessee River.

For its part, the new Confederation had the force of numbers working to its advantage. The threat of Indian attacks had dammed up westward expansion since 1775. After the war, Americans migrated by the thousands to three existing centers of Anglo settlement in the Old Southwest. By 1785, 10,000 recent migrants clustered along several rivers above Knoxville. Nearly three times that many newcomers had already staked claims to the rich land between Lexington and Louisville. In addition, another

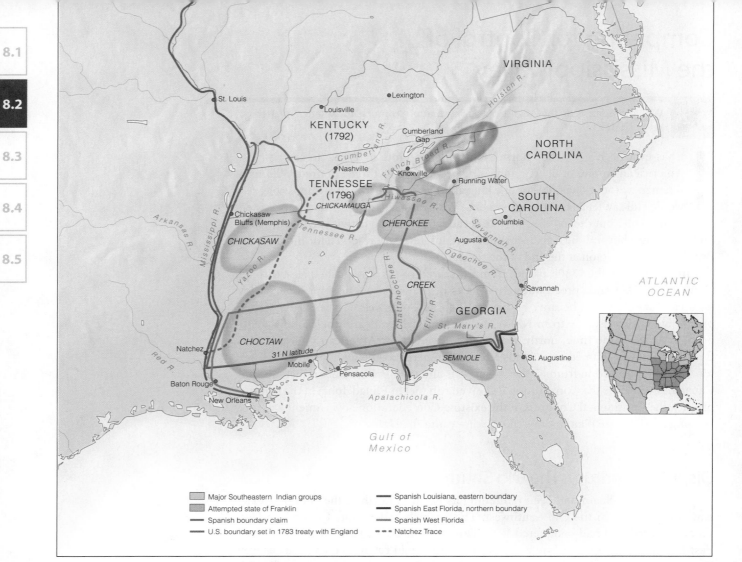

MAP 8.2 SOUTHERN LAND DEBATES AFTER 1783 Following the revolution, competing forces collided in the trans-Appalachian South. The United States claimed land reaching the Mississippi River down to 31 degrees latitude, and the Spanish claimed territory north to the Tennessee River. Although major Indian tribes continued to possess much of the region, coastal states also claimed sweeping jurisdiction. In Georgia, for instance, settlement remained confined near the Savannah River, but the state sold speculators large tracts as far west as the Yazoo River.

4,000 were clearing farms along the Cumberland River around Nashville. Aggressive Americans talked about pushing even farther west. They imagined establishing a foothold on the Mississippi at Chickasaw Bluffs (modern Memphis) or perhaps seizing Natchez or New Orleans.

Southern Claims and Indian Resistance

In the southern states, powerful land speculators pressed their legislatures to support expansion. Georgia, unlike many other states, had not relinquished its western lands to the Confederation. The state's 35-million-acre Yazoo claim stretched west from the Chattahoochee River (Georgia's present boundary with Alabama) to the Mississippi River and from the lower border of modern-day Tennessee to the thirty-first parallel. "I look forward to a time, not very far distant," wrote Judge George Walton, when Georgia "will be settled and connected . . . from the shores of the Atlantic to the banks of the Mississippi." By 1789, Walton had been elected governor of the state, and the land business boomed. During his tenure, Walton signed warrants for huge tracts up to 50,000 acres, sometimes selling unusable or even nonexistent acreage.

Unlike Georgians, pioneers from Virginia and the Carolinas faced a rugged mountain barrier. But they still trekked west through Cumberland Gap. In the decade after the war, backwoodsman Daniel Boone worked as a surveyor for these migrants in the trans-Appalachian region of Virginia that became Kentucky in 1792. During that same decade, North Carolina issued more land patents than it had created during the entire colonial era, most of them deeds for homesteads west of the mountains. Some of North Carolina's western landholders tried to create their own separate jurisdiction: the mountain state of Franklin. Without recognition from the Confederation government, their venture soon failed. Instead, all of North Carolina's western territory—from the Appalachians to the Mississippi—became the state of Tennessee in 1796.

Native American Southerners, living in all these lands, suddenly found themselves caught between the competing claims of Spain and the United States. The Cherokee, Creek, Choctaw, and Chickasaw—some 40,000 people—all debated which individuals and strategies to follow. Some responded to their new situation by selecting leaders with ties to European Americans. Among the Creek, for example, Alexander McGillivray rose to prominence. The son of a wealthy Scottish trader and a Creek woman, he had been raised on his father's Georgia plantation before becoming the Creek leader in 1782. He was well equipped to bargain with Spanish and American officials.

The renegade Cherokee warrior Dragging Canoe, who had split with tribal elders before the revolution broke out, offered a different approach. Hundreds of militant Indians, discouraged by the compromises of their leaders, had joined his band of guerrilla fighters known as the Chickamauga living along the Tennessee River. From this well-protected location—near where Alabama, Georgia, and Tennessee now meet—the Chickamauga recruited allies and led forays to stop American encroachment. But Dragging Canoe died in 1792 before he could build a strong alliance with Indians north of the Ohio River.

"We Are Now Masters": The Old Northwest

Native Americans in the North also struggled to maintain their way of life and resist the newcomers. But white Americans lost no time in claiming Indian domains ceded by Britain in the 1783 Treaty of Paris. "We are now Masters of this Island," General Philip Schuyler boasted to the Iroquois, "and can dispose of the Lands as we think proper." Britain refused to vacate western forts on the pretext that Americans still owed prewar debts to London merchants. Even so, the British could provide little material support to the region's Indians.

American delegations moved quickly to draft treaties with the Iroquois and the Ohio Valley tribes. Delegates bluntly asserted the right of the new U.S. government to Indian lands, treating the Native Americans as dependents rather than equals. The negotiators even took hostages to force the Indians to accept their terms. Ordinary Americans sealed these claims with a surge of migration into western Pennsylvania and beyond. "The Americans . . . put us out of our lands," Indian leaders complained to the Spanish in 1784, "extending themselves like a plague of locusts in the territories of the Ohio River which we inhabit."

Americans initially remained divided among themselves over who would control the region. Connecticut retained a "western reserve" of 4 million acres south of Lake Erie that it used to satisfy claims from the state's war veterans. Similarly, Virginia held onto land rights for an even larger "military district" to repay soldiers and war victims. But one by one, the states of Massachusetts, New York, Connecticut, and Virginia ceded large territorial claims to the Confederation government.

These western acquisitions transformed the Confederation into something more than a league of states. With lands of its own to organize, the Confederation government took on attributes of a sovereign ruling body. As territorial cessions increased, Congress put Thomas Jefferson in charge of a committee to draft "a plan for the temporary Government of the Western territory." Before he departed for Europe to replace

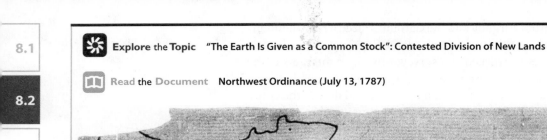

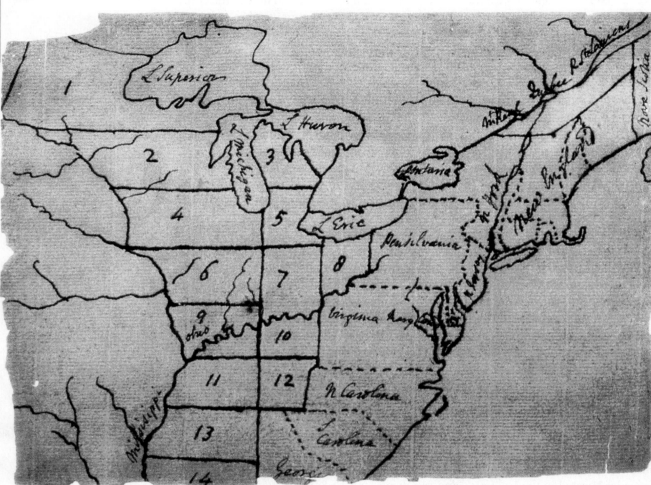

A sketch by Congressman Thomas Jefferson shows his proposal to divide the new interior territories into fourteen states, using established lines of longitude and latitude as convenient and orderly boundaries. By suggesting numerous compact states, Jefferson hoped to maximize the congressional voting strength of western farmers. Why did others, eager to limit future western power in Congress, push successfully for fewer, larger states?

SOURCE: University of Michigan, William L. Clements Library, Map Division

Benjamin Franklin as the American minister to France, Jefferson drew up a design for western land distribution.

After Jefferson sailed for France, his report became the basis for the Land Ordinance of 1785. Jefferson knew that in the South, where surveyors often staked out piecemeal claims on a first-come, first-served basis, the best property had gone to wealthy investors. Moreover, odd-shaped lots had prompted endless boundary litigation. To avoid these complications, the 1785 ordinance called for surveyors to lay out a grid of square townships, beginning at the point where the Ohio River flowed out of Pennsylvania. A township would contain 36 numbered sections, each 1 mile square (640 acres). The ordinance reserved the income from one valuable section near the heart of every township to support public education.

Orderly surveying and public education were just parts of Jefferson's plan. Hoping to populate the region with self-sufficient yeomen farmers, he proposed that the government give away land in small parcels. He envisioned self-government for these enterprising pioneers, not colonial status. For Jefferson, the more weight these independent farmers obtained in the American government the better, so he urged the rapid entry of numerous new territories into the Union on an equal footing with the thirteen original states. He suggested creating up to fourteen small, rectangular districts in the west. At least nine would be north of the Ohio River, and each could become a separate state with voting rights in Congress.

According to Jefferson's report, the first settlers arriving in a district were to form a temporary government. When the local population reached 20,000, residents could call a convention, frame a constitution, and send a delegate to Congress. When the district's population equaled the number of free inhabitants living in the smallest of the thirteen original states, that district could enter the Union if certain conditions were met. Each new state must agree to support a republican form of government, remain part of the Confederation, and accept a share of the federal debt. It must also agree to exclude slavery after 1800.

Congress accepted Jefferson's report, but then it modified the plan greatly. A few of his suggestions for territorial names (Michigania and Illinoia) attracted interest, but most, such as Saratoga and Polypotamia, were dropped. Jefferson's more substantial ideas, such as the use of a metric system for land measurement, also fared poorly. In its Land Ordinance of 1785, Congress removed his call for numerous districts, dismissed the notion of free land, and dropped the idea of ending slavery.

The Northwest Ordinance of 1787

The huge task of surveying the wilderness north of the Ohio River into neat geometric squares would take years to complete. Almost immediately—and long before the initial ordinance could take hold—political shifts produced an entirely new law from Congress: the Northwest Ordinance of 1787. This law determining how territories north of the Ohio River would be governed contained a number of additional changes. For example, it reversed direction on the slave question once again, introducing an immediate prohibition of slavery north of the Ohio River. However, it made arrangements to deport fugitive slaves back to their owners in slaveholding states.

In various ways, the new ordinance proved less democratic than earlier versions. Congress cut the possible number of new districts in the Old Northwest, specifying there could be only three to five new states. This move limited the potential political weight of the vast territory. In addition, the ordinance increased property requirements for citizens who wanted to vote or hold office. It also slowed the process by which new states could gain admission to the Union. Eventually, Congress granted statehood to five new entities, but the process took longer than half a century.

Most members of Congress feared democratic governance in the Old Northwest and the prospect of giving a strong voice to people with different regional interests. To retain control over the domain, they provided for the appointment of territorial officials—a governor, a secretary, and three judges—instead of allowing elected governments. Even when territorial legislatures formed, the governor would have veto power over their actions. James Monroe, head of the committee that moved the bill through Congress, wrote candidly to Jefferson, "It is in effect to be a colonial gover[nme]nt similar to wh[at] prevailed in these States previous to the revolution."

These changes benefited eastern speculators—some of whom were members of Congress—who hoped to control these lands for profit. In 1786, former army officers in New England, joined by five surveyors, organized the Ohio Company to buy up western land. They dispatched Massachusetts minister Manasseh Cutler to lobby Congress to sell a huge tract at bargain rates. Cutler joined forces with congressional insiders associated with another venture, the Scioto Company. Together, they engineered a deal providing 1.5 million acres to the Ohio Company and another 5 million acres for Scioto investors.

Whatever suspicious bargains surrounded congressional passage of the Northwest Ordinance of 1787, the new law still granted basic rights to western residents. These guarantees—following state bills of rights—included religious freedom, trial by jury, and access to common-law judicial proceedings. Most important, the western territories were assured of full entry into the Union as equal states rather than receiving dependent status as permanent colonies. This system established an orderly method for bringing new regions into the Union, starting when Vermont became the fourteenth state in 1791.

Debtor and Creditor, Taxpayer and Bondholder

8.3 Why did large bondholders care so deeply about what forces were in control of the state and national governments?

T he end of the Revolutionary War brought widespread economic depression. The money spent by foreign armies for goods and services dried up, and the split with Britain disrupted established patterns of commerce. When peace returned, merchants scrambled to find profitable markets and new trade routes. At the same time, those who had preserved their holdings or made money during the war paid to buy goods from abroad that had been scarce during the fighting. These foreign purchases drained hard currency away from the states and increased the Confederation's debt.

Citizens everywhere felt the brunt of the postwar slump as prices dropped and the money supply shrank. As credit tightened, merchants called in their loans and unpaid bills. Families in debt, especially poor artisans and subsistence farmers, suddenly faced the threat of foreclosure and loss of their property. They fought back in local elections, in state legislatures, and even in the streets. Violence broke out in state after state, from New Hampshire to Georgia, as hard-pressed people, many of them veterans, decried fiscal policies that favored wealthy bondholders. Heavy taxes were being used to pay annual interest on bonds held by members of the moneyed classes. When armed conflict erupted in Massachusetts, fear of wider rebellion helped prompt a drastic effort to restructure and strengthen the national government through a special, closed-door convention in Philadelphia.

New Sources of Wealth

In 1783, the British government managed to fire one parting shot at the former colonies. To nurture Britain's maritime trade and punish New England shippers, it restricted Americans from trading with the British West Indies. The move barred American ships from a key portion of Britain's imperial commerce, forcing merchants to seek out new avenues of trade. In 1784, an American vessel entered the Baltic Sea and established trade relations with Russia. Meanwhile, the Massachusetts ports of Nantucket and New Bedford stepped up their search for whales to provide oil for American lamps. Captains had no trouble finding sailors in need of work, and ships sailed wherever they sensed possible profits.

Early in 1783, a Savannah merchant named Joseph Clay commented that a "vast number" of slaves had fled the South in wartime. As rice plantations renewed production, African workers were "exceeding scarce and in demand." Sensing a profit, foreign slave traders shipped 15,000 Africans to Georgia and South Carolina by 1785. New England captains soon joined in, sailing ships to Africa in hopes of renewing a trade that had been interrupted during the war. Antislavery sentiment had increased with the idealism of the revolution, and several states, including Virginia, had outlawed slave imports. But these developments did not prevent American vessels from transporting Africans across the Atlantic. "The Negro business is a great object with us," Clay reported in 1784. "It is to the Trade of this Country, as the Soul to the body."

Financier Robert Morris took a global perspective, realizing that profits could be made by opening new trade routes to the Orient. The project would take an enormous investment—ten times the amount needed to send a ship to Europe—but the potential rewards were irresistible. Morris's first vessel, the *Empress of China*, left New York harbor for Canton by way of the Indian Ocean early in 1784. It carried almost 30 tons of ginseng root—procured from western Virginia—highly prized by the Chinese. The ship's cargo also included $20,000 in hard currency (a huge drain on New York's economy) and 2,600 furs.

In six months, the American vessel reached Canton, China's outlet for foreign commerce. "The Chinese had never heard of us," one sailor noted, "but we introduced ourselves as a new Nation" and gave them "a description of our Country." Chinese merchants welcomed trade with "the new people" and called their strange country "the flowery flag kingdom" because the stars on the American flag resembled blossoms. In May 1785, the *Empress of China* returned to New York loaded with tea, chinaware, and silk. Morris and his partners raked in a hefty 20 percent return on their investment.

Other traders took notice. In 1787, the Browns, wealthy merchants in Providence, diverted a slave ship from the African trade to the China tea trade. That same year, six Boston investors sent several vessels around Cape Horn to trade for furs on the American Northwest Coast, pioneering new Pacific routes for American ships. Among the Nootka Indians, Captain Robert Gray exchanged cloth and iron goods for sea otter pelts. Then he sailed the *Columbia* across the Pacific, pausing at Hawaii for supplies. Reaching Canton in 1789, Gray traded profitably and proceeded home through the Indian Ocean, making the *Columbia* the first American ship to circumnavigate the globe.

Because Gray's voyage affirmed the rewards of trade along the Northwest Coast, a diplomatic controversy flared the following year at Nootka Sound, on the west side of Vancouver Island. Although Spain protested British and American trading activities

ATACKTED at JUAN. DE. FUCA. STRAIT'S.

Shut out of British ports, adventurous American merchants launched global trading experiments after the revolution. This painting on glass shows Northwest Coast Indians menacing the American ship *Columbia* from their large war canoes in the waters north of Puget Sound. Cannon smoke above the deck suggests warning shots have been fired. Captain Robert Gray was conducting trade in sea otter pelts for transport across the Pacific Ocean to China, where the soft fur was highly valued. How and why might such an encounter have differed from similar events along North America's East Coast several centuries earlier?

SOURCE: George Davidson, *Attacked at Juan de Fuca Straits*, c. 1792.

in the area, Gray was back on the Northwest Coast by 1792. He entered a powerful stream—where Washington and Oregon now meet—and named it the Columbia River, after his ship. When he planted the American flag at the mouth of this major waterway, his action foreshadowed later territorial claims by the United States in the Oregon region.

While American merchants probed for new markets abroad, they also moved to strengthen their economic and political position at home. Some wealthy investors bought up a variety of loan certificates, paper notes, and wartime securities issued by state governments and the Continental Congress, paying only a small fraction of the original value. Certificates issued to soldiers at the end of the war became part of this speculative market when the original recipients sold their notes to prosperous speculators for needed cash. In Maryland, for example, the claims on $900,000 owed by the state became concentrated in the hands of only 318 people by 1790. Moreover, 16 of these people controlled more than half of the total value, and these wealthy investors took an increasing interest in political events. They realized that whoever controlled the reins of power at the state and national levels would determine how the various notes of credit might be redeemed. Speculators who had purchased numerous notes for a fraction of their face worth stood to reap enormous profits from any government that would pay interest on, and then buy back, all these paper arrangements at their original high value.

"Tumults in New England"

The few people who had acquired most of the paper securities wanted their holdings redeemed for hard money. But the majority of citizens, faced with rising debts amid an economic downturn, resented the heavy taxes needed to pay interest on the debt to these wealthy speculators. Favoring much easier credit, they urged their states to issue new paper money. But local elites wanted to limit paper money in ways that favored their new position as powerful creditors and holders of wartime certificates. Their opponents argued that issuing paper money could take the pressure off cash-strapped farmers and help retire enormous war debts. In seven states, these advocates of economic relief carried the day. State government presses put additional notes in circulation.

Local battles over debt, credit, and currency issues hit hardest in the Northeast. In Massachusetts, a legislature sympathetic to creditors consolidated the state's huge war debts in a way that placed extreme tax burdens on ordinary citizens. Also, Britain's ban on American commerce in the British West Indies undermined New England's economy. The fish, grain, and lumber from that region could no longer be sold to the Caribbean colonies in exchange for much-needed hard currency.

These changes had an immediate impact. In New Hampshire courts, debt cases rose sixfold from 1782 to 1785. The heavy costs of traveling to court and paying high legal fees pushed thousands of rural families into bankruptcy. Embittered farmers saw their livestock and household property seized and auctioned off at low prices. Hard times often spark drastic responses, and New England's pot soon boiled over. Early in 1787, Washington's secretary in Virginia noted that the "tumults, insurrections, and *Rebellion* in New England have of late much engrossed the minds of the people here."

Newspaper accounts told of disturbing events in Rhode Island. Rural politicians seeking relief for indebted farmers swept into power during the April 1786 election, routing rich Providence merchants from their longtime domination of the assembly. The newcomers quickly implemented their paper money platform. The Rhode Island region had a withered economy, and the state government carried a burdensome war debt. To address these matters, assemblymen approved a huge outlay of paper money. To ensure the plan's success, legislators declared that all creditors had to accept the money as legal tender.

Not surprisingly, creditors and speculators resented Rhode Island's currency law. They fumed at the new legislature's unwillingness to assume a share of the national debt and pay interest to wealthy bondholders, as other states had done. So rich merchants in Providence fought back, closing their stores rather than accept the new bills. Some even left the state to avoid being forced to accept debt payments in paper money. When judges who favored the merchants' cause finally declared the new statute unconstitutional, creditors everywhere sighed with relief. Their newspapers condemned the "Rogue Island" currency law as a dire example of the dangers of democracy.

Shays' Rebellion: The Massachusetts Regulation

In Massachusetts and New Hampshire, unlike Rhode Island, powerful merchants retained control over the state assemblies, and they resisted public pressure to generate more paper money. Instead, these creditors pushed to enforce debt collection by the courts. As in other states, wealthy speculators had bought up, at bargain rates, most of the public securities and certificates issued during the war. They anticipated huge profits if a government they controlled could redeem these notes, in gold and silver, at their full face value.

In New Hampshire, by 1785, securities valued at nearly £100,000 belonged to less than 1 percent of the state's total population. The wealthiest members of this elite had close ties to the prevailing government, situated in Exeter, near the coast. When farmers organized conventions to voice their economic grievances, merchants infiltrated and disrupted their meetings. In September 1786, 200 citizens, many of them armed war veterans, marched on Exeter to demand money reforms before conditions "drive us to a state of desperation." Officials organized cavalry units to confront the furious citizens, arresting their leaders from the crowd "as a butcher would seize sheep in a flock." The state's governor, General John Sullivan, suppressed the dissenters and issued a proclamation forbidding further conventions. He then wrote to the Massachusetts governor, James Bowdoin, offering to help crush similar unrest in the neighboring state.

Early in 1786, the Commonwealth of Massachusetts had imposed a heavy direct tax on its citizenry. Western farmers lacked sufficient cash and already faced a wave of foreclosures for debt. They protested the tax law at town meetings and county

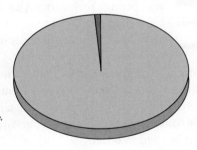

This pie chart depicts the entire population of New Hampshire in 1785 (approximately 125,000). The thin sliver represents the very small group of people, detailed below, who had bought up cheaply the notes issued to cover the state's war debts. They had a large stake in redeeming these securities at full face value.

Size of Investment	No. of Debt Holders	% of Debt Holders	Total Value of Debt	Average Face Value of Securities Held by Individuals in Each Group of Investors
Over £1,000	10	0.9	£16,278	£1,628
£500 to £999	24	2.1	£16,377	£682
£250 to £499	55	4.9	£20,958	£381
£100 to £249	125	11.2	£19,592	£157
£50 to £99	158	14.1	£11,065	£70
£1 to £49	748	66.8	£14,574	£19
	1,120	100.0	£98,844	

FIGURE 8.1 CONCENTRATION OF SECURITY NOTES IN THE HANDS OF A FEW: THE EXAMPLE OF NEW HAMPSHIRE IN 1785 New Hampshire had issued securities during the war, and, by 1785, like other new states, it was burdened with public debt. Since most people lacked cash, public securities were rapidly bought up by speculators for far less than their official value. Investors stood to profit handsomely if the various certificates could be redeemed at their full face value (nearly £100,000). This chart shows the startling degree to which these assets had become concentrated in the hands of a few people by 1785. Even among the few New Hampshire citizens holding securities (1,120), these assets were further concentrated. A mere 3 percent of this group—thirty-four men—controlled more than a third of this vast speculative investment.

conventions. When their complaints fell on deaf ears, they took action, "regulating" events as the North Carolina Regulators had done two decades earlier. The Massachusetts Regulation became known as Shays' Rebellion when a former army officer named Daniel Shays emerged as one of its popular leaders. At first, these New England Regulators focused on closing the courts. In August 1786, 1,500 farmers marched against the Court of Common Pleas in Hampshire County and shut it down. The next month, another band closed the court in Worcester.

The confrontation escalated as winter set in. By January, more than 1,000 Shaysites, knowing that their allies in New Hampshire had been defeated, moved to seize the federal arsenal in Springfield. But Governor Bowdoin had mobilized an army, financed largely by wealthy merchants in Boston. This private militia overpowered the Westerners and forced all who did not flee to sign an oath of allegiance. Disarmed but not silenced, the dissidents succeeded in extracting some relief from the legislature. They also managed to defeat Bowdoin in the next election and replace him with a more popular governor, John Hancock.

The unrest in New England played into the hands of those advocating a stronger national government. (Rumors even circulated that nationalists had provoked the violence to rally support for their cause.) In May 1787, Henry Knox expressed fear to Governor John Sullivan that "we are verging fast to anarchy." He urged Sullivan to send delegates from New Hampshire to a crucial meeting that was about to begin in Philadelphia.

Drafting a New Constitution

8.4 How did nationalist leaders use their political skills to bring about the Constitutional Convention in Philadelphia?

Even before Yorktown, Alexander Hamilton, Washington's youthful aide-de-camp, had proposed a convention to restructure the national government. Now he worked with another young nationalist, James Madison, and their energetic supporters to bring it about. Congress had made earnest efforts toward reform, but any changes to the Confederation's governing articles required approval from all thirteen states. Thus, vital amendments—which would let Congress regulate commerce, raise revenue, and establish a judiciary, for example—proved nearly impossible. For some powerful leaders, especially merchants and creditors, a major political revision seemed in order.

"Many Gentlemen both within & without Congress," wrote Madison, desire a "Convention for amending the Confederation." Still, it would take impressive leadership—Madison provided much of it—to seize the initiative and then generate enough momentum to change the rules of national government. Extensive compromise, both between elite factions and toward resistant popular forces, would be necessary at every stage. After all, it would take a gigantic push to engineer such a convention, to guide it to restructure the government along nationalist lines, and finally to persuade voting Americans to ratify the proposed changes and accept their legitimacy. To begin such a task, would-be reformers first had to convince the Confederation Congress to allow their revision plans to move forward. For that, they needed to recruit the enormous prestige of George Washington.

Philadelphia: A Gathering of Like-Minded Men

The path began at Mount Vernon in 1785, when Washington hosted commissioners appointed by Maryland and Virginia to resolve state boundary disputes regarding the Potomac River. During the gathering, these men (including James Madison) scheduled a broader meeting on Chesapeake trade for the next year at Annapolis, Maryland. The topic was regional, but they invited all the states to send representatives. Only twelve delegates from five states showed up at Annapolis in September 1786, but news of the unrest in New England prompted talk of a more extended meeting.

Alexander Hamilton, as a representative from New York, persuaded the other delegates at Annapolis to call for a convention in Philadelphia the following May to discuss commerce and other matters. Madison won endorsement for the proposal from the Virginia legislature and then from Congress. Reform-minded congressmen, such as James Monroe, saw an opportunity to amend and improve the existing Confederation structure. But when the states sent delegates to Philadelphia the following spring, many of the appointees thought that amendments might not go far enough. They were open to the more sweeping changes that Madison and other nationalists had in mind. So the gathering called to consider commercial matters and propose improvements to the Articles of Confederation soon became a private meeting to design and propose an entirely new structure for governing the United States.

Madison reached Philadelphia in early May 1787. He immediately began drafting plans for drastic change and lobbying delegates, some of whom came early to attend a secret gathering of the Society of the Cincinnati. On May 25, when representatives from seven states had arrived, they launched the convention and unanimously chose Washington as the presiding officer. Participants agreed that they would operate behind closed doors and each state delegation would have one vote. There would be no public discussion or official record of their proceedings. Soon, delegates had joined the gathering from twelve states. Only Rhode Island abstained from sending representatives. That state's leaders sensed an effort afoot to overthrow the Articles of Confederation and impose a stronger federal government, something they opposed.

The fifty-five delegates had much in common. All were white, male, and well educated, and many already knew one another. These members of the national elite included thirty-four lawyers, thirty public creditors, and twenty-seven members of the Society of the Cincinnati. More than a quarter of the participants owned slaves, and nearly a dozen had done personal business with financier Robert Morris of the Pennsylvania delegation. Not surprisingly, all seemed to agree that the contagion of liberty had spread too far. One called the current situation "an excess of democracy."

Specifically, these men feared recent legislation passed by state assemblies to assist hard-pressed citizens: laws that delayed tax collection, postponed debt payments, and issued paper money. Most delegates hoped to replace the existing Confederation structure with a national government capable of controlling finances and creating creditor-friendly fiscal policy. To be effective, they believed, a strengthened central government must have greater control over the states. Only Robert Yates and John Lansing of New York and Luther Martin of Maryland staunchly resisted expanding central power.

Many delegates, especially those from heavily populated states, thought the national legislature should be based on proportional representation according to population rather than each state receiving equal weight regardless of its numbers. Also, most wanted to see the single-house (unicameral) Congress of the Confederation replaced by an upper and lower house that would reflect the views and values of different social classes. John Adams had helped create such a two-house (bicameral) system in the Massachusetts constitution, thereby limiting pure democracy and giving more political power to propertied interests.

Besides calling for checks within the legislative branch itself, Adams had also laid out strong arguments for separating, and checking, the powers of each competing branch of government. For a sound and lasting government, Adams had argued, there should be **separation of powers**; the legislative branch should be balanced by separate executive and judicial branches that are equally independent. Most delegates agreed with this novel system of **checks and balances**, intended to add stability and remove corruption.

Separation of powers The novel idea that the powers of the three branches of government—legislative, executive, and judicial—should be kept separate from one another, so that each can check and balance the powers of the other two.

Checks and balances The rules controlling interactions among the executive, legislative, and judicial branches of government, making up a novel system designed to prevent any single branch from overreaching its powers, as set forth in the Constitution in 1787.

Compromise and Consensus

The Philadelphia gathering, which lasted through the entire summer, would later be known as the Constitutional Convention of 1787. Even as a consensus emerged within the small meeting, countless personal, practical, and philosophical differences persisted. Hamilton delivered a six-hour speech in which he staked out an extremely conservative position. He underscored "the imprudence of democracy" and stressed a natural separation between "the few and the many"—the "wealthy well born" and the "turbulent and changing" people. Hamilton's conservative oration called for the chief executive and the senators to be chosen indirectly, by elected representatives rather than by the people themselves, and he recommended that these high officials should serve for life. Such ideas undoubtedly appealed to many of his listeners, but all of the delegates knew that a majority of citizens would never accept such proposals. Pierce Butler of South Carolina invoked Solon in ancient Greece, "who gave the Athenians not the best government he could devise but the best they would receive."

This attentiveness of convention members to what the public would accept is illustrated by their approach to **suffrage** (the right to vote). Property ownership was no longer a universal voting requirement, and state constitutions varied on whether religion, race, or gender could determine eligibility. James Wilson of Pennsylvania, second only to Madison in working to build a practical nationalist majority in the convention, pointed out that "it would be very hard and disagreeable" for any person, once franchised, to give up the right to vote. Accordingly, the delegates proposed that in each state all those allowed to vote for any "branch of the state legislature" would also be permitted to cast ballots for members of the House of Representatives. But they shied away from accepting direct election for the Senate or the president, and they deferred suffrage matters to the states.

Suffrage The right to vote

Time and again during the 16-week convention, these like-minded men showed their willingness to bargain and compromise. Lofty principles and rigid schemes often gave way to balancing and improvisation. The unlikely creation of the **electoral college** for selecting a president is one example. Delegates who differed over the length for the chief executive's term of office and right to run for reelection also disagreed on the best method of presidential selection. Some suggested that ordinary voters should elect the president; others proposed that the state governors, or the national legislature, or even electors chosen by the lower house should choose the chief executive.

Electoral college An intricate system in which each state appoints electors, equal in number to its representation in Congress, to elect the president and vice president. The electoral college is a provision of the Constitution (Article II, Section 1) because the framers were unwilling to approve the direct election of president and vice president. This group, or "college," of electors still makes the selection, voting according to prior party commitments rather than individual choice.

Finally, the aptly named Committee on Postponed Matters cobbled together an acceptable system: a gathering (or "college") of chosen electors from each state would cast votes for the presidency. This electoral college plan had little precedent, but it managed to balance competing interests. Under the scheme, state legislatures would set the manner for selecting electors. The least populous states would get a minimum of three electoral votes, and states with more people would choose more electors in proportion to their numbers, giving them added weight in the decision. The people could also participate in the voting process, though only if their state legislatures called for it. If no candidate won a majority in the electoral college, the House of Representatives had the right to determine the president, with each state having one vote. The system was far from elegant or democratic, but it placated varied interests, and it won prompt approval.

Questions of Representation

As deliberations stretched across the long, hot summer of 1787, two central issues threatened to unravel the convention: political representation and slavery. Questions of representation pervaded almost every discussion, pitting the states with the largest populations, such as Virginia, Pennsylvania, and Massachusetts, against the less populated states. Madison's well-organized Virginians offered a comprehensive blueprint outlining a new national government that would have three separate branches. This design, called the "Virginia Plan," recommended a bicameral national legislature with proportional representation in each body. The House of Representatives would be chosen by popular election, the Senate by the lower house.

Madison's system clearly favored populous states. Not surprisingly, a coalition of small-state delegates led by William Paterson of New Jersey submitted an alternative "New Jersey Plan." This less sweeping revision built on the current Articles of Confederation. It called for a continuation of the current unicameral legislature, in which each state received an equal vote. A committee chaired by Benjamin Franklin finally broke the impasse between the two plans. The idea of an upper house, or Senate, would be retained, and each state, whatever its size, would hold two senate seats. Seats in the House of Representatives would be determined proportionally, according to the relative population of each state. Moreover, this lower house would have the power to initiate all bills dealing with finance and money matters.

To implement proportional representation in a fast-growing society, the delegates devised a radical innovation: a national census every ten years. This regular headcount in turn raised a thorny question. Should slaves—people enumerated in the census yet denied the rights of citizens—be counted in determining a state's proportional representation in the national government? Slaveholding states wanted their human property to count because that would give those states more representation. The convention resolved this dilemma in mid-July with a "three-fifths" formula that made every five enslaved people equivalent to three free people in apportionment matters.

In an ironic twist, the same week the Constitutional Convention delegates approved the notorious **three-fifths clause**, the existing government of the United States leaned in the opposite direction. Meeting in New York, members of the Confederation's Congress passed the Northwest Ordinance, which outlawed slavery in the new territory above the Ohio River. Because there was much contact between the two meetings, some scholars speculate that powerful Southerners agreed to give away the prospect of slavery north of the Ohio River in exchange for more support of slavery within the new plan taking shape in Philadelphia.

Slavery: The Deepest Dilemma

During the debate over the three-fifths clause, Madison commented that the greatest division in the United States "did not lie between the large & small States: it lay between the Northern & Southern," owing to "the effects of their having or not having slaves." This highly charged issue simmered beneath the surface for most of the summer. In late August, with most other matters resolved, delegates could no longer postpone questions surrounding slavery. Yet again, a committee deliberated, and a bargain was struck. This time, hundreds of thousands of human lives were at stake.

Planter delegates from Georgia and South Carolina refused to support any document that regulated the slave trade or curtailed slavery itself. They asserted that such a charter could never win acceptance at home. In part they were bluffing: constraints on slavery had wide popular appeal in the expanding backcountry of the Deep South. There, independent farmers outnumbered planters, ministers questioned slavery, and pioneers wanted national support in confronting powerful Indians. In Philadelphia, however, few delegates challenged the proslavery posturing, possibly because strong antislavery opinions could have prolonged or even deadlocked the convention. Weary participants were eager to complete their work and fearful of unraveling their hard-won consensus.

Rather than force the matter, even those who disapproved of slavery rushed to compromise, heaping a huge burden on future generations. Southern delegates dropped their protests against giving Congress the power to regulate international shipping. In exchange, the framers approved a clause protecting the importation of slaves for at least twenty years. They also added a provision governing fugitive slaves that required the return of "any person held to service or labor." Through a calculated bargain, delegates

Three-fifths clause A controversial clause of Article I, section 2, of the U.S. Constitution said that each slave would count as "three-fifths of all other Persons" when representatives and direct taxes were being apportioned to states according to population. Slaves had no rights of citizenship, but the clause gave southern slave states additional power in Congress. Section 2 of the Fourteenth Amendment did away with the clause in 1868.

👁 **Watch** the **Video**   **Slavery and the Constitution**

📖 **Read** the **Document**   **Quobna Ottobah Cugoano, An African Pamphleteer Attacks Slavery (1787)**

In a crucial decision, members of the Constitutional Convention chose to protect the slave trade and preserve slavery. One African American who had already taken matters in her own hands was Mumbet, a slave in Massachusetts and widow of a Revolutionary War soldier. In 1781, she sued for her freedom on the grounds that "all were born free and equal." Her court victory proved a landmark in New England. Proudly, she took the name Elizabeth Freeman. How does her case relate to Madison's assertion that the largest difference dividing the states "did not lie between the large & small States: it lay between the Northern & Southern," owing to "the effects of their having or not having slaves"?

had endorsed slavery and drawn the South into the Union on terms that suited that region's leaders. The word *slave* never appeared in the finished document.

In early September, the convention members put the finishing touches on their proposal and wondered whether Americans would accept it. Winning state-by-state approval would involve an uphill battle, especially given the absence of a bill of rights. George Mason, who had drawn up Virginia's Declaration of Rights eleven years earlier, reminded members that such a set of guarantees "would give great quiet to the people." But in the convention's closing days, many delegates resisted the notion, and all were eager to adjourn. They overwhelmingly voted down Mason's suggestion.

Without a bill of rights, Mason and Edmund Randolph of Virginia refused to endorse the final document, along with Elbridge Gerry of Massachusetts. Other delegates who dissented had already departed. Of the seventy-four delegates chosen at the convention's outset, fifty-five actually attended the proceedings, and only thirty-nine agreed to sign the finished plan. It was approved "by the unanimous consent of the States present" on September 17, 1787.

Ratification and the Bill of Rights

8.5   Why was a bill of rights, expected by citizens, omitted by the drafters of the Constitution and later added?

Committed nationalists now faced their most difficult task: winning public acceptance for an alternative structure that defied existing law. After all, the proposed constitution ignored the fact that the Articles of Confederation—the document governing the United States at the time—could be amended only with the approval of all thirteen states. Instead, the text drafted in Philadelphia stated that ratification (acceptance through voting) by conventions in any nine states would make the new document take effect in those places. Moreover, the proposed ratification process left no room for partial approval or suggested revisions. Each state, if it wanted to enter the debate at all, had to accept or reject the proposed frame of government as offered.

The Campaign for Ratification

The Confederation Congress had acquiesced in allowing the 1787 convention to occur in the first place. Most congressional representatives had expected the meeting to produce proposals for amending the current government, not discarding it. But now that the Philadelphia conclave had ended, the Congress sitting in New York City balked at endorsing the revolutionary document. To avoid a lengthy and troublesome debate, proponents of the new constitution urged Congress simply to receive the frame of government as a possible proposal and then transmit it to the states without an endorsement. Congress did so on September 28, 1787, and the document's advocates portrayed the unanimous vote as an expression of approval.

Supporters had no time to lose because Pennsylvania's assembly was set to adjourn on the next day. An early victory in that large and central state would be crucial in building momentum, so they rushed the congressional letter of transmittal from New York to Philadelphia. There, the assembly faction dominated by Robert Morris won a hasty vote to schedule a state ratifying convention. Over the next three months, Pennsylvania towns and counties elected delegates, a convention met, and the state voted to approve the new plan. Delaware's convention had approved it unanimously on December 7, and New Jersey and Georgia soon approved as well. By the end of January, Connecticut had also ratified. Other states called elections and scheduled conventions. Only Rhode Island, which had not sent delegates to the drafting convention, refused to convene a meeting to debate ratification.

By seizing the initiative early, the proponents of the new framework shaped the terms of debate. The drafters, anything but a cross-section of society, worked to portray themselves as such. They noted that their document began with the ringing phrase "We the people of the United States," a last-minute addition by Gouverneur Morris of New York. And Madison told the public that the text sprang from "*your* convention."

Most important, in a reversal of logic and contemporary usage, the nationalists who supported the new constitution took for themselves the respected name of **Federalists**. They gave their opponents the negative-sounding term **Anti-Federalists**. The Federalists then used their ties to influential leaders to wage a media war for public support. They dashed off letters and published essays praising the proposed constitution.

Federalists A coalition of nationalist leaders who favored creating a stronger central government to replace the Articles of Confederation. They labeled their opponents as Anti-Federalists in the late 1780s. The strongest essays endorsing their proposed new Constitution were entitled *The Federalist.*

Anti-Federalists A diverse and unsuccessful coalition that opposed ratification of the Constitution and feared the increased power of the proposed central government. The Anti-Federalists were named by their opponents, the Federalists.

The strongest advocacy came from Alexander Hamilton and James Madison. The two men composed eighty essays for the New York press under the pen name *Publius*. John Jay added five more, and in the spring of 1788, the collection appeared as a book titled *The Federalist*. In the most famous piece, "Number 10," Madison challenged the widely accepted idea that a republic must be small and compact to survive. Turning the proposition around, he argued that minority opinions would fare better in a large nation, where diverse competing interests would prevent a unified majority from exerting control.

Dividing and Conquering the Anti-Federalists

Opponents of the new plan found themselves on the defensive from the start. Many of them had supported some changes in government, and most conceded the presence of economic difficulties. But Federalist predictions of impending chaos seemed exaggerated. "I deny that we are in immediate danger of anarchy," one Anti-Federalist writer protested.

Richard Henry Lee, president of the Confederation Congress, condemned the Federalists as a noisy "coalition of monarchy men, military men, aristocrats and drones." Other prominent figures joined him in opposition: George Clinton in New York; Luther Martin in Maryland; and Patrick Henry, George Mason, and Benjamin Harrison in Virginia. Such notables became the spokespersons for a far wider array of Anti-Federalist skeptics.

Many opponents of the proposed constitution protested the plan's perceived threat to local political power. Despite Madison's reassurances in *Federalist* Number 10, they believed that local and state governments represented voters more fairly and responded to their needs more quickly than a distant national authority could. For some critics,

 Read the **Document**   Publius (James Madison), *The Federalist*, No. 10 (1788)

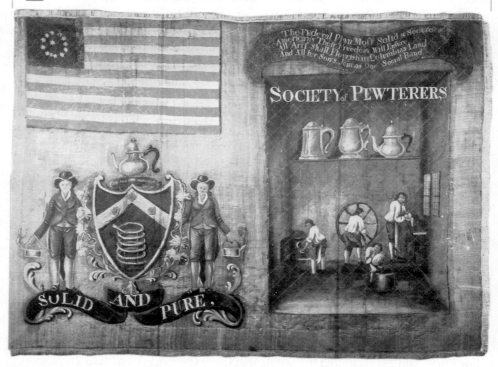

Celebrations in July 1788 hailed the new Constitution of the United States. "Columbus" on horseback led New York City's parade, followed by artisan groups. The silk banner of the pewterers proclaimed that under the Federal Plan, "All Arts Shall Flourish in Columbia's Land, And All Her Sons Join as One Social Band." Why did the name of Columbus, and the term "Columbia," suddenly gain such prominence in the celebrations of the new country's revolutionary generation?

SOURCE: Collection of the New-York Historical Society, (#1176)

Explore Ratification of the Constitution on MyHistoryLab

WHY DID RATIFICATION OF THE CONSTITUTION FACE OPPOSITION?

The early American republic found itself with a legal foundation based on the weak Articles of Confederation. Ratification of a new constitution, however, faced opposition up and down the new United States. For example, the inhabitants of cities, with economies linked tightly to commerce, were more likely to be divided on the issue, since the Constitution would provide the national government with more power over trade. Areas of the country with high populations of non-English Europeans, groups such as the Scots-Irish, often opposed ratification out of a concern that the document would give those of English descent more power. Ratified—often very narrowly— by all the states via constitutional conventions between 1787 and 1790, the new document provided the young nation with a more powerful and centralized federal government.

On September 17, 1787, after nearly four months of work, delegates to the Philadelphia convention approved the final draft of a new constitution. Nine months later, when New Hampshire became the ninth state to approve ratification, this constitution replaced the Articles of Confederation as the supreme law of the United States. Several states withheld approval until the addition of an explicit Bill of Rights had been assured.

RATIFICATION OF THE CONSTITUTION

State	Date of Ratification	Ratification Vote (yes–no)
Delaware	Dec. 8, 1787	30–0
Pennsylvania	Dec. 12, 1787	46–23
New Jersey	Dec. 18, 1787	38–0
Georgia	Jan. 2, 1788	26–0
Connecticut	Jan. 9, 1788	128–40
Massachusetts	Feb. 16, 1788	187–168
Maryland	April 28, 1788	63–11
South Carolina	May 23, 1788	149–73
New Hampshire	June 21, 1788	57–46
Virginia	June 25, 1788	89–79
New York	July 26, 1788	30–27
North Carolina	Nov. 21, 1789	184–77
Rhode Island	May 29, 1790	34–32

KEY QUESTIONS — Use **MyHistoryLab** *Explorer* to answer these **questions:**

Consequence ▶▶▶ *What was the relation between Loyalism in the Revolutionary War and subsequent views on ratification?*

Investigate area opinions on ratification in Loyalist strongholds.

Response ▶▶▶ *Did the level of slavery in an area affect opinion towards ratification?*

Map the level of opposition to ratification in slave-holding regions.

Analysis ▶▶▶ *What was the opinion in areas with a large German settler population?*

Conceptualize why members of this group and others saw the Constitution's adoption the way they did.

this belief expressed a radical democratic principle; for others it represented their provincial bias. In short, though they shared numerous fears of government potential for corruption and tyranny, Anti-Federalists remained too diverse and divided to speak with a single voice. They included subsistence farmers living far from urban markets and war veterans who saw their influence in republican government diminished by the proposed system. Many indebted people also opposed ratification, fearing that a strong national government would favor the interests of bondholders and foreign creditors ahead of the economic well-being of ordinary citizens.

If Anti-Federalists were numerous in the remote countryside and newly settled western regions, Federalists predominated in coastal commercial centers. Using a variety of tactics, they pressed their advantages in the fight to control state ratifying conventions. They lured prominent Anti-Federalist delegates with hints of high office, and they ridiculed vocal opponents as Shaysite extremists. In state after state, they forged coalitions linking commercial farmers living near towns and rivers with aspiring artisans and city-based entrepreneurs. Through intensive politicking, they garnered approval in Massachusetts in February 1788, but only by a thin margin (187 votes to 168 in the ratifying convention). This commitment from "the Bay State" helped to sway Maryland in April, South Carolina in May, and New Hampshire in June. The Federalists could now claim the nine states needed to implement their plan, and in July they staged parades to hail the new Constitution of the United States.

The approved Constitution promptly became the law of the land. But in Massachusetts, the Federalists had triumphed only by promising to add an explicit bill of rights that gave written protection for valued civil liberties. They had to make similar assurances to secure slim majorities in Virginia (89 to 79) and New York (30 to 27). North Carolina delegates, meeting in backcountry Hillsborough, had voted down the proposed frame of government at their first ratifying convention because it lacked a bill of rights. A second North Carolina convention, called in 1789, withheld approval until a bill of rights had actually been introduced into the first Federal Congress as proposed amendments to the Constitution. In 1790, Rhode Island narrowly voted approval for the new framework (34 to 32) rather than risk being left in economic and political isolation.

Adding a Bill of Rights

In a society consisting of almost 3 million people, the franchise remained a limited privilege, open primarily to white men with property. All told, only about 160,000 voters throughout the country took part in choosing representatives to the state ratifying conventions. And only about 100,000 of these people—less than 7 percent of the entire adult population—cast votes for delegates who supported the Constitution. Federalists knew, therefore, that they would have to fulfill their pledge to incorporate a bill of rights. Madison, goaded by Jefferson, promised Virginians that he would push for the inclusion of specific rights as amendments to the Constitution. He had several motives. First, he hoped to ensure his own election to the nation's new House of Representatives. Second, he wanted to head off talk of another convention "for a reconsideration of the whole structure of government."

Bill of Rights A set of amendments assuring basic rights, proposed by James Madison to help ensure acceptance of the newly drafted Constitution, and based on suggestions from the states. Ten of the twelve items passed by Congress were ratified by the states in 1791. Taken together, these first ten amendments to the Constitution became known as the Bill of Rights.

In compiling a list of protections, or bill of rights, Madison drew from scores of proposals for explicit amendments put forward by the state ratifying conventions. He selected those, mostly dealing with individual rights, that could pass a Federalist-dominated Congress and would not dilute any of the proposed new government's powers. He set aside suggestions for limiting the government's right to impose taxes, raise a standing army, or control the time and place of elections. True to his word, he pushed twelve less controversial statements through the Congress as constitutional amendments, despite congressional apathy and opposition. Within two years, three-fourths of the states ratified ten of these weighty pronouncements. Hence, the first ten amendments—the **Bill of Rights**—quickly became a permanent part of the U.S. Constitution.

Many of the protections provided by the Bill of Rights harked back to lessons learned in earlier struggles with Parliament. The ten amendments guarded the right of the people to bear arms, limited government power to quarter troops in homes, and banned unreasonable searches or seizures. They also ensured the right to trial by jury, outlawed excessive bail and fines, and prohibited "cruel and unusual punishments." The First Amendment secured freedom of speech and of the press, protected people's right to assemble and petition, and prohibited Congress from meddling in the exercise of religion. The Ninth and Tenth Amendments—brief, broad, and reassuring to Anti-Federalist doubters—implied sweeping protection for the rights of individuals and states. By securing these freedoms, Madison engineered a final set of compromises that ensured the acceptance and longevity of the Constitution he had done so much to frame.

Conclusion

The War for Independence exhausted the new nation. Managing the difficult task of demobilization and reconstruction consumed American energy and resources in the 1780s. So did the new western domain, where Americans had to balance prospects for national expansion against the military threats posed by European empires and Native American groups that claimed the region. Also, economic differences set aside during the war quickly reemerged; questions of wealth and property loomed large.

Therefore, when Confederation leaders imposed unprecedented taxes to pay off the war bonds gathered up by wealthy speculators, irate farmers and veterans protested that Congress was gouging "the Many" to enrich "the Few." These numerous dissenters pressured state governments to provide debt relief and issue paper money. But wealthy creditors reacted forcefully: these like-minded men maneuvered to create a new and stronger central government that could support their interests and override state-level economic measures favoring the common people. Sidestepping the existing government, they drafted a new constitution at a closed convention in Philadelphia in 1787, and they campaigned successfully for its ratification by 1789.

The reins of power had nearly slipped from the hands of established American leaders during the tumultuous 1770s. They had restored their secure grip on political affairs by the end of the 1780s in the face of bitter and varied opposition. But the fierce debate over ratification of the Constitution raised fresh uncertainties about the long-term survival of the union. Much hinged on selection of the initial president. Inevitably, George Washington emerged as the overwhelming favorite to become the first chief executive of the new republic.

Chapter Review

Beating Swords into Plowshares

8.1 Why did the prospect of a Newburgh conspiracy and the creation of the Society of the Cincinnati upset many Americans? p. 190

When officers at Newburgh hinted at a military takeover, Washington diffused this threat. But he took part in the Society of the Cincinnati, open only to American officers and their descendants. The organization struck many as a way to create a hereditary aristocracy with power to meddle effectively in politics.

Competing for Control of the Mississippi Valley

8.2 Why did control of the Mississippi Valley matter so much to Americans after the revolution? p. 195

Eastern inhabitants streamed into the Mississippi Valley after the war, bent on combating threats from Indians and encroaching colonial powers. Settlers and land speculators vied for rich tracts. The region's long-term value for these newcomers depended on establishing American control over the territory and asserting shipping rights on the Mississippi.

Debtor and Creditor, Taxpayer and Bondholder

8.3 Why did large bondholders care so deeply about what forces were in control of the state and national governments? p. 200

Bonds covering the national debt were bought up cheaply by postwar elites. Could wealthy bondholders receive annual interest on these paper holdings (paid from scarce public funds) and convince governments to redeem these depreciated notes at full face value? Only if they could control state legislatures and the Confederation Congress.

Drafting a New Constitution

8.4 How did nationalist leaders use their political skills to bring about the Constitutional Convention in Philadelphia? p. 204

Nationalists seeking a stronger federal government used a local boundary discussion (Mount Vernon, 1785) to prompt a regional trade meeting (Annapolis, 1786), which issued a call for a larger conference of state delegates (Philadelphia, 1787). That closed-door convention shifted from amending the Confederation structure to drafting an entirely new constitution.

Ratification and the Bill of Rights

8.5 Why was a bill of rights, expected by citizens, omitted by the drafters of the Constitution and later added? p. 209

The Constitution's framers omitted any list of explicit rights comparable to that of Virginia and other states. But with voting support for their plan at scarcely 7 percent of the total adult population, Federalist advocates promised to introduce a bill of rights, as constitutional amendments, to narrowly win state approvals.

Timeline

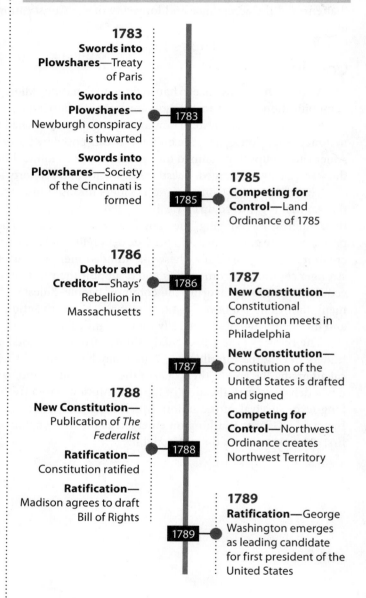

1783
Swords into Plowshares—Treaty of Paris

Swords into Plowshares—Newburgh conspiracy is thwarted — 1783

Swords into Plowshares—Society of the Cincinnati is formed — 1785

1785
Competing for Control—Land Ordinance of 1785

1786
Debtor and Creditor—Shays' Rebellion in Massachusetts — 1786

1787
New Constitution—Constitutional Convention meets in Philadelphia

New Constitution—Constitution of the United States is drafted and signed — 1787

Competing for Control—Northwest Ordinance creates Northwest Territory

1788
New Constitution—Publication of *The Federalist*

Ratification—Constitution ratified — 1788

Ratification—Madison agrees to draft Bill of Rights

1789
Ratification—George Washington emerges as leading candidate for first president of the United States — 1789

9 Revolutionary Legacies, 1789–1803

What happened if a slave tried to take advantage of the post-Revolution political climate and flee her owner? And what if that owner was George Washington, the country's first president? The story of Ona Judge reveals that slaves, as well as other Americans, did not wait long to test the new boundaries of citizenship.

In 1789, President Washington and his wife Martha moved from Virginia to New York and later to Philadelphia, the nation's first capital. When they arrived in Philadelphia, their household included seven enslaved workers, including mulatto teenager Ona Judge, the first lady's personal attendant. In the mid-1790s, Ona Judge escaped from the president's home and found her way to Portsmouth, New Hampshire. Later, Judge said she fled because she feared that she would be forced to return to the Washingtons' Mount Vernon estate in Virginia: "I knew that if I went back to Virginia, I should never get my liberty." In New Hampshire, Judge hoped, she would begin a new life of freedom.

In an effort to locate the young runaway, Washington enlisted the aid of a federal customs collector in

This is a detail from Edward Savage's portrait titled *The Washington Family*, painted around 1790. George Washington poses with his wife, Martha, his grandchildren, George Washington Parke Custis and Eleanor Parke Custis, and his enslaved valet. As reproduced here, the painting is flipped; in the original, the valet is on the right. George and Martha Washington owned more than 300 slaves, making them among the wealthiest planters in Virginia at the time. Some of their slaves escaped during the Revolutionary War. Together with Ona Judge, these men and women made a bid for freedom that reveals the power of revolutionary ideals for all people, but also the limitations of America's war for independence as a truly revolutionary struggle. How did the nation's first political leaders justify the ideal of freedom for some but not for others?

LEARNING OBJECTIVES

((Listen to Chapter 9 on MyHistoryLab

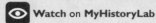 **Watch the Video Series on MyHistoryLab**

Learn about some key topics related to this chapter with the *MyHistoryLab Video Series: Key Topics in U.S. History.*

1 **Revolutionary Legacies: 1789–1803** This introductory video focuses on the post-Revolutionary years and the ways freedom expanded for some groups, but not others, including Native Americans and southern enslaved laborers. Although the voting population consisted almost entirely of white men, some privileged white women entered the public realm as writers, teachers, and as self-conscious mothers of future citizens. While the institution of bondage persisted and grew in the South, the northern states and territories eventually emancipated their slaves, adding to the population of free people of color.

 Watch on **MyHistoryLab**

People of Color: New Freedoms, New Struggles During the American Revolution, the British enlisted the willing aid of some African American men with promises of freedom. This video shows how the new nation preserved and in the process transformed the institution of slavery. While bondage gradually ended north of the Ohio River and the Mason-Dixon line, the need for slave labor increased in the South, with the invention of the cotton gin and the expansion of cotton cultivation into new territories. **2**

Watch on **MyHistoryLab**

3 **Continuity and Change in the West** After the American Revolution, war veterans and other settlers began moving west, not only into the western parts of the former thirteen colonies but also into the trans-Appalachian mountain region ceded to the new United States. This video describes the settlement of western lands in the years following the war, which provided new opportunities for the nation's whites but also bred new sources of conflict. Western settlers resented eastern privilege and federal taxation power, as evidenced by the Whiskey Rebellion.

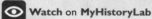 Watch on **MyHistoryLab**

Shifting Social Identities in the Post-Revolutionary Era Post-Revolutionary American politics emphasized an informed and virtuous citizenry. As this video reveals, a free press helped to ensure such ideals. Many ordinary Americans were eager to follow the major political debates of the day, take up various causes and reforms, and support parties. In the process, the Federalists' power diminished and gradually disappeared altogether. **4**

Watch on **MyHistoryLab**

Portsmouth and, in the process, ignored provisions of a law he had signed as president in 1793. The Fugitive Slave Act provided that any owner of a fugitive must receive authorization from a local judge in order to retrieve his or her property. The customs official eventually located Ona Judge and reported that she would return to Washington only if he freed her. She missed her family in Virginia and was willing to make a bargain with her master. The indignant president refused this offer. And so Ona Judge settled into life in New Hampshire. In 1797, she married John Staines, an African American sailor, and together they started a family.

Revolutionary ideals of freedom and equality were contagious. Ona Judge could not aspire to George Washington's wealth, power, or fame, but she could aspire to a life that would erase a central distinction that separated the two of them—the distinction between the slave and the free person. After the war, many different groups, such as enslaved people and indentured servants, sought to claim the freedom denied them by law or custom. New groups formed to challenge longstanding hierarchies that had shaped political and religious institutions. And new forms of social identity—such as "whiteness"—emerged, promoting certain forms of equality for some and imposing certain drastic forms of inequality on others.

Competing Political Visions in the New Nation

9.1 What were the disagreements between the Federalists and the Democratic-Republicans in domestic policy? In foreign policy?

The heirs of the Revolution continued to invoke the ideals of liberty and freedom, but those terms had different meanings for different groups of people. For some, the Revolution had been a complete success, liberating the colonists from dependence on the mother country and launching a new nation freed from aristocratic privilege. For others, the Revolution held out a promise of equal opportunity, the idea that even those born into modest circumstances might, through hard work, achieve great wealth and political influence. Still others saw the new federal government as an engine of equality powered by fiscal policy and the court system; in their view, the government should take concerted action to limit the ability of the few to exploit the labor of the many.

Most well-to-do white men embraced the ideal of equality under the law—but only for white men. They favored leaving intact certain hierarchies that sustained broad systems of inequality. For the most part, they agreed that women should not have the right to vote. The Constitution protected private property, even if that property was in the form

The city of Philadelphia played a pivotal role in the American war for independence. Representatives of the colonies signed the Declaration there on July 4, 1776, and representatives of the states crafted the Constitution there in 1787. Between 1790 and 1800, the city served as the capital of the United States. This painting of Congress Hall features a variety of Philadelphia citizens—individuals and families, young and old, men and women, black and white, the wealthy and persons of modest means, and a variety of workers going about their business. What does this out-of-doors scene suggest about the artist's view of the nature and prospects of the new nation?

Democratic-Republicans The political party that emerged after the Revolution to oppose the Federalists' support for a strong central government; favored states' rights and the agrarian way of life. Thomas Jefferson, a leader of the Democratic-Republicans, was elected president in 1800.

Two-party system A system of government characterized by two major political parties that compete with each other in "winner take all" elections.

Tariff A government tax on imported goods.

Monetary policy Government policies designed to affect the national economy through bank lending policies, interest rates, and control of the amount of money in circulation.

of human beings. The original United States Naturalization Law of 1790 limited naturalization to "free white persons," signifying that the federal government would endorse many forms of discrimination against people of color, enslaved and free. The blessings of citizenship, and civil liberties in general, would be reserved to free white men—and in some states, only to free white men who owned substantial amounts of property.

While many Americans heralded the birth of their new nation, domestic politics remained entwined with the great European powers, and political leaders continued to formulate public policies based upon the models offered by Great Britain and France. Specifically, some Americans found much to admire in British traditions of order and stability, traditions shaped by a strong central authority in the form of a monarchy. Other Americans derived inspiration from the French Revolution, which began in 1789. They believed that, for all its bloody excesses, the revolution represented an ideal of true democracy, an ideal at odds with entrenched privilege in the form of monarchies and aristocracies. The British model appealed to Federalists, supporters of a strong central government. In contrast, the French model appealed to Anti-Federalists, soon to be called **Democratic-Republicans**, supporters of the rights of the states and of the active participation of ordinary citizens in politics. These divergent views shaped both foreign and domestic policy in the 1790s.

Within this contentious atmosphere, George Washington assumed the presidency in 1789, backed by the unanimous endorsement of the electoral college. Neither the ratification of the Constitution nor Washington's election silenced the continuing debate over civil liberties and the nature of the national government. Responding to the concerns of the Anti-Federalists, Congress quickly passed ten amendments to the Constitution, collectively called the Bill of Rights. Ratified by the necessary number of states in 1791, the amendments were intended to protect white men from the power of government, whether local, state, or national. The Judiciary Act of 1789 established a national, federal court system that included a five-member Supreme Court and the office of attorney general, charged with enforcing the nation's laws.

Like other public figures of the time, Washington believed that ideological differences between political leaders should never become institutionalized in the form of separate parties. These leaders believed politicians should debate issues freely among themselves, without being bound by partisan loyalty to one view or political candidate over another. However, by the late 1790s, the intense rivalry between Alexander Hamilton, Washington's secretary of the treasury, and Thomas Jefferson, his secretary of state, had produced a **two-party system** that proved remarkably durable. Representing two competing political visions, Hamilton and his supporters (known as Federalists) and Jefferson and his supporters (called Democratic-Republicans) disagreed on foreign diplomacy and domestic economic policies. Hamilton advocated a strong central government that would promote commerce and manufacturing. In contrast, Jefferson favored states' rights bolstered by small, independent farmers who would serve as the nation's moral and political center.

In 1792, Washington ran for and won a second term. Four years later, Washington declined to run for a third term. His successor was his vice president, John Adams, an unabashed Federalist who rankled Jefferson and other more egalitarian-minded citizens. Between 1789 and 1800, the clash between the Federalists and the Democratic-Republicans reverberated in the halls of Congress, on the high seas, and in Indian country.

Federalism and Democratic-Republicanism in Action

An outspoken Federalist, Hamilton took bold steps to advance the commercial interests of the new nation. In 1789, as Washington's secretary of the treasury, he persuaded Congress to enact the first U.S. **tariff**, or tax, on imported goods. He argued this move would encourage home manufactures and raise money for the treasury.

Hamilton also sought to strengthen the federal government through **monetary policy**. At his prodding, in 1790 Congress agreed to fund the national debt—that is, to assume responsibility for repaying the government's creditors including paying interest on the debt (a total of $54 million). Congress also assumed responsibility for debts that the individual states had incurred during the Revolution. To pay for all this, federal officials stepped up debt collection and imposed new taxes on individuals. In 1791, Congress also issued a 20-year charter to the first Bank of the United States. Hamilton believed this institution, modeled after the Bank of England, would help stimulate the economy by circulating surplus funds held by the government.

An advocate of agricultural interests and the power of individual states, Jefferson disagreed with Hamilton on all these issues. Jefferson contrasted what he saw as the corrupting influence of manufactures, which enriched a few men, with the more whole-some and egalitarian existence enjoyed by modest farmers on the countryside. He feared that a strong central government would prove a threat to the liberties of free white men. Jefferson bitterly opposed the Bank of the United States, arguing that only the states could issue charters for financial institutions. He favored a lower tariff, arguing that high-priced imports hurt farmers and other small consumers. The leader of the Democratic-Republicans believed that the government should not interfere in the lives of its citizens by imposing new taxes on individual households or on imported goods. According to Jefferson, governments, like individuals, should exercise restraint in their spending and should avoid accumulating debt. Hamilton and Jefferson's opposing views of government shaped the American political party system for generations to come.

The different views epitomized by Hamilton and Jefferson found expression in American reactions to Europe's political turmoil surrounding the French Revolution. Since France had recently been a crucial wartime ally, most Americans at first sup-ported the dramatic events unfolding there in 1789. By imposing constitutional con-straints on their king, Louis XVI, the French seemed engaged in a heroic struggle much like that of the Patriots of 1776, who had challenged the enormous power of the British monarch. But when French radicals launched what became known as the Reign of Terror, American public opinion grew more critical.

In January 1793, leaders in Paris beheaded the French king and went on to execute aristocrats and presumed opponents of the revolution. In response, Federalist politi-cians argued that the bloody excesses in France should push American citizens toward a moderate and stable central government for the United States, more like that of Great Britain. Months later, when France and England went to war over territorial claims in Europe and the West Indies, American public opinion was divided. Fearing dangerous entanglements, President Washington issued a Proclamation of Neutrality at the outbreak of the war, but few Americans could resist taking sides.

Tensions between France and the United States took a turn for the worse when France's first envoy to the United States, Citizen Edmund Genêt, ignored the Neutrality Proclamation and tried to enlist American support for French designs on Spanish Flor-ida and British Canada. Nor did Britain endear itself to its former American subjects during these years. Pursuing French military forces in 1793, the British navy seized 300 American merchant ships plying the West Indian seas, forcing American sailors into service. In a practice known as **impressment**, British sea captains boarded American ships and captured sailors at gunpoint. Meanwhile, along the U.S. northwest border, British officials were supplying the Indians of the Ohio Confederacy with guns, alcohol, and encouragement in their fight against the Americans. Feeling squeezed by foreign powers in such ways, many Americans hoped that economic growth could assist the fledgling United States in resisting pressures from European rivals.

Impressment A policy that authorizes the seizure of persons or private property in the service of a government.

Planting the Seeds of Industry and Persistent Inequality

As debates swirled regarding American involvement in international affairs, questions arose over how to deal with the emerging industrial economy at home. Many Americans embraced technological innovations, especially those that spurred economic growth. Textile mills and flour mills constituted more efficient forms of production compared to traditional modes based on hand labor alone. At the same time, new machines, including the cotton gin, could spur both new and aggravated forms of social inequality.

During the late eighteenth century, most manufacturing still took place in individual households characterized by explicit hierarchies of skill, age, gender, and authority. Master artisans employed journeymen (skilled workers) and apprentices as well as their own wives and children. Throughout New England and the Mid-Atlantic, family businesses made everything from soap and candles to cloth and shoes.

In the 1790s, however, signs of a novel manufacturing economy emerged, especially in the region stretching from New England to New York, New Jersey, and Pennsylvania. This area had all the ingredients for an American Industrial Revolution: water power from rushing rivers, a faltering agricultural economy that western producers would soon eclipse, capital from successful merchants, and a dense population offering both workers and consumers.

Key individuals helped spark the early changes, including Samuel Slater, a 21-year-old English inventor who arrived in the United States in 1791. With financial support from Moses Brown, a wealthy merchant of Providence, Rhode Island, Slater constructed the first American machine for spinning cotton thread and launched his Steam Cotton Manufacturing Company in nearby Pawtucket. The nine boys and girls (ages 7 to 12) hired by Slater to operate the machinery were among America's first factory workers. They earned little pay for long hours of work in dark spinning rooms, while their meager earnings supplemented the income of their farmer-fathers in the countryside.

In 1793, another innovator, Massachusetts-born Eli Whitney, invented the cotton gin. This machine gave a tremendous boost to both the southern plantation economy and the fledgling northern industrial system. By quickly removing the seeds and other impurities from raw cotton, Whitney's cotton gin fostered the emergence of a new cotton economy. Southern planters expanded their holdings in land and slaves, rushing to meet the rising demand for cotton from mill owners in both England and New England. These planters forced enslaved men, women, and children to work at ever faster speeds to produce more cotton. For these workers, the cotton gin was a source of misery, not a source of either prosperity or "progress."

By the mid-1790s, Hamilton and his supporters were praising the nation's economic growth and regional specialization. Traditional products of the Atlantic seaboard—tar and turpentine in North Carolina, tobacco in the Chesapeake region, wheat in the Mid-Atlantic states—flourished once again, as early canal and turnpike construction encouraged new markets. In New England, shipbuilding prospered, free from earlier British restrictions, and the fishing and whaling fleets expanded. The forests of

---

Read the Document   Alexander Hamilton, "Report on Manufactures" (1791)

This logo advertises the Hampshire machine. A precursor of the canal lock, the machine consisted of a pulley that carried a canal barge in a cart up an inclined plane. Invented in 1795, it was used on the Connecticut River in western Massachusetts. However, it proved too cumbersome in the long run. Most canals used locks, sections closed off with gates so that the water level could be raised or lowered. Do you think that the "public and private good" constitutes a single objective or a set of competing ends?

SOURCE: Courtesy, American Canal and Transportation Center

Maine and New Hampshire produced wood for hulls, masts, planks, and barrels. In the Deep South, enslaved workers raised cotton, first in South Carolina and Georgia, later in the fertile lands of Alabama and Mississippi. Between 1792 and 1800, annual cotton production jumped from 3 million to 35 million pounds. The figure would soar to 93 million pounds by 1815, a testament not only to American-style mechanical ingenuity but also to the potential of the machine as a force for inequality.

Echoes of the American Revolution: The Whiskey Rebellion

Despite Hamilton's optimism about the economy, Washington's administration faced violent resistance to its policies in certain quarters. The federal government's power to tax its citizens had significant consequences for all segments of society. Would federal officials use that power in an even-handed way, to promote the well-being of all segments of society? Or would federal tax policy benefit certain groups at the expense of others? Would certain groups have more influence than others in shaping these policies?

In 1794, farmers and grain distillers in southwestern Pennsylvania refused to pay their federal taxes. This **Whiskey Rebellion** was the culmination of a lengthy rural protest against Hamilton's "hard money" policy. By favoring hard currency (coinage) over the more plentiful paper money, the government constricted financial credit. With less money to lend, creditors charged high interest rates for loans. Courts forced debtors such as small farmers to repay loans, even when money was extremely scarce. Those who could not pay their taxes or repay their loans faced foreclosure on their property.

Eager to strengthen the federal government and reduce the national debt, Hamilton devised a federal excise tax on whiskey. The plan was aimed at distillers rather than consumers, and it imposed a higher rate on small producers. Therefore, the tax fell especially hard on backcountry farmers, who distilled their bulky grain harvest into whiskey for efficient shipment to eastern markets. Using the tactics of the Stamp Tax rioters a generation earlier, western Pennsylvania farmers attacked officials and tarred and feathered a man charged with collecting the whiskey tax. They closed courts, blocked roads, and organized mass protests.

Hamilton, believing that a show of force would strengthen the federal government, urged the president to make western Pennsylvania a test case for enforcing the tax. In September, the government federalized 13,000 men from state militias to subdue the rebellion. To underscore the supremacy of the national government over the states, Washington personally led the troops into western Pennsylvania. However, when the soldiers arrived, they found that organized resistance had collapsed.

Washington claimed that the Whiskey Rebellion had been incited by ignorant men who twisted the facts with their "suspicions, jealousies, and accusations of the whole government." Yet he failed to gauge the extent of country dwellers' economic distress. By defying federal authority so openly, the farmers expressed the general grievances of westerners who felt underrepresented in state legislatures and the halls of Congress. Formal political equality, enshrined in the right to vote, was insufficient to guarantee western farmers formal influence in policy-making. The Whiskey Rebels revealed the deep current of resentment against Federalist policies that was running through rural America.

Securing Peace Abroad, Suppressing Dissent at Home

At the same time that Washington was dealing with unruly farmers, he also had to address international concerns. In 1794, the president sent Chief Justice John Jay to England to negotiate a key treaty. The negotiations were intended to resolve several problems: British forts in the Northwest Territory, British seizure of American ships and sailors in the West Indies, barriers to Americans trading freely with European belligerents in wartime, and American debts owed to British creditors.

Whiskey Rebellion Protest in 1794 by western Pennsylvania farmers and grain distillers who objected to a high federal tax on the whiskey they produced.

Watch the Video   George Washington: The Father of Our Country

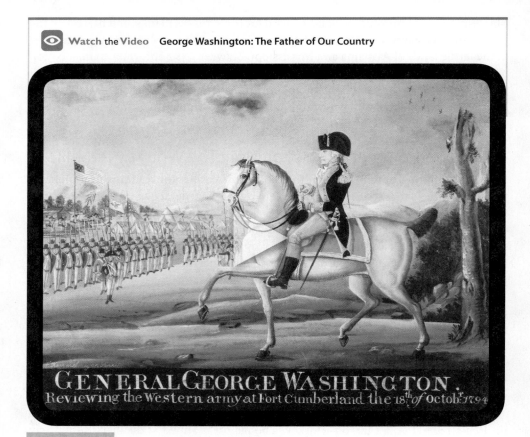

GENERAL GEORGE WASHINGTON.
Reviewing the Western army at Fort Cumberland the 18th of Octobr 1794

This 1794 painting seemingly evokes the American Revolution, when General Washington reviewed American troops. However, in this scene, President Washington is surveying some of the 13,000 state militiamen he commanded in an effort to suppress the Whiskey Rebellion in western Pennsylvania. Farmers objected to the new government tax on whiskey. With cries of "Liberty and No Excise," the protesters harassed federal tax collectors, reminiscent of anti–Stamp Act demonstrations three decades before. The Whiskey Rebellion melted away quickly. Critics objected to Washington's willingness to use such a huge force against protesting American citizens. Did the rebellion amount to a continuation of the Revolution? Why or why not?

SOURCE: Frederick Kemmelmeyer, *General George Washington Reviewing the Western Army at Fort Cumberland the 18th of October*, c. 1794. Winterthur Museum (58.2780)

Jay obtained a treaty but failed to extract meaningful compromises from the British government. England grudgingly agreed to evacuate its northern forts and to stop seizing American ships. Jay, however, acquiesced to English demands that individual Americans pay the debts they had owed to English creditors since before the Revolution. The Americans believed that their victory in the war exempted them from long-standing financial obligations to their English creditors. The Democratic-Republicans took alarm at Jay's concessions. In their view, the new agreement humiliated all Americans and threatened southern planters in particular.

Western agricultural interests also sought trade protections from Washington's administration. With the Pinckney Treaty of 1795 (the Treaty of San Lorenzo), they did better than their southern counterparts. Under this agreement, Spain allowed the United States to navigate the Mississippi River freely and to land goods at New Orleans free of taxes for three years.

With their eye on the next presidential election, the Democratic-Republicans began a vigorous campaign in favor of their own candidate, Virginia's Thomas Jefferson. They contrasted Jefferson, the friend of the small farmer, with the Federalists' choice, Vice President John Adams of Massachusetts, an advocate of strong central government run by the educated and wellborn. Jefferson's party expressed particular dismay over Washington's haste to crush the rebellious Pennsylvania farmers in 1794 and over Jay's Treaty. Backed by the New England states, Adams won the election, though narrowly. Because Jefferson received the second largest number of electoral votes—68 to Adams's 71—the Virginian became the new vice president according to the terms of the Constitution then in effect (Article II, Section 1).

Read the Document   The Alien and Sedition Acts (1798)

9.1

9.2

9.3

9.4

9.5

TABLE 9.1 THE ELECTION OF 1796

Candidate	Political Party	Electoral Vote
John Adams	Federalist	71
Thomas Jefferson	Democratic-Republican	68
Thomas Pinckney	Federalist	59
Aaron Burr	Democratic-Republican	30

In his farewell address, printed in newspapers but not delivered in person, Washington warned against the "insidious wiles of foreign influence" and against entangling alliances with foreign powers that could compromise America's independence and economic well-being. Nevertheless, upon assuming the presidency in 1797, Adams found that European powers still had a hold on American domestic and foreign relations. France began to seize American merchant vessels (300 of them by mid-1797) in retaliation for what it saw as favoritism toward England in Jay's Treaty. In October of that year, President Adams sent John Marshall and Elbridge Gerry to join the U.S. ambassador to France, Charles Pinckney, to negotiate a new treaty with France. However, French intermediaries (referred to only as X, Y, and Z in the Americans' dispatches) demanded that the three U.S. commissioners arrange for a loan of $12 million to France and pay a $250,000 bribe. Only then would the envoys be allowed to speak to the foreign minister, Charles Talleyrand. The sentiments of the American public, outraged at the idea of paying a bribe and willing to defend their new nation against all aggressors, were captured in the cry "Millions for defense, but not one cent for tribute." Adams called the commissioners home, ending the "XYZ Affair."

Federalists throughout the country called for war against France, and the Adams administration sought to shore up the country's military forces by creating the Navy Department and the Marine Corps. Hoping to rid U.S. coastal waters of French ships that were preying on American vessels, in May 1798, Congress authorized American captains to seize such armed "pirates" sent from the Republic of France. Over the next two years, the undeclared so-called Quasi War pitted the American navy against its French counterpart until the two nations signed a treaty, called the Convention of 1800, in Paris.

Conflicts also continued to simmer on the domestic front. The Federalist-dominated Congress passed the **Alien and Sedition Acts** in 1798 to suppress the rising chorus of criticism from rural people, Democratic-Republican leaders, and newspaper editors. Such dissent, Congress charged, amounted to sedition—an act of insurrection against the government. These new laws made it more difficult for immigrants to become resident aliens, gave the president the power to deport or imprison aliens, and branded as traitors any people (U.S. citizens included) who "unlawfully combine or conspire together, with intent to oppose any measure or measures of the government of the United States."

Even though the Alien and Sedition Acts were unconstitutional—they violated the First Amendment's guarantee of freedom of speech—the Federalist-dominated Supreme Court upheld them. Consequently, Democratic-Republicans were by definition guilty of treason, for they advocated policies and supported candidates opposed by the Federalists. The acts thus revealed the far-reaching potential of the party in power to divide the nation into two groups of citizens—those favored with the right of free speech and those denied that right.

Ten newspaper editors were convicted, and many others charged and jailed, under the Sedition Act. Some Democratic-Republican lawmakers also spent time in jail because their speech offended their partisan rivals. Congressman Matthew Lyon of Vermont (founder of a newspaper called Scourge of Aristocracy) went to prison for

Alien and Sedition Acts Laws enacted by the Federalist-dominated Congress in 1798 to limit the speech of their critics and to make it more difficult for immigrants to become citizens.

suggesting that President Adams showed "unbounded thirst for ridiculous pomp, foolish adulation, and selfish avarice."

In 1798 and 1799, the state legislatures of Kentucky and Virginia issued a series of resolutions condemning the Alien and Sedition Acts. Outraged at what they saw as the Federalists' blatant power grab, the two legislatures proposed that individual states had the right to declare such measures "void and of no force." Thomas Jefferson (for Kentucky) and James Madison (for Virginia) wrote the actual resolutions. As authors of the **Kentucky and Virginia Resolutions**, the two Founding Fathers unwittingly laid the theoretical framework for Southerners to attempt to nullify federal laws in the future.

People of Color: New Freedoms, New Struggles

9.2 In what ways did the legacy of the Revolution shape the lives of African Americans in the North and South?

Despite the rhetoric of equality, North American elites demonstrated a preoccupation with the idea of race as a means of categorizing people. Spanish officials in colonial New Mexico conducted a 1790 census that divided the population into groups based on ethnicity, with specific terms to designate varieties of mixed-race parentage. In the United States, a 1790 Naturalization law limited naturalized U.S. citizenship to free white persons, mocking the oft-heard claim that all people were equal under the law.

In the United States, the crosscurrents of the revolutionary legacy showed themselves most obviously in the status of African Americans. Most remained enslaved, and their numbers were increasing annually, due to the continuation of the Atlantic slave trade. African Americans like Ona Judge showed extraordinary resourcefulness in escaping slavery and claiming freedom. But even free African Americans faced an uphill struggle in their efforts to achieve political rights and economic well-being. Free people of color created educational and religious institutions that affirmed their sense of community and shared heritage. But persistent white prejudice, sanctioned by law, limited their employment options and condemned many black men and women to poverty. Lacking full citizenship rights, they saw the Revolution as an unfulfilled promise rather than a glorious achievement.

Blacks in the North

Between 1790 and 1804, all the northern states abolished slavery. On the surface, that development would seem to have been an affirmation of the Revolution, a ringing endorsement of the proposition that "all men are created equal." Nevertheless, the status of northern blacks reveals that liberation from slavery did not always guarantee equality in any meaningful sense of the word. Discriminatory laws denied black men the right to vote, and their children the right to attend public schools. Many northern whites, while abhorring the institution of slavery, persisted in seeing blacks as a separate—and unequal—group undeserving of the rights enjoyed by white people as a matter of course.

Some states, such as New York and New Jersey, abolished slavery gradually, stipulating that the children of slaves must serve a period of time (as long as 28 years in certain states) before they could gain their freedom. In 1800, over 36,500 blacks in the North were still enslaved, and some 47,000 were free. Pennsylvania did not liberate its last slave until 1847. Yet throughout the North, blacks—whether enslaved or free—were only a small percentage of the total population, ranging from less than 1 percent in Vermont to almost 8 percent in New Jersey. Most black men worked as farm hands or manual laborers, most black women as domestic servants or laundresses. Nevertheless, some whites saw black men as rivals for their jobs and as a threat to the well-being of the white population.

At both the state and national levels, most free blacks lacked basic citizenship rights. In 1792, two years after Congress limited naturalized U.S. citizenship to "free white persons," it restricted the militia to white men. State legislatures in New England and the Mid-Atlantic region imposed various other restrictions on free people of color. These measures limited blacks' right to vote, serve on juries, and move from place to place. Rectifying an "oversight" in their state constitutions, New Jersey and Connecticut later took special pains to disfranchise African American men. Massachusetts offered free blacks the most rights, including the right to vote (for men) and the right of blacks and whites to intermarry.

As slaves, blacks had served in a variety of skilled capacities in the North. Yet as free people, they faced mounting pressures in trying to live independently. Certain jobs, such as those with the federal postal service, remained closed to them by law. And municipal authorities refused to grant them licenses to ply their trades, such as wagon driving. Lacking the means to buy tools and equipment and the ability to attract white customers, many black artisans had to take menial jobs. Increasingly, free black men worked as laborers, sailors, and domestic servants, and black women worked mostly as domestic servants and laundresses.

Still, free blacks in the North set about creating their own households and institutions. They moved out of the garrets and back rooms in houses owned by whites and set up housekeeping on their own. In Boston in 1790, one in three African Americans lived outside white households; 30 years later, eight in ten did so. In response to efforts of white Methodists to segregate church seating, Philadelphia black leaders formed the Free African Society in 1787. The original articles of association called for monthly dues to maintain a mutual aid society that would benefit impoverished black people: "We, the free Africans and their descendants, of the City of Philadelphia, in the State of Pennsylvania, or elsewhere, do unanimously agree, for the benefit of each other, to advance one shilling in silver Pennsylvania currency a month." Founders of the group believed that since white officials refused to acknowledge their rights and needs, they must band together to help themselves. Discrimination on the part of whites also led to the founding in the early 1790s of the first independent black church in the North, St. Thomas Protestant Episcopal Church in Philadelphia. Black people also continued to celebrate their own festivals, typically featuring parades in which men, women, and

An anonymous artist captured this scene, probably in the slave quarters of a South Carolina plantation, in 1800. It is unknown what kind of entertainment or celebration the musicians and dancers are engaged in. The two men on the right are playing musical instruments of West African origin: a banjo and a *quaqua*, or skin-covered gourd used as a drum. On large lowcountry plantations especially, Africans and their descendants preserved traditional musical forms and social rituals. What were the criteria used by elite whites to assess the culture of subordinate groups, whether enslaved blacks or Native Americans?

children came together to display their finery, play drums and other African musical instruments, and proclaim their identity as a free people. The festivals gave blacks an opportunity to escape the confines of the workplace, even if only for a short time, and eat, drink, and dance with other people of color.

Manumissions in the South

Some southern slaves achieved freedom through legal means initiated by their owners. George Washington was not the only wealthy Southerner to move to free his own slaves in his will. In 1782, the Virginia state legislature lifted a 59-year-old ban on manumission, a process by which owners released selected people from bondage. Over the next ten years, approximately 10,000 Virginia slaves gained their freedom through manumission. Some planters believed that the Revolution was the will of God, and they came to believe that slavery violated their religious principles. Some, taking to heart the rhetoric of the Revolution, objected to the glaring contradiction between the ideal of liberty and the reality of bondage. In 1802, a Maryland woman freed her slaves because, she said, the institution went against "the inalienable Rights of Mankind."

In the Upper South, especially, private manumissions dramatically increased the free black population. There, the emergence of a more diversified economy, including craft shops and grist mills, had lowered slave prices and encouraged abolitionist sentiment among some lawmakers, clergy, and slave owners.

Virginia planters George Washington and Robert Carter were unusual in terms of the numbers of slaves they manumitted (several hundred) and their efforts to ease the transition to freedom for people who possessed neither land nor financial resources. Washington arranged apprenticeships for younger freed blacks and pensions for aged ones. In 1792, Carter granted his older slaves small plots of land. In general, however, newly emancipated men and women had difficulty finding employment as free workers. Nor was their freedom guaranteed: the 1782 Virginia manumission law provided that black debtors could be returned to slavery.

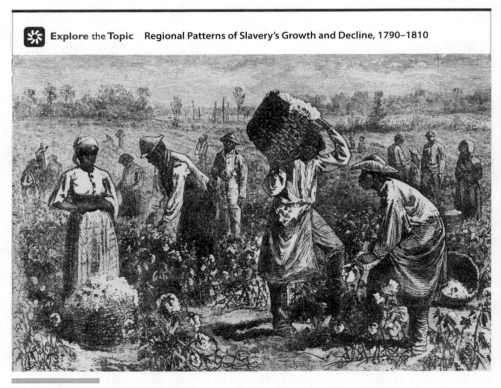

Explore the Topic   Regional Patterns of Slavery's Growth and Decline, 1790–1810

Believing that the ideals of the new nation were incompatible with the institution of human bondage, a few slaveholders freed their slaves after the Revolution. Nevertheless, the number of slaves in the South increased dramatically after the war. Why did southern whites fail to see slavery as an affront to the notion of equality?

Despite the growth in the free black population, the number of slaves actually increased in the Upper South, from over 520,000 in 1790 to almost 650,000 in 1810. In the South, slavery proved to be an extraordinarily durable institution. At the same time, the institution of bondage spread west with the nation.

Most dramatically, enslaved people themselves kept alive the rhetoric and ideals of the Revolution. In 1800, Gabriel, an enslaved blacksmith in Richmond, Virginia, plotted a rebellion to seize the city. His actions gave voice to the egalitarian principles articulated in Philadelphia in 1776, and again in Saint-Domingue in 1791, when slaves staged a bloody revolt against their French masters. (In 1804, the rebels renamed the country Haiti.) Gabriel's rebels used the words of the nation's founders to justify their actions, rallying around the cry "Death or Liberty." One even compared himself to George Washington in his struggle to "obtain the liberty of [his] countrymen." Gabriel's vengeful plans to kill all whites except abolitionists failed when informants betrayed him to Richmond authorities. The foiled slave rebellion in Virginia expressed enslaved people's desire to share in the freedom of the new nation.

Continuity and Change in the West

9.3 What were sources of conflict for people who lived in the Northwest Territory and the southern borderlands?

Blacks may have derived inspiration from the struggle against Great Britain, but as the nation expanded west, so did the institution of slavery and notions of white supremacy. Western communities tended to duplicate their eastern counterparts. The opening of federal lands proved a boon for speculators, who extended credit to homesteaders and profited from the sale of small land parcels. Some newcomers rapidly sank into debt when they were charged high prices for their purchases and forced to buy expensive supplies transported across the Appalachians. Nor did black Americans fare well, whether slave or free. Before 1800, many white families seeking a fresh start in the trans-Appalachian South took slaves with them into the new states of Kentucky and Tennessee. Even in the Northwest Territory (above the Ohio River), where slavery was prohibited by law, African American arrivals faced the same prejudices that shaped social relations in the East. Rather than extend the bounds of liberty, western settlement solidified ideas about white supremacy.

From the Canadian border to Georgia, the trans-Appalachian West had become a cultural battlefield. European Americans considered native ways to be distinctly inferior to their own; these whites believed that Indians should dress, pray, and work according to "white" standards. European Americans warred against Indians, but Indian leaders also disagreed bitterly with one another about how to respond. Should they defend their hunting grounds to the death or seek refuge elsewhere? For most, the answer was neither total resistance nor complete capitulation to an alien culture. Yet one generalization holds true for all inhabitants: the abundance of land and natural resources, combined with the clash of cultures and the prevalence of armed men of different backgrounds, made life particularly dangerous in the borderlands.

Land Speculation and Slavery

The West was not necessarily a place of boundless economic opportunity for all people who settled there. Eager investors and creditors thwarted many homesteaders' quest for cheap land. Schemes such as the Ohio Company of Associates foreshadowed the significance of land speculation in shaping patterns of settlement and property ownership farther west in later generations. With backing from wealthy investors, the Ohio Company quickly bought up tracts of land and then sold parcels to family farmers at inflated rates. A similar venture was initiated in Georgia in 1795, when speculators bribed state legislators for the right to resell huge tracts to the west of the state, land

 **Read the Document** Land Ordinance of 1785

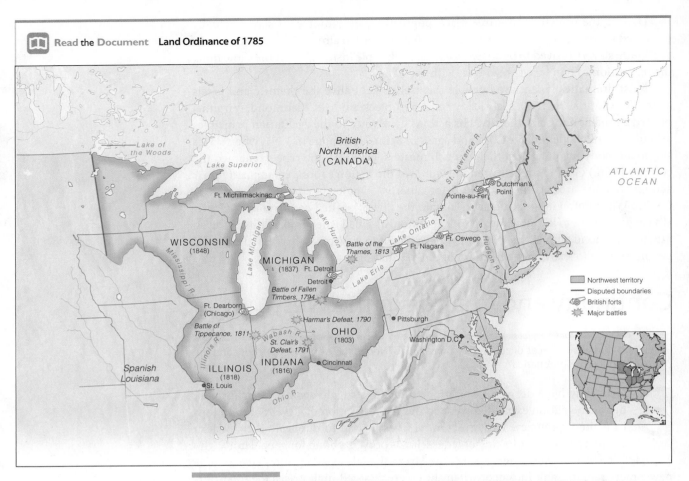

MAP 9.1 THE NORTHWEST TERRITORY After the Revolution, the Northwest Territory became a battleground. Indians—both long-term residents and newcomers—as well as European American squatters and speculators vied for control of the land. The Northwest Ordinance of 1787 provided for territorial governments before an area could apply for statehood. The present-day states of Ohio, Indiana, Michigan, Illinois, and Wisconsin were carved out of the Northwest Territory. All had gained statehood by 1848, but only after almost sixty years of bloodshed between Indians and U.S. troops in the region.

that the state did not even own. The state legislature passed the so-called Yazoo Act (named for a Georgia river) because of these bribes. The act resulted in the defrauding of thousands of buyers, whose land titles were worthless.

By protecting slavery and opening new territory to European American settlement, the new nation condemned southern blacks to a kind of legal bondage that stood in stark contrast to revolutionary principles. Many settlers relied on slave labor. By the late eighteenth century, Kentucky slaves numbered 40,000—more than 18 percent of the state's total population. On wilderness homesteads, where farmers owned just one or two slaves, African Americans faced a kind of isolation unknown on large plantations in the Southeast.

Patterns of land use directly affected the spread of slavery into the West. Despite eastern planters' use of European soil conservation techniques (crop rotation, use of manure as fertilizer), many of them had to contend with depleted soil in the Upper South. Generations of tobacco growers had worn out the land, depriving it of nutrients. As a result, many growers were forced to abandon tobacco. Some of them moved west into Indian lands in the Mississippi Territory to cultivate cotton. The scarcity of labor motivated slave owners to push workers to the limits of their endurance. Slaves cleared potential farmland of underbrush, rooted out tree stumps, and prepared the ground for cultivation. Once cotton could be planted, these same slaves worked in gangs under the sharp eye of a white overseer or black driver. Men, women, and children labored as human machines, forced to plant, hoe, and harvest as much cotton as possible, as quickly as possible.

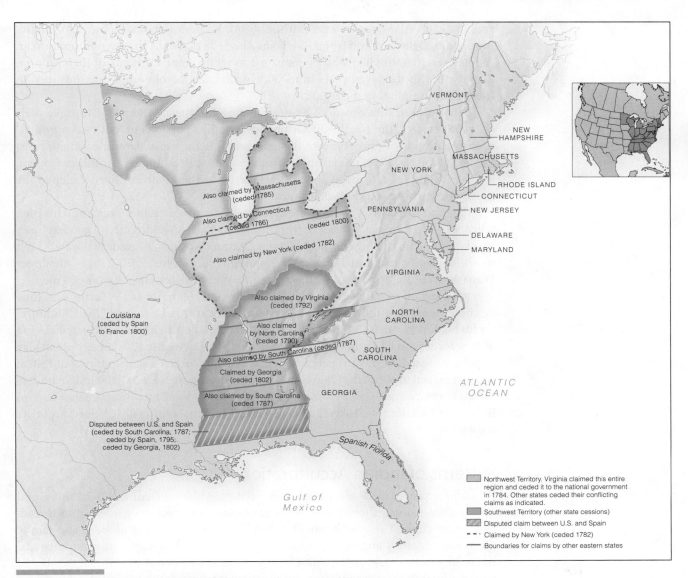

VERMONT

NEW
HAMPSHIRE

MASSACHUSETTS

NEW YORK

RHODE ISLAND

CONNECTICUT

NEW JERSEY

PENNSYLVANIA

DELAWARE

MARYLAND

Also claimed by Massachusetts
(ceded 1785)

Also claimed by Connecticut
(ceded 1786)

(ceded 1800)

Also claimed by New York (ceded 1782)

VIRGINIA

Louisiana
(ceded by Spain
to France 1800)

Also claimed by Virginia
(ceded 1792)

NORTH
CAROLINA

Also claimed
by North Carolina
(ceded 1790)

Also claimed by South Carolina (ceded 1787)

SOUTH
CAROLINA

Claimed by Georgia
(ceded 1802)

Also claimed by South Carolina
(ceded 1787)

GEORGIA

ATLANTIC
OCEAN

Disputed between U.S. and Spain
(ceded by South Carolina, 1787;
ceded by Spain, 1795;
ceded by Georgia, 1802)

Spanish Florida

Gulf of
Mexico

Northwest Territory. Virginia claimed this entire region and ceded it to the national government in 1784. Other states ceded their conflicting claims as indicated.

Southwest Territory (other state cessions)

Disputed claim between U.S. and Spain

Claimed by New York (ceded 1782)

Boundaries for claims by other eastern states

MAP 9.2 WESTERN LAND CLAIMS OF THE STATES Several of the original thirteen colonies, including Massachusetts, Connecticut, New York, Virginia, South Carolina, North Carolina, and Georgia, claimed land west of the Appalachian mountains. By 1802, these states had ceded their western lands to the federal government. The Land Ordinance of 1785 provided that this expanse be auctioned off in parcels no less than 640 acres each, with a minimum price of one dollar per acre—too expensive for many family homesteaders, thus opening the way for investors to purchase and profit. Hoping to raise money through land sales, the federal government did not object to speculation.

Many free people of color also found a less than hospitable welcome in the West. In 1802, delegates to the first Ohio territorial convention moved to restrict blacks' economic and political opportunities, even though fewer than 400 were living in Ohio at the time. Although slavery was outlawed in Ohio and other territories, blacks still lacked the right to vote. Soon after Ohio became a state in 1803, the legislature took steps to prevent the in-migration of free blacks altogether. In 1803, the territorial legislature of Indiana passed a "black law" prohibiting blacks or Indians from testifying in court against whites. Black families in the Northwest Territory were also vulnerable to kidnapping: some white men seized free blacks and sold them as slaves to plantation owners in the South.

Indian Wars in the Great Lakes Region

Native Americans residing in the Northwest Territory in the 1790s included peoples who had long occupied the Great Lakes region and the Upper Midwest, such as the Miami, Potawatomi, Menominee, Kickapoo, Illinois, Fox, Winnebago, Sauk, and Shawnee. Also present were refugees from the East: Ottawa, Ojibway, Wyandot, Algonquin, Delaware, and Iroquois who had been displaced by the Revolutionary War. As they resettled in villages, they managed to retain some elements of their cultural identity, but in the seven years immediately after the Revolution, thousands died in Indian-white clashes in the region.

What caused this violence? By encouraging European Americans to stake their claim to the area, the Northwest Ordinance inflamed passions on both sides: whites' determination to occupy and own the land, and Indians' equal determination to resist this incursion. In 1790, under orders from President Washington, Brigadier General Josiah Harmar led a force of about 1,500 men into the Maumee River Valley in the northwest corner of modern-day Ohio.

Orchestrating two ambushes in September, Miami chief Little Turtle and his men killed 183 of Harmar's troops, driving the general back in disgrace. The next year, Washington chose another officer, General Arthur St. Clair, to resume the fight. But when St. Clair's men met Little Turtle's warriors in November 1791 near the upper Wabash River, the Americans suffered an even greater defeat, losing over 600 men.

Washington tried once more to find a commander equal to Little Turtle. This time he chose General Anthony Wayne, a Revolutionary War hero dubbed "Mad Anthony" for his bold recklessness. Wayne mobilized a force of 3,000 men and constructed a string of new forts as well. At the battle of Fallen Timbers in August 1794, near present-day Toledo, hundreds of Indians perished before Wayne's forces. The withdrawal of British support helped to doom the Ohio Confederacy. On August 3, 1795, 1,100 Indian leaders met at Fort Greenville (in western Ohio) and ceded to the United States a vast tract of Indian land: all of present-day Ohio and most of Indiana. Little Turtle helped negotiate the agreement.

Patterns of Indian Acculturation

White newcomers made clear their belief that men should farm and herd sheep and cattle, while women should milk cows, raise chickens, tend the garden, spin thread, and weave cloth. These whites held that traditional native ways of work and family life made Indians "uncivilized" and hence undeserving of basic citizenship rights. According to this view, native cultures were inherently inferior or unequal to those of whites. Ultimately, white military and governmental officials had considerable power to enforce changes to those cultures, with or without the cooperation of native leaders.

However, Indian groups differed in their responses to the various attempts to persuade—or force—them to "acculturate" by adopting novel customs. At first, all learned from each other, as newly arrived settlers and indigenous peoples traded foodways, folk remedies, and styles of dress, adopting foreign habits while still retaining some old ways. Little Turtle himself chose among European American cultural traits; he drank tea and coffee, kept cows, and shunned leather breeches in favor of white men's clothing. The fact that his wife made butter suggested that she was skilled in the ways of European American homemakers.

Adopting some habits of European Americans—for example, liquor consumption—amounted to self-destruction. Alcohol was a prized trade item. Moreover, European Americans and Indians often used it to lubricate political negotiations and cultural rituals. Yet conflicts over liquor, and tensions vented under the influence of liquor, became increasingly common—and deadly. Some Indian leaders, such as Joseph Brant and Little Turtle, came to view the drinking of alcohol as a full-blown crisis among their people. Both believed that Indians must reject the white man's bottle if they were to survive.

But liquor was only one piece of a larger cultural puzzle, as the experience of the Cherokee, Chickasaw, Choctaw, Creek, and Seminole Indians in the southeastern United States revealed. The migration of whites into their hunting grounds rapidly depleted their game supply and devastated their crop fields. Unable to hunt efficiently for food, many in these groups took up new forms of agriculture after the Revolution,

Explore the Northwest Territory on MyHistoryLab

WHAT ROLE DID THE NORTHWEST TERRITORY PLAY IN AMERICAN HISTORY?

In 1787, the Northwest Ordinance transformed the course of expansion of the young United States. Previously, eastern states had claimed a huge swath of territory north of the Ohio River, but these states relinquished their claims and the Northwest Ordinance organized the settlement of these lands. Although the ordinance allowed new states to be carved out of this territory, the legislation expressly forbade slavery there. At the same time, lawmakers in 1787 ignored the fact that numerous Indian nations occupied these lands. Over the next decades, Indians formed the Western Indian Confederacy and battled U.S. settlers and soldiers for control of the region.

Clarksville, Indiana, was the first settlement in the Northwest Territory.

THE WESTERN INDIAN CONFEDERACY

Nation	
Anishinabe (Ojibwe)	Kickapoo
Wea	Kinkasha
Illinoi	
Ottawa	
Menominee	
Shawnee	
Lenape (Delaware)	
Miami	

KEY QUESTIONS   Use **MyHistoryLab** *Explorer* to **answer** these **questions:**

Analysis ▶▶▶ *Why might potential settlers in this area resent being governed by an East Coast state?*

Map the claims of the eastern states prior to the Northwest Ordinance of 1787.

Consequence ▶▶▶ *How did the outcome of the Northwest Indian War affect subsequent Native American land cessions?*

Chart the extent of land cessions in the Northwest Territory after 1795.

Comparison ▶▶▶ *How did the expansion of the U.S. population into the Northwest Territory compare to slavery's expansion in other areas?*

Map these two patterns to consider future possible conflict.

231

and they became known to whites as the Five Civilized Tribes. Women, who had traditionally tended crops using hoes, gave way in the fields to men, often using plows provided by the federal government. Protestant missionaries encouraged Indian women to learn to spin thread and weave cloth. For more than a generation, the willingness of these southern tribes to accommodate themselves to European American law and divisions of labor allowed them to stay in their homeland and retain key elements of their cultural identity.

In southwest and far west borderland areas, Spanish officials met with mixed success in their attempts to convert Indians to Christianity and encourage them to engage in sedentary farming. For example, between 1772 and 1804, Spanish priests established nineteen missions among the Chumash, hunter-gatherers living in permanent villages along the California coast. When large numbers of the Indians moved to these settlements, they forfeited their traditional kin and trade networks, and their distinctive culture began to fade. Birth rates plummeted due to disruptions in family life (more women than men lived in the missions), and mortality rates increased dramatically as contact with the Spanish introduced new diseases.

In contrast, along the Texas Gulf Coast, the Spanish made little headway in their efforts to bring the Karankawa Indians into the missions. Members of this nomadic tribe arrived at the mission gates only when their own food reserves were low; in essence, the Karankawa simply included the missions in their seasonal migrations between the Gulf Coast and the coastal plain.

Shifting Social Identities in the Post-Revolutionary Era

9.4 What kinds of traditional hierarchies were challenged by different groups of Americans in the wake of the Revolution? How successful were those challenges?

The nation's founders had argued for an egalitarian society, one in which people prospered according to their talents and ambition. Of course, their definition of egalitarianism encompassed only white men. Still, it was a revolutionary idea and led to challenges of social hierarchies after the Revolution. These hierarchies included the patriarchal (male-headed) family, established Protestant denominations, power systems based on social standing, and ideas about race and gender. Ordinary men and women penned letters to local newspapers, glorifying common laborers and questioning the claim to power of elite citizens.

In the early nineteenth century, voluntary reform organizations multiplied across the nation. As their numbers proliferated, both the possibilities and limitations of reform became clear. Some groups—for example, white working men—sought to advance their own self-interest without showing much concern for the plight of African American laborers. In other cases, people banded together to target the behavior of a specific group: drunkards, slave owners, the irreligious, or prostitutes. These moral reform groups welcomed diversity among members, as long as new converts supported the cause.

Artisan-Politicians and Menial Laborers

In the decades after the Revolution, residents of port cities along the eastern seaboard grew accustomed to public parades marking special occasions: a visit from George Washington, the ratification of the Constitution, the Fourth of July. Most of these parades consisted of groups of artisans marching together, carrying the banners of their respective occupations. As one example, the bricklayers' flag declared, "Both Buildings and Rulers Are the Works of Our Hands."

Interpreting History

A Farmer Worries About the Power of "THE FEW," 1798

"The **reason** why a **free government** has always **failed** is from the **unreasonable** demands and **desires** of the few."

A fter the Revolution, many ordinary Americans debated the challenges faced by the new nation. For example, C. William Manning, a tavern keeper and farmer in Massachusetts, in 1798 wrote an essay titled "The Key of Libberty." Manning warns about the power of "the few"—the wealthy and influential—over the power of "the many"—ordinary people who must work hard for a living.

"In the sweat of thy face shalt thou get thy bread, until thou return to the ground,"* is the irreversible sentence of Heaven on man for his rebellion. To be sentenced to hard labor during life is very unpleasant to human nature. There is a great aversion to it perceivable in all men; yet it is absolutely necessary that a large majority of the world should labor, or we could not subsist. For labor is the sole parent of all property; the land yields nothing without it, and there is no . . . necessary of life but what costs labor and is generally esteemed valuable according to the labor it costs. Therefore, no person can possess property without laboring unless he gets it by force or craft, fraud or fortune, out of the earnings of others.

But from the great variety of capacities, strength, and abilities of men, there always was and always will be a very unequal distribution of property in the world. Many are so rich that they can live without labor—also the merchant, physician, lawyer, and divine, the philosopher and schoolmaster, the judicial and executive officers, and many others who could honestly get a living without bodily labors. As all these professions require a considerable expense of time and property to qualify themselves therefore, . . . so all these professions naturally unite in their schemes to make their callings as honorable and lucrative as possible.

Also, as ease and rest from labor are reasoned among the greatest pleasures of life, pursued by all with the greatest avidity, and when attained at once create a sense of superiority; and as pride and ostentation are natural to the human heart, these orders of men generally associate together and look down with too much contempt on those that labor.

As the interests and incomes of the few lie chiefly in money at interest, rents, salaries, and fees, that are fixed on the nominal value of money, they are interested in having money scarce and the price of labor and produce as low as possible. . . .

But the greatest danger the many are under in these money matters is from the judicial and executive officers, especially so as their incomes for a living are almost wholly gotten from the follies and distress of the many—they being governed by the same selfish principles as other men are. They are the most interested in the distresses of the many of any in the nation; the scarcer money is and the greater the distresses of the many are, the better for them. . . .

This is the reason why they ought to be kept entirely from the legislative body; . . . For in all these conceived differences of interests, it is the business and duty of the legislative body to determine what is justice, or what is right and wrong; and it is the duty of every individual in the nation to regulate his conduct according to their decisions. . . .

The reason why a free government has always failed is from the unreasonable demands and desires of the few. They cannot bear to be on a level with their fellow creatures, or submit to the determinations of a legislature where (as they call it) the swinish multitude is fairly represented, but sicken at the idea, and are ever hankering and striving after monarchy or aristocracy, where the people have nothing to do in matters of government but to support the few in luxury and idleness.

For these and many other reasons, a large majority of those that live without labor are ever opposed to the principles and operation of a free government; and though the whole of them do not amount to one-eighth part of the people, yet, by their combinations, arts, and schemes, have always made out to destroy it sooner or later.

Questions for Discussion

1. According to Manning, why have attempts at "free government" failed in the past?
2. How do you think Manning would view the institution of slavery?
3. What is the significance of the fact that Manning never published his views? What does this fact tell us about the nature of political debates during this time?
4. Do you think Manning is referring to Federalists when he condemns "the few"? Why or why not?
5. Can you think of any individuals or groups of individuals whom Manning might have had in mind, as he warned about the power of the wealthy few?

SOURCE: C. William Manning, "The Key of Libberty" (1798), in *Major Problems in American History, Vol. 1: To 1877*, Elizabeth Cobbs Hoffman and Jon Gjerde (Houghton Mifflin, 2002), 170–171.

*Genesis 3:19

Proud of their role in the Sons of Liberty and other revolutionary organizations, bricklayers—along with tanners, carpenters, glassblowers, weavers, and other groups of artisans—proclaimed themselves the proud citizens of the new nation. American worker organizations built on a distinct revolutionary heritage that stressed the equality of all (white) freeborn men. These organizations promoted the view that free workers might contrast themselves with slaves, but they were not all equal to each other. According to this view, the majority of white men had fought in the Revolutionary War, while the majority of black men had remained enslaved during that conflict (ignoring the fact that the ranks of the continental Army had included black soldiers). Thus, even skilled free men of color could not hope to join the major workers' organizations that promoted the idea of "whiteness" as a powerful category of social identity.

Banding together according to craft, and across craft lines, skilled white workers claimed an equal place with their social betters in the governance of the new nation. Master artisans in several cities—including Boston, Albany, Providence, Portsmouth, Charleston, Savannah, and New York—created organizations called the General Society of Mechanics and Tradesmen that brought together skilled workers from a variety of fields. The proliferation of newspapers let these artisans participate in a new, more open public forum. Such participation in turn helped them to gain greater influence within local politics. In some towns, as many as 85 percent of adult men owned property of some kind and thus were eligible to vote. Indeed, artisans' organizations soon became quasi-political groups, extending their reach in ways that pre-Revolutionary trades-based associations had not.

But not all workers were so secure. The diggers who constructed the early canals of the 1790s included men from all walks of life: part-time farmers, indentured servants, slaves, and white transients. Moving around in search of work, they led an unsettled existence that contrasted greatly with the more predictable life of urban artisans. Canal diggers represented a transition workforce of sorts, bridging the worlds of traditional, outdoor work with the more disciplined, regimented pace of the factory.

The plight of menial laborers (in the countryside and the cities) suggests the ironies that accompanied the decline of indentured servitude and the rise of the "free laborer." To be sure, master artisans attained a degree of economic independence. But for men and women who lacked skills, money, and wealthy patrons, freedom often meant financial insecurity and, in some cases, reliance on public or private charity. Those who did find work usually had the kinds of jobs that came with the booming economy of the late eighteenth century: moving goods from one place to another, building new structures, and providing personal services for the merchants who profited from all this commercial activity.

Republican Mothers and Other Well-Off Women

The post-Revolutionary period was a time of flux for various groups of women as well as for male workers. Some well-educated women in the United States read English writer Mary Wollstonecraft's *Vindication of the Rights of Woman*, published in England and America in 1792. In that manifesto, Wollstonecraft argued that young men and women should receive the same kind of education. She objected to a special female curriculum that exclusively emphasized skills such as needlepoint and musical accomplishments; this "false system of education," she charged, left women in "a state of perpetual childhood."

In 1801, an anonymous "American Lady" published an essay titled "A Second Vindication of the Rights of Woman." In it, she claimed that "a good kitchen woman [that is, a household drudge], very seldom makes a desirable wife, to a man of any refinement." The anonymous "American Lady" and others who shared her opinion celebrated a new kind of woman—the **Republican mother**—who provided cultured companionship for her husband and reared her children to be virtuous, responsible

Republican mother A wife and mother whose primary role is caring for and socializing future citizens (her children); an ideal favored by some elites after the American Revolution.

members of society. This image of womanhood promoted the idea that well-off women should dedicate themselves to tending the home fires rather than aspiring to a more public role in business or politics.

Prior to the Revolution, women tended to bear many children, since additional hands were needed to labor in the fields. But as the sons of farmers became store managers and bookkeepers, they had less need for the unpaid labor of their own children. The decline in white women's fertility rates after the Revolution suggests that the economy had shifted. And some women could now buy products their grandmothers had made at home. In particular, a small but influential group of well-to-do women in the cities were shedding their roles as producers of candles, soap, and textiles. Instead, they became consumers of these staples and of luxury goods, and they managed household servants. "Republican mothers" participated in the public life of the new nation as the guardians of the home and the socializers of children.

But the idea of the "Republican mother" also suggested a more radical notion. If such a woman wanted to earn the respect accorded all intelligent human beings, she must strive for an education equal to that of men's. In the 1790s, a number of academies for "young ladies" opened in New England. These schools offered courses in such "womanly pursuits" as needlework, etiquette, and music. But many also offered a classical curriculum consisting of mathematics, foreign languages, and geography. This system of study encouraged young women to think for themselves. In this respect, female academies challenged the view that women were intellectually inferior to and necessarily dependent on men. At the same time, the spread of female academies introduced a new form of inequality separating well-to-do, well-educated women from their less fortunate counterparts.

A Loss of Political Influence: The Fate of Nonelite Women

The Revolution had given elite white women a rationale for speaking out in the realm of politics. These women were also the beneficiaries of their husbands' success at making a living in a post-Revolutionary world that afforded new and expanded opportunities for money-making among white men. At the same time, women in households outside of the world of commerce faced hardships that included, in some instances, the loss of political authority, and in most instances, unremitting toil and material deprivation.

Many Native American women, feeling the pressure of non-Indian cultures, found their traditional roles had been weakened by the end of the eighteenth century. For example, among the Cherokee, the introduction of a European American division of labor lessened women's customary political influence as leaders and diplomats. Most European Americans believed that only men should serve in positions of authority, and so Cherokee women felt pressed to refrain from taking part in political negotiations and to subordinate themselves to men.

In the West, Indian women bore the brunt of ongoing conflicts between their own people and European American settlers. In New Mexico, female Indian captives from Plains tribes (such as the Apache, Comanche, and Kiowa) became *indios servientes* in Hispanic households. In the East, Native American women dispossessed of their land pieced together a meager existence. For example, in Natick, Massachusetts, women turned to weaving and peddling baskets and brooms while their men scrounged for wage labor.

For some Americans, the postwar years brought unprecedented opportunities to buy, sell, and trade. However, commercial development, combined with race and gender discrimination, offered only modest possibilities for many impoverished women and women of color. Like other free blacks, Chloe Spear of Boston "worked early and late" at a number of jobs, such as laundering and ironing clothes. Eventually, she managed to purchase her own home. In Rhode Island, Elleanor Eldridge started her work career at age ten in 1795. Thereafter, she labored as a domestic servant, spinner, weaver, dairymaid, and nurse. She finally went into business, first as a soap boiler and then as a wallpaperer and house painter. However, like many free blacks, Eldridge remained vulnerable to the machinations of white men who tried to defraud her of her hard-won earnings.

Some white women also felt the effects of fluctuations in the market economy. In Philadelphia in the mid-1790s, two former servants—Polly Nugent (married to a blacksmith who had just lost his job) and Grace Biddle (newly widowed)—had to plead for assistance from their former mistress, Elizabeth Drinker. The city's "Bettering House" for indigent people housed men and women, blacks and whites. In the period after the Revolution, many women had neither the resources nor the opportunities to improve their lot.

The Election of 1800: Revolution or Reversal?

9.5	In what ways did the election of the Democratic-Republican Thomas Jefferson signal a new direction for the new nation?

The social turbulence of these years also played out in the political arena. The campaign of 1800 pitted Thomas Jefferson and his vice-presidential running mate, Aaron Burr, against the incumbent, John Adams, and his vice-presidential nominee, Charles Pinckney. Certain elements of the campaign were predictable. The Democratic-Republicans blasted Alexander Hamilton's economic policies and the Adams administration's military buildup. Jefferson's party also condemned the Alien and Sedition Acts, used to silence Adams's political opponents. For their part, the Federalists portrayed Jefferson as a godless supporter of the French Revolution. They also charged that he had fathered children by one of his slaves, Sally Hemings. (Two centuries later, the preponderance of evidence, including the Hemings family's oral traditions and DNA evidence, suggests that this assertion was true.)

Jefferson prevailed in the 1800 election, but his victory did not come easily. The electoral college allowed delegates to vote separately for president and vice president, and as a result Jefferson tied with Burr. Each man received seventy-three votes. Then the decision went to the House of Representatives, which was dominated by Federalists. After a series of tied votes, Jefferson finally gained a majority. His selection in February 1801 marked the orderly transfer of power from the Federalists to the Democratic-Republicans, a peaceful revolution in American politics.

As chief executive, Jefferson did little to change the direction of the country. Aware of his razor-thin victory, he retained many Federalist appointees. And his eagerness to expand the boundaries of the United States—which culminated in the Louisiana Purchase of 1803—solidified the Hamiltonian principles that favored commerce and trade over agrarian values.

The Enigmatic Thomas Jefferson

As the author of the Declaration of Independence, Thomas Jefferson had declared, "We hold these truths to be self-evident, that all men are created equal, that they are

TABLE 9.2 THE ELECTION OF 1800

Candidate	Political Party	Electoral Vote
Thomas Jefferson	Democratic-Republican	73
Aaron Burr	Democratic-Republican	73
John Adams	Federalist	65
Charles C. Pinckney	Federalist	64

endowed by their Creator with certain unalienable rights, that among these are life, liberty and the pursuit of happiness." To different groups of Americans living in a post-revolutionary United States, these words suggested several different views of equality, some of them contradictory. The theory of natural rights held that all people regardless of their station in life should enjoy certain basic rights and liberties. At the same time, many white Southerners interpreted freedom to mean the right to own private property (including other human beings) without the threat of governmental intrusion or arbitrary seizure. Most white men who endorsed the Declaration of Independence also believed that women, people of color, and Indians were fundamentally unequal—in intelligence and ability—and so justly left out of the new body politic. In contrast, persons in favor of women's rights and the abolition of slavery seized on Jefferson's words to promote a fuller, more expansive view of American equality.

Who was the man behind these stirring words? In 1800, Jefferson, the presidential candidate, wrote, "I have sworn upon the altar of God eternal hostility against every form of tyranny over the mind of man." Yet Jefferson's own views on ordinary people were less heroic. Specifically, his deep skepticism about African American equality and the viability of Indian cultures helped to justify violent assaults on both groups in the early nineteenth century.

Many Americans today know Jefferson as the author of the Declaration of Independence. But he also sought to defend slavery as a central institution in the new republic, and he regarded blacks as lacking in imagination and intelligence. Jefferson wrote much about the noble calling of the yeoman farmer. Yet he assigned the task of tilling the soil on his own estate (Monticello, near Charlottesville, Virginia) to his enslaved workers.

The president's views on Indians also did nothing to reverse the course of aggression in the West. He believed that land ownership created the stable institutions necessary for civilized behavior. Yet the system of private property, and the violent methods that whites used to enforce it, spelled the destruction of traditional Indian ways of life.

It is tempting to excuse Jefferson's prejudiced beliefs by saying he merely reflected his time. But in fact, a significant number of Jefferson's contemporaries were voicing their misgivings about slavery. While Jefferson acknowledged their arguments, he did not share their beliefs. A citizen of a transatlantic "republic of ideas," he corresponded with political thinkers—from John Adams to the Marquis de Lafayette—who understood the inherent tension between freedom for whites and slavery for blacks. Obviously, Jefferson knew that some of the northern states had written constitutions that incorporated the sentiments of the Declaration of Independence in ways that justified the abolition of slavery. Moreover, a notable number of Jefferson's wealthy Virginia compatriots (including George Washington) had chosen to free their slaves, either by their own hand or through provisions of their wills, to practice in their own households what they preached to British tyrants.

Jefferson lived in an age when revolutionary enthusiasm was sweeping the Western world. Challenges to slavery had rocked Europe; France outlawed the practice in 1794, although Napoleon later reinstated it. Abolition had also transformed the Western Hemisphere with the successful rebellion of the Saint-Domingue slaves in 1791. The United States provided the political theory and rhetoric to inspire abolitionists around the globe, but within the new nation, the debate over the institution of slavery continued to rage. The southern states, in particular, took decisive steps to solidify the institution within their own boundaries.

Protecting and Expanding the National Interest

As president, Jefferson reconsidered his original vision of the United States: a compact country in which citizens freely pursued modest agrarian interests without interference from the national government or distractions from overseas conflicts. Indeed, during his years in office, the federal government moved toward increasing its power.

Marbury v. Madison An 1803 Supreme Court decision establishing the right of the judiciary to declare acts of both the executive and legislative branches unconstitutional.

Just before Jefferson assumed the presidency, the Federalist-dominated Congress had strengthened the national court system by passing the Judiciary Act of 1801. The act created sixteen circuit (regional) courts, with a judge for each, and bolstered support staff for the judicial branch in general. President Adams appointed these judges (so-called midnight judges because they were appointed right before Jefferson took office). Before stepping down, Adams had also appointed Secretary of State John Marshall as chief justice of the Supreme Court.

Adams's last-minute acts had long-term consequences. Marshall remained on the bench for thirty-four years. He presided over the court when it rendered its landmark *Marbury v. Madison* decision in 1803, which established the judiciary's right to declare acts of both the executive and legislative branches unconstitutional. Chief Justice Marshall wrote: "It is emphatically the province and duty of the judicial department to say what the law is."

In the realm of international affairs, Jefferson asserted his own authority. Challenges from foreign powers prompted the Democratic-Republican president to take bold steps to protect U.S. economic and political interests abroad and along the country's borders. In 1801, Jefferson's administration launched a war against Barbary pirates in North Africa when Tripoli (modern-day Libya) demanded ransom money for kidnapped American sailors. (Together, the North African kingdoms of Tunis, Tripoli, Algeria, and Morocco were known as the Barbary States.) The war against Tripoli, which spanned four years, revealed the extent of U.S. trade interests even at this early point in the nation's history. The United States signed a peace treaty with Tripoli in 1805 and paid $60,000 for the release of the American captives.

At the beginning of the nineteenth century, the European powers continued their operations in the territory west of the United States. In 1801, General Napoleon Bonaparte persuaded the King of Spain to secretly cede the trans-Mississippi region called Louisiana to France. Retaining control of New Orleans, Spain denied Americans the right to use that city as a depository for goods awaiting shipment. In 1803, Jefferson sent his fellow Virginian, and prominent Anti-Federalist, James Monroe to Paris. Together with American ambassador Robert Livingston, Monroe set out to secure American trading rights to New Orleans. To the Americans' surprise, Napoleon agreed to sell the whole area to the United States. At the time, Louisiana included most of the territory between the Mississippi River and the Rocky Mountains—a total of 828,000 square miles. The United States agreed to pay $15 million for the Louisiana Purchase.

The Louisiana Purchase reversed the roles of Jefferson and his Federalist rivals. The president advocated territorial expansion, but his opponents remained suspicious of the move. Devoted to a strict interpretation of the Constitution, Jefferson traditionally favored limiting federal authority. Yet he sought to justify the purchase by pointing out that it would finally rid the area of European influence. He proposed shifting Indians from the Mississippi Territory (part of present-day Alabama and Mississippi) to the West so that American newcomers could have the eastern part of the country to themselves. For their part, the Federalists feared that Louisiana would benefit mainly agrarian interests and eventually dilute New England's long-standing political influence and power. They suspected Jefferson of attempting to expand the influence of his own political party.

Conclusion

In his first inaugural address, Jefferson suggested that both parties, despite their differences, shared similar views about the role of government and the importance of economic opportunity for ordinary people. Seeking unity after a partisan campaign, he reminded political leaders, "We are all Republicans, we are all Federalists." Indeed, most public officials at the time held a common suspicion of groups that professed religious beliefs that lay outside the mainstream of Protestantism or liberal Deism (a general belief in God without ties to a particular religious denomination). They considered slavery less a moral issue than a political matter that individual states must address. They united behind the idea that Indians, blacks, and women should have no formal voice in governing the nation.

Nevertheless, the post-Revolutionary era saw the rise of two opposing camps—those favoring local control and those supporting federal authority. Many people defined political interests in "either-or" terms: either the French system of political equality or the British monarchy; either the individual states or the federal government; either the farm or the factory. Such thinking promoted a narrow view of the United States, already a society of great economic and ethnic diversity.

Despite this ideological split, the new nation gave white men opportunities practically unknown in the rest of the world. Regardless of their background, many white men could aspire to own property, to enjoy impressive legal rights, and to participate in the political process. The federal government supported economic growth by facilitating territorial expansion, technological innovation, and the protection of private property. As much for the prosperity it promoted as for the noble ideas it nourished, the Revolution continued to inspire liberation movements within the United States and throughout the world.

Chapter Review

Competing Political Visions in the New Nation

9.1 What were the disagreements between the Federalists and the Democratic-Republicans in domestic policy? In foreign policy? p. 217

On the domestic front, Federalists supported a strong central government to promote order and stability. Democratic-Republicans favored the rights of the states and the active participation of ordinary citizens in politics. In foreign policy, the Federalists tended to side with the British and call for military buildup, while the Democratic-Republicans tended to support the French.

People of Color: New Freedoms, New Struggles

9.2 In what ways did the legacy of the Revolution shape the lives of African Americans in the North and South? p. 224

Slavery was abolished in the northern states between 1790 and 1804, but discriminatory laws kept black adults from voting and kept their children from attending public schools. Nevertheless, free blacks created their own households and institutions. In the South, some slaves achieved freedom through manumission, but the number of slaves actually increased in the Revolution's aftermath.

Continuity and Change in the West

9.3 What were sources of conflict for people who lived in the Northwest Territory and the southern borderlands? p. 227

Conflict in the West had economic and cultural dimensions. The opening of federal lands benefited speculators, who profited from extending credit and selling land to homesteaders. Many newcomers therefore sank into debt. The West also became a cultural battleground where European Americans clashed with Indians. White settlers took west with them their commitment to slavery and white supremacy.

Shifting Social Identities in the Post-Revolutionary Era

9.4 What kinds of traditional hierarchies were challenged by different groups of Americans in the wake of the Revolution? How successful were those challenges? p. 232

Americans challenged the hierarchies of the patriarchal family and power systems based on social standing, as well as established Protestant denominations and ideas about race and gender. Some groups, including skilled workers and well-to-do women, saw their influence increase, while ordinary workers, poor women, and African Americans made little headway during this era.

The Election of 1800: Revolution or Reversal?

9.5 In what ways did the election of the Democratic-Republican Thomas Jefferson signal a new direction for the new nation? p. 236

Despite his campaign rhetoric, Jefferson did little to change the direction of the county. He retained Federalist appointees and his Louisiana Purchase actually solidified the Hamiltonian principles of commercial development and territorial expansion. He also defended slavery and supported aggression against western Indians. Jefferson's election thus suggested that the two main parties shared many basic political ideas.

Timeline

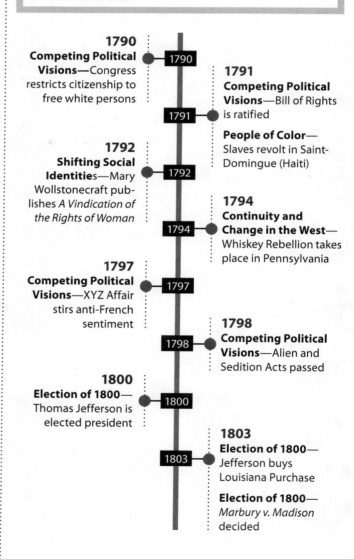

1790
Competing Political Visions—Congress restricts citizenship to free white persons — 1790

1791 — **1791**
Competing Political Visions—Bill of Rights is ratified

People of Color—Slaves revolt in Saint-Domingue (Haiti)

1792
Shifting Social Identities—Mary Wollstonecraft publishes *A Vindication of the Rights of Woman* — 1792

1794 — **1794**
Continuity and Change in the West—Whiskey Rebellion takes place in Pennsylvania

1797
Competing Political Visions—XYZ Affair stirs anti-French sentiment — 1797

1798 — **1798**
Competing Political Visions—Alien and Sedition Acts passed

1800
Election of 1800—Thomas Jefferson is elected president — 1800

1803 — **1803**
Election of 1800—Jefferson buys Louisiana Purchase

Election of 1800—*Marbury v. Madison* decided

10 Defending and Expanding the New Nation, 1804–1818

How did white Americans seek to enlarge the territory of the United States in the early nineteenth century? What was the fate of Indians who resisted this encroachment? The Creeks of the Southeast lost lives and land after whites—and rival Indians—defeated them in battle.

In 1813, a group of Creek warriors calling themselves Red Sticks (for their scarlet-painted weapons) prepared to attack a U.S. military encampment north of present-day Mobile, Alabama. In response, Andrew Jackson, a Tennessee militia leader, received a commission as major general. His mission was to retaliate against the Indians. At the time, the United States was engaged in a fierce war in an effort to protect the young country's territorial integrity. To the north and west, groups of Indians had joined with the British to halt American expansion. Jackson called Native Americans "blood thirsty barbarians." He often boasted about collecting the scalps of his Indian victims, and he relished his new assignment.

LEARNING OBJECTIVES

10.1	10.2	10.3	10.4
What were the domestic and international consequences of Britain's persistent challenges to U.S. territorial sovereignty and trade relations with other nations? p. 243	What were the political and economic interests of the United States, the Indian tribes, and Great Britain and why did those divergent interests clash during the War of 1812? p. 248	Did political and social realities justify the use of the term "the Era of Good Feelings" to describe the period after the War of 1812? p. 253	How did staple-crop production shape the labor, culture, and family lives of slaves? p. 259

An 1859 engraving shows the chief of the Creek "Red Sticks," William Weatherford (Red Eagle), surrendering to Andrew Jackson after the Battle of Horseshoe Bend in 1814. Jackson sought to exploit intra-tribal conflicts, enlisting the Creek White Sticks in his battle against the Red Sticks. During the War of 1812, Jackson also "recruited" Cherokee, Chickasaw, and Chocktaw fighters in the U.S. campaign against the British. Of that effort he later recalled, "I was directed to compel (by coercive measures if it became necessary) all the warriors of the four Southern Tribes to enroll themselves in our defense." As a result of the Treaty of Fort Jackson, the Creeks were forced to cede nearly 23 million acres of land to the United States—half of central Alabama and part of southern Georgia. On what bases did white military and political officials make distinctions among various Indian groups?

 Listen to Chapter 10 on MyHistoryLab

Watch the Video Series on MyHistoryLab

Learn about some key topics related to this chapter with the *MyHistoryLab Video Series: Key Topics in U.S. History.*

1 **The New Republic: 1789–1824** During the first quarter of the nineteenth century, the American republic expanded and explored its territory and fought a war with Great Britain and its Indian allies. The Industrial Revolution transformed the local economies of the New England and mid-Atlantic states. This video introduces a period when the bitter partisanship of the post-Revolutionary era had abated, leading some historians to call it the "Era of Good Feelings."

 Watch on MyHistoryLab

The Louisiana Purchase and Lewis and Clark One of the key events in the early history of the United States was the expedition of Meriwether Lewis and William Clark to explore and map the newly purchased Louisiana Territory. This video examines President Thomas Jefferson's decision to buy the territory from France for $15 million. **2**

Watch on MyHistoryLab

3 **The War of 1812** In 1812, with Great Britain preoccupied by fighting against Napoleonic France and its allies, the United States invaded Canada, triggering war. This video examines the reasons for war, including U.S. grievances against Great Britain—for impressing American merchant-ship seamen, for continuing to support Indian resistance to encroachment on their lands, and for failing to abandon its frontier forts.

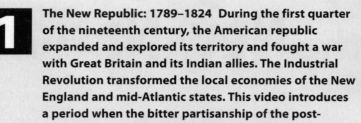 Watch on MyHistoryLab

The "Era of Good Feelings" American success in the War of 1812, combined with the election of James Monroe as president in 1816, led to the demise of the Federalist party. This video explains why some historians have called this period the "Era of Good Feelings," despite ongoing financial crises, sectional strife, and political conflicts. **4**

Watch on MyHistoryLab

Jackson's 3,500 troops laid waste to Creek territory. Regiments of Cherokee, Choctaw, and Chickasaw Indians helped them. During a monumental battle in March 1814, more than three-quarters of the defending Red Sticks and a number of Indian women and children died at Horseshoe Bend. In the treaty of the same name that followed, the Americans forced the Creek Nation to give up 2.3 million acres. The remnants of the Red Sticks fled to the swamps of Florida, where they joined additional Creeks, other Florida Indians, and numerous fugitive slaves in an emerging group known as the Seminoles.

A quarter century after the end of the Revolution, the United States sought to consolidate its gains in the face of multiple threats from within and outside its borders by resorting to violence. Indians were aggressively seeking to beat back white encroachment on their lands, while Great Britain was challenging U.S. sovereignty on the high seas and in the western territories. In the Great Lakes region, various tribes maintained political and military alliances with the British in Canada. A group of U.S. western political leaders, the "war hawks," felt contempt for the Indians, who believed that all land should be held in common, to be shared equally by all, as well as scorn for British monarchists, who favored aristocratic privilege over republicanism.

n this period, the United States met its most severe test to date: a war with Great Britain that raged from 1812 to 1815. The effects of this "Second American Revolution" were far-reaching. The conflict eliminated the British from the Old Northwest once and for all. The war also spurred industrialization and stimulated commerce. In the South, the cotton plantation system began to shape the political and economic life of the whole region, expanding human bondage in the process.

The dramatic events of the first two decades of the nineteenth century served both to solidify the standing of the United States in the world and to extend its borders at home. Yet, over time, it became clear that the greatest threat to the country and its self-proclaimed egalitarian ideals would come not only from the British monarchy and its allies the Indians but also from developments within the country itself. The institution of slavery mocked the nation's most noble ideals, and the campaign to eliminate the Indian threat unleashed a torrent of blood-letting that would continue for decades to come. The fate of the Red Sticks revealed that the U.S. drive for territorial expansion and commercial development would come at the expense of groups deemed "inferior" by whites.

A Contest over Land and Sea

10.1 What were the domestic and international consequences of Britain's persistent challenges to U.S. territorial sovereignty and trade relations with other nations?

n the election of 1804, Democratic-Republican Thomas Jefferson and his vice-presidential running mate, George Clinton, easily bested their Federalist opponents, Charles C. Pinckney and Rufus King. Developments overseas preoccupied Jefferson during his second term in office. England and France continued to challenge each other as the reigning powers of Europe. In 1805, the British navy, under the command of Lord Nelson, defeated the French and Spanish fleets in the Battle of Trafalgar off the coast of Spain. That same year, France reveled in its own triumph on land when Napoleon conquered the Austrian and Russian armies at the Battle of Austerlitz. Supreme on the seas, England in 1806 passed the Orders in Council, which specified that any country that wanted to ship goods to France must first send them to a British port and pay taxes on them.

President Jefferson sought to expand the boundaries of the new nation and to facilitate exploration of the vast new territory acquired from France. In 1804, he commissioned the first major transcontinental expedition to the Pacific. The purposes of the expedition were scientific and economic—to explore the land and to assess the prospects for trade and development. Yet tensions with Britain lingered, both on land and on the high seas. Many Americans believed that England's trade policies, combined with its persistent seizures of U.S. seamen, amounted to acts of economic and military aggression against the United States.

In early November 1804, a group of soldiers worked feverishly to construct a rough military garrison on the north bank of the Missouri River, near several Mandan Indian villages just west of modern Washburn, North Dakota. The soldiers knew they had to work quickly. Within a month, winter would descend on the northern Great Plains, and the temperature would plummet. In fact, not long after Fort Mandan was completed, the temperature registered 45 degrees below zero Fahrenheit.

The garrison provided shelter for the members of the **Lewis and Clark Expedition**, a party of exploration led by Meriwether Lewis and William Clark. Both captains in the U.S. Army, Lewis and Clark had been commissioned by President Thomas Jefferson

Lewis and Clark Expedition A "corps of discovery" commissioned by President Thomas Jefferson in 1804 to explore the newly acquired Louisiana Territory. Led by Meriwether Lewis and William Clark and lasting 28 months, the party reported on an array of subjects, including the cultural practices of western Indians and the natural features of the land, but failed to find a water route that would connect the Pacific Northwest to eastern markets.

TABLE 10.1 THE ELECTION OF 1804

Candidate	Political Party	Electoral Vote
Thomas Jefferson	Democratic-Republican	162
Charles C. Pinckney	Federalist	14

to explore the upper reaches of the newly acquired Louisiana Territory, which had doubled the size of the country. With the ultimate goal of reaching the Pacific Coast in what today is Oregon, their party spent the winter at Fort Mandan and joined the buffalo hunts and nightly dances sponsored by their hosts, the Mandan Indians. Between November 1804 and March 1805, Lewis and Clark also found time to record their observations on all manner of things natural and cultural. In their journals and their letters to President Jefferson, they described the language of the Hidatsa Indians and the beadwork of the Arikara, the medicinal properties of native plants, and the contours of the Missouri River. In a shipment prepared for the president, they included deer horns, pumice stones, and the pelt of a white weasel. Among an assortment of live animals, only a magpie and a prairie dog survived the journey to Washington, D.C.

Lewis and Clark's trek took 28 months to complete and covered 8,000 miles. Their expedition's purpose was partly scientific, but Jefferson had also commissioned them to chart a northwestern waterway passage to the Pacific coast. The president hoped to divert the profitable fur trade of the far Northwest away from British Canada and into the hands of Americans by locating a river connecting this larger Northwest directly to eastern U.S. markets. Jefferson also instructed Lewis and Clark to initiate negotiations with various Indian groups, to pave the way for miners and ranchers to move into the area.

Lewis and Clark's party consisted of a diverse group of people, including British and Irish enlisted men, and Lewis's African American slave, York. At Fort Mandan, the group picked up Toussaint Charbonneau, a French Canadian, and his fifteen-year-old wife, Sacajawea, a Shoshone Indian. The explorers came to rely on Sacajawea's skills as an interpreter. And because women never traveled with Indian war parties, Sacajawea's presence reassured suspicious Native Americans that the goal of the expedition was peaceful.

Although Lewis and Clark failed to find the northwestern passage to the Pacific that Jefferson had hoped for, they did send back dispatches about the rich natural resources, including rushing rivers, wide plains, and seemingly endless forests, that lay to the west of the Mississippi River. Many Americans swelled with pride at the natural bounty of their growing nation. Here was fertile and vast ground indeed for the fur trade, commercial development, staple-crop agriculture, and extensive settlements of Americans. Here was much to fight for, and much to defend.

The Embargo of 1807

Not content to control trade across the Atlantic as decreed by the 1806 Orders in Council, the British also seized sailors from American ships, claiming that these men were British seamen who had been lured away from their own vessels by American captains promising them higher wages. In some cases, these claims were probably true. However, U.S. political leaders charged that an estimated 6,000 U.S. citizens had been seized by the British navy between 1808 and 1811, including an unknown number of African Americans, many of whom were working as mariners. With limited economic opportunities on shore, black sailors accepted the danger and long absences from home, but neither black nor white sailors had bargained for enforced service in His Majesty's Royal Navy. Seizure, or impressment, reminded Americans of their pre–Revolutionary War days, when British "press gangs" prowled the docks of American port cities and seized colonial merchant sailors. In 1807, the tensions over impressment erupted into violence. Just 10 miles off the shore of Virginia, the American ship *Chesapeake* came under attack from a British vessel. British naval officers claimed that the Americans were harboring four British deserters. In the ensuing exchange of cannon fire, three Americans were killed and eighteen wounded. Jefferson demanded that England leave American sailors and ships alone, but he was rebuffed.

Embargo Act of 1807 A law passed by Congress, at the urging of President Thomas Jefferson, to halt the shipment of U.S. goods to Europe in response to British military and naval aggression.

President Jefferson decided to place an embargo on all exports to the European powers in an effort to force those nations to respect the rights of Americans on the high seas. The **Embargo Act of 1807** passed by Congress halted the shipment of goods from the United States to Europe. Because Europe—including England—relied heavily on American grain and timber, Jefferson hoped that the move would force England

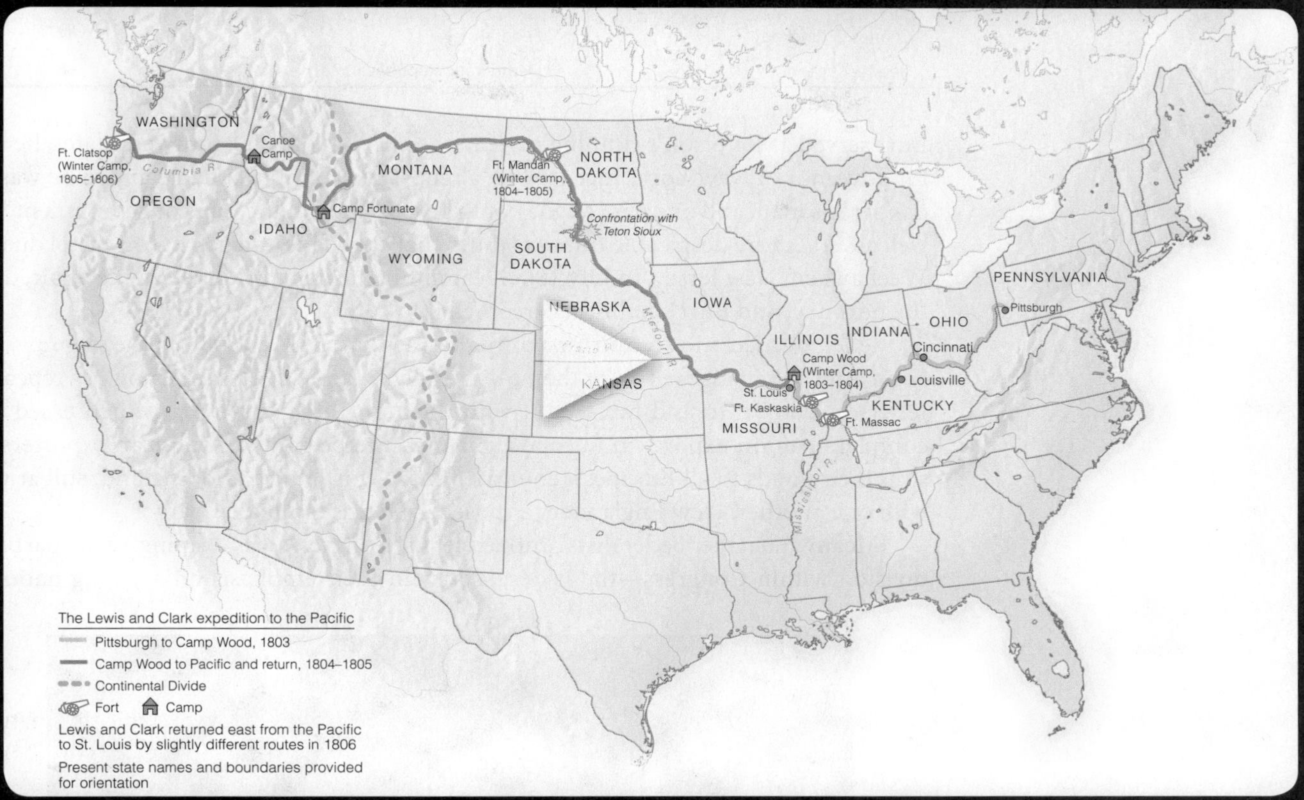

Watch the Video   Lewis and Clark: What Were They Trying to Accomplish?

10.1

10.2

10.3

10.4

MAP 10.1 LEWIS AND CLARK, 1803–1806 This map, showing the route of the Lewis and Clark Expedition, suggests the importance of interior waterways in facilitating travel and exploration in the West. Spain feared, rightly, that the Americans would use western rivers to establish trade links with the Indians and thereby challenge Spain's northern border with the United States.

to respect American independence. The president saw this measure as preferable to either war or capitulation to England. But the move aroused intense opposition in Federalist-dominated New England, where the regional economy depended heavily on foreign trade. As the effects of the embargo took hold, the New England grain growers saw the markets for their products dry up, and the timber industry suffered when local shipbuilding ground to a standstill. Southern tobacco and cotton planters faced similar hardship because of the embargo. By 1808, some of them had joined with Northerners to circumvent the embargo by moving their goods through Canada and then to Europe.

Yet Jefferson held his course, prodding Congress to enforce the unpopular act. His efforts provoked a backlash as New England politicians threatened to take their states out of the union. Despite all the uproar, the embargo did benefit Americans by promoting industrialization at home. At the same time, the embargo seemed only to intensify, not lessen, tensions between England and the United States.

On the Brink of War

The consequences of the Embargo of 1807 were some of the many challenges American political leaders faced during the first decade of the nineteenth century. Both the Federalists and the Democratic-Republicans suffered a blow to their leadership in 1804. That year, the Federalist party lost one of its original leaders with the death of Alexander Hamilton at the hand of his rival, Aaron Burr. Both successful New York attorneys, the two men had risen together through the political ranks in the 1780s and 1790s.

245

TABLE 10.2 THE ELECTION OF 1808

Candidate	Political Party	Electoral Vote
James Madison	Democratic-Republican	122
Charles C. Pinckney	Federalist	47
George Clinton	Democratic-Republican	6

Burr served as Jefferson's running mate in the election of 1800; four years later, he ran for governor of New York. Incensed by a report that Hamilton had claimed he was "a dangerous man, and one who ought not to be trusted with the reins of government," as well as "still more despicable rumors," Burr challenged his antagonist to a pistol duel at Weehawken, New Jersey, in July 1804. Hamilton, mortally wounded in the affair, died the next day, and Burr's political career fell into ruins.

Jefferson, declining to run for a third presidential term in 1808, left the stage as well. Soon after the inauguration of the new president, James Madison, Congress repealed Jefferson's embargo and replaced it with the Non-Intercourse Act, which eased the complete ban on exports to Europe. This measure permitted American exporters to ship their goods to all European countries except for France and England, still at war with one another. New Englanders opposed even this limited embargo.

Meanwhile, the Federalists' influence in Congress was waning. The partisan division within Congress—the Federalists, with their emphasis on a strong national

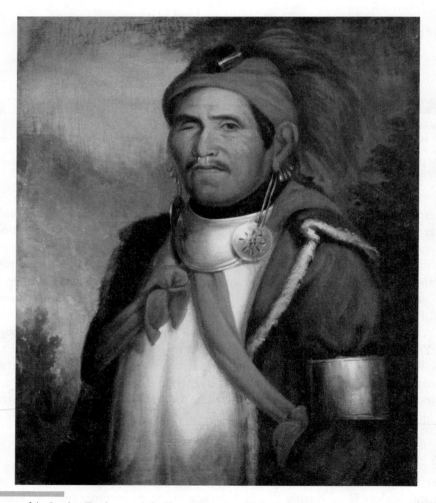

This image of the Prophet (Tenskwatawa), the Shawnee mystic and holy man, was based on an original 1824 painting by the artist Charles Bird King. Early in life, the Prophet suffered an accident with bows and arrows, losing his right eye. He and his older brother Tecumseh called on all Indians to resist the encroachment of their lands by whites and to renounce the way of life followed by whites, including the use of liquor. After the Indians' defeat at the Battle of Tippecanoe in 1811, the Prophet retreated to Canada. He returned to the United States in 1826. By that time, he no longer wielded influence as a leader of the Shawnee. Why did some tribes, and factions of tribes, resist the Prophet's call to fight for a sovereign Indian state?

government, against the localist Democratic-Republicans—gradually eased. By 1810, a different split had emerged—between young, hotheaded representatives from the West and their more conservative seniors from the eastern seaboard. The western group, or "**war hawks**," called on the nation to revive its former glory. Americans must uphold U.S. honor, they declared, by opposing European, especially British, claims to military dominance. The war hawks also yearned to vanquish the Indians who impeded settlement of the area west of the Mississippi.

War hawks Politicians who favor specific forms of military action as a tool of U.S. foreign policy.

Looking eastward, the war hawks saw an England determined to defile the honor of their young nation. Looking westward, these same men saw an equally threatening menace: the rise of an ominous Indian resistance movement that blended military strength with native spirituality. The movement was led by Shawnee brothers Tecumseh and Tenskwatawa (also known as the Prophet), who founded Prophet's Town in Indiana in 1808. They envisioned a sovereign Indian state and the preservation of Native American culture. Tenskwatawa spoke of a time and place where Indians would reject alcohol and scorn "the food of whites" as well as the "wealth and ornaments" of commercial trade. Tecumseh set out to deliver the message to as many Indian groups as possible, traveling the broad swath of territory from Florida to Canada.

Meanwhile, in 1809, the territorial governor of Indiana, William Henry Harrison, plied a group of Indian leaders with liquor, then got them to agree to sell 3 million acres to the U.S. government for just $7,600. Upon hearing of the deal, Tecumseh decried a new form of American aggression: "treaties" between U.S. officials and Indians who lacked the authority to sell their people's homeland. "All red men," Tecumseh proclaimed, must "unite in claiming a common and equal right in the land, as it was at first, and should be yet; for it never was divided, but belongs to all, for the use of each." This

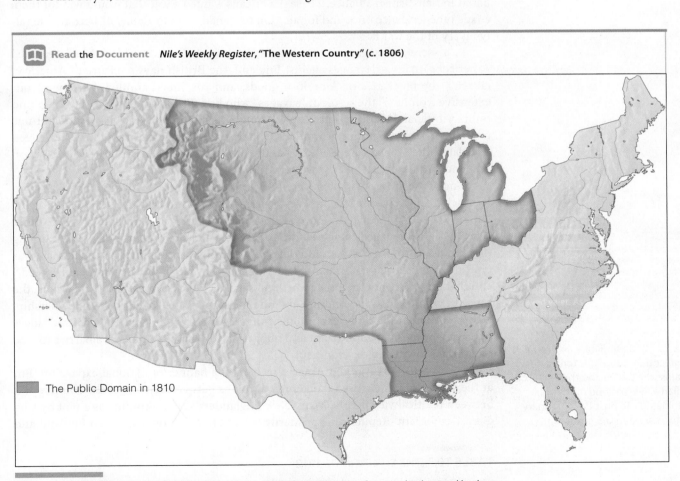

Read the Document *Nile's Weekly Register,* "The Western Country" (c. 1806)

The Public Domain in 1810

MAP 10.2 THE PUBLIC DOMAIN IN 1810 This map indicates the expanse of western lands owned by the U.S. government in 1810, after the Louisiana Purchase. American war veterans received land warrants in return for military service in the Revolutionary War and the War of 1812. A warrant entitled the bearer to settle a specific number of acres of unoccupied lands. Warrants could be transferred, sold, and traded like stocks and bonds. After the War of 1812, the government issued 29,186 land warrants for a total of 4.8 million acres.

view was dramatically at odds with the practice of holding private property and the idea that one of the hallmarks of a free society was the ability of men to buy and sell land.

In November 1811, Harrison led 1,000 U.S. soldiers in an advance on Prophet's Town. But before they could reach the settlement, several hundred Shawnees under the command of Tenskwatawa attacked their camp on the Tippecanoe River. The Indians suffered a sound defeat before the superior U.S. weapons, and Harrison burned Prophet's Town to the ground. Clearly, military technology, not just determination, would shape the western conflict. Yet, in the ensuing war, the Americans faced not just Indian foes, but also one of the mightiest military forces in the world—the British army and navy.

The War of 1812

10.2 What were the political and economic interests of the United States, the Indian tribes, and Great Britain and why did those divergent interests clash during the War of 1812?

The defeat of the Shawnees at Tippecanoe encouraged western war hawks' resolve to break the back of Indian resistance. But to achieve this goal, the United States would have to invade Canada and eliminate the British arms suppliers who had been trading with the Indians. Claiming the mantle of patriotism, western and southern members of the House of Representatives agitated for a war that would eliminate both the British threat on the high seas and the Canada-based Indian-British alliance. These Americans wanted a war that would win for them a true independence once and for all. "On to Canada! On to Canada!" became the rallying cry of the war hawks.

In a secret message sent to Congress on June 1, 1812, President Madison listed Americans' many grievances against England: the British navy's seizure of American citizens, the blockades of American goods, and continued conflict "on one of our extensive frontiers," the result of "savages" who had the backing of British traders and military officials. Madison left it up to Congress whether Americans would continue to endure these indignities or would act "in defense of their natural rights." Seventeen days later, the House voted 79 to 49 and the Senate voted 19 to 13 to declare war on England and, by extension, the western Indians.

One of the most outspoken war hawks was Speaker of the House Henry Clay from Kentucky. Clay epitomized the Westerners' desire to expand the boundaries of the United States, and he had organized Congressional supporters of that view. Like other war hawks, he engaged in aggressive and overheated rhetoric, at one point claiming that the militia of Kentucky could defeat all of British and French in Canada. He was typical too in his views of Indians, declaring that they were "not an improvable breed," and that they were not "as a race worth preserving." According to Clay and others, the Indians, with their strange culture and odd ideas about the equality of landownership, were a fair target for American military forces. Americans, with their "civilized" ideas of private property, had the right and obligation to remove Indians as a barrier to U.S. territorial growth and development.

War of 1812 A military and naval conflict that pitted U.S. forces against the British and their Indian allies. The end of the war eliminated the post-Revolutionary British threat to U.S. sovereignty.

The **War of 1812** united Americans behind a banner of national expansion. But at the same time, it exposed dangerous divisions between regions of the country and between political viewpoints. Many New Englanders saw the conflict as a plot by Virginia Democratic-Republicans primarily to aid France in opposition to England and

TABLE 10.3 THE ELECTION OF 1812

Candidate	Political Party	Electoral Vote
James Madison	Democratic-Republican	128
De Witt Clinton	Federalist	89

to add agrarian (that is, slave) states to the Union. In an ironic twist, the New England Federalists—usually staunch defenders of the national government—argued that states should control their own commerce and militias.

Pushing North

Although the Americans were better armed and organized than the western Indians, they were at a disadvantage when they took on the soldiers and sailors of the British Empire. The United States had not invested in its military and thus was ill-prepared for all-out war. The American navy consisted merely of a fleet of tiny gunboats constructed during the cost-conscious Jefferson administration. The charter for the Bank of the United States had expired in 1811, depriving the country of a vital source of financial credit. Suffering from a drop in tax revenues as a result of the embargo on foreign trade, the nation lacked the funds to train and equip the regular army and the state militias. Nevertheless, in the fall of 1812, the Americans launched an ambitious three-pronged attack against Canada, striking from Niagara, Detroit, and Lake Champlain. All three attempts failed miserably.

In the West in late 1812, Tecumseh (who had accepted a commission as a brigadier general in the British army) and British General Isaac Brock captured Detroit. Yet the Americans scored some notable successes in 1813. That September, Commodore Oliver H. Perry defeated a British fleet at Put-in-Bay on Lake Erie. Exhilarated, he declared, "We have met the enemy and they are ours." Perry's hard-won victory forced the British back into Canada, over Tecumseh's objections. General William Henry Harrison followed in hot pursuit. British Colonel Henry Proctor marched his troops to eastern Ontario, leaving Tecumseh to try holding the Americans at bay. At the Battle of the Thames that October, Harrison defeated the Indians. Many perished, Tecumseh among them.

Later that autumn, an American campaign against Montreal failed. The Americans trudged back into New York State, the British close behind them. Flush with their victory in Montreal, the British captured Fort Niagara and set Buffalo and other nearby towns aflame.

By mid-1814, the English and their allies had also crushed Napoleon in Europe. This success freed up 15,000 British troops, who promptly sailed for North America.

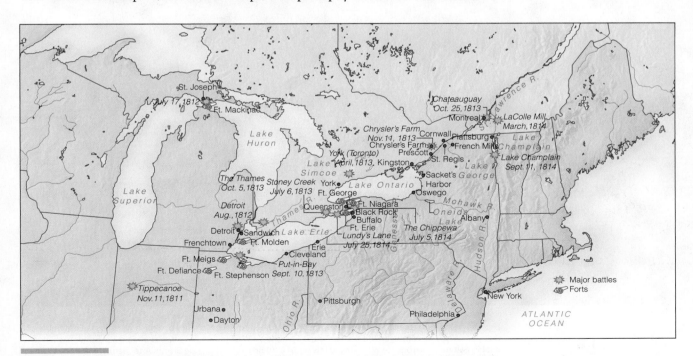

MAP 10.3 THE NORTHERN FRONT, WAR OF 1812 Much of the fighting of the War of 1812 centered in the Great Lakes region. It was there, the war hawks charged, that the British were inciting Indians to attack American settlements. Conducted in 1812 and 1813, the campaign against Canada was supposed to eliminate the British threat and, some Americans hoped, win Canadian territory for the United States.

249

Still, in July 1814, the Americans, under the leadership of Major General Jacob Brown and Brigadier General Winfield Scott, managed to defeat the British at the Battle of Chippewa, across the Niagara River from Buffalo. But by the end of that year, the Americans had withdrawn to their own territory and relinquished their goal of invading and conquering Canada. The arrival of fresh British troops forced the Americans to defend their own soil.

Fighting on Many Fronts

For the United States, the most humiliating episode of the war came with the British attack on the nation's capital. On August 24, 1814, the British army, backed by the Royal Navy, sailed into Chesapeake Bay. At the Battle of Bladensburg, Maryland, they scattered the American troops they encountered. The Redcoats then advanced to Washington, where they torched the Capitol building and the White House, causing extensive damage to both structures.

Residents of the capital city had received word that the British were advancing. On Sunday, August 21, public officials frantically packed up their books and papers. Private citizens gathered up their furniture and other belongings and left town. By Tuesday, the city stood nearly empty. As a ragtag American force succumbed to the British, a Baltimore newspaper reported, President Madison "retired from the mortifying scene, and left the city on horseback."

📖 Read the Document   **Francis Scott Key, "The Star-Spangled Banner" (1814)**

This engraving, published in 1814, depicts the bombardment of Fort McHenry by British warships in September of that year. When he witnessed the battle, Francis Scott Key, a Washington lawyer, was aboard a prisoner exchange boat in Baltimore Harbor. He was seeking release of a friend captured by the British. After penning the poem "The Star Spangled Banner," Key set the words to music, using the tune of a popular English drinking song. Congress declared the song the national anthem in 1931. The entire song has four verses (though only the first is usually sung). Each verse ends with a variation on this refrain: "O! say does that star-spangled banner yet wave, O'er the land of the free and the home of the brave?" What was the meaning of those words in 1814?

Yet the Americans rallied, pursued the British, and bested them in the Battle of Baltimore. This victory inspired an observer, Francis Scott Key, to write "The Star Spangled Banner" as he watched "the bombs bursting in air" over Baltimore's Fort McHenry. The Americans scored another crucial victory in September, when U.S. naval commander Thomas McDonough crushed the British fleet on Lake Champlain near Plattsburgh, New York.

In the Southeast, Tecumseh's message of Indian unity had resonated with particular force among Native Americans since the war broke out. However, some Cherokee and Chocktaw cast their lot with the United States. And even the Creek Nation was divided, with the pro-war Red Sticks facing opposition from some of their own people, the White Sticks, who counseled peace. These divisions among Indian tribes and nations were at odds with the prejudices of many whites, who tended to think of Indians as one large group, always united in their views on how to deal with whites. In fact, Indian leaders differed in substantial ways among themselves, including whether or not to go to war against the United States. Despite these divisions, the Red Sticks were a formidable opponent.

After Major General Andrew Jackson defeated the Red Sticks at Horseshoe Bend in March 1814, he next marched to New Orleans to confront the British. Knowing he would be facing some of Europe's finest soldiers, he assembled 7,000 men, U.S. soldiers and militiamen from the states of Louisiana, Kentucky, and Tennessee. Two Kentucky regiments consisted of free Negro volunteers, about 400 men in total. The Battle of New Orleans, fought on January 8, 1815, began with a ferocious assault by British soldiers. But within just half an hour, 2,000 of them lay dead or wounded. The Americans lost only 70 soldiers. Jackson's back-country sharpshooters had vanquished the army of Europe's greatest military power.

Jackson's diverse force of fighting men revealed that, when the defense of the country was at stake, whites could at times overcome their prejudicial views about black men serving in the military. Although most states still banned free men of color and enslaved men from their militias, black men could be welcomed into U.S. military ranks when their numbers were needed. Jackson pleaded for free blacks to enlist to help defend New Orleans against the British: "I call on free men of color to rally round the standard of the eagle, to defend all which is dear in existence. As sons of freedom, you are now called upon to defend our most inestimable blessing!" He also called upon planters to send their slaves to join his army and promised them their freedom in return. James Roberts was a black Revolutionary War veteran who had been freed but then sold back into slavery; he recalled that, when he heard Jackson's call to action, "Hardships, of whatever kind, or however severe, vanished into vapor at the sound of freedom."

Black men represented one-fifth of all American sailors who fought in the War of 1812. By the end of war, approximately 6,500 American prisoners of war were confined to Britain's dark Dartmoor Prison in Devonshire, England. About 15 percent of that number were black men, many of them crew members from privateers captured by British ships in the course of the war. Black people faced harsh discrimination at home; but in battle and on the high seas, their lives were equally at risk with those of their white comrades-in-arms.

The end of the war came in December 1814, when American and British negotiators signed a peace agreement. Jackson's victory at the Battle of New Orleans, then, came two weeks after the end of the war. Nevertheless, many Americans associated Jackson with the war's most decisive battle and most glorious victory. Although many Americans took pride in the defeat of the British at New Orleans, it was hardly the decisive battle of the war.

An Uncertain Victory

Before the Battle of New Orleans, in the fall of 1814, President Madison had decided to end the war. He dispatched John Quincy Adams, son of former president John Adams,

❋ Explore the War of 1812 on MyHistoryLab

WHAT BROUGHT ABOUT THE WAR OF 1812?

In the early 1800s, the United States felt threatened from forces within and outside its borders. The British had never completely withdrawn their troops from the Northwest Territory. Tensions with the former mother country grew when the British navy refused to respect the rights of neutral American ships. Claiming that some of the crew members aboard these ships were actually British seamen, the British navy impressed (seized) these men. Moreover, many years of U.S. encroachment on northwestern and southeastern Indian lands by both settlers and soldiers had antagonized the Native Americans living there. By 1812, the

During the War of 1812, Native American allies of the British army received bounties for the scalps of dead American combatants. Cartoons such as these inflamed anti-Indian sentiment among many Americans and led some U.S. military officials to approve and carry out massacres of Indian men, women, and children. *Library of Congress.*

United States was at war with both the British and with the Natives who lived in the Southeast and the Northwest.

NATIVE AMERICAN ALLIANCES DURING THE WAR OF 1812

Supplying Warriors Against the United States	U.S. Allies
Upper Creeks, Shawnees, Lenapes (Delawares), Miamis, Potawatomis, Ojibwes	Cherokees, Choctaws, Lower Creeks

KEY QUESTIONS Use **MyHistoryLab** *Explorer* to **answer** these **questions:**

Cause ▶▶▶ *In what areas was support for war with Britain strongest?*

Theorize the reasons for regional differences in the desire for conflict.

Consequence ▶▶▶ *Where had Native Americans been forced to cede lands?*

Consider how this might affect relations between Native Americans and settlers.

Analysis ▶▶▶ *Where were major battles fought, by whom, and with what outcomes?*

Understand the strategies of the various parties in the War of 1812.

to the Belgian city of Ghent to start negotiations. Representative Henry Clay and three other American envoys accompanied Adams. At first, English representatives at the meeting made two demands. The Americans, they said, must agree to the creation of an Indian territory in the upper Great Lakes region. They must also cede much of the state of Maine to England. The Americans refused, and the negotiations dragged on.

In the meantime, the New England states had grown increasingly impatient with what they called "Mr. Madison's war." As with the embargo, they saw the effort as a mistake and a threat to their regional commercial interests. In December 1814, Massachusetts, Connecticut, Rhode Island, New Hampshire, and Vermont sent delegates to a gathering in Hartford, Connecticut, to consider a course of action. The delegates demanded that the federal government give their states financial aid to compensate for the revenue they had lost as a result of disrupted trade. Some delegates even hinted that their states wanted to secede from the union. Although most delegates shied away from immediate action, the majority of them apparently wanted to leave open the possibility of secession.

Back in Ghent, the British had reversed their initial position by late December. They had lost recent battles in upper New York and in Baltimore and, as always, were still worried about new threats from France. They dropped their demands for territory and for an Indian buffer state in the upper Midwest. They also agreed to an armistice that, in essence, represented a draw: both combatants would retain the same territory they had possessed when the war began. The British made no concessions to the Americans' demands that they stop impressing American sailors and supplying the western Indians with arms or that they revoke the Orders in Council. Still, most U.S. citizens considered the war a great victory for the United States. After Congress ratified the **Treaty of Ghent**, which ended hostilities between the two nations in 1815, the Americans and the British never again met each other across a battlefield as enemies.

Treaty of Ghent Peace treaty signed by the United States and Great Britain in 1815, ending the War of 1812.

The "Era of Good Feelings"?

10.3 Did political and social realities justify the use of the term "the Era of Good Feelings" to describe the period after the War of 1812?

In 1816, the Democratic-Republicans nominated James Monroe for president, to run against Federalist candidate Rufus King. Although Monroe only narrowly won his party's endorsement, he soundly defeated King in the general election. Monroe benefited from several developments that had mortally wounded the Federalist party: the War of 1812 victory, presided over by a Democratic-Republican chief executive; the New England Federalists' flirtation with secession (and treason) during the war years; and the strong nationalist tendencies of both the Jefferson and Madison administrations, which had stolen the Federalists' thunder.

Addressing Congress in December 1817, President Monroe expressed optimism about the state of the nation. The country's boundaries were secure, and the Indians had little choice but to retreat farther and farther west. The president predicted that, shortly, "Indian hostilities, if they do not altogether cease, will henceforth lose their terror." Equally inspiring, the Americans had once again defied the British Empire and won. Two treaties with Britain—the Rush-Bagot of 1817 and the pending Convention

TABLE 10.4 THE ELECTION OF 1816

Candidate	Political Party	Electoral Vote
James Monroe	Democratic-Republican	183
Rufus King	Federalist	34

Interpreting History

Cherokee Women PETITION AGAINST FURTHER LAND SALES TO WHITES IN 1817

"Your mothers your sisters ask and beg of you not to part with any more of our lands"

In traditional Cherokee society, men took responsibility for foreign affairs while women focused on domestic matters, leading to a roughly equal division of labor. However, European American diplomats, military officials, and traders dealt primarily with Indian men. As a result, beginning in the eighteenth century, Cherokee women's traditional influence was eroding within their own communities. In this new world, Indian warriors wielded significant power.

Nevertheless, Cherokee women insisted on presenting their views during the crisis of 1817–1819, when men of the group were deciding whether to cede land to U.S. authorities and move west. The following petition was supported by Nancy Ward, a Cherokee War Woman. This honorific title was bestowed on women who accompanied and attended to the needs of war parties. Ward had supported the colonists' cause during the American Revolution.

AMOVEY [TENNESSEE] IN COUNCIL 2ND MAY 1817

The Cherokee Ladys now being present at the meeting of the Chiefs and warriors in council have thought it their duties as mothers to address their beloved Chiefs and warriors now assembled.

Our beloved children and head men of the Cherokee nation we address you warriors in council we have raised all of you on the land which we now have, which God gave to us to inhabit and raise provisions we know that our country has once been extensive but by repeated sales has become circumscribed to a small tract, and [we] never have thought it our duty to interfere in the disposition of it till now, if a father or mother was to sell all their lands which they had to depend on which their children had to raise their living on which would indeed be bad and to be removed to another country we do not wish to go to an unknown country [to] which we have understood some of our children wish to go over the Mississippi but this act of our children would be like destroying

In 1987, Wilma Mankiller became the first woman to be elected Principal Chief of the Cherokee Nation of Oklahoma. Would women in Nancy Ward's time have aspired to similar positions of leadership?

your mothers. Your mothers your sisters ask and beg of you not to part with any more of our lands, we say ours. [Y]ou are our descendants and take pity on our request, but keep it for our growing children for it was the good will of our creator to place us here and you know our father the great president [James Monroe], will not allow his white children to take our country away for if it was not they would not ask you to put your hands to paper for it would be impossible to remove us all for as soon as one child is raised, we have others in our arms for such is our situation and will consider our circumstance.

Therefore children don't part with any more of our lands but continue on it and enlarge your farms and cultivate and raise corn and cotton and we your mothers and sisters will make clothing for you which our father the president has recommended to us all we don't charge anybody for selling any lands, but we have heard such intentions of our children but your talks become true at last and it was our desire to forewarn you all not to part with our lands.

Nancy Ward to her children[:] warriors to take pity and listen to the talks of your sisters, although I am very old yet cannot but pity the situation in which you will hear of their minds. I have great many grand children which I wish they do well on our land.

In addition to Nancy Ward, twelve Cherokee women signed the petition. Their names suggest the varying degrees of assimilation to white ways on the part of Cherokees in general. Petitioners included Cun, o, ah, and Widow Woman Holder, as well as Jenny McIntosh and Mrs. Nancy Fields.

It is unclear what effect, if any, this petition had on Cherokee male leaders. The Cherokee nation did halt land cessions to whites between 1819 and 1835.

Questions for Discussion

1. How and why did motherhood confer authority on Cherokee women?
2. What is the significance and meaning of the land in Cherokee culture?
3. Does this petition provide evidence for the view that early nineteenth-century Cherokee men and women were adopting elements of European American culture? If so, what elements, and in what ways?

SOURCE: Cherokee Women to Cherokee Council, May 2, 1817, series 1, Andrew Jackson Presidential Papers.

of 1818—set the U.S.-Canadian border at the forty-ninth parallel and provided that the two countries would jointly occupy Oregon Territory for ten years.

Monroe called on Congress to acknowledge "the vast extent of territory within the United States [and] the great amount and value of its productions" and to facilitate the construction of roads and canals. It was this "happy situation of the United States," in Monroe's words, that ushered in what some historians call the **Era of Good Feelings**, a period relatively free of partisan political strife. Although voters continued to disagree over some issues of the day—such as the national bank, sectionalism, and internal improvements—they did not necessarily express those disagreements in the form of bitter partisan wrangling. Still, the term "good feelings" may fully apply only to a narrow group of enfranchised citizens, men who shared common beliefs about territorial expansion and economic development.

Era of Good Feelings A term used by historians to describe the presidency of James Monroe (1817–1825), when partisan tensions eased among voters and their political leaders.

Praise and Respect for Veterans After the War

American veterans of the War of 1812 won the praise of a grateful nation. Even the British expressed a grudging respect for Americans' fighting abilities. One British naval officer admitted, "I don't like Americans; I never did, and never shall." He had "no wish to eat with them, drink with them, or consort with them in any way." But, he added, he would rather not fight with "an enemy so brave, determined, and alert, as they have always proved." To reward veterans for their service, Congress offered them 160-acre plots of land in the territory between the Illinois and Mississippi rivers. These grants did much to encourage families to emigrate west and establish homesteads.

Some military heroes of the war parlayed their success into impressive political careers. Andrew Jackson won election to the presidency in 1828 and 1832, as did William Henry Harrison in 1840. Countless others earned recognition within their own communities, and European American veterans were not the only ones to gain status and influence as a result of the conflict. To some extent, at least, equality of sacrifice yielded equality of reward. For example, a Cherokee leader named The Ridge earned the gratitude of American officials for his contributions to the war effort. He had accepted the government's attempts to press the Cherokee to adopt European American ways; he had settled in a log cabin rather than in a traditional Cherokee dwelling when he married a Cherokee woman named Susanna Wickett in the early 1790s. During the war against the Red Sticks, The Ridge served under Andrew Jackson and earned the title of major. For the rest of his life, the Cherokee leader was known as Major Ridge. His wife devoted herself to tending an orchard, keeping a garden, and sewing clothes, tasks traditionally performed by European American but not Native American women. Eventually, the family prospered, bought African American slaves, and became Christians as well.

The Ridge's battlefield experiences earned him the respect of other Cherokee who embraced the "civilization" program that missionaries and government officials promoted. At the same time, The Ridge vehemently resisted U.S. officials' attempts to persuade the Cherokee to give up their lands to whites and move west. He believed that his people should adopt some elements of white culture but should also hold fast to their native lands in opposition to white settlers and politicians.

A Thriving Economy

The end of the War of 1812 saw an upsurge in internal migration. New Englanders, especially, pushed west in search of new economic opportunities that they lacked on the hilly, rocky farmland of their native states. The West beckoned with the promise of equal opportunity—if not equal results—for all individuals and families willing to work hard. Between 1800 and 1820, the population of Ohio grew from 45,000 to 581,000.

This engraving, c. 1819, shows women working in an early textile mill. Women and children composed the workforce of many early mills. This picture suggests the size of the intricate machinery, which dwarfs the women. For generations women had produced textiles at home, spinning thread and weaving cloth. For all factory operatives, these dark, cavernous places were new kinds of worksites—a striking contrast to the homes, shops, and fields where New Englanders traditionally had worked. How did the Industrial Revolution produce an emerging class system?

New means of transportation—and new means to fund them—facilitated the movement of goods and people. In 1807, an entrepreneur named Robert Fulton piloted the *Clermont*, his new kind of boat powered by steam, up the Hudson River from New York City. Steamboats traveled upriver, against the current, ten times faster than keelboats, which had to be pushed, pulled, or hauled by men or mules. Within a few years, therefore, such vessels were plying the Mississippi River and its major tributaries.

Improvements in land transportation stimulated economic growth. The profits that the Philadelphia and Lancaster Turnpike raked in by charging travelers tolls inspired other local private corporations to invest in roads. By 1810, several thousand such corporations were building roads up and down the East Coast. Funding came from a variety of sources, both public and private. Philadelphia textile mill owners financed transportation links with the city's hinterland (rural areas to the west) to carry their goods to the largest number of customers. Individual cities also invested in routes westward. The state of Virginia authorized a board of public works to expend funds for roads and other internal improvements. Western politicians flexed their political muscle in 1806 by securing congressional authorization for the building of the Cumberland (later National) Road, which snaked through the Allegheny Mountains and ended at the Ohio River.

The acceleration of commerce in the West, combined with the disruption in trade from Europe that had come with the Embargo of 1807 and the War of 1812, stimulated manufacturing throughout the United States. Philadelphia's growth proved particularly dazzling. During the war, the city's craft producers did not have to worry about foreign competition. Local merchant-financiers, who otherwise might have been pouring their money into trade ventures, began to invest in manufacturing. As early as 1808, the city's new factories had compensated for the glass, chemicals, shot, soap, lead, and earthenware that no longer flooded in from England. Philadelphia soon took the lead in production of all kinds, whether carried out in factories, artisans' shops, or private homes. Metalworking, ale brewing, and leather production counted among the array of thriving industries that made Philadelphia the nation's top industrial city in 1815. Still, in 1820 about two-thirds of all Philadelphia workers labored in small shops employing fewer than six people.

Transformations in the Workplace

Even the earliest stages of the Industrial Revolution transformed the way people lived and worked. Some crafts—for example, the production of leather, barrels, soap, candles, and newspapers—expanded from small shops with skilled artisans into larger establishments with unskilled wage earners. In these cases, production was reorganized; now wage earners under the supervision of a boss replaced apprentices and journeymen who had formerly worked alongside a master artisan. These workers performed a single task many times a day instead of using their specialized skills to see a production process through to completion.

New England rapidly became the center of mechanized textile production in the United States. By the late eighteenth century, Boston shippers were making handsome profits by supplying Alta California (the area north of San Diego, encompassing present-day California, Nevada, and parts of Arizona and Utah) with cloth, shoes, and tools; selling western otter pelts in China; and returning home laden with Chinese porcelains and silks. These profits helped to finance New England's mechanized textile industry. By 1813, seventy-six cotton mills housing over 51,000 spindles were operating within the vicinity of Providence, Rhode Island.

Faced with a shortage of adult men (many were moving west), New England mill owners sought other local sources of labor. The Rhode Island system of production had relied on child spinners working in small mills. This system gave way to the Lowell model, based in Waltham and Lowell, Massachusetts, which brought young women from the surrounding countryside to work in gigantic mills. Many of the women were eager to earn cash wages and to escape the routine of farm life. Still, New England mill owners realized that they had to reassure Yankee parents that their daughters would find the factories safe, attractive places to work. Mill owners offered the young women housing in dormitory-like boardinghouses staffed by older women, called matrons, who looked after them.

The Market Revolution

As new means of transportation facilitated the movement of ideas, goods, and people, natural barriers separating farms from towns and the West from the East began to crumble. Factory workers quickly and efficiently processed raw materials—leather into shoes, cotton into clothing. Wage earning gradually replaced family labor and indentured servitude as the dominant labor system in the North. Together, all of these rapid economic transformations in the early nineteenth century fueled what some scholars have called the **Market Revolution**. Driven by improvements in transportation, increasing commercialization, and the rise of factories, powerful economic changes affected ordinary Americans and their everyday routines at home and on the job.

The gradual changes of the Market Revolution were driven by investment. Wealthy New England merchants led the way, but a wide variety of private individuals and public institutions proved willing to invest their money and energy in new economic opportunities. Profits from foreign trade helped to build the textile factories that dotted

Market Revolution The combined effects of transportation innovation, technological change, and economic growth, especially during the first half of the nineteenth century.

257

✳ Explore the Topic   The Origins of the Industrial Revolution

Linking the East to the Midwest, the Erie Canal became the symbol of the "Market Revolution." With the expansion of commerce and increased migration among different groups, regional identities as well as barriers to trade crumbled. Some Americans believed that revolutions in transportation and industry heralded a new day of unlimited possibilities, for the country and for individuals. In what ways did these developments enhance equality among Americans? In what ways did they promote inequality? "View east of eastbound Lockport on the Erie Canal" by W. H. Bartlett, 1839.

the northeastern landscape. States and even towns used the money of taxpayers and private investors to build turnpikes and later to finance canals and railroads. Entrepreneurs pioneered the putting out system, a form of production (of hats and other forms of clothing, for example) that enlisted the efforts of single women in the cities, as well as farm families during the winter season. These workers received raw materials from a merchant-capitalist and engaged in piecework in return for wages. Combined public–private investment in new forms of business organization and technology spurred American economic growth.

These changes spilled over into American social and religious life, encouraging some people to adopt an optimistic worldview about the possibilities inherent in American life—possibilities that included moving from one place to another, making money by selling new products, altering the natural landscape to make way for canals or factories, and aspiring to buy goods rather than produce goods at home. Foreign visitors often commented on the "restlessness" of Americans, their "acquisitiveness," and their impatience with tradition.

Not all Americans adopted this new way of looking at the world, but almost all groups felt its effects. Slave owners pushed black men, women, and children to work even harder in the fields of the South so that more cotton and rice could be exported to northern and European markets. Western Indians suffered the effects of European American conquest, as whites chopped down forests and cleared the land for farms, violently displacing native populations in the process. In New England textile mills, women and children operated the machines that produced cloth. These operatives served as the vanguard of the Industrial Revolution in America.

By the second decade of the nineteenth century, America had clearly defined itself as a nation that embraced many different kinds of change in transportation and technology. Yet traditional forms of inequality and hierarchy endured, serving as distinguishing features of the Market Revolution.

The Rise of the Cotton Plantation Economy

10.4 How did staple-crop production shape the labor, culture, and family lives of slaves?

The growth and spread of the cotton economy redefined the institution of slavery, the southern political system, and, ultimately, all of American history. With the invention of the cotton gin and the acquisition of the Louisiana Territory, cotton production boomed, and the enslaved population expanded. About 700,000 slaves resided in the United States in 1790; just two decades later, that figure had jumped to 1.1 million.

The **Abolition Act of 1808** outlawed the importation of foreign slaves. Northern abolitionists had first called for an end to the international slave trade during the U.S. Constitutional debates of the late 1780s. Anti-slavery activists from New York, for example, argued that such traffic in human beings was repugnant to the "ideas of mankind which form the basis of the government of the United States." Yet even after the Act had passed, some southern plantation owners found ways to smuggle slaves into the country illegally. The expansion of the United States into the vast Louisiana Territory and the astounding profitability of cotton heightened the demand for labor. Slave traders in New Orleans responded by building a highly successful contraband market in foreign slaves and evading detection by the U.S. Marshals Service. Still, the Abolition Act forced an important shift as planters increasingly relied on natural reproduction among slaves and on the domestic slave trade—the forced migration of slaves from the upper South to the lower South.

The institution of slavery was marked by increasingly sharp regional variations, reflecting the impact of cotton cultivation on local economies. At the same time, the contours of an African American culture emerged. This culture had certain characteristics regardless of place, such as strong ties that bound nuclear and extended family members, rich oral and musical traditions heavily influenced by West African customs, and individual and collective resistance to slavery. White people as a group understood little of this culture; they viewed black people primarily as workers who would never become citizens. As U.S. military strength and nationalistic pride grew, southern planters imposed a harsher, more regimented system of slavery on the black population. The tension between the rhetoric of freedom and equality and the reality of slavery continued to shape southern—and American—life for the next four decades.

Abolition Act of 1808 Also called the Slave Trade Act, prohibited the importation of foreign slaves into the United States.

Regional Economies of the South

Throughout the South, shifts in production methods transformed the demographic and economic makeup of specific regions. For example, by the early nineteenth century, the Chesapeake tobacco economy had declined as a result of worn-out lands and falling prices. In its place arose a more diversified economy based on crafts, the cultivation of corn and wheat, and the milling of flour. Owners put enslaved men to work making barrels and horseshoes, while forcing their wives, sisters, and daughters to labor as spinners, weavers, dairymaids, personal servants, and livestock tenders.

The lower South states of Georgia and South Carolina also saw their economies change during this period. The indigo export business never recovered from the Revolution, since colonial cultivators of the plant had relied heavily on British subsidies to shore up their profits. European customers now had to turn to Louisiana and Central America for indigo. In contrast, the lowcountry (coastal) South Carolina rice economy recovered and flourished after the war. In a particularly rich rice district, All Saints Parish, one out of two slaves lived on a plantation with more than a hundred slaves in 1790; 30 years later, four out of five lived on such large establishments. In these areas, the plantation owners themselves often lived elsewhere, and black people constituted almost the entire population.

Adding to the wealth of South Carolina and Georgia was the rapid development of cotton cultivation, especially in the interior, away from the coast. There, prosperous cotton planters began to rival their lowcountry rice-growing counterparts in social status and political influence, and these slaveholders pushed steadily for further western expansion. Cotton planters rushed into the newly purchased Louisiana Territory after 1803. They accelerated an economic process that had begun in the late eighteenth century: the replacement of a frontier exchange economy with plantation agriculture. (Sugar dominated the New Orleans region; cotton, the rest of the lower Mississippi Valley.) By 1800, slaves in lower Louisiana were producing 4.5 million pounds of sugar annually.

The reaches of the lower Mississippi took on an increasingly multicultural flavor. A strong Spanish influence persisted as a vestige of colonial days. French-speaking planter-refugees and their slaves from revolutionary Saint-Domingue came to New Orleans while the city was still in French hands (1800 to 1803). Between 1787 and 1803, nearly 3,000 slaves arrived from Africa, Spanish West Florida, and the Chesapeake to be sold in New Orleans, followed by even larger numbers of slaves from the North after 1803. Slave owners who settled in Natchez, on the banks of the Mississippi River, grew cotton—and grew rich.

Black Family Life and Labor

By 1820, the enslaved population reached 1.5 million and continued to increase rapidly over the next four decades. Since importation of Africans ended officially in 1808, this number suggests a tremendous rate of natural increase. Some planters continued to buy slaves brought into the country illegally after 1808, but most of the increase stemmed from births. The preferences of both slave owners and slaves account for this development. Southern planters encouraged black women to bear many children. At the same time, enslaved African Americans valued the family as a social unit; family ties provided support and solace for a people deprived of fundamental human rights. Even under harsh conditions, black people fell in love, married (albeit informally, without the sanction of law), had children, and reared families. Despite the lack of protection from local, state, and national authorities, the slave family proved a remarkably resilient institution.

The stability of individual slave families depended on several factors, including the size and age of the plantation and the fortunes and life cycle of the slave owner's family. Very large or long-established plantations had more two-parent slave families than did the small or newer holdings, which tended to have more unrelated people. Slave families were broken up when whites died and their "property" was bequeathed to heirs. Slaves might also be sold or presented to other family members as gifts. Many slave families suffered disruption in response to the growing demand for slaves in the fresh cotton lands of Alabama and Mississippi. The forced migration from upper South to lower South necessarily severed kin ties, but slaves often reconstituted those ties in the form of symbolic kin relationships. Families adopted new, single members of the slave community, and the children called these newcomers "Aunt" or "Uncle." Since plantations functioned as slave labor camps, owners generally showed little or no inclination to take family relationships into account when they parceled out work assignments to men, women, and children. Rather, those assignments, and the conditions under which slaves performed them, reflected the size and crops of a particular plantation. During the period 1790 to 1860, an estimated 75 percent of slaves worked primarily as field hands. On large plantations the division of labor could be quite specialized. Men served as skilled carpenters, blacksmiths, and barrel makers, and women worked as cooks, laundresses, nursemaids, and personal maids.

Rice slaves continued to work under the task system. Each day, after they completed a specific assigned task, they spent their time as they chose, within limits. Even in the cotton-growing regions, where blacks labored under the regimented gang system, slaves tried to work for themselves in the little free time they had on Saturday afternoons and Sunday. In Louisiana, one white observer noted that the slave man returning to his living quarters after a long, hot day in the fields "does not lose his time. He goes to work at a bit of the land which he has planted with provisions for his own use, while his companion, if he has one, busies herself in preparing some for him, herself, and their children." Family members who grew or accumulated a modest surplus—of corn, eggs, vegetables—in some cases could sell their wares in a nearby market or to slaves on another plantation.

Some slaves took goods from their master's storeroom and barn and sold or traded them to other slaves or to poor whites. These transactions often took place under the cover of darkness. Planters complained of slaves who stole their cattle, hogs, chickens, sacks full of cotton, farm equipment, and stores of ham and flour. Thus, slaves' various forms of labor fell into at least three categories: work performed at the behest of and directly under the supervision of whites, labor performed by and for family members within the slaves' living quarters, and the sale (or sometimes clandestine exchange) of goods with masters, other slaves, and poor whites.

Resistance to Slavery

Slaves resisted the harsh demands made by their masters; that resistance took many forms, including cultural expression. In 1817, the New Orleans City Council decreed that enslaved men and women could sing and dance at a stipulated place—Congo Square—every Sunday afternoon. Thereafter, a variety of groups came together to make music. These groups included recent émigrés from Saint-Domingue and slaves newly imported from Africa; slaves from neighboring plantations, in town for the day; and New Orleans Creoles, enslaved and free people of color of Spanish or French colonial heritage. In towns and on plantations throughout the South, black people drew from West African musical traditions, using drums as well as banjo-like instruments, gourd

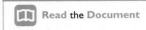 Read the Document Absalom Jones, Sermon on the Abolition of the International Slave Trade (1808)

From colonial times through the abolition of slavery in 1865, runaways were a persistent problem for slaveholders. This advertisement was published in the Centerville, Maryland, *Times and Eastern-Shore Public Advertiser*. Typically, the owner describes the runaways in terms of their height, skin color, and their distinguishing characteristics. Based on Robert Porter's description as given by his master, what were Porter's strategies to elude capture by authorities? Could he hope to blend into the population of free people of color?

Gullah A "pidgin," or blend of words and grammatical structures from West African languages and English, spoken by slaves in the South Carolina lowcountry.

rattles, and mandolins. Over the generations several uniquely American musical styles flowed from Congo Square and other southern gathering places: the blues, gospel, ragtime, jazz, swing, and rock and roll.

In their artistic expression, dress, hairstyles, and language, black people sought to preserve their cultural uniqueness and create an existence that slaveholders could not touch. In the South Carolina lowcountry, slaves spoke **Gullah**. Originally a pidgin—a blend of words and grammatical structures from West African languages and English—Gullah later developed into a more formal Creole language. Slaves throughout the United States also mixed West African religious beliefs with Christianity. In slave quarters, spiritual leaders not only preached a Christianity of equality but also told fortunes and warned away "haunts" (spirits of the dead).

Black resistance to slavery took many forms. Slaves might work carelessly in an effort to resist a master's or mistress's demands. During the course of their workday, some broke hoes and other farm implements. A cook might burn the biscuits, thus spoiling a special dinner party for her mistress. Striking out more directly, the African-influenced "conjurer"—often a woman who had a knowledge of plants and herbs—could wreak havoc on a white family by concocting poisons or encouraging disruptive behavior among other enslaved workers.

Slaves also stole goods from their masters and at times stole themselves by running away. (This practice was more common among young, unmarried men than among those who had family obligations.) Despite the extraordinary peril involved, some slaves revolted. In St. Charles and St. John the Baptist parishes in Louisiana, an 1811 revolt of 400 slaves cost two whites their lives and left several plantations in flames. The original participants, led by a free man of color, Charles Deslondes, acquired new members as they marched toward New Orleans. U.S. troops cut their advance short, killing 66 of them. In the Southeast in 1817 and 1818, 400 to 600 black fugitives converged on the swamps of central Florida, uniting with Indian refugees from the Red Stick War. Together, they raided Georgia plantations until Andrew Jackson and his soldiers halted them in April 1818.

To justify their own behavior, masters and mistresses created a number of myths about the black people they exploited. Whites had a vested interest in believing that their slaves felt gratitude toward them. Skilled in the so-called **deference ritual**, some slaves hid their true feelings and acted submissively in the presence of white people. Owners and overseers alike interpreted this behavior as a sign of black contentment.

Deference ritual A pattern of interaction between slaves and their masters with slaves hiding their true feelings while acting submissively in the presence of whites.

Although some planters boasted of their fatherly solicitude for their slaves, most slave owners harbored deep fears about the men and women they held in bondage. These fears explain the barbaric punishments that some owners inflicted on men, women, and children. Even in "respectable" Southern families, slave owners branded, mutilated, and beat enslaved workers for resisting discipline or to deliver a warning to other potentially defiant workers. In the slave South, American cries of freedom, equality, opportunity, and the blessings of citizenship rang hollow.

Conclusion

During the first two decades of the nineteenth century, striking historical developments stirred the spirit of American nationalism. The Louisiana Purchase magnified the natural wealth of the young nation, and the federal government encouraged citizens to exploit that wealth through trade and settlement. The Embargo of 1807 and the War of 1812 freed the country from the British menace in the Northwest Territory and on the high seas. The war also bolstered the American economy by stimulating technological innovation and the growth of manufacturing. Territorial expansion combined with economic development created new jobs for a burgeoning population.

Southern cotton planters and northern factory owners derived their newfound prosperity from very different sources: staple crop agriculture on one hand and the emerging industrial system on the other. At the same time, these two groups had much in common. As they expanded their operations, whether sprawling plantations or gigantic mill complexes, they displaced smaller landowners and raised land prices. Members of both elite groups proved restless entrepreneurs, eager to move around to find the freshest lands and the cheapest labor. Their personal wealth and their political power set them apart from the people under them—the slaves and wage earners—who produced that wealth. And both the southern "lords of the lash" and the northern "lords of the loom" depended on large numbers of slaves to grow cotton. Producing and processing cotton yielded tangible benefits for a few and created a new, harsher world of work for many.

Chapter Review

A Contest over Land and Sea

10.1 What were the domestic and international consequences of Britain's persistent challenges to U.S. territorial sovereignty and trade relations with other nations? p. 243

British impressment of American sailors, among other factors, led Jefferson to place an embargo on exports to European powers. This Embargo Act of 1807 aroused opposition from Federalists in New England and southern tobacco and cotton planters. British challenges to the United States also gave rise to Congressional war hawks.

The War of 1812

10.2 What were the political and economic interests of the United States, the Indian tribes, and Great Britain and why did those divergent interests clash during the War of 1812? p. 248

The United States hoped to eliminate the British threat on the high seas and win true independence once and for all. War hawks supported national expansion and called for an invasion of Canada. Indian tribes hoped to fend off white encroachment. The British wanted to weaken the United States and maintain control of the high seas and Canada.

The "Era of Good Feelings"?

10.3 Did political and social realities justify the use of the term "the Era of Good Feelings" to describe the period after the War of 1812? p. 253

The term, which referred to a relative lack of partisan strife during this period, only fully applied to enfranchised white men. The Market Revolution led to economic growth, but it also led to the replacement of skilled workers with unskilled workers and forced slaves to work harder. In the west, European Americans forcibly displaced Indians.

The Rise of the Cotton Plantation Economy

10.4 How did staple-crop production shape the labor, culture, and family lives of slaves? p. 259

Cotton slaves worked under the gang system, and rice slaves worked by the task. Family stability depended on the size and age of the plantation, and the life cycle of the slave owner's family. Forced migration led slaves to reconstitute family ties in the form of symbolic kin relationships. Through cultural expression, individual resistance, and, rarely, outright violent rebellion, slaves countered harsh demands made upon them.

Timeline

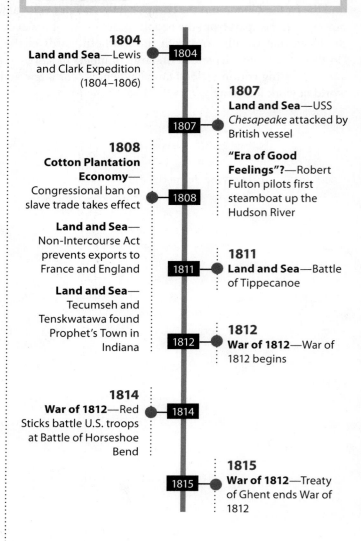

1804
Land and Sea—Lewis and Clark Expedition (1804–1806)

1804

1807
Land and Sea—USS *Chesapeake* attacked by British vessel

1807

"Era of Good Feelings"?—Robert Fulton pilots first steamboat up the Hudson River

1808
Cotton Plantation Economy—Congressional ban on slave trade takes effect

1808

Land and Sea—Non-Intercourse Act prevents exports to France and England

1811
Land and Sea—Battle of Tippecanoe

1811

Land and Sea—Tecumseh and Tenskwatawa found Prophet's Town in Indiana

1812

1812
War of 1812—War of 1812 begins

1814
War of 1812—Red Sticks battle U.S. troops at Battle of Horseshoe Bend

1814

1815
War of 1812—Treaty of Ghent ends War of 1812

1815

11
Society and Politics in the "Age of the Common Man," 1819–1832

How do we account for an **American political** vocabulary that evokes a rough-hewn, woodsman quality? Why do candidates hit the campaign *trail* and give *stump* speeches? Why do they support their party's platform with its *planks* (positions on the issues), and then, when elected, vote for *pork-barrel* projects that benefit their constituents at home?

Those terms had their origins in the third decade of the nineteenth century, when western settlers boasted of their rural roots and attacked what they considered centralized, eastern-based institutions of wealth and privilege. Representative of this boisterous political age was Tennessee politician David Crockett. As a candidate for office, Crockett was an unrivaled campaigner. He ran successfully for several offices, including local justice of the peace in 1818, state legislator in 1821 and 1823, and U.S. congressman in 1837, 1829, and 1833. The plainspoken Crockett knew how to play to a crowd and rattle a rival. He bragged about his skill as a bear hunter and ridiculed the fancy dress of his opponents. He condemned closed-door political caucuses (small groups of party insiders who hand-picked candidates) and praised grassroots democracy.

The Fairmont Water Works, a model of nineteenth-century engineering and civic architecture, pumped water from the Schuylkill River to supply Philadelphia. In operation for ninety-four years, from 1815 to 1909, the Fairmont has been designated a National Historic Landmark. During this period in American history, classical architecture was popular in America because it evoked the democratic ideals of ancient Greece. How did technological advances like the Fairmont Water Works transform urban living?

LEARNING OBJECTIVES

11.1 ((•

How did western expansion affect the nation's politics and economy in the 1820s?
p. 267

11.2 ((•

What were President Andrew Jackson's controversial views on the role of the federal government and the role of the chief executive?
p. 276

11.3 ((•

How did the work of Indians, free and enslaved African Americans, and women change during the "Age of the Common Man"?
p. 280

11.4 ((•

In what ways did Americans maintain a sense of community in the face of unprecedented migration and population growth?
p. 286

((• Listen to Chapter 11 on MyHistoryLab

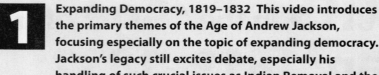 **Watch the Video Series on MyHistoryLab**

Learn about some key topics related to this chapter with the *MyHistoryLab Video Series: Key Topics in U.S. History.*

1 Expanding Democracy, 1819–1832 This video introduces the primary themes of the Age of Andrew Jackson, focusing especially on the topic of expanding democracy. Jackson's legacy still excites debate, especially his handling of such crucial issues as Indian Removal and the war against the national bank.

 Watch on MyHistoryLab

Andrew Jackson's Rise to Power This video discusses the path taken by Andrew Jackson from his early childhood to winning the presidency of the United States. Jackson represented the popular image of "everyman" to his contemporaries, though there is much more to the real Jackson than just the popular image. **2**

Watch on MyHistoryLab

3 The Indian Removal Act This video explores Andrew Jackson's order to remove Native American tribes from east of the Mississippi River to the Oklahoma Territory. Jackson believed that removal would allow the Cherokee to survive as a group, and at the time, this policy met with little resistance from non-Indians. However, Indian removal remains a controversial aspect of Jackson's historical legacy.

 Watch on MyHistoryLab

The "Monster Bank" This video expands our understanding of Andrew Jackson by explaining his dislike for the Bank of the United States, his efforts to destroy the bank, and the outcomes of that struggle. The Bank War remains one of the defining elements of Jackson's tenure in office, and a critical component of his reputation as a representative of the interests of the "common man." **4**

Watch on MyHistoryLab

Crockett claimed he could out-shoot, out-drink, and out-debate anyone who opposed him. If his opponent lied about him, why, then he would lie about himself: "Yes, fellow citizens, I can run faster, walk longer, leap higher, speak better, and tell more and bigger lies than my competitor, and all his friends, any day of his life." Crockett's blend of political theater and folksy backwoods banter earned him the allegiance of voters like him—men who, though having little formal education, understood the challenges of carving a homestead out of the dense thickets of Tennessee.

During the 1820s, European American settlers in the trans-Appalachian West transformed the style and substance of American politics. In 1790, 100,000 Americans (not including Indians) lived west of the Appalachians; half a century later that number had increased to 7 million, or about four out of ten Americans. In some respects "the common man" gained more influence and opportunity—through the move toward universal manhood suffrage (that is, removing restrictions on the right to vote) and a broad system of tax-supported public schools, for example. At the same time, African Americans found their access to these institutions closed, sometimes through violent means.

David Crockett preferred the nickname "Davy." He and other western voters believed that, in their ability to run and defend the country, they were the equals of any Easterner, no matter how well-born, well-educated, or wealthy. Yet, democracy had its limits during this period. While voter participation in elections soared, from 25 percent of eligible voters in 1824 to 50 percent in 1828, even most free people could

((• [icon] **Read** the Document   Davy Crockett, Advice to Politicians (1833)

John Gadsby Chapman painted this portrait of Davy Crockett in his artist's studio. How does Chapman convey Crockett's political ideas and his role in American politics in the 1820s and 1830s? What do the two dogs signify? Consider Crockett's nickname Davy in relation to the names of other early American political leaders. Can you think of other leaders (then or since) who chose to retain their nicknames, even when they ascended to the presidency?

not vote, including Native Americans, women, and people of color. Further complicating this age was the rise of distinct social classes, a class system that seemed to mock the idea of equality. Together, these tensions shaped American society and politics in the third decade of the nineteenth century.

The Politics Behind Western Expansion

11.1   How did western expansion affect the nation's politics and economy in the 1820s?

As the United States gained new territory through negotiation and conquest and people moved west, the nation felt the impact. President Monroe warned Europeans not to intervene any longer in the Western Hemisphere. Americans

MAP 11.1 THE MISSOURI COMPROMISE Missouri applied for statehood in 1819, threatening the balance between eleven free states and eleven slave states. According to a compromise hammered out in Congress, Missouri was admitted as a slave state, and Maine, formerly part of Massachusetts, was admitted as a free state. Slavery was banned above the 36°30′ parallel.

settling west of the Appalachian mountains rejoiced with the 1828 election of Andrew Jackson as president; here, they claimed, was a man who would battle eastern financiers and at the same time support white settlers' claims to Indian lands in the West. Jackson held out promise that ordinary people would have a political voice and access to expanding economic opportunities.

However, once in the West, settlers faced the same kinds of conflicts that increasingly preoccupied Easterners, especially those between masters and slaves and debtors and creditors. The West, then, duplicated fundamental kinds of inequality found in the East; moreover, with the growth of western land speculation and the institution of slavery, such inequality spread and expanded. In the process, issues related to racial and class differences in the West became matters of national and not just regional concern. Congressional debates over whether Missouri should be admitted to the Union as a slave state or as a free state sent shock waves throughout the country. Of the political conflict over the fate of slavery in the territories, the elderly Thomas Jefferson wrote, "This momentous question, like a firebell in the night, awakened and filled me with terror. I considered it at once as the death knell of the Union."

The Missouri Compromise

In 1819, the United States consisted of twenty-two states. Slavery was legal in half of them. In February of that year, the House of Representatives considered a bill to allow the people of Missouri Territory to write a constitution and form a government. These measures were steps necessary to the territory becoming a state. A representative from New York, James Tallmadge, offered an amendment (which would bear his name) to forbid the importation of slaves into the new state, and to free all slaves who had been born there when they reached the age of twenty-five. The Senate refused to agree, and the bill died. The following January, the House considered a similar bill, this one with an amendment proposed by another New York representative, John W. Taylor, that would admit Missouri as a slave state. This bill passed.

In the Senate, Rufus King of New York claimed that Congress had the ultimate authority to set laws governing slavery. However, his colleague William Pinckney of Maryland retorted that new states possessed the same rights as the original thirteen; that is, they could choose whether to allow slavery. Maine's application for admission to the Union suggested a way out of the impasse. Speaker of the House of Representatives Henry Clay of Kentucky successfully proposed a plan. Missouri would join the Union as a slave state at the same time that Maine, originally part of Massachusetts, would become the twenty-fourth state and be designated a free one. In the future, slavery would be prohibited from all Louisiana Purchase lands north of latitude 36°30', an area that included all territory north of present-day Missouri and Kansas. The House and Senate finally approved the compromise, which maintained the balance between the number of slave and free states.

The day Congress sealed the compromise, Secretary of State John Quincy Adams of Massachusetts walked home from the Capitol with Senator John C. Calhoun of South Carolina. The two men engaged in a muted but intense debate over slavery. Calhoun claimed that the institution "was the best guarantee to equality among the whites." Slavery, he asserted, demonstrated that all white men were equal to one another and superior to all blacks. Unnerved by Calhoun's comments, Adams concluded that the debate over Missouri had "betrayed the secret of [Southerners'] souls." By reserving backbreaking toil for blacks, wealthy planters fancied themselves aristocratic lords of the manor. Adams confided in his diary that night, "They look down upon the simplicity of a Yankee's manners, because he has no habits of overbearing like theirs and cannot treat negroes like dogs." Adams feared that North–South conflicts might someday imperil the nation itself.

Ways West

Missouri was just one of the territories west of the Mississippi River where the population had increased during this period. Some Americans moved west by choice, while others were forced to move. When whites moved, they often claimed that they were furthering the ideals of American equality; yet when they brought slaves with them, they were also expanding the boundaries of the slave economy. The federal government played an active part in the settlement of the West.

Through land grants and government financing of new methods of transportation, Congress encouraged European American migrants to push their way west and south. The Land Act of 1820 enabled Westerners to buy a minimum 80 acres at a price of $1.25 an acre in cash—even in those days, a bargain homestead. Built with the help of government legal and financial aid, new roads and canals, steamboats, and, after the early 1830s, railroads facilitated migration. Between 1820 and 1860, the number of steamboats plying the Mississippi River jumped from 60 to more than 1,000. Canals linked western producers to eastern consumers of grains and cattle and connected western consumers to eastern producers of manufactured goods. Shipping costs and times between Buffalo and New York shrank. Cities such as Rochester and Syracuse, New York; and Cincinnati, Ohio, flourished because of their geographic positions along key waterways.

Among the most significant of these waterways was the **Erie Canal**. Completed in 1825, this engineering marvel used eighty-three canal locks to link the Great Lakes directly to the East Coast by way of the Hudson River. Public acclaim was thunderous.

Erie Canal Waterway linking the New York cities of Troy and Albany, on the Hudson River, with Buffalo, on the eastern tip of Lake Erie; in the 1820s, the opening of the Erie Canal revolutionized trading between the Midwest and East Coast and established New York City as the most important financial center in the United States.

269

✳ Explore the Missouri Compromise on MyHistoryLab

WHY DID CONGRESS ADOPT THE MISSOURI COMPROMISE?

In 1787, disagreements between northern and southern delegates over the role of slavery in the new American Republic had almost derailed the framing of a new Constitution. As U.S. settlement expanded westward at the turn of the nineteenth century and new states began to join the Union, this regional divide over slavery only deepened. Many Northerners hoped to see the institution gradually eliminated in the U.S. Meanwhile, Southerners worried that eliminating slavery would destroy their economy. Because the North's larger population gave it an advantage in the House of Representatives, southern slave states depended on their equal representation in the Senate to block any attempts at abolition. Under such political conditions, anything that tipped the balance of power in the Senate threatened to tear the nation apart. The Missouri Compromise of

With the passage of the Missouri Compromise, the slave economy expanded west to the new state of Missouri. This early photo suggests the subordinate status of slaves in their style of dress and in the tasks they were forced to perform. In what other aspects of their lives were these men and women unequal to whites, no matter how poor?

SOURCE: Accessed at http://www.whitehouse.gov

1820 maintained this balance by admitting the slave state of Missouri to the Union alongside the free state of Maine. The compromise also attempted to prevent future conflict by drawing a line at 36°30' N latitude and then prohibiting slavery north of the line but permitting the admission of new slave states to the line's south.

BALANCE OF FREE AND SLAVE STATES PRIOR TO THE MISSOURI COMPROMISE OF 1820

	Free States	Slave States
Number of States in U.S.	11	11
U.S. Representatives	105	81
U.S. Senators	22	22

KEY QUESTIONS — Use MyHistoryLab *Explorer* to answer these questions:

Cause ▶▶▶ *What political factors triggered the Missouri Compromise?*

Map the regional spread and decline of slavery in the United States from 1790 to 1830.

Consequence ▶▶▶ *Why was the Missouri Compromise viewed as only a temporary solution?*

Map the spread of non-Indian settlement in the United States from 1790 to 1830.

Analysis ▶▶▶ *Why would slavery continue to be a divisive political issue in the United States?*

Map the economic and social differences that separated the North from South in 1820.

Upstate New York's economy thrived. And New York City, at the mouth of the Hudson, emerged as the most important port and financial center in the country.

Americans took a variety of routes west. In the 1820s, desperate planters moved out of the exhausted lands of the upper South (the states of Virginia and Maryland), the Carolinas, and Georgia, proceeding westward into Alabama, Arkansas, Louisiana, and Mississippi. This migration across the Appalachian Mountains furthered the nationalist idea of the "expansion of liberty and freedom," a view held by many white men regardless of political affiliation. Yet it also spread slavery. The sight of slave coffles—groups of men, women, and children bound together in chains, hobbling down a city street or a country road—became increasingly common in this western region. In 1821, Virginia, North Carolina, South Carolina, and Georgia had produced two-thirds of the nation's cotton crop; the rest came from recently settled areas. Just a dozen years later, the proportions shifted: Tennessee, Louisiana, Alabama, Mississippi, and Florida together produced two-thirds of all cotton, and the remaining one-third came from older areas.

European Americans also migrated across the border into Mexican territory. In 1821, Spain approved the application of a U.S. citizen, Moses Austin, to settle 300 American families on 200,000 fertile acres along the Colorado and Brazos river bottoms in southeastern Texas. Austin died soon after, but his son Stephen carried on his legacy. Within two years, the younger Austin had received permission (now from the government of newly independent Mexico) to bring in another 100 families. These

The rich bottomlands of the Mississippi Delta proved ideal for growing cotton. After the forced removal of Native Americans from the Old Southwest, slave owners established expansive plantations in the delta. This nineteenth-century illustration depicts slave life on a cotton plantation. How much work went into a cotton harvest? Does the illustration suggest the equality of hardship among enslaved workers, regardless of age or gender?

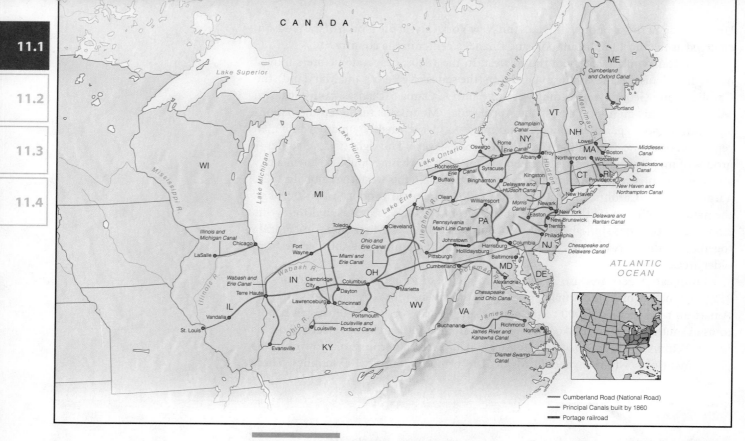

MAP 11.2 PRINCIPAL CANALS BUILT BY 1860 Many canals were expensive ventures and, in some cases, engineering nightmares. The Erie Canal had a competitive advantage because it snaked through the Mohawk Valley, the only major level pass through the mountain chain that stretched from Canada to Georgia. In contrast, the Pennsylvania Main Line Canal, which ran from Harrisburg to Pittsburgh, used a combination of inclined planes and steam engines in ten separate locations to haul boats up and down the Allegheny Mountains.

settlers, together with squatters, numbered about 1,500 people. Although the Mexican constitution prohibited slavery, some of the newcomers brought their slaves with them, and some free people of color came on their own. All these migrants from the United States called themselves **Texians** to distinguish themselves from the **Tejanos**, or Spanish-speaking residents of the region. These newly arrived Texians agreed to adopt the Roman Catholic faith and become citizens of Mexico. During the rest of the decade, 900 additional families sponsored by Austin arrived in Texas. They were followed by 3,000 more squatters. Mexican officials feared that they would lose authority over the mass of American newcomers within their borders.

The Panic of 1819 and the Plight of Western Debtors

In 1819, a financial panic swept across the nation, followed by an economic depression that hit western states and territories particularly hard. The Second Bank of the United States played a major role in triggering this economic downturn, which came to be called the Panic of 1819. Granted a twenty-year charter by Congress in 1816, the Second Bank resembled its predecessor, seeking to regulate the national economy through loans to state and local banks. In 1819, the bank clamped down on small, local **wildcat banks**, which had extended credit to many people who could not repay their loans. Many homesteaders were not self-sufficient farmers but producers of staple crops or proprietors of small enterprises. They relied on credit from banks and local private lenders. As a result, the bank's crackdown on wildcat banks had a devastating impact on western households. Debtors unable to meet their obligations had their mortgages foreclosed, their homes seized, and their crops and equipment confiscated.

Ruined by the Panic of 1819, many western farmers developed an abiding hatred of the Bank of the United States and a deep resentment of eastern financiers. These

Texians The name used by U.S.-born citizens who lived in the Mexican state of Texas.

Tejanos Spanish-speaking residents of the Mexican (and later, U.S.) state of Texas.

Wildcat banks Small banks that make loans unsupervised by the state or other financial institutions.

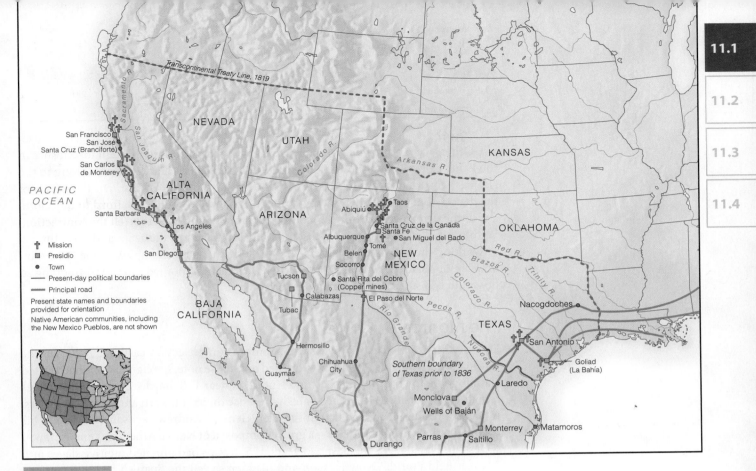

MAP 11.3 MEXICO'S FAR NORTHERN FRONTIER IN 1822 This map shows Mexico's far northern frontier in 1822. When Moses Austin died suddenly in 1821, the task of supervising the settlement of in-migrants from the United States fell to his son Stephen. The Mexican government authorized the younger Austin to act as impresario of the settlement. He was responsible for the legal and economic regulations governing the settlements clustered at the lower reaches of the Colorado and Brazos rivers.

Westerners believed that the federal government had actually increased levels of economic inequality among Americans by favoring the Second Bank of the United States (with a congressional charter) over local institutions. When the central bank cracked down on the wildcats, eastern creditors profited and western homesteaders lost their property. To western farmers, it seemed as if a financial system that was supposed to guarantee widespread access to credit among small farmers was instead further enriching the wealthiest Americans.

Davy Crockett's own family history suggests the plight of families dependent on bank credit to create homesteads out of western territory. The son of a propertyless squatter, Crockett had an intense fear of debt. Although he campaigned as a hunter and a farmer, he had built several enterprises on land he leased or owned on Shoal Creek in south-central Tennessee: a water-powered grist mill, a gunpowder factory (worked by slaves), an iron-ore mine, and a liquor distillery. For each venture, he had to borrow money from local creditors. Spending much of his time away from home, Crockett relied on his wife, Elizabeth, and his children to manage these businesses. (He had three children by his first wife, Polly, who died in 1815, and eventually would have a total of nine by Elizabeth.)

The depression of 1819 cut off Crockett's sources of credit, and in 1822, a flash flood swept away his grist mill and powder factory. Without milled grain, the distillery could no longer operate. Creditors immediately set upon the family, demanding payment of their debts. The Crocketts were fortunate enough to own land they could sell, using the proceeds to repay their debts and then moving farther west in Tennessee.

TABLE 11.1 THE ELECTION OF 1820

Candidate	Political Party	Electoral Vote
James Monroe	Democratic-Republican	231
John Quincy Adams	Democratic-Republican	1

Others were not so lucky. Small farmers who lost their land through foreclosure in the Panic of 1819 could not produce crops for the eastern market, contributing to the rise in the price of food. Deprived of credit, small shopkeepers also felt the effects of the depression. With rising unemployment, consumers could not afford to buy cloth, and as the demand for cotton fell, southern plantation owners, too, felt the contraction. Within a few years, Andrew Jackson would capitalize on the fears and resentments of working men, farmers, planters, and tradesmen, as he championed the "common man" in opposition to what debtors called the "eastern monied interests." In doing so he would transform the two-party system.

The Monroe Doctrine

Despite the troubled economy, James Monroe won reelection easily in 1820. On the international front, his second term opened on a tense note. Foreign nations had started claiming land or promoting their own interests near U.S. borders. The United States remained especially wary of the Spanish presence on its southern and western borders. In 1818, President Monroe had authorized General Andrew Jackson to broaden his assault on the Seminole Indians—a group composed of Native Americans and runaway slaves—in Florida. For the past two years, U.S. troops had pursued fugitive slaves into Spanish-held Florida. Now Jackson and his men seized the Spanish fort at Pensacola and claimed all of western Florida for the United States. The United States demanded that Spain either suppress the Seminole population or sell all of east Florida to the United States. With the Transcontinental Treaty of 1819, Spain gave up its right to both Florida and Oregon (although Britain and Russia still claimed land in Oregon). In 1822, General Jackson became the first governor of Florida Territory.

Farther north, in 1821 the emperor of Russia, Czar Alexander I, forbade non-Russians from entering the territory north of the fifty-first parallel and the open sea 100 miles off the coast of what is now Canada and Alaska. The Russians had established trading posts up and down that coast, some almost as far south as San Francisco Bay. Meanwhile, rumors circulated that European monarchs were planning new invasions of Latin America.

Fearful of an alliance among Russia, Prussia, Austria, Spain, and France, President Monroe and Secretary of State John Quincy Adams formulated a policy that became a landmark in American diplomatic history. Adams rejected a British proposal that Great Britain and the United States join forces to oppose a further Spanish encroachment in Latin America. He convinced Monroe that the United States must stand alone against the European powers—Spain in the south and Russia in the northwest—if it hoped to protect its own interests in the Western Hemisphere. In his annual message to Congress in December 1823, the president declared that the era of Europe's colonization of the Americas had ceased. Henceforth, he said, foreign nations would not be allowed to intervene in the Western Hemisphere.

Monroe Doctrine Policy announced by President James Monroe in 1823 that the era of European colonization of the Americas had ceased; warned foreign powers, especially Russia, Spain, and Britain, that the United States would not allow them to intervene in the Western Hemisphere.

The United States conceived the **Monroe Doctrine** as a self-defense measure aimed specifically at Russia, Spain, and Britain. With the Russo-American Treaty of 1824, Russia agreed to pull back its claims to the area north of 54°40', the southern tip of the present-day Alaska panhandle. However, the United States did not have the naval power to back up the Monroe Doctrine with force. The doctrine was at first more a statement of principle than a blueprint for action, intended to discourage European powers from political or military meddling in the Western Hemisphere. The doctrine would have greater international significance in the late nineteenth century, when the United States developed the military might to enforce it.

Andrew Jackson's Rise to Power

The election of 1824 provided a striking contrast to the bland affair four years earlier in which Monroe had been elected. In 1824, the field of presidential nominees was crowded, suggesting a party system in disarray. Although all the candidates called themselves "Democratic-Republicans," the label meant little more than the fact that most politicians sought to distance themselves from the outmoded "Federalist" label, which hearkened back to the post-Revolutionary period rather than pointing forward to the nation's new challenges. Nominees included Secretary of State John Quincy Adams, Representative Henry Clay of Kentucky, and Andrew Jackson, now a senator from Tennessee. Jackson received the highest number of electoral votes (ninety-nine), but no candidate achieved a majority. As a result, the election went to the House of Representatives.

Clay withdrew from the race. He had promised Jackson his support but then endorsed Adams, whom the House subsequently elected. When Adams named Clay secretary of state, Jackson's supporters cried foul. The election, they charged, amounted to nothing more than a corrupt deal between two political insiders.

Haunted by these charges, Adams served his four-year term under a cloud of public distrust. A member of a respected New England family and the son of former president John Adams, the new chief executive had served with distinction in Monroe's cabinet. Still, Adams proved ill suited to the rough-and-tumble world of what came to be called the New Democracy. Adams advocated a greater federal role in internal improvements and public education, a variation on Henry Clay's "American System," a set of policies which promoted a national bank, public funding of canals and turnpikes, and a high tariff to protect domestic manufactures.

Adams's party, now calling itself the **National Republicans**, faced a formidable challenge in the election of 1828. Having seethed for four long years, Andrew Jackson's supporters (the Democratic-Republicans) now urged "the people" to reclaim the White House. The campaign was a nasty one. Jackson's opponents attacked his personal morality and that of his wife and his mother. Jackson's supporters countered with the charge that Adams himself was corrupt and that he and his cronies must be swept from office.

Jackson won a stunning victory, with his supporters hailing the well-to-do slaveholder as the president of the "common" (meaning white) man. In office, Jackson tightened his party's grip on power by introducing a national political spoils system. Through this process, successful candidates rewarded their supporters with jobs and tossed their rivals out of appointed offices. The spoils system let the Democratic-Republicans—now called the Democrats—build a nationwide political machine. Not surprisingly, it also provided fertile ground for corruption and fueled the debate over the use and limits of federal authority.

National Republicans A political party, led by John Adams in the 1820s, that favored a greater federal role in funding internal improvements and public education; forerunner of the Whigs, formed in opposition to President Andrew Jackson.

TABLE 11.2 THE ELECTION OF 1824

Candidate	Political Party	Popular Vote (%)	Electoral Vote
John Quincy Adams	Democratic-Republican	30.5	84
Andrew Jackson	Democratic-Republican	43.1	99
William H. Crawford	Democratic-Republican	13.1	41
Henry Clay	Democratic-Republican	13.2	37

TABLE 11.3 THE ELECTION OF 1828

Candidate	Political Party	Popular Vote (%)	Electoral Vote
Andrew Jackson	Democratic	56.0	178
John Quincy Adams	National Republican	44.0	83

Some commentators disapproved of what they considered the excessively lively inauguration gala for President Jackson in 1829. One described the affair this way: "On their arrival at the White House, the motley crowd clamored for refreshments and soon drained the barrels of punch, which had been prepared, in drinking to the health of the new Chief Magistrate. A great deal of glassware was broken, and the East Room was filled with a noisy mob." In contrast to the disapproval of some people, others hailed the inauguration gala as the dawning of a new era that promised people of modest means the same access to political influence and power previously enjoyed only by their social betters. What different groups of people are represented in the crowd outside the White House?

Federal Authority and Its Opponents

11.2 What were President Andrew Jackson's controversial views on the role of the federal government and the role of the chief executive?

When Americans defeated the British in the War of 1812, they ensured the physical security of the new nation. However, the war's end left a crucial question unanswered: what role would federal authority play in a republic of states? During Andrew Jackson's tenure, Congress, the chief executive, and the Supreme Court all jockeyed for influence over one another and over the states. Jackson claimed a broad popular mandate to increase the power of the presidency, and he used it to end the charter of the Second Bank of the United States.

At the same time, militant southern sectionalists regarded the growth of federal executive and judicial power with alarm. If the president could impose a high tariff on the states and if the Supreme Court could deny the states the authority to govern Indians within their own borders, might not high-handed federal officials someday also threaten the South's system of slavery?

Judicial Federalism and the Limits of Law

In a series of notable cases, the Supreme Court, under the leadership of Chief Justice John Marshall, sought to limit states' power to control people and resources within their own boundaries. In *McCulloch v. Maryland* (1819), the Court supported Congress's decision to grant the Second Bank of the United States a twenty-year charter. The state of Maryland had imposed a high tax on notes issued by the bank. Declaring that "the power to tax involves the power to destroy," the Supreme Court ruled the state's action unconstitutional. The court justices held that, although the original Constitution did not mention a national bank, Congress retained the authority to create such an institution. This fact implied that Congress also had the power to preserve it. This decision relied on what came to be called a "loose construction" of the Constitution to justify "implied powers" of the government, powers not explicitly stated in the Constitution.

In 1832, a case involving the rights of the Cherokee nation brought the Court head to head with President Jackson's own brand of federal muscle-flexing. With the expansion of cotton cultivation into upland Georgia in the early nineteenth century, white residents of that state increasingly resented the presence of their Cherokee neighbors. At the same time, some Cherokee worked and worshipped in ways similar to European Americans: They cultivated farmland, converted to Christianity, and established a formal legal code. On July 4, 1827, Cherokee leaders met in convention to devise a republican constitution. In the grand tradition of the Patriots of 1776, the group proclaimed the Cherokee a sovereign nation, responsible for its own affairs and free of the dictates of individual (U.S.) states.

In aiming to create an independent nation, these Cherokee leaders rejected the idea that they should aspire to U.S. citizenship—that they should become equal to white men in their ability to own property, vote, and run for office under the flag of the United States. Rather, they hoped to create their own nation that was equal to the United States, a sovereignty entity that could make its own laws and govern its own people free from outside influence. The Cherokee nation would be neither subject to nor equal to the states, but equal to the United States itself.

By the late 1820s, however, many white people, including the president, were calling for the removal of the Cherokee from the Southeast. The 1829 discovery of gold in the Georgia hills brought 10,000 white miners to Cherokee territory in a gold rush that the Indians called the "Great Intrusion." President Jackson saw the very existence of the Cherokee nation as an affront to his authority and a hindrance to Georgia's economic well-being. He resented the fact that the Cherokee considered themselves a sovereign nation, independent of the U.S. president. Jackson, in fact, favored removing all Indians from the Southeast to make way for whites. He declared that Georgia should be rid of "a few thousand savages" so that "towns and prosperous farms" could develop there. In 1830, with the president's backing, Congress passed the Indian Removal Act. The act provided for "an exchange of lands with the Indians residing in any of the states or territories, and for their removal west of the river Mississippi."

Outraged by this naked land grab, the Cherokee nation refused to sign the removal treaties specified by Congress as part of the Indian Removal Act. In a petition to Congress in 1830, members of the group declared, "We wish to remain on the land of our fathers. We have a perfect and original right to claim this, without interruption or molestation." In an effort to protect their land titles, the Cherokee first tried to take their case to Georgia courts, but Georgia refused to allow them to press their claim. The Georgia legislature maintained that it had authority over all the Indians living within the state's borders and that the Cherokee nation lacked jurisdiction over its own people. The Cherokee nation appealed to the Supreme Court.

The Cherokee hoped that the Supreme Court would support their position that they were an independent entity, not bound by the laws of Georgia. In a set of cases—*Cherokee Nation v. Georgia* (1831) and *Worcester v. Georgia* (1832)—the Court agreed that Georgia's authority did not extend to the Cherokee nation. The Court proclaimed that Indian self-governing bodies were "domestic dependent nations" under the authority of the U.S. government, not the individual states. Under this ruling, Georgia lacked the authority to force Indians from their land. More generally, the states must defer to the federal government in issues related to the welfare and governance of the Indians. The governor of Georgia rejected these Supreme Court rulings, as did Jackson. Of the *Worcester* decision, Jackson declared, "John Marshall has made his decision. Now let him enforce it." In 1832, the president instead sent troops to Georgia to begin forcing the Indians out of their homeland.

Read the Document *Nile's Weekly Register*, "Memorial of the Cherokee Nation" (1830)

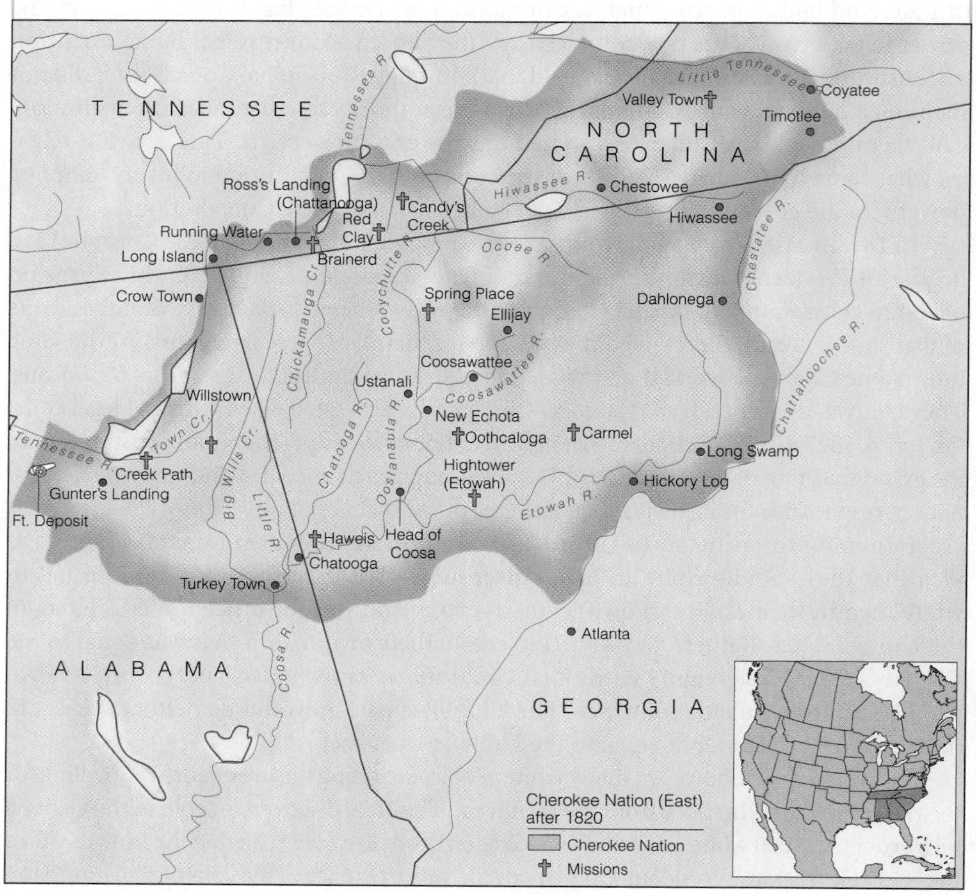

MAP 11.4 THE CHEROKEE NATION AFTER 1820 This map shows the Cherokee nation on the eve of removal to Indian Territory (present-day Oklahoma). The discovery of gold in the region sparked a constitutional battle over control of Cherokee land. In 1832, the Supreme Court ruled that the federal government had ultimate authority over Indian nations. The state of Georgia ignored the ruling and sought to enforce its own laws in Cherokee territory.

The "Tariff of Abominations"

Besides engineering the removal of the Cherokee, Jacksonian Democrats continued the post–War of 1812 policy of high tariffs. In 1828, they pushed through Congress legislation that raised fees on imported manufactured products and raw materials such as wool. Facing a disastrous decline in cotton prices after the Panic of 1819, Southerners protested: to survive, they had to both sell their cotton on the open world market and buy high-priced supplies from New England or Europe. In their view, the higher the tariff on English goods, the less likely the English were to continue to purchase their cotton from southern planters. Southerners dubbed the 1828 legislation the "Tariff of Abominations."

A renewal of the tariff four years later moderated the 1828 rates. But by this time, South Carolina politicians were in no mood to sit back and accept what they saw as the arrogant wielding of federal power. They drew on past precedents in developing a theory called **nullification**—the idea that individual states had the authority to reject, or nullify, specific federal laws. The Virginia and Kentucky Resolutions of 1798 and 1799 and the Hartford Convention of New England states, during the War of 1812, had previously raised this issue of state sovereignty.

Nullification The doctrine that a state has the right to ignore or nullify certain federal laws with which it disagrees.

The nullification crisis began when politicians led by Senator John C. Calhoun met in a convention in 1832 and declared the tariff "null and void" in South Carolina. But Jackson struck back swiftly. In his Nullification Proclamation of December 10, 1832, he argued that states' rights did not include nullification of federal laws or secession from the Union. The president then sent a token military and naval force to South Carolina to intimidate the nullifiers. Henry Clay, now senator from Kentucky, brokered a compromise agreement: a 10 percent reduction in the Tariff of 1832 over a period of eight years. This compromise finally eased tensions, and the South Carolina nullifiers retreated for the time being. However, they continued to maintain "that each state of the Union has the right, whenever it may deem such a course necessary . . . to secede peaceably from the Union."

The "Monster Bank"

A similar struggle unfolded over the power of the federal government regarding a central bank. The repository of federal funds ($10 million), the Bank of the United States in the 1830s had thirty branches and controlled the money supply by dictating how state banks should repay their loans: in paper notes or in currency. As a central (though privately held) institution, the bank also aided economic growth and development by extending loans to commercial enterprises.

In 1832, Jackson vetoed a bill that would have renewed the charter of the Second Bank of the United States, which was due to expire in 1836. Somewhat contradictorily, Jackson claimed to represent the interests of small borrowers such as farmers, but he also advocated hard money (currency in the form of gold or silver, not paper or credit extended by banks). Traditionally, small lenders objected to hard-money policies, which kept the supply of currency low and interest rates for borrowers high. Jackson also objected to the bank's work as a large commercial institution. For example, he blamed the bank for precipitating the Panic and Depression of 1819 by withholding credit from small banks, causing them to recall their loans and, in some cases, fail.

Jackson condemned the bank as a "monster" intent on devouring working people and enriching a few eastern financiers and foreign creditors (a fourth of the bank's holdings were owned by non-U. S. citizens). In his veto message he emphasized the theme that the bank sustained and even deepened insidious forms of inequality among white men. He declared, "It is to be regretted that the rich and powerful too often bend the acts of government to their selfish purposes. Distinctions in society will always exist under every just government. Equality of talents, of education, or of wealth can not be produced by human institutions." He continued: "In the full enjoyment of the gifts of Heaven and the fruits of superior industry, economy, and virtue, every man is equally entitled to protection by law; but when the laws undertake to add to these natural and just advantages artificial distinctions, to grant titles, gratuities, and exclusive privileges, to make the rich richer and the potent more powerful, the humble members of society—the farmers, mechanics, and laborers—who have neither the time nor the means of securing like favors to themselves, have a right to complain of the injustice of their Government." In other words, government existed to promote equality of opportunity—individual achievement accomplished through hard work and ambition. In fact, though, he charged, the bank was making the rich richer and the poor poorer.

By vetoing the bank bill, Jackson angered members of Congress and his own cabinet. They had urged him to recharter the bank because they believed the credit system was necessary for economic progress and expansion. Convinced that Jackson had overextended his reach, his opponents seized on the issue as a sign of the chief executive's political vulnerability. However, Congress upheld Jackson's veto of the Second Bank

TABLE 11.4 THE ELECTION OF 1832

Candidate	Political Party	Popular Vote (%)	Electoral Vote
Andrew Jackson	Democratic	55.0	219
Henry Clay	National Republican	42.4	49
John Floyd	Independent	—	11
William Wirt	Anti-Masonic	2.6	7

(the bank closed when its charter expired in 1836). Nominated for president by the National Republicans in 1832, Henry Clay drew support from merchants who had benefited from Bank of the United States loans and from the sizable contingent of Jackson haters. But Jackson won in a landslide, carrying not only his stronghold, the West, but also the South and substantial parts of New York, Pennsylvania, and New England.

While in office, Jackson used his veto power a total of twelve times. All his predecessors *combined* had used it just ten times. When his opponents finally formed a political party in 1834, they called themselves **Whigs**, after the English antimonarchist party. In choosing this name, their intention was to ridicule "King Andrew." The Whigs opposed the man who had built up the power of the presidency in defiance of Congress and the Supreme Court.

Americans in the "Age of the Common Man"

11.3 How did the work of Indians, free and enslaved African Americans, and women change during the "Age of the Common Man"?

I n the early 1830s, a wealthy Frenchman named Alexis de Tocqueville visited the United States and wrote about the contradictions he saw. In his book *Democracy in America* (published in 1835), Tocqueville noted that the United States lacked the rigid hierarchy of class privilege that characterized European nations. With universal white manhood suffrage, white men could vote and run for office regardless of their class or religion. However, Tocqueville also noted some sore spots in American democratic values and practices. He commented on the plight of groups deprived of the right to vote; their lack of freedom stood out starkly in the otherwise egalitarian society of the United States. He sympathized with the southeastern Indians uprooted from their homelands. He raised the possibility that conflicts between blacks and whites might eventually lead to bloodshed. He even contrasted the situation of young unmarried white women, who seemed so free-spirited, with that of wives, who appeared cautious and dull. He concluded, "In America a woman loses her independence forever in the bonds of matrimony." Tocqueville saw America for what it was: a blend of freedom and slavery, of independence and dependence.

Wards, Workers, and Warriors: Native Americans

Population growth in the United States—and on the borderlands between the United States and Mexican territory—put pressure on Indian societies. Yet different cultural groups responded in different ways to this pressure. Some, like the Cherokee, conformed to European American ways and became sedentary farmers. Others were forced to work for whites. Still others either waged war on white settlements and military forces or retreated farther and farther from European American settlements in the hope of avoiding clashes with the intruders.

Nevertheless, prominent whites continued to denigrate the humanity of all Indians. In the 1820s, Henry Clay claimed that Indians were "essentially inferior to the Anglo-Saxon race ... and their disappearance from the human family will be no great loss to the world." In 1828, the House of Representatives Committee on Indian Affairs surveyed the Indians of the South and concluded that "an Indian cannot work" and that all Indians were lazy and notable for their "thirst for spirituous liquours." According to the committee, when European settlers depleted reserves of wildlife, Indians as a group would cease to exist.

Members of the Cherokee nation bitterly denounced these assertions. "The Cherokees do not live upon the chase [for game]," they pointed out. Neither did

Alexis de Tocqueville (1805–1859) employed the perspective of an outsider to contrast patterns of European social and economic inequality with Americans' widespread belief in equality; one of his observations: "Among a democratic people, where there is no hereditary wealth, every man works to earn a living . . . Labor is held in honor; the prejudice is not against but in its favor." At the same time, Tocqueville believed that a commitment to radical equality could breed materialism and selfish individualism. How did many white Americans reconcile their belief in equality—that "labor is held in honor" —with their support for the institution of slavery?

the Creek, Choctaw, Chickasaw, or Seminole—the other members of the Five Civilized Tribes, so called for their varying degrees of conformity to white people's ways.

In parts of California, Spanish missionaries conquered Indian groups, converted them to Christianity, and then forced them to work in the missions. In missions up and down the California coast, Indians worked as weavers, tanners, shoemakers, bricklayers, carpenters, blacksmiths, and other artisans. Some herded cattle and raised horses. Indian women cooked for the mission, cleaned, and spun wool. They wove cloth and sewed garments.

But even Indians living in or near missions resisted the cultural change imposed by the intruders. Catholic missionaries complained that Indian women such as those of the Chumash refused to learn Spanish. The refusal among some Indians to completely assimilate signaled persistent, deep-seated conflicts between Native groups and incoming settlers. In 1824, a revolt among hundreds of newly converted Indians at the mission La Purísima Concepción north of Santa Barbara revealed a rising militancy among Native peoples.

After the War of 1812, the U.S. government had rewarded some military veterans with land grants in the Old Northwest. Federal agents tried to clear the way for these new settlers by ousting Indians from the area. Overwhelmed by the number of whites, some Indian groups such as the Peoria and Kaskaskia gave up their lands to the interlopers. Others took a stand against the white intrusion. In 1826 and 1827, the Winnebago attacked white families and boat pilots living near Prairie du Chien, Wisconsin. Two years later, the Sauk chief Black Hawk (known to Indians as Ma-ka-tai-me-she-kia-kiak) assembled a coalition of Fox, Winnebago, Kickapoo, and Potawatomi. Emboldened by the prospect of aid from British Canada, they clashed with federal troops and raided farmers' homesteads and miners' camps.

In August 1832, a force of 1,300 U.S. soldiers and volunteers struck back, killing 300 Indian men, women, and children encamped on the Bad Axe River in western Wisconsin. The massacre, the decisive point of what came to be called the Black Hawk War, marked the end of armed Indian resistance north of the Ohio River and east of the Mississippi.

Slaves and Free People of Color

In the 1820s, the small proportion of free blacks within the southern population declined further. Southern whites perceived free blacks, like Indians, as an unwelcome and dangerous presence, especially given the possibility that they would conspire with enslaved people to spark a rebellion. For these reasons, some states began to outlaw

SE·QUO·YAH.

Philadelphia Published by Key & Biddle

Artist Charles Bird King painted this portrait of Sequoyah while the Indian leader was in Washington, D.C., in 1828. Government officials honored him for developing a written form of the Cherokee language. He is wearing a medal presented to him by the Cherokee nation in 1825. He later settled permanently in Sallisaw, in what is today Sequoyah County, Oklahoma. What was the political and cultural significance of this new, written form of the Cherokee language? What was the difference between the goal of Cherokee sovereignty on the one hand, and the ideal of full, equal American citizenship for the Cherokee people on the other?

private manumissions (the practice of individual owners freeing their slaves) and to force free blacks to leave the state altogether.

One free black who inspired such fears was Denmark Vesey. Born on the Danish-controlled Caribbean island of St. Thomas in 1767, Vesey was a literate carpenter as well as a religious leader. In 1799, he won $1,500 in a Charleston, South Carolina, lottery and used some of the money to buy his freedom. In the summer of 1822, a Charleston court claimed to have unearthed evidence of a "diabolical plot" hatched by Vesey together with plantation slaves from the surrounding area.

Yet the historical record strongly suggests that no plot ever existed. Black "witnesses" who feared for their own lives provided inconsistent and contradictory testimony to a panel of judges. Authorities never located any material evidence of a planned uprising, such as stockpiles of weapons. Under fire from other Charleston elites for rushing to judgment, the judges redoubled their efforts to embellish vague rumors of black discontent into a tale of a well-orchestrated uprising and to implicate growing numbers of black people. As a result of the testimony of several slaves, thirty-five black men were hanged and another eighteen were exiled outside the United States. Of those executed, Vesey and twenty-three other men said nothing to support even the vaguest charges of the court.

In the North, some blacks were granted the right to vote after emancipation in the late eighteenth century; however, many of those voting rights were lost in the early nineteenth century. New Jersey (in 1807), Connecticut (1818), New York (1821), and Pennsylvania (1838) all revoked the legislation that had let black men cast ballots. Free northern blacks continued to suffer under a number of legal restrictions. Most were not citizens and therefore perceived themselves as oppressed like the slaves in the South.

A new group of black leaders in the urban North began to link their fate to that of their enslaved brothers and sisters in the South. In Boston, North Carolina–born David Walker published his fiery *Walker's Appeal to the Coloured Citizens of the World* in 1829. Walker called for all blacks to integrate fully into American society, shunning racial segregation whether initiated by whites or by blacks themselves. Reminding his readers of the horrors of the slave trade, he declared that black people were ready to die for freedom: "I give it as a fact, let twelve black men get well armed for battle, and they will kill and put to flight fifty whites."

Northern black leaders disagreed among themselves on the issues of integration and black separatism—for example, whether blacks should create their own schools or press for inclusion in the public educational system. A few leaders favored leaving the country altogether, believing that black people would never find peace and freedom in the United States. Founded by whites in New Jersey in 1817, the American Colonization Society (ACS) paid for a small number of black Americans to settle in Monrovia, later named Liberia, on the west coast of Africa. The ACS drew support from a variety of groups, including whites in the upper South who wanted to free their slaves but believed that blacks and whites could not live in the same country, as well as some slaves and free people of color convinced that colonization would give them a fresh start. A small number of American-born blacks settled in Liberia. However, most black activists rejected colonization. They had been born on American soil, and their forebears had been buried there. Maria Stewart, a black abolitionist and public speaker in Boston, declared, "Before I go [to Africa] the bayonet shall pierce me through."

Northern whites sought to control black people and their movements. Outspoken black men and women such as Walker and Stewart alarmed northern whites who feared that if blacks could claim decent jobs, white people would lose their own jobs. African Americans who worked outdoors as wagon drivers, peddlers, and street sweepers were taunted and in some cases attacked by whites who demanded deference from blacks in public. In October 1824, a mob of white men invaded a black neighborhood in Providence, Rhode Island. They terrorized its residents, destroyed buildings, and left the place "almost entirely in ruins." The catalyst for the riot had come a few days before, when a group of blacks had refused to yield the inside of the sidewalk—a cleaner place to walk—to white passersby.

In the South, whites in 1831 took steps to reinforce the institution of slavery, using both violent and legal means. That year, Nat Turner, an enslaved preacher and mystic,

Interpreting History
Eulalia Pérez Describes HER WORK IN A CALIFORNIA MISSION, 1823

"The **duties** of the **housekeeper** were many."

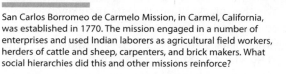

B orn to Spanish parents in Baja California, Eulalia Pérez was a widow with five daughters when she became the chief housekeeper for the San Gabriel Mission in the early 1820s. She secured her position by winning a cooking competition between herself and two other Spanish women. Here she gives an account of her many duties in the mission.

I made several kinds of soup, a variety of meat dishes and whatever else happened to pop into my head that I knew how to prepare. . . .

Because of all this, employment was provided for me at the mission. At first they assigned me two Indians so that I could show them how to cook. . . .

The missionaries were very satisfied; this made them think more highly of me. I spent about a year teaching those two Indians. I did not have to do the work, only direct them, because they already had learned a few of the fundamentals.

After this, the missionaries conferred among themselves and agreed to hand over the mission keys to me. This was in 1821, if I remember correctly. . . .

The duties of the housekeeper were many. In the first place, every day she handed out the rations for the mess hut. To do this she had to count the unmarried women, bachelors, day-laborers, vaqueros [cowboys]. . . . Besides that, she had to hand out daily rations to the heads of households. In short, she was responsible for the distribution of supplies to the Indian population and to the missionaries' kitchen. She was in charge of the key to the clothing storehouse where materials were given out for dresses for the unmarried and married women and children. Then she also had to take care of cutting and making clothes for the men.

Furthermore, she was in charge of cutting and making the vaqueros' outfits, from head to foot—that is, for the vaqueros

San Carlos Borromeo de Carmelo Mission, in Carmel, California, was established in 1770. The mission engaged in a number of enterprises and used Indian laborers as agricultural field workers, herders of cattle and sheep, carpenters, and brick makers. What social hierarchies did this and other missions reinforce?

who rode in saddles. Those who rode bareback received nothing more than their cotton blanket and loin-cloth, while those who rode in saddles were dressed the same way as the Spanish-speaking inhabitants; that is, they were given shirt, vest, jacket, trousers, hat, cowboy boots, shoes and spurs; and a saddle, bridle and lariat for the horse. Besides, each vaquero was given a big silk or cotton handkerchief, and a sash of Chinese silk or Canton crepe, or whatever there happened to be in the storehouse.

They put under my charge everything having to do with clothing. I cut and fitted, and my five daughters sewed up the pieces. When they could not handle everything, the father was told, and then women from the town of Los Angeles were employed, and the father paid them.

Besides this, I had to attend to the soap-house, . . . to the wine-presses, and to the olive-crushers that produced oil, which I worked in myself. . . .

I handled the distribution of leather, calf-skin, chamois, sheep-skin, Morocco leather, fine scarlet cloth, nails, thread, silk, etc.—everything having to do with the making of saddles, shoes and what was needed for the belt- and shoe-making shops.

Every week I delivered supplies for the troops and Spanish-speaking servants. These consisted of beans, corn, garbanzos, lentils, candles, soap and lard. To carry out this distribution, they placed at my disposal an Indian servant named Lucio, who was trusted completely by the missionaries.

When it was necessary, some of my daughters did what I could not find the time to do.

Questions for Discussion

1. What were some of the things produced at the mission?
2. Why did the position of housekeeper confer such high status?
3. What other kinds of workers in the mission does Pérez mention?
4. How does this account reveal some of the larger purposes of Spanish missions? In what ways were these missions colonial as well as religious enterprises?

SOURCE: Eileen Boris and Nelson Lichtenstein, eds., *Major Problems in the History of American Workers*, 2nd ed. (New York: Houghton Mifflin, 2002), 93–95.

led a slave revolt in Southampton, Virginia. In the 1820s, the young Turner had looked skyward and had seen visions of "white spirits and black spirits engaged in battle . . . and blood flowed in streams." Turner believed that he had received divine instructions to lead other slaves to freedom, to "arise and prepare myself, and slay my enemies with their own weapons." In August, he and a group of followers that eventually numbered eighty moved through the countryside, killing whites wherever they could find them. Ultimately, nearly sixty whites died at the hands of Turner's rebels. Turner himself managed to evade capture for more than two months. After he was captured, he was tried, convicted, and executed.

In the wake of the Turner revolt, a wave of white hysteria swept the South. In Virginia, near where the killings had occurred, whites assaulted blacks with unbridled fury. The Virginia legislature seized the occasion to defeat various antislavery proposals. Thereafter, all the slave states moved to strengthen the institution of slavery. For all practical purposes, public debate over slavery ceased throughout the American South.

Legal and Economic Dependence: The Status of Women

Regardless of where they lived, enslaved women and Indian women had almost no rights under either U.S. or Spanish law. However, legal systems in the United States and the Spanish borderlands differed in their treatment of women. In the United States, most of the constraints that white married women had experienced in the colonial period still applied in the 1820s. A husband controlled the property that his wife brought to the marriage, and he had legal authority over their children. Indeed, the wife was considered her husband's possession. She had no right to make a contract, keep money she earned, vote, run for office, or serve on a jury. In contrast, in the Spanish Southwest, married women could own land and conduct business on their own. At the same time, however, husbands, fathers, and local priests continued to exert much influence over the lives of these women.

European American women's economic subordination served as a rationale for their political inferiority. The "common man" concept rested on the assumption that men had the largest stake in society because only they owned property. That stake made them responsible citizens.

Yet women contributed to the economy in myriad ways. For example, almost all adult women worked. In the colonial period, society had highly valued women's labor in the fields, the garden, and the kitchen. However, in the early nineteenth century, work was becoming increasingly identified as labor that earned cash wages. This attitude proved particularly common in the Northeast, where increasing numbers of workers labored under the supervision of a boss. As this belief took root, men began valuing women's contributions to the household economy less and less. If women did not earn money, many men asked, did they really work at all?

In these years, well-off women in the northeastern and mid-Atlantic states began to think of themselves as consumers and not producers of goods. They relied more and more on store-bought cloth and household supplies. Some could also afford to hire servants to perform housework for them. Privileged women gradually stopped thinking of their responsibilities as making goods or processing and preparing food. Rather, their main tasks were to manage servants and create a comfortable home for their husbands and children.

In contrast, women in other parts of the country continued to engage in the same forms of household industry that had characterized the colonial period. In Spanish settlements, women played a central role in household production. They made all of their family's clothes by carding, spinning, and weaving the wool from sheep. They tanned cowhides and ground blue corn to make tortillas, or *atole*. They produced their own candles and soap, and they plastered the walls of the home. In the Spanish mission of San Gabriel, California, the widow Eulalia Pérez cooked, sewed, ministered to the ill, and instructed children in reading and writing. At Mission San Diego, Apolonaria Lorenzana worked as a healer and cared for the church sacristy and priestly vestments.

Indian women also engaged in a variety of essential tasks. Sioux and Mandan women, though of a social rank inferior to men, performed a great deal of manual labor in their own villages. They dressed buffalo skins that the men later sold to traders. They collected water and wood, cooked, dried meat and fruit, and cultivated maize (corn), pumpkins, and squash with hoes made from the shoulder blades of elk. These women worked collectively within a network of households, rather than individually within nuclear families.

Some women worked for cash wages during this era. New England women and children, for example, were the vanguard of factory wage-earners in the early manufacturing system. In Massachusetts in 1820, women and children constituted almost a third of all manufacturing workers. In the largest textile factories, they made up fully 80 percent of the workforce.

The business of textile manufacturing took the tasks of spinning thread and weaving cloth out of the home and relocated those tasks in factories. The famous "Lowell mill girls" are an apt example. Young, unmarried white women from New Hampshire, Vermont, and Massachusetts, these workers moved to the new company town of Lowell, Massachusetts, to take jobs as textile machine operatives. In New England, thousands of young men had migrated west, tipping the sex ratio in favor of women and creating a reserve of female laborers. But to attract young women to factory work, mill owners had to reassure them (and their parents) that they would be safe and well cared for away from home. To that end, they established boarding houses where employees could live together under the supervision of a matron—an older woman who served as their mother-away-from-home. Many young women valued the friendships they made with their co-workers and the money they made in the mills. Some of these women sent their wages back home so that their fathers could pay off the mortgage or their brothers could attend school.

Most ordinary women received little in the way of formal education. Yet elite young women had expanded educational opportunities, beginning in the early nineteenth century. Emma Willard founded a female academy in Troy, New York, in 1821, and Catharine Beecher established the Hartford (Connecticut) Female Seminary two years later. For the most part, such schools catered to the daughters of wealthy families, young women who would never have to work in a factory to survive. Hailed as a means to prepare young women to serve as wives and mothers, the schools taught geography, foreign languages, mathematics, science, and philosophy, as well as the "female" pursuits of embroidery and music.

Out of this curriculum designed especially for women emerged women's rights activists, women who keenly felt both the potential of their own intelligence and the degrading nature of their social situation. Elizabeth Cady, an 1832 graduate of the Troy Female Seminary, later went on to marry Henry B. Stanton and bear seven children. But by the 1840s, she strode onto the national stage as a tireless advocate of women's political and economic rights.

Ties That Bound a Growing Population

11.4 In what ways did Americans maintain a sense of community in the face of unprecedented migration and population growth?

As the nation expanded westward, population growth and migration patterns disrupted old bonds of community. When people left their place of birth, they often severed ties with their family and original community. New forms of social cohesion arose to replace these traditional ties. New religions sought to make sense of the changing political and economic landscape. High literacy rates among the population created a new community of readers—a dispersed audience for periodicals as well as for a new, uniquely American literature. Finally, opinion makers used the printed word to spread new ideas and values across regional boundaries. These ideas, such as glorification of male ambition, helped knit together far-flung segments of the population, men and women who began to speak of an "American character."

New Visions of Religious Faith

New forms of religious faith arose in response to turbulent times. During the Indian Wars in the Old Northwest, a Winnebago prophet named White Cloud helped Black Hawk create a **coalition** of Winnebago, Potawatomi, Kickapoo, Sauk, and Fox Indians. A mystic and medicine man, White Cloud preached against white people and exhorted

Coalition An alliance of parties, factions, or nations.

his followers to defend their way of life, an Indian way that knew no tribal boundaries. White Cloud, the religious leader, and Black Hawk, the military leader, surrendered together to federal troops on August 27, 1832, their alliance signifying the spiritual component in the Indians' militant resistance to whites. Through the rest of the nineteenth century, a number of Indian groups found inspiration, and in some cases common ground, in the teachings of Indian religious leaders.

New religious enthusiasms took hold in other parts of the country as well. In the late 1820s and early 1830s, the **Second Great Awakening** swept western New York. The fervor of religious revivals so heated the region that people began to call it "the Burned-Over District." Huge crowds of people of various Protestant denominations attended week-long prayer meetings, sat together on the "anxious bench" for sinners, and listened, transfixed, as new converts told of their path to righteousness.

What explains this wave of religious enthusiasm? A major factor was a clergyman named Charles Grandison Finney, who managed to tap into the wellspring of hope and anxiety of the time. A former lawyer, Finney preached that people were moral free agents, fully capable of deciding between right and wrong and doing good in the world. Finney's message had great appeal during this period of rapid social, economic, and technological change. In New England and New York, for example, canals were bringing new kinds of goods to rural areas and longtime residents were departing for the Midwest. Traditional social relationships seemed threatened.

Throughout the country, religious institutions also grappled with questions about slavery. As the fear of possible black uprisings spread, white clergy in the South began to turn away from their former willingness to convert anyone. Instead, they began seeking respectability in the eyes of the well-to-do, slave-owning class. Incorporating masculine imagery into their sermons, they strove to reinforce the power of husband over wife, parent over child, and master over slave, relations that defined the typical plantation household. Nevertheless, even southern denominations had to acknowledge a core tension in their beliefs—the Christian idea that all people were equal in the eyes of God seemed at odds with the persistent subordination of enslaved men and women. The Reverend Charles Colcock Jones, a Presbyterian minister in Liberty County, Georgia, advocated missionary work among slaves but ran into opposition from his fellow slaveholders, who worried that Christianizing black people would inspire among them dangerous views of equality. Jones acknowledged, "The feelings of men being excited, those who had undertaken the religious instruction of the Negroes were looked upon with suspicion and some of them were obliged to quit the field. It was not considered that a separation might be made between the *religious* and the *civil* condition and interests of a people; and that a minister could confine himself to the one without interfering at all with the other."

Elsewhere, some church leaders sought to purge Christianity of what they saw as its too-worldly nature and to revive the early, simple church that Jesus and his disciples had established. On April 6, 1830, a young farmer named Joseph Smith founded the Church of Jesus Christ of Latter-Day Saints (also called the Mormons) in Fayette, New York. Smith said that, in a vision, an angel named Moroni presented him with the text of a holy book originally written by a Native American historian more than 1,400 years earlier. The text was called the *Book of Mormon*. Together with the Old and New Testaments, it formed the basis of a new faith. Over the next few years, the Mormon Church grew rapidly, claiming 8,000 members by the mid-1830s. However, the young church also aroused intense hostility among mainstream Protestant denominations that regarded the new group's theology and textual inspiration with suspicion. It was almost impossible for religious institutions to escape the worldly realm of politics and social fragmentation.

Literate and Literary America

Around the same time, a young widow named Sarah Hale broke new ground for women. In 1821, she became the first woman to edit an American periodical when she accepted responsibility for editing the Boston-based *Ladies Magazine*, later renamed *Godey's Lady's Book*. Once a hat maker but now a published poet and novelist, Hale

Second Great Awakening A series of Protestant religious revivals that began in the 1790s and continued through the 1820s. Prominent revivalists such as Charles Grandison Finney sought to link the life of the spirit with political action and reform efforts.

portrayed women as especially devout and thus powerful: men might claim as their domain "the government and the glory of the world," she wrote in 1832, "but nevertheless, what man shall become depends upon the secret, silent influence of women." That influence, Hale and other men and women like her believed, derived from women's roles as nurturers and caretakers. Thousands of similar magazines—most short-lived—appeared between 1825 and 1850.

Just as sentimental fiction and poetry attracted a large readership among women, a number of male writers staked their claim to emerging American literature. Washington Irving, James Fenimore Cooper, and William Cullen Bryant all explored regional histories and landscapes in their works. In *Rip Van Winkle* (1819) and the *Legend of Sleepy Hollow* (1820), Irving wrote about the legends of upstate New York. Cooper explored the western New York middle ground contested by the British, Americans, French, and Indians in the late eighteenth century in such works as *The Spy* (1821) and *The Last of the Mohicans* (1826). Bryant, inspired by the sight of the Illinois plains in 1832, penned "The Prairies," a praise-song to the vast plains as beautiful and "quick with life."

Along with this new American literary tradition, small towns across the nation began publishing newspapers to educate, inform, and entertain readers. News stories about national elections and legislation, about foreign monarchs and conflicts, reached log cabins in the West as well as elegant townhouses in Boston and Philadelphia. Wrote Washington Irving in 1820, "Over no nation does the press hold a more absolute control than over the people of America, for the universal education of the poorest classes makes every individual a reader." Widely distributed newspapers, books, and magazines promoted a set of values that writers claimed described an enduring American character. The ideal American supposedly was ambitious—ready to seize opportunity wherever it could be found—and at the same time devoted to home and family. In fact, these values strongly resembled those adopted by the British middle classes during this period. Indeed, the United States spawned its own brand of middle-class sensibility called Victorianism, after the English queen who reigned from 1837 to 1901.

Five core values defined early American Victorianism. First, the Victorians believed in the significance of the individual. People should be judged on the basis of their character, not on the circumstances of their birth. This belief, however, generally applied only to white men. Second, individuals should have the freedom to advance as far as their talents and ambition took them; no person should claim advantages over others by virtue of a noble title or aristocratic lineage. Third, work was intrinsically noble, whether performed by a canal digger wielding a pick-axe or a merchant using a quill pen. All people, regardless of their trade, deserved to reap the fruits of their labor. Fourth, everyone should exercise self-control and restraint in activities such as drinking and engaging in sexual relations. Finally, men and women occupied separate but complementary spheres. American society could be orderly and stable only if men could find a haven from the heartless world of work in their own homes. There, wives tended the hearth and infused the household with their love, self-sacrifice, and religious devotion.

These core values of American Victorianism had far-reaching implications, and in certain respects unanticipated consequences, for the way middle-class people thought and talked about equality. The notion that individuals must be judged on their merits alone and not on the circumstances of their birth challenged the legal subordination of whole groups of people, including women, blacks, and Indians. The inherent nobility of productive labor seemed to suggest that the job a person did was less important than the pride and skill with which he or she performed it: Why then should the conscientious domestic servant be deemed inferior to the careless factory foreman? Too, the conscience served as an equalizing force within each person—the emotional force that pulled everyone in the same direction—toward righteous behavior. And finally, complementary spheres between men and women highlighted their different roles in society but also revealed that neither gender was better than the other; men and women were equally worthy of respect, equally necessary to a well-functioning family and well-ordered society. In the coming years, the ironies and contradictions of Victorian ideology would cause seismic shocks through all of the United States.

In this portrait of the Rev. John Atwood and his family, painted by the artist Henry F. Darby in 1845, family members are reading the Bible. What do the parlor furnishings tell us about this family? How many Bibles are in evidence? In some households, no doubt, the father read from the Bible to assembled family members. What does this scene tell us about relations among family members? What can we infer about the family's religious practices? Does this family portrait reveal competing ideals about equality in antebellum (pre-Civil War) America?

Conclusion

Western settlement infused American politics with raw energy in the 1820s. Andrew Jackson was the first in a long line of presidents who boasted of their humble origins and furthered their careers by denouncing what they called the privileges enjoyed by wealthy Easterners. The challenges faced by western settlers in establishing homesteads and paying their debts emerged as national, not purely local, issues. Through the sheer force of his personality, Andrew Jackson exemplified these dramatic changes in the political landscape. Almost single-handedly, he extended the limits of executive power and remade the American party system in the process.

At the same time, the contradictions in Jacksonian politics became ever more glaring. As the nation expanded its borders and diversified its economy, distinctions between social classes sharpened. The country also staked its claim to foreign territory, using violence to advance democratic values. Meanwhile, the North and South eyed each other with increasing distrust. And the contrast between those who moved from place to place voluntarily and those who were forced to move became even more striking.

Chapter Review

The Politics Behind Western Expansion

11.1 How did western expansion affect the nation's politics and economy in the 1820s? p. 267

Westward expansion provoked a national debate over the spread of slavery. New turnpikes and canals facilitated migration, which in turn spurred trade, the growth of the cotton economy, land speculation, and indebtedness among homesteaders. The United States sought to protect and expand its territory in opposition to European powers.

Federal Authority and Its Opponents

11.2 What were President Andrew Jackson's controversial views on the role of the federal government and the role of the Chief Executive? p. 276

Defying the Supreme Court, Jackson supported the forcible removal of southeastern Indians to western territory. Defying South Carolina politicians, he took a strong stand against the idea of nullification. Defying Congress, he vetoed the renewal of the charter of the Second Bank of the United States.

Americans in the "Age of the Common Man"

11.3 How did the work of Indians, free and enslaved African Americans, and women change during the "Age of the Common Man"? p. 280

The disappearance of Native hunting grounds forced Indian groups to alter their traditional patterns of work. African Americans suffered as a result of the expansion of the cotton economy and whites' fears of possible slave rebellions. As the vanguard of the Industrial Revolution, some white women took jobs as factory workers.

Ties That Bound a Growing Population

11.4 In what ways did Americans maintain a sense of community in the face of unprecedented migration and population growth? p. 286

New reform associations and new religions emerged to create new communities. High literacy rates produced readers of newspapers, books, magazines, and a national literature that extolled "the American character." Groups of men and women in various parts of the country were bound together by Victorian values.

Timeline

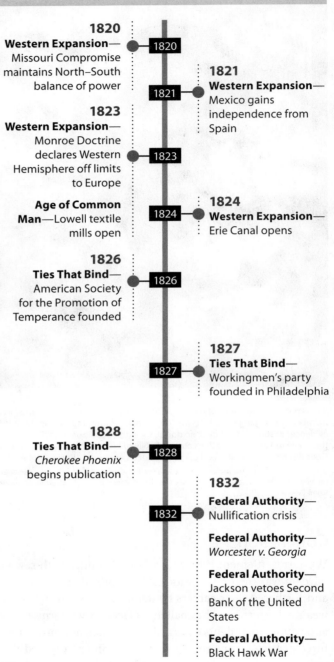

1820
Western Expansion—Missouri Compromise maintains North–South balance of power
`1820`

`1821`
1821
Western Expansion—Mexico gains independence from Spain

1823
Western Expansion—Monroe Doctrine declares Western Hemisphere off limits to Europe
`1823`

Age of Common Man—Lowell textile mills open
`1824`
1824
Western Expansion—Erie Canal opens

1826
Ties That Bind—American Society for the Promotion of Temperance founded
`1826`

`1827`
1827
Ties That Bind—Workingmen's party founded in Philadelphia

1828
Ties That Bind—*Cherokee Phoenix* begins publication
`1828`

`1832`
1832
Federal Authority—Nullification crisis

Federal Authority—*Worcester v. Georgia*

Federal Authority—Jackson vetoes Second Bank of the United States

Federal Authority—Black Hawk War

12 Peoples in Motion, 1832–1848

Why would a young woman journey from Scandinavia to America's rural Midwest to work as a domestic servant? Would the opportunities in the land of plenty outweigh all of the hardships?

This young woman was called Jannicke Saehle. In the spring of 1847, she left her home in Bergen, a city on the western coast of Norway, and boarded a ship bound for New York City. By the summer, she had settled in Koshkonong, Wisconsin, a rapidly growing settlement of Norwegian immigrants farming the fertile prairie. Saehle was eager to make a new life for herself in America. In September 1847, she wrote of her good fortune in a letter to her family back in Norway, describing "the superabundance of food" in her new home.

Indeed, Saehle conveyed the great opportunity that awaited immigrants to America through her detailed description of the tasty meals she was now enjoying. Working as a servant in a tavern, she had "food and drink in abundance," and dined on the same fare served to the guests; for breakfast, "chicken, mutton [lamb], beef, or pork, warm or cold wheat bread, butter, white cheese, eggs, or small

A family of Norwegian immigrants to the United States in the 1880s poses outside their wooden cabin. Many immigrants lived in modest circumstances but hoped that they would eventually prosper in their new home. Newcomers sought to take advantage of the country's cheap and abundant land, free public-school system, and tradition of religious freedom so that they and their children could partake fully and equally in American life, alongside native-born citizens. What resources might these immigrants have possessed to manage a move from faraway Norway?

LEARNING OBJECTIVES

12.1 ((•
What caused some groups to migrate voluntarily? Why were others forced to move against their will? p. 293

12.2 ((•
Why did debates over the rights (or lack thereof) of workers, slaves, and immigrants lead to the rise of new political organizations? p. 300

12.3 ((•
What were the major reform movements of the 1830s and 1840s? What were the various strategies used by reformers to effect social change? p. 305

12.4 ((•
Why was seizing the land that would become the state of Texas so important to so many Americans? p. 309

((• Listen to Chapter 12 on MyHistoryLab

👁 Watch the Video Series on MyHistoryLab

Learn about some key topics related to this chapter with the *MyHistoryLab Video Series: Key Topics in U.S. History.*

1 **Manifest Destiny Marches West: 1832–1858** This video addresses topics associated with the westward migration of diverse groups of people—foreign immigrants as well as eastern migrants—across the nineteenth-century American landscape. It includes discussion of manifest destiny as a justification for seizing Indian lands. All groups found that moving across the continent was an arduous undertaking.

👁 Watch on **MyHistoryLab**

The Oregon Trail Focusing on the Oregon Trail, this video describes the overland routes of migration among non-Native settlers of the West. Settlers traveled in wagon trains or smaller groups. Among the challenges they faced were the hostility of Native Americans, harsh terrain and unpredictable weather, and a constant struggle to locate food and water. **2**

Watch on **MyHistoryLab** 👁

3 **War with Mexico** The United States went to war with Mexico in January 1846. Over the next two years, the United States conducted a series of successful military campaigns to claim a huge amount of territory from Mexico.

👁 Watch on **MyHistoryLab**

Treaty of Guadalupe Hidalgo This video discusses the peace treaty between the United States and Mexico that ended the U.S.-Mexican War (1846–1848). Mexico ceded its claim to Texas and the United States extended its boundaries into territories that comprised what is now New Mexico, Arizona, Utah, Nevada, and California. **4**

Watch on **MyHistoryLab** 👁

pancakes, the best coffee, tea, cream and sugar." For supper, she feasted on "warm biscuits, and several kinds of cold wheat bread, cold meats, bacon, cakes, preserved apples, plums, and berries, which are eaten with cream." Saehle felt heartbroken to see excess food thrown to the chickens and pigs, for, she wrote, "I think of my dear ones in Bergen, who like so many others must at this time lack the necessaries of life."

Jannicke Saehle was one of the more than 13,000 immigrants from Norway, Sweden, and Denmark who arrived in the United States in the 1840s. Patterns of settlement and employment among immigrant groups varied widely. For example, while many Scandinavians settled in the rural Midwest, most Irish immigrants lacked the resources to move much further west than the eastern seaboard ports where they landed.

D uring this period, the United States was home to many peoples in motion. Some migrants and immigrants traveled long distances eager to take advantage of the demand for labor, the promise of religious freedom, or abundant fertile farmland. In contrast, groups of Indians in the Southeast and Midwest and slaves in the upper South were forced at gunpoint to move from one region of the country to another.

Population movements and economic change generated new forms of group identity. Reformers embraced a variety of strategies in order to achieve what they considered improvements in American society—a public school system, rights for women, the abolition of slavery. In politics, the so-called Second Party system had emerged by 1836, as Jacksonian Democrats squared off against the Whigs on familiar issues, including tariffs and new systems of transportation.

To Jannicke Saehle, the United States was a place where no one need go hungry. Yet some Americans saw not a bounteous land for all, but a site of conflict among various groups, and turned to violence to advance their causes. Within the larger society, physical force seemed to be an acceptable means of both resolving disputes and expanding the nation's boundaries.

Mass Migrations

12.1 What caused some groups to migrate voluntarily? Why were others forced to move against their will?

When foreign visitors called Americans a "restless" people, they were referring to patterns of both immigration to and migration within the country. Between 1830 and 1850, 2.3 million immigrants entered the United States, up from a total of 152,000 during the two previous decades. Most newcomers came from Ireland, Germany, England, Scotland, and Scandinavia. In the United States itself, individuals and families moved around the country with almost dizzying frequency in search of better jobs. They migrated from rural to urban areas, from one city to another, out West and then back to the East. In the late 1840s, almost half of all urban residents moved within a twelve-month period. For the country as a whole, an estimated one family in five moved every year, and on average, every family moved once every five years. Many westward migrants had enough money to move overland and buy a homestead once they arrived in Wisconsin or Oregon. However, much of the population turnover in urban areas stemmed from landless people's relentless quest for higher wages and cheaper places to rent.

Some people moved because other people forced them to—under the crack of a whip and in manacles. Slave traders in the upper South transported thousands of enslaved men, women, and children to the lower South for sale "on the block." U.S. soldiers forced Indians to walk from their homelands in the southeast to Indian Territory (now the state of Oklahoma). In the less-settled West, however, older identities of race and ethnicity sometimes gave way to new identities forged from mixed cultures.

Europeans marveled at Americans' apparent willingness to search out new opportunities. But to some Americans, moving meant the death of dreams and the loss of hope for a better life.

Newcomers from Western Europe

During this period, hardships in western Europe led to increased immigration to the United States, especially from Ireland and the German states. For the long-suffering people of Ireland, life had become more precarious than ever by the early nineteenth century. Over the generations, small farm plots had been subdivided among heirs to the point that most holdings consisted of fewer than 15 acres each. At the same time, the population of Ireland had grown exponentially—to more than 4 million people in 1800. England treated Ireland like a colony that existed purely for the economic gain of the mother country (or, in the eyes of the Irish, an occupying power). A series of English laws and policies mandated that farmers export most of the island's grain and cattle, leaving the impoverished people to subsist mainly on a diet of potatoes.

Then, beginning in 1845, a blight devastated the potato crop. In the next five years, 1 million people died. Under the weight of imperious British rule, the Irish people seemed destined for poverty and political oppression. John Mitchel, an Irish nationalist and critic of English rule, linked Irish economic hardship (and the famine in particular) to British policies that deprived the Irish of food other than potatoes. Mitchel objected to British pronouncements that the famine was an act of God. He declared, "But potatoes failed in like manner all over Europe, yet there was no famine save in Ireland. The British account of the matter, then, is, first a fraud; second a blasphemy. The Almighty, indeed, sent the potato blight, but the English created the famine." In 1845, the great Irish migration began. Between 1845 and 1850, 1 million people fled to the United States.

Large numbers of poor Irish had settled in the United States even before the potato famine of the mid-1840s. In the 1820s, about 50,000 such immigrants arrived; the following decade saw a spike in numbers to more than 200,000. Then as the 1840s and 1850s unfolded, 1.7 million Irish men, women, and children emigrated to the United States. This exodus continued over the next century as more than 4.5 million Irish arrived.

By the 1870s, the Irish constituted fully 20 percent of the population of New York City, 14 percent of Philadelphia, and 22 percent of Boston (the "hub of Gaelic America"). Most Irish immigrants remained along the eastern seaboard, since they lacked the resources to move farther inland. The newcomers quickly formed mutual aid associations and other community organizations. In cities across America, the Sisters of Mercy, a Roman Catholic order founded in Dublin, established homes to provide lodging for single women and day nurseries for the children of working mothers.

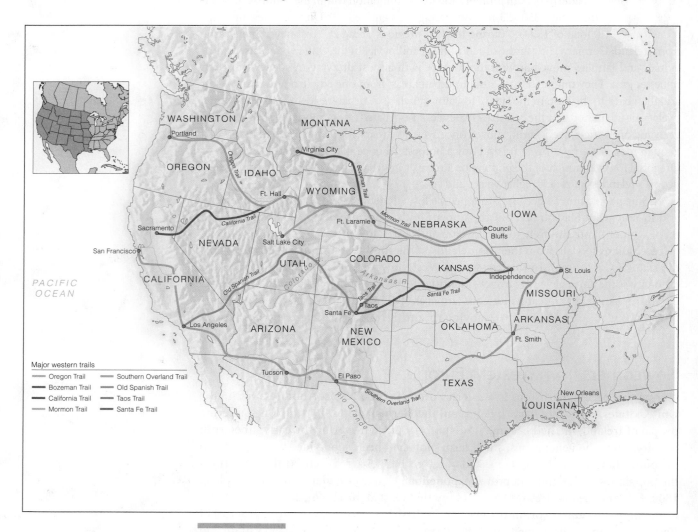

MAP 12.1 WESTERN TRAILS This map shows the major trails followed by western emigrants in the nineteenth century. Settlers endured long and dangerous journeys. For example, beginning at Independence, Missouri, and stretching to Portland, Oregon, the Overland Trail was 2,000 miles long. Covering the entire trail could take four to six months. Wagon trains had to traverse rocky terrain, scale mountains, and ford rivers. Along the way, outposts such as Fort Laramie and Fort Hall gave travelers a chance to refresh their supplies, rest their livestock, and repair their wagons. Though resentful of such incursions, Indians rarely attacked large wagon trains.

The Irish newcomers soon realized that their struggle against poverty, discrimination, and religious persecution would not end in the United States. The arrival of large numbers of Irish immigrants in the 1830s threatened the jobs of native-born Protestants, who reacted with resentment and violence. Employers posted signs outside their doors reading "No Irish Need Apply." Despised for their Roman Catholicism and their supposed clannishness, the Irish competed with African Americans for the low-paying jobs at the bottom of the economic ladder. In 1834, a mob destroyed the Ursuline convent in Charlestown, near Boston, after terrifying the women and children residents and ransacking the building.

Nevertheless, by the 1850s, the Irish had gained a measure of influence. They filled many high positions in the U.S. Catholic Church and became active in the Democratic party. They believed that their white skin entitled them to distance themselves from blacks and lay claim to full American citizenship.

The hardship endured by the Irish in the early nineteenth century mirrored the political and economic distress of many other people living in Europe at the time. In the revolutions of 1848 in France, the German states, the Austrian Empire, and parts of Italy, people struck out against monarchy and called for constitutional government. The Germans immigrated in especially dramatic numbers, with more than half a million arriving in the United States between 1831 and 1850. Those numbers exploded in the next few decades, as a failed uprising against the authoritarian Prussian state in 1848 led many German intellectuals, farmers, and workers to flee the region. Across western Europe, rising unemployment and dramatic population increases made food scarce in both rural and urban areas, further stimulating immigration across the Atlantic.

The Slave Trade

Forced migration of enslaved workers increased during this period as the slave trade became big business. Many wealthy traders made regular trips between the upper and lower South. Traders transported men, women, and children by boat down the eastern seaboard or down the Mississippi River or chained and forced them to walk as much as 20 miles a day for seven or eight weeks at a time. Eventually, slaves stood on the block in the markets of New Orleans, Natchez, Charleston, and Savannah, where white men inspected them for health, strength, and compliance.

Between 1800 and 1860, the average price of slaves quadrupled, revealing a growing demand for bound labor. As many as one out of every ten slave children in the upper South was sold to the lower South (many to cotton planters) between 1820 and 1860. Slave households in Virginia bore the brunt of these forced separations. There, an estimated three-quarters of the people sold never saw their spouse, parents, or children again.

It was sometimes worse if they did. Moses Grandy, standing on a sidewalk one day, saw his wife in chains, in a coffle passing by. He recalled the scene in his 1844 autobiography:

> Mr. Rogerson was with them on his horse, armed with pistols. I said to him, "For God's sake, have you bought my wife?" He said he had; when I asked him what she had done, he said she had done nothing, but that her master wanted money. He drew out a pistol and said that if I went near the wagon where she was, he would shoot me. I asked for leave to shake hands with her which he refused, but said I might stand at a distance and talk with her. My heart was so full that I could say very little. . . . I have never seen or heard from her from that day to this. I loved her as I love my life.

Voluntary migrations of African Americans formed the counterpoint of the slave trade as runaways and free people of color made their way out of the old slave states. An estimated 50,000 enslaved workers tried to escape each year, but few made it to the North and freedom. Some southern free people of color headed to northern cities. By 1850, more than half of all Boston blacks had been born outside Massachusetts.

Of those migrants, about one-third had been born in the South, most in Virginia, Maryland, and the District of Columbia. Slave runaways who lived in fear of their safety and their lives eluded census takers, but by mid-century as many as 600 fugitives lived in Boston.

Regardless of their place of origin, many migrants took up residence with other blacks, who helped ease the newcomers' transition to city life. These boarding arrangements strengthened ties between the enslaved and the free communities. For example, when authorities arrested the runaway George Latimer in Boston in 1842, free blacks in that city took immediate action. They posted signs condemning the police as "human kidnappers." Some tried to wrench him physically from his captors. Still others sponsored protest meetings in the local African Baptist Church and made common cause with white lawyers sympathetic to abolition. Finally, a group of blacks and whites raised enough money to buy Latimer from his owner and free him.

Meanwhile, throughout the urban North, whites began eyeing blacks' jobs. Irish immigrants in particular desperately sought work. Skilled black workers found it increasingly difficult to ply their trades as cooks, hotel and boat stewards, porters, brick makers, and barbers. In 1838, 656 black artisans in Philadelphia reported that they had to abandon their work because white customers would no longer patronize them. White factory owners in Philadelphia preferred white laborers. In that same city, a bustling site of machine shops and textile factories, almost no blacks did industrial labor of any kind. For black people, freedom from slavery did not guarantee equality with white people in jobs or political influence.

Trails of Tears

Like enslaved blacks, many Indians were forced to migrate. Throughout the 1830s, the U.S. government pursued the policy of removing Indians from the Southeast by treaty or by force. The 1832 Treaty of Payne's Landing, negotiated by the Seminole Indians and James Gadsden, a representative of Secretary of War Lewis Cass, aimed to force the Seminole out of Florida and into Indian Territory (present-day Oklahoma). The federal government promised to give individual Indians cash, plus blankets for the men and dresses for the women, in exchange for their lands. Government authorities also hoped to recapture the large number of runaway slaves who had sought refuge in Seminole villages, deep in the swamps of central Florida.

Three years later, many of the Indians had departed for the West. But a small number withdrew deeper into the Everglades and held their ground. They were led by a young man named Osceola, who with his followers waged a **guerrilla war** (based on ambush tactics) against better-armed U.S. troops. Osceola's resistance, called the Second Seminole War, dragged on for seven years. Eventually, the government forced 3,000 Seminole to move West, but not until it had spent $20 million, and 1,500 U.S. soldiers had lost their lives.

Guerrilla war A conflict fought not on the basis of conventional warfare but, rather, by mobilizing small groups of fighters who attack and harass superior forces.

The Choctaw of the southern Alabama–Mississippi region, the Chickasaw directly to the north of them, the Creek in central Georgia and Alabama, and the Cherokee of north Georgia suffered the same fate in the 1830s. The Creek remained bitterly divided among themselves on the issue of removal, as did the Cherokee. Major Ridge, his son John Ridge, and Elias Boudinot, leaders of a new political group called the Treaty party of the Cherokee nation, urged their people to give up their homeland and rebuild their nation in the West. John Ross and others like him opposed the Ridges and Boudinot. The Cherokee must remain in Georgia at all costs, Ross insisted. He claimed that he spoke for a majority of Cherokee. To silence him, the U.S. government threw him in prison. Then it concluded negotiations with the Treaty party, which agreed to sell Cherokee land to the federal government for $5 million. Elias Boudinot said, "We can die, but the great Cherokee Nation will be saved." Within a few years, the Ridges and Boudinot died at the hands of anti–Treaty party Cherokee assassins.

In 1838, General Winfield Scott, with 7,000 troops under his command, began rounding up the citizens of the Cherokee nation. U.S. troops held men, women, and

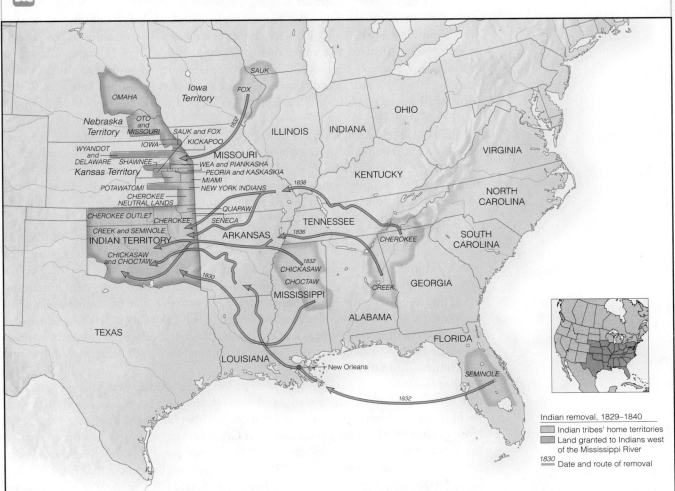

MAP 12.2 INDIAN REMOVAL This map shows the routes of forced migration of the Five Civilized Tribes in the 1830s. By the 1870s, several groups of Plains Indians, including the Cheyenne, Arapaho, Comanche, and Kiowa, had joined them in Indian Territory (present-day Oklahoma).

children in concentration camps before forcing them to march west. During the period from 1838 to 1839, nearly 16,000 Indians were forced by federal authorities to make a journey from their homeland in the Southeast to western territory. The Indians called this journey the Trail on Which We Cried, also known as the **Trail of Tears**. Four thousand of them died of malnutrition and disease in the course of the 116-day forced march. Federal troops confiscated or destroyed the material basis of Cherokee culture: sawmills, cotton gins, barns, homes, spinning wheels, meetinghouses, flocks, herds, and the printing press used to publish the *Cherokee Phoenix*. They often forcibly separated families. A soldier who participated in the operation saw children "separated from their parents and driven into the stockade with the sky for a blanket and the earth for a pillow."

U.S. officials claimed that troops had carried out the removal with "great judgment and humanity." However, an internal government report completed in 1841 revealed that the United States had reneged on even its most basic treaty promises: "Bribery, perjury, and forgery, short weights, issues of spoiled meat and grain, and every conceivable subterfuge was employed by designing white men." Many government agents seized goods such as blankets and food intended for Indians and sold these goods for profit. Military authorities suppressed the report, and the public never saw it.

Trail of Tears The name Cherokee Indians gave to their forced removal from the Southeast to the West in 1838 and 1839 as part of the federal government's Indian removal policy. During the journey, U.S. troops destroyed the material basis of Cherokee culture and separated many families; over 4,000 Indians died.

Migrants in the West

For many native-born migrants seeking a new life west of the Mississippi, the road proved neither smooth nor easy. For example, as the Mormon community moved west from New York, it met with religious persecution. The founder of the church, Joseph Smith, aroused the anger of his neighbors in Nauvoo, Illinois. They took alarm at the Nauvoo Legion, a military company formed to defend the Mormon community. They also heard rumors (for the most part true) that Smith and other Mormon leaders engaged in plural marriage or polygamy, allowing men to marry more than one wife.

In 1844, the Nauvoo Legion destroyed the printing press owned by a group of rebellious church members who objected to what they considered Smith's authoritarian tactics. Civil authorities charged Smith and his brother Hyrum with the destruction of private property and arrested and jailed the two men in the nearby town of Carthage. In June 1844, an angry mob of non-Mormons broke into the jail and lynched the brothers.

By 1847, Brigham Young, who had inherited the mantle of leadership from Smith, determined that the Mormons could not remain in Illinois. He feared, rightly, that non-Mormons, whether citizens or civil officials, would not accord the new religion the respect and protection enjoyed by other older, mainstream religious denominations. Migrants, some of them pushing handcarts loaded with personal belongings, set out for the West. By 1852, 10,000 Mormons had settled in Salt Lake City in what is present-day Utah. With their large numbers and church-inspired discipline, the community prospered. They created an effective irrigation system and turned the desert into a thriving agricultural community.

But the Mormons had not settled an uninhabited wilderness. Around Salt Lake, Canadian trappers, Paiute Indians, and Spanish speakers from New Mexico crossed paths, some to hunt, others to gather roots and berries, herd sheep, or trade captives. A Christmas dinner celebrated near Great Salt Lake around this time revealed the multicultural mix of western life. The dinner guests included a Maine-born trader, a Frenchman married to a Flathead woman, and various other intermarried Cree, Snake, and Nez Perce Indians. The group feasted on the meat of elk and deer, a flour pudding, cakes, and strong coffee. After the meal, the women cleared the table. The men smoked pipes and then went outside and conducted target practice with their guns.

European Americans also migrated to the Northwest during this period. Protestant missionaries initially settled Oregon beginning in 1834. But in contrast to the Mormons, these northwestern colonists found themselves in the midst of hostile Native Americans. One young doctor and his wife from western New York, Marcus and Narcissa Whitman, established a mission near present-day Walla Walla, Washington. More than a thousand more emigrants from the East followed the Whitmans to Oregon during the "Great Migration" of 1843.

The U.S. government aided this westward movement when it commissioned its Topographical Corps of Engineers to survey the Oregon Trail. That task fell to an expedition headed by John Charles Frémont in 1843–1844. The expedition's final report had immense practical value for the emigrants, for it mapped the way west and provided crucial information about pasture, sources of water, and climate.

Some settlers established successful homesteads in Oregon, but the settlements founded by missionaries were fragile affairs. Discouraged and overwhelmed by homesickness, Narcissa Whitman eagerly awaited copies of the latest *Mothers' Magazine* sent to her by female relatives in the East. After 1843, the influx of newcomers brought her some consolation but also brought outbreaks of measles, to which the Native Americans had no immunity. An ensuing epidemic among the Cayuse claimed many lives. In 1847, blaming the missionaries for the deaths of their people, several Indians attacked the Whitman mission, killing twelve whites, including Narcissa and Marcus Whitman.

This picture of the Whitman mission at Waiilatpu, Oregon, in 1845 shows the missionaries' house on the left, a mill in the background, a blacksmith shop in the right center, and a gathering place for worshippers on the far right. By this time, the Whitmans had turned their attention from converting Indians to preaching to European American emigrants recently arrived from the East. Like other missionaries, the Whitmans believed Indians were capable of converting to Christianity—that no matter what their cultural differences with whites, Indians would respond to the appeal of well-meaning proselytizing efforts. What were some of the barriers to the couple's mission among the Cayuse Indians?

New Places, New Identities

Like the West, the Midwest and the borderlands between U.S. and Spanish territories were meeting places for many different cultures. Leaving established communities behind, some migrants challenged rigid definitions of who was black, Indian, Hispanic, or European American. Moving from one place to another enabled—or forced—people to adopt new individual and group identities.

People who fell into one racial category in the East sometimes acquired new identities in the West. Some people classified as "black" in the South became "white" outside the region. For example, the Commonwealth of Virginia classified the light-skinned George and Eliza Gilliam as black. Beginning their married life near Petersburg, they were well aware of Virginia's tightening restrictions on free people of color and their uncertain future in Virginia, where local officials knew who they were and who their parents were. In 1831, the couple decided to make a new life for themselves in western Pennsylvania. Eliza died in 1838, and George remarried nine years later. He prospered over the course of his lifetime. He worked as a doctor and druggist and invested in and sold real estate. George and his second wife, Frances, who was white, eventually moved to Illinois, and the couple finally settled in Missouri. Several of the Gilliam children attended college in Ohio. In 1870, the census listed the value of his estate at $95,000 (the equivalent of $2 million today). Public records in Pennsylvania, Illinois, and Missouri listed family members as white. Outside the slave South, the Gilliams managed to reinvent themselves and embrace opportunities sought by many other Americans in this era of migration.

Throughout the West, migrants forged new identities as a matter of course. For example, many people straddled more than one culture in the western borderlands.

In 1828, Mexican military officer José María Sánchez described the Tejano settlers (Spanish-speaking natives of Mexico) he met in the province of Tejas (Texas): "Accustomed to the continued trade with the North Americans, they have adopted their customs and habits, and one may say truly that they are not Mexican except by birth, for they even speak Spanish with a marked incorrectness." In other provinces of northern Mexico, European American Protestant traders and travelers mingled with Catholic native Spanish speakers.

In parts of the West, traditional social identities yielded to new ones, based less on a single language or ethnicity than on a blend of cultures and new ways of making a living from the land. The 1830s and 1840s marked the height of the Rocky Mountain fur trade. The trade could generate huge profits for the eastern merchants who controlled it. Individual trappers fared more modestly, ranging freely across national boundaries and cultures, going wherever the bison, bear, and beaver took them. These men demonstrated a legendary ability to navigate among Spanish, French, European American, and Native American communities. Westerners coined new terms to describe the people representative of new kinds of cultural identity within trading communities. Some white men became "white Indians," and the children they had with Indian women were called "métis" (mixed bloods). William Sherley "Old Bill" Williams, a convert to the religion of the Osage Indians of the southeastern Plains, was not unusual in the ways he crossed cultural boundaries. He married an Osage woman, and when she died, he wed a New Mexican widow. His third wife was a Ute woman. Williams's life story suggests the ways that Indian and Hispanic women could serve as cultural mediators between native peoples and European American traders.

A Multitude of Voices in the National Political Arena

12.2 Why did debates over the rights (or lack thereof) of workers, slaves, and immigrants lead to the rise of new political organizations?

The increasing diversity of the American population, combined with specialized regional economies, also heightened tensions within and between different groups and sections of the country. The Second Party system, which replaced the Federalist–Anti-Federalist rivalry of the early nineteenth century, was characterized by intense competition between the Jacksonian Democrats and anti-Jackson Whigs. But this new system could not accommodate the old or new conflicts based on race, religion, ethnicity, regional loyalties, and political beliefs. Social and cultural disputes between nativists and immigrants, and between abolitionists and defenders of slavery, spilled out of the courthouse and the legislative hall and into the streets. Public demonstrations ran the gamut from noisy parades to bloody clashes. During these displays, resentments between ethnic and religious groups, arguments over political issues, and opposition to reformers often blended together.

Whigs, Workers, and the Panic of 1837

One polarizing elected official, Andrew Jackson—ill with tuberculosis—did not run for a third term in 1836. The Democrats nominated Jackson's vice president and friend Martin Van Buren of New York for president. The Jackson haters, led by Senator Henry Clay and other congressmen, formed a political party called the Whigs. They drew their support from several groups: advocates of Clay's American System (policies that supported a national bank, public funding of canals and turnpikes, and protective tariffs), states' rights Southerners opposed to Jackson's heavy-handed use of national power, and merchants and factory owners in favor of the Second Bank of the United States.

Evangelical Protestants from the middle classes also joined the anti-Jackson forces; they objected to his rhetoric stressing class differences because they believed that individual religious conviction, not a group's material status, should shape politics and society. Still somewhat disorganized, these allied groups fielded three candidates: Hugh White of Tennessee, Senator Daniel Webster of Massachusetts, and General William Henry Harrison of Indiana. Benefiting from the Whigs' disarray, Van Buren narrowly won the popular vote but swept the electoral college.

12.1

12.2

12.3

12.4

Evangelical Protestants
Christians who emphasize the importance of personal faith, as well as seeking new converts.

During this period, political candidates of all persuasions in northeastern cities began to court the allegiance of workers aligned with a new trade union movement. People worried about making a living tended to favor the Democratic party, which spoke against class privilege and the wealthy. In the late 1820s and early 1830s, a variety of trade organizations had formed to advance the interests of skilled workers (the "producing classes," they called themselves). These unions pressed for a ten-hour workday, the abolition of debtors' prisons and paper money (so that workers would receive their wages in hard currency rather than bank notes), and higher wages.

The founding of the National Trades Union (NTU) in 1834 made workers more politically visible. The union represented workers as diverse as jewelers, butchers, bookbinders, and factory workers. The first president of the group, Ely Moore, a New York printer, told the members that they must guard their liberties carefully, and actively seek to participate in the political process. He declared, "Even in this fair land of freedom, where our written constitutions have so wisely provided limitations to power, and securities for rights, the *twin fiends, intolerance* and *aristocracy*, presume to rear their hateful crests [heads]." In Philadelphia in the early 1830s, the local NTU organization, called the General Trades Union, consisted of fifty trade societies and sponsored a number of successful strikes.

The NTU and its affiliates represented enough workers that both the Whigs and the Democrats professed allegiance to the union. On the campaign trail, many politicians professed support for the NTU's demands. However, once elected, few of those politicians went out of their way to represent the interests of skilled workers over other groups, such as farmers.

A major depression, the **Panic of 1837**, created even larger troubles for the trade union movement. Brought on by overspeculation—in canals, turnpikes, railroads, and slaves—the panic deepened when large grain crops failed in the West. British creditors worsened matters when they recalled loans they had made to American customers. The depression lasted until the early 1840s and devastated the NTU and its constituent organizations. Up to one-third of all Americans lost their jobs when businesses failed. Those fortunate enough to keep their jobs were in no position to press for higher wages. Not until the Civil War era did members of the laboring classes recapture political momentum at the national level.

Panic of 1837 Economic crisis and depression caused by a combination of overspeculation— in canals, turnpikes, railroads, and slaves—and a large failure of grain crops in the West.

Suppression of Antislavery Sentiment

Enslaved black workers were also at the center of contention in these years. In 1831, a Boston journalist named William Lloyd Garrison launched *The Liberator*, a newspaper dedicated to "immediate emancipation" of all slaves. Two years later, a group of sixty blacks and whites formed the American Anti-Slavery Society. That same year,

TABLE 12.1 THE ELECTION OF 1836

Candidate	Political Party	Popular Vote (%)	Electoral Vote
Martin Van Buren	Democratic	50.9	170
William Henry Harrison	Whig	36.6	73
Hugh L. White	Whig	9.7	26
Daniel Webster	Whig	2.7	14
W. P. Magnum	Independent	—	11

Great Britain had abolished slavery in the British West Indies. This move encouraged like-minded Americans eager to cooperate with their British counterparts to abolish slavery everywhere. In the United States, the abolitionist movement enlisted the energies of a dedicated group of people who believed not only that slavery was immoral but also that the federal government must take immediate steps to destroy this "peculiar institution."

Northern communities of free people of color, as well as white women and men, provided moral and financial support to the society. All the supporters showed a great deal of courage within a larger American society indifferent to the issue of slavery. Well-to-do black leaders, including Henry Highland Garnet, Charles Lenox Remond, and his sister Sarah Parker Remond, spoke out on behalf of southern blacks in chains. Fugitive slaves, including Frederick Douglass, Solomon Northup, and William and Ellen Craft, electrified northern abolitionist audiences with their firsthand accounts of the brutality of slavery and of their own daring escapes from bondage.

Douglass became the most famous fugitive slave in America. Born in Maryland in 1818, he labored in Baltimore and rural Maryland. When, as a youth, he learned to read and write, a whole new world of possibility opened up to him. In 1838, he made his escape by disguising himself as a sailor, forging a pass for himself, and fleeing to the North. Trained as a ship caulker, Douglass faced job discrimination in the shipyards of New Bedford, Massachusetts, where he and his wife Anna settled soon after he escaped from slavery. He soon became a leading abolitionist speaker, editor, and activist. Not content to condemn southern slaveholders exclusively, he also criticized northern employers for not hiring blacks. His autobiography, *Narrative of the Life of Frederick Douglass, An American Slave, Written by Himself,* was published in 1845. Douglas was a fierce champion of equality for people of color and all women. He declared, "I would unite with anybody to do right and with nobody to do wrong."

A few white women also became active in the abolitionist cause. Sarah and Angelina Grimké, for example, left the household of their slave-owning father in Charleston, South Carolina, and moved to Philadelphia. The Grimké sisters spoke before groups composed of men and women, blacks and whites in the North, an act offensive to many other whites. They were struck by what they perceived to be the similar legal constraints of slaves and white women. White men considered both groups to be unworthy of citizenship rights, childlike in their demeanor, well-suited for domestic service, and inherently unintelligent and overly emotional.

Abolitionist activities provoked outrage not only from southern slave owners but also from anti-abolitionists and their allies in Congress—in other words, most northern whites. In Washington, D.C., the House of Representatives imposed a gag rule on antislavery petitions, forbidding them to be read aloud or entered into the public record. Supporters of slavery also resorted to violence. In 1834, a mob of whites attacked a school for young women of color operated by a white teacher, Prudence Crandall, near New Haven, Connecticut. A local paper charged that the school was fostering "levelling [egalitarian] principles, and intermarriage between whites and blacks." The next year in Boston, a different mob attacked the *Liberator* founder, William Lloyd Garrison, tying a rope around him and parading him through the streets of that city while onlookers jeered. In 1837 in Alton, Illinois, a group of whites murdered outspoken abolitionist Rev. Elijah P. Lovejoy. Hounded out of Missouri because of his antislavery pronouncements, Lovejoy had moved directly across the river to Alton, in free-state Illinois, where he published the *Alton Observer* and organized the Illinois Anti-Slavery Society. Antiblack riots broke out in New York City, Philadelphia, and Cincinnati in 1834, and again in Philadelphia in 1842. Indeed, white workers attacked blacks so often in the 1830s and 1840s that bricks and stones became known as "Irish confetti" because of the way immigrants used them as weapons.

Still, these dramatic episodes had little noticeable impact on the two major political parties. In 1840, the Democrats renominated Van Buren, although many people blamed him for the depression. Eager to find a candidate as popular as Andrew Jackson, the Whigs selected William Henry Harrison; his supporters called him "Old Tippecanoe" in

TABLE 12.2 THE ELECTION OF 1840

Candidate	Political Party	Popular Vote (%)	Electoral Vote
William Henry Harrison	Whig	53.1	234
Martin Van Buren	Democratic	46.9	60
James G. Birney	Liberty	<1	—

recognition of his defeat of Indians at the battle of the same name in 1811. As Harrison's running mate, the Whigs chose John Tyler, who had been both governor of and a senator from Virginia. To counter their reputation as well-heeled aristocrats, which in fact they were, the Whigs promoted Harrison as a simple, humble man living in a log cabin and drinking hard cider. They rallied around the slogan "Tippecanoe and Tyler Too."

By this time, the Whigs had gained strong support among wealthy southern planters, who worried that Van Buren would not protect their interests in slavery. Harrison won the election, but he contracted pneumonia at his inauguration and died within one month of taking office. Ridiculed as "His Accidency," Tyler assumed the presidency and soon lost his core constituency, Whigs who favored a strong central government, by vetoing bills for both a national bank and higher tariffs. The new president represented members of the Whig party who were ardent supporters of states' rights. As a result, he proved a poor standard-bearer for the numerous nationalist-minded Whigs. Tyler learned a hard lesson: that members of his own party were a loose coalition of groups with varying views on a range of issues rather than a unified party bound to a single idea or principle.

Abolitionists could claim few victories, either real or symbolic, during these years. However, they did take heart from the *Amistad* case. In 1839, Spanish slave traders attempted to transport fifty-three illegally purchased Africans to Havana, Cuba, on a ship named *Amistad*. En route to Havana, the Africans, under the leadership of a young man named Cinqué, rebelled, killed the captain, and took over the ship. Soon after, U.S. authorities captured the ship off the coast of Long Island. President Van Buren wanted to send the blacks to Cuba. However, a federal district court judge in Hartford, Connecticut, ruled that because the African slave trade had been illegal since 1808, the Africans had been wrongfully enslaved. The U.S. government appealed the case to the Supreme Court.

To raise funds for the *Amistad* case, Philadelphia black leader Robert Purvis paid to have Cinqué's portrait painted; then antislavery activists sold copies for $1 each. In 1841, former president John Quincy Adams argued the Africans' case before the high court. The court ruled in their favor. Of the original fifty-three men, women, and children, thirty-five had survived the ordeal, and they returned to Africa. Slavery advocates and abolitionists alike pondered the question: Could the law be used to dismantle slavery?

Nativists as a Political Force

Immigration, like slavery, aroused strong feelings. Among the active players on the political scene in the early nineteenth century were the **nativists**, who opposed immigration and immigrants. Nativists held that immigrants should be denied the equal rights and privileges enjoyed by white male native-born Americans—that the newcomers should be denied the right to vote and the right to pursue economic opportunities in the form of certain kinds of jobs. Nativists, like people prejudiced against blacks, believed that if subordinate groups enjoyed the blessings of American citizenship, then white native-born men would lose both social status and political influence.

The immigrants who came to the United States were a varied group in terms of their jobs, religion, and culture. Some farmed homesteads in Michigan, and others worked in northeastern factories. But to nativists, these distinctions made little difference: all immigrants were foreigners and thus unwelcome. Some nativists were also

Nativists American citizens born in the United States who opposed further immigration, especially from anywhere outside northwestern Europe.

Temperance A social movement embracing either total opposition to alcohol consumption or support for its moderate use.

temperance advocates calling for the prohibition of alcohol; they objected to the Irish drinking in taverns and the Germans drinking in their *Biergarten*. Protestants worried that large numbers of Catholic immigrants would be loyal to the pope in Rome, the head of the Roman Catholic Church, and thus undermine American democracy. Members of the working classes, black and white, feared the loss of their jobs to desperate newcomers who would accept low, "starvation" wages. But nativists objected just as much when immigrants kept to themselves—in their Catholic schools or in their German *Turnverein* (gymnastics clubs). They also complained when immigrants participated in U.S. politics as individual voters and members of influential voting blocs.

Samuel F. B. Morse, the artist and inventor, was among the most vocal nativists. In the early 1840s, he ceased painting portraits and turned his creative energies to developing a form of long-distance electric communication. Congress financed construction of the first telegraph line, which ran from Washington to Baltimore. In May 1844, Morse sent a message in code, "What hath God wrought!" and the modern telegraph was born. The precursor of all later communication innovations, the telegraph revolutionized the spread of information and tied the country together.

Morse was convinced that Catholic immigrants in particular (mostly the Irish) were a grave threat to American democracy. In his book *Imminent Dangers to the Free Institutions of the United States* (1835), Morse charged that Catholics favored "monarchical power" over republican governments. Catholicism was like a cancer, he wrote: "We find it spreading itself into every nook and corner of the land; churches, chapels, colleges, nunneries and convents are springing up as if by magic every where." In his fears, Morse expressed nostalgia for a simpler past, even as his technical ingenuity paved the way for the modern world. In 1844, an openly nativist political organization, the American Republican party, elected six of its candidates to Congress and dozens of others to local political offices. In 1849, nativists founded the Order of the Star-Spangled Banner. Also called the Know-Nothing party, the group got its name by cautioning its members to profess ignorance when asked about its existence.

In some cases, anti-Catholic prejudices in particular helped to justify territorial expansion. Many U.S. Protestants believed the government was justified in seizing the

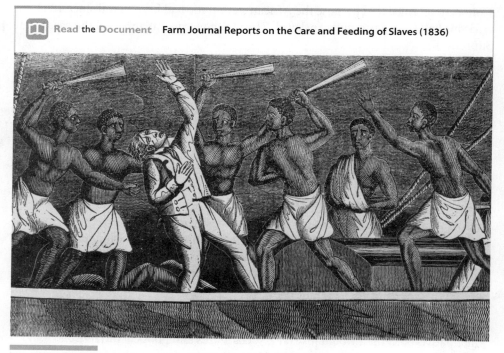

Read the Document **Farm Journal Reports on the Care and Feeding of Slaves (1836)**

This 1840 illustration shows slaves attacking and killing the captain of the *Amistad*. Initially charged with his murder, the Africans were held in New Haven, Connecticut, until a U.S. Supreme Court ruling led to their release and return to Africa in 1842. Abolitionists hailed the eventual freeing of the *Amistad* captives as one of their few successes in the fight against slavery before the Civil War. Why do you think the justice system worked to the benefit of these slaves, but not slaves living in the United States at the time?

land of Spanish-speaking Catholics in the West. They claimed religious and cultural superiority over Hispanos. As Protestant explorers, traders, and travelers reported on their experiences in the Southwest, their condemnation of Mexican Roman Catholics set the stage for the U.S. conquest of northern Mexico in the late 1840s.

Reform Impulses

12.3 What were the major reform movements of the 1830s and 1840s? What were the various strategies used by reformers to effect social change?

In August 1841, writer Lydia Maria Child recorded a striking scene in New York City: a march sponsored by the Washington Society, a temperance group, was snaking its way through the streets. The procession stretched for two miles and consisted of representatives from "all classes and trades." The marchers carried banners depicting streams and rivers (the pure water favored over liquor) and poignant scenes of the grateful wives and children of reformed drunkards. Stirred by the martial sounds of trumpets and drums, Child wrote that the music was "the voice of resistance to evil." She added, "Glory to resistance! for through its agency men become angels."

Inspired by faith in the perfectibility of human beings and heartened by the rapid pace of technological progress, many Americans set about trying to "make angels out of men," in Child's words. In the process, some reformers promoted radical new ideas about equality, ideas that had significant consequences for antebellum America. For example, some reformers believed in the equality of the spirit—the idea that regardless of a person's gender, skin color, or place or circumstances of birth—all individuals were equal in the sight of God and hence were worthy of at least decent treatment, if not the full blessings of American citizenship. Some reformers also acted on the idea that all people, no matter what their behavior, had the capability of becoming better and more moral persons if they set their minds to it.

Different reform associations employed different strategies to promote personal and social change, including targeting personal habits such as dress and diet, conventional beliefs about sexuality and the status of women, and institutions such as schools, churches, and slavery. Their efforts often brought women out of the home and into public life. Yet not all Americans shared the reformers' zeal, and even those who did rarely agreed about the appropriate means to transform society.

Public Education

In the eyes of some Americans, a growing nation needed new forms of tax-supported schooling. As families moved from one area of the country to another, public education advocates pointed out, children should be able to pick up in one school where they had left off in another. Members of a growing middle class wanted to provide their children with schooling beyond basic literacy instruction (reading and writing skills) and had the resources to do so.

Horace Mann, a Massachusetts state legislator and lawyer, was one of the most prominent educational reformers. In 1837, Mann became secretary of the first state board of education. He stressed the notion of a **common school system** available to all boys and girls regardless of class or ethnicity. In an increasingly diverse nation, schooling promoted the acquisition of basic knowledge and skills. But it also provided instruction in what Mann and others called American values: hard work, punctuality, and sobriety.

By the 1840s, public school systems attended by white children had cropped up across the North and the Midwest. Local school boards eagerly tapped into the energies of women as teachers. School officials claimed that women were naturally nurturing and could serve as "mothers away from home" for small children. Furthermore, schools could pay women only a fraction of what men earned. Between the 1830s and 1840s, the number of female schoolteachers in Massachusetts jumped more than 150 percent. In 1846, writer and educator Catharine Beecher created a Board of National Popular Education, which sent unmarried female New England teachers to the Midwest.

Common school system
Tax-supported public education to provide elementary schooling free to young children.

305

Despite the lofty goals of Mann and other reformers, public schooling did not offer a "common" experience for all American children. Almost exclusively, northern white children benefited from public school systems. Slightly more than one-third of all white children attended school in 1830; twenty years later, the ratio had increased to more than one-half. In northern cities, these proportions were considerably higher; there reformers were able to provide elementary-school instruction for relatively large numbers of white children, both immigrant and native-born.

By contrast, few black children had the opportunity to attend public schools. In the South, slave children were forbidden by law to learn to read and write. Recalled one former slave many years later, "dey [owners] didn't teach 'em nothin' but wuk [work]." By the 1830s, schools for even the children of free people of color had to meet in secret. In the North, many black households needed the labor of children to survive, resulting in black school-attendance rates well below those of whites. Throughout the Northeast and Midwest, black children remained at the mercy of local officials, who decided whether they could attend the schools their parents' tax dollars helped to support.

All over the country, education remained an intensely grassroots affair, belying the reformers' call for uniform systems. Local communities raised money for the teacher's salary, built the schoolhouse, and provided wood to heat the building. Southern states did not develop uniform public education systems until the late nineteenth century. Lacking local, popular support for tax-supported schooling, poor white children remained illiterate, while wealthy parents hired tutors for their own children or sent them to private academies.

An increase in the literate population resulted in an increased demand for higher education. Between 1830 and 1850, the number of colleges more than doubled (46 to 119). Founded in 1837, Mount Holyoke, a college for women in Massachusetts, and Oberlin in Ohio, which accepted black men as well as white and black women, were unusual for their liberal admission policies. Lyceums—informal lectures offered by speakers who traveled from place to place—attracted hordes of adults regardless of their formal education. By the mid-1830s, approximately 3,000 local lecture associations, mostly in New England and the Midwest, were sponsoring such series. In addition, local agricultural fairs offered informal practical instruction to rural people.

Formal training for professionals such as physicians and lawyers also changed during this period. By the 1830s, almost all states required that doctors be licensed. The only way to attain such a license was to attend medical school, and these schools excluded women. In regions of the country where medical schools appeared, the self-taught midwife gradually yielded to the formally educated male physician. In contrast, in rural communities of black and white Southerners, Native Americans, and Hispanos, women continued to practice time-honored ways of midwifery and healing.

Alternative Visions of Social Life

The crosscurrents of reform showed up clearly in debates not only about education, but also about sexuality, the family, and the proper role of women. For example, reformer Sylvester Graham argued that even husbands and wives must monitor their sexual activity. Sexual excess between husband and wife, he claimed, caused ills ranging from headaches, chills, and impaired vision, to loss of memory, epilepsy, insanity, and "disorders of the liver and kidneys." Graham also promoted a diet of special crackers made of wheat flour (now called Graham crackers) and fruit (in place of alcohol and meat) in addition to a regimen of plain living reinforced with cold showers.

Other reformers disagreed with Graham's notion that people must repress their sexuality to lead a good and healthy life. Defying conventional standards of morality, sponsors of a number of experimental communities discouraged marriage-based monogamy (a legal commitment between a man and a woman to engage in sexual relations only with each other) and made child-rearing the responsibility of the entire community rather than the responsibility of just the child's parents. These communities were communitarian—seeking to break down exclusive relations between husband and wife, parent and child, employer and employee—in an effort to advance the well-being of the whole group, not just individuals within it. These communities were also **utopian**, seeking to forge new kinds of social relationships that would, in the eyes of the reformers, serve as a model for the larger society.

Many of these communities explicitly challenged mainstream views related to property ownership and the system of wage labor as well as rules governing relations between the sexes.

Utopian Relating to communities organized to strive for ideal social and political conditions.

Explore the Topic   Making School Attendance Mandatory

Reformers often pursued their causes zealously, convinced that the well-being of individuals—and indeed, all of American society—was at stake. This Currier and Ives print depicts an antebellum temperance crusader conducting a holy war against liquor. Together with other girls and women in protective armor, she leads a "grand charge" against the makers and distributors of alcohol. While some reformers embraced a number of different issues, others believed that a single cause—public education, communitarianism, dress and diet reform, abolitionism— deserved priority among Americans seeking to change society for the better.

The Scottish industrialist and socialist Robert Owen founded New Harmony in Indiana in 1825, basing his experiment on principles of "cooperative labor." In 1826, Owen released his "Declaration of Mental Independence," which condemned private property, organized religion, and marriage. By this time, 900 persons had joined the New Harmony order.

Several other prominent communitarian experiments that challenged conventional marital relations were vehemently criticized, and participants were sometimes physically attacked by their neighbors. Salt Lake City Mormons, who practiced plural marriage, continued to meet intense hostility from outsiders. Another group, the Oneida Community, founded in upstate New York near Utica in 1848 by John Humphrey Noyes, went even further than the Mormons in advocating an alternative to monogamy. At its peak, Oneida consisted of 300 members who endorsed the founder's notion of "complex marriage," meaning communal sexual unions and community-regulated parent-child relations. Charges of adultery eventually forced Noyes to flee the country and seek refuge in Canada.

Networks of Reformers

Many moral reforms overlapped with and reinforced each other. For example, women's rights advocates often supported temperance. Husbands who drank, they pointed out, were more likely to abuse their wives and children. Sarah and Angelina Grimké gained prominence as both abolitionists and advocates for women's rights. They also followed Sylvester Graham's program, and for a short time, they sported "bloomers" (loose-fitting pants popularized by dress reformer Amelia Bloomer) in place of cumbersome dresses.

Dorothea Dix spearheaded a major reform effort that gained the support of a variety of politicians and activists. As a young woman, Dix had worked as a teacher and writer. In 1836, she visited England, where she met several prominent British reformers. Five years later, she volunteered to teach a Sunday school class for women at an East Cambridge jail not far from Boston. Her first day there, in March 1841, changed her life—and the face of American antebellum reform—forever.

Dix found among the inmates not only women accused of prostitution and vagrancy, but also women who were clearly mentally ill. All of them were miserable, shivering in the cold. Dix was horrified that insane persons were imprisoned with criminals. She set out on a campaign to investigate the conditions under which the mentally ill were confined. Over the next eighteen months, she investigated every prison, almshouse, and asylum in Massachusetts. She kept careful notes, which later formed the basis of her petitions, or "memorials," demanding better treatment for all insane persons. At one place, she found people "confined in *cages, closets, cellars, stalls, pens! Chained, naked, beaten with rods,* and *lashed* into obedience." Dix presented her findings to the Massachusetts state legislature. Heartened by the public outcry she had inspired, she widened her investigation to include the states of Rhode Island and New York. In the late 1840s, she traveled to another dozen states in the South, Mid-Atlantic, and Midwest.

Some women argued that the United States must change its laws and customs to allow women the full legal rights and economic opportunities enjoyed by native-born white men. The organized women's rights movement drew its greatest inspiration from the abolitionist cause. Elizabeth Cady Stanton, for example, and other American women attended the 1840 World Anti-Slavery Convention in London. Male leaders of the British and Foreign Anti-Slavery Society relegated the women delegates to a balcony and excluded them from the formal deliberations. Eight years later, Cady Stanton worked with Lucretia Mott, a Quaker minister; Susan B. Anthony, a women's rights activist; and other similarly inclined men and women to organize a women's rights convention at Seneca Falls, New York.

Women's rights advocates made some progress independent of the abolitionist movement. For instance, in 1839, Mississippi passed the nation's first Married Women's Property Law. The ruling was intended to protect the fortunes of the married daughters of wealthy planters. In 1848, both New York and Pennsylvania passed legislation giving married women control over any real property (land) or personal property they brought to marriage.

Massachusetts resident Margaret Fuller explored many reform impulses of the day during her brief life (1810–1850). Educated in the classics by her father at home in Cambridge, in the 1830s she embraced a new intellectual sensibility called Transcendentalism. Fuller cultivated friendships with two other famous Transcendentalists living in the Boston area: Ralph Waldo Emerson and Henry David Thoreau. Transcendentalists believed in the primacy of the spirit and the essential harmony between people and the natural world. They took their inspiration from European Romantics, who celebrated the beauty of nature in art, music, and literature. In 1845, Fuller published *Woman in the Nineteenth Century*, one of the first feminist essays written by an American. "I would have Woman lay aside all thought, such as she habitually cherishes, of being led and taught by men," wrote Fuller. She then embraced the role of investigative journalist, writing about the plight of slaves, Indians, and imprisoned women for the *New-York Tribune*.

The United States Extends Its Reach

12.4 Why was seizing the land that would become the state of Texas so important to so many Americans?

Efforts to reform society at home went hand in hand with a determination to expand the nation's borders, especially in the Southwest. In the mid-1840s, the editor of the *New York Morning News* declared that the United States had a "manifest destiny" to "overspread the continent" and claim the "desert wastes." Those inhabiting the "desert wastes"—Mexican settlers and a variety of Indian groups—apparently would have little say in the matter. The term **manifest destiny** soon became a catchall phrase, justifying American efforts not only to conquer new territory but also to seek out new markets for its goods across the oceans. Supporters of manifest destiny believed that white Americans were a superior, exceptional people, and that they had the right to place their own economic and territorial interests over those of other, supposedly "inferior" peoples.

Manifest destiny The idea, first promoted in the 1840s, that the United States had a God-given right to expand its territory; used to justify territorial growth, expansion of economic markets, and conquest.

The Lone Star Republic

In the early 1830s, the Mexican government became alarmed by the growing number of American emigrants to Texas. Worried that the settlers would refuse to pledge allegiance to Mexico, that country closed the Texas border to further in-migration. By 1835, only one out of every eight residents of Texas was a Tejano (that is, a native Spanish speaker); the rest, numbering 30,000, hailed from the United States. The U.S.-born Texians, together with some prominent Tejanos, had become increasingly well armed and militant. They organized volunteer patrols to attack Indian settlements. These forces became the precursor of the Texas Rangers, a statewide organization of law enforcement officers.

In 1836, the Texians decided to press for independence from Mexico. Only by becoming a separate nation, they believed, could they trade freely with the United States, establish their own schools, and collect and spend their own taxes. The pro-independence Texians included Davy Crockett, who had moved there in late 1835. A few months later, Crockett and other armed Texians retreated to a Spanish mission in San Antonio called the Alamo. In March 1836, a military force led by Antonio Lopez de Santa Anna, president of the Republic of Mexico and a general in the army, battled them for thirteen days. All 187 Texians died at the hands of Santa Anna and his men; the Mexican leader lost 600 of his own troops. Historians disagree on whether all of the Alamo defenders died fighting or if some were executed by Mexican soldiers.

In April, a force of Texians and their Tejano allies, including military leader Juan Seguin, surprised Santa Anna and his men at the San Jacinto River and killed another 600 of them. The victors captured Santa Anna and declared themselves a new nation. Sam Houston, former U.S. congressman from Tennessee and commander-in-chief of the Texian army, became president of the Republic of Texas (also called the Lone Star Republic) in 1837. Some Tejanos who objected to Mexican high-handedness joined in supporting the new republic, including José Antonio Navarro, Francisco Ruiz, and Lorenzo de Zavala, who became its vice president.

In the northern territories of Mexico, many Spanish speakers had long felt abandoned by the Mexican government, which had made no provisions for their self-government and, as in the case of Texas, inhibited trade relations with the United States. Although other Mexican provinces protested the way they were treated by the government, Texas was the only Mexican state to launch a successful rebellion against Mexico.

The independence of Texas did not necessarily promote the freedom and equality of all peoples within the borders of the Lone Star Republic. U.S.-born white Texians regarded themselves as superior to Tejanos, even those who had lived on the land for many generations, and their new republic superior to Mexico. More specifically, Texas's successful bid for independence raised the fears of U.S. abolitionists and imperiled blacks living in the new republic. In contrast to Mexico, which had abolished slavery in 1829, Texas approved a constitution that not only legalized slavery but also prohibited free blacks from living in the country. Greenbury Logan, a black man who owned a farm near Austin, petitioned to stay. He wrote, "Every privilege dear to a free man is taken away." But **vigilantes** forced him to leave. They also forced out many Tejanos. Among them was Juan Seguin, who had helped defeat Santa Anna at the Battle of San Jacinto and was now the mayor of San Antonio. Not until 1981 did another Tejano, Henry Cisneros, hold the office of mayor of the city of San Antonio.

Vigilantes People who seek to take the law into their own hands and punish or intimidate alleged criminals or persons who resist a certain social order (for example, white supremacy).

The Election of 1844

As an independent republic, Texas became a hotly contested political issue in the United States. During the election of politicians began to debate whether the United States should annex Texas. Van Buren was outspoken in his opposition to the idea. As a result, the frankly expansionist Democrats spurned the former president as a candidate and nominated James K. Polk of Tennessee. They called for the "reannexation" of Texas and the "reoccupation" of Oregon. Their rallying cry became "Fifty-Four Forty or Fight," a reference to their desire to own the area (expressed in terms of its longitude and latitude coordinates) claimed by the British in present-day Canada south of Alaska and west of the Continental Divide. Kentucky congressman Henry Clay received the Whig nomination after he announced he was against the **annexation** of Texas. But under pressure from Southerners, he later changed his mind, to the disgust of party leaders.

Annexation Addition of territory that had belonged to one nation into another nation.

Neither the Democrats nor the Whigs had shown an interest in addressing the issue of slavery directly in the last presidential election. Yet in 1844, the controversy over the annexation of Texas made it impossible for the two parties to ignore the growing controversy over bound labor. Under the banner of the young Liberty party, some abolitionists charged that territorial expansion would mean the continued growth and prosperity of the slave system; they pointed to the public pronouncements of southern planters, who were outspoken in their desire to expand their slaveholdings into the fertile lands of eastern Texas.

For their part, Democrats and Whigs believed, correctly, that most voters would ignore slavery when they cast their ballots. Thus members of both parties tried to silence both sides of the slavery debate. They turned a deaf ear to the proslavery advocates on one hand and squelched Northern abolitionist opinion by ignoring petitions to Congress on the other. In the end, Polk won the election. The expansionists had elected one of their most ardent champions to the highest office in the land.

Still, Polk was not interested in going to war with Great Britain over the vast territory of Oregon. In 1846, the two countries reached a compromise. Britain would accept the 49th parallel as the border between Canada and the United States and retain the disputed islands off

TABLE 12.3 THE ELECTION OF 1844

Candidate	Political Party	Popular Vote (%)	Electoral Vote
James K. Polk	Democratic	49.6	170
Henry Clay	Whig	48.1	105
James G. Birney	Liberty	2.3	—

Interpreting History
Senator John C. Calhoun Warns Against
INCORPORATING MEXICO INTO THE UNITED STATES

"I know **further,** sir, that we have **never** dreamt of incorporating into **our** Union **any** but the **Caucasian** race—the **free** white race."

In January 1848, Senator John C. Calhoun delivered a speech to President Polk and to his fellow lawmakers, urging them to resist calls to incorporate all of a conquered Mexico into the United States. Calhoun favored the spread of slavery into new territories, but here he expresses the fear that residents of Mexico were incapable of becoming suitable U.S. citizens for "racial" reasons.

It is without example or precedent, either to hold Mexico as a province, or to incorporate her into our Union. . . . We have conquered many of the neighboring tribes of Indians, but we never thought of holding them in subjection—never of incorporating them into our Union. They have either been left as an independent people amongst us, or been driven into the forests.

I know further, sir, that we have never dreamt of incorporating into our Union any but the Caucasian race—the free white race. To incorporate Mexico, would be the first instance of the kind of incorporating an Indian race; for more than half of the Mexicans are Indians, and the other half is composed chiefly of mixed tribes. I protest such a union as that! . . .

Sir, it is a remarkable fact, that in the whole history of man, as far as my knowledge extends, there is no instance whatever of any civilized colored races being found equal to the establishment of free popular government. . . . Are we to associate with ourselves as equals, companions, and fellow-citizens, the Indians and mixed race of Mexico? Sir, I should consider such a thing as fatal to our institutions.

Calhoun then moves to dispute the notion that Mexico can begin as a territory and then work its way up to statehood.

You can establish a Territorial Government for every State in Mexico. . . . You can appoint governors, judges, and magistrates. You can give the people a subordinate government, allowing them to legislate for themselves, whilst you defray the cost. So far as the law goes, the thing is done. There is no analogy between this and our Territorial Governments. Our Territories are only an offset of our own people, or foreigners from the same regions from which we came. They are small in number. They are

incapable of forming a government. It would be inconvenient for them to sustain a government, if it were formed; and they are very much obliged to the United States for undertaking the trouble, knowing that, on the attainment of their majority—when they come to manhood—at twenty-one—they will be introduced to an equality with all other members of the Union. It is entirely different with Mexico. You have no need of armies to keep your Territories in subjection. But when you incorporate Mexico, you must have powerful armies to keep them in subjection. You may call it annexation, but it is a forced annexation, which is a contradiction in terms, according to my conception. You will be involved, in one word, in all the evils which I attribute to holding Mexico as a province. . . . How long will it be before Mexico will be capable of incorporation into our Union? Why, if we judge from the examples before us, it will be a very long time. Ireland has been held in subjection by England for seven or eight hundred years, and yet still remains hostile, although her people are of kindred race with the conquerors. . . . [A]nd never will the time come, in my opinion, Mr. President, that these Mexicans will be reconciled to your authority. . . . Of all nations of the earth they are the most pertinacious—have the highest sense of nationality—hold out the longest, and often even with the least prospect of effecting their object.

We make a great mistake, sir, when we suppose that all people are capable of self-government. We are anxious to force free government on all; and I see that it has been urged in a very respectable quarter, that it is the mission of this country to spread civil and religious liberty over all the world, and especially this continent. It is a great mistake. None but people advanced to a very high state of moral and intellectual improvement are capable, in a civilized state, of maintaining free government; and amongst those who are so purified, very few, indeed, have had the good fortune of forming a constitution capable of endurance.

Calhoun also warns that "these twenty-odd Mexican States" would eventually have power in Congress. He asks his listeners whether they would want their own states "governed by" these peoples.

Portrait of John C. Calhoun by Charles Bird King, c. 1818–1825.
SOURCE: Centre DES Archives D'Outre-MER

Questions for Discussion

1. Why does Calhoun assume that, if the United States incorporates Mexico into its territory, the federal government "must have powerful armies to keep them [Mexicans] in subjection"?
2. On what basis does Calhoun reject the idea of Mexican territories becoming future states?
3. How might Calhoun's more extreme expansionist colleagues—those in favor of seizing all of Mexico—have countered his arguments?

SOURCE: Clyde A. Milner, ed., *Major Problems in the History of the American West: Documents and Essays* (1989), pp. 219–221.

the coast of Vancouver. The United States settled for one-half of its original claim to Oregon. Thereafter, it was free to turn its full attention to extending its southern and western borders.

War with Mexico

Texian leaders wanted to become part of the United States. In 1845, as one of his last acts as president, Tyler invited Texas to become the twenty-eighth state. He also understood that annexing Texas was a way to goad Mexico into open hostilities; Mexico had warned the United States that such a move would mean war. A joint resolution of both houses of Congress confirmed Texas statehood in December 1845.

The boundaries between Mexico and the new state of Texas remained in dispute. Mexico recognized the Nueces River as the boundary for Texas. In contrast, Texians

((• 📖 Read the Document Thomas Corwin, Speech Against the Mexican War (1847)

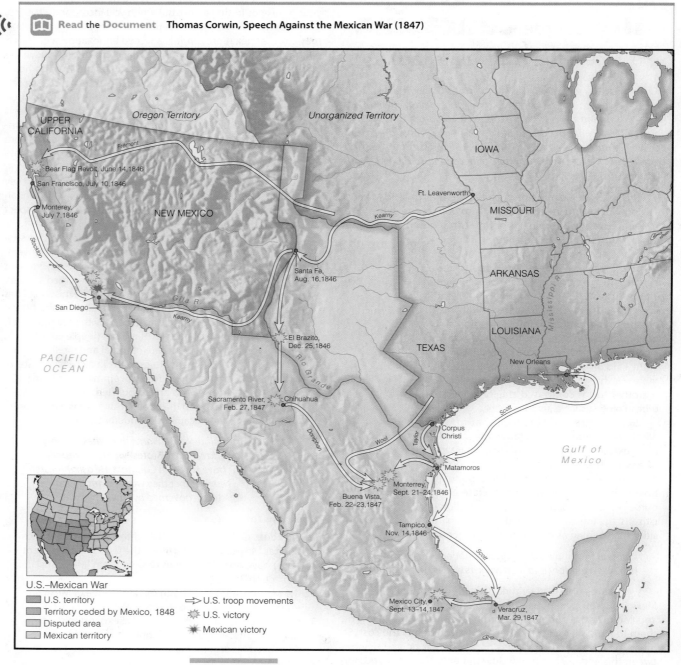

MAP 12.3 THE U.S.-MEXICAN WAR During the U.S.-Mexican War, American troops marched deep into the interior of Mexico. General Winfield Scott raised the American flag over Mexico City on September 14, 1847. The treaty that concluded the war was named after the village of Guadalupe Hidalgo, a few miles north of the Mexican capital. The U.S. army withdrew the last of its troops from foreign soil in July 1848.

and U.S. politicians envisioned the boundary a hundred miles to the south at the Rio Grande. Complicating matters further, the new president, James K. Polk, had sent an envoy, John Slidell, to purchase California and a disputed section of Texas from Mexico. Mexico refused the deal. Nevertheless, around this time, Polk wrote in his diary that if he could not acquire all of New Mexico and California through diplomatic negotiation, he was determined to obtain them by force. The stage was set for war.

Armed conflict broke out in January 1846. U.S. troops, under the command of General Zachary Taylor (a veteran of wars against Tecumseh, the Seminole, and Black Hawk), clashed with a Mexican force near the mouth of the Rio Grande near Matamoros. Taylor had deliberately moved his troops across the Nueces River into disputed territory; his intention was to provoke an armed response from Mexico. A skirmish ensued, eleven Americans were killed, and Taylor pulled back. Polk used this military action as justification for a declaration of war against Mexico. The president declared, "American blood has been shed on American soil."

Not all Americans supported the war. Transcendentalists such as Henry David Thoreau objected to what they saw as a naked land grab. Refusing to pay taxes for what he considered a war to expand slavery, Thoreau went to jail. Nativists also objected to the war, fearing that the United States would have to assimilate thousands of Indians and Spanish-speaking Roman Catholics. Some members of Congress, including a newly elected U.S. Representative from Illinois named Abraham Lincoln, also condemned Polk's "act of aggression."

Predictably, opponents of slavery were among Polk's most outspoken critics. Soon after the outbreak of war, Representative David Wilmot of Pennsylvania attached an amendment to a bill appropriating money for the war. Called the Wilmot Proviso, the measure declared that "neither slavery nor involuntary servitude shall ever exist" in territories the United States acquired from Mexico. Though a member of the Democratic party, Wilmot spoke primarily as a white Northerner; he wanted to preserve the West for "the sons of toil of my own race and color." Wilmot's views show how racial prejudice and antislavery sentiment coexisted in the minds of many white Northerners. The House approved the proviso, but the Senate did not. Southern Democrats claimed that Congress had no right to deprive slaveholders of their private property anywhere in the nation.

Meanwhile, Polk launched a three-pronged campaign against Mexico. He sent Taylor into northern Mexico and ordered General Stephen Watts Kearny into New Mexico and then into California. Following the third directive of the campaign, General in Chief of the U.S. Army Winfield Scott coordinated an amphibious landing of 10,000 soldiers at Veracruz, on the Gulf of Mexico coast. Mexican forces tried to defend their homeland using guerrilla tactics. But U.S. soldiers overcame them in part by terrorizing civilians. Scott acknowledged that the men under his command had "committed atrocities to make Heaven weep and every American of Christian morals blush for his country. . . . Murder, robbery and rape of mothers and daughters in the presence of tied-up males of the families."

In September 1847, Mexico City surrendered, and the war ended. Mexico had been in no shape to resist superior U.S. firepower. The United States paid for Scott's victory with 13,000 lives and $100 million. The Mexicans lost 20,000 lives. In the Treaty of Guadalupe Hidalgo (approved by the Senate in 1848), Mexico agreed to give up its claims to Texas. The United States gained all of Texas and half of the territory of Mexico: the area west of Texas, comprising present-day New Mexico, Arizona, Utah, Nevada, and California. Male residents of areas formerly held by Mexico were given one year to decide whether to stay in the United States and become citizens or return to Mexico. They were also entitled to retain their titles to the land, a provision that proved difficult to enforce in the face of European American land hunger.

The U.S. government paid Mexico $18.25 million. Of that amount, $15 million was designated as payment for land lost; the rest was restitution to U.S. citizens who might bring claims against Mexico for damaged or destroyed property during the war. Americans had conflicting views of the treaty. Abolitionists saw it as a blood-drenched gift from American taxpayers to slaveholders. Others argued that Polk had squandered a rare opportunity to seize all of Mexico.

✳ Explore the War with Mexico on MyHistoryLab

WHAT DID THE TEXAS REVOLUTION AND U.S. -MEXICAN WAR MEAN FOR AMERICAN EXPANSION?

In the 1830s, the Mexican government encountered resistance from some of the people living in its northern state of Texas. The state was home to increasing numbers of U.S. settlers (called Texians) who were dissatisfied with Mexican rule. In 1836, Texians rebelled and formed their own independent Republic of Texas. In 1845, the United States annexed Texas, which became the twenty-eighth state. The following year, disputed land claims led to war between the United States and Mexico. In 1848 U.S. forces defeated the Mexican army, and wrested from that country huge territorial gains as part of the provisions of the Treaty of Guadalupe Hidalgo.

When the United States annexed Texas, it triggered a territorial dispute that became the U.S. -Mexican War (1846 to 1848). This print depicts General Zachary Taylor, who repulsed a larger Mexican army, at the Battle of Buena Vista, February 22–23, 1847. *Library of Congress.*

MAJOR BATTLES OF THE U.S. -MEXICAN WAR

Battle	Date	Victor
Battle of Palo Alto	May 8, 1846	U.S.
Battle of Resaca de la Palma	May 9, 1846	U.S.
Battle of Monterrey	Sep. 21–24, 1846	U.S.
Battle of San Pasqual	Dec. 6, 1846	Mexico
Battle of Rio San Gabriel	Jan. 8, 1847	U.S.
Battle of Buena Vista	Feb. 22–23, 1847	U.S.
Battle of Sacramento River	Feb. 27, 1847	U.S.
Battle of Veracruz	March 29, 1847	U.S.
Battle of Cerro Gordo	April 18, 1847	U.S.
Battle of Mexico City	Sept. 13–14, 1847	U.S.

KEY QUESTIONS   Use **MyHistoryLab** *Explorer* to **answer** these **questions:**

Context ▶▶▶ *What was the political situation in Mexico leading up to its war with the United States?*

Map the nation's transformations between the 1820s and 1840s.

Response ▶▶▶ *How did the Texas Revolution unfold?*

Understand the progress, troop movements, and major battles.

Consequence ▶▶▶ *What did the acquisition of Mexican territory mean for the institution of slavery in the United States?*

Consider the potential implications for the extension of slavery.

This painting shows the U.S. Navy going up the Tuxpan River in Mexico during the U.S.-Mexican War. Located on the Gulf Coast halfway between Veracruz and Tampico, Tuxpan was the last significant Mexican port to be seized by U.S. forces by the spring of 1847. Commodore M. C. Perry assembled a formidable force of marines and infantry to take over the town on April 19, 1847. How do you think different groups of Americans reacted to the U.S. victory over Mexico? Consider, for example, free people of color in the northern United States, proponents of manifest destiny, and people of Mexican descent living in Texas.

Conclusion

In the 1830s and 1840s, mass population movements affected almost every aspect of American life. Immigrants from western Europe helped to swell the nation's labor force in midwestern farming communities and eastern cities. The arrival of the Roman Catholic Irish provoked a backlash among native-born Protestants and spawned a nativist political movement. Reformers in the United States and Europe went back and forth across the Atlantic, exchanging ideas related to women's rights, abolition, and utopian communities. As European Americans pushed the boundaries of the country west and south, they clashed with Indians and with foreign powers that claimed those lands as their own. Thus migration and immigration had profound consequences for American politics, ideas, society, and economics.

Most striking was the restlessness among land-hungry slave owners and antislavery forces alike. The war with Mexico in general, and the clash over the Wilmot Proviso in particular, opened a new chapter in the debate over slavery. In considering the proviso, congressmen gave up their party loyalties as Democrats or Whigs and began to think of themselves as Northerners and Southerners. When Wilmot proclaimed that he wanted to preserve the West for his "own color," he revealed that even antislavery Northerners did not necessarily embrace black people as equals. When Southerners indicated that even the vast expanse of Texas would not satisfy their desire for land, they revealed that the conflict over slavery was far from over. In fact, that conflict was about to enter a new and ominous stage.

Chapter Review

Mass Migrations

12.1 What caused some groups to migrate voluntarily? Why were others forced to move against their will? p. 293

Groups who moved voluntarily hoped to take advantage of economic opportunities and religious freedom in the United States. In contrast, slave traders sold slaves from the Upper South to planters in the Lower South. The U.S. government removed Indians from the southeastern United States in order to clear the region for white settlement.

A Multitude of Voices in the National Political Arena

12.2 Why did debates over the rights (or lack thereof) of workers, slaves, and immigrants lead to the rise of new political organizations? p. 300

Workers joined trade unions like the National Trades Union in order to press for better wages and conditions. Opponents of slavery organized groups like the American Antislavery Society. Debates over immigration led many native-born white Americans to join nativist organizations, which sought to curb the rights of immigrants.

Reform Impulses

12.3 What were the major reform movements of the 1830s and 1840s? What were the various strategies used by reformers to effect social change? p. 305

Major reform movements of the 1830s and 1840s included public education, utopian communities, abolitionism, and women's rights. Reformers targeted personal habits, laws, conventional beliefs about sexuality and the status of women, and institutions such as schools, churches, and slavery.

The United States Extends Its Reach

12.4 Why was seizing the land that would become the state of Texas so important to so many Americans? p. 309

Many Americans believed that the United States had a "manifest destiny" to expand to the Pacific Ocean. At the same time, seizing Texas would force the country to grapple with slavery. Southern slaveholders hoped to expand slavery westward, while abolitionists, including members of the new Liberty party, opposed this expansion of slavery.

Timeline

1835
United States Extends Reach—Texas revolts against Mexico

1836
Reform Impulses—Congress passes gag rule on antislavery petitions

1837
Multitude of Voices—Panic of 1837

1838
Mass Migrations—Cherokee removal begins; Trail of Tears

1844
Mass Migrations—Mormon leader Joseph Smith killed by mob in Nauvoo, Illinois

1845
Multitude of Voices—Frederick Douglass, *Narrative of the Life of Frederick Douglass*

1846
United States Extends Reach—Great Britain cedes southern part of Oregon Country to United States
United States Extends Reach—U.S.-Mexican War begins

1848
United States Extends Reach—Treaty of Guadalupe Hidalgo ends U.S.-Mexican War
Multitude of Voices—Women's rights convention in Seneca Falls, New York

13 The Crisis over Slavery, 1848–1860

How would the valuable natural resources of the United States be divided? As the young nation expanded its boundaries, these resources came not only from the land itself but also from riches beneath it. In a country of seemingly boundless opportunities, what role did slavery play in politics and the economy?

On January 24, 1848, Henry William Bigler took a break from building a sawmill for John Sutter in California's Sacramento Valley and penned in his pocket diary, "This day some kind of mettle was found . . . that looks like goald."

Gold! News of the discovery at Sutter's mill spread like wildfire. In 1849, immigrants from all over the world and migrants from all over the United States began to pour into the foothills of the Sierra Nevada Mountains. In the process these "Forty-Niners" were

Chinese and European American miners pan for gold in the Auburn Ravine in California in 1852. Within a few years, individual miners would be replaced by machines that extracted the precious metal from rivers and mountains. Although this photo suggests a rough equality among the men and the work they were doing, the Chinese miners were subject to a discriminatory Foreign Miners Tax. What accounts for that tax? How are cultural differences between these two groups of men inscribed in their clothing and on their persons?

LEARNING OBJECTIVES

13.1	13.2	13.3	13.4
To what extent, and in what ways, were U.S. regional economies interdependent by 1860? Were certain regions, or groups of people, outside the emerging national economy? p. 319	In what ways did the American ideal of individualism clash with the group stereotypes and prejudices enshrined in 1850s law and customs? p. 324	How could white Southerners dominate all three branches of the national government and still perceive themselves on the defensive, under siege? p. 329	During the 1850s, what specific events and developments pushed the nation toward armed conflict? p. 336

((• Listen to **Chapter 13** on **MyHistoryLab**

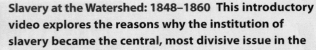 Watch the Video Series on MyHistoryLab

Learn about some key topics related to this chapter with the *MyHistoryLab Video Series: Key Topics in U.S. History.*

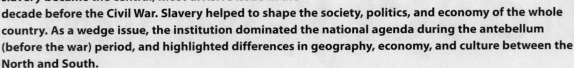

1 **Slavery at the Watershed: 1848–1860** This introductory video explores the reasons why the institution of slavery became the central, most divisive issue in the decade before the Civil War. Slavery helped to shape the society, politics, and economy of the whole country. As a wedge issue, the institution dominated the national agenda during the antebellum (before the war) period, and highlighted differences in geography, economy, and culture between the North and South.

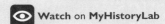 **Watch** on MyHistoryLab

The Compromise of 1850 The Compromise of 1850 was a critical development on the path to civil war. This video shows that the compromise became the U.S. Congress's signature piece of legislation during the 1850s. Lawmakers aimed to deal with a host of issues, including the expansion of slavery into territories and new states such as California, and the enforcement of a new, far-reaching Fugitive Slave Act. The debates surrounding the compromise featured aging legislators such as Henry Clay, Daniel Webster, and John C. Calhoun, as well as younger leaders, including Stephen Douglas, who would one day face a formidable political rival named Abraham Lincoln. **2**

Watch on MyHistoryLab

3 **The *Dred Scott* Decision** The Supreme Court's *Dred Scott v. Sandford* decision of 1857 is the subject of this video. Chief Justice Roger B. Taney wrote the majority opinion in this controversial case. His argument went beyond any previous legal justification for denying rights not only to slaves but also to free people of color. The case stemmed from Scott's attempt to free himself and his family from their owner, once they were on free soil in the North. Although Scott lost in court, the decision fueled the growing abolitionist movement, and further divided the country over the issue of slavery.

 **Watch** on MyHistoryLab

The Lincoln–Douglas Debates In 1858, Illinois senator Stephen Douglas, a popular and established politician, faced a challenge from a newcomer, Abraham Lincoln, who represented a new political party, the Republicans. During the course of the campaign, they held a series of debates on critical issues such as slavery and states' rights. All over the country, newspapers covered the debates with interest. This video explains how Lincoln gained a national reputation and, in the process, won for himself a national following. Although he lost his bid for Douglas's Senate seat, Lincoln had positioned himself for a run for the presidency in 1860. One of the opponents he defeated in that contest was Stephen Douglas of Illinois.

Watch on MyHistoryLab

thrown in close proximity to each other. Yet if most were committed to staking their own claim in the gold fields, legal barriers prevented certain groups from sharing in the profits.

California came to be part of the United States as a result of the U.S.–Mexican War. In the 1848 Treaty of Guadalupe Hidalgo, Mexico agreed to hand over 530,000 square miles (called the Mexican Cession), an expanse that stretched from Texas northwest to California. In addition to the land, the nation added to its population large numbers of men, women, and children already living in the area—13,000 Spanish speakers and 100,000 Indians (all former Mexican citizens) in California alone.

A s a result of the **Compromise of 1850**, California entered the Union as a free state. Nevertheless, the principle of free labor was often violated. In 1850, the state enacted a law that provided for the indenture or apprenticeship of Indian children

Compromise of 1850
Congressional legislation that provided that California would enter the Union as a free state that year and that New Mexico and Utah would eventually submit the slavery question to their voters. As part of this compromise, the federal government abolished the slave trade in Washington, D.C.

to white men for indeterminate periods of time. The law also allowed for the hiring out, to the highest bidder, of adult Indians deemed guilty of vagrancy. The state's Fugitive Slave Law of 1852 decreed that, regardless of his or her current status, a black person who entered the state and thereafter attempted to remain on free soil was a fugitive slave. Moreover, soon after the discovery of gold, the state of California enacted a discriminatory Foreign Miners Tax, a measure leveled with special force against Chinese and Mexican miners. Although the Treaty of Guadalupe Hidalgo guaranteed U.S. citizenship rights to Mexicans, those rights were not enforced under the law. In California, the Gold Rush ignited a wider debate about the role of African Americans, Native Americans, and noncitizens in sharing the bounty of the nation's riches.

Continued European American migration into the Midwest, the Great Plains, and the Southwest intensified conflicts over land with Native Americans and Latinos. Rapid population growth, the coming together of many different cultures, and dramatic economic changes all fueled the conflict over slavery. All over the nation, Americans gradually united around a radical proposition: that there could be no compromise on the issue of whether human beings could be held as property.

Regional Economies and Conflicts

13.1 To what extent, and in what ways, were U.S. regional economies interdependent by 1860? Were certain regions, or groups of people, outside the emerging national economy?

I t is tempting to view the decade of the 1850s with an eye toward the impending firestorm of 1861. However, in the early 1850s, few Americans could have anticipated the Civil War. At midcentury, the United States was going through a period of rapid transition. New developments such as railroads, the factory system, and more efficient farm equipment led to significant changes in regional economies and began to give form to an emerging national economy.

Migration into the Midwest accelerated. Slavery shaped the lives of all Southerners, though most whites were not plantation owners or slaveholders. In the North, an emerging free labor ideology gained the support of growing numbers of voters. Meanwhile, annexation of land in the Southwest and West and the conquest of Indians on the Plains produced wrenching social upheavals for Native Americans in those regions. Despite the country's great regional diversity in terms of local economies and the predominance of certain cultural groups, the whole nation was forced to confront the problems of labor and property ownership in a rapidly changing society. How did a person's race, gender, ethnicity, or personal wealth shape his or her citizenship rights?

Native American Economies Transformed

On the Plains, Indians confronted dramatic transformations in their way of life. Forced to relocate from the Southeast to Indian Territory (present-day Oklahoma), the Five Southern ("Civilized") Tribes, the Cherokee, Choctaw, Creek, Chickasaw, and Seminole, grappled with the task of rebuilding their political institutions. By the 1850s, the Cherokee had established a new capital at Talequah, along with public schools. They published a Cherokee newspaper (the *Advocate*) and created a flourishing print culture in their own language.

In the 1850s, U.S. officials negotiated treaties with various Plains Indian groups to enable European Americans to move west without fear of attack. Most settlers were bent on heading straight for California or the Northwest, traversing the Plains, which they called the Great American Desert in the mistaken belief that the absence of trees there demonstrated the infertility of the soil. The Fort Laramie Treaty of 1851 and the Treaty of Fort Atkinson three years later provided that the government could build roads and establish forts along western trails and that, in return, Indians would be compensated with supplies and food for their loss of hunting rights in the region. A young Cheyenne woman, Iron Teeth, recalled "the government presents" to her people in these terms: "We were given beef, but we did not care for this kind of meat. Great piles of bacon were stacked upon the prairies and distributed to us, but we used it only to make fires or to grease robes for tanning." She and her family sought out other items from government trading posts: "brass kettles, coffee-pots, curve-bladed butcher knives, boxes of black and white thread."

As whites moved west in large numbers to (in the words of a popular song) "scrape the mountains clean and drain the rivers dry," they disregarded U.S. treaties and tribal boundaries and overran the fragile settlements of Indians. Taking leave of the Fort Laramie conclave of 1851, Cut Nose of the Arapaho declared, "I will go home satisfied. I will sleep sound, and not have to watch my horses in the night, or be afraid for my women and children. We have to live on these streams and in the hills, and I would be glad if the whites would pick out a place for themselves and not come into our grounds." But within a generation, the Plains Indians were besieged by the technology, weaponry, and the sheer numbers of newcomers heading west.

Land Conflicts in the Southwest

To the southwest, the United States had gained control over a vast expanse of land, provoking legal and political conflicts over the rights and labor of the people who lived there, both natives and newcomers. Under the terms of the Treaty of Guadalupe Hidalgo, Mexico ceded not only California but also the province of New Mexico, territory that included the present-day states of New Mexico, Arizona, Utah, Nevada, and western Colorado. In 1853, the United States bought an additional tract of land from Mexico: 19 million acres located in the area south of the Gila River (in present-day New Mexico and Arizona). Overseen by the U.S. secretary of war, a Mississippi planter named Jefferson Davis, the agreement was called the **Gadsden Purchase** (after James Gadsden, a railroad promoter and one of the American negotiators).

In Texas, newly arrived European Americans battled native Tejanos (people of Mexican origin or descent) for political and economic supremacy. White migrants from the South brought their slaves with them to the region, claiming that the institution of slavery was crucial for commercial development. German immigrants came to central and east Texas, founding towns with German names such as Fredericksburg, Weimar, and Schulenburg. During the 1850s, commercial farming continued to replace subsistence homesteading as the cattle industry spread and the railroads penetrated the region. Although European Americans monopolized the courts and regional political institutions, Tejanos retained cultural influence throughout Texas, dominating the cuisine and styles of music and architecture.

Some Spanish-speaking residents in the Southwest reacted forcefully when U.S. courts disregarded the land titles held by Californios and Tejanos. In the early 1850s, California authorities battled Mexican social bandits such as Joaquin Murrieta, who, with his men, raided European American settlements. Murrieta and others argued that they were justified in stealing from privileged European Americans who, they claimed, disregarded the lives and property of Mexicans. In 1859, in the Rio Grande Valley of Texas, tensions between the Tejano majority and groups of European American law enforcement officers known as the Texas Rangers erupted into full-scale warfare. Juan Cortina, who had fought on the side of Mexico during the Mexican War, orchestrated attacks on European Americans and their property in the vicinity of Brownsville. U.S. retaliation led to Cortina's War, pitting the Mexican leader against a young U.S. colonel, Robert E. Lee. Cortina became a hero to Tejanos. "You have been robbed of your property, incarcerated, chased, murdered, and hunted like wild beasts," he declared. "To me is entrusted the work of breaking the chains of your slavery."

Ethnic and Economic Diversity in the Midwest

Compared to the Southwest, the Midwest revealed a distinctive social make-up shaped by the European immigrants and the New Englanders who settled there. The Yankee Strip (named for the Northeasterners who migrated there) ran through northern Ohio,

Gadsden Purchase A total of 30,000 square miles of land (located in present-day southern Arizona and southwestern New Mexico) purchased by the United States from Mexico in 1853.

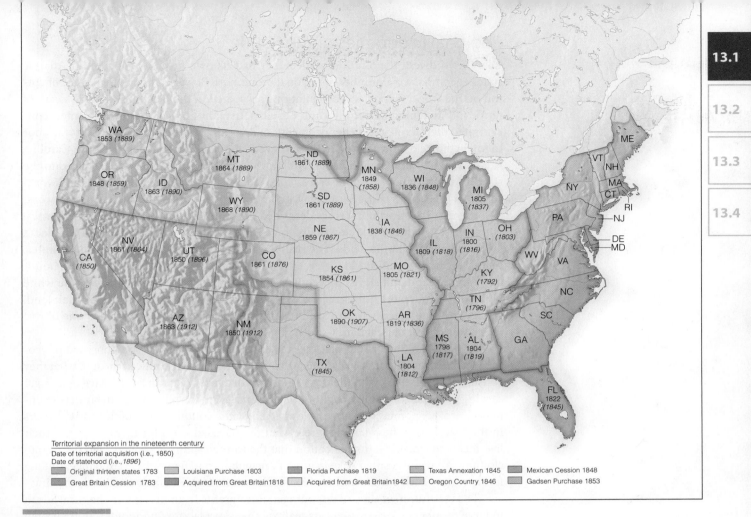

MAP 13.1 TERRITORIAL EXPANSION IN THE NINETEENTH CENTURY As a result of the Mexican War (1846–1848), the United States won the territory west of Texas by conquest. In 1853, James Gadsden, U.S. ambassador to Mexico, received congressional approval to pay Mexico $15 million for 30,000 square miles in present-day southern Arizona and New Mexico. That year marked the end of U.S. continental expansion.

Indiana, and Illinois and encompassed the entire states of Michigan, Wisconsin, and Minnesota. Here migrants from New England settled and established public schools and Congregational churches. Immigrants from western Europe also made a home in this region—the Germans, Belgians, and Swiss in Wisconsin, the Scandinavians in Minnesota. At times, cultural conflict wracked even the smallest rural settlements. In some Wisconsin villages, equally matched numbers of Yankees and Germans contended for control over the local public schools, with the group in power posting notices for school board elections in its own language, hoping that its rivals would not show up at the polls.

The lower Midwest, including the southern portions of Ohio, Indiana, and Illinois, retained strong cultural ties to the South, from which many settlers had migrated. Though residing in free states, they maintained broad support for the institution of slavery. In some cases, they outnumbered their Yankee counterparts and managed to shape the legal system in a way that reflected a distinct anti-black bias. For example, Indiana's state constitution prohibited blacks from voting, making contracts with whites, and testifying in trials that involved whites, and it also prohibited black migrants from entering the state.

Most rural Midwestern households followed the seasonal rhythms characteristic of traditional systems of agriculture. However, by the mid-nineteenth century, family farming had become dependent on expensive machinery and hostage to the national and international grain markets. John Deere's steel plow (invented in 1837) and Cyrus McCormick's horse-drawn mechanical reaper (patented in 1854) boosted levels of grain production. Improved agricultural efficiency meant that the Midwest, both upper and lower, was fast becoming the breadbasket of the nation.

Regional Economies of the South

Like the Midwest, the South at midcentury had its own diversity. The South Atlantic states encompassed a number of regional economies. Bolstered by the high price of cotton on the world market, slave plantations prospered in the Black Belt, a wide swath of fertile soil stretching west from South Carolina. In many areas of the South, planters concentrated their money and energy on cotton, diverting slaves from nonagricultural labor to toil in the fields. During the 1850s, enslaved Virginia sawmill laborers, South Carolina skilled artisans, and Georgia textile mill operatives all found themselves reduced to the status of cotton hands. In some cases, white laborers took their places in mills and workshops. In other parts of the South, slaves combined field work with nonagricultural work.

Increasingly, northern critics described the South as a land of economic extremes, with wealthy planters enjoying their white-columned mansions while degraded blacks slaved obediently in the fields. The reality was more complicated. Even among whites, there were huge variations in material conditions and daily experiences. A large amount of wealth in land and slaves was concentrated among a small percentage of the white population, and many non-slaveholding whites were tenant farmers, leasing their land, mules, and implements from wealthy planters. In some areas, as many as one of five farms was operated by tenant farmers.

At the same time, about half the total southern white population consisted of yeoman farmers, families that owned an average of 50 acres and produced most of what they consumed themselves, with the occasional help of a hired hand (a leased slave or a wage-earning white person). In up-country Georgia and South Carolina, yeoman farmers maintained local economies that were little affected by the cotton culture of the great planters in the Black Belt. These families grew what they needed: corn for themselves and their livestock and small amounts of cotton that the women spun, wove, and then sewed into clothing. Men and women alike labored in neighborhood networks of exchange, trading farm produce such as milk and eggs for services such as shoemaking and blacksmithing.

The institution of slavery discouraged immigrants from moving to the rural South in large numbers. German artisans realized that slave labor would undercut their own wages, and Scandinavian farmers understood that they could not compete with large planters in terms of landowning or slave owning. However, the ethnic diversity of southern port cities offered a striking contrast to the countryside, where native-born Protestants predominated. In 1860, 54 percent of all skilled workers and 69 percent of unskilled workers in Mobile, Alabama, were immigrants.

Throughout the slave states, black people continued to challenge the underpinnings of white supremacy. On the back roads of the plantation counties, late at night, poor workers of both races colluded to deprive the planter elite of their ill-gotten gain. Slaves swapped hams pilfered from smokehouses and bags of cotton lifted from storehouses for cash and goods offered by landless whites.

Southern blacks were a diverse group. In the cities, planters allowed highly skilled slaves to hire themselves out and keep part of the money they earned for themselves. In their pride of craft and in their relative freedom to come and go as they pleased, these people inhabited a world that was neither completely slave nor completely free. Located primarily in the upper South and in the largest towns, communities composed of free people of color supported churches and clandestine schools, mocking the white notion that all black people possessed a childlike temperament that rendered them incapable of caring for themselves.

A Free Labor Ideology in the North

In reaction to the southern slave system, the rural areas of the Northeast and Mid-Atlantic spawned a potent free-labor ideology, which held that workers should reap what they sowed, unfettered by legal systems of slavery and indentured servitude. Free labor advocates glorified the family farmer, the sturdy landowner of modest means, the husband and father who labored according to the dictates of the season and owed his soul—and his vote and the land he tilled—to no master. Nevertheless, the reality that sustained this ideal was eroding in the North during the 1850s.

Maine textile workers, with their shuttles, pose for a formal portrait around 1860. Some early New England textile mills, such as those in Lowell, Massachusetts, hired young unmarried white women exclusively, most from the surrounding rural areas. Although women factory workers developed a collective identity distinct from that of middle-class wives, most young, native-born women eventually married and withdrew from the paid labor force. How does this photo reveal the cultural and demographic sameness of this particular labor force? Why would an employer seek to hire workers of a similar cultural background in terms of religion, age, marital status, and racial identity?

More and more Northerners were earning wages by working for bosses, rather than tilling their own land. Faced with competition from Midwestern farmers and burdened by unfavorable growing conditions imposed by rocky soil and a long winter, New Englanders were migrating to nearby towns and mill villages and to the West. By 1860, the region's textile and shoemaking industries were largely mechanized. From New Hampshire to Rhode Island, growing numbers of water-powered factories perched along the fall line, where rivers spilled swiftly out of the foothills and into the coastal plain. The all-white factory workforce included men and women, adults and children, Irish Catholics and native-born Protestants, failed farmers and young men and women eager to leave the uncertain, hardscrabble life of the countryside for the promise of the mill towns and the seaport cities.

Although Northerners in general contrasted themselves to the "backward slave South," their region of the country retained elements of unfree labor systems. New Jersey did not officially emancipate the last of its slaves until 1846, and throughout the North, vestiges of slavery lingered through the mid-nineteenth century. As a group of disproportionately poor people, blacks in New England, the Mid-Atlantic, and the Midwest were vulnerable to labor exploitation, including indentured servitude and a system of "apprenticeship" whereby black children were taken from their parents and forced to work for whites.

Many non-slave workers did not receive pay for their labor. As is the case today, wives and mothers throughout the country performed almost all of their work in the home without monetary compensation, although the measure of a white man was calculated more and more in cash terms. On farms and in textile mills such as those of Pawtucket, Rhode Island, children played a key role in the livelihood of individual households but received little or nothing in cash wages. Some members of the white working classes began to condemn "wage slavery," a system that deprived them of what they considered a fair reward for their labors and left them at the mercy of merchant capitalists and factory bosses. These workers charged that they were paid so little by employers that their plight was similar to that of black slaves in the South.

While different regions developed specialized economies, these regions relied on each other for the production of staple crops and manufactured goods. The result was a national economy. Southern slaves produced the cotton processed in New England textile mills. Midwestern farmers grew the grain that fed eastern consumers. California Forty-Niners discovered the gold that expanded the national currency supply. Yet these patterns of economic interdependence were insufficient to resolve the persistent political question: which groups of people were entitled to American citizenship, with all the rights and privileges that the term implied?

Individualism Versus Group Identity

13.2 In what ways did the American ideal of individualism clash with the group stereotypes and prejudices enshrined in 1850s law and customs?

In every region of the country, discriminatory ideas and practices increasingly exerted force. People were defined ever more strongly on the basis of their nationality, language, religion, and skin color. They were more and more limited in their legal status and the jobs they could obtain. Degrading images of legally vulnerable groups—blacks, Chinese, Hispanos—became a part of popular culture, in the songs people sang and the pictures they saw in books and magazines. Through these means, native-born Americans of British stock sought to distance themselves from people of color and from immigrants.

Paradoxically, some writers began to highlight the idea of American individualism during this time. Such authors extolled what they considered the universal qualities embedded in American nationhood. They believed that the United States consisted not of distinctive and competing groups, but of a collection of individuals, all bent on pursuing their own self-interest, variously defined. They believed that the "representative" American was ambitious and acquisitive, eager to make more money and buy new things.

Yet not everyone could afford to embrace this optimistic form of individualism. Many who were marginalized found emotional support, and in some cases even political power, in a strong group identity. For example, on the Plains, the Sioux Indians resisted the idea that U.S. officials could carve up territory and sell land to individual farmers at the expense of a people that pursued the buffalo across artificial political boundaries. During negotiations at Fort Laramie in 1851, Black Hawk, a leader of the Oglala Sioux, condemned the whites with his understatement, "You have split my land and I don't like it." In contrast to the Plains Indians, who wanted no role in American politics, African Americans and white women strove for full citizenship rights. These groups looked forward to the day when each person was accorded the same rights and was free to pursue his or her own talents and ambitions.

Putting into Practice Ideas of Social Inferiority

Everywhere, European American men sought to achieve or preserve the most stable, well-paying, and appealing jobs for themselves. By promoting ideas related to the

Just as American writers explored questions of national identity, American artists portrayed everyday scenes related to the vitality of American enterprise and democracy. This painting, *Raftsmen Playing Cards* (1847), was one from George Caleb Bingham's series of pictures of Missouri river men. A contemporary observer speculated that the youth on the right is "a mean and cunning scamp, probably the black sheep of a good family, and a sort of vagabond idler." Large rivers such as the Missouri and Mississippi remained powerful symbols of freedom in the American imagination. What do the jug on the left, the pair of shoes on the right, and the card players in the middle suggest about the nature of work that these raftsmen do?

SOURCE: George Caleb Bingham, *Raftsmen Playing Cards*, 1847. Saint Louis Art Museum, Ezra H. Linley Fund

supposed inferiority of African Americans, Hispanos, and immigrants, European American men could justify barring these groups from the rights of citizenship and landownership as well as from non-menial kinds of employment. In California, U.S. officials justified the exclusion of blacks, Indians, Chinese, and the poorest Mexicans from citizenship rights by claiming that members of these groups were nonwhite or, in the words of one state judge writing in 1854, "not of white blood." (Of course, the concept of "white blood" has no scientific basis because the different blood types—A, B, AB, and O—are found among all peoples.)

The precarious social status of various groups was revealed in patterns of their work. In California, white men pursued opportunities on farms and in factories while increasing numbers of Chinese men labored as laundrymen and domestic servants. Indians toiled as field hands under white supervision. In rural Texas, Anglos established plantations and ranches, while more and more Mexicans worked as vaqueros (cowboys), shepherds, sidewalk vendors, and freighters. In Massachusetts mill towns, white men and women served as the forefront of an industrial labor force, while many African Americans of both sexes and all ages were confined to work in kitchens and outdoors as sweepers, cart drivers, and hawkers of goods.

Despite the divergent regional economies that shaped them, emerging ideologies of racial inferiority were strikingly similar. European Americans stereotyped all Chinese, Mexicans, and African Americans as promiscuous, crafty, "degraded," and intellectually inferior to whites. Such prejudices, in places as diverse as Boston, San Antonio, and San Francisco, prevented many people of color from reaching the limits of their own talents in mid–nineteenth-century America.

"A Teeming Nation"—America in Literature

Ideas about ethnic and racial difference coexisted with notions of American individualism, which stressed forms of universal equality. The variety of voices that gave

325

Interpreting History

Professor George Howe ON THE SUBORDINATION OF WOMEN

"She may **strive** for the **mastery, but** to **rule** with the hand of **power** was **never designed** for her."

Antebellum southern elites prized what they called "natural" hierarchical social relations: the authority of fathers and husbands over daughters and wives, parents over children, rich over poor, and whites over blacks. According to slaveholders, clergy, and scholars, these relationships provided social stability and ensured that the weak and dependent would receive care from the rich and powerful. In July 1850, George Howe, professor of Biblical literature at the Theological Seminary at Columbia, South Carolina, addressed the graduating class of a private women's academy. Howe suggested that the roles of women (elite white women) were enduring and never-changing.

THE ENDOWMENTS, POSITION AND EDUCATION OF WOMAN. AN ADDRESS DELIVERED BEFORE THE HEMANS AND SIGOURNEY SOCIETIES OF THE FEMALE HIGH SCHOOL AT LIMESTONE SPRINGS

The duties of life to all human beings are arduous, its objects are noble—each stage of its progress is preparatory to some other stage, and the whole a preparation to an interminable existence, upon which, in one sense, we are hereafter to enter, and in another, have already entered. Others may slightly regard the employments, trials and joys of the school girl. I am disposed to put on them a higher value. Our wives, sisters, and our mothers were in the same position yesterday. You will occupy a like [position] with them tomorrow. Whatever of virtue, of patient endurance, of poignant suffering, of useful labor, of noble impulse, of generous endeavor, of influence exerted on society for its good, has been exhibited in their example, in a few short years we shall see exhibited also in yours.

To woman, . . . there must be ascribed . . . acuteness in her powers of perception, . . . instincts . . . and emotions. When these are powerfully excited there is a wonderful vigor and determination of will, and a ready discovery of expedients to accomplish her wishes. She has readier sympathies, her fountain of tears is nearer the surface, but her emotions may not be so constant and permanent as those of man. She has greater readiness and tact, purer and more noble and unselfish desires and impulses, and a higher degree of veneration for the virtuous and exalted, and when she has found

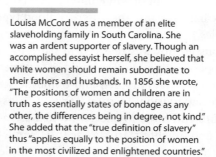

Louisa McCord was a member of an elite slaveholding family in South Carolina. She was an ardent supporter of slavery. Though an accomplished essayist herself, she believed that white women should remain subordinate to their fathers and husbands. In 1856 she wrote, "The positions of women and children are in truth as essentially states of bondage as any other, the differences being in degree, not kind." She added that the "true definition of slavery" thus "applies equally to the position of women in the most civilized and enlightened countries."

the way of truth, a heart more constant and more susceptible to all those influences which come from above. To the gentleness and quiet of her nature, to its affection and sympathy, that religion which pronounces its benediction on the peace-makers and the merciful, which recommends to them the ornament of a meek and quiet spirit, which, in the sight of the Lord, is of a great price, addresses itself with more force and greater attraction than it addresses man. Born to lean upon others, rather than to stand independently by herself, and to confide in an arm stronger than hers, her mind turns more readily to the higher power which brought her into being. . . .

Providence, then, and her own endowments mark out the proper province of woman. In some cases she may strive for the mastery, but to rule with the hand of power was never designed for her. When she thus unsexes herself she is despised and detested by man and woman alike. England's Queen Victoria at the present moment, if not more feared, is far more beloved in the quiet of her domestic life, than Elizabeth was, the most feared of her female Sovereigns.

Howe ends his address by drawing an implicit comparison between the South and the North. Like many Southerners, he associated the North with labor radicalism, abolitionism, and challenges to the "natural" position of women.

When women go about haranguing promiscuous assemblies of men, lecturing in public, either on infidelity or religion, on slavery, on war or peace—when they meet together in conventions and pass resolutions on grave questions of State—when they set themselves up to manufacture a public opinion for their own advantage and exaltation—when they meet together in organized bodies and pass resolutions about the "rights of woman," and claim for her a voice and a vote in the appointment of civil rulers, and in the government, whether of Church or State, she is stepping forth from her rightful sphere and becomes disgusting and unlovely, just in proportion as she assumes to be a man.

Questions for Discussion

1. Does Professor Howe believe that women are naturally inferior to men? Why or why not?
2. Why would Howe argue against citizenship rights for women, including the right to vote and serve on juries?
3. What were the tensions implicit in white women's status, considering that they were neither full citizens like their husbands nor slaves like the workers who toiled on their behalf?

SOURCE: George Howe, *The Endowments, Position and Education of Woman. An Address Delivered Before the Hemans and Sigourney Societies of the Female High School at Limestone Springs*, July 23, 1850 (Columbia, SC: I. C. Morgan, 1850), pp. 5, 9, 10–11.

expression to the national ideals of personal striving and ambition suggested the growth, energy, and vitality of the United States in the 1850s. In the Northeast, writers such as Ralph Waldo Emerson, Henry David Thoreau, Herman Melville, and Walt Whitman promoted a robust sensibility attuned to the challenges posed by the rigors of both the external world of natural beauty and the inner world of the spirit.

Some forms of literature offered an explicit critique of American materialism. According to Emerson, people were too concerned about possessions; as he put it, things were "in the saddle," riding everyone. During the 1850s, Thoreau's work became more explicitly focused on nature, as in his book *Walden* (1854). An appreciation of the wonders of nature—wonders that could be felt and tasted, as well as seen—amounted to a powerful force of democratization; anyone and everyone could participate. In turn, Thoreau actively supported the abolition of slavery; his love of nature formed the foundation of his belief in the universal dignity of all people in general and the cause of freedom for black people in particular.

In contrast, other writers celebrated busy-ness, whether in the field or workshop. In the introduction to his book of poetry titled *Leaves of Grass* (1855), Walt Whitman captured the restlessness of a people on the move: "Here is not merely a nation but a teeming nation of nations. Here is action . . . magnificently moving in vast masses." To Whitman, the expansiveness of the American landscape mirrored the American soul, "the largeness and generosity of the spirit of the citizen." His sensuous "Song of Myself" constituted an anthem for all Americans poised, gloriously diverse in their individuality, to exploit the infinite possibilities of both body and spirit.

Challenges to Individualism

Many men and women remained skeptical of—and, in some cases, totally estranged from—the wondrous possibilities inherent in Whitman's phrase "Me, Me going in for my chances." In northern cities, individualism promoted the kind of creative genius necessary for technological innovation and dynamic economic change, but it had little meaning for Native Americans in the West, most of whom were desperately seeking a collective response to new threats in the form of cattle ranchers and the U.S. cavalry. On the Great Plains, groups such as the Mandan and Pawnee performed ceremonies and rituals that celebrated kinship and village life above the individual.

African Americans in the North forged a strong sense of group identity. Though they rejected notions of white people's "racial" superiority, blacks had little choice but to think of themselves as a group separate and distinct from whites. In northern cities, blacks took in boarders and joined mutual-aid societies in order to affirm the collective interests of the larger black community. In contrast, well-to-do whites were increasingly emphasizing the sanctity of the nuclear family, composed solely of parents and children. Charismatic black Boston preacher Maria Stewart denounced the twin evils of racial and gender prejudice for condemning all black women to a life of menial labor: "How long shall the fair daughters of Africa be compelled to bury their minds and talents beneath a load of iron pots and kettles?"

Some groups of women embraced a collective identity of womanhood, although the definition of that identity took several forms. In the North, writers such as Catharine Beecher articulated a vision of female self-sacrifice fueled by family obligations and emotional relationships. Beecher declared that self-sacrifice formed the "grand law of the system" by which women should live their lives. Informed by religious devotion and sustained by labors of love in the home, this female world offered an alternative to the masculine individualism necessary for profit-seeking, whether on the family farm or in the bank or textile mill. Middle-class women believed they could take pride in rearing virtuous citizens and caring for overworked husbands. Sarah Willis Parton (Fanny Fern) cautioned her readers in a series of sketches published in 1853 (*Fern Leaves from Fanny's Portfolio*) that marriage is "the hardest way on earth of getting a living. You never know when your work is done."

Other groups of women cherished different kinds of aspirations. Organizers of the country's first conference devoted to the status of women, the Seneca Falls Convention

((• 📖 **Read** the **Document**   **Lucretia Mott, Declaration of Sentiments and Resolutions (1848)**

Isabella Baumfree was born into slavery in New York State in 1797. Thirty years later, she escaped from bondage and became a preacher. In 1843, she changed her name to Sojourner Truth. A powerful orator, she spoke on behalf of abolition and urged white women's rights activists to embrace the cause of enslaved women. Truth sold small cards, called *cartes de visite*, to support herself. On this card, a portrait taken in 1864, she notes that she must sell her image ("the Shadow") to make a living. Some activists during this period argued that white women and all enslaved men and women suffered some similar kinds of prejudices and legal liabilities. At the 1848 Seneca Falls Convention, organized by Lucretia Mott and Elizabeth Cady Stanton, the delegates declared, "All men and women are created equal." How might Sojourner Truth have perceived the "equality" of all women with each other?

held in upstate New York in 1848, derived inspiration from the abolitionist movement and protested the efforts of white men to exclude women from formal participation in it. In their demands for women's rights, Elizabeth Cady Stanton and Lucretia Mott linked the plight of the slave with the plight of free women, arguing that white men exploited and denigrated members of both groups. Though some delegates believed that women's rights should only be pursued in religious and social contexts, Stanton insisted that their activism extend into the political realm. Over the objections of Lucretia Mott and others, Stanton boldly called upon her fellow delegates to fight for the right of women to vote. In the midst of this debate, Stanton received crucial support from African American leaders such as Frederick Douglass and Sojourner Truth. Douglass, who published the antislavery newspaper the *North Star* in nearby Rochester, spoke forcefully in favor of female suffrage at Seneca Falls. Denying women the vote, he argued, had for too long resulted in the "maiming and repudiation of one-half of the moral and intellectual power of the government of the world." Delegates to Seneca Falls eventually approved a document called the "Declaration of Sentiments," modeled after the Declaration of Independence: "We hold these truths to be self-evident: that all men and women are created equal." This group of women claimed for themselves a revolutionary heritage and all the rights and privileges of citizenship: to own property in their own names, to vote, to attend schools of higher learning, and to participate "in the various trades, professions, and commerce." Seneca Falls and the declaration it inspired gave rise to the women's rights movement in the United States, a movement that eventually won the vote for women some 70 years later.

Many women, including enslaved workers throughout the South and hard-pressed needleworkers toiling in cramped New York City tenements, could not devote themselves full time to the care of hearth and home, nor could they aspire to a career of public agitation. In her autobiographical novel *Our Nig; or, Sketches from the Life of a Free Black, in a Two-Story White House, North* (1859), Harriet Wilson wrote bitterly of the fate of women such as her mother, a woman "early deprived of parental guardianship, far removed from relatives . . . left to guide her tiny boat over life's surges alone and inexperienced." Like the book's main character, Alfrado, Wilson herself had suffered at the hands of tyrannical white women employers, but at the end of the story Alfrado achieves a measure of dignity and independence for herself by setting up a small business. She thus offered an explicit challenge to both the arrogance of propertied white men and the homebound sentimentality of wealthy white women.

The Paradox of Southern Political Power

13.3 How could white Southerners dominate all three branches of the national government and still perceive themselves on the defensive, under siege?

At the center of debates about hierarchies and equality, the institution of slavery needed to expand to survive. Decades of intensive cultivation were exhausting the cotton fields in the South. The planter elite was counting on the admission of new territories as slave states to preserve their threatened power in Congress. To slave owners, northern-sponsored efforts to block their expansion amounted to a death sentence for all that the white South held dear. In defense of the slave system, the white South had to mount a strong offense, or die.

Slaveholders' anxieties indicated that the United States was being pulled in two directions. In the North, a growing, dynamic economy pointed toward expanding economic opportunities for both immigrants and the native-born, as new forms of technology created new jobs. In the South, white slaveholders sought to preserve their traditional staple-crop economy, an economy that demanded not innovation, but more land and more slaves. This tension provoked growing calls for equality from whites in the North, and persistent calls to preserve slavery at all costs from whites in the South.

In the early 1850s, proslavery forces maintained firm control over all branches of the federal government. This derived in large part from the "three-fifths clause" of the Constitution, which gave disproportionate representation to the slave states, where each slave was counted as three-fifths of a person. Nevertheless, southern planters felt increasingly defensive as the country expanded westward. They warned against "the abolition excitement," which would necessarily upset the delicate balance between slave and free states. Gradually, this tension between southern strength and southern fears led to the fraying and then unraveling of the Jacksonian American party system, which had relied on a truce maintained between Whigs and Democrats on the issue of slavery. A new party, the Republicans, fused the democratic idealism and economic self-interest of native-born Northerners in such a powerful way that white Southerners believed that the institution of slavery was in danger of succumbing to the Yankee onslaught. And so a clash of ideas gradually slipped out of the confines of the polling place and into the realm of armed conflict.

The Party System in Disarray

In 1848, eight years after the appearance of the antislavery Liberty party, cracks in the second two-party system of Whigs versus Democrats opened wider with the founding

329

TABLE 13.1 THE ELECTION OF 1848

Candidate	Political Party	Popular Vote (%)	Electoral Vote
Zachary Taylor	Whig	47.4	163
Lewis Cass	Democratic	42.5	127
Martin Van Buren	Free-Soil	10.1	—

of the Free-Soil party. Free-Soilers challenged the prevailing notion that the Whigs and Democrats could continue to smooth over the question of slavery in the territories with a variety of patchwork policies and piecemeal compromises. The Free-Soil platform promoted a forthright no-slavery-in-the-territories policy and favored the Wilmot Proviso (introduced in Congress in 1846), which would have banned slavery from all land acquired as a result of the Mexican War. In the presidential election of 1848, the Free-Soil party nominated former President Martin Van Buren, Democrat of New York. At the same time, Free-Soilers extended their appeal to the Whig party by supporting federal aid for internal improvements, free western homesteads for settlers, and protective tariffs for northern manufacturers.

Nevertheless, the two major parties persisted in avoidance politics. The Democrats nominated General Lewis Cass, the "father of **popular sovereignty**," a doctrine allowing citizens of new states to decide for themselves whether to permit slavery within their borders. The Whigs put forth General Zachary Taylor, although the Louisiana slaveholder and Mexican War veteran had never held elected office. Taylor managed to parlay his military record into a close win in the fall of 1848. But Taylor died after a year and a half as president and was replaced by his vice president, Millard Fillmore.

In 1849, white Southerners confronted a disturbing reality. Although slave owners controlled the presidency and the Supreme Court and outnumbered the North in the House of Representatives, California's application for statehood in 1849 raised the specter of an unbalanced federal system consisting of 16 free states and 15 slave states. The abolitionist threat appeared in other guises as well: the territories of Utah and New Mexico apparently preparing to ban slavery once they became states, abolitionists clamoring for the immediate **emancipation** (that is, freedom from bondage) of all slaves, and black men and women, including former slave Harriet Tubman, working with abolitionists in the upper South and the North to facilitate the escape of slaves through a network of safe stops called the **Underground Railroad**. The "railroad" consisted of Northerners, white and black, who sheltered fugitives from slavery in their flight to the North or, in some instances, to Canada.

The Compromise of 1850

Against this backdrop of sectional controversy, Congress debated the terms under which California would enter the Union in 1850. A young Democratic senator from Illinois, Stephen Douglas, helped cobble together the Compromise of 1850, under which California would enter the Union as a free state that year. New Mexico and Utah would eventually submit the slavery question to voters and thus put the idea of popular sovereignty to a practical test. The federal government would abolish the slave trade in Washington, D.C. (a move that did not affect the status of slaves already living there), and shore up the Fugitive Slave law of 1793 with a new, harsher measure.

The **Fugitive Slave Law of 1850** essentially did away with the notion of the North as free territory, for it required local and federal law enforcement agents to retrieve runaways no matter where they sought refuge in the United States. Blacks were denied a trial or the right to testify on their own behalf. Fugitive slave commissioners earned $10 for each runaway they returned to a claimant. By compelling ordinary citizens to aid in the capture of alleged fugitives, the law brought the issue of slavery to the doorstep of northern whites.

Popular sovereignty The idea that residents of a state should be able to make decisions on crucial issues, such as whether or not to legalize slavery.

Emancipation National or state-sponsored program to free slaves.

Underground Railroad A secret network of abolitionists developed during the antebellum period to help slaves escape and find refuge, many in the North or in Canada.

Fugitive Slave Law of 1850 Congressional legislation that required local and federal law enforcement agents to retrieve runaways no matter where they sought refuge in the United States.

TABLE 13.2 THE ELECTION OF 1852

Candidate	Political Party	Popular Vote (%)	Electoral Vote
Franklin Pierce	Democratic	50.9	254
Winfield Scott	Whig	44.1	42
John P. Hale	Free-Soil	5.0	—

The compromise left some political leaders bitterly disappointed. Senator William H. Seward of New York argued that Congress must answer to a "higher law" than the Constitution, and he denounced supporters of the new measure as "traitors to the cause of freedom." He believed that the compromise would solidify the institution of human bondage. As a result, he and others formed an offshoot of the Whig Party called the "Conscience Whigs," who vowed to use the political process to fight against slavery.

Despite these dramatic events, the presidential campaign of 1852 was a lackluster affair. The Democrats nominated an unknown lawyer, Franklin Pierce. Although he hailed from New Hampshire, Pierce supported slavery. The Whigs turned their back on the undistinguished President Fillmore and chose as their nominee General Winfield Scott, who had gained fame during the Mexican War. Yet the Whigs split into regional factions during the election, Northerners resenting Scott's support of the Fugitive Slave Law and Southerners doubting his devotion to slavery. This split foreshadowed the end of national political parties and the emergence of regional parties, an ominous development indeed.

The Violent Politics of Expansionism

The interests of the South's planters affected not only domestic politics, but debates and policies related to foreign affairs as well. Even as Congress was heatedly discussing the Compromise of 1850, Southerners were contemplating ways to extend their reach across and even beyond the continental United States. They wanted to find new, fresh, fertile lands for cotton cultivation, and they hoped to incorporate those lands into the United States. Such expansion would also help to bolster the political power of slave owners in Congress by someday adding new slave states to the Union.

In 1848, President Polk had made a gesture to buy Cuba from Spain, an offer that was rebuffed but one that did not discourage two privately financed expeditions of proslavery Americans from making forays into Cuba in an effort to seize the island by force on behalf of the United States. In 1854, the American ambassadors to Great Britain, France, and Spain met in Ostend, Belgium, and issued a statement declaring that, if Spain would not sell Cuba, the United States would be justified in taking control of the island. According to the Americans, the Monroe Doctrine gave license to the United States to rid the Western Hemisphere of European colonial powers. Noting that two of the three ambassadors hailed from slave states, abolitionists charged that the Ostend Manifesto was just one more ploy to extend the power of slaveholders throughout the Northern Hemisphere.

In 1855, a young proslavery American adventurer, Tennessee-born William Walker, gathered a band of fifty-eight mercenaries and managed to capture Granada, Nicaragua. Declaring himself president of Nicaragua, Walker encouraged the institution of slavery and won U.S. recognition for his regime in 1856. Walker was driven out of the country a year later, but his arrogance and bold move helped set the stage for the Nicaraguan anti-American movement that would resurface in the twentieth century.

The Gadsden Purchase of 1853 marked the end of westward land acquisition on the continent, but in a commercial sense, expansion continued past the edge of the continental United States. Americans saw the Pacific Ocean as a trade route and East Asia as a trading partner. Commodore Matthew Perry commanded a fleet of U.S. Navy ships that steamed into Tokyo Harbor in 1853. The treaty Perry helped arrange with Japan in 1854 protected American whaling ships, sailors, and merchants in that part of the world and opened the door to an increase in trade later in the century.

By the mid-1850s, the uniting of the continent into what would eventually become the forty-eight contiguous states was a source of sectional tension as well as national pride. Fewer and fewer Northerners supported what they considered pro-slavery charades, so-called legislative compromises. And the territory of Nebraska, poised on the brink of statehood, forced national lawmakers to confront again the political problem of the expansion of slavery. Once more Senator Douglas from Illinois stepped in to fill the breach. Douglas believed that mutual accommodation between North and South demanded a constant process of negotiation and flexibility on both sides. Thus he argued that the gigantic territory be split into two new states, Kansas and Nebraska, whose respective voters would decide the issue of slavery for themselves. His proposal necessitated that part of the Missouri Compromise of 1820, the part that forbade slavery above the 36°30′ line, would have to be repealed.

The Kansas–Nebraska Act became law in 1854, enraging northern Free-Soilers by dismantling the 1820 agreement. They became convinced that what they called the Slave Power Conspiracy would stop at nothing until slavery overran the entire nation. The measure also had a profound effect on the Plains Indians, for it deprived them of fully one-half the land they had been granted by treaty. Specifically, the act wrought havoc on the lives of Ponca, Pawnee, Arapaho, and Cheyenne on the southern and central plains. European American settlers poured into the region, provoking Indian attacks. In September 1855, 600 American troops staged a retaliatory raid against an Indian village, Blue Water, in Nebraska, killing 85 Sioux and leading to an escalation in violence between Indians and settlers in the area.

In their impatience with the two major parties, Free-Soilers were not alone in the early 1850s. The nativist American party, or Know-Nothings, condemned the growing political influence of immigrants, especially Roman Catholics. With its ranks filled with former Whigs, the party tapped into a deep wellspring of resentment against immigrants on the part of urban, native-born workers as well as Protestant farmers anxious about retaining their influence in public affairs. The party wanted to limit the political participation of all foreign-born men by denying them the right to vote, whether or not they became U.S. citizens.

The Republican Alliance

The rapid rise of the Know-Nothings further indicated that voters had grown disillusioned with the two-party system. Confirmation of that fact appeared on March 20, 1854, in the small town of Ripon, Wisconsin, when a group of disaffected Whigs created the **Republican party**. One core idea informed the party: that slavery must not be allowed to spread into the western territories. From this base, the Republicans built an organization so powerful that it would capture the presidency within six years.

The genius of the Republican party resided in its ability to create and maintain an alliance between groups with vastly different goals. Now forced by the Fugitive Slave Act of 1850 to serve slaveholders (by returning runaway slaves to them) and fearful of the potential of slaveholding Southerners to capture their party, some northern Democrats cast their lot with the Republicans. From the ranks of antislavery men—the long-suffering adherents of the Liberty and Free-Soil parties—came another wing of the Republicans. These party members openly proclaimed their belief in the power of the federal government to halt the relentless march of slavery and ensure that, throughout the land, free soil would be tilled by free labor, free men and women.

Republican party Founded in 1854, this political party began as a coalition of Northerners who opposed the extension of slavery into the western territories.

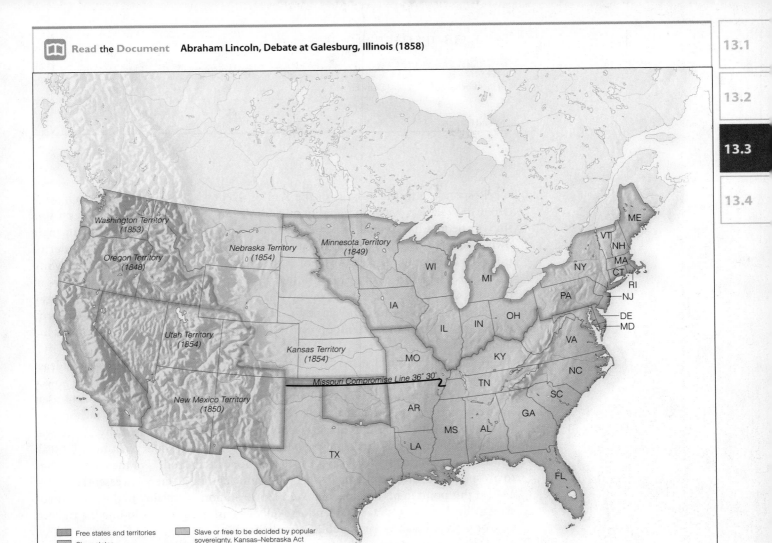

MAP 13.2 THE KANSAS–NEBRASKA ACT, 1854 Stephen A. Douglas, senator from Illinois, proposed the Kansas–Nebraska Act of 1854. Douglas hoped to ensure that any transcontinental railroad route would run through Illinois and benefit his constituents. To secure southern support for the measure, proponents of the bill repealed part of the Missouri Compromise of 1820. As a result of the act, settlers displaced many Plains Indians from their lands. In the mid-1850s, the territory of Kansas became engulfed in an internal civil war that pitted supporters of slavery against abolitionists.

Yet antislavery Republicans were by no means unified on major issues apart from the extension of slavery. Many Northerners were willing to tolerate slavery as long as it could be confined to the southern states; they cared little or nothing for the rights of black people, slave or free. In fact, in the Midwest, Republicans saw no contradiction in calling for the end of slavery in one breath and for the end of black migration to the area in the next. They feared that as job competitors, blacks would force whites to work for less money than they were accustomed to, or would push whites out of jobs altogether.

From the ranks of the newly formed Illinois state Republican party emerged a formidable leader. Born in 1809 in Kentucky, Abraham Lincoln came from a modest background and followed a checkered path into Illinois Whig politics: from youthful plow-hand and log-splitter, to local postmaster and county surveyor, and finally self-taught lawyer and member of the state legislature (1834–1842). Although his 6-foot 4-inch frame and humble background drew ridicule from wealthy people—a Philadelphia lawyer described him as "a tall rawly boned, ungainly back woodsman, with coarse, ill-fitting clothing"—Lincoln made good use of his oratorical gifts and political ambition in promoting the principles of free soil.

TABLE 13.3 THE ELECTION OF 1856

Candidate	Political Party	Popular Vote (%)	Electoral Vote
James Buchanan	Democratic	45.3	174
John C. Frémont	Republican	33.1	114
Millard Fillmore	American	21.6	8

Responding to the passage of the Kansas–Nebraska Act in 1854, Lincoln pondered the relation between equality and free-labor ideology. His key concern was that all people have equal opportunities to work hard and to prosper from their own labor. He wrote, "Advancement—improvement in condition—is the order of things in a society of equals. As labor is the common burden of our race [i.e., white people], so the effort of some to shift their share of the burden on to the shoulders of others is the great durable curse of the [black] race." According to Lincoln, slavery degraded all people, white and black, because the system was inherently corrupt, providing privileges for some and oppressing others regardless of their natural talents or abilities.

Above, all Lincoln stressed the role of ambition as common to all people (at least all men): "Free labor has the inspiration of hope; pure slavery has no hope. The power of hope upon human exertion and happiness is wonderful. The slave-master himself has a conception of it, and hence the system of tasks among slaves. The slave whom you cannot drive with the lash to break seventy-five pounds of hemp in a day, if you will task him to break a hundred, and promise him pay for all he does over, he will break you an hundred and fifty. You have substituted hope for the rod." For the United States to prosper, Lincoln argued, equality of opportunity among all men was essential. However, at this point in his life, Lincoln confined his notion of equality to the abolition of slavery; he did not go so far as to endorse full citizenship rights (including the right to vote or send one's children to public schools) for blacks.

The presidential election of 1856 revealed the full dimension of the national political crisis. The Democrats nominated James Buchanan, a "dough-face" (i.e., proslavery Northerner) from Pennsylvania, with John Breckinridge of Tennessee as his running mate. In their platform, they took pains to extol the virtue of sectional compromise on the slavery issue, by this time a very unpopular position. Meanwhile, the enfeebled Whigs could do little but stand by helplessly and declare as their "fundamental article of political faith, an absolute necessity for avoiding geographical parties," another plank decidedly out of favor with a growing number of voters. The Know-Nothings cast their lot with former President Millard Fillmore, offering voters little more than an anti-immigrant platform.

Drawing on support from members of the Free-Soil and Whig parties, the Republicans nominated John C. Frémont of California for president. Their platform stated in no uncertain terms the party's opposition to the extension of slavery, as well as Republican support for a transcontinental railroad and other federally sponsored internal improvements such as roads and harbors. The document also included the bold, noble rhetoric—in favor of "the blessings of liberty" and against "tyrannical and unconstitutional laws"—that would be the hallmark of the Republican party in the decade to come. Buchanan won the election, but Frémont's carrying eleven of the sixteen northern states boded well for the Republican party and ill for the slaveholders' union. In Illinois, Frémont had benefited from the tireless campaigning of Abraham Lincoln, who electrified ever-growing crowds of people with the declaration that "the Union must be preserved in the purity of its principles as well as in the integrity of its territorial parts." The founding of the Republican party, with its unabashed pro-Union, antislavery stand, signaled that the days of political compromise on the issue of human bondage were rapidly coming to an end.

Explore the Sectional Crisis on MyHistoryLab

HOW DID THE NATION INCREASINGLY FRACTURE DURING THE SECTIONAL CRISIS?

Between 1790 and 1860, the United States witnessed dramatic growth in both population and territory. Politicians hoped to compromise on the issue of slavery. For example, the Missouri Compromise of 1820 sought to make sure that, even with introduction of new states, the number of slave and "free" senators in the U.S. Senate would remain even. Nevertheless, tensions persisted in the western territories, where settlers fought among themselves over whether a territory (and future state) should allow slavery. Northern farmers hoped to keep the western territories free of slavery, so they could move to this area with their families and not have to compete for land and labor with slaveholders living there.

When abolitionists petitioned the House of Representatives to curtail and eliminate slavery, pro-slavery congressmen responded with a series of gag rules to prevent antislavery petitions from being read. *Library of Congress.*

SLAVES AS TOTAL POPULATION PERCENTAGE IN SLAVE-HOLDING STATES

State	Percent
Alabama	45%
Arkansas	26%
Delaware	2%
Florida	44%
Georgia	44%
Kentucky	20%
Louisiana	47%
Maryland	13%
Mississippi	55%
Missouri	10%
North Carolina	33%
South Carolina	57%
Tennessee	25%
Texas	30%
Virginia	31%

KEY QUESTIONS Use **MyHistoryLab** *Explorer* to **answer** these **questions:**

Comparison ▶▶▶ *How did the demographics of the North differ from the South?*

Explore the populations of the two regions based on census results.

Consequence ▶▶▶ *What impact did slavery have on immigration to the South?*

Map the percentage of foreign-born immigrants in the United States.

Analysis ▶▶▶ *In what areas did more people live in towns and cities during this time?*

Theorize what effects differences in levels of urban population had on area economies.

The Deepening Conflict over Slavery

13.4 During the 1850s, what specific events and developments pushed the nation toward armed conflict?

Only a small subset of Americans—adult white men—participated directly in the formation of new political parties that set the terms for congressional debates over territorial expansion and slavery. Nevertheless, during the 1850s, increasing numbers of ordinary people were drawn into the escalating conflict over the South's "peculiar institution" as some Northerners mounted concerted challenges, violent as well as peaceful, to the Fugitive Slave Law. The western territory of Kansas became a bloody battleground as abolitionists and proslavery forces fought for control of the new state government. Sites of struggle over the slavery issue also included the streets of Boston, the Supreme Court of the United States, political rallies in Illinois, and a federal arsenal in Harpers Ferry, Virginia. No longer would the opposing sides confine their disagreements to congressional debates over the admission of new states. Nor would words be the only weapons. The country was rushing headlong into nationwide armed conflict.

The Rising Tide of Violence

The Fugitive Slave Law of 1850 caused fear and alarm among many Northerners. In response to the measure, some African Americans, hiding in northern cities, fled to Canada, often with the aid of conductors on the Underground Railroad. Abolitionists, white and black, made dramatic rescue attempts on behalf of men and women sought by their self-proclaimed southern owners. In Boston in 1851, a waiter named Shadrach Minkins was seized at work and charged with running away from a Virginia slaveholder. During a court hearing to determine the merits of the case, a group of blacks stormed in, disarmed the startled authorities, and, in the words of a sympathetic observer, "with a dexterity worthy of the Roman gladiators, snatched the trembling prey of the slavehunters, and conveyed him in triumph to the streets of Boston." Shadrach Minkins found safety in Montreal, Canada, and a Boston jury refused to convict his lawyers, who had been accused of masterminding his escape. The spectacular public rescue of Minkins, and other such attempts, both successful and unsuccessful, throughout the North, brought the issue of slavery into the realm of public performance in northern towns and cities.

Gradually, the war of words over slavery cascaded out of small-circulation abolitionist periodicals and into the consciousness of a nation. In particular, author Harriet Beecher Stowe managed to wed politics and sentiment in a most compelling way. Her novel *Uncle Tom's Cabin* (1852) sold more than 300,000 copies within ten months and a million copies over the next seven years. The book, originally serialized in a magazine, *The National Era*, introduced large numbers of Northerners to the sufferings of an enslaved couple, Eliza and George. Slavery's greatest crime, in Stowe's eyes, was the forced severance of family ties between husbands and wives, parents and children.

Southern slaveholders were outraged at Stowe's attempt to portray their way of life as an unmitigated evil. A South Carolina slave-holding woman, Louisa McCord, wrote, "We proclaim it [slavery], on the contrary, a Godlike dispensation, a providential caring for the weak, and a refuge for the portionless." Another Southerner, George Fitzhugh, took this argument to its logical conclusion. In his book *Cannibals All! Or, Slaves Without Masters* (1857), Fitzhugh claimed that civil society demanded the enslavement of the masses, whether white or black: "Some were born with saddles on their backs, and others booted and spurred to ride them—and the riding does them good." Fitzhugh also argued that slaves, whom he claimed were cared for by benevolent planters, were better off than northern factory workers, whom he asserted were exploited and neglected by indifferent employers.

👁 **Watch the Video** **Harriet Beecher Stowe and the Making of** *Uncle Tom's Cabin*

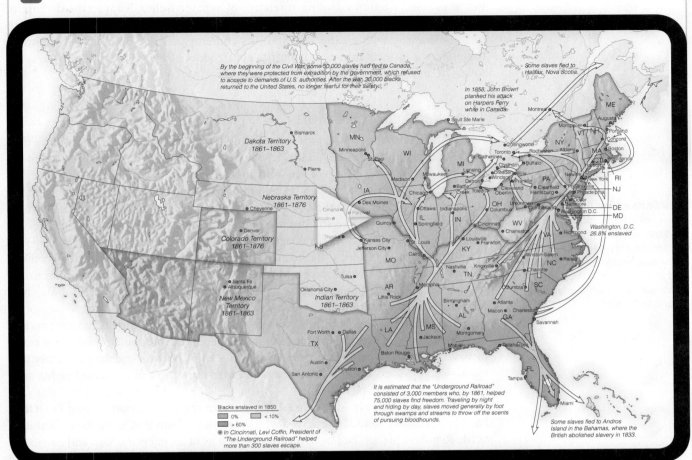

By the beginning of the Civil War, some 50,000 slaves had fled to Canada, where they were protected from extradition by the government, which refused to accede to demands of U.S. authorities. After the war, 30,000 blacks returned to the United States, no longer fearful for their safety.

In 1858, John Brown planned his attack on Harpers Ferry while in Canada.

Some slaves fled to Halifax, Nova Scotia.

It is estimated that the "Underground Railroad" consisted of 3,000 members who, by 1861, helped 75,000 slaves find freedom. Traveling by night and hiding by day, slaves moved generally by foot through swamps and streams to throw off the scents of pursuing bloodhounds.

Washington, D.C. 26.8% enslaved

Some slaves fled to Andros Island in the Bahamas, where the British abolished slavery in 1833.

Blacks enslaved in 1850
- 0%
- < 10%
- > 60%
- In Cincinnati, Levi Coffin, President of "The Underground Railroad" helped more than 300 slaves escape.

MAP 13.3 THE UNDERGROUND RAILROAD The Underground Railroad consisted of a network of people who helped fugitives in their escape from slavery en route to the North or Canada. Harriet Tubman made an estimated thirteen separate trips to the South to help an estimated seventy slaves escape to freedom.

Meanwhile, the territory of Kansas was becoming engulfed in a regional civil war. Proslavery settlers, aided and abetted by their compatriots (called Border Ruffians) from Missouri, installed their own territorial government at Shawnee Mission in 1855. Opposing these proslavery settlers were the Free-Soilers, some of whom had organized into abolitionist groups, such as the New England Emigrant Aid Company, and armed themselves with rifles.

This dangerous situation soon gave way to terrorism and insurrection on both sides. In 1855, in retaliation for a proslavery raid on the "Free-Soil" town of Lawrence, Kansas, an Ohio abolitionist named John Brown, together with his four sons and two other men, hacked to death five proslavery men at Pottowatamie Creek. The massacre only strengthened the resolve of proslavery advocates, who in the next year drew up a constitution for Kansas, which effectively nullified the principle of popular sovereignty over the issue of slavery. Called the **Lecompton Constitution**, the document decreed that voters might approve or reject slavery, but even if they chose to reject it, any slaves already in the state would remain slaves under the force of law. By throwing his support behind the Lecompton Constitution, President Buchanan alienated members of his own party in the North, and the Democrats descended into North–South factionalism.

The spilling of blood over slavery was not confined to the Kansas frontier. In 1856, Senator Charles Sumner of Massachusetts, an outspoken abolitionist, delivered a speech on the floor of the U.S. Senate condemning "The Crime Against Kansas" (the Lecompton Constitution) and the men who perpetrated it, men he characterized as "hirelings picked from the drunken spew and vomit of an uneasy civilization," men

Lecompton Constitution A Kansas state constitution drawn up by proslavery advocates in 1857; sought to nullify the doctrine of popular sovereignty in the state, decreeing that even if voters rejected slavery, any slaves already in the state would remain enslaved under the force of law.

who (like his own colleague Senator Butler of South Carolina) loved slavery the way that degenerates loved their prostitutes. Shortly after this speech, Congressman Preston S. Brooks of South Carolina, a relative of Senator Butler, leapt to the defense of the white South and attacked Sumner on the floor of the Senate, beating him into unconsciousness with a cane. Abolitionists contemplated the necessity of defending themselves and their interests, from the courtrooms of New England and the small towns of the West to the halls of Congress itself.

The *Dred Scott* Decision

Dred Scott v. Sandford The 1857 case in which the Supreme Court held that residence on free soil did not render a slave a free person, for black people, enslaved and free, had (in the words of the court) "no rights which the white man was bound to respect."

Across the street from the Capitol, proceedings in the Supreme Court were more civil but no less explosive. In 1857, a former slave named Dred Scott sued in federal court, claiming that he was a citizen of Missouri and a free man. Scott maintained that he had become free once his master had taken him onto free soil (the state of Illinois and the territory of Wisconsin). In the case of **Dred Scott v. Sandford** (1857), the court ruled that even residence on free soil did not render a slave a free person, for, regardless of their status, black people had "no rights which the white man was bound to respect." With this single decision, Chief Justice Roger B. Taney and the Court threw off the hard-won balance between slave and free states. In effect, the Court declared unconstitutional the Compromise of 1820, which had banned slavery in the region north of Missouri's southern boundary, because, the justices held, slave owners could not be deprived of their property without due process. This decision threatened the precarious freedom of the South's quarter million free people of color and extended the reach of slavery into the North. The court's decision seemed to foreclose the possibility that black people regardless of legal status could ever aspire to full and equal rights anywhere in the United States.

Most white people residing outside the South never read the Court's ruling, but if they had, they probably would have agreed with the justices' claim that, since the earliest days of the Republic, blacks "had been regarded as beings of an inferior order, and altogether unfit to associate with the white race, either in social or political relations." At the same time, northern opinion makers warned that the decision made Northerners complicit in the slave system. Of the "slave power," the *Cincinnati Daily Commercial* thundered, "It has marched over and annihilated the boundaries of the states. We are now one great homogeneous slaveholding community." Even nonabolitionists had good reason to fear the long-term implications of the ruling, for it suggested that the institution of slavery was about to spill out of the confines of the South and into the rest of the country. Free white men and women feared competing with slaves in the workplace, whether in the West or East. These concerns increased with the onset of a depression in 1857 in the Northeast and the Midwest, as the mining of California gold produced inflation in the East.

The Lincoln–Douglas Debates

Against this backdrop of economic turmoil and political conflict, the congressional elections of 1858 assumed great significance. In particular, the Senate contest in Illinois pitted incumbent Stephen A. Douglas against challenger Abraham Lincoln. In a series of seven public debates, the two men debated the political conflict over slavery as it had been shaped during the tumultuous decade after the Mexican War. Though no friend of the abolitionists, Douglas was quickly falling from favor within the Democratic party; the Supreme Court had nullified his proposal for popular sovereignty in the territories, and he had parted ways from his brethren from the South when he denounced Kansas's Lecompton Constitution.

Lincoln ridiculed the doctrine of popular sovereignty, which he maintained was as thin as the "soup that was made by boiling the shadow of a pigeon that had starved to death." He had no desire to root out slavery in the South, but, "I have said, and I repeat, my wish is that the further spread of [slavery] may be arrested, and that it may be placed where the public mind shall rest in the belief that it is in the course of ultimate extinction." According to a reporter present, this last remark provoked great applause. And this was no minor confrontation between two candidates; it is estimated that in six of the seven debates, the two men spoke before crowds exceeding 10,000 people each. Lincoln lost the election (in which blacks were not allowed to vote as a matter of Illinois law), but, more significantly, he won the loyalty of Republicans all over the North and put the white South on notice that the days of compromise were almost over. Meanwhile, with the admission as free states of Minnesota in 1858 and Oregon in 1859, Congress began to reflect a distinct antislavery bias.

Harpers Ferry and the Presidential Election of 1860

On a Sunday night in October 1859, John Brown and nineteen other men (including at least five African Americans) launched a daring attack on the federal arsenal in Harpers Ferry, Virginia. They had received guns and moral support from some of the North's leading abolitionists, and their plan was to raid the arsenal and distribute firearms to slaves in the surrounding area, thereby inciting a general rebellion that, they hoped, would engulf the rest of the South. The Virginia militia and a U.S. Marines force, commanded by Lieutenant Colonel Robert E. Lee, captured Brown and his surviving followers, but not before the insurrectionist had killed seven people and injured ten others. Brown was convicted of treason against the United States for his raid on the federal arsenal, murder, and inciting an insurrection. On December 2, 1859, before being led to the gallows, Brown handed a scrap of paper to one of his guards: "I John Brown am now quite *certain* that the crimes of this *guilty land: will* never be purged *away:* but with Blood." Brown failed as the instigator of a slave rebellion, but he succeeded as a prophet.

The raid on Harpers Ferry cast a shadow over the party conventions held in the summer of 1860. By then it was apparent that the national party system had all but disintegrated. Southerners in effect seceded from the Democratic party by walking out of their Charleston convention rather than supporting Stephen Douglas as candidate for president. Within a few weeks, representatives of the party from the North and from the South reconvened in separate conventions in Baltimore. Northerners gave the nod to Douglas and Southerners chose as their standard-bearer John C. Breckinridge, a proponent of extending slavery into the territories and annexing Cuba. Representing the discredited strategy of compromise was the candidate of the Constitutional Union party, John Bell of Tennessee.

In Chicago, the Republicans lined up behind Abraham Lincoln and agreed on a platform that had something for everybody, including measures to boost economic growth (as promoted by Henry Clay's American System earlier in the century): a proposed protective tariff, a transcontinental railroad, internal improvements, and free homesteads for western farmers. The Republicans renounced the Know-Nothings. Lincoln himself took the lead in admonishing Republicans who sought to curtail the voting rights of European immigrants, such as the Germans and Scandinavians.

Yet Republicans gave little hope to other groups demanding the rights and protection that flowed from American citizenship. Spanish-speaking residents of California, Chinese immigrants, free people of color throughout the North, Indian tribes from North Carolina to the northwestern states, the wives and daughters of men all over the country—these groups were not included in the Republicans' grand design for a country based on the principles of free labor.

Abraham Lincoln was elected president in 1860, although he received support from only 40 percent of the men who cast ballots. Lincoln won the electoral college, and he also received a plurality of the popular vote. However, ten states in the South had refused to list him on the ballot; in that region of the country, he received almost no votes. Stephen Douglas won almost 30 percent of the popular vote; together, Douglas and Breckenridge outpolled Lincoln (2.2 million votes to 1.85 million). Nevertheless, the new president had swept New England, New York, Pennsylvania, and the upper Midwest. The regional interests of North and South took precedence over national

Explore the Topic The Expansion of Slavery in the Deep South, 1840 to 1860

Augustus Washington, son of a former slave, took this picture of John Brown in 1846, thirteen years before the raid on Harpers Ferry, Virginia. A pioneer daguerreotypist, Washington operated a successful studio in Hartford, Connecticut. Based on Brown's bold act, many white Southerners feared that *all* northern whites and blacks were committed to the violent overthrow of the slave system. Was that indeed the case? Does this photo convey Brown's fierce determination to challenge slaveholders and free the slaves?

TABLE 13.4 THE ELECTION OF 1860

Candidate	Political Party	Popular Vote (%)	Electoral Vote
Abraham Lincoln	Republican	39.8	180
Stephen A. Douglas	Democratic	29.5	12
John C. Breckinridge	Democratic	18.1	72
John Bell	Constitutional Union	12.6	39

political parties. By the end of 1860, South Carolina had seceded from the Union, and the nation headed toward war.

Conclusion

During the 1850s, ordinary Americans on both sides of the slavery issue began to feel that the institution of slavery had relevance to their lives. In the slave states, black workers remained yoked to a system that denied their humanity and mocked the integrity of their families. In the non-slave states, free people of color understood that northern racial prejudice was but a variation of the slaveholders' theme of domination.

340

New England farm families looking to move west were convinced that western home-steads would not improve their economic security if these homesteads were surrounded by plantations cultivated by large numbers of enslaved workers.

Republicans promoted a future full of hope, a future that would fulfill the long-thwarted promise of the young country as a republic of equal opportunity for all male citizens regardless of their ethnicity or skin color. At the same time, following the lead of Abraham Lincoln, many Republicans defined "equality" narrowly, as freedom from slavery only, and not necessarily as full and equal access to a wide range of citizenship rights, including the right to vote, run for office, or serve on a jury. Indeed, Republicans could express at the same time both anti-slavery sentiments and anti-black prejudices. Thus proponents of "free" states in the West often supported laws that discriminated against black people in their efforts to get an education, find a job, and move from place to place.

Yet this rhetoric of equality among whites carried different meanings for different groups of Southerners. The owners of large plantations were desperate to preserve their enslaved labor forces, and they were also hungry for fresh lands and renewed political power; these men scrambled to maintain their own privileges in face of growing north-ern influence in Congress. In contrast, non-slaveholding farmers sought to produce all household necessities themselves and remain independent of the worldwide cotton market economy so crucial to the wealth of slave masters and mistresses. Nevertheless, many southern whites, rich and poor, stood allied, determined to take up arms to pro-tect their families and their distinctive southern "way of life."

On the eve of the Civil War, complex forces roiled an ethnically diverse society. Ultimately, the North and South marched into combat, each side united enough to mobilize huge armies. However, wartime strains would expose fault lines in the free-labor coalition as well as in the slaveholders' republic.

Chapter Review

Regional Economies and Conflicts

13.1 To what extent, and in what ways, were U.S. regional economies interdependent by 1860? Were certain regions, or groups of people, outside the emerging national economy? p. 319

In the West, whites took land from Indians and left them as subservient players in a white-dominated economy. The Midwest consisted of diverse farms. The northern economy was based on free labor but still retained elements of inequality. Slavery dominated the South. Slaves and Indians saw few benefits from this new economy.

Individualism versus Group Identity

13.2 In what ways did the American ideal of individualism clash with the group stereotypes and prejudices enshrined in 1850s law and customs? p. 324

Many European American men held stereotypical views about the supposed inferiority of African Americans, Hispanos, and immigrants to justify barring these groups from the rights of citizenship, land ownership, and higher-paying jobs. Black men and women and white women, among others, formed groups to agitate for the rights of individuals.

The Paradox of Southern Political Power

13.3 How could white Southerners dominate all three branches of the national government and still perceive themselves on the defensive, under siege? p. 329

White Southerners argued that "abolitionist excitement" would disturb the balance between slave and free states, especially once California applied for statehood (1849). They feared that the free labor culture of the North, with its innovation and economic opportunities, would jeopardize the staple-crop economy of the South, which was dependent on slavery.

The Deepening Conflict over Slavery

13.4 During the 1850s, what specific events and developments pushed the nation toward armed conflict? p. 336

Conflict arose over the Fugitive Slave Law and the rescue of fugitive slaves in Boston; the Kansas–Nebraska Act of 1854 and its bloody aftermath; the Supreme Court's *Dred Scott* decision; John Brown's raid of Harpers Ferry, Virginia; and the election of Abraham Lincoln in 1860.

Timeline

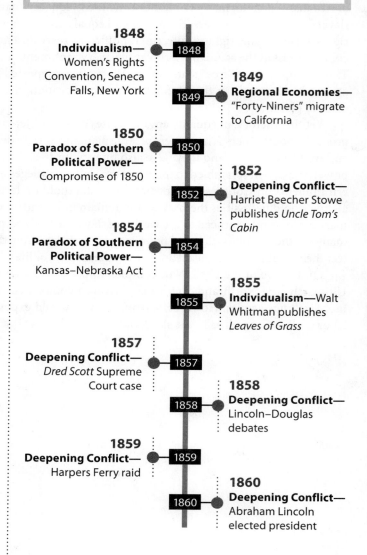

1848
Individualism— Women's Rights Convention, Seneca Falls, New York — 1848

1849
Regional Economies— "Forty-Niners" migrate to California — 1849

1850
Paradox of Southern Political Power— Compromise of 1850 — 1850

1852
Deepening Conflict— Harriet Beecher Stowe publishes *Uncle Tom's Cabin* — 1852

1854
Paradox of Southern Political Power— Kansas–Nebraska Act — 1854

1855
Individualism— Walt Whitman publishes *Leaves of Grass* — 1855

1857
Deepening Conflict— *Dred Scott* Supreme Court case — 1857

1858
Deepening Conflict— Lincoln–Douglas debates — 1858

1859
Deepening Conflict— Harpers Ferry raid — 1859

1860
Deepening Conflict— Abraham Lincoln elected president — 1860

14 "To Fight to Gain a Country": The Civil War

What would cause white **Southerners** to consider a group of fugitive slaves to be a dire threat to the would-be Confederate nation?

Pensacola, Florida, was the site of a dramatic court-martial trial in April 1862, when five men were found guilty of treasonous acts against the Confederate States of America. "Possessed of information well calculated to aid the enemy," and thus capable of "giving intelligence" to the enemy, the defendants had endangered the security of Confederate troops stationed in the area, according to the chief prosecutor.

All of the defendants—George, Robert, Stephen, Peter, and William—were runaway slaves. The specific charges lodged against them read, "That the said slaves are intelligent beings possessing the faculties of conveying information which would prove useful to the enemy and detrimental to the Confederate States." The charges suggest that the Confederates were forced to repudiate elements of their own proslavery beliefs, which held that black people were childlike, incapable of acting on their own, and grateful for the guidance and protection of southern whites.

Prosecuting officers believed that "strong measures were needed to prevent the nefarious

Sgt. F. L. Baldwin, a Union soldier, poses with an American flag as a backdrop. Black soldiers wore the Union uniform proudly. However, many of them received unequal pay compared to their white counterparts; white men received $13 a month, while black men received only $7. This form of discrimination was not overturned until late in the war. Despite these hardships and indignities, approximately 179,000 black soldiers served in the Union army. As black men fought for freedom, what were the various meanings of this uniform?

LEARNING OBJECTIVES

14.1	14.2	14.3	14.4	14.5
How did the North and South prepare for war, and how did those preparations reflect each side's strategy for fighting—and winning—the war? p. 345	What obstacles did the South face in defending its territory against northern invaders? p. 352	In what ways did black people, in the North and in the South, enslaved and free, shape the course of the fighting? p. 357	How did developments on the battlefield affect politics in both the North and South? p. 359	During the last months of the war, what factors contributed to the defeat of the Confederacy? p. 364

((• Listen to Chapter 14 on **MyHistoryLab**

👁 Watch the Video Series on MyHistoryLab

Learn about some key topics related to this chapter with the *MyHistoryLab Video Series: Key Topics in U.S. History.*

1 **The Civil War: 1861–1865** This video provides an overview of the American Civil War. The North and South clashed over the issue of slavery, in particular, and the nature of states' rights, in general. The war led to the destruction of slavery. Still, debates over the relation between the federal government and the states continue to rage today.

👁 Watch on MyHistoryLab

The Emancipation Proclamation As soon as war broke out, abolitionists began to press President Lincoln to free the slaves. This video looks at unofficial wartime challenges to the slave system even before the president announced the Emancipation Proclamation on January 1, 1863. The proclamation, an executive order, declared that all slaves in Confederate territory on that date were legally free. **2**

Watch on MyHistoryLab 👁

3 **Gettysburg: A Turning Point** In the summer of 1863, General Robert E. Lee sought to capitalize on the momentum achieved by Confederate forces at the battle of Chancellorsville. He led the Army of Northern Virginia into south-central Pennsylvania in an attempt to outflank Union forces and ultimately capture Washington, D.C. This video explores the crucial battle of Gettysburg fought in early July 1863, a turning point in the war.

👁 Watch on MyHistoryLab

The Surrender at Appomattox Court House Union Generals Ulysses S. Grant and William T. Sherman successfully led northern forces, eventually breaking the resistance of Confederate armies. This video examines the last year and a half of the war, culminating in General Lee's surrender at Appomattox Court House, Virginia, in April 1865. **4**

Watch on MyHistoryLab 👁

activities of "spys [*sic*] whether white or black." These officials therefore were unprepared for the firestorm of criticism that followed the announcement of the verdict. The owner of the slaves, General Jackson Morton, expressed outrage that two of his workers were marked for summary execution. Morton denounced the hearing as "vulgar and improper."

Though at a distinct disadvantage compared to the North in terms of troops, supplies, and industrial might, the white South managed to fight on for four long, bloody years. At the same time, black people were waging their own war. Nearly 200,000 black men from the North and South served in the Union army or navy during the war; they fought for freedom and for full citizenship rights. Nevertheless, as the institution of slavery crumbled throughout the South, blacks found the goal of equality with whites to be elusive.

The Republican conduct of the war revealed the party's nationalistic principles. Yet not all groups embraced a strong federal government. The Lincoln administration met bitter resistance from Indian tribes throughout the Midwest and Southwest. In eastern cities, Irish immigrants violently objected to the military draft. The Civil War, then, pitted diverse groups against each other over the issues of slavery, territorial expansion, federal power, and local control—all at a cost of nearly 700,000 lives.

Mobilization for War, 1861–1862

14.1 How did the North and South prepare for war, and how did those preparations reflect each side's strategy for fighting—and winning—the war?

On December 20, 1860, less than eight weeks after Abraham Lincoln was elected president of the United States, South Carolina seceded from the Union, determined, in the words of its own Declaration of Independence, to "resume her separate and equal place among nations." By February 1, 1861, Mississippi, Florida, Alabama, Georgia, Louisiana, and Texas (all states dependent on slave-based staple-crop agriculture) had also withdrawn from the United States of America. Three days later, representatives of the seven states met in Montgomery, Alabama, and formed the **Confederate States of America**. They also adopted a new constitution for their new nation. Though modeled after that of the United States, this document invoked the power of "sovereign and independent states" instead of "we, the people." Delegates to the Montgomery convention elected as their president Jefferson Davis, a wealthy Mississippi planter with an impressive record of public service. Davis was a graduate of West Point, a veteran of the Mexican War, and a former U.S. congressman, senator, and secretary of war.

Confederate States of America The would-be new nation formed in February 1861 by seven southern states—South Carolina, Mississippi, Florida, Alabama, Georgia, Louisiana, and Texas—in a bid for independence from the United States of America. By late spring 1861, the Confederacy also included Virginia, Arkansas, Tennessee, and North Carolina.

The Secession Impulse

In some respects, the Civil War seems difficult to explain, for the two sides shared a great deal. Most of the people in the North and South were English-speaking Protestants with deep roots in the culture of the British Isles. Together they celebrated a revolutionary heritage, paying homage to George Washington and the other Founding Fathers.

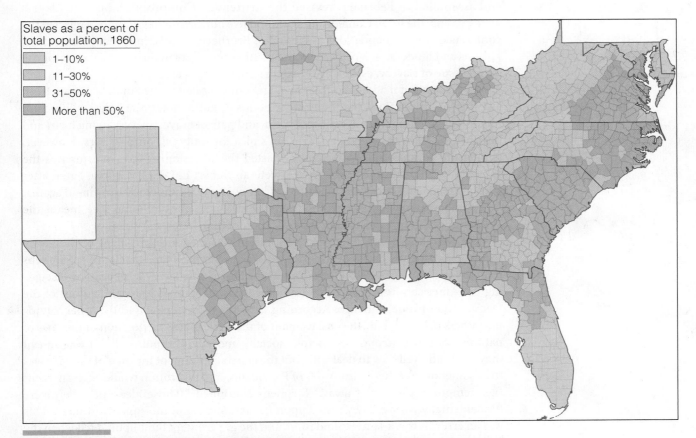

Slaves as a percent of total population, 1860

- 1–10%
- 11–30%
- 31–50%
- More than 50%

MAP 14.1 SLAVERY IN THE UNITED STATES, 1860 In the South, the areas of the greatest concentration of slaves were also the areas of greatest support for the Confederacy. During the war, the Appalachian mountain region and the upper Piedmont—the area between the mountains and the broad coastal plain—were home to people loyal to the Union and to people who became increasingly disaffected with Confederate policies as the war dragged on.

Secession The process by which the southern states withdrew from the Union; white men in each of the eleven states that eventually joined the Confederacy elected delegates to a secession convention that decided the question of whether to remain in or leave the Union.

Why, then, was the white South, especially the slave South, so fearful of Abraham Lincoln? Although Lincoln enjoyed a broad electoral college victory, he won only 40 percent of the popular vote. Lincoln had made it clear that, as president, he would possess neither the authority nor the desire to disturb slavery as it existed in the South. However, he summed up his philosophy before the **secession** crisis this way: "As I would not be a *slave*, so I would not be a *master*. This expresses my idea of democracy. Whatever differs from this . . . is not democracy."

Not surprisingly, then, southern elites felt threatened by Lincoln in particular and the Republicans in general, pointing to the new president's oft-repeated promise to halt the march of slavery into the western territories. Although he was in no position to achieve this goal by executive order, Lincoln did have the power to expand the Republican base in the South by dispensing patronage jobs to a small group of homegrown abolitionists. He could also make appointments to the Supreme Court as openings became available. The Republican party was not a majority party; it was a sectional party of the North and the upper Midwest. But this sectional party had managed to seize control of the executive branch of government, tipping the antebellum balance of power between slave and free states decisively in favor of the North. Slave owners feared that John Brown's 1859 raid on the federal arsenal at Harpers Ferry, Virginia, was just the first in a series of planned attacks on the slave South (see Chapter 13).

Two last-ditch efforts at compromise failed to avert a constitutional crisis. In December 1860, as South Carolina was seceding and other states were preparing to join it, neither northern Republicans nor lower South Democrats showed any interest in a series of proposed constitutional amendments that would have severely curtailed the federal government's ability to restrict the interstate slave trade or the spread of slavery. Called the Crittenden Compromise (after its sponsor, Senator John J. Crittenden, a Whig from Kentucky), this package of proposed amendments was defeated in the Senate on January 16, 1861. A peace conference, organized by the Virginia legislature and assembled in February, revised the Crittenden Compromise, but key players were missing: the seven Confederate states and five northern states. Congress rejected the conference's recommendations at the end of February. By this time, many Americans, radicals and moderates, Northerners and Southerners, were in no mood to compromise on the issue of slavery, especially its extension into the West.

In his inaugural address of March 4, Lincoln appealed to the South to refrain from any drastic action, invoking the historic bonds of nationhood, the "mystic chords of memory, stretching from every battle-field, and patriot grave, to every living heart and hearthstone." For the most part, Lincoln's plea for unity fell on deaf ears. However, among the Southerners who initially resisted the secessionists' call to arms was the West Point graduate and Mexican War veteran Robert E. Lee of Virginia. Later, after Virginia seceded, Lee cast his lot with the Confederacy: "I cannot raise my hand against my birthplace, my home, my children," he declared. By his home, Lee meant the Commonwealth of Virginia, not the collection of disaffected states.

On March 21, Alexander Stephens, recently named vice president of the newly formed Confederate States of America, gave a speech in Savannah, Georgia. Stephens outlined the principles behind the formation of the Confederacy. He began by discussing the American Revolution, especially the ideas of Thomas Jefferson, author of the Declaration of Independence. According to Stephens, Jefferson and the other founding fathers believed that "the enslavement of the African was in violation of the laws of nature; that it was wrong in principle, socially, morally, and politically. It was an evil they knew not well how to deal with, but the general opinion of the men of that day was that, somehow or other in the order of Providence, the institution would be evanescent [i.e., temporary] and pass away." Stephens continued, "Those ideas, however, were fundamentally wrong. They rested upon the assumption of the equality of races. This was an error. It was a sandy foundation, and the government built upon it fell when the 'storm came and the wind blew.'"

Stephens contended that the Confederacy's "foundations are laid, its corner-stone rests, upon the great truth that the negro is not equal to the white man; that slavery

MAP 14.2 THE SECESSION OF SOUTHERN STATES, 1860–1861 The southern states seceded from the Union in stages, beginning with South Carolina in December 1860. Founded on February 4, 1861, the Confederate States of America initially consisted of only that state and six Deep South states. The four upper South states of Virginia, Arkansas, Tennessee, and North Carolina did not leave the Union until mid-April, when Lincoln called for 75,000 troops to put down the civil rebellion. The slave states of Delaware, Maryland, Kentucky, and Missouri remained in the Union, but each of those states was bitterly divided between Unionists and Confederate sympathizers.

subordination to the superior race is his natural and normal condition. This, our new government, is the first, in the history of the world, based upon this great physical, philosophical, and moral truth." The foundation of the Confederacy, then, was the idea of the fundamental inequality between blacks and whites.

Stephens and other leading Confederates were outspoken in their determination not only to preserve the institution of slavery but also to convince the world that slavery was a necessary institution in terms of managing and controlling black labor. Indeed, in early April, the Confederacy was a rhetorical powerhouse, full of blustering firebrands. But it was also a poor excuse for an independent nation, with only one-third of the U.S. population and almost no industrial capacity. Over the next few weeks, as the seven Confederate states attempted to coax the upper South to join their revolution, Lincoln emerged as an unwitting ally in their effort.

Located in Charleston Harbor, Fort Sumter was one of two Union forts in southern territory, and in the spring of 1861, it was badly in need of supplies. On April 12, Lincoln took the moral high ground by sending provisions but not troops to the fort. The Confederates found the move provocative nonetheless and began firing on the fort. After a 33-hour Confederate bombardment, the heavily damaged fort surrendered without a fight. In response, many white Southerners, such as Mary Boykin Chesnut, the wife of a high Confederate official, cheered and embraced the "pomp and circumstance of glorious war."

Three days after the capture of Fort Sumter, Lincoln (anticipating a conflict no longer than 90 days) called for 75,000 northern volunteers to quell a civil uprising "too powerful to be suppressed by the ordinary course of judicial proceedings." By the end of the month, he had ordered a blockade of southern seaports. Condemning these moves as acts of "northern aggression," the upper South, including Virginia (deprived of its western part, which now formed a new state called West Virginia), Tennessee,

Interpreting History
A Virginia Slaveholder Objects TO THE
IMPRESSMENT OF SLAVES

> "If a **man's** wagon and **team** should be **impress'd** into **Service,** can his **slave** be impress'd to drive the **said** team?"

D uring the Civil War, some southern slave owners bitterly resisted Confederate slave impressment policies. On December 4, 1861, John B. Spiece, an Albemarle County, Virginia, slaveholder and lawyer, wrote to the Confederate attorney general and protested government policy.

Dr Sir, Although a stranger to you, yet in consequence of the excitement and distress in this section of the country, in reference to a certain matter; I am constrained to address you, not merely on my own account; but on behalf of a large number of most respectable citizens. . . .

A practice has prevailed for some considerable time in *this* section of the country of impressing into service of the confederate army, the horses wagons and *slaves* belonging to the people.

The "Press masters" will go to their houses, and drag off their property to Just Such an extent as they choose; until it has not only created great excitement and distress; but bids fair to produce wide spread ruin. And I am told that these "Press masters" are paid by the Government the enormous price of *two dollars and fifty cents for each team which they impress;*—hence their anxiety and untiring exertions to increase the number;—thus making thirty or forty dollars pr day—

While I do not controvert the right of the Government to impress into its service *wagons and teams;* yet I do controvert the right to impress *Slaves*—It does seem to me that no one can be impress'd into military service of any kind, unless he is subject to military duty: because this whole business is relating to the Army, and is purely a military matter.—

The people in this section of the country are much attached to their slaves, and treat them in a humane manner—consequently they are exceedingly pained at having them dragged off at this inclement season of the year, and exposed to the severe weather in the mountains of north western Virginia. . . . Some have already died, and others have returned home afflicted with Typhoid fever, which has spread through the family to a most fatal and alarming extent.—

I am a practicing lawyer myself, but these "Press masters" will hear nothing from any one residing amongst the people.—

Therefore Sir, in consequence of the distress produced by the causes before mentioned, I am constrained to write to you; requesting you if you please, to give your opinion upon the questions involved.

To wit—If a man's wagon and team should be impress'd into Service, can his slave be impress'd to drive the said team—

Secondly—If a man has neither wagon or team can his slave be impress'd to drive some other team (*some* of the "Press masters" yield this *last* point, whilst others do not, and contend that they can impress just as many slaves as they choose from any plantation, taking all the negro men if they think proper.)—

Some few of the people have not been able to sow their grain this fall:—and there is deep dissatisfaction amongst the people—therefore I deem it proper and expedient that the authorities should know it—

Spiece goes on to cite the laws of the Commonwealth of Virginia, as amended in 1860, "by which it seems there is no power to impress Slaves." In the absence of Confederate congressional legislation to that effect, he argues, government authorities lack the legal right to take slaves from their owners. Spiece concludes his letter by suggesting that in taking slaves far from their homes, Confederate authorities were endangering the security of the would-be new nation.

There is also a serious evil in impressing slaves for the service in North western Virginia:—whilst there they get to talking with *Union men* in disguise, and by that means learn the original cause of the difficulty between North & South: then return home and inform other negroes:—not long since one of my neighbors negro men went to his master, and desired to let him go again to the north western army—adding "I wish you to let me go further than I went before["]—I have the honor to be most respectfully your Obt Servt.

It is unknown whether Confederate officials responded to Spiece's letter.

These slaves are unloading ships at City Point, Virginia. Field hands impressed to work in Confederate factories, on wharves, and in mines experienced a new way of life off the plantation and out of the sight of their owners. The South's need to mobilize for war challenged traditional rhetoric about black people's abilities. The war forced southern whites to seek multiple ways to exploit blacks as workers. How did these developments challenge the core principles of slavery, which held that plantation discipline was at the heart of the institution?

Questions for Discussion

1. How does John Spiece demonstrate his talents as a lawyer in this letter?

2. How does Spiece suggest that slave impressment might actually undermine the security of the Confederacy?

3. In what ways does Spiece's reaction to slave impressment suggest changes in, or challenges to, southern planters' ideology of paternalism?

SOURCE: Ira Berlin, Barbara J. Fields, Thavolia Glymph, Joseph P. Reidy, and Leslie S. Rowland, eds., *Freedom: A Documentary History of Emancipation, 1861–1867,* Series 1, Vol. 1, *The Destruction of Slavery* (1985), pp. 782–783.

Arkansas, and North Carolina, all seceded from the Union by May 20. Grateful for the newfound loyalty of Virginia and eager to appropriate the Tredegar Iron Works in Richmond, the Confederacy moved its capital from down-at-the-heels Montgomery to elegant Richmond on May 11.

Certain segments of the southern population demonstrated that they would withhold their support from the Confederacy. However, southern Unionists did not necessarily agree with northern Republicans' antislavery sentiments. Yeoman farmers in the up-country were non-slaveholders determined to maintain household self-sufficiency; they did not share the planters' interests in maintaining the cotton staple-crop economy, but neither did they want to see the institution of slavery destroyed. Louisiana sugar planters, many of whom owned large numbers of slaves, depended on world markets for their profits and feared that war would disrupt trade with other nations. These groups and others, including people in the hill country east of Tennessee, all voted for Unionist delegates to their respective state constitutions that chose secession. Enslaved black workers, of course, could hardly be counted on to defend those who kept them in bondage. The Border States of Missouri, Kentucky, Maryland, and Delaware remained within the Union, although among their residents were many outspoken people who openly sympathized with the South.

Preparing to Fight

Poised to battle each other, the South and the North faced similar challenges. Both sides had to inspire—or force—large numbers of men to fight. Both had to produce massive amounts of cannon, ammunition, and food. And both had to devise military strategies that would, they hoped, ensure victory. In early 1861, white Southerners were boasting of the stockpiles of cotton that, if needed, would serve as leverage for military support, diplomatic recognition, and financial assistance from the great European powers. Plantations brimming with hogs and corn, it was hoped, would sustain both masters and slaves, in contrast to the North, where cotton mills would lie idle and workers would soon descend to poverty and starvation.

From the beginning of the war, Confederates aimed for a strategy calculated to draw on their strengths. They would fight a purely defensive war with small units of troops deployed around the South's 6,000-mile border. Seasoned officers such as Robert E. Lee and Thomas J. Jackson would lead the charge to crush Union armies that ventured into Confederate territory. Finally, the South could command more than 3 million black people (a third of its total population of 9 million), all of whom, it was assumed, would do the bidding of planters and military men. Whereas the North would have to conquer the South to preserve the Union, the Confederacy would only have to survive to win its independence.

At first, the North was inclined to think little past the numbers: in 1860, it possessed 90 percent of the manufacturing capacity and three-quarters of the 30,000 railroad miles in the United States. Its population, 22 million, dwarfed that of the South. The North retained control of the (admittedly less than formidable) U.S. Navy and all other resources of the federal government, including a bureaucratic infrastructure to facilitate troop deployment and communication. Its diversified economy yielded grain as well as textiles; it could not only mobilize a large army but count on feeding it as well.

Early on, the North had a plan, but one that could hardly be dignified by the term *strategy*. It would defend its own territory from southern attack and target Confederate leaders, under the assumption that latent Union sentiment in the South would arise to smash the rebellion before it went too far. Union gunboats positioned along the East Coast and up and down the Mississippi River would seal off the Confederacy from foreign supply lines. The North would also launch a political offensive calculated to undermine Confederate sympathizers by bolstering Unionist sentiment everywhere. Lincoln, for example, continued to appeal to slaveholders loyal to the Union, whether those slaveholders lived in the Border States or deep in the heart of the Confederacy.

Confederates claimed that they were heirs of the noble ideas of the American Revolution. They argued that the tariff on imported goods was a form of taxation imposed on the South without its consent. White Southerners denounced what they called northern "tyranny" and "oppression." Northerners also invoked a Revolutionary heritage to justify their cause. However, they downplayed the issue of unjust taxation and instead stressed the glories of the Union—in Lincoln's words, "the last, best hope of mankind" in an age of kings and emperors.

Barriers to Southern Mobilization

On July 21, 1861, at Manassas Junction (Bull Run), about 30 miles southwest of Washington, D.C., Union and Confederate forces encountered each other on the field of battle for the first time. This was the fight that earned Thomas "Stonewall" Jackson his nickname and burnished his reputation, for Union troops skirmished briefly with the enemy and then turned and fled back to the capital, disgraced. In the coming weeks, Northerners gave up the idea that the effort to suppress the rebels would be an easy one, and Lincoln began to reorganize the country's officer corps and fortify its armies.

To win this initial victory, the Confederates had relied on the massing of several huge forces: those of Generals Joseph Johnston and P.G.T. Beauregard, as well as Stonewall Jackson. Consequently, southern military strategists decided they must continue to defend southern territory while going on the offensive against the Yankees (the "offensive-defensive" strategy was used for the duration of the conflict). In other matters, however, the South learned life-and-death lessons more slowly. Only gradually did the central paradox of the Confederate nation become abundantly clear: that a country founded on an agrarian ideal of "states' rights" needed to industrialize its economy and centralize its government operations to defeat the Union.

The first weeks of the war revealed that the South would pursue its antebellum aims of conquering western territory for slavery. An early victory of Texas forces over Union troops in New Mexico led to the formation of what slaveholders in that region called the Confederate Territory of Arizona. Over the next year, the Confederates launched successful assaults on the cities of Albuquerque and Santa Fe, in present-day New Mexico. However, southern troops amounted to little more than a band of plunderers; in Rio Abajo, for example, farmers and ranchers switched their allegiance to the Union after the rebels raided their homesteads.

Deprived of money raised from customs duties (the U.S. Navy blockade brought a halt to established patterns of overseas trade), the Confederacy relied on floating bonds ($400 million worth), raising taxes, and a 10 percent tax on farm produce. The Confederate Treasury printed money at a furious rate ($1 billion over the course of the conflict), but its value declined precipitously; near the end of the war, one Confederate dollar was worth only 1.6 cents.

Raising a volunteer army and impressing slave labor (forcing slaves to labor for the military) met with stiff resistance from various quarters of southern society. For yeoman farm families, long defensive of the independence of their own households, Confederate mobilization efforts came as a rude shock. Antebellum Southerners believed that white fathers should protect and retain control over their dependents at all times. Planters expressed a well-founded fear that slaves impressed for a wide range of tasks, whether saltmaking or chopping trees or tending brick kilns, were difficult to control now that plantation discipline had been loosened. When the Confederate call for volunteers failed to produce the number of soldiers (and menial laborers) needed to fight the Union, the Richmond government in March 1862 implemented a military conscription law (all men between ages 18 and 35—later it became 45—were called up for three years of service). The law exempted certain kinds of workers, such as railroad employees, schoolteachers, miners, and druggists, and allowed the buying of **substitutes** by draftees who could afford the $300 price for them. This last type of exemption allowed wealthy men to pay someone to fight in their place.

Substitute During war, a man paid to serve in combat in another man's place.

Some white Southerners complained bitterly that the Confederate government instituted policies that were fundamentally unfair and that favored the wealthy and well-connected. In a letter to the *Atlanta Southern Confederacy* in October, 1862, one writer declared, "I tell you that the worst enemy our young republic has is the spirit that pervades to an alarming extent of extracting from the poor and needy to build up the rich and powerful." He and others objected to the practice of military substitutes; the exemptions won by a favored few; and the **20-slave law**, which provided that plantations with twenty or more slaves could petition to have one white man (a planter or an overseer) exempt from army service. Even slaveholders criticized Confederate policies when they denounced slave impressment practices that seemed to target poorer counties while letting richer ones avoid giving up their bound workers to "press masters." The implementation of Confederate manpower policies, then, seemed to mock the antebellum ideal of the equality of all southern white men regardless of their station in life.

Heavy-handed government policies also provoked anger among principled states' rights advocates such as governors Joseph Brown of Georgia and Zebulon Vance of North Carolina. Brown exempted large numbers of men from the draft, claiming that the Confederacy posed a greater threat to states' rights than did the Union. On January 1, 1862, 209,852 southern men were present for duty. Yet the northern force was more than twice as large, with 527,204.

20-slave law Legislation passed by the Confederate Congress in October 1862 that exempted from military service one white man for every twenty slaves on a plantation.

Indians and Immigrants in the Service of the Confederacy

Just as the Confederates failed in their attempt to use fully the labor of enslaved workers, so they failed to reap much gain from the vaunted military prowess of Indians, especially those in Indian Territory (present-day Oklahoma). In 1861, southern military officials appealed to the Cherokee and the other Five Tribes for support, promising them arms and protection from Union forces in return. Only gradually and reluctantly did Cherokee leader John Ross commit his men to the Confederacy: "We are in the situation of a man standing alone upon a low naked spot of ground, with the water rising all around him." More devoted to the Confederate cause was Cherokee leader Stand Watie, who, backed by many Cherokee slaveholders, proceeded to mobilize what he called the "United Nations of Indians" as a fighting force on behalf of the Confederacy. Among those responding to the call to arms were Chocktaw and Chickasaw men, who formed Company E of the 21st Mississippi Regiment, "the Indian Brigade."

Although Indian Territory was considered of great strategic value to the Confederacy, southern military officials at times expressed frustration with the traditional battle tactics of Indian warriors. They were unused to military encounters that pitted long, straight rows of men on foot against each other. At the Battle of Elkhorn Tavern (Pea Ridge) in March 1862, Indian troops abandoned the battlefield in the face of cannon fire, leading their commander, Albert Pike, to demand that in the future they be "allowed to fight in their own fashion" rather than "face artillery and steady infantry on open ground." By the summer of 1862, the Confederacy had lost its advantage in Indian Territory; the Cherokee and Creek were divided in their loyalties, with some joining Union forces. By this time, the Comanche and Kiowa, resentful of the Confederacy's broken promises (guns and money diverted from them), had joined Union troops and were threatening to invade Texas.

Like Native Americans, immigrants and ethnic minorities in the South were divided in their loyalties. A Jewish lawyer and slaveholder, Judah Benjamin, served as a cabinet member and trusted adviser to Jefferson Davis. Prominent southern military officers included some from Ireland, Prussia, and France. German and Irish workmen from southern cities helped fill the ranks of the Confederate army, as did an estimated 2,500 Hispanos. But ethnic loyalties could also disrupt services deemed necessary to Confederate manufacturing and transportation. The Confederate railroad director in Selma, Alabama, contended with a labor force of immigrants (most probably from Germany and Ireland), men who "do not feel identified in any great degree with the South" and who demanded high wages. They were constantly threatening to run away to Union lines, where they believed they could make more money and enjoy the luxuries denied them in war-torn Alabama.

The Course of War, 1862–1864

What obstacles did the South face in defending its territory against northern invaders?

When the time came to marshal resources in the service of the national state, Northerners were at a distinct advantage over the states' rights men who dominated the Confederacy. Not only did the Union have more resources, but the Republicans' support for the centralization and consolidation of power also facilitated the war-mobilization process. In Congress, the Republicans took advantage of their new majority status and expanded federal programs in the realm of the economy, education, and land use. However, like Davis, Lincoln encountered vehement opposition to his wartime policies. Meanwhile, on the battlefield, Union losses were mounting. The United States confronted an uncertain fate.

The Republicans' War

Worried about disloyalty in the vicinity of the nation's capital, on April 27, 1861, Lincoln gave General Winfield Scott the power to suspend the writ of *habeas corpus* (a legal doctrine designed to protect the rights of people arrested) in Baltimore. By the end of the year, this policy, which allowed the incarceration of people not yet charged with a crime, was being applied in almost all of the loyal United States. Chief among those targeted were people suspected of interfering with war mobilization of men and supplies. Democrats stepped up their opposition to the president, denouncing him as a tyrant and a dictator. Meanwhile, from the other side of the political spectrum, abolitionists expressed their frustration with the administration's conciliatory policy toward the South in general and toward Unionist slaveholders in particular. Lincoln insisted that his objective was "to save the Union, and . . . neither to save or destroy slavery."

Wartime manufacturing and commerce proved to be a boon to entrepreneurs. In Cleveland, a young commission-house operator named John D. Rockefeller was earning enough money to hire a substitute to serve in the army for him. In the middle of the war, he shifted his business from trading grain, fish, water, lime, plaster, and salt to refining the crude oil (used in kerosene lamps) recently discovered in western Pennsylvania. War profiteers seized their opportunities in both the North and the South. In 1862, the *Southern Cultivator*, a magazine published in Augusta, Georgia, ran an article titled "Enemies at Home," denouncing the "vile crew of speculators" who were selling everything from corn to cloth at exorbitant prices.

Republicans' willingness to centralize wartime operations led in 1861 to the formation of the U.S. Sanitary Commission, which recruited physicians, trained nurses, raised money, solicited donations, and conducted inspections of Union camps on the front. During the war, as many as 20,000 white and black women served as nurses, cooks, and laundresses in Union military hospitals. Black women worked primarily in the latter two categories. A long-time advocate of reform on behalf of the mentally ill during the antebellum period, Dorothea Dix, served as superintendent of nurses.

The Republicans believed that the federal government should actively promote economic growth and educational opportunity, and they enacted measures previously thwarted by Democratic presidents and Congresses. In July 1862, the **Homestead Act** granted 160 acres of western land to each settler who lived on and made improvements to the land for five years. Congress also passed the **Morrill Act**, which created a system of land-grant colleges. (Many of these colleges eventually became major public universities, including Colorado State University, Kansas State University, and Utah State University.) Also approved in 1862, the **Pacific Railroad Act** appropriated to the Union Pacific and the Central Pacific railroads a 400-foot right-of-way along the Platte River route of the Oregon Trail and lent them $16,000 to $48,000 (depending on the terrain) per mile.

Homestead Act Legislation passed in 1862 that granted 160 acres of land free to each settler who lived on and made improvements to government land for five years.

Morrill Act Legislation passed by Republican Congress in 1862 to create a system of agricultural (land-grant) public colleges.

Pacific Railroad Act Legislation that granted to the Union Pacific and the Central Pacific railroads cash subsidies and a 400-foot right of way along the Platte River route of the Oregon Trail.

During the first year and a half of war, Union military strategy reflected a prewar Republican indifference to the rights and welfare of both northern and southern blacks. With the exception of radical abolitionists such as Frederick Douglass, few Northerners saw the war as a fight to liberate the slaves. In September 1861, Lincoln revoked a directive released by General John Frémont that would have authorized the seizure of property and the emancipation of slaves owned by Confederates in the state of Missouri. The president feared that such a policy would alienate slaveholders who were considering switching their allegiance to the Union. Later that fall, the capture of Port Royal, South Carolina, allowed Union soldiers to treat blacks as "contraband of war," denying slaveholders their human property but failing to recognize blacks as free people with rights.

As Union forces pushed deeper into Confederate territory, U.S. officers devised their own methods for dealing with the institution of slavery. By early 1862, the North had set its sights on the Mississippi River valley, hoping to bisect the Confederacy and cut off supplies and men bound from Texas, Arkansas, and Louisiana to the eastern seaboard. In February, General Ulysses S. Grant captured Fort Henry and Fort Donelson on the Tennessee and Cumberland rivers, the Union's first major victory of the war; in April, New Orleans fell to Admiral David Farragut. In New Orleans, General Benjamin Butler attempted to retain the loyalty of Unionist slaveholders by returning runaway slaves to them. This policy was not always greeted with enthusiasm within Union ranks. A Massachusetts soldier, restless under the command of an officer sympathetic to "slave catching brutes," vowed, "I never will be instrumental in returning a slave to his master in any way shape or manner."

👁 **Watch the Video**   **The Meaning of the Civil War for Americans**

The bodies of soldiers lie where they fell on September 17, 1862, the single day that claimed the largest number of lives in the Civil War. Like many other battles of the war, Antietam was shaped by the physical features of the battlefield itself, with soldiers on both sides seeking cover in small groves of trees and behind rocks, road ruts, and fences made of stone and wood. Although Union troops outnumbered their Confederate opponents (87,000 men to 45,000), battlefield strategy on both sides played a large part in the outcome, to some extent compensating for the unequal number of combatants in the Union and southern armies. The number of Union soldiers killed, wounded, missing, or captured was about 12,000; Confederates losses numbered about 11,000. In what ways did battlefield tactics work to minimize the North's overwhelming advantages in terms of men and matériel?

The Ravages of War

In the summer of 1862, the South suffered a hemorrhaging of its slave population as the movement of Union troops up and down the eastern seaboard opened the floodgates to runaways. Yet over the course of the summer, the Confederacy persevered on the battlefield, aided by the failure of Union armies to press their advantage. In June, General George McClellan was turned back on the outskirts of Richmond, which convinced Lincoln not only of the incompetence of his chief general but also of the value of a less forgiving approach toward the South. But General John Pope, brought in from the western campaign to command the 50,000-man Army of the Potomac, did little better.

Read the Document   **Clara Barton, Memoirs about Medical Life at the Battlefield (1862)**

Kate Cumming of Mobile, Alabama, earned the gratitude of the Confederacy for her work as a hospital matron during the war. Before and during the Civil War, many people believed that respectable women should not work in hospitals. Physicians claimed that women were likely to faint at the sight of blood and that they were not strong enough to turn patients over in their beds. Yet, as the war progressed, more and more northern and southern women defied these stereotypes and served in hospitals as nurses, administrators, and comforters of the ill and dying. Noted Cumming soon after she first entered a hospital, "The foul air from this mass of human beings at first made me giddy and sick, but I soon got over it." Still, in southern hospitals, soldiers and enslaved workers handled much of the direct patient care. How did necessity encourage some women to expand their traditional roles during wartime?

In other parts of the country, the Yankee war against the Confederates spilled over into savage campaigns against Indian tribes. An uprising among the Santee Sioux in Minnesota killed 500 whites before the state militia quashed the rebellion at Wood Lake in the fall of 1862. General James H. Carleton routed the Texas Confederates who had been occupying New Mexico and Arizona, and then provided what he called a "wholesome lesson" to the Mescalero Apache and Navajo who had been menacing Spanish American *placitas* (communities) in the area. Carleton's Union soldiers forced the Mescaleros to accept reservation status at Bosque Redondo in the Pecos River valley. Meanwhile, Colonel Kit Carson conducted a campaign of terrorism against the Navajo, burning hogans and seizing crops and livestock, claiming that "wild Indians could be tamed." Many of the survivors undertook the "Long Walk" to Bosque Redondo, a forced march reminiscent of the Cherokee Trail of Tears a generation before.

The bloodiest day of the war occurred on September 17, 1862, on the banks of Antietam Creek near Sharpsburg, Maryland. The Battle of Antietam claimed 20,000 lives and resulted in a Union victory, although a costly one. To journalists and soldiers alike, battles could offer stirring sights of long rows of uniformed men arrayed against each other, their arms at the ready, regimental flags unfurled in the wind. Yet for the women of Shepardstown, Maryland, left to clean up after the Antietam slaughter, there was no talk of the glory of war, only a frantic, round-the-clock effort to feed the Confederates and bind their wounds. Surveying the battlefield wreckage, one observer, Maria Blunt, lamented the carnage: not only the dead but also men "without arms, with one leg, with bandaged sides and backs; men in ambulances, wagons, carts, wheelbarrows, men carried on stretchers or supported on the shoulder of some self-denying comrade." All over the South, white women established temporary hospitals in barns, private homes, and churches and mourned each human sacrifice to the cause: "A mother—a wife—a sister had loved him."

The extraordinarily high casualty rate in the war stemmed from several factors. Confederates and Federals alike fought with new kinds of weapons (rifles and sharpshooters accurate at up to 1,000 yards) while troops massed in old-style (that is, close) formation. Soft minié balls punctured and lodged in limbs, leading to high rates of amputation that in turn fostered deadly infections. One Alabama soldier observed in 1862, "I believe the Doctors kills more than they cour [cure]." In fact, twice as many Civil War soldiers died of infection and disease—diarrhea, dysentery, typhoid, pneumonia, and malaria—as were killed in combat.

The Emancipation Proclamation

Appalled by the loss of life but heartened by the immediate outcome of Antietam, Lincoln took a bold step. In September, he announced that on January 1, 1863, he would proclaim all slaves in Confederate territory free. Lincoln used the **Emancipation Proclamation** to bolster northern morale by infusing the conflict with moral purpose and at the same time to further the Union's interests on the battleground by encouraging southern blacks to join the U.S. army. The measure left slavery intact in the loyal Border States and in all territory conquered by the Union. Consequently, nearly 1 million black people were excluded from its provisions. Skeptical of the ability of blacks and whites to live together, Lincoln remained committed to the colonization of freed blacks outside the United States (in Central America or the West Indies).

At the same time, the Emancipation Proclamation provided Lincoln with an opportunity to engage in soaring rhetoric that drew a stark contrast between freedom and slavery. In late 1862, he declared, "In giving freedom to the slave, we assure freedom to the free—honorable alike in what we give, and what we preserve. We shall nobly save, or meanly lose, the last best hope of earth." Here Lincoln was suggesting that real freedom would endure only when slavery was dead; in that sense, he implied, the fates of northern and southern whites were linked to the fate of the slaves. By destroying slavery, the North would reaffirm its ideal of freedom for all. Lincoln was

Emancipation Proclamation An executive order issued by President Abraham Lincoln on January 1, 1863, declaring that all slaves living in states or areas controlled by the Confederate States of America were now free. The proclamation did not affect the status of slaves in Union-held areas.

Explore the Topic   The Limits of the Emancipation Proclamation

President Lincoln released the Emancipation Proclamation on January 1, 1863. In the last weeks of 1862, many abolitionists, including Frederick Douglass, feared that Lincoln would bow to pressure from conservatives in the North and break his promise to go forward with it. Soon after midnight on New Year's Eve, Douglass and others were overjoyed to hear the news that the proclamation was official. This illustration, by political cartoonist Thomas Nast (1965), envisions a somewhat optimistic future for African Americans in the United States. Given the proclamation's limits (in terms of how many slaves were actually freed), why did Douglass term it a "moral bombshell" aimed at the Confederacy?

not only an idealist, however; throughout the war, he remained sensitive to northern public opinion, and he had realized by late 1862 that the majority of white Northerners would support the Emancipation Proclamation. He had not arrived at a point where he could promote the cause of full citizenship rights for blacks; rather, he conceived "equality" broadly to mean that all people would be equally free from bondage.

In the congressional elections of 1862, the Democrats had picked up strength in New York, Pennsylvania, and Ohio and carried Illinois. The lower Midwest in general harbored large numbers of Democrats who opposed the war (especially now that it was an "abolition war") and called for peace with the South; these so-called Copperheads disrupted Union enlistments and encouraged military desertions. The Emancipation Proclamation electrified abolitionists, but the war effort and the growing casualties were taking their toll among the laboring classes. Especially aggrieved were the working people who paid higher taxes (relative to those paid by the wealthy) to keep the war machine running, and the dockworkers and others who lost their livelihoods when trade with foreign countries ceased. Their resentment boiled over in the summer of 1863.

Persistent Obstacles to the Confederacy's Grand Strategy

From the beginning of the war, the North's effort to blockade 3,500 miles of southern coastline met with fierce resistance on the high seas. The South made up in resourcefulness what it lacked in a navy, relying for supplies on swift steamers manned by privateers (British arms smuggled onto remote southern beaches could bring up to 700 percent in profits). Seemingly invincible Confederate ships such as the ironclad *Merrimack* and the well-fortified British-built ships *Alabama* and *Florida* prowled the southeastern seaboard, sinking Union vessels and protecting the blockade runners. Nevertheless, by December 1861, Union forces had established beachheads in Confederate territory up and down the East Coast.

In November 1861, Union naval forces intercepted a British packet ship, the *Trent*, and seized two Confederate diplomats, James Mason and John Slidell, who were en route to London and Paris, where they planned to plead the South's case in a bid to gain diplomatic recognition. To avoid a rift with England, Lincoln and Secretary of State William H. Seward released the two men. In the process, Mason and Slidell lost whatever influence they might have had with European governments, and Lincoln enjoyed the praise of the British public for his moderation in handling the *Trent* affair.

More generally, Confederate hopes for diplomatic recognition foundered on the shoals of European politics and economics, in England and in the Western Hemisphere. English textile mills drew on their own immense prewar stockpiles of raw cotton and sought out new sources of fiber in Egypt and elsewhere. Also, English workers flexed their political muscle in a successful effort to forestall recognition of the slaveholders' nation. Early in the war, the Confederates, who counted 2,500 Hispanos among their ranks, recognized the strategic importance of Mexico, both as a trade route for supplies and as a means of access to ports. In approaching Mexican President Benito Juarez for aid in late 1861, however, Confederate envoy John T. Pickett discovered that, although Mexicans still smarted from their defeat on their own land 13 years before, the Juarez administration remained an ally of the United States.

By the summer of 1862, Britain and France were inclined to mediate peace in favor of Confederate independence, for the two powers assumed that the South's impressive victories in Virginia and Tennessee signaled a quick end to the war. Nevertheless, the Confederacy's autumn setbacks of Antietam and Perryville (in Kentucky), combined with ennobling rhetoric of the soon-to-be-announced Emancipation Proclamation, proved that the Union was still very much alive. The diplomatic recognition the white South so desperately craved remained elusive.

The Other War: African American Struggles for Liberation

In what ways did black people, in the North and in the South, enslaved and free, shape the course of the fighting?

From the onset of military hostilities, African Americans, regardless of whether they lived in the North or the South, perceived the Civil War as a fight for freedom. Although they allied themselves with Union forces, they also recognized the limitations of Union policy in ending slavery. Therefore, blacks throughout the northern and southern states were forced to take action to free themselves as individuals, families, and communities. Twenty-year-old Charlie Reason recalled his daring escape from a Maryland slave master and his decision to join the famous 54th Massachusetts Infantry composed of black soldiers: "I came to fight *not* for my country, I never had any, but to gain one." Soon after the 54th's assault on Fort Wagner (outside Charleston Harbor) in July 1863, Reason died of an infection contracted when one of his legs had to be amputated. In countless ways, black people throughout the South fought to gain a country on their own terms. Moreover, they fought to gain a country in which they would not only be liberated from the chains of slavery, but also one in which they would enjoy all the full and equal blessings of U.S. citizenship.

Enemies Within the Confederacy

Slaveholding whites were shocked when they could not always count on the loyalty of "petted" domestics. Soon after the war began, South Carolina's Mary Boykin Chesnut had expressed unease about the enigmatic behavior of one of her trusted house slaves, Laurence, asking herself of all her slaves, "Are they stolidly stupid or wiser than we

👁 **Watch the Video** **What Caused the Civil War?**

All over the South, black people watched and waited for opportunities to claim their own freedom. The movement of Union troops into an area often prompted slaves to flee from the plantation. Individuals and extended families sought safety behind Union lines or in nearby towns or cities, or began the quest for long-lost loved ones. What are some of the factors that blacks as individuals and family members considered in deciding whether to stay on or flee from a plantation?

are, silent and strong, biding their time?" A few months later, Chesnut's cousin was murdered while sleeping, bludgeoned by a candlestick; the cousin's slaves William and Rhody were charged with the crime. Of her own mulatto servant, one of Chesnut's women friends remarked, "For the life of me, I cannot make up my mind. Does she mean to take care of me—or to murder me?" Now rising to the surface, such fears put whites on alert, guarding against enemies in their midst.

Yet no single white man or woman could halt the tide of freedom. Given the chance to steal away at night or walk away boldly in broad daylight, black men, women, and children left their masters and mistresses, seeking safety and paid labor behind Union lines. Throughout the South, black people waited and watched for an opportunity to flee from plantations, their actions depending on the movement of northern troops and the disarray of the plantations they lived on. In July 1862, the Union's Second Confiscation Act provided that the slaves of rebel masters "shall be deemed captives of war and shall be forever free," prompting Union generals to begin employing runaway male slaves as manual laborers. Consequently, military authorities often turned away women, children, older adults, and the disabled, leaving them vulnerable to spiteful masters and mistresses. For black men pressed into Union military and menial labor service, and for their families still languishing on plantations, "freedom" came at a high price indeed.

The Ongoing Fight Against Prejudice in the North and South

In the North, the Emancipation Proclamation spurred the enlistment of black men in the Union army and navy. Eventually, about 33,000 northern blacks enlisted, following the lead of their brothers-in-arms from the South. For black northern soldiers, military service opened up a wider world. Some learned to read and write in camp, and almost all felt the satisfaction of contributing to a war that they defined in stark terms of freedom versus slavery. They wore their uniforms proudly.

Union wartime policies revealed, however, that African Americans would continue to fight prejudice on many fronts. Some northern whites approved recruiting blacks, reasoning that for each black man killed in battle, one white man would be spared. Until late in the war, black soldiers were systematically denied opportunities to advance through the ranks and were paid less than whites. Although they showed loyalty to the cause in disproportionate numbers compared with white men, most blacks found themselves barred from taking up arms at all, relegated to fatigue work deemed dangerous and degrading to whites. They intended to labor for the Union, but, in the words of a black soldier from New York, "Instead of the musket it is the spade and the Whelbarrow and the Axe cuting in one of the horable swamps in Louisiana stinking and misery." For each white Union soldier killed or mortally wounded, two died of disease; the ratio for blacks was one to ten.

Many northern military strategists and ordinary enlisted men showed indifference at best, contempt at worst, for the desire of black fugitives to locate lost loved ones and begin to labor on their own behalf. In the course of the war, Union experiments with free black labor—on the South Carolina Sea Islands under the direction of northern missionaries, and in Louisiana, under the direction of generals Nathaniel Banks and Benjamin Butler—emphasized converting the former slaves into staple crop wage workers under the supervision of Yankees. Some of these whites, in their eagerness to establish "order" in former Confederate territory, saw blacks only as exploitable labor—if not cannon fodder, then hands to dig ditches and grow cotton.

Former slave Susie King Taylor recalled the heady, dangerous days of 1862, when she fled from Savannah and found refuge behind Union lines off the coast of Georgia. Despite the soldiers' scant pay and poor treatment in the First South Carolina Volunteers (later known as the 33rd United States Colored Cavalry), Taylor gained a great deal of satisfaction from conducting a school for black children on St. Simon's Island and performing a whole host of tasks for the fighting men, from cleaning rifles to washing clothes and tending the ill. She understood that her own contributions to the war effort showed "what sacrifices we can make for our liberty and rights."

The Emancipation Proclamation did not materially change the day-to-day experiences of any slaves within southern territory, though many derived hope from the Union's new-found commitment to the abolition of bondage. That commitment changed the nature of the war from 1863 onward.

Battle Fronts and Home Fronts in 1863

14.4   How did developments on the battlefield affect politics in both the North and South?

In 1863, the North abandoned the strategy of conciliation in favor of an effort to destroy the large southern armies and deprive the Confederacy of its slave labor force. By this time, the war was causing tremendous hardship among ordinary white folk in the South. Meanwhile, Lincoln found himself caught between African American freedom fighters who resented the poor treatment they received from many white commanders, and white Northerners who took their opposition to the war in general and the military draft in particular into the streets. Deprivation at home and the mounting casualty rates on the battlefields were reshaping the fabric of American society, North and South. In both sections, issues of fairness and equality of sacrifice prompted not only ongoing debates about the nature of the conflict but also violent reaction among some groups who felt they were paying more than their fair share of the burdens of war.

Disaffection in the Confederacy

The Civil War assaulted Southerners' senses and their land. Before the war, slave owners and their allies often contrasted the supposed tranquility of their rural society with the rude, boisterous noisiness of the North. According to this view, the South was a peaceful place of contented slaves toiling in the fields, whereas the North was the site of workers striking, women clamoring for the vote, and eccentric reformers delivering street-corner harangues.

The war exploded on the southern landscape with ferocious force, and the rumble of huge armies on the march shook southern society to its foundations. For the first time, many Southerners smelled the acrid odor of gunpowder and the stench of rotting bodies. They heard the booms of near and distant cannon and the mournful sounds of church bells tolling for the dead. They saw giant encampments of soldiers cover what used to be cotton fields. Seemingly overnight, both armies constructed gorge-spanning train trestles and huge riverside docks and warehouses, all in preparation for conflict. As soldiers withdrew from the battlefield, they left behind a scarred and blood-spattered land, cornfields mowed down, fires smoldering in their wake.

These sights and sounds were especially distressing to Southerners who objected to the war as a matter of principle or because of its disastrous effects on their households. Scattered throughout the South were communities resistant to the policies of what many ordinary whites considered the Richmond elite—the leaders of the Confederacy. In western North Carolina, a group calling themselves Heroes of America declared their loyalty to the Union. In southern Mississippi, the "Free State of Jones [County]" raised troops for the Yankee army. Throughout the rural South, army deserters were welcomed home by their impoverished wives and children; it is estimated that during much of the war, as many as one-third of all Confederate soldiers were absent without leave at any particular time.

Groups of poor women resisted the dictates of the Davis administration, wealthy men and women who flaunted an extravagant wartime lifestyle of lavish dinners and parties. Women from Virginia to Alabama protested a Confederate 10 percent "tax-in-kind" on produce grown by farmers and the food shortages that reached crisis proportions. In April 1863, several hundred Richmond women, many of them wives of Tredegar Iron Works employees, armed themselves with knives, hatchets, and pistols and ransacked stores in search of food: "Bread! Bread! Our children are starving while the rich roll in wealth."

Whereas some white women resisted the Confederacy, others leaped to the fore to provide essential goods and services to the beleaguered new nation. Virginia's Belle Boyd kept track of Union troop movements and served as a spy for Confederate armies. Poor women took jobs as textile factory workers, and their better-educated sisters found employment as clerks for the Confederate bureaucracy. Slaveholding women busied themselves running plantations, rolling bandages, and knitting socks for soldiers. Still, many women thought their labors were in vain. Of the Confederacy's stalled progress, Georgia's Gertrude Thomas noted, "Valuable lives lost and nothing accomplished."

The Tide Turns Against the South

In the fall of 1862, Lincoln replaced General McClellan with General Ambrose E. Burnside and then General Joseph ("Fighting Joe") Hooker. In early May 1863, Lee and Jackson encountered Hooker at Chancellorsville, Virginia. The battle left Hooker reeling, but it also claimed the life of Jackson, mistakenly shot by his own men on May 2 in the early evening twilight. The South had lost one of its most ardent champions.

Lee decided to press his advantage by invading Pennsylvania and, it was hoped, encouraging northern Peace Democrats and impressing the foreign powers. The ensuing clash at Gettysburg was a turning point in the war. Drawn by reports of a cache of much-needed shoes, Confederate armies converged on the town, in the south-central part of the state and across the border from Maryland. Union forces pursued. In a three-day battle that began on July 1, the 92,000 men under the command of General George G. Meade were arrayed against the 76,000 troops of Robert E. Lee.

((• 📖 Read the Document   Abraham Lincoln, Gettysburg Address (1863)

A photograph of President Lincoln at Gettysburg, a few hours before he delivered his famous speech to dedicate the Soldiers' National Cemetery in that Pennsylvania town. (His face is toward the camera, near the top of the crowd, left of center.) By this time, in what way had the Emancipation Proclamation changed the nature of the war? Did Lincoln's address refer to that fact?

Gettysburg later came to represent the bloody consequences of a war fought by men with modern weapons under commanders with a premodern military sensibility. On the last day of the battle, the men under Confederate Major General George Pickett moved slowly into formation, passing hastily dug graves and the fragments of bodies blown to bits the day before. At 3 p.m., a mile-wide formation of 15,000 men gave the rebel yell and charged three-quarters of a mile across an open field to do battle with Union troops well fortified behind stone walls. Within half an hour, Pickett had lost two-thirds of his soldiers and all 13 of his colonels. The battle's three-day toll was equally staggering: 23,000 Union and 28,000 Confederate soldiers wounded or killed. Fully one-third of Lee's army was dead or wounded.

What made the soldiers of both sides fight on under these conditions? Some remained devoted to a cause. Others cared less about the Confederacy or the Union and more about proving their manhood and upholding their family's honor. Still others sought to memorialize comrades slain in battle or to conform to standards of discipline drilled into them. Some prayed merely to survive.

The Union victory at Gettysburg on July 3 brought rejoicing in the North. The next day, General Ulysses S. Grant captured Vicksburg on the Mississippi River, a move that earned him the rank of lieutenant general (conferred by Congress). Within a year, he assumed the position of supreme commander of the Union armies.

Civil Unrest in the North

Not all segments of northern society joined in the celebration. Even principled supporters of the Union war effort were growing weary of high taxes and inflated consumer prices, not to mention the sacrifices of thousands of husbands, sons, and brothers. In

✳ Explore the Civil War on MyHistoryLab

WHAT BROUGHT THE UNITED STATES TO CIVIL WAR?

By 1860, the North and South had come to see each other as aggressive and unyielding on the subject of slavery. Although small farmers predominated in both regions, the two sides had developed different economies and cultures over the years. The South employed slave labor to produce staple crops such as rice and cotton. In contrast, the North had begun to industrialize and pay its workers a daily wage. In December 1860, South Carolina responded to the election of Abraham Lincoln as president by seceding from the Union. Eventually, eleven states left the Union to form the Confederate States of America. The ensuing conflict claimed the lives of nearly 700,000 men, more

Union soldiers pose with a captured Confederate canon. *Library of Congress*.

RESOURCES OF THE UNION AND THE CONFEDERACY, 1861

	Industrial Workers	Factories	Railroad Tracks (miles)
Union	1,300,000	110,000	22,000
Confederacy	110,000	1,800	9,000

American (Union and Confederate) fatalities than in all other U.S. wars combined. The war preserved the Union and destroyed slavery, but conflicts over the role of the federal government would persist well into the future.

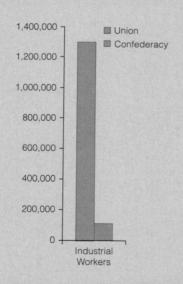

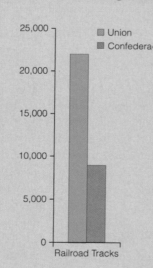

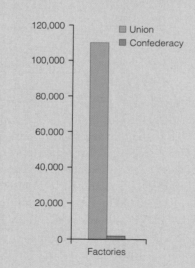

KEY QUESTIONS   Use **MyHistoryLab** *Explorer* to **answer** these **questions:**

Comparison ▶▶▶ *How did the South's population density contrast to that of the North?*

Map area data based on census information.

Response ▶▶▶ *Where were the major Civil War battles fought?*

Consider different regional strategies that affected military campaigns.

Analysis ▶▶▶ *How did the North win the Battle of Gettysburg?*

Examine the course of this decisive battle.

May, federal soldiers had arrested the defiant and outspoken Copperhead Clement Vallandigham at his home in Dayton, Ohio. Subsequently convicted of treason (he had declared the conflict "a war for the freedom of blacks and the enslavement of whites"), Vallandigham was banished to the South.

Following a military draft imposed on July 1, 1863, the northern white working classes erupted. Enraged at the wealthy who could buy substitutes, resentful of the Lincoln administration's high-handed tactics, and determined not to fight on behalf of their African American competitors in the workplace, laborers in New York City, Hartford, Troy, Newark, and Boston (many of them Irish) went on a rampage. The **New York City draft riot** of July 11–15 was especially savage as white men directed their wrath against black men, women, and children. Members of the mob burned the Colored Orphan Asylum to the ground and then mutilated their victims, before the federal government deployed 20,000 troops to New York to quell the violence and discourage other men from resisting the draft elsewhere. On August 19, the draft resumed.

In some quarters, the New York city draft riot hardened native-born Americans' views of Irish immigrants, themselves the victims of harsh forms of prejudice on the part of employers and public officials. Some conservative observers warmed to the cause of black civil rights at the same time they stepped up their denunciations of all Irish. A writer in the northern magazine *Atlantic* in 1864 denigrated the "Celtic race" by comparing members of that "race" with blacks: "The emancipated negro is at least as industrious and thrifty as the Celt, takes more pride in self-support, is far more eager for education, and has fewer vices. It is impossible to name any standard for the full rights of citizenship which will give a vote to the Celt and exclude the negroes." In the North, as well as the South, the war exposed traditional patterns of inequality, but also created new ones. Neither region could claim that even its white citizens enjoyed full equality with each other.

The draft riots of 1863 served as a stark reminder to northern blacks that, even though they were free, they were vulnerable to discriminatory treatment and even violence. The wives of black Union soldiers especially suffered in the North, where the army's unequal pay policies had a crushing effect on families and friends back home; as the men of the all-black Massachusetts 55th Regiment noted, "We left our Homes our Familys Friends & Relatives most Dear to take as it ware our Lives in our Hands To Do Battle for God & Liberty." For married recruits, the ensuing hardships endured by their wives and children clouded the decision to refuse all pay until this wrong could be righted. Rachel Ann Wicker, the wife of William Wicker, a 32-year-old farmer from Troy, Ohio, described her frustration in a letter addressed to "Mr. President Andrew." (Governor Andrew of Massachusetts passed it along to Lincoln in Washington.) Wicker demanded "to know the reason why our husbands and sons who enlisted in the 55 Massichusette regiment have not Bin paid off." Writing on behalf of herself, her mother, and all others "suffering for the want of money to live on," she pointed out that wartime inflation had trebled the cost of goods and services on the home front. Nevertheless, even if prices had remained the same, "thin it a Piece of injustice to that those soldiers there 15 months with out a cent of Money." In Washington, officials of the treasury and war departments remained unmoved.

The Desperate South

Meanwhile, the South had to contend not only with dissent and disaffection at home but also with the stunning battle and territorial losses it suffered at Gettysburg and Vicksburg. On August 21, Jefferson Davis proclaimed a day of "fasting, humiliation and prayer." Even as Davis was invoking the name of the Almighty, 450 rebels under the command of William Clarke Quantrill were destroying the town of Lawrence, Kansas (long a hotbed of abolitionist sentiment), and killing 150 of its inhabitants. With the exception of Quantrill and John Singleton Mosby (whose squads of men roamed northern Virginia attacking Union posts and troops in 1863), Confederate military leaders shunned guerrilla warfare, preferring to meet the enemy on a field of

New York City draft riot A July 1863 violent protest against the government passage of a military conscription law; whites attacked black men, women, and children and burned the city's Colored Orphan Asylum.

honor. The desperate Quantrill raid on Lawrence demonstrated that the Confederate cause was, if not lost, then losing in the late summer of 1863.

Before the year was out, Davis faced other setbacks as well. Grant's successes at Missionary Ridge and Lookout Mountain in Tennessee caused both France and England to draw back from offering overt support to the Confederacy in the form of sales of navy warships or diplomatic recognition. The Confederate president had long counted on securing the support of the great European powers; now those hopes were dashed.

Dedicating the national cemetery at Gettysburg on November 19, 1863, Lincoln delivered a short address that affirmed the nation's "new birth of freedom" and its commitment that "the government of the people, by the people, for the people, shall not perish from the earth." Lincoln's speech is one of the great rhetorical masterpieces of American politics. In it, he elevated the Civil War from a military conflict exclusively to a great moral struggle against slavery. In the South, more and more whites were flagging in their conviction that the system of bondage was worth the ultimate sacrifice in terms of their own lives and the welfare of their families.

The Prolonged Defeat of the Confederacy, 1864–1865

14.5 During the last months of the war, what factors contributed to the defeat of the Confederacy?

By 1864, northern generals, with Lincoln's blessing, had decided to fight a "hard war" against their tenacious enemy. Union troops were authorized to live off the land (denying southern civilians the necessities of life in the process), to seize livestock and other supplies indiscriminately, and to burn everything that the Confederates might find useful. The purposes of this strategy were twofold: to irreparably harm what was left of Confederate morale, and to facilitate the movement of northern troops through hostile territory. If northern troops could sever the area west of Georgia from the Confederacy and take Richmond and destroy its surrounding armies, the Union would be safe at last.

"Hard War" Toward African Americans and Indians

The policy of "hard war" should not be confused with total war, characterized by state-approved terrorism against civilians. However, Confederate policies toward black soldiers and Union policies toward Indian insurgents in the West did show elements of total war against particular segments of the population. In April 1864, Confederate General Nathan Bedford Forrest destroyed Fort Pillow, a Union garrison on the Mississippi River.

After surrendering, black soldiers were systematically murdered. Wounded survivors were bayoneted or burned to death. Among southern generals, conventions of war (providing for the detention and exchange of prisoners of war) did not apply to African American soldiers.

Nor were Indians accorded the minimal respect shown to most white combatants. In the early fall of 1864, a group of Cheyenne and Arapaho were camped along Sand Creek in the southeastern corner of Colorado. Black Kettle, a chief of the Cheyenne, had received promises from Union Colonel John M. Chivington and others stationed at Camp Weld in Denver that the two sides would remain at peace with each other. Therefore, on the morning of November 29, 1864, when Black Kettle saw Chivington leading a Colorado volunteer militia toward his settlement, he waved a white flag and stood his ground.

Chivington did not come in peace. That day he and his men massacred 125 to 160 Indians, mostly women, children, and old people, returning later to mutilate the bodies. In response, the Sioux, Arapaho, and Cheyenne launched their own campaigns against white migrants traveling the South and North Platte trails. Chivington declared that it was "right and honorable" to kill Indians, even children, using any means.

"Father Abraham"

The election of 1864 proceeded without major incident, although Lincoln faced some opposition within his own party. Together with his new running mate, a former slave owner from Tennessee named Andrew Johnson, Lincoln benefited from a string of preelection military victories won for him by Admiral David G. Farragut at Mobile, Alabama, and by General Philip Sheridan in Virginia's Shenandoah Valley. As a result, he defeated the Democratic nominee, his own former general, George McClellan, who managed to garner 45 percent of the popular vote. One of the keys to Lincoln's success was the "peace platform" that the Democrats had drafted at their convention the summer before. Support among Union soldiers for "Little Mac" dropped precipitously as a result, and Lincoln won three-quarters of the army's vote.

Despite his limited military experience, Lincoln possessed a strategic sense superior to that of many of his generals. He played down his own military experience, making light of his minor part in the Black Hawk War of 1832. In that conflict, he reminisced, he had engaged in "charges upon wild onions . . . [and] bloody struggles with the Musquetoes." However, he cared deeply about ordinary soldiers and talked with them whenever he had the opportunity. In return, Union troops gave "Father Abraham" their loyalty on the battlefield and, especially during the election of 1864, at the ballot box.

The Last Days of the Confederacy

Union General William Tecumseh Sherman's forces overtook Atlanta in September 1864 and swept southeast toward the coast, living off the land and denying Confederate soldiers and civilians alike food and supplies along the way. En route to Savannah, Sherman's men liberated **Andersonville Prison**, a 26-square-acre Confederate camp that held 33,000 prisoners in the summer of 1864. Unable to feed their own armies and so unwilling to commit large supplies of food to the prison, the Confederates, under

Andersonville Prison A Georgia prisoner-of-war camp that held as many as 33,000 Union prisoners at one time. Commanded by Henry Wirz, the prison was infamous for the large number of northern soldiers who died there of starvation, disease, and exposure to the elements.

In September 1864, the Indian chiefs Black Kettle and White Antelope (front row, center), with other Cheyenne and Arapaho leaders, met with Colonel John M. Chivington at Camp Weld, Colorado. The purpose of the meeting was to secure a truce between the Indians and European Americans in the area. Two months later, Chivington attacked an encampment of these Indians on the banks of Sand Creek, about 100 miles southeast of Denver. How did different groups of Indians respond to the Civil War and to the Republicans' nationalistic efforts in general?

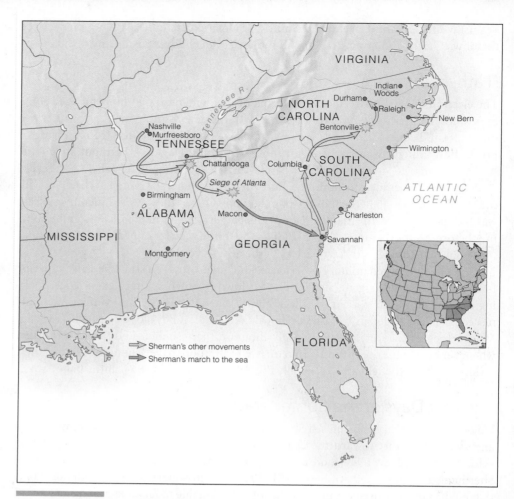

■■■■■■ **MAP 14.3 SHERMAN'S MARCH TO THE SEA, 1864–1865** General William T. Sherman's famous march to the sea marked the final phase of the Union effort to divide and conquer the Confederacy. Sherman's men burned Atlanta to the ground in September 1864. In late December, they made their triumphant entry into the city of Savannah. Sherman followed a policy of "hard war" in these final months of the war; he ordered his troops to seize from civilians any food and livestock they could use and to destroy everything else, whether rail lines, houses, or barns. White Southerners expressed outrage over these tactics. Still, Sherman never systematically attacked civilians, a characteristic of the Union's "total war" against Native American peoples in the West.

the command of Henry Wirz, stood by while 13,000 died of starvation, disease, and exposure. Wirz was the only Confederate officer to be tried, convicted, and executed for war crimes by the U.S. government.

After presenting Lincoln with the "Christmas gift" of Savannah in December, Sherman took his 60,000 troops north, slogging through swamps and rain-soaked terrain to confront the original secessionists. Later, he recalled with satisfaction, "My aim then was to whip the rebels, to humble their pride, to follow them to their inmost recesses, and make them fear and dread us." By mid-February, South Carolina's state capital, Columbia, was in flames. African American troops were among the triumphant occupiers of the charred city.

By early April 1865, Grant had overpowered Lee's army in Petersburg, Virginia. Withdrawing, Lee sent a telegram to Davis, who was attending church in Richmond, warning him that the fall of the Confederate capital was imminent. Davis and almost all other whites fled the city. Arriving in Richmond on April 3, only hours after the city had been abandoned, was the commander in chief of the Union army, Abraham Lincoln. Lincoln calmly walked the streets of the smoldering city (set afire by departing Confederates), flanked by a group of ten sailors. Throngs of black people greeted the president, exclaiming, "Glory to God! Glory! Glory! Glory!" When a black man kneeled to thank Lincoln, the president said, "Don't kneel to me. That is not right. You must kneel to God only, and thank Him for the liberty you will enjoy hereafter."

TABLE 14.1 THE ELECTION OF 1864

Candidate	Political Party	Popular Vote (%)	Electoral Vote
Abraham Lincoln	Republican	55.0	212*
George B. McClellan	Democratic	45.0	21

*Eleven secessionist states did not participate.

On April 9, Lee and his demoralized and depleted army of 35,000 men found themselves outnumbered by Grant and Meade, and Lee surrendered his sword at Appomattox Court House in northern Virginia. Union officials ensured rebel soldiers of protection from future prosecution for treason, and allowed the cavalry to keep their horses for use in spring planting. When the ragtag members of the so-called Stonewall Brigade—men who had entered the war with Stonewall Jackson four years before—came forward to lay down their arms, the Union army gave them a salute of honor, acknowledging their bravery.

One of the last casualties of the war was Abraham Lincoln. Watching a comedy with his wife, Mary, at Ford's Theater in Washington on the night of April 14, Lincoln was assassinated by John Wilkes Booth, a Confederate loyalist fearful that the president was bent on advancing "nigger citizenship." Lincoln lingered through the night but died the next morning. Booth was caught and shot within a matter of days. Of the departed president, Secretary of War Edwin M. Stanton is reported to have said, "Now he belongs to the ages."

Conclusion

Rather than asking why the South lost the Civil War, we might wonder why it took the North four years to win it. Despite all the political dissent and social conflict in the white South, despite the crumbling of the institution of slavery and the lack of support from the European powers, the Confederacy was able to mobilize huge armies under the command of brilliant tacticians such as Lee and Jackson. The war was fought on the battlefield by regiments of soldiers, not on the sea by navies or in the countryside by guerrillas. Therefore, as long as Confederate generals could deploy troops and outwit their foes during brief but monumental clashes, the Confederacy could survive to fight another day.

The South had entered the war armed with a states' rights ideology that held that all whites in the region were unified in support of slavery and that blacks were passive and childlike in their dependence on whites. The course of the war exposed the fallacy of this ideology. Even at the outset of the war, white Southerners differed in their support for the Confederacy, and as the conflict dragged on, many poor whites believed they were sacrificing more for the cause than were their social betters. Blacks proved aggressive in fighting for their freedom, wreaking havoc on plantation discipline and on southern military strategy. And too, many Confederates were forced to accept the fact that in order to fight the war successfully, principled states' rights supporters must yield to those politicians advocating a more centralized effort in behalf of mobilizing for war and fighting the enemy.

In terms of soldiers' lives lost—620,000—the Civil War was by far the costliest in the nation's history. Adding the deaths of slaves who toiled for the Confederate armies, the number of people who died as a result of the Civil War reaches 700,000. (The death toll among American military personnel in the Revolution was 26,000; in World War I, 116,000; in World War II, 400,000; in Vietnam, 58,000.) At the end of the war, the Union was preserved and slavery was destroyed. Yet, in their quest for true freedom, African Americans soon learned that military hostilities were but one phase of a wider war, a war to define the nature of American citizenship and its promise of liberty and equality. Thus, April 1865 marked not so much a final judgment as a transition to new battlefields.

Chapter Review

Mobilization for War, 1861–1862

14.1 How did the North and South prepare for war, and how did those preparations reflect each side's strategy for fighting—and winning—the war? p. 345

Confederates planned to fight a defensive war along their 6,000-mile border and to rely on the labor of their 3 million slaves. The North held the advantage in manufacturing and railroad miles, and it controlled the U.S. Navy and the federal government. It counted on Unionists in the South to halt the rebellion before it went too far.

The Course of War, 1862–1864

14.2 What obstacles did the South face in defending its territory against northern invaders? p. 352

The Union had greater resources, and the Republicans' centralized government facilitated mobilization. Confederate leaders had to coordinate strategy across a vast region, and they had to contend with runaway slaves fleeing to Union lines. The South also failed to gain diplomatic recognition and formal aid from European powers.

The Other War: African American Struggles for Liberation

14.3 In what ways did black people, in the North and in the South, enslaved and free, shape the course of the fighting? p. 357

Many slaves in the South fled for Union lines as soon as possible. There they worked as menial laborers for the military, but also served as scouts and spies. In the North, about 33,000 free black men enlisted in the federal army. Like their counterparts in the South, northern blacks encountered discriminatory treatment in the military.

Battle Fronts and Home Fronts in 1863

14.4 How did developments on the battlefield affect politics in both the North and South? p. 359

The death and destruction of war directly affected the lives of many in the South. Poor women in particular led protests against the Davis administration. In the North, many whites endured high taxes, inflated consumer prices, and the deaths of friends and family. Draft riots targeting African Americans occurred in a number of cities in 1863.

The Prolonged Defeat of the Confederacy, 1864–1865

14.5 During the last months of the war, what factors contributed to the defeat of the Confederacy? p. 364

Initiating a "hard war" against the South in 1864, William Tecumseh Sherman marched Union forces through Georgia and the Carolinas, living off the land. In early April 1865, Grant overpowered Lee's army at Petersburg. Outnumbered by Grant and Meade, Lee surrendered at Appomattox Court House on April 9.

Timeline

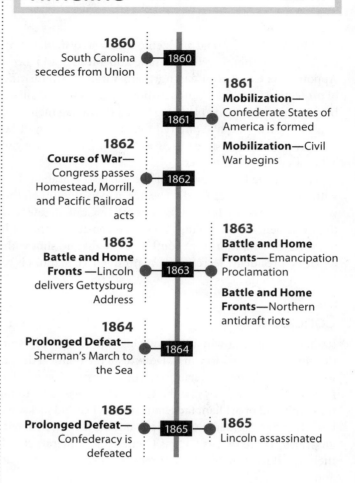

368

15 Consolidating a Triumphant Union, 1865–1877

Why did a procession of **black children** through the streets of Savannah, Georgia, in January 1865 cause so much excitement?

The day of jubilee had come at last! In late December 1864, African American men, women, and children rejoiced when the troops of Union General William Tecumseh Sherman liberated the city. Savannah's black community immediately formed its own school system under the sponsorship of a new group, the Savannah Education Association (SEA). On the morning of January 10, 1865, just two weeks after Sherman's forces entered the city, several hundred black children gathered at the First African Baptist Church. From there they processed in a group to the Old Bryant Slave Mart where, surrounded by the trappings of slavery—whips, handcuffs, bills of receipt—they commenced their studies as free children.

An illustration in *Harper's Weekly*, from December 15, 1866, shows African American pupils in a schoolroom in Charleston, South Carolina. After the Civil War, many southern black communities created, or enlarged and solidified, their own institutions, including schools and churches. At the same time, these communities pressed for full and equal citizenship rights. Was there a conflict between their goals of cultural and economic autonomy on the one hand and integration into the American body politic on the other? Why or why not?

LEARNING OBJECTIVES

15.1 ((•
How did various groups of Northerners and Southerners differ in their vision of the postwar South? p. 371

15.2 ((•
What human and environmental forces impeded the Republican goal of western expansion? p. 381

15.3 ((•
What were some of the inconsistencies in, and unanticipated consequences of, Republican notions of equality and federal power? p. 386

((• Listen to Chapter 15 on MyHistoryLab

Watch the Video Series on MyHistoryLab

Learn about some key topics related to this chapter with the *MyHistoryLab Video Series: Key Topics in U.S. History.*

 1 **Reconstruction and Its Missed Opportunities: 1865–1877** This overview video introduces critical issues related to Reconstruction, the period after the Civil War when the former Confederate states were reintegrated into the Union. Freedpeople embraced their rights as American citizens, and black men began to run for office and in other ways participate actively in the political life of the South and the nation as a whole. Presidents Abraham Lincoln, Andrew Johnson, and Ulysses S. Grant differed in their approaches to Reconstruction. Moreover, the Republican party was split on whether southern states should be *restored* to their former condition or *reconstructed* (i.e., have their basic governmental and social structures transformed).

 Watch on MyHistoryLab

The Amendments of Freedom In the years after the Civil War, Congress passed, and the states ratified, the Thirteenth, Fourteenth, and Fifteenth Amendments to the Constitution. These measures ended slavery, guaranteed the rights of citizenship to former slaves, and extended the right to vote to black men. This video describes the Freedmen's Bureau, a governmental agency formed in March 1865 and charged with overseeing the transition of former slaves from bondage to freedom. Despite the efforts of the federal government, several southern states passed Black Codes in 1865, intending to reduce freedpeople to a form of slavery. By 1867, Republicans had changed course and instituted Radical, or Congressional, Reconstruction, which put an end to those codes and enacted a more stringent set of requirements for states that had not yet rejoined the Union. **2**

Watch on MyHistoryLab

 3 **Presidential Reconstruction** This video explains how President Lincoln established the precedent of Presidential Reconstruction through his conviction that the Civil War was an armed rebellion on the part of U.S. citizens, not a conflict between the United States and a foreign country (the Confederacy). Even before the spring of 1865, Lincoln began to ponder the ways in which the war might be brought to an end and the rebellious southern states brought back into the Union. As commander-in-chief, he claimed for himself sweeping powers in this regard. His successor, Andrew Johnson, encountered stiff resistance from fellow Republicans, who felt he dealt too leniently with the former Confederate states. Johnson was impeached by the House, but not convicted by the Senate.

 Watch on MyHistoryLab

The Compromise of 1877 Twelve years of Reconstruction came to an end in 1877, when a bipartisan congressional committee considered disputed returns from the presidential election of 1876. The committee decided that the Republican Rutherford B. Hayes would be awarded the presidency and that all federal troops should be withdrawn from the South, ending Reconstruction. This video examines the Compromise of 1877, the political deal that made Hayes's victory possible. **4**

Watch on MyHistoryLab

The old slave market was just one of several schools opened by the SEA, which aimed to provide elementary schooling for 1,000 children. By late March, the group's leaders were hoping to receive aid from the U.S. Bureau of Refugees, Freedmen, and Abandoned Lands, a government agency created earlier that month to ease the transition between slavery and freedom for more than 3.5 million black people. Many southern blacks believed that a hallmark of freedom was the freedom to learn to read and write.

:D: uring the months and years immediately after the war, a major conflict raged between supporters of African American rights and supporters of southern white privilege. Republican congressmen hoped to *reconstruct* the South by enabling African Americans to own land and to become full citizens. Southern freedpeople sought to free themselves from white employers, landlords, and clergy, and to establish control over their own workplaces, families, and churches. In contrast, President Andrew Johnson appeared bent on *restoring* the antebellum power relations that made southern blacks dependent on white landowners.

After the war, the U.S. government sought to weld the whole nation into one political and economic unit. On the Plains and in the Northwest, Indians resisted white efforts to force them to abandon their nomadic way of life and take up sedentary farming. At the same time, the Civil War hardened the positions of the two major parties. The Republicans remained in favor of a strong national government and promoted a robust partnership between private enterprise and the federal government. The Democrats tended to support states' rights, which included regulating relations between employers and employees, whites and blacks.

The postwar years, now called the **Reconstruction era**, saw a spirited, often bitter, national debate about the meaning of equality as that concept applied to the rights of African Americans, women, workers, and Indians. Many whites argued that "equality" was not an absolute condition but, rather, a matter of degree; for example, just because freedmen were no longer slaves, should they be able to vote, sit on juries, or run for office? Women were not slaves, but should they be allowed to hold property and vote? The ongoing debate over these questions suggested that the military defeat of the South had only begun the process of consolidating the Union, North and South, East and West.

Reconstruction era The twelve years after the Civil War when the U.S. government took steps to integrate the eleven states of the Confederacy back into the Union.

The Struggle over the South

15.1 How did various groups of Northerners and Southerners differ in their vision of the postwar South?

The Civil War had a devastating impact on the South in physical, social, and economic terms. Estimates of fatalities among southern soldiers amounted to 260,000 men, as many as 33 percent of the total who marched off to war. The region had lost an estimated $2 billion in investments in slaves; modest homesteads and grand plantations alike lay in ruins; and gardens, orchards, and cotton fields were barren. More than 3 million former slaves eagerly embraced freedom, but the vast majority lacked the land, cash, and credit necessary to build family homesteads for themselves. Hoping to achieve social and economic self-determination, African American men and women traveled great distances, usually on foot, in efforts to locate loved ones and reunite families that had been separated during slavery. At the same time, landowning whites considered black people primarily as a source of agricultural labor; these whites resisted the idea that freedpeople should be granted citizenship rights.

In the North, Republican lawmakers disagreed among themselves how best to punish the defeated but defiant rebels. President Abraham Lincoln had indicated early that after the war the government should bring the South back into the Union quickly and painlessly. His successor wanted to see members of the southern planter elite humiliated, but resisted the notion that freedpeople should become independent of white landowners. In Congress, moderate and radical Republicans argued about how far the government should go in ensuring the former slaves' freedom. Nevertheless, most white Republicans agreed among themselves that black people should return to tilling the soil on plantations owned by their former masters.

During this period, the question of "equality" was a complicated one. Some whites, Northerners and Southerners, argued that the former slaves were completely equal to white people now that they were free. These whites believed that freedom from slavery did not necessarily mean that black people should be able to vote, hold office, or send their children to taxpayer-supported schools. Radical Republicans and blacks in general held that the federal government should guarantee certain basic rights that would provide freedpeople with a measure of economic opportunity, and some went further to suggest that meaningful economic opportunity would require a program of land re-distribution from former Confederates to former slaves. For their part, black people resisted a return to the gang system of labor, which seemed too close to the system of bondage they hoped to leave behind. Yet few whites, regardless of political loyalties, supported the notion of "social equality," which they defined as the ability of whites and blacks to become close friends on equal terms or to marry each other. A contest over the meaning of "equality" and "rights" shaped the postbellum (postwar) years in both the North and the South.

Wartime Preludes to Postwar Policies

Wartime experiments with African American free labor in Union-occupied areas foreshadowed bitter postwar debates. As early as November 1861, Union forces had occupied the Sea Islands off Port Royal Sound in South Carolina. In response, wealthy cotton planters fled to the mainland. Over the next few months, three groups of northern civilians landed on the Sea Islands with the intention of guiding blacks in the transition from slave to free labor. Teachers arrived intent on creating schools, and missionaries hoped to start churches. A third group, representing Boston investors, had also settled on the Sea Islands to assess economic opportunities; by early 1862, they decided to institute a system of wage labor that would reestablish a staple crop economy and funnel cotton directly into northern textile mills. The freed slaves, however, preferred to grow crops for their families to eat rather than cotton to sell, relying on a system of barter and trade among networks of extended families. Their goal was to break free of white landlords, suppliers, and cotton merchants.

Meanwhile, in southern Louisiana, the Union capture of New Orleans in the spring of 1862 enabled northern military officials to implement their own free (that is, non-slave) labor system. General Nathaniel Banks proclaimed that U.S. troops should forcibly relocate blacks to plantations "where they belong"; there they would continue to work for their former owners in the sugar and cotton fields, but now for wages supposedly negotiated annually. The Union army would compel blacks to work if they resisted doing so. In defiance of these orders, however, some blacks went on strike for higher wages, and others refused to work at all. Moreover, not all Union military men relished the prospect of forcing blacks to work on the plantations where they had been enslaved. Thus, federal policies returning blacks to plantations remained contested even within the ranks of the army itself.

The Lincoln administration had no hard-and-fast policy to guide congressional lawmakers looking toward the postwar period. In December 1863, the president outlined his Ten Percent Plan. This plan would allow former Confederate states to form new state governments once 10 percent of the men who had voted in the 1860 presidential election had pledged allegiance to the Union and renounced slavery. Congress instead passed the Wade-Davis Bill, which would have required a majority of southern voters in any state to take a loyalty oath affirming their allegiance to the United States. By refusing to sign the bill before Congress adjourned, Lincoln vetoed the measure (through a **pocket veto**). However, the president approved the creation of the **Freedmen's Bureau** in March 1865. The bureau was responsible for coordinating relief efforts on behalf of blacks and poor whites loyal to the Union, for sponsoring schools, and for implementing a labor contract system on southern plantations. At the time of his assassination, Lincoln seemed to be leaning toward giving the right to vote to southern black men.

Pocket veto An indirect veto of a legislative bill made when an executive (such as a president or governor) simply leaves the bill unsigned, so that it dies after the adjournment of the legislature.

Freedmen's Bureau Federal agency created by Congress in March 1865 and disbanded in 1869. Its purposes were to provide relief for Southerners who had remained loyal to the Union during the Civil War, to support black elementary schools, and to oversee annual labor contracts between landowners and field hands.

Presidential Reconstruction, 1865–1867

When Andrew Johnson, the seventeenth president of the United States, assumed office in April 1865 after Lincoln's death, he brought his own agenda for the defeated South. Throughout his political career, Johnson had seen himself as a champion of poor white

((• 📖 **Read the** Document   **Jourdon Anderson to His Former Master (1865)**

Freedmen's Bureau agents distributed rations to former slaves and southern whites who had remained loyal to the Union. Agents also sponsored schools, legalized marriages formed under slavery, arbitrated domestic disputes, and oversaw labor contracts between workers and landowners. The bureau faced many challenges; it was chronically understaffed, and many freedpeople lived on isolated plantations, far from the scrutiny of bureau agents. But by 1869 the bureau had ceased to exist. This photo shows the bureau office in Petersburg, Virginia. Can you speculate about the way this building was used before and during the war? How do you think southern whites reacted to the various roles and responsibilities of bureau agents?

farmers in opposition to the wealthy planter class. A man of modest background, he had been elected U.S. senator from Tennessee in 1857. He alone among southern senators remained in Congress and loyal to the Union after 1861. Lincoln first appointed Johnson military governor of Tennessee when that state was captured by the Union in 1862 and then tapped him as his running mate for the election of 1864.

Soon after he assumed the presidency, Johnson disappointed congressional Republicans who hoped that he would serve as a champion of the freedpeople. The new president had no interest in black equality. He welcomed back into the Union those states reorganized under Lincoln's Ten Percent Plan. He advocated denying the vote to wealthy Confederates, though he would allow individuals to come to the White House to beg the president for special pardons. Johnson also outlined a fairly lenient plan for readmitting the other rebel states into the Union. Poor whites would have the right to vote, but they must convene special state conventions that would renounce secession and accept the Thirteenth Amendment abolishing slavery. Further, they must repudiate all Confederate debts. The president opposed granting the vote to former slaves; he believed that they should continue to toil as field workers for white landowners.

Johnson failed to anticipate the speed and vigor with which former Confederate leaders would move to reassert their political authority. In addition, he did not gauge accurately the resentment of congressional Republicans, who thought his policies toward the defeated South were too forgiving. The southern states that took advantage of Johnson's reunification policies passed so-called **Black Codes**. These state laws were an ill-disguised attempt to institute a system of near-slavery. They aimed to penalize "vagrant" blacks, defined as those who did not work in the fields for whites, and to deny blacks the right to vote, serve on juries, or in some cases even own land. The Black Code of Mississippi restricted the rights of a freedperson to "keep or carry fire-arms," ammunition, and knives and to "quit the service of his or her employer before the expiration of his or her term of service without good cause." The vagueness of this last provision threatened any blacks who happened not to be working under the supervision of whites at any given moment. People arrested under the Black Codes faced imprisonment or forced labor.

Black Codes Southern state laws passed after the Civil War to limit the rights and actions of newly liberated African Americans.

Interpreting History

A Georgia Planter APPEALS TO A FREEDMEN'S BUREAU OFFICER

"Poor white women have to work—so should all poor people—or else stealing must be legalized."

In April 1866, M. C. Fulton, a white planter living near Thomson, Georgia, wrote to Brigadier General Davis Tillson, the head of the Freedmen's Bureau in Georgia, appealing for help in getting black women workers back to work in the fields in time for spring cotton planting.

Dear Sir—Allow me to call your attention to the fact that most of the Freedwomen who have husbands are not at work—never having made any contract at all—their husbands are at work, while they are as nearly as idle as it is possible for them to be, pretending to spin—knit or something that really amounts to nothing for their husbands have to buy them clothing. . . .

Now these women have always been used to working out & it would be far better for them to go to work for reasonable wages & their rations—both in regard to health & in furtherance of their family wellbeing. . . . It is impossible for one man to do this [work] & maintain his wife in idleness without stealing more or less of their support, whereas if their wives (where they are able) were at work for rations & fair wages—which they can all get; the family could live in some comfort and more happily—besides their labor is a very important percent of the labor of the South. . . .

Now & then there is a woman who is not able to work in the field—or has 3 or 4 children at work & can afford to live on her childrens labor—with that of her husband—Even in such a

case it would be better she should be at work—Generally however most of them should be in the field—Could not this matter be referred to your agents[?] They are generally clever men and would do right. I would suggest that you give this matter your favorable consideration & if you can do so to use your influence to make these idle women go to work. You would do them & the country a service besides gaining favor & the good opinion of the people generally.

I beg you will not consider this matter lightly for it is a very great evil & one that the Bureau ought to correct—if they wish the Freedmen & women to do well. . . . I am very respectfully your ob[edien]t servant

M. C. Fulton

Fulton added a postscript:

These idle women are bad examples to those at work & they are often mischief makers—having no employment their brain becomes more or less the Devil's workshop as is always the case with idle people—black or white. . . .

Such people are generally a nuisance—& ought to be reformed if possible or forced to work for a support. . . . Poor white women have to work—so should all poor people—or else stealing must be legalized—or tolerated for it is the twin sister of idleness. . . .

After the Civil War, many rural southern blacks, such as those shown here, continued to toil in cotton fields owned by whites. As sharecroppers, these workers made very little in cash wages, and even when they did accumulate some money, many learned that whites would not sell them land. What were the limits of Reconstruction as a federal program designed to assist freed slaves to become truly free?

Questions for Discussion

1. How does Fulton define "idleness"? Why does he believe that women who stay home and care for their families are not really working?

2. Is Fulton making a race-based or a class-based argument in his appeal to Tillson? Explain.

3. Does Fulton have good reason for assuming—or hoping—that Tillson will be responsive to this letter?

SOURCE: M. C. Fulton to Brig. Gen. Davis Tillson, 17 April 1866, Unregistered Letters.

At the end of the Civil War, congressional Republicans were divided by their commitment (or lack thereof) to various forms of black equality. Radicals wanted to use strong federal measures to advance black people's civil rights and economic independence. In contrast, moderates were more concerned with the free market and private property rights; they took a hands-off approach regarding former slaves. But members of both groups reacted with outrage to the Black Codes. Moreover, when the legislators returned to the Capitol in December 1865, they were in for a shock: among their new colleagues were four former Confederate generals, five colonels, and other high-ranking members of the Confederate elite, including former Vice President Alexander Stephens, now under indictment for treason. All of these rebels were duly elected senators and representatives from southern states. In a special session called for December 4, a joint committee of fifteen lawmakers (six senators and nine members of the House) voted to bar these men from Congress.

By January 1865, both houses of Congress had approved the Thirteenth Amendment to the Constitution, abolishing slavery. The necessary three-fourths of the states ratified the measure by the end of the year. However, President Johnson was becoming more openly defiant of his congressional foes who favored aggressive federal protection of black civil rights. He vetoed two crucial pieces of legislation: an extension and expansion of the Freedmen's Bureau and the Civil Rights Bill of 1866. This latter measure was an unprecedented piece of legislation. It called on the federal government—for the first time in history—to protect individual rights against the willful indifference of the states (as manifested, for example, in the Black Codes). Congress managed to override both vetoes by the summer of 1866.

In June of that year, Congress passed the Fourteenth Amendment. This amendment guaranteed the former slaves citizenship rights, punished states that denied citizens the right to vote, declared the former rebels ineligible for federal and state office, and voided Confederate debts. This amendment was the first to use gender-specific language, guarding against denying the vote "to any of the male inhabitants" of any state.

Even before the war ended, certain groups of Northerners had moved south, and the flow increased in 1865. Black and white teachers volunteered to teach the former slaves to read and write. Some Northerners journeyed south to invest in land and become planters in the staple crop economy. White southern critics called all these migrants **carpetbaggers**. This derisive term suggested that the Northerners hastily packed their belongings in rough bags made of carpet scraps and then rushed south to take advantage of the region's devastation and confusion. To many freedpeople, whether they worked for a carpetbagger or a Southerner, laboring in the cotton fields was but a continuation of slavery.

Some former southern (white) Whigs, who had been reluctant secessionists, now found common ground with northern Republicans who supported government subsidies for railroads, banking institutions, and public improvements. This group consisted of some members of the humbled planter class as well as men of more modest means. Southern Democrats, who sneered at any alliances with the North, scornfully labeled these whites **scalawags** (the term referred to a scrawny, useless type of horse on the Scottish island of Scalloway).

Soon after the war's end, southern white vigilantes launched a campaign of violence and intimidation against freedpeople who dared to resist the demands of white planters and other employers. Calling itself the Ku Klux Klan, a group of Tennessee war veterans soon became a white supremacist terrorist organization and spread to other states. In May 1866, violence initiated by white terrorists against blacks in Memphis, Tennessee, left forty-six freedpeople and two whites dead, and in July, a riot in New Orleans claimed the lives of thirty-four blacks and three of their white allies. These bloody encounters demonstrated the lengths to which ex-Confederates would go to reassert their authority and defy the federal government.

Back in Washington, Johnson vetoed the Fourteenth Amendment, traveling around the country and urging the states not to ratify it. He argued that policies related to black suffrage should be decided by the states. The time had come for reconciliation between the North and South, maintained the president. (The amendment would not be adopted until 1868.) Johnson's opposition to the amendment revealed how thoroughly questions of black equality had become enmeshed in postbellum politics. Those questions did not necessarily reveal a partisan divide, however; the views of Johnson and other conservative Republicans were similar to those of southern Democrats in many respects.

Congressional Republicans fought back. In the election of November 1866, they won a two-thirds majority in both houses of Congress. These numbers allowed them to claim a mandate from their constituents and to override any future vetoes by the president. Moderates and radicals together prepared to bypass Johnson to shape their own Reconstruction policies.

Carpetbaggers A negative term applied by Southerners to Northerners who moved to the South after the Civil War to pursue political or economic opportunities.

Scalawag A negative term applied by southern Democrats after the Civil War to any white Southerner who allied with the Republican party.

✳ Explore Reconstruction on MyHistoryLab

HOW DID RECONSTRUCTION AFFECT AFRICAN AMERICANS IN THE SOUTH?

The Civil War ended in April 1865, and by the end of the year slavery would be formally abolished with the passage of the Thirteenth Amendment to the Constitution. Americans vehemently disagreed among themselves about the future of the southern states, in particular, and the United States, in general. Many white Southerners aimed to reestablish a staple crop economy that relied on landless black agricultural workers. Some northern whites wanted to guarantee blacks economic independence through land grants and the right to vote; others felt that former slaves should be left to fend for themselves. For their part, African Americans hoped to reconstitute their families, farm their own land, send their children to school, and participate in the larger community as free and equal U.S. citizens.

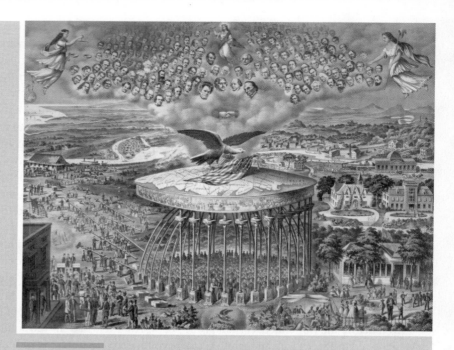

This 1867 allegorical lithograph portrays a heavenly reconciliation among those men of both sides who lost their lives in the Civil War (including President Lincoln, to the left of the figure of Jesus at the top in the center). An eagle symbolizing the nation oversees the rebuilding of the Union, restoring the country to peace and prosperity. Can you see evidence of the artist's view of black people's roles in the newly unified nation? *Library of Congress*.

RECONSTRUCTION AMENDMENTS TO THE CONSTITUTION

Amendment	Summary	Date
Thirteenth	Abolishes slavery	December 6, 1865
Fourteenth	Ensures equal rights and protections to every person born or naturalized in the United States	July 9, 1868
Fifteenth	Prohibits the denial of the right to vote based on race	February 3, 1870

KEY QUESTIONS   Use MyHistoryLab *Explorer* to answer these questions:

Analysis ▶▶▶ *How did voting patterns for Republicans evolve during the Reconstruction period?*

Chart voting patterns to understand reasons behind voting trends.

Comparison ▶▶▶ *How did literacy rates differ between African Americans and Euro-Americans in the South?*

Theorize how this might affect black disenfranchisement.

Response ▶▶▶ *What was the landholding situation for African Americans at the end of the nineteenth century?*

Map land tenure to see discrepancies with whites.

The Postbellum South's Labor Problem

While policymakers maneuvered in Washington, black people throughout the postbellum South aspired to labor for themselves and gain independence from white overseers and landowners. Yet white landowners persisted in regarding blacks as field hands who must be coerced into working. With the creation of the Freedmen's Bureau in 1865, Congress intended to form an agency that would mediate between these two groups. Bureau agents encouraged workers and employers to sign annual labor contracts designed to eliminate the last vestiges of the slave system. All over the South, freed men, women, and children would contract with an employer on January 1 of each year. They would agree to work for either a monthly wage, an annual share of the crop, or some combination of the two.

According to the Freedmen's Bureau, the benefits of the annual labor contract system were clear. Employers would have an incentive to treat their workers fairly—to offer a decent wage and refrain from physical punishment. Disgruntled workers could leave at the end of the year to work for a more reasonable landowner. In the postbellum South, however, labor relations were shaped not by federal decree but by a process of negotiation that pitted white landowners against blacks who possessed little but their own labor.

For instance, blacks along the Georgia and South Carolina coast were determined to cultivate the land on which their forebears had lived and died. They urged General Sherman to confiscate the land owned by rebels in the area. In response, in early 1865, Sherman issued Field Order Number 15, mandating that the Sea Islands and the coastal region south of Charleston be divided into parcels of 40 acres for individual freed families. He also decreed that the army might lend mules to these families to help them begin planting. Given the provisions of this order, many freed families came to expect that the federal government would grant them "forty acres and a mule."

As a result of Sherman's order, 20,000 former slaves proceeded to cultivate the property once owned by Confederates. Within a few months of the war's end, however, the War Department bowed to pressure from white landowners and revoked the order. The War Department also provided military protection for whites to return and occupy their former lands. In response, a group of black men calling themselves Commissioners from Edisto Island (one of the Sea Islands) met in committee to protest to the Freedmen's Bureau what they considered a betrayal. Writing from the area in January 1866, one Freedmen's Bureau official noted that the new policy must be upheld but regretted that it had brought the freedpeople into "collision" with "U.S. forces."

The Commissioners from Edisto Island, together with black people all over the South, recognized the hollowness of their freedom—the limits to their "equality"—without the ability to own land. Lacking cash or credit, they had few options but to return to the cotton fields, now as sharecroppers. Lacking literacy skills, they could not aspire to many of the better jobs that whites held. The Freedmen's Bureau, the chief government agency that was supposed to ensure a measure of fairness in white landowners' relations with black workers, was short-lived.

During its brief life (1865 to 1868), the Freedmen's Bureau compiled a mixed record. The individual agents represented a broad range of backgrounds, temperaments, and political ideas. Some were former abolitionists who considered northern-style free labor to be "the noblest principle on earth." These men tried to ensure safe and fair working arrangements for black men, women, and children. In contrast, some agents had little patience with the freedpeople's drive for self-sufficiency. Some bureau offices became havens for blacks seeking redress against abusive or fraudulent labor practices, but other offices had little impact on the postwar political and economic landscape. For agents without means of transportation (a reliable horse), plantations scattered throughout the vast rural South remained outside their control. Because white landowners crafted the wording and specific provisions of labor contracts, the bureau agents who enforced such agreements often served the interests of employers rather than laborers.

The outlines of sharecropping, a system that defined southern cotton production until well into the twentieth century, were visible just a few years after the Civil War.

Poor families, black and white, contracted annually with landlords, who advanced them supplies, such as crop seed, mules, plows, food, and clothing. Fathers directed the labor of their children in the fields. At the end of the year, many families remained indebted to their employer and, thus, entitled to nothing and obliged to work another year in the hope of repaying the debt. If a sharecropper's demeanor or work habits displeased the landlord, the family faced eviction.

Single women with small children were especially vulnerable to the whims of landlords in the postbellum period. Near Greensboro, North Carolina, for example, planter Presley George Sr. settled accounts with his field worker Polly at the end of 1865. For her year's expenses, Polly was charged a total $69 for corn, cloth, thread, and board for a child who did not work. By George's calculations, Polly had earned exactly $69 for the labor she and her three children (two sons and a daughter) performed in the course of the year, leaving her no cash of her own. Under these harsh conditions, freedpeople looked to each other for support and strength.

Building Free Communities

Independence in the workplace was not the only concern of freedpeople. Soon after the war's end, southern blacks set about organizing themselves as an effective political force and as free communities devoted to the social and educational welfare of their own people. Differences among blacks based on income, jobs, culture, and skin color at times inhibited institution-building. Some black communities found themselves divided by class, with blacks who had been free before the war (including many literate and skilled light-skinned men) assuming leadership over illiterate field hands. In New Orleans, a combination of factors contributed to class divisions among people of African heritage. During the antebellum period, light-skinned free people of color, many of whom spoke French, were much more likely to possess property and a formal education than were enslaved people, who were dark-skinned English speakers. After the Civil War, the more privileged group pressed for public accommodations laws, which would open the city's theaters, opera, and expensive restaurants to all blacks for the first time. However, black churches and social organizations remained segregated according to class. Few black people expected that the end of slavery would usher in a time and place where all blacks would be equal to one another in terms of their wealth or material condition.

For the most part, postbellum black communities united around the principle that freedom from slavery should also mean full citizenship rights: the ability to vote, own land, and educate their children. These rights must be enforced by federal firepower: "a military occupation will be absolutely necessary," declared the blacks of Norfolk, "to protect the white Union men of the South, as well as ourselves." Freedpeople in some states allied themselves with white yeomen who had long resented the political power of the great planters and now saw an opportunity to use state governments as agents of democratization and economic reform.

Networks of freedpeople formed self-help organizations. Like the sponsors of the Savannah Education Association, blacks throughout the South formed committees to raise funds and hire teachers for neighborhood schools. Small Georgia towns, such as Cuthbert, Albany, Cave Spring, and Thomasville, with populations no greater than a few hundred, raised up to $70 per month and contributed as much as $350 each for the construction of school buildings. Funds came from the proceeds of fairs, bazaars, and bake sales; subscriptions raised by local school boards; and tuition fees. In the cash-starved postbellum South, these amounts represented a great personal and group sacrifice for the cause of education.

All over the South, black families charted their own course. They elected to take in orphans and elderly kin, pool resources with neighbors, and arrange for mothers to stay home with their children. These choices challenged the power of former slaveholders and the influence of Freedmen's Bureau agents and northern missionaries and teachers. At the same time, in seeking to attend to their families and to provide for themselves,

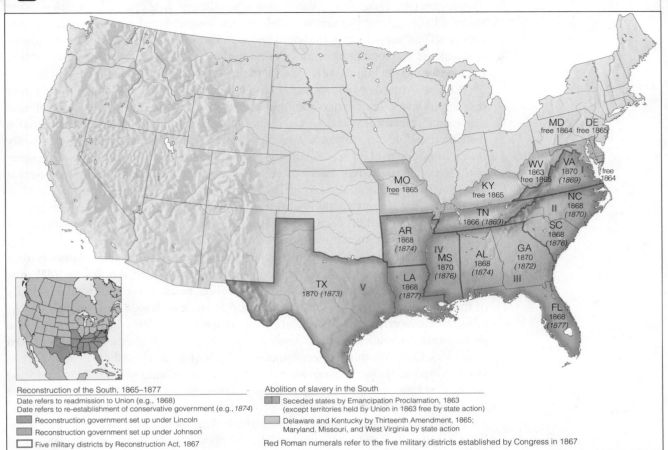

Reconstruction of the South, 1865–1877
Date refers to readmission to Union (e.g., 1868)
Date refers to re-establishment of conservative government (e.g., *1874*)
- Reconstruction government set up under Lincoln
- Reconstruction government set up under Johnson
- Five military districts by Reconstruction Act, 1867

Abolition of slavery in the South
- Seceded states by Emancipation Proclamation, 1863 (except territories held by Union in 1863 free by state action)
- Delaware and Kentucky by Thirteenth Amendment, 1865; Maryland, Missouri, and West Virginia by state action

Red Roman numerals refer to the five military districts established by Congress in 1867

MAP 15.1 RADICAL RECONSTRUCTION Four of the former Confederate states, Louisiana, Arkansas, Tennessee, and Virginia, were reorganized under President Lincoln's Ten Percent Plan in 1864. Neither this plan nor the proposals of Lincoln's successor, Andrew Johnson, provided for the enfranchisement of former slaves. In 1867 Congress established five military districts in the South and demanded that newly reconstituted state governments implement universal manhood suffrage. By 1870, all of the former Confederate states had rejoined the Union, and by 1877, all of those states had installed conservative (i.e., Democratic) governments.

southern blacks resembled members of other mid-nineteenth-century laboring classes who valued family ties over the demands of employers and landlords.

Tangible signs of the new emerging black communities infuriated most southern whites. A schoolhouse run by blacks proved threatening in a society where most white children had little opportunity to receive an education. Black communities were also quick to form their own churches, rather than continue to occupy an inferior place in white churches. Other sights proved equally unsettling: on a main street in Charleston, an armed black soldier marching proudly or a black woman wearing a fashionable hat and veil, the kind favored by white women of the planter class. These developments help to account for the speed with which whites organized themselves in the Klan and various other vigilante groups, aiming to preserve "the supremacy of the white race in this Republic."

Congressional Reconstruction: The Radicals' Plan

The rise of armed white supremacist groups in the South helped spur congressional Republicans to action. On March 2, 1867, Congress seized the initiative. A coalition led by two radicals, Senator Charles Sumner of Massachusetts and Congressman Thaddeus Stevens of Pennsylvania, prodded Congress to pass the **Reconstruction Act of 1867**. The purpose of this measure was to purge the South of disloyalty once and for all. The act stripped thousands of former Confederates of voting rights. The former Confederate states would not be readmitted to the Union until they had ratified the Fourteenth

Reconstruction Act of 1867 An act that prevented the former Confederate states from entering the Union until they had ratified the Fourteenth Amendment and written new constitutions that guaranteed black men the right to vote. It also divided the South (with the exception of Tennessee, which had ratified the Fourteenth Amendment) into five military districts and stationed federal troops throughout the region.

Amendment and written new constitutions that guaranteed black men the right to vote. The South (with the exception of Tennessee, which had ratified the Fourteenth Amendment in 1866) was divided into five military districts. Federal troops were stationed throughout the region. These troops were charged with protecting Union personnel and supporters in the South and with restoring order in the midst of regional political and economic upheaval. In essence, the radicals' plan yoked southern states' readmission to the Union with a pledge to protect the political equality of blacks.

Congress passed two additional acts specifically intended to secure congressional power over the president. The intent of the Tenure of Office Act was to prevent the president from dismissing Secretary of War Edwin Stanton, a supporter of the radicals. The other measure, the Command of the Army Act, required the president to seek approval for all military orders from General Ulysses S. Grant, the army's senior officer. Grant also was a supporter of the Republicans. Both of these acts probably violated the separation of powers doctrine as put forth in the Constitution. Together, they would soon precipitate a national crisis

During the Reconstruction period, approximately 2,000 black men of the emerging southern Republican party served as local elected officials, sheriffs, justices of the peace, tax collectors, and city councilors. Many of these leaders were of mixed ancestry, and many had been free before the war. They came in disproportionate numbers from the ranks of literate men, such as clergy, teachers, and skilled artisans. In Alabama, Florida, Louisiana, Mississippi, and South Carolina, black men constituted a majority of the voting public. Throughout the South, 600 black men won election to state legislatures. However, nowhere did blacks control a state government, although they did predominate in South Carolina's lower House. Sixteen black Southerners were elected to the U.S. Congress during Reconstruction. Most of those elected to Congress in the years immediately after the war were freeborn. However, among the nine men elected for the first time after 1872, six were former slaves. All of these politicians exemplified the desire among southern blacks to become active, engaged citizens.

Newly reconstructed southern state legislatures provided for public school systems, fairer taxation methods, bargaining rights of plantation laborers, racially integrated transportation systems and accommodations, and public works projects, especially railroads. These measures reflected the priorities among Republicans—to pass legislation that would, first, promote economic development and, second, yield a rough equality of economic opportunity among workers regardless of status or skin color. Enjoying a public education and some modest measure of job security should not be advantages for a favored few, black and white, Republicans argued. Some Democrats, hoping to appeal to poor white constituents on the one hand or to railroad interests on the other, at times joined with Republicans to pass certain measures.

Nevertheless, the legislative coalitions forged between Northerners and Southerners, blacks and whites, were uneasy and, in many cases, less than productive. Southern Democrats (and later, historians sympathetic to them) claimed that Reconstruction governments were uniquely corrupt, with some carpetbaggers, scalawags, and freed-people vying for **kickbacks** from railroad and construction magnates. In fact, whenever state legislatures sought to promote business interests, they opened the door to the bribery of public officials. In this respect, northern as well as southern politicians were vulnerable to charges of corruption. In the long run, southern Democrats cared less about charges of legislative corruption and more about the growing political power of local black Republican party organizations.

In Washington in early 1868, President Johnson forced a final showdown with Congress. He replaced several high military officials with more conservative men. He also fired Secretary of War Stanton, in apparent violation of the Tenure of Office Act. Shortly thereafter, in February, a newly composed House Reconstruction Committee impeached Johnson for ignoring the act, and the Senate began his trial on March 30. The president and Congress were locked in an extraordinary battle for political power.

The final vote was thirty-five senators against Johnson, one vote short of the necessary two-thirds of all senators' votes needed for conviction. Nineteen senators voted to acquit Johnson of the charges. Nevertheless, to win acquittal, he had had to promise

Kickbacks Money paid illegally in return for favors (for example, to a politician by a person or business that has received government contracts).

TABLE 15.1 THE ELECTION OF 1868

Candidate	Political Party	Popular Vote (%)	Electoral Vote
Ulysses S. Grant	Republican	52.7	214
Horatio Seymour	Democratic	47.3	80

moderates that he would not stand in the way of congressional plans for Reconstruction. Johnson essentially withdrew from policymaking in the spring of 1868. That November, with Republicans urging Northerners to "vote as you shot" (that is, to cast ballots against the former Confederates), Ulysses S. Grant was elected president.

Political reunion was an uneven process, but one that gradually eroded the newly won rights of former slaves in many southern states. By the end of 1868, Arkansas, North Carolina, South Carolina, Louisiana, Tennessee, Alabama, and Florida had met congressional conditions for readmission to the Union, and two years later, Mississippi, Virginia, Georgia, and Texas followed. The Fifteenth Amendment, passed by Congress in 1869 and ratified by the necessary number of states a year later, granted all black men the right to vote. However, in some states, such as Louisiana, reunification gave Democrats license to engage in wholesale election fraud and violence toward freed men and women. In 1870–1871, a congressional inquiry into the Klan exposed pervasive and grisly assaults on Republican schoolteachers, preachers, and prospective voters, black and white. The Klan also targeted men and women who refused to work like slaves in the fields. In April 1871, Congress passed the Ku Klux Klan Act, which punished conspiracies intended to deny rights to citizens. But Klan violence and intimidation had already taken their toll on Republican voting strength.

Claiming Territory for the Union

15.2 What human and environmental forces impeded the Republican goal of western expansion?

While blacks and whites, Northerners and Southerners clashed over power in the South, poet Walt Whitman celebrated the "manly and courageous instincts" that propelled a brave, adventurous people westward. Whitman hailed the march across the prairies and over the mountains as a cavalcade of progress. He and other Americans believed that the postbellum migration fulfilled a mission of national regeneration begun by the Civil War. Kansas's population grew by 240 percent in the 1860s, Nebraska's by 355 percent.

To unite the entire country together as a single economic and political unit was the Republican ideal. The railroads in particular served as vehicles of national integration. When the Central Pacific and Union Pacific met at Promontory Point, Utah, in 1869, the hammering of the spike that joined the two railroads produced a telegraphic signal received simultaneously on both coasts, setting off a national celebration.

Meanwhile, regular units of U.S. cavalry, including two regiments of blacks, were launching attacks on Indians on the Plains, in the Northwest, and in the Southwest. Between 1865 and 1890, U.S. military forces conducted a dozen separate campaigns against western Indian peoples and met Indian warriors in battle or attacked Indian settlements in more than 1,000 engagements.

In contrast to African Americans, who adamantly demanded their rights as American citizens, defiant western Indians battled a government to which they owed no allegiance. Indians did not lobby for the right to vote, sit on juries, or run for office; the notion of "equality" with whites meant little to them. They preferred to live apart from white society and to manage their own affairs rather than to push for political integration into the United States.

With this 1870 photograph, the Kansas Pacific Railroad advertised the opportunity for western travelers to shoot buffalo from the comfort and safety of their railroad car. The company's official taxidermist shows off his handiwork. Railroad expansion facilitated the exploitation of natural resources while promoting tourism. What groups of people might be eager to take advantage of the buffalo-hunting services offered by the Kansas Pacific Railroad?

Federal Military Campaigns Against Western Indians

In 1871 the U.S. government renounced the practice of seeking treaties with various Indian groups. This change in policy opened the way for a more aggressive effort to subdue Native populations. It also hastened the expansion of the reservation system, an effort begun in the antebellum period to confine specific Indian groups to specific territories.

On the Plains, clashes between Indians and U.S. soldiers persisted after the Civil War. In 1867 at Medicine Lodge Creek in southern Kansas, the United States signed a treaty with an alliance of Comanche, Kiowa, Cheyenne, Arapaho, and Plains Apache. This treaty could not long withstand the provocation posed by the railroad, as Indians continued to attack the surveyors, supply caravans, and military escorts that preceded the railroad work crews. The year before, the Seventh U.S. Cavalry, under the command of Lieutenant Colonel George Custer, had been formed to ward off Indian attacks on the Union Pacific, snaking its way across the central Plains westward from Kansas and Nebraska. In November 1868, Custer destroyed a Cheyenne settlement on the Washita River, in present-day Oklahoma. Custer's men murdered women and children, burned tipis, and destroyed 800 horses.

The Apache managed to elude General George Crook until 1875. Crook employed some of these Apache to track down the war chief Geronimo of the Chiricahua. Like many other Indian leaders, Geronimo offered both religious and military guidance to his people. He believed that a spirit would protect him from the white man's bullets and from the arrows of Indians in league with government troops. Yet Geronimo was tricked into an initial surrender in 1877 and was held in irons for several months before gaining his release and challenging authorities for another nine years.

In 1874 Custer took his cavalry into the Black Hills of the Dakotas. Supposedly, the 1868 Treaty of Fort Laramie had rendered this land off-limits to whites. Custer's mission was to offer protection for the surveyors of the Northern Pacific Railroad and to force Indians onto reservations as stipulated in the 1868 treaty. However, the officer lost no time trumpeting the fact that Indian lands were filled with gold. This report prompted a rush to the Black Hills, lands sacred to the Sioux. Within two years, 15,000 gold miners had illegally descended on Indian lands to seek their fortunes. The federal government proposed buying the land, but leaders of the Sioux, including Red Cloud, Spotted Tail, and Sitting Bull, spurned the offer.

During the morning of June 25, 1876, Custer and his force of 264 soldiers attacked a Sun Dance gathering of 2,500 Sioux and Cheyenne on the banks of the Little Big Horn River in Montana. Custer foolishly launched his attack without adequate backup, and he and his men were easily overwhelmed and killed by Indian warriors, led by the Oglala Sioux Crazy Horse and others. Reacting to this defeat, U.S. military officials reduced the Lakota and Cheyenne to wardship status, ending their autonomy.

Indians throughout the West maintained their distinctive ways of life during these turbulent times. Horse holdings, so crucial for hunting, trading, and fighting, varied from group to group, with the Crow wealthy in relation to their Central Plains neighbors the Oglala and the Arikara. Plains peoples engaged in a lively trading system. They exchanged horses and their trappings (bridles and blankets) for eastern goods such as kettles, guns, and ammunition. Despite their differences in economy, these groups held similar religious beliefs about an all-powerful life force that governed the natural world. People, plants, and animals were all part of the same order.

The Postwar Western Labor Problem

In 1865 the owners of the Central Pacific Railroad seemed poised for one of the great engineering feats of the nineteenth century. In the race eastward from California, they would construct trestles spanning vast chasms and roadbeds traversing mountains and deserts. Government officials in Washington were eager to subsidize the railroad. What the owners lacked was a dependable labor force. The Irish workers who began the line in California struck for higher wages in compensation for brutal, dangerous work. These immigrants dropped their shovels and hammers at the first word of a gold strike nearby— or far away. As a result, in 1866 the Central Pacific had decided to tap into a vast labor source by importing thousands of Chinese men from their native Guangdong province.

The Chinese labored to extend the railroad tracks eastward from Sacramento, California, up to ten miles a day in the desert, only a few feet a day in the rugged Sierra Nevada Mountains. In nerve-wracking feats of skill, they lowered themselves in woven baskets to implant nitroglycerine explosives in canyon walls. Chinese laborers toiled through snowstorms and blistering heat to blast tunnels and cut passes through granite mountains. With the final linking of the railroad in Utah in 1869, many Chinese sought work elsewhere in the West.

Read the Document   Chinese Six Companies, Letter to President Grant (1876)

Chinese construction workers labor on the Central Pacific Railroad, around 1868. Many Chinese immigrants toiled as indentured laborers, indebted to Chinese merchant creditors who paid for their passage to California. Isolated in all-male work camps, crews of railroad workers retained their traditional dress, language, and diet. After the completion of the Transcontinental Railroad in 1869, some immigrants returned to China, and others dispersed to small towns and cities throughout the West. From this photo, can you speculate about the engineering challenges faced by builders of western railroads?

Signed in 1868, the Burlingame Treaty, named for Anson Burlingame, an American envoy to China, had supposedly guaranteed government protection for Chinese immigrants as visitors, traders, or permanent residents. Most immigrants were men. (Six out of ten California Chinese women were listed in the 1870 census as prostitutes, most the victims of their compatriots.) Yet the treaty did not inhibit U.S. employers, landlords, and government officials from discriminating against the Chinese.

By 1870, 40,000 Chinese lived in California and represented fully one-quarter of the state's wage earners. They found work in the cigar, woolen-goods, and boot and shoe factories of San Francisco; in the gold mining towns, now as laundry operators rather than as miners as they had before the Civil War; and in the fields as agricultural laborers. White workers began to cry unfair competition against this Asian group that was becoming increasingly integrated into the region's economy.

As a group, Chinese men differed from California Indians, who remained trapped in the traditional agricultural economy of unskilled labor. Whites appropriated Indian land and forced many men, women, and children to work as wage earners for large landowners. Deprived of their familiar hunting and gathering lands, and wracked by disease and starvation, California Indians had suffered a drastic decline in their numbers by 1870, from 100,000 to 30,000 in twenty years.

Land Use in an Expanding Nation

The Union's triumph in 1865 prompted new conflicts and deepened long-standing ones over the use of the land in a rich, sprawling country. In the South, staple crop planters began to share political power with an emerging elite, men who owned railroads and textile mills. Despairing of ever achieving antebellum levels of labor efficiency, some landowners turned to mining the earth and the forests for saleable commodities. These products, obtained through extraction, included phosphate (used in producing fertilizer), timber, coal, and turpentine. Labor in extractive industries complemented labor in the plantation economy. Sharecroppers alternated between tilling cotton fields in the spring and harvesting the crop in the fall, while seeking employment in sawmills and coal mines in the winter and summer.

As European Americans settled in the West and Southwest, they displaced natives who had been living there for generations. For example, the U.S. court system determined who could legally claim property. Western courts also decided whether natural resources such as water, land, timber, and fish and game constituted property that could be owned by private interests. In the Southwest, European American settlers, including army soldiers who had come to fight Indians and then stayed, continued to place Hispanic land titles at risk. Citing prewar precedents, American courts favored the claims of recent squatters over those of long-standing residents. In 1869, with the death of her husband (who had served as a general in the Union army), Maria Amparo Ruiz de Burton saw the large ranch they had worked together near San Diego slip out of her control. The first Spanish-speaking woman to be published in English in the United States, de Burton was a member of the Hispanic elite. Nevertheless, she had little political power. California judges backed the squatters who occupied the ranch.

As they controlled more land and assumed public office, some European Americans in the Southwest exploited their political connections and economic power. In the 1870s, the so-called Santa Fe Ring wrested more than 80 percent of the original Spanish grants of land from Hispanic landholders in New Mexico. An alliance of European American lawyers, businesspeople, and politicians, the Santa Fe Ring defrauded families and kin groups of their land titles and speculated in property to make a profit. Whereas many ordinary Hispanic settlers saw land—with its crops, pasture, fuel, building materials, and game—as a source of livelihood, groups such as the Santa Fe Ring saw land primarily as a commodity to be bought and sold.

Seemingly overnight, boom towns sprang up wherever minerals or timber beckoned: southern Arizona and the Rocky Mountains west of Denver, Virginia City in western Nevada, the Idaho-Montana region, and the Black Hills of South Dakota. In all these

TABLE 15.2 ESTIMATES OF RAILROAD CROSSTIES USED AND ACRES OF FOREST
CLEARED, 1870–1910

Year	Miles of Track	Ties Renewed Annually (millions)	Ties Used on New Construction (millions)	Total Ties Annually (millions)	Acres of Forest Cleared (thousands)
1870	60,000	21	18	39	195
1880	107,000	37	21	58	290
1890	200,000	70	19	89	445
1900	259,000			91	455
1910	357,000			124	620

SOURCE: Michael Williams, *Americans and Their Forests* (1989), 352. Cambridge University Press.

places, increasing numbers of workers operated sophisticated kinds of machinery, such as rock crushers. When the vein was exhausted or the forests depleted, the towns went bust.

Railroads facilitated not only the mining of minerals but also the growth of the cattle-ranching industry. Rail connections between the Midwest and East made it profitable for Texas ranchers to pay cowboys to drive their herds of long-horned steers to Abilene, Ellsworth, Wichita, or Dodge City, Kansas, for shipment to stockyards in Chicago or St. Louis. Cattle drives were huge; an estimated 10 million animals were herded north from Texas alone between 1865 and 1890. They offered employment to all kinds of men with sufficient skills and endurance. Among the cowhands were African American horsebreakers and gunmen and Mexicans skilled in the use of the *reata* (lasso). Blacks made up about 25 percent and Hispanos about 15 percent of all cowboy outfits.

In knitting regional economies together, federal land policies were crucial to the Republican vision of a developing nation. The Mineral Act of 1866 granted title to millions of acres of mineral-rich land to mining companies, a gift from the federal government to private interests. The Timber Culture Act of 1873 allotted 160 acres to individuals in selected western states if they agreed to plant one-fourth of the acreage with trees. Four years later, the Desert Land Act provided cheap land if buyers irrigated at least part of their parcels.

The exploitation of western resources raised many legal questions: Must ranchers pay for the prairies their cattle grazed on and the trails they followed to market? How could one "own" a stampeding buffalo herd or a flowing river? What was the point of holding title to a piece of property if only the timber, oil, water, or minerals (but not the soil) were of value? The Apex Mining Act of 1872 sought to address some of these issues. This law legalized traditional mining practices in the West by validating titles approved by local courts. According to the law, a person who could locate the apex of a vein (its point closest to the surface) could lay claim to the entire vein beneath the surface. The measure contributed to the wholesale destruction of certain parts of the western landscape as mining companies blasted their way through mountains and left piles of rocks in their wake. It also spurred thousands of lawsuits as claimants argued over what constituted an apex or a vein.

It was during this period that a young Scottish-born naturalist named John Muir began to explore the magnificent canyons and mountains of California. He contrasted nature's majesty with the artificial landscape created by and for humans. In the wilderness, there is nothing "truly dead or dull, or any trace of what in manufactories is called rubbish or waste," he wrote; "everything is perfectly clean and pure and full of divine lessons."

Muir was gratified by the creation of the National Park system during the postwar period. Painters and geologists were among the first Easterners to appreciate the spectacular vistas of the western landscape. In 1864 Congress set aside a small area within California's Yosemite Valley for public recreation and enjoyment. Soon after the war, railroad promoters forged an alliance with government officials in an effort to block commercial development of particularly beautiful pockets of land. Northern Pacific Railway financier Jay Cooke lobbied hard for the government to create a 2-million-acre park in what is today the northwest corner of Wyoming. As a result, in March 1872,

Congress established Yellowstone National Park. Tourism would continue to serve as a key component of the western economy.

Muir and others portrayed the Yosemite and Yellowstone valleys as wildernesses, empty of human activity. In fact, both areas had long provided hunting and foraging grounds for Native peoples. Yellowstone had been occupied by the people now called the Shoshone since the fifteenth century. This group, together with the Bannock, Crow, and Blackfoot, tried to retain access to Yellowstone's meadows, rivers, and forests after it became a national park. However, U.S. policymakers and military officials persisted in their efforts to mark off territory for specific commercial purposes, while Indians were confined to reservations.

Buying Territory for the Union

Before the war, Republicans had opposed any federal expansionist schemes that they feared might benefit slaveholders. However, after 1865 and the outlawing of slavery, some Republican lawmakers and administration officials advocated the acquisition of additional territory. Secretary of State William Seward led the way in 1867 by purchasing Alaska from Russia. For $7.2 million (about 2 cents an acre), the United States gained 591,004 square miles of land. Within the territory were diverse indigenous groups—Eskimo, Aleut, Tlingit, Tsimshian, Athabaskan, and Haida—and a small number of native Russians. Though derided at the time as "Seward's icebox," Alaska yielded enough fish, timber, minerals, oil, and water power in the years to come to prove that the original purchase price was a tremendous bargain.

The impulse that prompted administration support for the Alaska purchase also spawned other plans for territorial acquisitions. In 1870 some Republicans joined with Democrats in calling for the annexation of the Dominican Republic. These congressmen argued that the tiny Caribbean country would make a fine naval base, provide investment opportunities for American businesspeople, and offer a refuge for southern freedpeople. The abolitionist Frederick Douglass argued in favor of annexation as a way for the United States to establish a foothold in the Caribbean and thereby "strike a blow at slavery wherever it may exist in the tropics"—especially in the Spanish colony of Cuba.

However, influential Senator Charles Sumner warned against a takeover without considering the will of the Dominican people, who were currently involved in their own civil war. Some congressmen, in a prelude to foreign policy debates of the 1890s, suggested that the dark-skinned Dominican people were unequal to whites in intelligence and ambition and were therefore incapable of appreciating the blessings of American citizenship. In 1871 an annexation treaty failed to win Senate approval.

In facilitating western expansion, Republicans upheld the ideal that prosperity would come to all people who worked hard. Indians were not part of the Republican vision of western prosperity. But other groups also questioned the Republican vision as it affected their own interests.

The Republican Vision and Its Limits

15.3 What were some of the inconsistencies in, and unanticipated consequences of, Republican notions of equality and federal power?

After the Civil War, victorious Republicans envisioned a nation united in the pursuit of prosperity. All citizens would be free to follow their individual economic self-interest and to enjoy the fruits of honest toil. In contrast, some increasingly vocal and well-organized groups saw the expansion of legal rights, and giving black men the right to vote in particular, as only initial, tentative steps on the path to an all-inclusive citizenship. Women, industrial workers, farmers, and African Americans made up overlapping constituencies pressing for equal political rights and economic opportunity. Together they challenged the mainstream Republican view that defeat of the rebels and destruction of slavery were sufficient to guarantee prosperity for everyone.

Partnerships between government and business also produced unanticipated consequences for Republicans committed to what they believed was the collective good. Some politicians and business leaders saw these partnerships as opportunities for private gain. Consequently, private greed and public corruption accompanied postwar economic growth. Thus, Republican leaders faced challenges from two very different sources: people agitating for civil rights and people hoping to reap personal gain from political activities.

Postbellum Origins of the Women's Suffrage Movement

After the Civil War, the nation's middle class, which had its origins in the antebellum period, continued to grow. Dedicated to self-improvement and filled with a sense of moral authority, many middle-class Americans (especially Protestants) felt a deep cultural connection to their counterparts in England. Indeed, the United States produced its own "Victorians," so called for the self-conscious middle class that emerged in the England of Queen Victoria during her reign from 1837 to 1901.

At the heart of the Victorian sensibility was the ideal of domesticity: a harmonious family living in a well-appointed home, guided by a pious mother and supported by a father successful in business. Famous Protestant clergyman Henry Ward Beecher and his wife were outspoken proponents of this domestic ideal. According to Eunice Beecher, women had no "higher, nobler, more divine mission than in the conscientious endeavor to create a *true home*."

Yet the traumatic events of the Civil War only intensified the desire among a growing group of American women to participate fully in the nation's political life. They wanted to extend their moral influence outside the narrow and exclusive sphere of the home. Many women believed that they deserved the vote and that the time was right to demand it.

In 1866 veteran reformers Elizabeth Cady Stanton, Susan B. Anthony, and Lucy Stone founded the Equal Rights Association to link the rights of white women and African Americans. Nevertheless, in 1867, Kansas voters defeated a referendum proposing suffrage for both blacks and white women. This disappointment convinced some former abolitionists that the two causes should be separated—that women should wait patiently until the rights of African American men were firmly secured. Frederick Douglass declined an invitation to a women's suffrage convention in Washington, D.C., in 1868. He explained, "I am now devoting myself to a cause [if] not more sacred, certainly more urgent, because it is one of life and death to the long enslaved people of this country, and that is: negro suffrage." But African American activist and former slave Sojourner Truth warned, "There is a great stir about colored men getting their rights, but not a word about the colored women; and if colored men get their rights, and not colored women get theirs, there will be a bad time about it."

In 1869 two factions of women parted ways and formed separate organizations devoted to women's rights. The more radical wing, including Cady Stanton and Anthony, bitterly denounced the Fifteenth Amendment because it gave the vote to black men only. They helped to found the National Woman Suffrage Association (NWSA), which argued for a renewed commitment to the original Declaration of Sentiments passed in Seneca Falls, New York, two decades earlier. They favored married women's property rights, liberalization of divorce laws, opening colleges and trade schools to women, and a new federal amendment to allow women to vote. Lucy Stone and her husband, Henry Blackwell, founded the rival American Woman Suffrage Association (AWSA). This group downplayed the larger struggle for women's rights and focused on the suffrage question exclusively. Its members supported the Fifteenth Amendment and retained ties to the Republican party. The AWSA focused on state-by-state campaigns for women's suffrage.

In 1871 the NWSA welcomed the daring, flamboyant Victoria Woodhull as a vocal supporter, only to renounce her a few years later. Woodhull's political agenda ranged from free love and dietary reform to legalized prostitution, working men's rights, and women's suffrage. (In the nineteenth century, free love advocates denounced what they called a sexual double standard, one that glorified female chastity while tolerating male promiscuity.) In 1872 one of Woodhull's critics successfully challenged her. Woodhull spent a month in jail as a result of the zealous prosecution by vice reformer Anthony Comstock, a clergyman who objected to her public discussions and writings on sexuality. Comstock assumed the role of an outspoken crusader against vice. A federal law passed in 1873, and named after him, equated information related to birth control with pornography, banning this and other "obscene material" from the mails.

Susan B. Anthony used the 1872 presidential election as a test case for women's suffrage. She attempted to vote and was arrested, tried, and convicted as a result. By this time, most women suffragists, and most members of the NWSA for that matter, had become convinced that they should focus on the vote exclusively; they therefore accepted the AWSA's policy on this issue. In the coming years, they would avoid other related causes with which they might have allied themselves, including black civil rights and labor reform.

Workers' Organizations

Many Americans benefited from economic changes of the postwar era. Railroading, mining, and heavy industry helped fuel the national economy and in the process boosted the growth of the urban managerial class. In the Midwest, many landowning farmers prospered when they responded to an expanding demand for grain and other staple crops. In Wisconsin, wheat farmers cleared forests, drained swamps, diverted rivers, and profited from the booming world market in grain. Yet the economic developments that allowed factory managers and owners of large wheat farms to make a comfortable living for themselves did not necessarily benefit agricultural and manufacturing wage-workers.

Indeed, during this period growing numbers of working people, in the countryside and in the cities, became caught up in a cycle of indebtedness. In the upcountry South (above the fall line, or Piedmont), formerly self-sufficient family farmers sought loans from banks to repair their war-damaged homesteads. To qualify for these loans, the farmer had to plant cotton as a staple crop, to the neglect of corn and other foodstuffs. Many sharecroppers, black and white, received payment in the form of credit only; for these families, the end-of-the-year reckoning yielded little more than rapidly accumulating debts. Midwestern farmers increasingly relied on bank loans to purchase expensive threshing and harvesting machinery.

Several organizations founded within five years of the war's end offered laborers an alternative vision to the Republicans' brand of individualism and nationalism. In 1867 Oliver H. Kelly, a former Minnesota farmer now working in a Washington office, organized the National Grange of the Patrons of Husbandry, popularly known as the **Grange**. This movement sought to address a new, complex marketplace increasingly dominated by railroads, banks, and grain elevator operators. The Grange encouraged farmers to form cooperatives that would market their crops and to challenge discriminatory railroad rates that favored big business.

Founded in Baltimore in 1866, the National Labor Union (NLU) consisted of a collection of craft unions and claimed as many as 600,000 members at its peak in the early 1870s. The group welcomed farmers as well as factory workers and promoted legislation for an eight-hour workday and the arbitration of industrial disputes.

In 1873 a nationwide depression threw thousands out of work and worsened the plight of debtors. Businesspeople in agriculture, mining, the railroad industry, and manufacturing had overexpanded their operations. The free-wheeling loan practices of major banks had contributed to this situation. The inability of these businesspeople to repay their loans led to the failure of major banks. With the contraction of credit, thousands of small businesses went bankrupt. The NLU did not survive the crisis.

However, by this time, a new organization had appeared to champion the cause of the laboring classes in opposition to lords of finance. Founded in 1869 by Uriah Stephens and other Philadelphia tailors, the Knights of Labor eventually aimed to unite industrial and rural workers, the self-employed and the wage earner, blacks and whites, and men and women.

Grange An organization founded by Oliver H. Kelly in 1867 to represent the interests of farmers by pressing for agricultural cooperatives, an end to railroad freight discrimination against small farmers, and other initiatives. Its full name was National Grange of the Patrons of Husbandry.

The Knights were committed to private property and to the independence of the farmer, the entrepreneur, and the industrial worker. The group banned from its ranks "nonproducers," such as liquor sellers, bankers, professional gamblers, stockbrokers, and lawyers.

This period of depression also laid the foundation for the Greenback Labor party, organized in 1878. Within three years after the end of the Civil War, the Treasury had withdrawn from circulation $100 million in wartime paper currency ("greenbacks"). With less money in circulation, debtors found it more difficult to repay their loans. The government also ceased coining silver dollars in 1873, despite the discovery of rich silver lodes in the West. To add insult to injury, the Resumption Act (1875) called for the government to continue to withdraw paper greenbacks. Thus, hard money became dearer, and debtors became more desperate. In 1878 the new Greenback Labor party managed to win 1 million votes and elect fourteen candidates to Congress. The party laid the foundation for the Populist party that emerged in the 1890s.

Several factors made coalition building among these American workers difficult. One was the nation's increasingly multicultural workforce. Unions, such as the typographers, were notorious for excluding women and African Americans, a fact publicized by both Frederick Douglass and Susan B. Anthony, to no avail. In 1869 shoe factory workers (members of the Knights of St. Crispin) went on strike in North Adams, Massachusetts. They were soon shocked to see seventy-five Chinese strikebreakers arrive by train from California. Their employer praised the new arrivals for their "rare industry." The shoemakers' strike collapsed quickly after the appearance of what the workers called this "Mongolian battery." Employers would continue to manipulate and divide the laboring classes through the use of ethnic, religious, and racial prejudices.

Political Corruption and the Decline of Republican Idealism

Out of the new partnership between politics and business emerged an extensive system of bribes and kickbacks. Greedy politicians of both parties challenged the Republicans' high-minded idealism.

In the early 1870s, the *New York Times* exposed the schemes of William M. "Boss" Tweed. Tweed headed Tammany Hall, a New York City political organization that courted labor unions and contributed liberally to Catholic schools and charities. Tammany Hall politicians routinely used bribery and extortion to fix elections and bilk taxpayers of millions of dollars. One plasterer employed on a city project received $138,000 in "payment" for two days' work. After the *Times* exposé, Tweed was prosecuted and convicted. His downfall attested to the growing influence of newspaper reporters.

Another piece of investigative journalism rocked the political world in 1872. In 1867 major stockholders of the Union Pacific Railroad had formed a new corporation, called the Crédit Mobilier, to build railroads. Heads of powerful congressional committees received shares of stock in the new company. These gifts of stock were bribes to secure the legislators' support for public land grants favorable to the new corporation. The *New York Sun* exposed a number of the chief beneficiaries in the fall of 1872, findings confirmed by congressional investigation. Among the disgraced politicians was Grant's vice president, Schuyler Colfax.

The 1872 presidential election pitted incumbent Grant against the Democratic challenger, *New York Tribune* editor Horace Greeley. Many Republicans, disillusioned with congressional corruption and eager to press forward with civil service reform, endorsed the Democratic candidate. Greeley and his Republican allies decried the patronage (or "spoils") system by which politicians rewarded their supporters with government jobs. Nevertheless, Grant won the election.

By 1872, after four bloody years of war and seven squandered years of postwar opportunity, the federal government seemed prepared to hand the South back to unrepentant rebels. The North showed what one House Republican called "a general apathy among the people concerning the war and the negro." The **Civil Rights Act of 1875** guaranteed blacks equal access to public accommodations and transportation. Yet this

Civil Rights Act of 1875
Congressional legislation that guaranteed black people access to public accommodations and transportation; the Supreme Court declared the measure unconstitutional in 1883.

Watch the Video Democracy and Corruption: The Rise of Political Machines

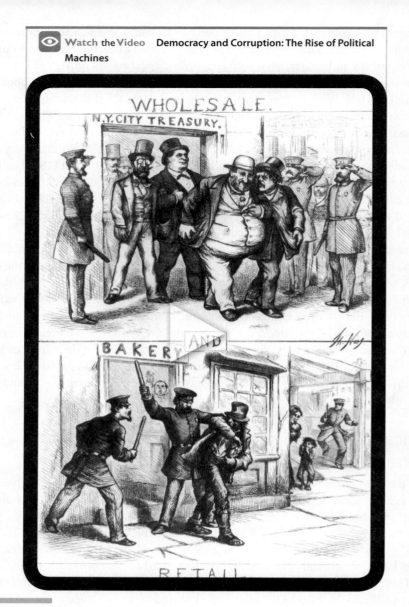

In 1871 Thomas Nast drew a series of cartoons exposing the corruption of New York City Democratic boss William M. Tweed and his political organization, Tammany Hall. In this drawing, published in *Harper's Weekly* in 1871, Nast depicts Tweed and his cronies engaging in a "wholesale" looting of the New York City treasury with the assistance of compliant police officers. Those same officers stand ready to crack down on the impoverished father who robs a bakery to feed his family. By portraying Tweed as an enemy of the poor, Nash ignored the fact that the political boss gained a large following among immigrant voters. What message was Nast trying to convey about the nature of urban political machines and the corruption they spawned?

act represented the final, half-hearted gesture of radical Republicanism. The Supreme Court declared the measure unconstitutional in 1883 on the grounds that the government could protect only political and not social rights. White Southerners reasserted their control over the region's political economy.

The presidential election of 1876 intensified public cynicism about deal making in high places. A dispute over election returns led to what came to be known as the Compromise of 1877. In the popular vote, Democrat Samuel J. Tilden outpolled Republican Rutherford B. Hayes, a former Ohio governor. However, when the electoral votes were counted, the Democrat had only 184, one short of the necessary number. Nineteen of the twenty votes in dispute came from Louisiana, South Carolina, and Florida, and these three states submitted two new sets of returns, one from each of the two main parties. A specially appointed congressional electoral commission, the Committee of Fifteen, was charged with resolving the dispute. It divided along partisan lines. The eight Republicans outvoted the seven Democrats to accept the Republican set of returns from Florida.

TABLE 15.3 THE ELECTION OF 1872

Candidate	Political Party	Popular Vote (%)	Electoral Vote
Ulysses S. Grant	Republican	55.6	286
Horace Greeley	Democratic, Liberal Republican	43.9	66

To break the logjam, the Democrats agreed that Hayes could assume office in return for the withdrawal of all remaining federal troops from the South. The Republicans tacitly agreed that their work there was finished and that blacks in the region should fend for themselves. Hayes declined to enforce the Civil Rights Act of 1875. White Southerners were free to uphold the principle of states' rights that had been traditionally invoked to deny blacks their rights in the region. Thus the Civil War failed to solve one of the most pressing issues of the day—the relation between federal and state power in protecting the rights of individuals.

Conclusion

During the dozen or so years after the Civil War, both northern Republicans and southern Democrats registered a series of spectacular wins and crushing losses. Though humiliated by the Union victory, southern white supremacists eventually won for themselves the freedom to control their own local and state governments. As landlords, sheriffs, and merchants, these men defied the postwar federal amendments to the Constitution and deprived African Americans of basic citizenship rights. By the end of Reconstruction, northern Republicans had conceded local power to their former enemies. Even an aggressive nationalism, it turned out, could accept traditional southern hierarchies: white over nonwhite, rich over poor.

Yet the Civil War was not only a fight between whites. During the conflict, black people had served as combatants in the struggle for freedom. They saw the war in different terms than did northern white Republicans and southern white Democrats. After the war, blacks pursued full citizenship rights while attempting to maintain institutional and cultural autonomy from white people regardless of political affiliation. In their quest, freed men and women met with mixed success. Black men gained the (formal) right to vote. Yet white Republicans, both in Congress and in southern state legislatures, proved to be disappointing allies to blacks who found themselves, increasingly, at the mercy of white vigilantes and other terrorist groups. During the Reconstruction period, blacks consolidated their families, established their own churches, and sought to work on their own terms in the fields. Yet lacking money and credit, they found it difficult to buy land and in the process achieve true independence from white landowners, bankers, and politicians.

At the end of Reconstruction, Republicans remained in firm control of national economic policy. The white South had secured its right to conduct its own political affairs, but the Republican vision of economic growth and development had become the law of the land. This vision was a guiding principle of historic national and, increasingly, international significance. Economic innovation in particular proved to be a force of great unifying power, stronger even than all the federal military forces deployed during and after the Civil War.

Read the Document **Samuel Tilden, Speech to the Manhattan Club Conceding the Election (1876)**

TABLE 15.4 THE ELECTION OF 1876

Candidate	Political Party	Popular Vote (%)	Electoral Vote
Rutherford B. Hayes	Republican	48.0	185
Samuel J. Tilden	Democratic	51.0	184

Chapter Review

The Struggle over the South

15.1 How did various groups of Northerners and Southerners differ in their vision of the postwar South? p. 371

Congressional Republicans united in opposition to President Johnson's conciliatory approach toward the South. They pushed for basic civil rights and a measure, at least, of economic independence for African Americans. White Southerners opposed black rights and sought to maintain their control over African American labor. Black Southerners, on the other hand, desired land ownership and freedom from white supervision. They set about reuniting their families, providing for themselves, and organizing themselves as an effective political force.

Claiming Territory for the Union

15.2 What human and environmental forces impeded the Republican goal of western expansion? p. 381

Republicans had to clear western land of the Indians who lived there and who fought to maintain their distinctive ways of life. Republicans also wanted to subsidize railroads to aid westward expansion, and owners, who lacked a dependable labor force, solved this problem by exploiting the labor of Chinese immigrants. Traversing mountains and canyons required the use of sophisticated engineering techniques. To manage the land and natural resources, Republicans passed legislation favorable to expansion, such as the Apex Mining Act of 1872.

The Republican Vision and Its Limits

15.3 What were some of the inconsistencies in, and unanticipated consequences of, Republican notions of equality and federal power? p. 386

Most Republicans believed that the defeat of the Confederacy and the destruction of slavery were sufficient to guarantee prosperity for everyone. Women, industrial workers, farmers, and African Americans, however, challenged this notion and pressed for equal political rights and economic opportunity. Partnerships between government and business produced unanticipated consequences, as private greed and public corruption accompanied economic growth.

Timeline

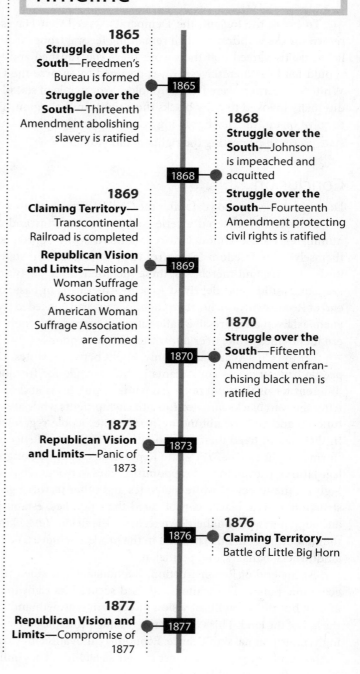

1865
Struggle over the South—Freedmen's Bureau is formed
Struggle over the South—Thirteenth Amendment abolishing slavery is ratified

1865

1868
Struggle over the South—Johnson is impeached and acquitted
Struggle over the South—Fourteenth Amendment protecting civil rights is ratified

1868

1869
Claiming Territory—Transcontinental Railroad is completed
Republican Vision and Limits—National Woman Suffrage Association and American Woman Suffrage Association are formed

1869

1870
Struggle over the South—Fifteenth Amendment enfranchising black men is ratified

1870

1873
Republican Vision and Limits—Panic of 1873

1873

1876
Claiming Territory—Battle of Little Big Horn

1876

1877
Republican Vision and Limits—Compromise of 1877

1877

The Declaration of Independence

In Congress, July 4, 1776

The Unanimous Declaration of the Thirteen United States of America

When, in the course of human events, it becomes necessary for one people to dissolve the political bonds which have connected them with another, and to assume, among the powers of the earth, the separate and equal station to which the laws of nature and of nature's God entitle them, a decent respect to the opinions of mankind requires that they should declare the causes which impel them to the separation.

We hold these truths to be self-evident: That all men are created equal; that they are endowed by their Creator with certain unalienable rights; that among these are life, liberty, and the pursuit of happiness; that, to secure these rights, governments are instituted among men, deriving their just powers from the consent of the governed; that whenever any form of government becomes destructive of these ends, it is the right of the people to alter or to abolish it, and to institute new government, laying its foundation on such principles, and organizing its powers in such form, as to them shall seem most likely to effect their safety and happiness. Prudence, indeed, will dictate that governments long established should not be changed for light and transient causes; and accordingly all experience hath shown that mankind are more disposed to suffer, while evils are sufferable, than to right themselves by abolishing the forms to which they are accustomed. But when a long train of abuses and usurpations, pursuing invariably the same object, evinces a design to reduce them under absolute despotism, it is their right, it is their duty, to throw off such government, and to provide new guards for their future security. Such has been the patient sufferance of these colonies; and such is now the necessity which constrains them to alter their former systems of government. The history of the present King of Great Britain is a history of repeated injuries and usurpations, all having in direct object the establishment of an absolute tyranny over these states. To prove this, let facts be submitted to a candid world.

He has refused his assent to laws, the most wholesome and necessary for the public good.

He has forbidden his governors to pass laws of immediate and pressing importance, unless suspended in their operation till his assent should be obtained; and, when so suspended, he has utterly neglected to attend to them.

He has refused to pass other laws for the accommodation of large districts of people, unless those people would relinquish the right of representation in the legislature, a right inestimable to them, and formidable to tyrants only.

He has called together legislative bodies at places unusual, uncomfortable, and distant from the depository of their public records, for the sole purpose of fatiguing them into compliance with his measures.

He has dissolved representative houses repeatedly, for opposing, with manly firmness, his invasions on the rights of the people.

He has refused for a long time, after such dissolutions, to cause others to be elected; whereby the legislative powers, incapable of annihilation, have returned to the people at large for their exercise; the state remaining, in the mean time, exposed to all the dangers of invasions from without and convulsions within.

He has endeavored to prevent the population of these states; for that purpose obstructing the laws for naturalization of foreigners; refusing to pass others to encourage their migration hither, and raising the conditions of new appropriations of lands.

He has obstructed the administration of justice, by refusing his assent to laws for establishing judiciary powers.

He has made judges dependent on his will alone, for the tenure of their offices, and the amount and payment of their salaries.

He has erected a multitude of new offices, and sent hither swarms of officers to harass our people and eat out their substance.

He has kept among us, in times of peace, standing armies, without the consent of our legislatures.

He has affected to render the military independent of, and superior to, the civil power.

He has combined with others to subject us to a jurisdiction foreign to our constitution, and unacknowledged by our laws, giving his assent to their acts of pretended legislation:

For quartering large bodies of armed troops among us;

For protecting them, by a mock trial, from punishment for any murder which they should commit on the inhabitants of these states;

For cutting off our trade with all parts of the world;

For imposing taxes on us without our consent;

For depriving us, in many cases, of the benefits of trial by jury;

For transporting us beyond seas, to be tried for pretended offenses;

For abolishing the free system of English laws in a neighboring province, establishing therein an arbitrary government, and enlarging its boundaries, so as to render it at once an example and fit instrument for introducing the same absolute rule into these colonies;

For taking away our charters, abolishing our most valuable laws, and altering fundamentally the forms of our governments;

For suspending our own legislatures, and declaring themselves invested with power to legislate for us in all cases whatsoever.

He has abdicated government here, by declaring us out of his protection and waging war against us.

He has plundered our seas, ravaged our coasts, burned our towns, and destroyed the lives of our people.

He is at this time transporting large armies of foreign mercenaries to complete the works of death, desolation, and tyranny already begun with circumstances of cruelty and perfidy scarcely paralleled in the most barbarous ages, and totally unworthy the head of a civilized nation.

He has constrained our fellow-citizens, taken captive on the high seas, to bear arms against their country, to become the executioners of their friends and brethren, or to fall themselves by their hands.

He has excited domestic insurrection among us, and has endeavored to bring on the inhabitants of our frontiers the merciless Indian savages, whose known rule of warfare is an undistinguished destruction of all ages, sexes, and conditions.

In every stage of these oppressions we have petitioned for redress in the most humble terms; our repeated petitions have been answered only by repeated injury. A prince, whose character is thus marked by every act which may define a tyrant, is unfit to be the ruler of a free people.

Nor have we been wanting in our attentions to our British brethren. We have warned them, from time to time, of attempts by their legislature to extend an unwarrantable jurisdiction over us. We have reminded them of the circumstances of our emigration and settlement here. We have appealed to their native justice and magnanimity; and we have conjured them, by the ties of our common kindred, to disavow these usurpations, which would inevitably interrupt our connections and correspondence. They, too, have been deaf to the voice of justice and of consanguinity. We must, therefore, acquiesce in the necessity which denounces our separation, and hold them, as we hold the rest of mankind, enemies in war, in peace friends.

We, therefore, the representatives of the United States of America, in General Congress assembled, appealing to the Supreme Judge of the world for the rectitude of our intentions, do, in the name and by the authority of the good people of these colonies, solemnly publish and declare, that these United Colonies are, and of right ought to be, FREE AND INDEPENDENT STATES; that they are absolved from all allegiance to the British crown, and that all political connection between them and the state of Great Britain is, and ought to be, totally dissolved; and that, as free and independent states, they have full power to levy war, conclude peace, contract alliances, establish commerce, and do all other acts and things which independent states may of right do. And for the support of this declaration, with a firm reliance on the protection of Divine Providence, we mutually pledge to each other our lives, our fortunes, and our sacred honor.

JOHN HANCOCK

New Hampshire
Josiah Bartlett
William Whipple
Matthew Thornton

Massachusetts
John Adams
Samuel Adams
Robert Treat Paine
Elbridge Gerry

New York
William Floyd
Philip Livingston
Francis Lewis
Lewis Morris

Rhode Island
Stephen Hopkins
William Ellery

New Jersey
Richard Stockton
John Witherspoon
Francis Hopkinson
John Hart
Abraham Clark

Pennsylvania
Robert Morris
Benjamin Rush
Benjamin Franklin
John Morton
George Clymer
James Smith
George Taylor
James Wilson
George Ross

Delaware
Caeser Rodney
George Read
Thomas McKean

Maryland
Samuel Chase
William Paca
Thomas Stone
Charles Carroll of Carrollton

North Carolina
William Hooper
Joseph Hewes
John Penn

Virginia
George Wythe
Richard Henry Lee
Thomas Jefferson
Benjamin Harrison
Thomas Nelson Jr.
Francis Lightfoot Lee
Carter Braxton

South Carolina
Edward Rutledge
Thomas Heyward Jr.
Thomas Lynch Jr.
Arthur Middleton

Connecticut
Roger Sherman
Samuel Huntington
William Williams
Oliver Wolcott

Georgia
Button Gwinnett
Lyman Hall
George Walton

The Articles of Confederation

Between the States of New Hampshire, Massachusetts Bay, Rhode Island and Providence Plantations, Connecticut, New York, New Jersey, Pennsylvania, Delaware, Maryland, Virginia, North Carolina, South Carolina, Georgia

Article 1

The stile of this confederacy shall be "The United States of America."

Article 2

Each State retains its sovereignty, freedom and independence, and every power, jurisdiction, and right, which is not by this confederation expressly delegated to the United States, in Congress assembled.

Article 3

The said states hereby severally enter into a firm league of friendship with each other for their common defence, the security of their liberties and their mutual and general welfare; binding themselves to assist each other against all force offered to, or attacks made upon them, or any of them, on account of religion, sovereignty, trade, or any other pretence whatever.

Article 4

The better to secure and perpetuate mutual friendship and intercourse among the people of the different states in this union, the free inhabitants of each of these states, paupers, vagabonds, and fugitives from justice excepted, shall be entitled to all privileges and immunities of free citizens in the several states; and the people of each State shall have free ingress and regress to and from any other State, and shall enjoy therein all the privileges of trade and commerce, subject to the same duties, impositions, and restrictions, as the inhabitants thereof respectively; provided, that such restrictions shall not extend so far as to prevent the removal of property, imported into any State, to any other State of which the owner is an inhabitant; provided also, that no imposition, duties, or restriction, shall be laid by any State on the property of the United States, or either of them.

If any person guilty of, or charged with treason, felony, or other high misdemeanor in any State, shall flee from justice and be found in any of the United States, he shall, upon demand of the governor or executive power of the State from which he fled, be delivered up and removed to the State having jurisdiction of his offence.

Full faith and credit shall be given in each of these states to the records, acts, and judicial proceedings of the courts and magistrates of every other State.

Article 5

For the more convenient management of the general interests of the United States, delegates shall be annually appointed, in such manner as the legislature of each State shall direct, to meet in Congress, on the 1st Monday in November in every year, with a power reserved to each State to recall its delegates, or any of them, at any time within the year, and to send others in their stead for the remainder of the year.

No State shall be represented in Congress by less than two, nor by more than seven members; and no person shall be capable of being a delegate for more than three years in any term of six years; nor shall any person, being a delegate, be capable of holding any office under the United States, for which he, or any other for his benefit, receives any salary, fees, or emolument of any kind.

Each State shall maintain its own delegates in a meeting of the states, and while they act as members of the committee of the states.

In determining questions in the United States, in Congress assembled, each State shall have one vote.

Freedom of speech and debate in Congress shall not be impeached or questioned in any court or place out of Congress: and the members of Congress shall be protected in their persons from arrests and imprisonments, during the time of their going to and from, and attendance on Congress, except for treason, felony, or breach of the peace.

Article 6

No State, without the consent of the United States, in Congress assembled, shall send any embassy to, or receive any embassy from, or enter into any conference, agreement, alliance, or treaty with any king, prince, or state; nor shall any person, holding any office of profit or trust under the United States, or any of them, accept of any present, emolument, office or title, of any kind whatever, from any king, prince, or foreign state; nor shall the United States, in Congress assembled, or any of them, grant any title of nobility.

No two or more states shall enter into any treaty, confederation, or alliance, whatever, between them, without the consent of the United States, in Congress assembled, specifying accurately the purposes for which the same is to be entered into, and how long it shall continue.

No State shall lay any imposts or duties which may interfere with any stipulations in treaties entered into by the United States, in Congress assembled, with any king, prince, or state, in pursuance of any treaties already proposed by Congress to the courts of France and Spain.

No vessels of war shall be kept up in time of peace by any State, except such number only as shall be deemed necessary by the United States, in Congress assembled, for the defence of such State or its trade; nor shall any body of forces be kept up by any State, in time of peace, except such number only as, in the judgment of the United States, in Congress assembled, shall be deemed requisite to garrison the forts necessary for the defence of such State; but every State shall always keep up a well regulated and disciplined militia, sufficiently armed and accoutred, and shall provide, and constantly have ready for use, in public stores, a due number of field pieces and tents, and a proper quantity of arms, ammunition and camp equipage.

No State shall engage in any war without the consent of the United States, in Congress assembled, unless such State be actually invaded by enemies, or shall have received certain advice of a resolution being formed by some nation of Indians to invade such State, and the danger is so imminent as not to admit of a delay till the United States, in Congress assembled, can be consulted; nor shall any State grant commissions to any ships or vessels of war, nor letters of marque or reprisal, except it be after a declaration of war by the United States, in Congress assembled, and then only against the kingdom or state, and the subjects thereof, against which war has been so declared, and under such regulations as shall be established by the United States, in Congress assembled, unless such States be infested by pirates, in which case vessels of war may be fitted out for that occasion, and kept so long as the danger shall continue, or until the United States, in Congress assembled, shall determine otherwise.

Article 7

When land forces are raised by any State for the common defence, all officers of or under the rank of colonel, shall be appointed by the legislature of each State respectively, by whom such forces shall be raised, or in such manner as such State shall direct; and all vacancies shall be filled up by the State which first made the appointment.

Article 8

All charges of war and all other expences, that shall be incurred for the common defence or general welfare, and allowed by the United States, in Congress assembled, shall be defrayed out of a common treasury, which shall be supplied by the several states, in proportion to the value of all land within each State, granted to or surveyed for any person, as such land and the buildings and improvements thereon shall be estimated according to such mode as the United States, in Congress assembled, shall, from time to time, direct and appoint.

The taxes for paying that proportion shall be laid and levied by the authority and direction of the legislatures of the several states, within the time agreed upon by the United States, in Congress assembled.

Article 9

The United States, in Congress assembled, shall have the sole and exclusive right and power of determining on peace and war, except in the cases mentioned in the 6th article; of sending and receiving ambassadors; entering into treaties and alliances, provided that no treaty of commerce shall be made, whereby the legislative power of the respective states shall be restrained from imposing such imposts and duties on foreigners as their own people are subjected to, or from prohibiting the exportation or importation of any species of goods or commodities whatsoever; of establishing rules for deciding, in all cases, what captures on land or water shall be legal, and in what manner prizes, taken by land or naval forces in the service of the United States, shall be divided or appropriated; of granting letters of marque and reprisal in times of peace; appointing courts for the trial of piracies and felonies committed on the high seas, and establishing courts for receiving and determining, finally, appeals in all cases of captures; provided, that no member of Congress shall be appointed a judge of any of the said courts.

The United States, in Congress assembled, shall also be the last resort on appeal in all disputes and differences now subsisting, or that hereafter may arise between two or more states concerning boundary, jurisdiction or any other cause whatever; which authority shall always be exercised in the manner following: whenever the legislative or executive authority, or lawful agent of any State, in controversy with another, shall present a petition to Congress, stating the matter in question, and praying for a hearing, notice thereof shall be given, by order of Congress, to the legislative or executive authority of the other State in controversy, and a day assigned for the appearance of the parties by their lawful agents, who shall then be directed to appoint, by joint consent, commissioners or judges to constitute a court for hearing and determining the matter in question; but, if they cannot agree, Congress shall name three persons out of each of the United States, and from the list of such persons each party shall alternately strike out one, in the petitioners beginning, until the number shall be reduced to thirteen; and from that number not less than seven, nor more than nine names, as Congress shall direct, shall, in the presence of Congress, be drawn out by lot; and the persons whose names shall be drawn, or any five of them, shall be commissioners or judges to hear and finally determine the controversy, so always as a major part of the judges who shall hear the cause shall agree in the determination; and if either party shall neglect to attend at the day appointed, without shewing reasons which Congress shall judge sufficient, or, being present, shall refuse to strike, the Congress shall proceed to nominate three persons out of each State, and the secretary of Congress shall strike in behalf of such party absent or refusing; and the judgment and sentence of the court to be appointed, in the manner before prescribed, shall be final and conclusive; and if any of the parties shall refuse to submit to the authority of such court, or to appear or defend their claim or cause, the court shall nevertheless proceed to pronounce sentence or judgment, which shall, in like manner, be final and decisive, the judgment or sentence and other proceedings being, in either case, transmitted to Congress, and lodged among the acts of Congress for the security of the parties concerned: provided, that every commissioner, before he sits in judgment, shall take an oath, to be administered by one of the judges of the supreme or superior court of the State where the cause shall be tried, "well and truly to hear and determine the matter in question, according to the best of his judgment, without favour, affection, or hope of reward": provided, also, that no State shall be deprived of territory for the benefit of the United States.

All controversies concerning the private right of soil, claimed under different grants of two or more states, whose jurisdictions, as they may respect such lands and the states which passed such grants, are adjusted, the said grants, or either of them, being at the same time claimed to have originated antecedent to such settlement of jurisdiction, shall, on the petition of either party to the Congress of the United States, be finally determined, as near as may be, in the same manner as is before prescribed for deciding disputes respecting territorial jurisdiction between different states.

The United States, in Congress assembled, shall also have the sole and exclusive right and power of regulating the alloy and value of coin struck by their own authority, or by that of the respective states; fixing the standard of weights and measures throughout the United States; regulating the trade and managing all affairs with the Indians not members of any of the states; provided that the legislative right of any State within its own limits be not infringed or violated; establishing and regulating post offices from one State to another throughout all the United States, and exacting such postage on the papers passing through the same as may be requisite to defray the expences of the said office; appointing all officers of the land forces in the service of the United States, excepting regimental officers; appointing all the officers of the naval forces, and commissioning all officers whatever in the service of the United States; making rules for the government and regulation of the said land and naval forces, and directing their operations.

The United States, in Congress assembled, shall have authority to appoint a committee to sit in the recess of Congress, to be denominated "a Committee of the States," and to consist of one delegate from each State, and to appoint such other committees and civil officers as may be necessary for managing the general affairs of the United States, under their direction; to appoint one of their number to preside; provided that no person be allowed to serve in the office of president more than one year in any term of three years; to ascertain the necessary sums of money to be raised for the service of the United States, and to appropriate and apply the same for defraying the public expences; to borrow money or emit bills on the credit of the United States, transmitting, every half year, to the respective states, an account of the sums of money so borrowed or emitted; to build and equip a navy; to agree upon the number of land forces, and to make requisitions from each State for its quota, in proportion to the number of white inhabitants in such State; which requisitions shall be binding; and, thereupon, the legislature of each State shall appoint the regimental officers, raise the men, and cloathe, arm, and equip them in a soldier-like manner, at the expence of the United States; and the officers and men so cloathed, armed, and equipped, shall march to the place appointed and within the time agreed on by the United States, in Congress assembled; but if the United States, in Congress assembled, shall, on consideration of circumstances, judge proper that any State should not raise men, or should raise a smaller number than its quota, and that any other State should raise a greater number of men than the quota thereof, such extra number shall be raised, officered, cloathed, armed, and equipped in the same manner as the quota of such State, unless the legislature of such State shall judge that such extra number cannot be safely spared out of the same, in which case they shall raise, officer, cloathe, arm, and equip as many of such extra number as they judge can be safely spared. And the officers and men so cloathed, armed, and equipped, shall march to the place appointed and within the time agreed on by the United States, in Congress assembled.

The United States, in Congress assembled, shall never engage in a war, nor grant letters of marque and reprisal in time of peace, nor enter into any treaties or alliances, nor coin money, nor regulate the value thereof, nor ascertain the sums and expences necessary for the defence and welfare of the United States, or any of them: nor emit bills, nor borrow money on the credit of the United States, nor appropriate money, nor agree upon the number of vessels of war to be built or purchased, or the number of land or sea forces to be raised, nor appoint a commander in chief of the army or navy, unless nine states assent to the same; nor shall a question on any other point, except for adjourning from day to day, be determined, unless by the votes of a majority of the United States, in Congress assembled.

The Congress of the United States shall have power to adjourn to any time within the year, and to any place within the United States, so that no period of adjournment be for a longer duration than the space of six months, and shall publish the journal of their proceedings monthly, except such parts thereof, relating to treaties, alliances or military operations, as, in their judgment, require secrecy; and the yeas and nays of the delegates of each State on any question shall be entered on the journal, when it is desired by any delegate; and the delegates of a State, or any of them, at his, or their request, shall be furnished with a transcript of the said journal, except such parts as are above excepted, to lay before the legislatures of the several states.

Article 10

The committee of the states, or any nine of them, shall be authorized to execute, in the recess of Congress, such of the powers of Congress as the United States, in Congress assembled, by the consent of nine states, shall, from time to time, think expedient to vest them with; provided, that no power be delegated to the said committee for the exercise of which, by the articles of confederation, the voice of nine states, in the Congress of the United States assembled, is requisite.

Article 11

Canada acceding to this confederation, and joining in the measures of the United States, shall be admitted into and entitled to all the advantages of this union; but no other colony shall be admitted into the same, unless such admission be agreed to by nine states.

Article 12

All bills of credit emitted, monies borrowed and debts contracted by, or under the authority of Congress before the assembling of the United States, in pursuance of the present confederation, shall be deemed and considered as a charge against the United States, for payment and satisfaction whereof the said United States and the public faith are hereby solemnly pledged.

Article 13

Every State shall abide by the determinations of the United States, in Congress assembled, on all questions which, by this confederation, are submitted to them. And the articles of this confederation shall be inviolably observed by every State, and the union shall be perpetual; nor shall any alteration at any time hereafter be made in any of them, unless such alteration be agreed to in a Congress of the United States, and be afterwards confirmed by the legislatures of every State.

These articles shall be proposed to the legislatures of all the United States, to be considered, and if approved of by them, they are advised to authorize their delegates to ratify the same in the Congress of the United States; which being done, the same shall become conclusive.

The Constitution of the United States of America

Preamble

We the People of the United States, in Order to form a more perfect Union, establish Justice, insure domestic Tranquility, provide for the common defence, promote the general Welfare, and secure the Blessings of Liberty to ourselves and our Posterity, do ordain and establish this Constitution for the United States of America.

Article I

Section 1

All legislative Powers herein granted shall be vested in a Congress of the United States, which shall consist of a Senate and House of Representatives.

Section 2

The House of Representatives shall be composed of Members chosen every second Year by the People of the several States, and the Electors in each State shall have the Qualifications requisite for Electors of the most numerous Branch of the State Legislature.

No Person shall be a Representative who shall not have attained to the Age of twenty five Years, and been seven Years a Citizen of the United States, and who shall not, when elected, be an inhabitant of that State in which he shall be chosen.

Representatives and direct Taxes shall be apportioned among the several States which may be included within this Union, according to their respective Numbers, *which shall be determined by adding to the whole Number of free Persons, including those bound to Service for a Term of Years, and excluding Indians not taxed, three fifths of all other Persons.** The actual Enumeration shall be made within three Years after the first Meeting of the Congress of the United States, and within every subsequent Term of ten Years, in such Manner as they shall by Law direct. The Number of Representatives shall not exceed one for every thirty Thousand, but each State shall have at Least one Representative; *and until such enumeration shall be made, the State of New Hampshire shall be entitled to chuse three, Massachusetts eight, Rhode-Island and Providence Plantations one, Connecticut five, New York six, New Jersey four, Pennsylvania eight, Delaware one, Maryland six, Virginia ten, North Carolina five, South Carolina five, and Georgia three.*

When vacancies happen in the Representation from any State, the Executive Authority thereof shall issue Writs of Election to fill such Vacancies.

The House of Representatives shall chuse their Speaker and other Officers; and shall have the sole Power of Impeachment.

Section 3

The Senate of the United States shall be composed of two Senators from each State, *chosen by the Legislature thereof,* for six Years; and each Senator shall have one Vote.

Immediately after they shall be assembled in Consequence of the first Election, they shall be divided as equally as may be into three Classes. The Seats of the Senators of the first Class shall be vacated at the Expiration of the second Year, of the second Class at the Expiration of the fourth Year, and of the third Class at the Expiration of the

*Passages no longer in effect are printed in italic type.

sixth Year so that one third may be chosen every second Year; and if Vacancies happen by Resignation, or otherwise, during the Recess of the Legislature of any state, the Executive thereof may make temporary Appointments until the next Meeting of the Legislature, which shall then fill such Vacancies.

No Person shall be a Senator who shall not have attained to the Age of thirty Years, and been nine Years a Citizen of the United States, and who shall not, when elected, be an Inhabitant of that State for which he shall be chosen.

The Vice President of the United States shall be President of the Senate, but shall have no Vote, unless they be equally divided.

The Senate shall chuse their other Officers, and also a President *pro tempore*, in the Absence of the Vice President, or when he shall exercise the Office of President of the United States.

The Senate shall have the sole Power to try all Impeachments. When sitting for that Purpose, they shall be on Oath or Affirmation. When the President of the United States is tried the Chief Justice shall preside: And no Person shall be convicted without the Concurrence of two thirds of the Members present.

Judgment in Cases of Impeachment shall not extend further than to removal from Office, and disqualification to hold and enjoy any Office of honor, Trust or Profit under the United States: but the Party convicted shall nevertheless be liable and subject to Indictment, Trial, Judgment and Punishment, according to Law.

Section 4

The Times, Places and Manner of holding Elections for Senators and Representatives, shall be prescribed in each State by the Legislature thereof; but the Congress may at any time by Law make or alter such Regulations, except as to the Places of chusing Senators.

The Congress shall assemble at least once in every Year, *and such Meeting shall be on the first Monday in December, unless they shall by Law appoint a different Day.*

Section 5

Each House shall be the Judge of the Elections, Returns and Qualifications of its own Members, and a Majority of each shall constitute a Quorum to do Business; but a smaller Number may adjourn from day to day, and may be authorized to compel the Attendance of absent Members, in such Manner, and under such Penalties as each House may provide.

Each House may determine the Rules of its Proceedings, punish its Members for disorderly Behaviour, and, with the Concurrence of two thirds, expel a Member.

Each House shall keep a Journal of its Proceedings, and from time to time publish the same, excepting such Parts as may in their Judgment require Secrecy; and the Yeas and Nays of the Members of either House on any question shall, at the Desire of one fifth of those Present, be entered on the Journal.

Neither House, during the Session of Congress, shall, without the Consent of the other, adjourn for more than three days, nor to any other Place than that in which the two Houses shall be sitting.

Section 6

The Senators and Representatives shall receive a Compensation for their Services, to be ascertained by Law, and paid out of the Treasury of the United States. They shall in all Cases, except Treason, Felony and Breach of the Peace, be privileged from Arrest during their Attendance at the Session of their respective Houses, and in going to and returning from the same; and for any Speech or Debate in either House, they shall not be questioned in any other Place.

No Senator or Representative shall, during the Time for which he was elected, be appointed to any civil Office under the Authority of the United States, which shall have been created, or the Emoluments whereof shall have been encreased during such time, and no Person holding any Office under the United States, shall be a Member of either House during his Continuance in Office.

Section 7

All Bills for raising Revenue shall originate in the House of Representatives; but the Senate may propose or concur with Amendments as on other Bills.

Every Bill which shall have passed the House of Representatives and the Senate, shall, before it become a Law, be presented to the President of the United States; If he approve he shall sign it, but if not he shall return it, with his Objections to the House in which it shall have originated, who shall enter the Objections at large on their Journal, and proceed to reconsider it. If after such Reconsideration two thirds of that House shall agree to pass the Bill, it shall be sent, together with the Objections, to the other House, by which it shall likewise be reconsidered, and if approved by two thirds of that House, it shall become a Law. But in all such Cases the Votes of both Houses shall be determined by yeas and Nays, and the Names of the Persons voting for and against the Bill shall be entered on the Journal of each House respectively. If any Bill shall not be returned by the President within ten Days (Sundays excepted) after it shall have been presented to him, the Same shall be a Law, in like Manner as if he had signed it, unless the Congress by their Adjournment prevent its Return, in which Case it shall not be a Law.

Every Order, Resolution, or Vote to which the Concurrence of the Senate and House of Representatives may be necessary (except on a question of Adjournment) shall be presented to the President of the United States; and before the Same shall take Effect, shall be approved by him, or being disapproved by him, shall be repassed by two thirds of the Senate and House of Representatives, according to the Rules and Limitations prescribed in the Case of a Bill.

Section 8

The Congress shall have Power To lay and collect Taxes, Duties, Imposts and Excises, to pay the Debts and provide for the common Defence and general Welfare of the United States; but all Duties, Imposts and Excises shall be uniform throughout the United States;

To borrow Money on the credit of the United States;

To regulate Commerce with foreign Nations, and among the several States, and with the Indian Tribes;

To establish an uniform Rule of Naturalization, and uniform Laws on the subject of Bankruptcies throughout the United States;

To coin Money, regulate the Value thereof, and of foreign Coin, and fix the Standard of Weights and Measures;

To provide for the Punishment of counterfeiting the Securities and current Coin of the United States;

To establish Post Offices and post Roads;

To promote the Progress of Science and useful Arts, by securing for limited Times to Authors and Inventors the exclusive Right to their respective Writings and Discoveries;

To constitute Tribunals inferior to the supreme Court;

To define and punish Piracies and Felonies committed on the high Seas, and Offences against the Law of Nations;

To declare War, grant Letters of Marque and Reprisal, and make Rules concerning Captures on Land and Water;

To raise and support Armies, but no Appropriation of Money to that Use shall be for a longer Term than two Years;

To provide and maintain a Navy;

To make Rules for the Government and Regulation of the land and naval Forces;

To provide for calling forth the Militia to execute the Laws of the Union, suppress Insurrections and repel Invasions;

To provide for organizing, arming, and disciplining, the Militia, and for governing such Part of them as may be employed in the Service of the United States, reserving to the States respectively, the Appointment of the Officers, and the Authority of training the Militia according to the discipline prescribed by Congress;

To exercise exclusive Legislation in all Cases whatsoever, over such District (not exceeding ten Miles square) as may, by Cession of particular States, and the Acceptance of Congress, become the Seat of the Government of the United States, and to exercise like Authority over all Places purchased by the Consent of the Legislature of the State in which the Same shall be, for the Erection of Forts, Magazines, Arsenals, dock-Yards, and other needful Buildings;—And

To make all Laws which shall be necessary and proper for carrying into Execution the foregoing Powers, and all other Powers vested by this Constitution in the Government of the United States, or in any Department of Officer thereof.

Section 9

The Migration or Importation of such Persons as any of the States now existing shall think proper to admit, shall not be prohibited by the Congress prior to the Year one thousand eight hundred and eight, but a Tax or duty may be imposed on such Importation, not exceeding ten dollars for each Person.

The Privilege of the Writ of Habeas Corpus shall not be suspended, unless when in Cases of Rebellion or Invasion the public Safety may require it.

No Bill of Attainder or ex post facto Law shall be passed.

No Capitation, or other direct, Tax shall be laid, unless in Proportion to the Census or Enumeration herein before directed to be taken.

No Tax or Duty shall be laid on Articles exported from any State.

No Preference shall be given by any Regulation of Commerce or Revenue to the Ports of one State over those of another: nor shall Vessels bound to, or from, one State, be obliged to enter, clear, or pay Duties in another.

No Money shall be drawn from the Treasury, but in Consequence of Appropriations made by Law; and a regular Statement and Account of the Receipts and Expenditures of all public Money shall be published from time to time.

No Title of Nobility shall be granted by the United States: And no Person holding any Office of Profit or Trust under them, shall, without the Consent of the Congress, accept of any present, Emolument, Office, or Title, of any kind whatever, from any King, Prince, or foreign State.

Section 10

No State shall enter into any Treaty, Alliance, or Confederation; grant Letters of Marque and Reprisal; coin Money; emit Bills of Credit; make any Thing but gold and silver Coin a Tender in Payment of Debts; pass any Bill of Attainder, ex post facto Law, or Law impairing the obligation of Contracts, or grant any Title of Nobility.

No State shall, without the Consent of the Congress, lay any Imposts or Duties on Imports or Exports, except what may be absolutely necessary for executing its inspection Laws: and the net Produce of all Duties and Imposts, laid by any State on Imports or Exports, shall be for the Use of the Treasury of the United States; and all such Laws shall be subject to the Revision and Controul of the Congress.

No State shall, without the Consent of Congress, lay any Duty of Tonnage, keep Troops, or Ships of War in time of Peace, enter into any Agreement or Compact with another State, or with a foreign Power, or engage in War, unless actually invaded, or in such imminent Danger as will not admit of delay.

Article II
Section 1

The executive Power shall be vested in a President of the United States of America. He shall hold his Office during the Term of four Years, and, together with the Vice President, chosen for the same Term, be elected, as follows:

Each State shall appoint, in such Manner as the Legislature thereof may direct, a Number of Electors, equal to the whole Number of Senators and Representatives to which the State may be entitled in the Congress: but no Senator or Representative, or Person holding an Office of Trust or Profit under the United States, shall be appointed an Elector.

The Electors shall meet in their respective States, and vote by Ballot for two Persons, of whom one at least shall not be an Inhabitant of the same State with themselves. And they shall make a List of all the Persons voted for, and of the Number of Votes for each; which List they shall sign and certify, and transmit sealed to the Seat of the Government of the United States, directed to the President of the Senate. The President of the Senate shall, in the Presence of the Senate and House of Representatives, open all the Certificates, and the Votes shall then be counted. The Person having the greatest Number of Votes shall be the President, if such Number be a Majority of the whole number of Electors appointed; and if there be more than one who have such Majority, and have an equal Number of Votes, then the House of Representatives shall immediately chuse by Ballot one of them for President; and if no Person have a Majority, then from the five highest on the List the said House shall in like Manner chuse the President. But in chusing the President, the Votes shall be taken by States, the Representation from each State having one Vote; A quorum for this Purpose shall consist of a Member or Members from two thirds of the States, and a Majority of all the States shall be necessary to a Choice. In every Case, after the Choice of the President, the Person having the greatest Number of Votes of the Electors shall be the Vice President. But if there should remain two or more who have equal Votes, the Senate shall chuse from them by Ballot the Vice President.

The Congress may determine the time of chusing the Electors, and the Day on which they shall give their Votes; which Day shall be the same throughout the United States.

No person except a natural born Citizen, *or a Citizen of the United States, at the time of the Adoption of this Constitution,* shall be eligible to the Office of President; neither shall any Person be eligible to that Office who shall not have attained to the Age of thirty five Years, and been fourteen Years a Resident within the United States.

In Case of the Removal of the President from Office, or of his Death, Resignation, or Inability to discharge the Powers and Duties of the said Office, the Same shall devolve on the Vice President, and the Congress may by Law provide for the Case of Removal, Death, Resignation or Inability, both of the President and Vice President, declaring what Officer shall then act as President, and such Officer shall act accordingly, until the Disability be removed, or a President shall be elected.

The President shall, at stated Times, receive for his Services, a Compensation, which shall neither be encreased nor diminished during the Period for which he shall have been elected, and he shall not receive within that period any other Emolument from the United States, or any of them.

Before he enter on the Execution of his Office, he shall take the following Oath or Affirmation:—"I do solemnly swear (or affirm) that I will faithfully execute the Office of President of the United States, and will to the best of my Ability, preserve, protect and defend the Constitution of the United States."

Section 2

The President shall be Commander in Chief of the Army and Navy of the United States, and of the Militia of the several States, when called into the actual Service of the United States; he may require the Opinion, in writing, of the principal Officer in each of the executive Departments, upon any Subject relating to the Duties of their respective Offices, and he shall have Power to grant Reprieves and Pardons for Offences against the United States, except in Cases of Impeachment.

He shall have Power, by and with the Advice and Consent of the Senate, to make Treaties, provided two thirds of the Senators present concur; and he shall nominate, and by and with the Advice and Consent of the Senate, shall appoint Ambassadors, other public Ministers and Consuls, Judges of the supreme Court, and all other Officers of the United States, whose Appointments are not herein otherwise provided for, and which shall be established by Law: but the Congress may by Law vest the Appointment of such inferior Officers, as they think proper in the President alone, in the Courts of Law, or in the Heads of Departments.

The President shall have Power to fill up all Vacancies that may happen during the Recess of the Senate, by granting Commissions which shall expire at the End of their next Session.

Section 3

He shall from time to time give to the Congress Information of the State of the Union, and recommend to their Consideration such Measures as he shall judge necessary and expedient; he may, on extraordinary Occasions, convene both Houses, or either of them, and in Case of disagreement between them, with Respect to the Time of Adjournment, he may adjourn them to such Time as he shall think proper; he shall receive Ambassadors and other public Ministers; he shall take Care that the Laws be faithfully executed, and shall Commission all the officers of the United States.

Section 4

The President, Vice President and all civil Officers of the United States, shall be removed from Office on Impeachment for, and Conviction of, Treason, Bribery or other high Crimes and Misdemeanors.

Article III
Section 1

The judicial Power of the United States, shall be vested in one supreme Court, and in such inferior Courts as the Congress may from time to time ordain and establish. The Judges, both of the supreme and inferior Courts, shall hold their offices during good Behaviour, and shall, at stated Times, receive for their Services, a Compensation, which shall not be diminished during their Continuance in Office.

Section 2

The judicial Power shall extend to all Cases, in Law and Equity, arising under this Constitution, the Laws of the United States, and Treaties made, or which shall be made, under their Authority;—

to all Cases affecting Ambassadors, other public Ministers and Consuls;—to all Cases of admiralty and maritime Jurisdiction;—to Controversies to which the United States shall be a Party;—to Controversies between two or more States;—*between a State and Citizens of another State;*—between Citizens of different States;—between Citizens of the same State claiming Lands under Grants of different States, and between a State, or the Citizens thereof, and foreign States, Citizens or Subjects.

In all Cases affecting Ambassadors, other public Ministers and Consuls, and those in which a State shall be Party, the supreme Court shall have original Jurisdiction. In all the other Cases before mentioned, the supreme Court shall have appellate Jurisdiction, both as to Law and Fact, with such Exceptions, and under such Regulations as the Congress shall make.

The Trial of all Crimes, except in Cases of Impeachment, shall be by Jury; and such Trial shall be held in the State where the said Crimes shall have been committed; but when not committed within any State, the Trial shall be at such Place or Places as the Congress may by Law have directed.

Section 3

Treason against the United States, shall consist only in levying War against them, or in adhering to their Enemies, giving them Aid and Comfort. No person shall be convicted of Treason unless on the Testimony of two Witnesses to the same overt Act, or on Confession in open Court.

The Congress shall have Power to declare the Punishment of Treason, but no Attainder of Treason shall work Corruption of Blood, or Forfeiture except during the Life of the Person attainted.

Article IV
Section 1

Full Faith and Credit shall be given in each State to the public Acts, Records, and judicial Proceedings of every other State. And the Congress may by general Laws prescribe the Manner in which such Acts, Records and Proceedings shall be proved, and the Effect thereof.

Section 2

The Citizens of each State shall be entitled to all Privileges and Immunities of Citizens in the several States.

A Person charged in any State with Treason, Felony, or other Crime, who shall flee from Justice, and be found in another State, shall on Demand of the executive Authority of the State from which he fled, be delivered up, to be removed to the State having Jurisdiction of the Crime.

No Person held to Service or Labour in one State, under the Laws thereof, escaping into another, shall, in Consequence of any Law or Regulation therein, be discharged from such Service or Labour, but shall be delivered up on Claim of the Party to whom such Service or Labour may be due.

Section 3

New States may be admitted by the Congress into this Union; but no new State shall be formed or erected within the Jurisdiction of any other State; nor any State be formed by the Junction of two or more States, or Parts of States, without the Consent of the Legislatures of the States concerned as well as of the Congress.

The Congress shall have Power to dispose of and make all needful Rules and Regulations respecting the Territory or other

Property belonging to the United States; and nothing in this Constitution shall be so construed as to Prejudice any Claims of the United States, or of any particular States.

Section 4

The United States shall guarantee to every State in this Union a Republican Form of Government, and shall protect each of them against Invasion; and on Application of the Legislature, or of the Executive (when the Legislature cannot be convened) against domestic violence.

Article V

The Congress, whenever two thirds of both Houses shall deem it necessary, shall propose Amendments to this Constitution, or, on the Application of the Legislatures of two thirds of the several States, shall call a Convention for proposing Amendments, which, in either Case, shall be valid to all Intents and Purposes, as Part of this Constitution, when ratified by the Legislatures of three fourths of the several States, or by Conventions in three fourths thereof, as the one or the other Mode of Ratification may be proposed by the Congress; Provided *that no Amendment which may be made prior to the Year One thousand eight hundred and eight shall in any Manner affect the first and fourth Clauses in the Ninth Section of the first Article;* and that no State, without its Consent, shall be deprived of its equal Suffrage in the Senate.

Article VI

All Debts contracted and Engagements entered into, before the Adoption of this Constitution, shall be as valid against the United States under this Constitution, as under the Confederation.

This Constitution, and Laws of the United States which shall be made in Pursuance thereof; and all Treaties made, or which shall be made, under the Authority of the United States, shall be the supreme Law of the Land; and the Judges in every State shall be bound thereby, any Thing in the Constitution or Laws of any State to the Contrary notwithstanding.

The Senators and Representatives before mentioned, and the Members of the several State Legislatures, and all executive and Judicial Officers, both of the United States and of the several States, shall be bound by Oath or Affirmation, to support this Constitution; but no religious Test shall ever be required as a Qualification to any Office of public Trust under the United States.

Article VII

The Ratification of the Conventions of nine States, shall be sufficient for the Establishment of this Constitution between the States so ratifying the Same.

Done in Convention by the Unanimous Consent of the States present the Seventeenth Day of September in the Year of our Lord one thousand seven hundred and Eighty seven and of the Independence of the United States of America the Twelfth* IN WITNESS whereof We have hereunto subscribed our Names,

GEORGE WASHINGTON
President and Deputy from Virginia

Delaware
George Read
Gunning Bedford Jr.
John Dickinson
Richard Bassett
Jacob Broom

Maryland
James McHenry
Daniel of St. Thomas Jenifer
Daniel Carroll

Virginia
John Blair
James Madison Jr.

North Carolina
William Blount
Richard Dobbs Spraight
Hugh Williamson

South Carolina
John Rutledge
Charles Cotesworth Pinckney
Charles Pinckney
Pierce Butler

Georgia
William Few
Abraham Baldwin

New Hampshire
John Langdon
Nicholas Gilman

Massachusetts
Nathaniel Gorham
Rufus King

Connecticut
William Samuel Johnson
Roger Sherman

New York
Alexander Hamilton

New Jersey
William Livingston
David Brearley
William Paterson
Jonathan Dayton

Pennsylvania
Benjamin Franklin
Thomas Mifflin
Robert Morris
George Clymer
Thomas FitzSimons
Jared Ingersoll
James Wilson
Gouverneur Morris

Amendments to the Constitution

Amendment I

Congress shall make no law respecting an establishment of religion, or prohibiting the free exercise thereof; or abridging the freedom of speech, or of the press; or the right of the people peaceably to assemble, and to petition the Government for a redress of grievances.

Amendment II

A well regulated Militia being necessary to the security of a free State, the right of the people to keep and bear Arms, shall not be infringed.

---

*The Constitution was submitted on September 17, 1787, by the Constitutional Convention, was ratified by conventions of the several states at various dates up to May 29, 1790, and became effective on March 4, 1789.

Amendment III

No Soldier shall, in time of peace be quartered in any house, without the consent of the Owner, nor in time of war, but in a manner to be prescribed by law.

Amendment IV

The right of the people to be secure in their persons, houses, papers, and effects, against unreasonable searches and seizures, shall not be violated, and no Warrants shall issue, but upon probable cause, supported by Oath or affirmation, and particularly describing the place to be searched, and the persons or things to be seized.

Amendment V

No person shall be held to answer for a capital, or otherwise infamous crime, unless on a presentment or indictment of a Grand Jury, except in cases arising in the land or naval forces, or in the Militia, when in actual service in time of War or public danger; nor shall any person be subject for the same offense to be twice put in jeopardy of life or limb; nor shall be compelled in any criminal case to be a witness against himself, nor be deprived of life, liberty, or property, without due process of law; nor shall private property be taken for public use, without just compensation.

Amendment VI

In all criminal prosecutions, the accused shall enjoy the right to a speedy and public trial, by an impartial jury of the State and district wherein the crime shall have been committed, which district shall have been previously ascertained by law, and to be informed of the nature and cause of the accusation; to be confronted with the witnesses against him; to have compulsory process for obtaining witnesses in his favor, and to have the Assistance of Counsel for his defence.

Amendment VII

In Suits at common law, where the value in controversy shall exceed twenty dollars, the right of trial by jury shall be preserved, and no fact tried by a jury, shall be otherwise re-examined in any Court of the United States, than according to the rules of the common law.

Amendment VIII

Excessive bail shall not be required, nor excessive fines imposed, nor cruel and unusual punishments inflicted.

Amendment IX

The enumeration in the Constitution, of certain rights, shall not be construed to deny or disparage others retained by the people.

Amendment X*

The powers not delegated to the United States by the Constitution, nor prohibited by it to the States, are reserved to the States respectively, or to the people.

---

*The first ten amendments (the Bill of Rights) were ratified and their adoption was certified on December 15, 1791.

Amendment XI [Adopted 1798]

The Judicial power of the United States shall not be construed to extend to any suit in law or equity, commenced or prosecuted against one of the United States by Citizens of another State, or by Citizens or Subjects of any Foreign State.

Amendment XII [Adopted 1804]

The Electors shall meet in their respective states, and vote by ballot for President and Vice President, one of whom, at least, shall not be an inhabitant of the same state with themselves; they shall name in their ballots the person voted for as President, and in distinct ballots the person voted for as Vice President, and they shall make distinct lists of all persons voted for as President, and of all persons voted for as Vice President, and of the number of votes for each, which lists they shall sign and certify, and transmit sealed to the seat of the government of the United States, directed to the President of the Senate;—President of the Senate shall, in the presence of the Senate and House of Representatives, open all the certificates and the votes shall then be counted;—The person having the greatest number of votes for President, shall be the President, if such number be a majority of the whole number of Electors appointed; and if no person have such majority, then from the persons having the highest numbers not exceeding three on the list of those voted for as President, the House of Representatives shall choose immediately, by ballot, the President. But in choosing the President, the votes shall be taken by states, the representation from each state having one vote; a quorum for this purpose shall consist of a member or members from two-thirds of the states, and a majority of all the states shall be necessary to a choice. And if the House of Representatives shall not choose a President whenever the right of choice shall devolve upon them, before *the fourth day of March* next following, then the Vice President shall act as President, as in the case of the death or other constitutional disability of the President.—The person having the greatest number of votes as Vice President, shall be the Vice President, if such number be a majority of the whole number of Electors appointed, and if no person have a majority, then from the two highest numbers on the list, the Senate shall choose the Vice President; a quorum for the purpose shall consist of two-thirds of the whole number of Senators, and a majority of the whole number shall be necessary to a choice. But no person constitutionally ineligible to the office of President shall be eligible to that of Vice President of the United States.

Amendment XIII [Adopted 1865]

Section 1

Neither slavery nor involuntary servitude, except as a punishment for crime whereof the party shall have been duly convicted, shall exist within the United States, or any place subject to their jurisdiction.

Section 2

Congress shall have power to enforce this article by appropriate legislation.

Amendment XIV [Adopted 1868]

Section 1

All persons born or naturalized in the United States, and subject to the jurisdiction thereof, are citizens of the United States and of the State wherein they reside. No State shall make or enforce any law which shall abridge the privileges or immunities of citizens of the United States; nor shall any State deprive any person of life, liberty, or property, without due process of law; nor deny to any person within its jurisdiction the equal protection of the laws.

Section 2

Representatives shall be apportioned among the several States according to their respective numbers, counting the whole number of persons in each State, excluding Indians not taxed. But when the right to vote at any election for the choice of electors for President and Vice President of the United States, Representatives in Congress, the Executive and Judicial officers of a State, or the members of the Legislature thereof, is denied to any of the male inhabitants of such State, being twenty-one years of age, and citizens of the United States, or in any way abridged, except for participation in rebellion, or other crime, the basis of representation therein shall be reduced in the proportion which the number of such male citizens shall bear to the whole number of male citizens twenty-one years of age in such State.

Section 3

No person shall be a Senator or Representative in Congress, or elector of President and Vice President, or hold any office, civil or military, under the United States, or under any State, who, having previously taken an oath, as a member of Congress, or as an officer of the United States, or as a member of any State legislature, or as an executive or judicial officer of any State, to support the Constitution of the United States, shall have engaged in insurrection or rebellion against the same, or given aid or comfort to the enemies thereof. But Congress may by a vote of two-thirds of each House, remove such disability.

Section 4

The validity of the public debt of the United States, authorized by law, including debts incurred for payment of pensions and bounties for services in suppressing insurrection or rebellion, shall not be questioned. But neither the United States nor any State shall assume or pay any debt or obligation incurred in aid of insurrection or rebellion against the United States, or any claim for the loss or emancipation of any slave; but all such debts, obligations and claims shall be held illegal and void.

Section 5

The Congress shall have power to enforce, by appropriate legislation, the provisions of this article.

Amendment XV [Adopted 1870]

Section 1

The right of citizens of the United States to vote shall not be denied or abridged by the United States or by any State on account of race, color, or previous condition of servitude.

Section 2

The Congress shall have power to enforce this article by appropriate legislation.

Amendment XVI [Adopted 1913]

The Congress shall have power to lay and collect taxes on incomes, from whatever source derived, without apportionment among the several States, and without regard to any census or enumeration.

Amendment XVII [Adopted 1913]

The Senate of the United States shall be composed of two Senators from each State, elected by the people thereof, for six years; and each Senator shall have one vote. The electors in each State shall have the qualifications requisite for electors of the most numerous branch of the State legislatures.

When vacancies happen in the representation of any State in the Senate, the executive authority of such State shall issue writs of election to fill such vacancies: *Provided*, That the legislature of any State may empower the executive thereof to make temporary appointments until the people fill the vacancies by election as the legislature may direct.

This amendment shall not be so construed as to affect the election or term of any Senator chosen before it becomes valid as part of the Constitution.

Amendment XVIII [Adopted 1919, repealed 1933]

Section 1

After one year from the ratification of this article the manufacture, sale, or transportation of intoxicating liquors within, the importation thereof into, or the exportation thereof from the United States and all territory subject to the jurisdiction thereof for beverage purposes is hereby prohibited.

Section 2

The Congress and the several States shall have concurrent power to enforce this article by appropriate legislation.

Section 3

This article shall be inoperative unless it shall have been ratified as an amendment to the Constitution by the legislatures of the several States, as provided in the Constitution, within seven years from the date of the submission hereof to the States by the Congress.

Amendment XIX [Adopted 1920]

The right of citizens of the United States to vote shall not be denied or abridged by the United States or by any State on account of sex.

Congress shall have power to enforce this article by appropriate legislation.

Amendment XX [Adopted 1933]

Section 1

The terms of the President and Vice President shall end at noon on the 20th day of January, and the terms of Senators and Representatives at noon on the 3d day of January, of the years in which such terms would have ended if this article had not been ratified and the terms of their successors shall then begin.

Section 2

The Congress shall assemble at least once in every year, and such meeting shall begin at noon on the 3d day of January, unless they shall by law appoint a different day.

Section 3

If, at the time fixed for the beginning of the term of the President, the President elect shall have died, the Vice President elect shall become President. If a President shall not have been chosen before the time fixed for the beginning of his term, or if the President elect shall have failed to qualify, then the Vice President elect shall act as President until a President shall have qualified; and the Congress may by law provide for the case wherein neither a President elect nor a Vice President elect shall have qualified, declaring who shall then act as President, or the manner in which one who is to act shall be selected, and such person shall act accordingly until a President or Vice President shall have qualified.

Section 4

The Congress may by law provide for the case of the death of any of the persons from whom the House of Representatives may choose a President whenever the right of choice shall have devolved upon them, and for the case of the death of any of the persons from whom the Senate may choose a Vice President whenever the right of choice shall have devolved upon them.

Section 5

Sections 1 and 2 shall take effect on the 15th day of October following the ratification of this article.

Section 6

This article shall be inoperative unless it shall have been ratified as an amendment to the Constitution by the legislatures of three fourths of the several States within seven years from the date of its submission.

Amendment XXI [Adopted 1933]

Section 1

The eighteenth article of amendment to the Constitution of the United States is hereby repealed.

Section 2

The transportation or importation into any State, Territory, or possession of the United States for delivery or use therein of intoxicating liquors in violation of the laws thereof, is hereby prohibited.

Section 3

This article shall be inoperative unless it shall have been ratified as an amendment to the Constitution by conventions in the several States, as provided in the Constitution, within seven years from the date of the submission hereof to the States by the Congress.

Amendment XXII [Adopted 1951]

Section 1

No person shall be elected to the office of the President more than twice, and no person who has held the office of President, or acted as President, for more than two years of a term to which some other person was elected President shall be elected to the office of the President more than once. But this Article shall not apply to any person holding the office of President when this Article was proposed by the Congress, and shall not prevent any person who may be holding the office of President, or acting as President, during the term within which this Article becomes operative from holding the office of President or acting as President during the remainder of such term.

Section 2

This article shall be inoperative unless it shall have been ratified as an amendment to the Constitution by the legislatures of three-fourths of the several States within seven years from the date of its submission to the States by the Congress.

Amendment XXIII [Adopted 1961]

Section 1

The District constituting the seat of Government of the United States shall appoint in such manner as the Congress shall direct:

A number of electors of President and Vice President equal to the whole number of Senators and Representatives in Congress to which the District would be entitled if it were a State, but in no event more than the least populous State; they shall be in addition to those appointed by the States, but they shall be considered, for the purposes of the election of President and Vice President, to be electors appointed by a State; and they shall meet in the District and perform such duties as provided by the twelfth article of amendment.

Section 2

The Congress shall have power to enforce this article by appropriate legislation.

Amendment XXIV [Adopted 1964]

Section 1

The right of citizens of the United States to vote in any primary or other election for President or Vice President, for electors for President or Vice President, or for Senator or Representative in Congress, shall not be denied or abridged by the United States or any state by reason of failure to pay any poll tax or other tax.

Section 2

The Congress shall have the power to enforce this article by appropriate legislation.

Amendment XXV [Adopted 1967]

Section 1

In case of the removal of the President from office or his death or resignation, the Vice President shall become President.

Section 2

Whenever there is a vacancy in the office of the Vice President, the President shall nominate a Vice President who shall take the office upon confirmation by a majority vote of both houses of Congress.

Section 3

Whenever the President transmits to the President pro tempore of the Senate and the Speaker of the House of Representatives his written declaration that he is unable to discharge the powers and duties of his office, and until he transmits to them a written declaration to the contrary, such powers and duties shall be discharged by the Vice President as Acting President.

Section 4

Whenever the Vice President and a majority of either the principal officers of the executive departments or of such other body as Congress may by law provide, transmit to the President pro tempore of the Senate and the Speaker of the House of Representatives their written declaration that the President is unable to discharge the powers and duties of his office, the Vice President shall immediately assume the powers and duties of the office as Acting President.

Thereafter, when the President transmits to the President pro tempore of the Senate and the Speaker of the House of Representatives his written declaration that no inability exists, he shall resume the powers and duties of his office unless the Vice President and a majority of either the principal officers of the executive department or of such other body as Congress may by law provide, transmit within four days to the President pro tempore of the Senate and the Speaker of the House of Representatives their written declaration that the President is unable to discharge the powers and duties of his office. Thereupon Congress shall decide the issue, assembling within 48 hours for that purpose if not in session. If the Congress, within 21 days after receipt of the latter written declaration, or, if Congress is not in session, within 21 days after Congress is required to assemble, determines by two-thirds vote of both houses that the President is unable to discharge the powers and duties of his office, the Vice President shall continue to discharge the same as Acting President; otherwise, the President shall resume the powers and duties of his office.

Amendment XXVI [Adopted 1971]

Section 1

The right of citizens of the United States, who are 18 years of age or older, to vote shall not be denied or abridged by the United States or any state on account of age.

Section 2

The Congress shall have the power to enforce this article by appropriate legislation.

Amendment XXVII [Adopted 1992]

No law, varying the compensation for the services of the Senators and Representatives shall take effect, until an election of Representatives shall have intervened.

PRESIDENTIAL ELECTIONS

Year	Candidates	Parties	Popular Vote	Electoral Vote	Voter Participation
1789	**George Washington**		a	69	
	John Adams			34	
	Others			35	
1792	**George Washington**		a	132	
	John Adams			77	
	George Clinton			50	
	Others			5	
1796	**John Adams**	Federalist	a	71	
	Thomas Jefferson	Democratic-Republican		68	
	Thomas Pinckney	Federalist		59	
	Aaron Burr	Dem.-Rep.		30	
	Others			48	
1800	**Thomas Jefferson**	Dem.-Rep.	a	73	
	Aaron Burr	Dem.-Rep.		73	
	John Adams	Federalist		65	
	C. C. Pinckney	Federalist		64	
	John Jay	Federalist		1	
1804	**Thomas Jefferson**	Dem.-Rep.	a	162	
	C. C. Pinckney	Federalist		14	
1808	**James Madison**	Dem.-Rep.	a	122	
	C. C. Pinckney	Federalist		47	
	George Clinton	Dem.-Rep.		6	
1812	**James Madison**	Dem.-Rep.	a	128	
	De Witt Clinton	Federalist		89	
1816	**James Monroe**	Dem.-Rep.	a	183	
	Rufus King	Federalist		34	
1820	**James Monroe**	Dem.-Rep.	a	231	
	John Quincy Adams	Dem.-Rep.		1	

aElectors selected by state legislatures.

United State Presidential Election Results from 1788 to 2012 are from the National Archives and Records Administration, United States Government. http://www.archives.gov/federal-register/electoral-college/votes/index.html

Year	Candidates	Parties	Popular Vote	Electoral Vote	Voter Participation
1824	**John Quincy Adams**	Dem.-Rep.	108,740 (30.5%)	84	26.9%
	Andrew Jackson	Dem.-Rep.	153,544 (43.1%)	99	
	William H. Crawford	Dem.-Rep.	46,618 (13.1%)	41	
	Henry Clay	Dem.-Rep.	47,136 (13.2%)	37	
1828	**Andrew Jackson**	Democratic	647,286 (56.0%)	178	57.6%
	John Quincy Adams	National Republican	508,064 (44.0%)	83	
1832	**Andrew Jackson**	Democratic	687,502 (55.0%)	219	55.4%
	Henry Clay	National Republican	530,189 (42.4%)	49	
	John Floyd	Independent		11	
	William Wirt	Anti-Mason	33,108 (2.6%)	7	
1836	**Martin Van Buren**	Democratic	765,483 (50.9%)	170	57.8%
	William Henry Harrison	Whig		73	
	Hugh L. White	Whig	739,795 (49.1%)	26	
	Daniel Webster	Whig		14	
	W. P. Magnum	Independent		11	
1840	**William Henry Harrison**	Whig	1,274,624 (53.1%)	234	80.2%
	Martin Van Buren	Democratic	1,127,781 (46.9%)	60	
	J. G. Birney	Liberty	7,069	—	
1844	**James K. Polk**	Democratic	1,338,464 (49.6%)	170	78.9%
	Henry Clay	Whig	1,300,097 (48.1%)	105	
	J. G. Birney	Liberty	62,300 (2.3%)	—	
1848	**Zachary Taylor**	Whig	1,360,967 (47.4%)	163	72.7%
	Lewis Cass	Democratic	1,222,342 (42.5%)	127	
	Martin Van Buren	Free-Soil	291,263 (10.1%)	—	
1852	**Franklin Pierce**	Democratic	1,601,117 (50.9%)	254	69.6%
	Winfield Scott	Whig	1,385,453 (44.1%)	42	
	John P. Hale	Free-Soil	155,825 (5.0%)	—	
1856	**James Buchanan**	Democratic	1,832,955 (45.3%)	174	78.9%
	John C. Frémont	Republican	1,339,932 (33.1%)	114	
	Millard Fillmore	American	871,731 (21.6%)	8	
1860	**Abraham Lincoln**	Republican	1,865,593 (39.8%)	180	81.2%
	Stephen A. Douglas	Democratic	1,382,713 (29.5%)	12	
	John C. Breckinridge	Democratic	848,356 (18.1%)	72	
	John Bell	Union	592,906 (12.6%)	39	
1864	**Abraham Lincoln**	Republican	2,213,655 (55.0%)	212[b]	73.8%
	George B. McClellan	Democratic	1,805,237 (45.0%)	21	
1868	**Ulysses S. Grant**	Republican	3,012,833 (52.7%)	214	78.1%
	Horatio Seymour	Democratic	2,703,249 (47.3%)	80	
1872	**Ulysses S. Grant**	Republican	3,597,132 (55.6%)	286	71.3%
	Horace Greeley	Dem.; Liberal Republican	2,834,125 (43.9%)	66[c]	
1876	**Rutherford B. Hayes**[d]	Republican	4,036,298 (48.0%)	185	81.8%
	Samuel J. Tilden	Democratic	4,300,590 (51.0%)	184	
1880	**James A. Garfield**	Republican	4,454,416 (48.5%)	214	79.4%
	Winfield S. Hancock	Democratic	4,444,952 (48.1%)	155	
1884	**Grover Cleveland**	Democratic	4,874,986 (48.5%)	219	77.5%
	James G. Blaine	Republican	4,851,981 (48.2%)	182	
1888	**Benjamin Harrison**	Republican	5,439,853 (47.9%)	233	79.3%
	Grover Cleveland	Democratic	5,540,309 (48.6%)	168	
1892	**Grover Cleveland**	Democratic	5,556,918 (46.1%)	277	74.7%
	Benjamin Harrison	Republican	5,176,108 (43.0%)	145	
	James B. Weaver	People's	1,041,028 (8.5%)	22	

[b]Eleven secessionist states did not participate.
[c]Greeley died before the electoral college met. His electoral votes were divided among the four minor candidates.
[d]Contested result settled by special election.

Year	Candidates	Parties	Popular Vote	Electoral Vote	Voter Participation
1896	**William McKinley**	Republican	7,104,779 (51.1%)	271	79.3%
	William Jennings Bryan	Democratic People's	6,502,925 (47.7%)	176	
1900	**William McKinley**	Republican	7,207,923 (51.7%)	292	73.2%
	William Jennings Bryan	Dem.-Populist	6,358,133 (45.5%)	155	
1904	**Theodore Roosevelt**	Republican	7,623,486 (57.9%)	336	65.2%
	Alton B. Parker	Democratic	5,077,911 (37.6%)	140	
	Eugene V. Debs	Socialist	402,283 (3.0%)	—	
1908	**William H. Taft**	Republican	7,678,908 (51.6%)	321	65.4%
	William Jennings Bryan	Democratic	6,409,104 (43.1%)	162	
	Eugene V. Debs	Socialist	420,793 (2.8%)	—	
1912	**Woodrow Wilson**	Democratic	6,293,454 (41.9%)	435	58.8%
	Theodore Roosevelt	Progressive	4,119,538 (27.4%)	88	
	William H. Taft	Republican	3,484,980 (23.2%)	8	
	Eugene V. Debs	Socialist	900,672 (6.0%)	—	
1916	**Woodrow Wilson**	Democratic	9,129,606 (49.4%)	277	61.6%
	Charles E. Hughes	Republican	8,538,221 (46.2%)	254	
	A. L. Benson	Socialist	585,113 (3.2%)	—	
1920	**Warren G. Harding**	Republican	16,152,200 (60.4%)	404	49.2%
	James M. Cox	Democratic	9,147,353 (34.2%)	127	
	Eugene V. Debs	Socialist	919,799 (3.4%)	—	
1924	**Calvin Coolidge**	Republican	15,725,016 (54.0%)	382	48.9%
	John W. Davis	Democratic	8,386,503 (28.8%)	136	
	Robert M. La Follette	Progressive	4,822,856 (16.6%)	13	
1928	**Herbert Hoover**	Republican	21,391,381 (58.2%)	444	56.9%
	Alfred E. Smith	Democratic	15,016,443 (40.9%)	87	
	Norman Thomas	Socialist	267,835 (0.7%)	—	
1932	**Franklin D. Roosevelt**	Democratic	22,821,857 (57.4%)	472	56.9%
	Herbert Hoover	Republican	15,761,841 (39.7%)	59	
	Norman Thomas	Socialist	881,951 (2.2%)	—	
1936	**Franklin D. Roosevelt**	Democratic	27,751,597 (60.8%)	523	61.0%
	Alfred M. Landon	Republican	16,679,583 (36.5%)	8	
	William Lemke	Union	882,479 (1.9%)	—	
1940	**Franklin D. Roosevelt**	Democratic	27,244,160 (54.8%)	449	62.5%
	Wendell L. Willkie	Republican	22,305,198 (44.8%)	82	
1944	**Franklin D. Roosevelt**	Democratic	25,602,504 (53.5%)	432	55.9%
	Thomas E. Dewey	Republican	22,006,285 (46.0%)	99	
1948	**Harry S. Truman**	Democratic	24,105,695 (49.5%)	304	53.0%
	Thomas E. Dewey	Republican	21,969,170 (45.1%)	189	
	J. Strom Thurmond	State-Rights Democratic	1,169,021 (2.4%)	38	
	Henry A. Wallace	Progressive	1,156,103 (2.4%)	—	
1952	**Dwight D. Eisenhower**	Republican	33,936,252 (55.1%)	442	63.3%
	Adlai E. Stevenson	Democratic	27,314,992 (44.4%)	89	
1956	**Dwight D. Eisenhower**	Republican	35,575,420 (57.6%)	457	60.6%
	Adlai E. Stevenson	Democratic	26,033,066 (42.1%)	73	
	Other	—	—	1	
1960	**John F. Kennedy**	Democratic	34,227,096 (49.9%)	303	62.8%
	Richard M. Nixon	Republican	34,108,546 (49.6%)	219	
	Other	—	—	15	
1964	**Lyndon B. Johnson**	Democratic	43,126,506 (61.1%)	486	61.7%
	Barry M. Goldwater	Republican	27,176,799 (38.5%)	52	

Year	Candidates	Parties	Popular Vote	Electoral Vote	Voter Participation
1968	**Richard M. Nixon**	Republican	31,770,237 (43.4%)	301	60.6%
	Hubert H. Humphrey	Democratic	31,270,533 (42.7%)	191	
	George Wallace	American Indep.	9,906,141 (13.5%)	46	
1972	**Richard M. Nixon**	Republican	47,169,911 (60.7%)	520	55.2%
	George S. McGovern	Democratic	29,170,383 (37.5%)	17	
	Other	—	—	1	
1976	**Jimmy Carter**	Democratic	40,828,587 (50.0%)	297	53.5%
	Gerald R. Ford	Republican	39,147,613 (47.9%)	241	
	Other	—	1,575,459 (2.1%)	—	
1980	**Ronald Reagan**	Republican	43,901,812 (50.7%)	489	52.6%
	Jimmy Carter	Democratic	35,483,820 (41.0%)	49	
	John B. Anderson	Independent	5,719,722 (6.6%)	—	
	Ed Clark	Libertarian	921,188 (1.1%)	—	
1984	**Ronald Reagan**	Republican	54,455,075 (59.0%)	525	53.3%
	Walter Mondale	Democratic	37,577,185 (41.0%)	13	
1988	**George H. W. Bush**	Republican	48,886,000 (53.4%)	426	57.4%
	Michael S. Dukakis	Democratic	41,809,000 (45.6%)	111	
1992	**William J. Clinton**	Democratic	43,728,375 (43.0%)	370	55.0%
	George H. W. Bush	Republican	38,167,416 (38.0%)	168	
	H. Ross Perot	Independent	19,237,247 (19.0%)	—	
1996	**William J. Clinton**	Democratic	47,401,185 (49.2%)	379	48.8%
	Robert Dole	Republican	39,197,469 (40.7%)	159	
	H. Ross Perot	Reform	8,085,294 (8.4%)		
	Ralph Nader	Green	684,871 (<1%)	—	
2000	**George W. Bush**	Republican	50,456,002 (47.9%)	271	51.2%
	Al Gore	Democratic	50,999,897 (48.4%)	266[e]	
	Ralph Nader	Green	2,882,955 (2.7%)	—	
	Other	—	834,774 (<1%)	—	
2004	**George W. Bush**	Republican	62,040,610 (50.7%)	286	55.3%
	John Kerry	Democratic	59,028,444 (48.3%)	251	
	Ralph Nader	Independent	465,650 (<1%)	—	
2008	**Barack Obama**	Democratic	69,456,897 (52.9%)	365	
	John McCain	Republican	59,934,814 (45.7%)	173	
2012	**Barack Obama**	Democratic	65,446,032 (51.0%)	332	57.5%
	Mitt Romney	Republican	60,589,084 (47.4%)	206	
	Gary Johnson	Libertarian	1,273,168 (<1.0%)		
	Jill Stein	Green	464,510 (<1.0%)		

[e]One District of Columbia Gore elector abstained.

20-slave law Legislation passed by the Confederate Congress in October 1862 that exempted from military service one white man for every twenty slaves on a plantation.

Abolition Act of 1808 Also called the Slave Trade Act, prohibited the importation of foreign slaves into the United States.

Age of Enlightenment This term is applied to the century stretching from the late seventeenth to the late eighteenth century, when generations of European writers, scientists and philosophers began to question the predominance of organized religion and elevate the use of rational argument and scientific investigation. In the American colonies, the practical experimenter Benjamin Franklin came to epitomize this new Age of Reason.

Alien and Sedition Acts Laws enacted by the Federalist-dominated Congress in 1798 to limit the speech of their critics and to make it more difficult for immigrants to become citizens.

Almshouse Such establishments to care for the indigent of a locality had existed in Europe since the Middle Ages. They appeared in the British colonies in the eighteenth century, as towns grew larger and society became more stratified. In Christian tradition, *alms* constituted money or services donated to care for the poor.

Andersonville Prison A Georgia prisoner-of-war camp that held as many as 33,000 Union prisoners at one time. Commanded by Henry Wirz, the prison was infamous for the large number of northern soldiers who died there of starvation, disease, and exposure to the elements.

Annexation Addition of territory that had belonged to one nation into another nation.

Anti-Federalists A diverse and unsuccessful coalition that opposed ratification of the Constitution and feared the increased power of the proposed central government. The Anti-Federalists were named by their opponents, the Federalists.

Archaic The second long stage of North American habitation, covering about 7,000 years, from roughly 8,000 B.C.E. to 1000 B.C.E. (or from 10,000 to 3,000 years ago). During this period, inhabitants adapted to diverse local environments, gathering plants and hunting smaller animals than during the previous Paleo-Indian period.

Archipelago A group of islands, such as the Hawaiian archipelago.

Asiento A contract negotiated by the Spanish crown (between 1595 and 1789) with other European powers such as Portugal, France, England, and the Netherlands to provide a fixed number of slaves annually to Spain's American colonies for a set payment.

Atlatl A weighted, handheld device that enabled early Native Americans to throw spears with added power and velocity.

Babel A city described in the Old Testament where constructing a tower was made impossible by the confusion of varied languages. This term from the Book of Genesis is used to describe any scene of clamor and confusion.

Balanced government This idealized form of governance (based on the ideas of Aristotle) was supposed to avoid the pitfalls created by monarchy ("tyranny"), aristocracy ("oligarchy"), and democracy ("mobocracy").

Barracoon An enclosure or barrack used for the confinement of slaves before their forced deportation from the African coast.

Basque The Basque region of southwest France, bordering the Pyrenees and the Atlantic Bay of Biscay, was famous for its fishing fleet and its experienced sailors.

Bill of Rights A set of amendments assuring basic rights, proposed by James Madison to help ensure acceptance of the newly drafted Constitution, and based on suggestions from the states. Ten of the twelve items passed by Congress were ratified by the states in 1791. Taken together, these first ten amendments to the Constitution became known as the Bill of Rights.

Black Codes Southern state laws passed after the Civil War to limit the rights and actions of newly liberated African Americans.

Burgess A representative elected to the popular branch of the colonial legislature in either Virginia or Maryland.

Cabal A close group or faction united in some plan or secret intrigue to foster their own interests and views.

Cajuns The Louisiana word for French-speaking people from Acadia (Nova Scotia) who were forced to migrate south in 1755 during the French and Indian War. Many of these refugees eventually moved to French Louisiana, where they have had a lasting impact on the culture.

Carpetbaggers A negative term applied by Southerners to Northerners who moved to the South after the Civil War to pursue political or economic opportunities.

Checks and balances The rules controlling interactions among the executive, legislative, and judicial branches of government, making up a novel system designed to prevent any single branch from overreaching its powers, as set forth in the Constitution in 1787.

Civil Rights Act of 1875 Congressional legislation that guaranteed black people access to public accommodations and transportation; the Supreme Court declared the measure unconstitutional in 1883.

Coalition An alliance of parties, factions, or nations.

Coffle A procession or train of enslaved prisoners, bound together for travel (from the Arabic word for "caravan").

Columbian Exchange The significant two-way interchange of plants, animals, microbes, and people that occurred once Christopher Columbus established regular contact by sea between the Eastern and Western Hemispheres. For thousands of years before 1492, despite occasional encounters, these two separate and different "worlds" had remained isolated from each other.

Comanchería The area dominated by the Comanche Indians during the second half of the eighteenth century, after they acquired the horse and conquered the Plains Apache. This vast domain, shown on Map 5.1, covered much of the southern plains and embraced large parts of five modern western states.

Common school system Tax-supported public education to provide elementary schooling free to young children.

Compromise of 1850 Congressional legislation that provided that California would enter the Union as a free state that year and that New Mexico and Utah would eventually submit the slavery question to their voters. As part of this compromise, the federal government abolished the slave trade in Washington, D.C.

Confederate States of America The would-be new nation formed in February 1861 by seven southern states—South Carolina, Mississippi, Florida, Alabama, Georgia, Louisiana, and Texas—in a bid for independence from the United States of America. By late spring 1861, the Confederacy also included Virginia, Arkansas, Tennessee, and North Carolina.

Coverture French term for the dependent and legal status of a woman during marriage. Under English law, the male family head received legal rights, and his wife lost independent status, becoming, in legal terms, a *femme covert*.

Czar The title for a male ruler, or king, of Russia during the centuries before the Russian Revolution of 1917.

De facto Latin phrase meaning "in reality," sometimes applied to a government that is exercising real power, though it has not been legally constituted.

Deference ritual A pattern of interaction between slaves and their masters with slaves hiding their true feelings while acting submissively in the presence of whites.

Democratic-Republicans The political party that emerged after the Revolution to oppose the Federalists' support for a strong central government; favored states' rights and the agrarian way of life. Thomas Jefferson, a leader of the Democratic-Republicans, was elected president in 1800.

Diaspora The dispersion of a population abroad, whether forced or voluntary. The term is often applied to Jewish settlement outside the eastern Mediterranean region, and to the spread of Africans across the Americas, as a result of the Atlantic slave trade.

Dred Scott v. Sandford The 1857 case in which the Supreme Court held that residence on free soil did not render a slave a free person, for black people, enslaved and free, had (in the words of the court) "no rights which the white man was bound to respect."

Edict of Nantes This decree, issued at Nantes in 1598 by King Henry IV of France, granted political rights and limited toleration to French Protestants, or Huguenots.

Electoral college An intricate system in which each state appoints electors, equal in number to its representation in Congress, to elect the president and vice president. The electoral college is a provision of the Constitution (Article II, Section 1) because the framers were unwilling to approve the direct election of president and vice president. This group, or "college," of electors still makes the selection, voting according to prior party commitments rather than individual choice.

Emancipation National or state-sponsored program to free slaves.

Emancipation Proclamation An executive order issued by President Abraham Lincoln on January 1, 1863, declaring that all slaves living in states or areas controlled by the Confederate States of America were now free. The proclamation did not affect the status of slaves in Union-held areas.

Embargo Act of 1807 A law passed by Congress, at the urging of President Thomas Jefferson, to halt the shipment of U.S. goods to Europe in response to British military and naval aggression.

Encomienda The Spanish *encomienda* system, imposed in Spain's American empire, requiring Indian communities to supply labor or pay tribute to a local colonial overlord (identified as an *encomendero*).

Encomienda The Spanish *encomienda* system, imposed in Spain's American empire, requiring Indian communities to supply labor or pay tribute to a local colonial overlord (identified as an *encomendero*).

Enumerated articles Colonial products listed (enumerated) in the Navigation Act of 1660, such as tobacco, sugar, and indigo, had to pass through an English port before reexport to Europe, to aid the domestic economy.

Era of Good Feelings A term used by historians to describe the presidency of James Monroe (1817–1825), when partisan tensions eased among voters and their political leaders.

Erie Canal Waterway linking the New York cities of Troy and Albany, on the Hudson River, with Buffalo, on the eastern tip of Lake Erie; in the 1820s, the opening of the Erie Canal revolutionized trading between the Midwest and East Coast and established New York City as the most important financial center in the United States.

Evangelical Protestants Christians who emphasize the importance of personal faith, as well as seeking new converts.

Federalists A coalition of nationalist leaders who favored creating a stronger central government to replace the Articles of Confederation. They labeled their opponents as Anti-Federalists in the late 1780s. The strongest essays endorsing their proposed new Constitution were entitled *The Federalist*.

Federation An alliance or compact between political units that agree to surrender certain powers to a central authority while still retaining other powers.

Flotilla Any sizeable fleet of ships, or, more specifically, a naval term for a unit consisting of two or more squadrons of small warships.

Freedmen's Bureau Federal agency created by Congress in March 1865 and disbanded in 1869. Its purposes were to provide relief for Southerners who had remained loyal to the Union during the Civil War, to support black elementary schools, and to oversee annual labor contracts between landowners and field hands.

Fugitive Slave Law of 1850 Congressional legislation that required local and federal law enforcement agents to retrieve runaways no matter where they sought refuge in the United States.

Gadsden Purchase A total of 45,535 square miles of land (located in present-day southern Arizona and southwestern New Mexico) purchased by the United States from Mexico in 1853.

Gentry An English term for the land-owning social class of well-to-do elite who possessed wealth and power, but lacked the hereditary titles of the nobility.

Globalization The process of integration—economic, but also cultural—of different parts of the world into a more unified system of trade and communication.

Grange An organization founded by Oliver H. Kelly in 1867 to represent the interests of farmers by pressing for agricultural cooperatives, an end to railroad freight discrimination against small farmers, and other initiatives. Its full name was National Grange of the Patrons of Husbandry.

Great Awakening The title that was applied, in retrospect, to the interdenominational Christian revival that swept Britain's North American colonies between the 1730s and the 1750s, inspired at first by the preaching of Jonathan Edwards and George Whitefield. (A religious revival in the early nineteenth century became known as the Second Great Awakening.)

Guerrilla war A conflict fought not on the basis of conventional warfare but, rather, by mobilizing small groups of fighters who attack and harass superior forces.

Gullah A "pidgin," or blend of words and grammatical structures from West African languages and English, spoken by slaves in the South Carolina lowcountry.

Headright Under the headright system, English colonial governments granted a fixed amount of land, usually 50 acres, to any head of household for every family member or hired hand that person brought into the colony. Sometimes fewer acres were granted for women and children on the grounds that they would clear and plant less land.

Homestead Act Legislation passed in 1862 that granted 160 acres of land free to each settler who lived on and made improvements to government land for five years.

Huguenots The term applied to Protestants living in Catholic France. In 1685, King Louis XIV revoked the Edict of Nantes, which had assured protection to this minority. Despite a royal ban on Huguenot emigration, thousands fled to other parts of Europe and many families migrated to North America.

Iberian Relating to Europe's Iberian peninsula, the location of Spain and Portugal.

Impressment A policy that authorizes the seizure of persons or private property in the service of a government.

Indenture A document binding one person to work for another for a given period of time. Indentured servants received food, shelter, and clothing, plus "freedom dues" when their terms of service ended to help them get started independently.

Iroquois League A Native American confederacy, located in central New York, originally composed of the Cayuga, Mohawk, Oneida, Onondaga, and Seneca Indians, and later including the Tuscarora as well.

Isthmus A narrow strip of land connecting two larger land areas (such as the isthmus of Panama).

Itinerant minister During the era of the Great Awakening, some Protestant ministers practiced itinerancy; that is, they traveled widely and spoke to diverse communities, rather than being committed to one particular geographical parish or Protestant denomination.

Kachina An Indian religious system, inspired by Mesoamerican traditions, and present in the American Southwest for more than 800 years; the kachina cult used masks for group performances associated with rain, curing, fertility, warfare, and the ancestors. Among many Pueblo and Hopi Indians, this tradition was epitomized by kachina (or katsina) dolls.

Kachina An Indian religious system, inspired by Mexican traditions, and present in the American Southwest for more than 800 years. The kachina cult used masks for group performances associated with rain, curing, fertility, warfare, and the ancestors. Among many Pueblo and Hopi Indians, this tradition was epitomized by kachina (or katsina) dolls.

Kayak A highly maneuverable, decked-in canoe used by Native Alaskans for travel and hunting. The light frame is covered with skins, and the paddle has a blade at each end. Popular modern versions of this traditional boat are made with canvas or fiberglass.

Kentucky and Virginia Resolutions Resolutions issued by two state legislatures in 1798 in response to the Alien and Sedition Acts passed by Congress; proclaimed that individual states had the right to declare such measures "void and of no force."

Kickbacks Money paid illegally in return for favors (for example, to a politician by a person or business that has received government contracts).

Lecompton Constitution A Kansas state constitution drawn up by pro-slavery advocates in 1857; sought to nullify the doctrine of popular sovereignty in the state, decreeing that even if voters rejected slavery, any slaves already in the state would remain enslaved under the force of law.

Lewis and Clark Expedition A "corps of discovery" commissioned by President Thomas Jefferson in 1804 to explore the newly acquired Louisiana Territory. Led by Meriwether Lewis and William Clark and lasting 28 months, the party reported on an array of subjects, including the cultural practices of western Indians and the natural features of the land, but failed to find a water route that would connect the Pacific Northwest to eastern markets.

Manifest destiny The idea, first promoted in the 1840s, that the United States had a God-given right to expand its territory; used to justify territorial growth, expansion of economic markets, and conquest.

Manumission A formal emancipation from slavery; the act (by an individual owner or government authority) of granting freedom to an enslaved person or persons.

Marbury v. Madison An 1803 Supreme Court decision establishing the right of the judiciary to declare acts of both the executive and legislative branches unconstitutional.

Market Revolution The combined effects of transportation innovation, technological change, and economic growth, especially during the first half of the nineteenth century.

Mercantilism A commercial policy that sought to achieve economic self-sufficiency and a favorable balance of trade (often by planting colonies) in order to promote a country's prosperity, strength, and independence. Rival European imperial powers favored the strategy of mercantilism in the seventeenth and eighteenth centuries.

Mercenaries Soldiers (such as the German Hessians who served for the British in the Revolutionary War) who fight for pay rather than for any devotion to a specific cause.

Mesoamerica The transitional region between North and South America, composed of Mexico and Central America.

Mestizo A person of mixed European and American Indian ancestry.

Middle passage For European slave ships, the middle passage was the second of three legs in the triangular round-trip voyage from Europe to Africa to America and back to Europe. For enslaved Africans, the middle passage came to mean not only the transatlantic journey itself, but the entire process of removal from an African homeland and ultimate sale to an American master.

Monetary policy Government policies designed to affect the national economy through bank lending policies, interest rates, and control of the amount of money in circulation.

Monroe Doctrine Policy announced by President James Monroe in 1823 that the era of European colonization of the Americas had ceased; warned foreign powers, especially Russia, Spain, and Britain, that the United States would not allow them to intervene in the Western Hemisphere.

Morrill Act Legislation passed by Republican Congress in 1862 to create a system of agricultural (land-grant) public colleges.

Mulatto A person of mixed European and African ancestry; the first-generation offspring of a Caucasian and a Negroid parent.

National Republicans A political party, led by John Adams in the 1820s, that favored a greater federal role in funding internal improvements and public education; forerunner of the Whigs, formed in opposition to President Andrew Jackson.

Nativists American citizens born in the United States who opposed further immigration, especially from anywhere outside northwestern Europe.

New York City draft riot A July 1863 violent protest against the recent passage of a northern military conscription law; whites attacked black men, women, and children and burned the city's Colored Orphan Asylum.

Nullification The doctrine that a state has the right to ignore or nullify certain federal laws with which it disagrees.

Ordnance Cannons, artillery, and by extension general military supplies, including weapons, ammunition, combat vehicles, and tools.

Outrigger canoe Polynesian mariners in Southeast Asia developed large canoes with one or more lateral support floats, known as outriggers, that gave stability for ocean sailing. They used such canoes to reach Hawaii.

Pacific Railroad Act Legislation that granted to the Union Pacific and the Central Pacific railroads cash subsidies and a 400-foot right of way along the Platte River route of the Oregon Trail.

Paleo-Indians The earliest human inhabitants of North America, who first migrated to the continent from Siberia more than 15,000 years ago. Faced with a warming climate and the disappearance of many large game animals roughly 10,000 years ago (8,000 B.C.E.), their descendants learned to hunt smaller animals and adapted to varied local conditions during the Archaic Period (to c. 1000 B.C.E.).

Panic of 1837 Economic crisis and depression caused by a combination of overspeculation—in bridges, canals, and turnpikes—and a large failure of grain crops in the West.

Patronage system Any structure where individuals—in order to obtain a post, retain it, or advance—must rely more on inside connections and networks of friends than upon superior competence, effort, or dedication.

Pest house In colonial times, a shelter to quarantine those possibly infected with contagious diseases (such as newcomers arriving in American ports from Africa or Europe) to prevent the spread of shipborne pestilence.

Pocket veto An indirect veto of a legislative bill made when an executive (such as a president or governor) simply leaves the bill unsigned, so that it dies after the adjournment of the legislature.

Popular sovereignty The idea that residents of a state should be able to make decisions on crucial issues, such as whether or not to legalize slavery.

Privateers A term for private ships (and their owners) licensed by government to engage in warfare at sea and to keep the profits of their raids, easing the burden on the navy to build ships, train officers, and pay sailors.

Privateers Ships (and their crew members) licensed to harass enemy shipping in wartime.

Prize money The proceeds earned by privateers from the capture and sale of enemy cargo and vessels. This money was divided among the ship's investors, officers, and crew, providing an incentive to join the war effort.

Quitrent A fixed annual tax, included in many colonial land grants, paid by the recipient to the donor.

Reconstruction Act of 1867 An act that prevented the former Confederate states from entering the Union until they had ratified the Fourteenth Amendment and written new constitutions that guaranteed black men the right to vote. It also divided the South (with the exception of Tennessee, which had ratified the Fourteenth Amendment) into five military districts and stationed federal troops throughout the region.

Reconstruction era The twelve years after the Civil War when the U.S. government took steps to integrate the eleven states of the Confederacy back into the Union.

Redemption system An eighteenth-century arrangement in which potential migrants in Europe signed up with an agent who agreed to pay for their Atlantic passage. Reaching America, the newcomer signed a pact to work for several years for an employer. In exchange for much-needed labor, the employer agreed to pay back the shipper, "redeeming" the original loan that had been made to the immigrant "redemptioner."

Redress A remedy for a wrong; a correction or reparation. As a verb, to redress means to correct, to set right, or to remove the cause of a grievance.

Republican mother A wife and mother whose primary role is caring for and socializing future citizens (her children); an ideal favored by some elites after the American Revolution.

Republican party Founded in 1854, this political party began as a coalition of Northerners who opposed the extension of slavery into the western territories.

Restoration Era Royalist supporters restored the English monarchy in 1660. Charles II became king and the Stuart dynasty resumed its rule of England until Charles's successor, the pro-Catholic James II, was forced into exile in 1688.

Sachem Algonquin Indian term for a Native American leader or chief.

Saltwater slaves This term applied to Africans in America who had personally endured the transatlantic middle passage. It distinguished them from their descendants, the "country-born slaves" who had grown up in America from birth.

Scalawag A negative term applied by southern Democrats after the Civil War to any white Southerner who allied with the Republican party.

Secession The process by which the southern states withdrew from the Union; each of the eleven states that eventually joined the Confederacy elected delegates to a secession convention that decided the question of whether to remain in or leave the Union.

Second Great Awakening A series of Protestant religious revivals that began in the 1790s and continued through the 1820s. Prominent revivalists such as Charles Grandison Finney sought to link the life of the spirit with political action and reform efforts.

Separation of powers The novel idea that the powers of the three branches of government—legislative, executive, and judicial—should be kept separate from one another, so that each can check and balance the powers of the other two.

Shallop A shallow-draft, undecked vessel, roughly 30 feet in length, holding more than a dozen sailors and suitable for rowing and sailing in rivers and bays.

Social stratification The schematic arrangement of a population into a ranking of horizontal social layers (strata), or an identifiable hierarchy of classes within a society.

Substitute During war, a man paid to serve in combat in another man's place.

Suffrage The right to vote.

Tariff A government tax on imported goods.

Tejanos Spanish-speaking residents of the Mexican (and later, U.S.) state of Texas.

Temperance A social movement embracing either total opposition to alcohol consumption or support for its moderate use.

Temperance A social movement embracing either total opposition to alcohol consumption or support for its moderate use.

Texians The name used by U.S.-born citizens who lived in the Mexican state of Texas.

Three-fifths clause A controversial clause of Article I, section 2, of the U.S. Constitution said that each slave would count as "three-fifths of all other Persons" when representatives and direct taxes were being apportioned to states according to population. Slaves had no rights of citizenship, but the clause gave southern slave states additional power in Congress. Section 2 of the Fourteenth Amendment did away with the clause in 1868.

Tithe A levy or donation (generally a tenth part) given to provide support, usually for a church.

Trading factory The overseas trading outposts built by competing European empires became known as factories, since each was run by a *factor*, or manager. Along the west coast of Africa, from Senegal to Angola, such posts played a central role in the Atlantic slave trade.

Trail of Tears The name Cherokee Indians gave to their forced removal from the Southeast to the West in 1838 and 1839 as part of the federal government's Indian removal policy. During the journey, U.S. troops destroyed the material basis of Cherokee culture and separated many families; over 4,000 Indians died.

Treaty of Ghent Peace treaty signed by the United States and Great Britain in 1815, ending the War of 1812.

Two-party system A system of government characterized by two major political parties that compete with each other in "winner take all" elections.

Underground Railroad A secret network of abolitionists developed during the antebellum period to help slaves escape and find refuge, many in the North or in Canada.

Unicameral A legislative body that has only one chamber, or house.

Utopian Relating to communities organized to strive for ideal social and political conditions.

Vigilantes People who seek to take the law into their own hands and punish or intimidate alleged criminals or persons who resist a certain social order (for example, white supremacy).

War hawks Politicians who favor specific forms of military action as a tool of U.S. foreign policy.

War of 1812 A military and naval conflict that pitted U.S. forces against the British and their Indian allies. The end of the war eliminated the post-Revolutionary British threat to U.S. sovereignty.

Whigs A national political party formed in 1834 in opposition to the presidency of Andrew Jackson and his policy of expanding the power of the president. The Whigs favored congressional funding for internal improvements and other forms of federal support for economic development.

Whiskey Rebellion Protest in 1794 by western Pennsylvania farmers and grain distillers who objected to a high federal tax on the whiskey they produced.

Wildcat banks Small banks that make loans unsupervised by the state or other financial institutions.

USZ61-1182]; 216: U.S. Senate Historical Office; 217: Fotose-arch/Getty Images; 220: Winterthur Museum; 222: © World History Archive/Alamy; 225: Hulton Archive/Getty Images; 226: Ilene MacDonald/Alamy; 231

CHAPTER 10 Picture History/Newscom; 241: Library of Congress Prints and Photographs Division[LC-USZ62-17372]; 242: National Portrait Gallery, Smithsonian Institution/Art Resource, NY; 246: Library of Congress Photographs and Prints Division[LC-USZ62-61]; 250: Library of Congress Prints and Photographs Division[LC-DIG-ppm-sca-31111]; 252: Peter Turnley/CORBIS; 254: SSPL/Science Museum/Art Resource, NY; 256: akg-images/The Image Works; 258: Chicago History Museum[ICHi-22005]; 261

CHAPTER 11 Richard T. Nowitz/Corbis; 265: Library of Congress Prints and Photographs Division[LC-DIG-ppm-sca-32639]; 266: Davy Crockett, Harry Ransom Humanities Research Center, The University of Texas at Austin/Harry Ransom Humanities Research Center; 267: Bob Pardue - SC/Alamy; 270: North Wind Picture Archives/Alamy; 271: Robert Cruikshank 1789-1856/Library of Congress Prints and Photographs Division [LC-USZC4-970]; 276: Chasseriau, Theodore (1819-56)/The Art Gallery Collection/Alamy; 281: Everett Collection Inc/Alamy; 282: Thomas Barrat/Shutterstock; 284: Henry F. Darby, American, 1829-1897 The Reverend John Atwood and His Family, 1845 Oil on canvas 183.2 x 244.47 cm (72 1/8 x 96 1/4 in.) Museum of Fine Arts, Boston Gift ofMaxim Karolik for the M. and M. Karolik Collection of American Paintings, 1815-1865 62.269; 289

CHAPTER 12 Minnesota Historical Society; 291: Scotts Bluff National Monument; 292: Scotts Bluff National Monument; 299: Library of Congress Prints and Photographs Division[LC-USZ62-52577]; 304: Currier & Ives/Cartoon Prints, American/Popular Graphic Arts/Library of Congress Prints and Photographs Division/[LC-USZ62-683]; 307: King, Charles Bird (1785-1862) (attr.) John Caldwell Calhoun (1782-1850), Statesman. ca. 1818-25. Oil on canvas. 76.2 x 63.5 cm./National Portrait Gallery, Smithsonian Institution/Art Resource, NY; 311: Library of Congress Prints and Photographs Division[LC-USZC4-2957]; 314: Henry Walke (1808-1896), The U. S. Naval Expedition Under Comore. M. C. Perry, Ascending the Tuspan River, Toned lithograph with applied watercolor, Amon Carter Museum of American Art, Fort Worth, Texas, 1976.33.2; 315

CHAPTER 13 Courtesy of the California History Room, California State Library, Sacramento, California; 317: Glasshouse Images/Alamy; 318: American Textile History Museum, Lowell, Ma; 323: George Caleb Bingham, American, 1811–1879; Raftsmen Playing Cards, 1847; oil on canvas; 28 1/16 x 38 1/16 in. (71.3 x 96.7 cm); Saint Louis Art Museum, Bequest of Ezra H. Linley by exchange 50:1934; 325: Evert A. and George L. Duyckinck, eds. Cyclopaedia of American Literature (1855), vol. 2, p. 251./Library Company fo Philadelphia; 326: Bettmann/Corbis; 328: Library of Congress Prints and Photographs Division[LC-USZ62-9916]; 335: The Ohio Historical Society; 340

CHAPTER 14 Chicago History Museum[ICHi-22172]; 343: Library of Congress Prints and Photographs Division[LC-DIG-pga-02091]; 344: Library of Congress Prints and Photographs Division[LC-DIG-cwpb-01748]; 348: Alexander Gardner 1821-1882/Library of Congress Prints and Photographs Division [LC-DIG-cwpb-01097]; 353: The Museum of the Confederacy Richmond, Virginia; 354: Thomas Nast, 1863/Library of Congress Prints and Photographs Division[LC-USZ62-130778]; 356: Timothy O'Sullivan/Library of Congress Prints and Photographs Division[LC-B8171-518]; 358: Library of Congress Prints and Photographs Division[LC-B8184-10454]; 361: Library of Congress Prints and Photographs Division[LC-DIG-cwpb-01571]; 362: SPC Plains Cheyenne BAE 26-47 00388800, National Anthropological Archives, Smithsonian Institution; 365

CHAPTER 15 The Library of Congress[LC-USZ62-117666]; 369: Library of Congress Prints and Photographs Division[LC-DIG-cwpbh-00952]; 370: Historical/Corbis; 373: Library of Congress Prints and Photographs Division[LC-USZ62-45067]; 374: Library of Congress Prints and Photographs Division Washington, D.C. [LC-DIG-pga-01366]; 376: Robert Benecke. DeGolyer Library, SMU; 382: The California History Room, California State Library, Sacramento, California.; 383: Thomas Nast/Library of Congress Prints and Photographs Division; 390

All Maps are owned and copyrighted by Pearson Education, Upper Saddle River, NJ unless otherwise noted.

Index

Entries followed by *f, t, m,* and *i* refer to figures, tables, maps, and illustrations, respectively.